EssexWorks.
For a better quality of life

Essex County Council

Please return this book on or before the date shown above. To
renew go to www.essex-gov.uk/libraries, ring 0846 803 7628 or
go to any Essex library.

1 9 MAY 2016

– 4 APR 2016

...YLEIGH

FOR LONDONERS
timeout.com

D0191359

Time Out Guides Ltd
Universal House
251 Tottenham Court Road
London W1T 7AB
United Kingdom
Tel: +44 (0)20 7813 3000
Fax: +44 (0)20 7813 6001
Email: guides@timeout.com
www.timeout.com

Published by Time Out Guides Ltd, a wholly owned subsidiary of Ti
Time Out and the Time Out logo are trademarks of Time Out Group Ltd.

This edition first published in Great Britain in 2012 by Ebury Publishing
A Random House Group Company
20 Vauxhall Bridge Road, London SW1V 2SA

Random House Australia Pty Ltd 20 Alfred Street, Milsons Point, Sydney, New South Wales 2061, Aus

Random House New Zealand Ltd 18 Poland Road, Glenfield, Auckland 10, New Zealand

Random House South Africa (Pty) Ltd Isle of Houghton, Corner Boundary Road & Carse O'Gowrie,
Houghton 2198, South Africa

Random House UK Limited Reg. No. 954009

Distributed in USA by Publishers Group West
1700 Fourth Street, Berkeley, California 94710

Distributed in Canada by Publishers Group Canada
250A Carlton Street, Toronto, Ontario M5A 2L1

For further distribution details, see www.timeout.com.

ISBN: 978-1-84670-267-9

A CIP catalogue record for this book is available from the British Library.

Printed and bound by in Great Britain by Butler Tanner & Dennis, Frome, Somerset.

The Random House Group Limited supports The Forest Stewardship Council (FSC®), the leading
international forest certification organisation. Our books carrying the FSC label are printed on FSC® certified
paper. FSC is the only forest certification scheme endorsed by the leading environmental organisations,
including Greenpeace. Our paper procurement policy can be found at www.randomhouse.co.uk/environment

Time Out carbon-offsets its flights with Trees for Cities (www.treesforcities.org).

MIX
Paper from
responsible sources
FSC® C023561

DISCOVER IT

Disney
PRESENTS

THE LION KING

THE AWARD-WINNING MUSICAL

Visit www.thelionking.co.uk or call 0844 871 3000

LYCEUM THEATRE

21 Wellington Street, London ⊖ Covent Garden

Andile Gumbi as 'Simba'. Photo by Simon Turtle. © Disney

Time Out Guides Limited
Universal House
251 Tottenham Court Road
London W1T 7AB
Tel + 44 (0)20 7813 3000
Fax + 44 (0)20 7813 6001
Email guides@timeout.com
www.timeout.com

Editorial
Editor Cath Phillips
Researchers William Crow, Emily Baker
Proofreader John Watson
Indexer William Crow

Editorial Director Sarah Guy
Series Editor Cath Phillips
Editorial Manager Holly Pick
Management Accountants Margaret Wright, Clare Turner

Design
Art Editor Pinelope Kourmouzoglou
Senior Designer Kei Ishimaru
Group Commercial Senior Designer Jason Tansley

Picture Desk
Picture Editor Jael Marschner
Picture Desk Assistant/Researcher Ben Rowe

Advertising
New Business & Commercial Director Mark Phillips
Sales Director St John Betteridge
Account Managers Deborah Maclaren & team
@ The Media Sales House

Marketing
Senior Publishing Brand Manager Luthfa Begum
Guides Marketing Manager Colette Whitehouse
Group Commercial Art Director Anthony Huggins

Production
Group Production Manager Brendan McKeown
Production Controller Katie Mulhern-Bhudia

Time Out Group
Chairman & Founder Tony Elliott
Chief Executive Officer David King
Chief Operating Officer Aksel Van der Wal
Editor-in-Chief Tim Arthur
Chief Technical Officer Remo Gettini
Group Financial Director Paul Rakkar
Group General Manager/Director Nichola Coulthard
UK Chief Commercial Officer David Pepper
Time Out International Ltd MD Cathy Runciman

Contributors
Neighbourhoods, Restaurants & cafés, Pubs & bars and Shops written by Jessica Cargill Thompson, Simon Coppock, Sarah Guy, Ronnie Haydon, Cath Phillips, Holly Pick, Ben Rowe, Jennifer Scott.
Additional writing, interviews and research by William Crow, Emily Baker, Sarah Guy.
The Editor would like to thank Zena Alkayat, Sonya Barber, Douglas Benford, Abby Blanch, Ariana Blanch and Hunnie & Koko the spaniels, Dan Collins, Guy Dimond, Dave Faulkner, Susie Giles, Loren Harway, Anthony Huggins, Zoe Kamen, Adam LeeDavies, Charmaine Mok, Katie Mulhern-Bhudia, Lara Pawson, Chris Pierre, Danica Priest, Julian Richards, Christian Sabe, Gabriel Tate, Daniele Turi, Patrick Welch, Colette Whitehouse, Susie Williams.

Maps by JS Graphics (john@jsgraphics.co.uk).

Cover photography Scott Wishart, retouching Pinelope Kourmouzoglou. Taken at Medcalf, 40 Exmouth Market, EC1R 4QE (7833 3533).

Photography pages 3, 24, 73, 97, 103, 121, 122, 125, 153, 183, 188, 283, 285, 311, 335, 339 Ben Rowe; 7, 62, 66, 87, 143, 173 (bottom), 225, 332, 250 Britta Jaschinski; 8 Food From The Sky; 9, 26, 46, 49, 106, 109, 163 (right), 288, 301 Rob Greig; 17, 21, 65, 69 (top left), 174, 176 Michelle Grant; 19, 169, 209, 260 Scott Wishart; 29, 164, 192 Gemma Day; 32, 120 Olivor Knight; 37 (left), 45, 241, 243, 271 Nigel Tradewell; 37 (right), 88, 255 Belinda Lawley; 43 Laurence Davis; 55, 115, 119, 129, 180, 203, 258 (top), 265 Jonathan Perugia; 58, 76, 108, 133, 163 (left), 187, 258 (bottom) Ed Marshall; 59, 69 (bottom right), 214 (top and right) Alys Tomlinson; 61 r.nagy; 63, 158, 214 (bottom left), 217, 327, 328 Tricia de Courcy Ling; 69 (top right), 84 Jitka Hynkova; 69 (bottom left), 111, 113, 135, 149 (left), 190, 199, 234, 336 Ming Tang-Evans; 75, 136, 194, 244, 274, 286, 317 Heloise Bergman; 78 Christina Theisen; 81 Nick Ballon; 91 Jael Marschner; 94, 179 (bottom), 204 Celia Topping; 123 Gordon Rainsford; 128, 142, 161 Michael Franke; 144 Elisabeth Blanchet; 149 (right), 185 Olivia Rutherford; 155 Ben Gilman; 157 Chris Brown; 173 (top) Bikeworldtravel; 175 Lisa Payne; 179 (top) Susie Reu, 208 Andrew Brackenbury; 231 Tove K Breitstein; 263 Morley von Sternberg; 267 ODA; 293 www.simonleigh.com.

Contents

How local can you go?

Food from the Sky, Crouch End

From neighbourhood forums to busy cafés, one-off shops to own-grown blogs, art festivals to street art, Londoners are lapping up all things local. **Jessica Cargill Thompson** investigates.

Something's going on all across London, from Brixton to Stoke Newington, East Dulwich to Walthamstow. People are paying closer attention to where they live, spending more time in their own postcodes, enjoying what's on offer locally. Instead of heading into town for a night out, they're visiting local restaurants, bars, theatres and cinemas; making their own entertainment by setting up local comedy clubs, film clubs, wine clubs and knitting clubs; organising art and music festivals in the local park or community centre; and generally bringing together like-minded locals and relishing the cheap(er) fun on their own doorsteps.

Postcode patriotism is worn loud and proud on T-shirts, canvas shoppers, mugs, and necklaces. Vintage and replica bus blinds displaying stops on your route home are a fashionable way of announcing your local credentials.

Visit some of the capital's more 'villagey' neighbourhoods during the week and you'll find their characterful cafés are full – not just with parents with buggies, but also with home-workers lugging laptops, would-be entrepreneurs writing business plans, web designers meeting clients, actors reading scripts, artisans swapping tips and tittle-tattle, and community groups discussing plans of action.

This is partly down to a change in working patterns, as people look for ways to have a more flexible lifestyle or to make it easier to look after children. At the end of 2011, more than 14 per cent of UK workers were classified as self-employed or home-workers, according to the Office of National Statistics. It's partly the economic downturn that is encouraging a new era of 'make do and mend' austerity, but the nationwide interest in such things as local, seasonal produce and 'food miles' is also fuelling a focus on what's available around the corner.

And as we start to spend more time in our neighbourhoods, we begin to care more about them. This doesn't just mean campaigning about speed bumps, but turning wasteland into community gardens, public squares or playgrounds, establishing Free Schools or breathing new life into an all-but-forgotten velodrome. Take

Walthamstow, where the community has rallied behind the long-running campaign to bring back the local cinema (the only one in the borough), though earlier attempts to save its famous dog track were unsuccessful.

Angela Burgess started ultra-local magazine *SE22* in 2005 as a way of keeping East Dulwich residents informed about what was going on all around them. 'I developed a real passion for the area and wanted to share that,' she says. 'The feedback I receive is fabulous. I have been approached by many mums saying the children's activities pages have been a life-saver, and I know people who get together with their friends and mark up the events they want to go to for the next month.'

Such has been the appetite for all things local that *SE22* has since been joined by sister publications *SE21* (covering Dulwich Village and West Dulwich) and *SE23* (Forest Hill and Honor Oak). And Burgess reckons other south London neighbourhoods, such as Blackheath, are ripe for a similarly detailed treatment. She's also behind East Dulwich's annual fair on Goose Green (coinciding with the wider Dulwich Festival), which has local bands performing, local cafés cooking, local artisans selling and local businesses and voluntary groups setting out their stalls.

Of course, shopping is one of the key ways that people can express their interest in their home turf. Middle-class residents now want their high streets to look as they might have done in the 1950s – with a proper butcher, fishmonger, greengrocer, artisanal baker and cheese seller, all of whom know their customers – even if they want a giant supermarket somewhere nearby too. The 'shop local' campaign has encouraged this trend, boosted independent traders and given some people the courage to start their own business or community-oriented venture.

A drive to regenerate Wood Street in E17 has included offering small local independent traders units for free or reduced rents, and asking local artists to design promotional artwork. In Hackney, Growing Communities (www.growingcommunities.org) has a team of volunteers nurturing salad greens and other vegetables on a variety of sites across the borough, then distributing the results via their popular veg box scheme. Capital Growth funding has been used to install

A PINT OF WANDLE, PLEASE

Walk into any London pub and you'd probably expect to see Fuller's London Pride or Young's Bitter on handpump at the bar. But increasingly these days, you might be offered the choice of Sambrook's Wandle or Redemption's Trinity. The latest craze for all things local in London is focused on the humble pint.

The number of independent microbreweries that have opened in the past few years is staggering. Meantime Brewery was an early bird, launching in Greenwich back in 2000, but it's got a lot of competition now from the likes of the Kernel Brewery (Bermondsey), Redchurch and London Fields (both Hackney), Sambrooks (Battersea), Redemption (Tottenham), Camden Town (actually in Kentish Town), and the East London Brewing Company (Leyton). All make a point of celebrating their origins and environs, with beer names such as Hoxton Stout, Wandle and Hackney Hopstar. And the number of stockists across the capital – whether pubs or shops – is growing. What could be better than drinking a pint of London Fields Bitter, in London Fields itself, only yards from where it was brewed?

For details of the microbreweries, their beers and where you can find them, visit:
www.camdentownbrewery.com
www.eastlondonbrewing.com
www.londonfieldsbrewery.co.uk
www.redemptionbrewing.co.uk
www.sambrooksbrewery.co.uk
www.thekernelbrewery.com
www.theredchurchbrewery.com

raised beds on unused land at the London College of Fashion to grow all sorts of crops, including, it's hoped, dye plants for use by the fashion students. Other Hackney operations have got in on the act; Fabrications shop-cum-art-gallery on Broadway Market runs upcycling and craft workshops, for exampe, while the nearby E5 Bakehouse teaches people to make their own bread.

Crouch End, with a big population of families and creatives, no tube and an impressive clocktower, is another enclave of proud residents working the villagey vibe. The bleak rooftop of the local Budgens has been commandeered for use as a roof garden (www.foodfromthesky.org.uk), again run by volunteers. The shop sells the salad leaves, tomatoes, herbs, strawberries and other produce grown overhead – less than ten metres from soil to shelf, it's got to be a record – alongside other popular locally made brands.

In Brixton, the 'shop local' mantra has been taken to another level by a number of different schemes designed to encourage and support local trade and production. For starters, there's the Brixton Pound (www.brixtonpound.org), a local currency that can be spent at local shops and market stalls, designed to keep money within SW9. Creatives in the area (not just Brixton, but also Stockwell, Camberwell, Clapham and Herne Hill) can sell online through new umbrella outfit Makerhood (www.brixton. makerhood.com). Run by volunteers on a not-for-profit basis, the website hosts virtual 'stalls', as well as an actual monthly market on Brixton Station Road.

'We wanted to create the traditional village model, where people live locally and have skills and exchange them locally and also meet people locally,' says co-founder Kristina Glushkova. 'Although we intended the scheme as a website only, it has led to lots of offline community events that we hadn't expected, such as craft-making sessions and business development workshops.'

There are about 30 sellers on the website now – and they're no longer just individuals, but a collective. It's given people who have creative but not commercial skills the confidence to start their own business, and set up a microeconomic enterprise that keeps money in the area. There's definitely a recognition that buying

something that's locally produced is more meaningful and enjoyable.'

What Makerhood shows too is that the internet has been hugely instrumental in galvanising communities, paradoxical though that may seem. Every self-respecting neighbourhood now has its own online discussion forum where people can swap recommendations for builders, sell their kids' old bikes, sound off about dustbin collections, and indulge in a bit of electronic curtain twitching. It's the village pub, noticeboard, post office, school gates and garden fence rolled into one.

One of the most active local network forums in the country is the East Dulwich Forum (www.eastdulwichforum.co.uk). Here, the circling of a helicopter over Peckham Rye can, within the hour, draw a flurry of comments speculating on what could be going on. Recent discussion about a controlled parking zone drew more than 1,300 comments (and more than 30,000 'views') – far more people than you'd get turning up to a council meeting in a church hall. (A map of hyper-local sites can be found at Openly Local: http://openlylocal. com/hyperlocal_sites).

Local passions are also voiced in the growing number of blogs reporting on the minutiae of life in a particular area. There are food blogs, shopping blogs, literary blogs, walking blogs, news blogs, mum blogs and even spoof blogs – no blade of civic-park grass or cup of locally brewed coffee is left un-commented-upon.

Twitter has also become in important part of the mix, as a valuable marketing tool for local businesses and as a watercooler substitute and real-time IT help-desk for homeworkers. It's a way to 'meet' your neighbours. It can alert you to new places before they've opened, give you a heads-up on traffic problems, and help crowd-source urgent information such as 'does anywhere round here sell camping gas canisters?' or '@localrestaurant Any tables for 2 left for tonight?' You can find out what's happening on your high street at that very moment, without having to leave the house, right down to the detail of what guest ale has just been put on at your local pub.

But the key thing is that all this online activity acts as a spur to offline activity – to people actually leaving their houses, meeting their neighbours, and getting involved in where they live. So what's stopping you?

About the Guide

How the guide is arranged

Thanks to centuries of haphazard growth and various changes in the division and administration of the capital's districts, London is a defiantly disordered city. To cope with contradictory postcode lines, electoral wards and borough boundaries, we've divided this guide into 25 chapters, each focusing on one borough.

The most central boroughs (City of Westminster, City of London, Tower Hamlets, Hackney, Islington, Camden, Kensington & Chelsea, Hammersmith & Fulham, Lambeth, Wandsworth, Southwark and Lewisham) are covered in their entirety; in slightly more outlying boroughs, such as Greenwich and Brent, neighbourhoods closest to central London are covered; in outer boroughs such as Waltham Forest and Redbridge only key areas are covered. Each chapter is broken down by neighbourhood, with guides to restaurants and cafés, bars and pubs, shops and other essentials within the borough.

Neighbourhoods

Inevitably, neighbourhoods don't neatly follow borough boundaries. In cases where one district straddles two or more boroughs, we have included it in the most suitable chapter. Knightsbridge, for example, straddles both Kensington & Chelsea and Westminster, but is included in the former. We've provided a map of each borough in the relevant chapter, plus an overview map (on pages 14-15) of all the boroughs covered in the guide.

Amenities & essentials

No guide to London's amenities can be completely comprehensive: we have tried to select the best each borough has to offer. Addresses, telephone numbers and websites were all correct as we went to press, most listings for large chains are omitted.

Sport & fitness covers all publicly funded sports centres plus key private facilities. Schools covers all state secondary schools plus landmark private schools. Local estate agents are listed within each chapter.

While every effort has been made to ensure the accuracy of information in this guide, the publishers cannot accept responsibility for any errors it may contain.

Statistics

Our statistics come from a variety of sources. Borough populations, housing stock figures and recycling statistics are from Capital Waste Facts (www.capital wastefacts.com), which has collected data from a variety of sources; ethnic origins are taken from 'Resident Population Estimates by Ethnic Group (Percentages) (2001 - 2009)' from the Office for National Statistics (ONS); student and retiree figures from the 2001 Census (www.statistics.gov.uk); crime figures from the 'Recorded Crime for Seven Key Offences 2009/10' report by Research Development & Statistics Directorate (RDS); and average property prices from the Land Registry's House Price Index for October 2011 (www1.landregistry.gov.uk/house-prices). Council tax datacomes from the individual councils.

Let us know what you think

We hope you enjoy this book and we'd like to know what you think of it. Email us at guides@timeout.com.

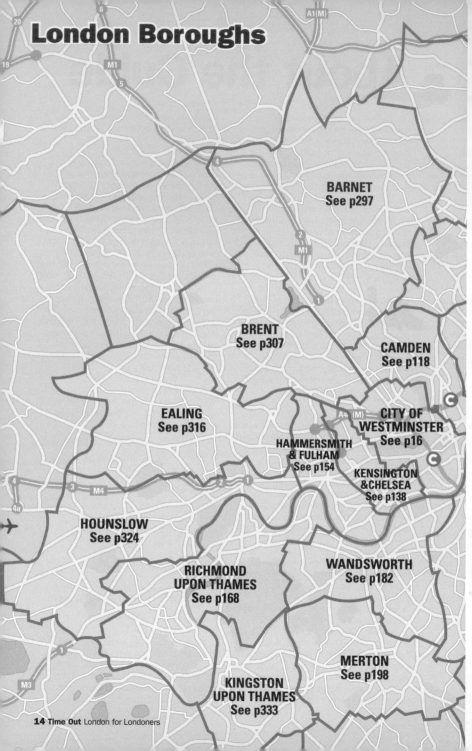

London Boroughs

BARNET
See p297

BRENT
See p307

CAMDEN
See p118

EALING
See p316

CITY OF WESTMINSTER
See p16

HAMMERSMITH & FULHAM
See p154

KENSINGTON & CHELSEA
See p138

HOUNSLOW
See p324

RICHMOND UPON THAMES
See p168

WANDSWORTH
See p182

MERTON
See p198

KINGSTON UPON THAMES
See p333

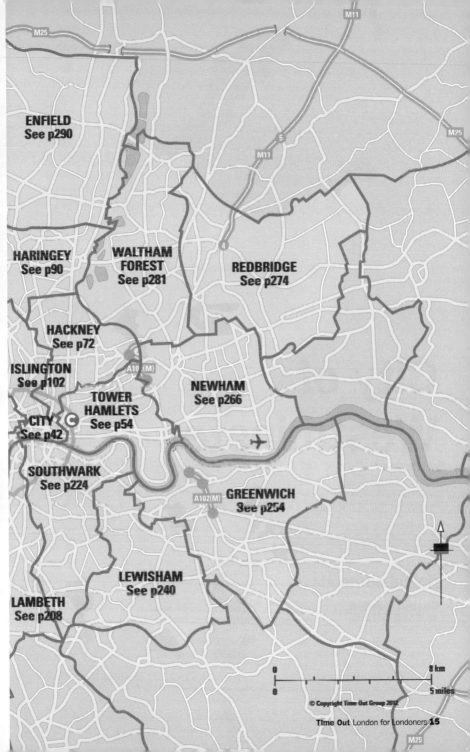

ENFIELD
See p290

HARINGEY
See p90

WALTHAM FOREST
See p281

REDBRIDGE
See p274

HACKNEY
See p72

ISLINGTON
See p102

NEWHAM
See p266

CITY
See p42

TOWER HAMLETS
See p54

SOUTHWARK
See p224

GREENWICH
See p254

LEWISHAM
See p240

LAMBETH
See p208

0   8 km
0   5 miles

© Copyright Time Out Group 2012

'It's like everything in Soho is made out of blue touch paper: one minute it can be quiet and serene, the next it can explode into mayhem.'

Michelle & Tania, Maison Bertaux

City of Westminster

Power, wealth and fame in their most concentrated forms shape the City of Westminster's landscape. Set against a backdrop of much-snapped tourist sights is the busily working, living city, its creative centre earning more than £15 billion a year. Beyond the West End and the corridors of power lies the hectic transport hub of Victoria, along with airy Hyde Park, historic Paddington and, just along the canal, poetic Little Venice.

Neighbourhoods

Covent Garden and the Strand

Though high on every tourist's visiting agenda, Covent Garden is more than an entertainment centre. True, the area is synonymous with the Royal Opera House, hosts daily alfresco entertainment on its central piazza, is surrounded by theatres and has one of London's most popular museums (the Transport Museum). True, too, that it is always thronged with shoppers and merrymakers. Yet there's a big residential community as well, and many independent businesses.

Thirty-five years ago, Covent Garden was still a busy fruit and veg market (to see what it was like, watch Hitchcock's 1972 thriller *Frenzy*). When the wholesale market was moved to Nine Elms, this prime site was in line for redevelopment – roads, office blocks and business hotels were planned.

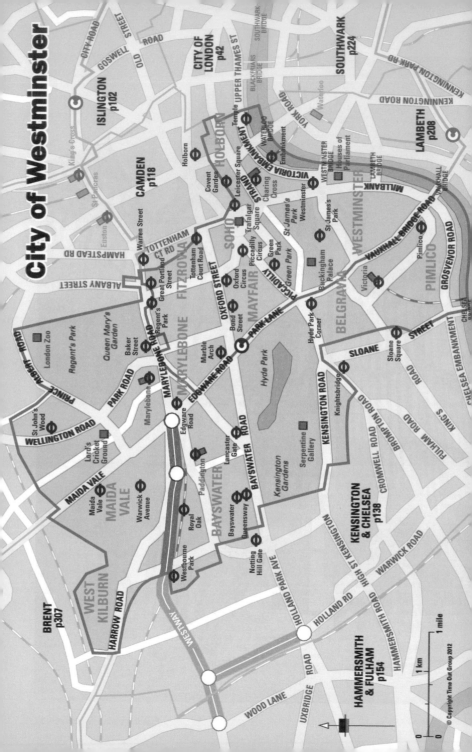

Fortunately, the locals demonstrated and squatted properties, kicking up such a fuss that the area was saved. Today, the residents are a pleasant mix of people. Sure, there's the odd multi-million-pound apartment for sale, but the denizens of such places share amenities with long-term residents and those living in the local Peabody Trust housing, such as Daveys Court on Bedfordbury. More desirable residential areas can be found at Ching Court, off Shelton Street, and the flats opposite Phoenix Garden, a delightful wildlife garden built on an old car park on Stacey Street (enter from St Giles Passage).

Away from the largely pedestrianised streets and community squares, towards Charing Cross Road, the lights of Theatreland meld into the neon of Leicester Square – only worth a visit if you want cheap same-day theatre tickets from the tkts booth, or to catch a film at the only cinema right-minded folk can afford hereabouts, the Prince Charles. Despite serious redevelopment by Westminster Council, it remains a tourist trap, largely shunned by Londoners.

Covent Garden's southern border, the Strand, is rather dull by comparison. Connecting Westminster to the City, the area's saving grace is Somerset House, whose galleries are a peaceful antidote to the overcrowded ice-rink that becomes its centrepiece every winter. The Savoy hotel (open again after a £100 million restoration project) has always attracted rich tourists and expense-accounters, but, come dusk, the homeless still bed down in doorways along the Strand.

Soho and Chinatown

Slippery Soho is a hard place to pin down. Its outline is marked in boisterous fashion by four Circuses: Oxford, St Giles, Cambridge and Piccadilly. The district within – and its southern annex Chinatown – is residential, touristy, intellectual and historically complex, all at the same time.

You'll need to mug up on it. Many Londoners still think it's all about sex and sleaze. Fact is, Soho is a diverse part of the West End that has always been more notable for its hostelries than its sexual favours. Certainly, since censorship laws were relaxed and licensed lap-dancing and strip clubs became more widespread, Soho's sex industry has petered out. It now

consists of a few hardy venues around Berwick Street, which is more popular for its daily street market than its 'fresh new models'. Soho also never lost its hardy residential community. Many residents live above shops and restaurants, which means they must live with challenging levels of noise.

One success story is the restoration of the historic Marshall Street baths, reopened in 2010 as a leisure centre; the Grade II-listed building retains its barrel-vaulted roof and marble floors.

South of Shaftesbury Avenue is the domain of the LCCA (London Chinatown Chinese Association), centred on Gerrard Street; you can't miss its ersatz oriental street trimmings. The Chinese community first opened restaurants and shops here in the 1950s; Chinatown's way of life, like much of Soho, was established in the halcyon days of cheap rents and slummy streets. Today, these streets are valuable real estate.

The Crossrail development is having a huge impact on the area – the legendary Astoria on Charing Cross Road was just one casualty of the project, and the distinctive royal blue Crossrail hoarding is now a familiar sight at the Tottenham Court Road end of Soho. Work here is due to be completed in 2017.

Touristy **Covent Garden Market**.

Holborn

Camden and the City of London muscle in on this purposeful area of central London, where a short walk can take you to the heart of the British legal system (the Inns of Court), to the West End (Covent Garden is but a block away) or to some of London's great museums and seats of learning (the British Museum, the Hunterian Museum, the London School of Economics).

Residential, Holborn is not. There are student halls of residence on High Holborn, where apartment blocks and conversions also yield affordable private homes of the two-bed, one bath variety. Near High Holborn, the Bourne Estate, local authority-owned but Grade II-listed, can sometimes offer one-bed flats around the £350,000 mark, but they're snapped up quickly. Most of Holborn's more affordable property tends to be on the Covent Garden side of Kingsway. Here, flats – often in big Victorian buildings such as decommissioned primary schools – make up the stock. Minutes from Holborn tube, crossing the border into Camden borough, quiet Macklin Street and Newton Street have a number of such conversions. Queen Square, north of High Holborn, is also a favoured (expensive) residential area. Mostly, however, property around here – especially anywhere near beautiful Lincoln's Inn Fields – is likely to cost around £1 million, and there are very few unconverted houses.

Amusingly, given the price of property, nearby Carey Street provides its own euphemism for being in debt ('on Carey Street'), which comes from the fact that the back entrance to the Royal Courts of Justice is on it. Debtors were clearly expected to shuffle in through the back door. On a brighter (even twinkly) note, Carey Street is home to the Seven Stars pub, known for its food, atmosphere and glamorous proprietor, the one and only Roxy Beaujolais.

Mayfair

You have to be ultra-rich to afford a home in Mayfair, London's most blue-blooded district, where a two-bed apartment might cost about £3 million. If you're not into looks, or cat-swinging, there are some modern red-brick blocks around Shepherd Market, where a studio would cost about £400,000.

Bordered by the weighty thoroughfares of Piccadilly, Park Lane and Oxford Street, Mayfair's posh squares and salubrious streets seem by turns hushed and imperious. No nightingales sing in Berkeley Square, but the historic Guinea pub, a delightfully unpretentious drinking den on the north-east corner of Bruton Place, will put a song in your heart. Shepherd Market is Mayfair's real-life bit, still dealing in the pleasures of life. It's named after an early 18th-century food market and famed for its prostitutes (although there are fewer here these days). There are chocolate shops, good restaurants and a couple of nice little boozers. Nearby Farm Street is the kind of residential area most Londoners, if they're truthful, would admit to aspiring to. The pretty local library, on South Audley Street, speaks of a lucky, literate residential community.

West of Park Lane is the wonderful expanse of Hyde Park. Here you'll find Speakers' Corner, beloved of loons and free-speech advocates, and the Serpentine Gallery, host of adventurous modern art

Highs & Lows

▲ **City centre** If you want to feel like you're in the beating heart of the capital, this has got to be the borough to live in.
Accessibility The City of Westminster has more tube stations than any other London borough – 30 in all.
Cutting-edge libraries Busy borrowers in Westminster libraries can use self-service checkouts that read your library card, allowing you to take out books without dealing with cardigan-wearing librarians.

Noise levels People living in Soho or Covent Garden have always had to contend with late-night shenanigans, but since the law forced smokers outside the problem has become much louder.
Big money for titchy flats You'll have to search long and hard to find anything approaching a bargain.
Refuse collectors The lorries seem to be out 24/7. There's an awful lot of rubbish to pick up every day in this part of town, and Westminster City Council is conscientious about its collection. ▼

Budget bites: **Canela**, a Portuguese/Brazilian café in Covent Garden. See p28.

and architecture. As Hyde Park becomes Kensington Gardens, it enters the Royal Borough of Kensington & Chelsea.

Marylebone

Twenty or so years ago, Marylebone was a reasonably affordable part of Westminster. You could pick up a two-bedroom flat for about £300,000. Today, Marylebone rents and property prices match those of its expensive neighbours. The rebranding of the pretty High Street – despite having Oxford Street just to the south, it could belong to an affluent provincial town – into desirable 'Marylebone Village' has been a roaring success. Now everyone wants a piece of Marylebone and its lovely quiet squares.

The area isn't all luxury cashmere babywear and Nigella's favourite cheese shop, though. Radiating out from the village are less appealing streets. When it first grew up, this parish – St Mary by the Bourn – was known for its criminal population, many of whom ended up swinging from Tyburn gallows, where Marble Arch is now. Although nowhere is exactly rough around here, the thunderingly busy Marylebone Road is not a particularly pleasant place to linger. However, it does have a splendid old town hall – Westminster Council House – which is both the local library and a

classic London wedding venue, its steps always strewn with rose petals and rice.

Lisson Grove, which heads north-west from here, was once all slums: 'it wasn't fit for a pig to live in!' (*Pygmalion*). Much of the housing stock is ex-council. While the large Lisson Green Estate overlooking the canal can be intimidating, the streets between Lisson Grove and Edgware Road are more enticing. There are bargains to be had, but visit the area at different times of day so you know what you're getting into. Still on the Grove (but at the other end of the market), the gated Belvedere development has two-bed flats for £500,000, and there's a small supply of bijou Georgian houses. Otherwise, you might want to look into buying one of the houseboats on the canal.

Bell Street is one of the more interesting roads hereabouts, with the area's only art gallery (the Lisson), plus a couple of second-hand bookshops. The other standout is Church Street, which has a weekend market but is otherwise almost completely given over to antiques shops, drawn by Alfie's Antique Market with its fine rooftop café.

New building in the as-yet-unprettified quarter of Baker Street, such as the redevelopment of the old Marks & Spencer building, is throwing more housing into the Marylebone mix. Much of it is expensive – but then, you would be living next to the

formal flower beds, waterfowl lakes and playing fields of Regent's Park, and close to London Zoo.

Fitzrovia

Portland Place, the home of the BBC's Broadcasting House, separates Marylebone from medialand. Fitzrovia is a district that lies east of Great Portland Street, bordered by Euston Road to the north, Oxford Street to the south and Tottenham Court Road to the east. The name comes from Fitzroy Square (on the Camden side), built by one Honourable Charles Fitzroy in the 18th century.

Unlike its neighbours, Marylebone and Bloomsbury, in which lofty terraces, crescents and squares were created by empire-building wealthy landowners, Fitzrovia was developed on a smaller scale by minor landowners. This left the streets feeling less well organised, but the area has a low-key, arty, crafty and business-like vibe. There are a few fashion wholesale businesses, an increasing number of new-media offices, a giant hole where the old Middlesex Hospital was (now moved to University College Hospital on Euston Road), the famous BT Tower, and loads of restaurants, cafés and pubs.

The Fitzrovia Neighbourhood Association on Tottenham Street is used by local organisations for meetings. The association was established (with the battle cry 'The people live here') in the 1970s, when the area's residents stood up against would-be developers, and is in action today as a prime mover in the battle against unsympathetic development of the Middlesex Hospital site.

Westminster and St James's

The wider borough is called the City of Westminster, but this inner circle, built up around the Abbey, takes the Westminster name for itself. Happily snapping tourists throng around Parliament Square and its star sights year round. It's a conservation area designated by UNESCO as a World Heritage Site, and central Westminster is kept spick and span for guests. The tube station is clean and impressively modern, and the made-over and traffic-calmed central precinct, Trafalgar Square, is London's 'best room', site of the Mayor of London's series of free seasonal festivals and events. Here, the famous Norwegian spruce is put up with much ceremony every

winter before Christmas, and a very slowly changing art exhibition is hosted on Sir Charles Barry's statulesss Fourth Plinth: for 2012, it's Elmgreen & Dragset's boy on a rocking horse, cast in bronze; 2013 sees a giant cockerel in ultramarine blue by Katharina Fritsch.

Connecting the two public squares is Whitehall, where tourists derive huge pleasure from photographing themselves with Household Cavalry troopers. This is a po-faced land of civil servants, and the ministries that line the road (as well as the heavily guarded, security-gated Downing Street) are strictly off-limits.

Going west from here, gorgeous St James's Park, famed for its waterfowl (notably the pelicans), is far prettier than Green Park, which provides a pleasant walk to a seat of privilege, rather than power: Buckingham Palace. The network of elderly streets bounded by the parks, Vauxhall Bridge Road and Millbank (home to the headquarters of the Security Service, MI5), are peaceful, atmospheric and largely residential. You can tell if someone important lives in one of the houses if there's an armed policeman outside.

Moving through Peter Street, Old Pye Street and Marsham Street returns you to community Westminster. There are Peabody estates for low-paid key workers round here – it can't be bad having Westminster Abbey as your local church.

Victoria

Like many areas in Zone 1, Victoria is defined by its transport terminuses. The streets around them are crowded, dominated by backpackers, package tourists, commuters and various other scuttlers on their way somewhere else. The transitory nature of the area has long encouraged residents to insist they live in less frenetic-sounding neighbouring areas – Pimlico, Belgravia, even Westminster. Victoria Street, the main street linking Parliament Square to Victoria station is full of chain stores, with only the 1903 Roman Catholic cathedral offering interest (to Catholics and those looking to enjoy the fabulous views from the campanile).

Badly needed redevelopment of Victoria station, notably the tube station, is underway: completion is set for 2018, so people arriving here face a messy introduction to the capital for a while yet.

Pimlico

Pimlico started off very smartly, with Thomas Cubitt building white stucco dwellings and garden squares for Lord Grosvenor in 1825. When land was sold off and charitable housing body the Peabody Trust built estates for the poor here, the smart money lost interest. After World War II, large public housing estates were built on the area's bombsites and fine houses were converted into flats, so all pretence to exclusivity was lost for decades.

Still, Pimlico is central, and pockets of Zone 1 smartness give the whole district panache. In fact, property of any calibre is expensive here. Pimlico's extensive Westminster Council housing stock, all managed by CityWest Homes, includes the Lillington Gardens Estate. Off Tachbrook Street, this high-density, low-rise, red-brick estate, built in the 1970s, has Grade II-listed status. Hide Tower, on Regency Street, was built in the late 1950s and is run by a tenant management organisation. Its flats have fantastic views over London and attract high prices. Hide competes with nearby Tate Britain as the area's most recognisable building since landmark brutalist building Pimlico School was demolished in 2010.

Down by the river is Dolphin Square, a self-contained village of pieds-à-terre for important (and wealthy) people. The fortress-like, red-brick 1930s block has a health club, smart restaurant and a little art deco parade of shops. Such exclusivity is absent in the Westminster Boating Base, with headquarters on the river, just across Grosvenor Road. This charitable trust has been teaching urban youth the joys of watersports for more than 30 years.

Belgravia

Pimlico and Victoria folk enjoy the reflected glory their proximity to Belgravia affords them. Belgravia, however, remains aloof. Like Mayfair, it gets its blue blood from the aristocratic Grosvenor family who still own much of it. Richard Grosvenor, second Marquess of Westminster, commissioned Thomas Cubitt to develop it in the 1820s; Belgrave and Eaton Squares, with their white stucco mansions, are the result. Today, the responsibility for managing the estate falls to Gerald, sixth Duke of Westminster, and Grosvenor is an international property group.

The area has never been anything other than posh. When World War II initiated the decline of whacking great Belgravian homes, the mansions were simply converted for use as embassies and institutes; today, the super-rich are reclaiming the stucco palaces as desirable homes.

It's a refined, rarefied area, and the shops, restaurants, mews houses and garden squares all reflect this. Around Elizabeth Street, toward Ebury Street and the Sloaney end of Pimlico Road, are shops of privilege, but Peabody social housing also has a foothold – in the shape of a gorgeously

Denbigh Street in **Pimlico**, also known as 'Stuccoville'.

picturesque balconied terrace: Lumley Flats on the Pimlico Road. Otherwise, anything vaguely vulgar, such as supermarkets, office blocks and entertainment venues, has been kept firmly out of the enchanted garden. One advantage of Belgravia's refusal to join the real world is the fact that pubs originally built as modest affairs (for servants of the resident aristocracy) have not been superseded by big chain boozers.

Bayswater

Westminster's most multifaceted district, Bayswater is a pleasing mix of once-grand mansions, hotels, architecturally significant pleasure palaces and great places to eat and drink. Being Westminster, there's nowhere really cheap to live, although the odd run-down bedsit in some of the scruffier terraces around Queensborough Terrace might be good value. Bayswater's big council estate, Hallfield, designed by Sir Denys Lasdun, gives its residents spectacular views over west London from top-floor flats that are very much in demand on the private market.

Queensway is Bayswater's backbone and is one big, noisy conservation area. The splendid Edwardian Whiteleys shopping centre, the largest in central London, is located here. The rest of the street is full of Middle Eastern cafés and restaurants. To the south lie Kensington Gardens and the excellent playground dedicated to the memory of the late Princess of Wales. The built-up areas of Paddington and Bayswater both gain from their proximity to these royal green acres, which merge to the east with Hyde Park. At the northern end of Queensway lies the beautiful Porchester Centre, one of the few surviving examples of the Victorian Turkish baths that once proliferated in Britain. West of Queensway, on Moscow Road, the Greek Orthodox Cathedral of St Sophia, with its Byzantine icons and golden mosaics, adds to the area's cosmopolitan charm.

North of Bayswater lies Westbourne Green, a high priority area for Westminster Council's regeneration plans. Its challenging position between Harrow Road and the Westway does the place few favours, but impressive openings, such as the Westminster Academy secondary school and Stowe Community Centre, are bringing new hope to an area dominated by high-rise council homes. See www.westbourne green.com for more details.

Paddington

Strange as it may seem, only a few years ago the most noteworthy aspect of chaotic Paddington was its station, a lofty example of Victorian engineering, built to the specifications of Isambard Kingdom Brunel, the glazed roof giving shelter to thousands of commuters and a small bronze statue of a certain bear. Today, all the excitement is beyond the station. The swankily rejuvenated Paddington Basin, once a neglected body of water forming the terminus of the Grand Junction Canal, is now desirable real estate. It has walkways, pedestrian-friendly towpaths and new bridges that allow strollers to circumnavigate the whole basin for the first time in its history. Look out for the Rolling Bridge, built in eight triangular sections that can be curled up to allow water traffic to pass. (This happens every Friday at noon.) The whole area is surrounded by gorgeous, gleaming new-builds, one of which is the new Marks & Spencer headquarters.

Away from this 21st-century ideal of waterside living, inland Paddington, once deplored for its overcrowding and vice, is still plagued by traffic chaos and a preponderance of rather down-at-heel terraces. The northern edge of the district has the Westway roaring through it (as well as Paddington Green high-security police station, where terrorist suspects are questioned). North of the Westway, the Paddington Green conservation area is centred on St Mary's Church and the children's hospital. The surrounding streets have some 19th-century stucco houses and well-tended mansion flats that date from the mid 20th century.

Going south, Westbourne Terrace, towards Bayswater, was hailed as the finest street in London in its heyday. It still has some fantastically handsome houses that, in common with those on many of the roads running from Paddington to Hyde Park, command high prices.

Maida Vale

When Robert Browning coined the term 'Little Venice', he was describing the point where the Paddington arm of the Grand Union Canal meets the Regent's Canal. South Maida Vale's most poetic citizen is remembered forever at friendly Browning's Pool, where pelargonium-adorned

narrowboats contain cafés, galleries and the Puppet Theatre Barge. Continuing west on the canal path leads the unwary to the rather less attractive Westbourne Green and its tower blocks. Instead stroll east along the towpath, which will bring you to Regent's Park.

The area around Little Venice and Clifton Gardens is an affluent part of town. The houses are tall, white stucco and the shops are geared to the luxury market. More affordable accommodation is available north-west towards Paddington Recreation Ground, at Maida Vale's northerly extreme. Here, Kilburn craic starts to impinge on Maida Vale's sanity. Elgin Avenue bisects the district west to east, and the pretty, residential roads that lead off it are lined by solid Victorian terraces with wrought-iron balconies and by handsome blocks of well-proportioned mansion flats. It's a quiet, cosy part of the world, with few shops and businesses. The handsome flats of Westside Court and pretty Delaware Road are much sought after.

St John's Wood

Smart, desirable and pricey, St John's Wood is a northerly outpost of Westminster that's just too quirky to be labelled a mere suburb. Although its stucco villas, opacious 19th-century housing and well-maintained purpose-built apartment buildings – the last dating from careful 1950s redevelopment – all reek of provincial prosperity, the Wood has global appeal. The biggest attraction is Lord's Cricket Ground, which keeps the area busy all summer. The second biggest is the Fab Four association: the famous Abbey Road recording studios and *that* zebra crossing. St John's Wood High Street has a good number of independent stores, as well as top-end chains. The area has always been wealthy, and its proximity to gracious Regent's Park keeps house prices high. More affordable property can be found in the apartment blocks along busy St John's Wood Road, but these are more often available as short-term lets.

West Kilburn

As you travel north, the City of Westminster's furthest-flung district seems too ordinary to be of the same borough; indeed, road signs announce the imminent onset of Brent. At West Kilburn's heart is the Queen's Park Estate, built from 1874 as dwellings for labourers. It is now extremely popular with people who feel the need to be associated, by postcode, with trendy Ladbroke Grove and Notting Hill in the Royal Borough of Kensington & Chelsea. The houses on the estate are small, but the exteriors are ornate and they are beautifully put together. Some heartache ensues when children happen along and residents have to move to bigger, still more expensive houses around Kensal Rise. At least here, young families are near enough to the large, family-friendly Corporation of London Queen's Park on the other side of the railway tracks. Elsewhere in West Kilburn, there are tall blocks of council flats, which save the district from excessive ponciness.

Restaurants & cafés

Westminster locals have some of the capital's finest dining on their doorstep. For starters, check out what's below; for the whole menu, see the *Time Out London Eating & Drinking Guide* or, for the latest openings, check out *Time Out* magazine.

Soho's restaurants run the gamut from sleek and chic (dim sum specialist Yauatcha) to heartily fuss-free (sausage, pie and mash merchant Mother Mash), covering countless cuisines and specialities along the way. Stalwarts include L'Escargot Marco Pierre White (classic French), Andrew Edmunds (Modern European) and Gay Hussar (Hungarian). More recent additions such as Arbutus (Modern European), Hix (British) and Barshu (Sichuan) have also made their mark on the neighbourhood. Laid-back breakfast, lunch and snack options are provided by the likes of the Breakfast Club, Hummus Bros and the various branches of Fernandez & Wells.

Old-school Italian Vasco & Piero's Pavilion has been joined by the fashionable Polpo and Bocca di Lupo. Other communities are also represented: Caribbean (Jerk City); Korean (Myung Ga); North American (Bodean's, Spuntino); Japanese (Kulu Kulu); and Indian (Masala Zone for value, Red Fort for class).

Many more oriental choices lie south of Shaftesbury Avenue. Chinatown cannot lay claim to producing London's best Chinese food, but locals have the likes of dim sum specialist Imperial China and newcomer Manchurian Legends at their disposal.

Along Long Acre and into Covent Garden, tourist traps abound, although there are plenty of quality places to eat if you know where to look: unpretentious British restaurant Great Queen Street, for starters. For a handy lunchtime pit-stop Portuguese/Brazilian café Canela is the ticket, while Rock & Sole Plaice and Food for Thought serve up fish and chips and veggie fare, respectively. You'll find celeb hangouts J Sheekey (fish) and the Ivy (Modern European) on suitably discreet backstreets, and hot new openings the Delaunay (grand European brasserie) and Mishkin's (a hip take on a Jewish deli) are within a few streets of each other. Upmarket chains include the Carluccio's flagship on Garrick Street and modern Mexican restaurant Wahaca nearby. Near the river, in Somerset House, there's a big branch of Fernandez & Wells, plus Tom's Kitchen and Tom's Deli.

Upmarket Mayfair hosts some of Britain's most celebrated chefs: Gordon Ramsay at Claridge's; Michel Roux at Le Gavroche. Other excellent examples of haute cuisine here include the inventive Greenhouse restaurant and Gordon Ramsay-owned Maze. Mayfair is also where to find classic Scott's (fish), inventive Wild Honey, and smart Japanese (Nobu), Indian (Tamarind) and Chinese (China Tang) restaurants. Towards Piccadilly, the swanky must-visits include Bentley's Oyster Bar & Grill and glam grand-café the Wolseley.

Marylebone is less showy, but there's plenty of excellent (and far more affordable) eating to be had. Cafés are a forte, notably the one at La Fromagerie (*see p36*) and, in Regent's Park, the retro-chic Garden Café. A branch of Thai canteen Busaba Eathai and family-friendly Giraffe also provide quick bites. Top Italian Locanda Locatelli is on Seymour Street; other highlights include smashing fish and chips at the Golden Hind, a decent kosher restaurant (Reuben's) and Oliver Peyton's gallery restaurant the Wallace. Towards Marble Arch, in the Cumberland Hotel, is Gary Rhodes's fine-dining restaurant Rhodes W1.

Fitzrovia's dining district is centred on Charlotte Street, on the border between Westminster and Camden. Away from Charlotte Street but firmly in the City of Westminster, is Riding House Café (brasserie), Özer (classy Turkish) and restaurant-bar-deli Villandry.

Westminster contains a few choice venues. Cinnamon Club is one of London's best posh Indian restaurants; Bank Westminster is good for crowd-pleasing Modern European fare. St James's, meanwhile, has a rarefied vibe, as exemplified by the very grand Wiltons; Green's is in a similar upmarket vein. Inn The Park is a breakfast-to-dinner British restaurant in leafy St James's Park.

Primarily a residential area, Pimlico has a smattering of restaurants, including Seafresh (fish and chips), Rex Whistler Restaurant at Tate Britain (Mod Euro), the Orange (gastropub) and Tinello (smart Italian). In Belgravia, restaurants have a quietly sophisticated appeal. Sardinian-influenced fish restaurant Olivomare is a choice destination, as is first-rate Chinese venue Hunan. Close by is classic French eaterie Roussillon, while further up towards Eccleston Street are Olivo (sister to Olivomare) and gastropub the Ebury.

Celeb-favourite the Cow gastropub is officially in the City of Westminster, though it feels more like Notting Hill than Bayswater. Queensway, meanwhile, holds some superb Chinese restaurants, including the flagship venue of dim sum specialist Royal China. Other good bets include Assaggi (Italian), Hereford Road (British) and, in Whiteleys, Le Café Anglais (Modern European).

The development of Paddington Basin has given the area's dining a much-needed boost in the form of beautiful Chinese restaurant Pearl Liang. Malaysian venue Satay House is another excellent eaterie. For further choices, head for the Edgware Road, where Middle Eastern is the gastronomic strength: try the late-opening Ranoush Juice Bar for kebabs and juices. Also here is Mandalay, London's only Burmese restaurant.

Maida Vale's restaurants cater to affluent locals. Try Raoul's (daytime brunch, night-time Mediterranean) or Red Pepper (pizza and pasta). There's also a branch of bakery Baker & Spice. Eateries along St John's Wood High Street feed well-heeled shoppers, who ogle pastries at Maison Blanc or tuck into Jewish dishes at Harry Morgan's.

Andrew Edmunds *46 Lexington Street, W1F 0LW (7437 5708).*
Arbutus *63-64 Frith Street, W1D 3JW (7734 4545, www.arbutusrestaurant.co.uk).*

Clifton Nurseries in Maida Vale, London's oldest garden centre.

Assaggi *1st floor, 39 Chepstow Place, W2 4TS (7792 5501).*
Baker & Spice *20 Clifton Road, W9 13U (7289 2499, www.bakerandspice.uk.com).*
Bank Westminster *45 Buckingham Gate, SW1E 6BS (7630 6644, www.bank restaurants.com).*
Barshu *28 Frith Street, W1D 5LF (7287 6688, www.bar-shu.co.uk).*
Bentley's Oyster Bar & Grill *11-15 Swallow Street, W1B 4DG (7734 4756, www.bentleys oysterbarandgrill.co.uk)*
Bocca di Lupo *12 Archer Street, W1D 7BB (7734 2223, www.boccadilupo.com).*
Bodean's *10 Poland Street, W1F 8PZ (7287 7575, www.bodeansbbq.com).*
Breakfast Club *33 D'Arblay Street, W1F 8EU (7434 2571, www.thebreakfastclubcafes.com).*
Busaba Eathai *8-13 Bird Street, W1U 1BU (7518 8080, www.busaba.com).*
Le Café Anglais *8 Porchester Gardens, W2 4DB (7221 1415, www.lecafeanglais.co.uk).*
Canela *33 Earlham Street, WC2H 9LS (7240 6926, www.canelacafe.com).*

Carluccio's Caffè *26 Garrick Street, WC2E 9BH (7836 0990, www.carluccios.com).*
China Tang *The Dorchester, 53 Park Lane, W1K 1QA (7629 9988, www.thedorchester.com).*
Cinnamon Club *Old Westminster Library, 30-32 Great Smith Street, SW1P 3BU (7222 2555, www.cinnamonclub.com).*
Cow *89 Westbourne Park Road, W2 5QH (7221 0021, www.thecowlondon.co.uk).*
Delaunay *55 Aldwych, WC2B 4BB (7499 8558, www.thedelaunay.com).*
Ebury *11 Pimlico Road, SW1W 8NA (7730 6784, www.theebury.co.uk).*
L'Escargot Marco Pierre White *48 Greek Street, W1D 4EF (7439 7474, www.lescargot restaurant.co.uk).*
Fernandez & Wells
www.fernandezandwells.com; Somerset House, Strand, WC2R 0RN (7420 9408); 16A St Anne's Court, W1F 0BH (7494 4242); 43 Lexington Street, W1F 9AL (7734 1546); 73 Beak Street, W1F 9RS (7287 8124).
Food for Thought *31 Neal Street, WC2H 9PR (7836 0239/9072).*

Garden Café *Inner Circle, Regent's Park, NW1 4NU (7935 5729, www.thegardencafe.co.uk).*
Le Gavroche *43 Upper Brook Street, W1K 7QR (7408 0881, www.le-gavroche.co.uk).*
Gay Hussar *2 Greek Street, W1D 4NB (7437 0973, www.gayhussar.co.uk).*
Giraffe *6-8 Blandford Street, W1U 4AU (7935 2333, www.giraffe.net).*
Golden Hind *73 Marylebone Lane, W1U 2PN (7486 3644).*
Gordon Ramsay at Claridge's *Claridge's, Brook Street, W1K 4HR (7499 0099, www.gordonramsay.com).*
Great Queen Street *32 Great Queen Street, WC2B 5AA (7242 0622).*
Greenhouse *27A Hay's Mews, W1J 5NY (7499 3331, www.greenhouserestaurant.co.uk).*
Green's *36 Duke Street, SW1Y 6DF (7930 4566, www.greens.org.uk).*
Harry Morgan's *29-31 St John's Wood High Street, NW8 7NH (7722 1869, www.harryms.co.uk).*
Hereford Road *3 Hereford Road, W2 4AB (7727 1144, www.herefordroad.org).*
Hix *66-70 Brewer Street, W1F 9UP (7292 3518, www.hixsoho.co.uk).*
Hummus Bros *88 Wardour Street, W1F 0TH (7734 1311, www.hbros.co.uk).*
Hunan *51 Pimlico Road, SW1W 8NE (7730 5712, www.hunanlondon.com).*
Imperial China *White Bear Yard, 25A Lisle Street, WC2H 7BA (7734 3388, www.imperial-china.co.uk).*
Inn The Park *St James's Park, SW1A 2BJ (7451 9999, www.innthepark.co.uk).*
The Ivy *1-5 West Street, WC2H 9NQ (7836 4751, www.the-ivy.co.uk).*
Jerk City *189 Wardour Street, W1F 8ZD (7287 2878, www.jerkcity.co.uk).*
J Sheekey *28-34 St Martin's Court, WC2N 4AL (7240 2565, www.j-sheekey.co.uk).*
Kulu Kulu *76 Brewer Street, W1F 9TX (7734 7316).*
Locanda Locatelli *8 Seymour Street, W1H 7JZ (7935 9088, www.locandalocatelli.com).*
Maison Blanc *37 St John's Wood High Street, NW8 7NG (7586 1982, www.maison blanc.co.uk).*
Manchurian Legends *12 Macclesfield Street, W1D 5BP (7437 8785, www.manchurian legends.com).*
Mandalay *444 Edgware Road, W2 1EG (7258 3696, www.mandalayway.com).*
Masala Zone *9 Marshall Street, W1F 7ER (7287 9966, www.masalazone.com).*
Maze *10-13 Grosvenor Square, W1K 6JP (7107 0000, www.gordonramsay.com).*

Mishkin's *25 Catherine Street, WC2B 5JS (7240 2078, www.mishkins.co.uk).*
Mother Mash *26 Ganton Street, W1F 7QZ (7494 9644, www.mothermash.co.uk).*
Myung Ga *1 Kingly Street, W1B 5PA (7734 8220, www.myungga.co.uk).*
Nobu *Metropolitan Hotel, 19 Old Park Lane, W1K 1LB (7447 4747, www.nobu restaurants.com).*
Olivo *21 Eccleston Street, SW1W 9LX (7730 2505, www.olivorestaurants.com).*
Olivomare *10 Lower Belgrave Street, SW1W 0LJ (7730 9022, www.olivorestaurants.com).*
Orange *37 Pimlico Road, SW1W 8NE (7881 9844, www.theorange.co.uk).*
Özer *5 Langham Place, W1B 3DG (7323 0505, www.ozerrestaurant.com).*
Pearl Liang *8 Sheldon Square, W2 6EZ (7289 7000, www.pearlliang.co.uk).*
Polpo *41 Beak Street, W1F 9SB (7734 4479, www.polpo.co.uk).*
Ranoush Juice Bar *43 Edgware Road, W2 2JR (7723 5929).*
Raoul's *13 Clifton Road, W9 1SZ (7289 7313, www.raoulsgourmet.com).*
Red Fort *77 Dean Street, W1D 3SH (7437 2525, www.redfort.co.uk).*
Red Pepper *8 Formosa Street, W9 1EE (7266 2708, www.theredpepper.net).*
Reuben's *79 Baker Street, W1U 6RG (7486 0035, www.reubensrestaurant.co.uk).*
Rex Whistler Restaurant at Tate Britain *Tate Britain, Millbank, SW1P 4RG (7887 8825, www.tate.org.uk).*
Rhodes W1 *The Cumberland, Great Cumberland Place, W1H 7DL (7616 5930, www.rhodesw1.com).*
Riding House Café *43-51 Great Titchfield Street, W1W 7PQ (8968 0202, www.ridinghousecafe.co.uk).*
Rock & Sole Plaice *47 Endell Street, WC2H 9AJ (7836 3785).*
Roussillon *16 St Barnabas Street, SW1W 8PE (7730 5550, www.roussillon.co.uk).*
Royal China *13 Queensway, W2 4QJ (7221 2535, www.royalchinagroup.co.uk).*
Satay House *13 Sale Place, W2 1PX (7723 6763, www.satay-house.co.uk).*
Scott's *20 Mount Street, W1K 2HE (7495 7309, www.caprice-holdings.co.uk).*
Seafresh Fish Restaurant *80-81 Wilton Road, SW1V 1DL (7828 0747, www.fish andchipsinlondon.com).*
Tamarind *20 Queen Street, W1J 5PR (7629 3561, www.tamarindrestaurant.com).*
Tinello *87 Pimlico Road, SW1W 8PH (7730 3663, www.tinello.co.uk).*

Tom's Deli *Somerset House, Strand, WC2R 1LA (www.somersethouse.org.uk).*

Tom's Kitchen *South Wing, Somerset House, Strand, WC2R 1LA (7845 4646, www.toms kitchen.co.uk).*

Vasco & Piero's Pavilion *15 Poland Street, W1F 8QE (7437 8774, www.vascosfood.com).*

Villandry *170 Great Portland Street, W1W 5QB (7631 3131, www.villandry.com).*

Wahaca *www.wahaca.co.uk; 66 Chandos Place, WC2N 4HG (7240 1883); 80 Wardour Street, W1F 0TF (7734 0195).*

Wallace *Wallace Collection, Hertford House, Manchester Square, W1U 3BN (7563 9505, www.peylonandbyrne.co.uk).*

Wild Honey *12 St George Street, W1S 2FB (7758 9160, www.wildhoneyrestaurant.co.uk).*

Wiltons *55 Jermyn Street, SW1Y 6LX (7629 9955, www.wiltons.co.uk).*

Wolseley *160 Piccadilly, W1J 9EB (7499 6996, www.thewolseley.com).*

Yauatcha *15-17 Broadwick Street, W1F 0DL (7494 8888, www.yauatcha.com).*

Bars & pubs

Westminster attracts a massive influx of revellers – provincials, tourists and local workers; club kids, bar-crawlers and gay-scene posers – so for residents the dream of a cosy local where everyone knows your name can seem destined to remain just that. It doesn't take too much surface-scratching to sort the wheat from the chaff, though. Below are a few essentials, for more, consult *Time Out London's Best Bars*.

Out-of-towners flock to the big-name locations – Covent Garden, Leicester Square, Soho – with predictable crowd-inducing, nitrokeg-downing results. Venture just a few streets from Covent Garden Piazza, however, and there are plenty of drinking holes worth sinking into for the evening. Traditional old boozers such as the Lamb & Flag (packed to its bare beams after 5pm) and the ultra-cosy Cross Keys are good places to start. Benelux bar Lowlander has a relaxed vibe and great beers, while just off the Strand are two newer subterranean venues – Bedford & Strand (sophisticated wine bar) and CellarDoor (tiny, mirrored bar in a converted public toilet). Also near the Strand are friendly pub the Nell Gwynne and below-street-level wine bar Gordon's. Near Leicester Square, basement wine bar

the Cork & Bottle is a good escape from the hordes, as is Gallic venue Le Beaujolais.

Soho draws hedonists of all persuasions from across London, the UK and beyond – and it's diverse enough to accommodate the lot. The gay scene is focused on the west end of Old Compton Street, around the Admiral Duncan, Comptons of Soho and, north up Wardour Street, Village Soho; lesbians have the Candy Bar. Barflies should try the likes of Milk & Honey (non-members need to book ahead), Two Floors, Mark's Bar and the Experimental Cocktail Club; pub fans will enjoy historic old boozers the French House, the Old Coffee House and the lovely little Dog & Duck. For something a bit different, show off your talents in one of the private karaoke rooms at Lucky Voice.

Holborn has several drinking dens to be proud of, including the gorgeous Seven Stars and gastropub the Bountiful Cow (both owned by local name Roxy Beaujolais). Former journalists' pub the Edgar Wallace has great real ales; for something slicker, try the dramatic Lobby Bar in the One Aldwych hotel.

In Mayfair, swanky hotel bars rule: try Claridge's Bar, the Donovan Bar, the David Collins-designed Connaught Bar or Galvin at Windows. Alternatively, join young royals and trustafarians at pricey Hawaiian club Mahiki.

Marylebone residents have plenty to choose from; notable choices include the patriotic Windsor Castle on Crawford Place (one of two such named pubs in the vicinity) or the traditional Golden Eagle (complete with round-the-piano pub singalongs). For a touch of swank, try the Langham Hotel's Artesian.

Some of Fitzrovia's best bars are officially in Camden, but among those in the City of Westminster are the Sanderson's Long Bar and DJ bar the Social. Alternatively, sink a pint at the cosy Newman Arms or bargain Sam Smith's boozers the Cock Tavern and Champion.

In Westminster, politicians cram into Parliament Street's Red Lion, complete with a (currently broken) division bell, while the bar at the Cinnamon Club (*see p29*) offers a sophisticated place to unwind. Zander Bar at Bank Westminster is also worth a look. St James's has the old-school pub vibe sewn up with three Lions to its name – two Red (on Crown Passage and Duke of York Street)

FILLING THE TOWN WITH ARTISTS

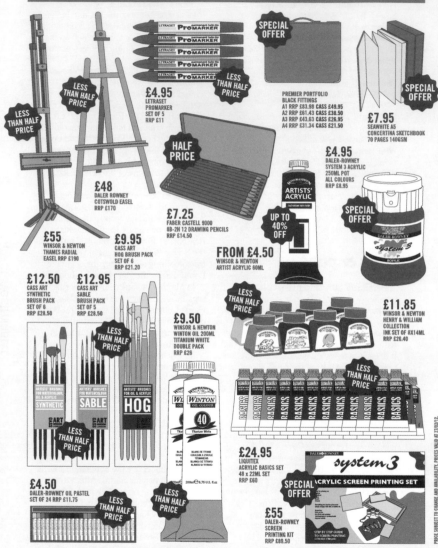

£4.95
LETRASET
PROMARKER
SET OF 5
RRP £11

SPECIAL OFFER

PREMIER PORTFOLIO
BLACK FITTINGS
A1 RRP £83.98 CASS £49.95
A2 RRP £61.43 CASS £38.50
A3 RRP £43.63 CASS £26.95
A4 RRP £31.34 CASS £21.50

SPECIAL OFFER

£7.95
SEAWHITE A5
CONCERTINA SKETCHBOOK
70 PAGES 140GSM

LESS THAN HALF PRICE

LESS THAN HALF PRICE

HALF PRICE

£48
DALER ROWNEY
COTSWOLD EASEL
RRP £170

£7.25
FABER CASTELL 9000
8B–2H 12 DRAWING PENCILS
RRP £14.50

£4.95
DALER-ROWNEY
SYSTEM 3 ACRYLIC
250ML POT
ALL COLOURS
RRP £8.95

SPECIAL OFFER

UP TO 40% OFF

£55
WINSOR & NEWTON
THAMES RADIAL
EASEL RRP £190

£9.95
CASS ART
HOG BRUSH PACK
SET OF 6
RRP £21.20

FROM £4.50
WINSOR & NEWTON
ARTIST ACRYLIC 60ML

£12.50
CASS ART
SYNTHETIC
BRUSH PACK
SET OF 6
RRP £28.50

£12.95
CASS ART
SABLE
BRUSH PACK
SET OF 5
RRP £28.50

LESS THAN HALF PRICE

£11.85
WINSOR & NEWTON
HENRY & WILLIAM
COLLECTION
INK SET OF 6X14ML
RRP £26.40

LESS THAN HALF PRICE

£9.50
WINSOR & NEWTON
WINTON OIL 200ML
TITANIUM WHITE
DOUBLE PACK
RRP £26

LESS THAN HALF PRICE

SYNTHETIC

SABLE

HOG

WINTON
OIL COLOUR
40
Titanium White

BASICS

LESS THAN HALF PRICE

£24.95
LIQUITEX
ACRYLIC BASICS SET
48 x 22ML SET
RRP £60

£4.50
DALER-ROWNEY OIL PASTEL
SET OF 24 RRP £11.75

LESS THAN HALF PRICE

LESS THAN HALF PRICE

SPECIAL OFFER

£55
DALER-ROWNEY
SCREEN
PRINTING KIT
RRP £89.50

system 3
ACRYLIC SCREEN PRINTING SET

STEP BY STEP GUIDE
TO SCREEN PRINTING

PRICE SUBJECT TO CHANGE AND AVAILABILITY. PRICES VALID AT 27/02/12.

CASS PROMISE – CREATIVITY AT THE LOWEST PRICES. WE'RE CONFIDENT OUR PRICES CAN'T BE BEATEN

FLAGSHIP STORE: 66-67 COLEBROOKE ROW, ISLINGTON N1
ALSO AT: 13 CHARING CROSS RD WC2 (NEXT TO THE NATIONAL GALLERY),
58-62 HEATH STREET HAMPSTEAD NW3, 220 KENSINGTON HIGH ST W8
AND 24 BERWICK ST W1. ALL STORES OPEN 7 DAYS WWW.CASSART.CO.UK

and one Golden. On the Mall, the ICA Bar serves up a slice of contemporary culture with its drinks.

Pimlico pubs are quiet affairs, frequented by affluent locals and office workers: typical is the Morpeth Arms. Chimes bar-restaurant has a laudable choice of ciders, while Millbank Lounge offers a surprising oasis of calm in hotel-bar form. In Belgravia, the Lanesborough's Library Bar and the Blue Bar at the Berkeley are classy places to sip a cocktail before you head off to a first-rate boozer, such as charming time-warp pub the Nag's Head.

The fast-regenerating Bayswater and Paddington areas offer tiny Fuller's pub the Victoria and the cosy Mitre. Over in Little Venice, don't miss the fabulous Bridge House. Across the water, the beautiful Prince Alfred has great food and drink, while, near Warwick Avenue tube, the Warrington is a splendid affair, with leather sofas and fine British cooking. St John's Wood also houses a few prime drinking establishments. Among them, bucolic hangout the Clifton is down-to-earth and welcoming. Westminster's West Kilburn enclave is best served by Little Venice venues, or the drinking dens of Kensal Green and Queen's Park.

Admiral Duncan 54 Old Compton Street, W1D 5PA (7437 5300).
Artesian Langham Hotel, 1C Portland Place, W1B 1JA (7636 1000, www.artesian-bar.co.uk).
Le Beaujolais 25 Litchfield Street, WC2H 9NJ (7240 3776).
Bedford & Strand 1A Bedford Street, WC2E 9HH (7836 3033, www.bedford-strand.com).
Blue Bar The Berkeley, Wilton Place, SW1X 7RL (7235 6000, www.the-berkeley.co.uk).
Bountiful Cow 51 Eagle Street, WC1R 4AP (7404 0200, www.thebountifulcow.co.uk).
Bridge House 13 Westbourne Terrace Road, W2 6NG (7266 4326, www.thebridgehouse littlevenice.co.uk).
Candy Bar 4 Carlisle Street, W1D 3BJ (7287 5041, www.candybarsoho.com).
CellarDoor Zero Aldwych, WC2E 7DN (7240 8848, www.cellardoor.biz).
Champion 12-13 Wells Street, W1T 3PA (7323 1228).
Chimes 26 Churton Street, SW1V 2LP (7821 7456, www.chimes-of-pimlico.co.uk).
Claridge's Bar Claridge's, 49 Brook Street, W1A 4HR (7629 8860, www.claridges.co.uk).
Clifton 96 Clifton Hill, NW8 0JT (7372 3427, www.cliftonstjohnswood.com).
Cock Tavern 27 Great Portland Street, W1W 8QE (7631 5002).
Comptons of Soho 51-53 Old Compton Street, W1D 6HJ (3238 0163, www.faucetinn.com).
Connaught Bar The Connaught, Carlos Place, W1K 2AL (7499 7070, www.theconnaught hotellondon.com).
Cork & Bottle 44-46 Cranbourn Street, WC2H 7AN (7734 7807, www.thecorkandbottle.co.uk).
Cross Keys 31 Endell Street, WC2H 9BA (7836 5185, www.crosskeyscoventgarden.com).
Dog & Duck 18 Bateman Street, W1D 3AJ (7494 0697, www.nicholsonspubs.co.uk).
Donovan Bar Brown's Hotel, Albemarle Street, W1S 4BP (7493 6020, www.brownshotel.com).
Edgar Wallace 40 Essex Street, WC2R 3JF (7353 3120).
Experimental Cocktail Club 13A Gerrard Street, W1D 5PS (7434 3559, www.chinatown ecc.com).
French House 49 Dean Street, W1D 5BG (7437 2477/2799, www.frenchhousesoho.com).
Galvin at Windows 28th floor, London Hilton, 22 Park Lane, W1K 1BE (7208 4021, www.galvinatwindows.com).
Golden Eagle 59 Marylebone Lane, W1U 2NY (7935 3228).
Golden Lion 25 King Street, SW1Y 6QY (7925 0007).
Gordon's 47 Villiers Street, WC2N 6NE (7930 1408, www.gordonswinebar.com).
ICA Bar The Mall, SW1Y 5AH (7930 8619, www.ica.org.uk).
Lamb & Flag 33 Rose Street, WC2E 9EB (7497 9504).
Library Bar The Lanesborough, 1 Lanesborough Place, Hyde Park Corner, SW1X 7TA (7259 5599, www.lanesborough.com).
Lobby Bar One Aldwych, Aldwych, WC2B 4RH (7300 1000, www.onealdwych.com).
Long Bar The Sanderson, 50 Berners Street, W1T 3NG (7300 5588, www.sandersonlondon.com).
Lowlander 36 Drury Lane, WC2B 5RR (7379 7446, www.lowlander.com).
Lucky Voice 52 Poland Street, W1F 7NQ (7439 3660, www.luckyvoice.co.uk).
Mahiki 1 Dover Street, W1S 4LD (7493 9529, www.mahiki.com).
Mark's Bar 66-70 Brewer Street, W1F 9UP (7292 3518, www.marksbar.co.uk).
Milk & Honey 61 Poland Street, W1F 7NU (7065 6840, www.mlkhny.com).
Millbank Lounge Doubletree by Hilton, 30 John Islip Street, SW1P 4DD (7630 1000, http://doubletree1.hilton.com).

City of Westminster

Mitre *24 Craven Terrace, W2 3QH*
(7262 5240, www.mitrelancastergate.com).
Morpeth Arms *58 Millbank, SW1P 4RW*
(7834 6442, www.youngs.co.uk).
Nag's Head *53 Kinnerton Street, SW1X 8ED*
(7235 1135).
Nell Gwynne *1-2 Bull Inn Court, WC2R 0NP*
(7240 5579).
Newman Arms *23 Rathbone Street, W1T 1NG*
(7636 1127, www.newmanarms.co.uk).
Old Coffee House *49 Beak Street,*
W1F 9SF (7437 2197).
Prince Alfred & Formosa Dining Rooms
5A Formosa Street, W9 1EE (7286 3287,
www.theprincealfred.com).
Red Lion *23 Crown Passage, off Pall Mall,*
SW1Y 6PP (7930 4141).
Red Lion *2 Duke of York Street, SW1Y 6JP*
(7321 0782, www.fullers.co.uk).
Red Lion *48 Parliament Street, SW1A 2NH*
(7930 5826, www.fullers.co.uk).
Seven Stars *53 Carey Street, WC2A 2JB*
(7242 8521).
Social *5 Little Portland Street, W1W 7JD*
(7636 4992, www.thesocial.com).
Two Floors *3 Kingly Street, W1B 5PD*
(7439 1007, www.barworks.co.uk).
Victoria *10A Strathern Place, W2 2NH*
(7724 1191, www.fullers.co.uk).
Village Soho *81 Wardour Street, W1D 6QD*
(7478 0530, www.village-soho.co.uk).
Warrington *93 Warrington Crescent, W9 1EH*
(7286 8421, www.faucetinn.com).
Windsor Castle *29 Crawford Place, W1H 4LJ*
(7723 4371).
Zander Bar *Bank Westminster, 45 Buckingham*
Gate, SW1E 6BS (7630 6644, www.bank
restaurants.com).

Shops

Westminster wins out as London's all-embracing shopping centre. Below are the highlights; consult *Time Out London's Best Shops* for more ideas.

Jostling, maddening Oxford Street is the unlovely but convenient retail backbone of the city. The Centre Point end is dominated by cheap clothes shops and tacky gift emporia, but move west towards Oxford Circus and the choice improves. The massive Topshop flagship squats on the north-eastern corner of the Circus, sharing premises with its smaller sister Miss Selfridge. The line-up of global and national fashion chains continues towards

Marble Arch. Pedestrianised St Christopher's Place, with its upmarket chains and designer shops, is a welcome respite from the crush. It emerges at Wigmore Street, brimming with swanky kitchen, bathroom and furniture showrooms, and the sleek Margaret Howell store.

While most of the city's department stores congregate on Oxford Street, Fenwick, known for its accessories and lingerie, perches demurely on nearby Bond Street, and Fortnum & Mason, whose 300th birthday nip-and-tuck in 2007 included the expansion of its famous food hall, is on Piccadilly. John Lewis is king for homeware, haberdashery and other basics, but Selfridges wins hands-down for its exciting displays and all-encompassing selection of clothes, food and gadgets. Down on Regent Street, Liberty may have physically downsized, losing its annex, but its stock gets better all the time, especially the menswear.

Formerly dowdy Regent Street has been revitalised by the arrival of the Apple Store, funky Anthropologie and an influx of new mid-range fashion chains, such as H&M's offshoot COS (great for luxurious basics). Carnaby Street has also undergone a gradual transformation. A few years back, this iconic strip had descended into tacky studded-collar/novelty-hat territory. Now, it's a decent destination for branded streetwear. Don't miss Kingly Court – the small shopping centre houses numerous one-off boutiques and is notable for vintage fashion. There are more small shops on cobbled Newburgh Street, running parallel and east of Carnaby Street.

In Soho, Berwick Street Market's traders hawk fruit and veg alongside shops selling cut-price fabric, household goods and the less wholesome wares of the bordering red-light district. The area is still known for indie record stores, although there have been recent closures. The original Broadwick Street outpost of luxury lingerie chain Agent Provocateur is at home in this slightly louche locality.

Continuing east towards Covent Garden, Neal Street and the streets radiating from Seven Dials heave with streetwear and limited-edition trainers. Monmouth Street is great for a browse, with Kiehl's skincare, Poste Mistress shoes, print queen Orla Kiely's flagship and London's chicest erotic emporium, Coco de Mer. Nearby,

Neal's Yard Dairy is pungent with farmhouse cheeses, while the yard itself has organic pioneer Neal's Yard Remedies. Covent Garden Piazza has acquired more luxury shops in recent years, although it still contains charming oddities such as Benjamin Pollock's Toyshop with its wonderful model theatres.

While for most people Charing Cross Road is inextricably linked with books – due to the famous Foyles and several dusty second-hand stores (though fewer than there used to be) – not everyone is aware of Cecil Court. A pedestrian alley connecting Charing Cross Road and St Martin's Lane, it is lined with specialist book and print dealers.

Mayfair is the traditional home of tailors (Savile Row) and shirtmakers (Jermyn Street), and there are posh jewellers and designer names galore on Bond Street and environs, from Stella McCartney's flagship townhouse to Rupert Sanderson's footwear emporium. Browns – five interconnecting shops on South Molton Street – has showcased its mix of big-league labels and rising stars for nearly 40 years (see also its sale shop, Labels for Less). For avant-garde fashion just up the road from Savile Row's august tailors, try B Store.

The old arcades – Burlington, Piccadilly and the Royal – offer elegant browsing, while nearby is Rei Kawakubo's 21st-century take on London's old covered markets, Dover Street Market, where Comme collections join uber-designer concessions. Venerable specialists survive in St James's Street, including Swaine Adeney Brigg, purveyor of upper-crust accessories, and old-fashioned chemist DR Harris with its lovely traditional toiletries.

South-west in Belgravia, charming Elizabeth Street offers delicious breads (Poilâne), rare perfumes (Les Senteurs), designer hats (Philip Treacy) and a chic dog boutique (Mungo & Maud). Nearby, in Pimlico, is a branch of Daylesford Organic amid a number of chi chi antiques shops. Victoria has Cardinal Place shopping centre. Its shops, interspersed with lunch options, seem geared towards well-groomed local office workers: Zara, L'Occitane, Hawes & Curtis shirtmakers. Bayswater is home to Edwardian shopping centre Whiteleys, which retains beautiful original features, but its 50-odd retail spaces are mainly used by chains (there's also an

Odeon and a branch of bowling bar All Star Lanes). Middle Eastern food stores on and around Edgware Road include the well-stocked Green Valley. North-west of Bayswater, near the border with Kensington & Chelsea, boutiques proliferate around Westbourne Grove.

To the north, Marylebone High Street has become an established shopping enclave and weekend hangout for both well-heeled denizens and non-residents. Foodies are well catered for by rustic deli-and-cheese specialist La Fromagerie, rare-breed butcher Ginger Pig and quality choc shop Rococo, plus a Sunday-morning farmers' market in the car park behind Waitrose. There's a lovely old bookshop (Daunt) and lots of middle- to upmarket clothing chains. The contemporary jewellery at Cox & Power and Kabiri dazzles; Fresh satisfies beauty needs; and the Conran Shop and Skandium provide chic furnishings. On Saturdays, Cabbages & Frocks (a small general market) sets up in the cobbled yard of St Marylebone Parish Church. Don't bypass Marylebone Lane, where interesting shops include Tracey

Neuls West (iconoclastic footwear), laid-back boutique KJ's Laundry and century-old deli Paul Rothe & Son.

North of Marylebone Road, at the eastern end of Church Street, Alfie's Antique Market has stalls selling all sorts, from 20th-century Italian furniture to glam vintage fashion. The number of surrounding antiques shops has grown, making this one of London's best hunting grounds. There's also a large general street market that's at its best on Saturday.

In St John's Wood, the High Street has a pleasant, villagey atmosphere. The usual upmarket fashion chains and high-class food stores are here, including quality butcher Kent & Sons and branches of Carluccio's and Maison Blanc. Maida Vale's shops mainly cater to (affluent) domestic needs. Some of the best are Raoul's Deli, Sheepdrove Organic Farm Family Butcher and superior wine merchant the Winery, plus venerable Clifton Nurseries.

Agent Provocateur 6 Broadwick Street, W1F 8HL (7439 0229, www.agentprovocateur.com).
Alfie's Antique Market 13-25 Church Street, NW8 8DT (7723 6066, www.alfies antiques.com).
Anthropologie 158 Regent Street, W1B 5SW (7529 9800, www.anthropologie.co.uk).
Apple Store 235 Regent Street, W1B 2EL (7153 9000, www.apple.com).
Benjamin Pollock's Toyshop 44 The Market, WC2E 8RF (7379 7866, www. pollocks-coventgarden.co.uk).
Browns 24-27 South Molton Street, W1K 5RD (7514 0016, www.brownsfashion.com).
Browns Labels for Less 50 South Molton Street, W1K 5SB (7514 0052, www.browns fashion.com).
B Store 21 Kingly Street, W1B 5QA (7734 6846, www.bstorelondon.com).
Burlington Arcade Piccadilly, W1 (7630 1411, www.burlington-arcade.co.uk).
Cabbages & Frocks Market St Marylebone Parish Church Grounds, Marylebone High Street, W1 (7794 1636, www.cabbagesand frocks.co.uk).
Cardinal Place Victoria Street, SW1 (www.cardinalplace.co.uk).
Cecil Court Cecil Court, WC2 (www.cecil court.co.uk).
Clifton Nurseries 5A Clifton Villas, W9 2PH (7289 6851, www.clifton.co.uk).
Coco de Mer 23 Monmouth Street, WC2H 9DD (7836 8882, www.coco-de-mer.co.uk).

Conran Shop 55 Marylebone High Street, W1U 5HS (7723 2223, www.conran.com).
COS 222 Regent Street, W1B 5BD (7478 0400, www.cosstores.com).
Cox & Power 35C Marylebone High Street, W1U 4QA (7935 3530, www.coxandpower.com).
Daunt Books 83-84 Marylebone High Street, W1U 4QW (7224 2295, www.daunt books.co.uk).
Daylesford Organic 44B Pimlico Road, SW1W 8LP (7881 8060, www.daylesford organic.com).
Dover Street Market 17-18 Dover Street, W1S 4LT (7518 0680, www.doverstreet market.com).
DR Harris 29 St James's Street, SW1A 1HB (7930 3915, www.drharris.co.uk).
Fenwick 63 New Bond Street, W1A 3BS (7629 9161, www.fenwick.co.uk).
Fortnum & Mason 181 Piccadilly, W1A 1ER (7734 8040, www.fortnumandmason.co.uk).
Foyles 113-119 Charing Cross Road, WC2H 0EB (7437 5660, www.foyles.co.uk).
Fresh 92 Marylebone High Street, W1U 4RD (7486 4100, www.fresh.com).
La Fromagerie 2-6 Moxon Street, W1U 4EW (7935 0341, www.lafromagerie.co.uk).
Ginger Pig 8-10 Moxon Street, W1U 4EW (7935 7788, www.thegingerpig.co.uk).
Green Valley 36-37 Upper Berkeley Street, W1H 5QF (7402 7385).
John Lewis 300 Oxford Street, W1A 1EX (7629 7711, www.johnlewis.co.uk).
Kabiri 37 Marylebone High Street, W1U 4QE (7224 1808, www.kabiri.co.uk).
Kent & Sons 59 St John's Wood High Street, NW8 7NL (7722 2258, www.kents-butchers.co.uk).
Kiehl's 29 Monmouth Street, WC2H 9DD (7240 2411, www.kiehls.com).
Kingly Court Carnaby Street, opposite Broadwick Street, W1B 5PW (7333 8118, www.carnaby.co.uk).
KJ's Laundry 74 Marylebone Lane, W1U 2PW (7486 7855, www.kjslaundry.com).

TRANSPORT

Tube stations, rail stations and main bus routes dozens of tube, rail and bus services run through the City of Westminster; for maps and service information, visit www.tfl.gov.uk
River commuter and leisure boat services run east and west through London, with piers at the Savoy, Embankment, Westminster and Millbank

Upmarket developments now surround **Paddington Basin**. See p25.

Liberty *Regent Street, W1B 5AH (7734 1234, www.liberty.co.uk).*

Margaret Howell *34 Wigmore Street, W1U 2RS (7009 9009, www.margarethowell.co.uk)*

Marylebone Farmers' Market *Cramer Street car park, behind Marylebone High Street, W1U 4EA (7833 0338, www.lfm.org.uk).*

Miss Selfridge *36-38 Great Castle Street, W1W 8LG (7927 0158, www.missselfridge.com).*

Mungo & Maud *79 Elizabeth Street, SW1W 9PJ (7022 1207, www.mungoandmaud.com).*

Neal's Yard Dairy *17 Shorts Gardens, WC2H 9AT (7240 5700, www.nealsyarddairy.co.uk).*

Neal's Yard Remedies *www.nealsyardremedies.com; 15 Neal's Yard, WC2H 9DP (7379 7222); 45 St John's Wood High Street, NW8 7NJ (7586 1647).*

Orla Kiely *31-33 Monmouth Street, WC2H 9DD (7240 4022, www.orlakiely.com).*

Paul Rothe & Son *35 Marylebone Lane, W1U 2NN (7935 6783).*

Philip Treacy *69 Elizabeth Street, SW1W 9PJ (7730 3992, www.philiptreacy.co.uk).*

Piccadilly Arcade *SW1Y 6NH (7647 3000, www.piccadilly-arcade.com).*

Poilâne *46 Elizabeth Street, SW1W 9PA (7808 4910, www.poilane.fr).*

Poste Mistress *61-63 Monmouth Street, WC2H 9EP (7379 4040).*

Raoul's Deli *8-10 Clifton Road, W9 1SS (7289 6649, www.raoulsgourmet.com).*

Rococo *45 Marylebone High Street, W1U 5HG (7935 7780, www.rococochocolates.com).*

Rupert Sanderson *19 Bruton Place, W1J 6LZ (7491 2260, www.rupertsanderson.co.uk).*

Selfridges *400 Oxford Street, W1A 1AB (0800 123400, www.selfridges.com).*

Les Senteurs *71 Elizabeth Street, SW1W 9PJ (7730 2322, www.lessenteurs.com).*

Sheepdrove Organic Farm Family Butcher *5 Clifton Road, W9 1SZ (7266 3838, www.sheepdrove.com).*

Skandium *86 Marylebone High Street, W1U 4QS (7935 2077, www.skandium.com).*

Stella McCartney *30 Bruton Street, W1J 6LG (7518 3100, www.stellamccartney.co.uk).*

Swaine Adeney Brigg *54 St James's Street, SW1A 1JT (7409 7277, www.swaine adeney.co.uk).*

Topshop *214 Oxford Street, W1W 8LG (0844 848 7487, www.topshop.com).*

Tracey Neuls West *29 Marylebone Lane, W1U 2NQ (7935 0039, www.tn29.com).*

Whiteleys *151 Queensway, W2 4YN (7229 8844, www.whiteleys.com).*

Winery *4 Clifton Road, W9 1SS (7286 6475, www.thewineryuk.com).*

Arts & attractions

Cinemas & theatres

There's an incredible number of cinemas and theatres in the City of Westminster, most clustered in the district around Shaftesbury Avenue. We give just an overview below; for more – plus the latest developments, reviews and practical information – consult the 'Film' and 'Theatre' sections of the weekly *Time Out* magazine, or visit www.timeout.com.

Adelphi Theatre *Strand, WC2R 0NS (0844 412 4651, www.reallyuseful.com).*

Curzon *0330 500 1331, www.curzoncinemas. com; Mayfair, 38 Curzon Street, W1J 7TY; Soho, 99 Shaftesbury Avenue, W1D 5DY.*

Dominion Theatre *Tottenham Court Road, W1T 7AQ (7927 0900, www.dominiontheatre. org.uk).*

Everyman *0871 906 9060, www.everyman cinema.com; Baker Street, W1U 6TJ; 215 Sutherland Avenue, W9 1RU.*

Lyceum Theatre *Wellington Street, WC2E 7RQ (7420 8100, www.londontheatredirect.com).*

Novello Theatre *Aldwych, WC2B 4LD (0844 482 5170, www.delfontmackintosh.co.uk).*

Odeon *0871 224 4007, www.odeon.co.uk; 24-26 Leicester Square, WC2H 7LQ; 40 Leicester Square, WC2H 7LP; 11-18 Panton Street, SW1Y 4DP; 135 Shaftesbury Avenue, WC2H 8AH.*

Open Air Theatre *Regent's Park, NW1 4NR (0844 375 3460, box office 0844 826 4242, www.openairtheatre.org). Alfresco theatre, perfect for summery Shakespeare romps.*

Piccadilly Theatre *16 Denman Street, W1D 7DY (0844 871 7627, www.atgtickets.com).*

Prince Charles Cinema *7 Leicester Place, WC2H 7BP (7494 3654, www.princecharles cinema.com). The best value in town for releases ending their first run elsewhere.*

Prince of Wales Theatre *Coventry Street, W1D 6AS (0844 482 5115, www.delfont mackintosh.co.uk).*

Puppet Theatre Barge *Little Venice, opposite 35 Blomfield Road, W9 2PF (7249 6876, www.puppetbarge.com).*

Queen's Theatre *Shaftesbury Avenue, W1D 6BA (0844 482 5160, www.delfont mackintosh.co.uk).*

St Martin's Theatre *West Street, WC2H 9NZ (0844 499 1515, www.londontheatredirect.com).*

Shaftesbury Theatre *210 Shaftesbury Avenue, WC2H 8DP (7379 5399, www.shaftesburytheatre.com).*

Theatre Royal Drury Lane *Catherine Street, WC2B 5JF (0844 412 4660, www.london theatredirect.com).*

Victoria Palace Theatre *Victoria Street, SW1E 5EA (0844 248 5000, www.victoria palacetheatre.co.uk).*

Galleries & museums

Westminster is the site of most of London's principal museums, galleries and tourist attractions. Below is a selection; for a more complete guide, see the *Time Out London Guide*, consult the 'Art' and 'Around Town' sections of *Time Out* magazine or visit www.timeout.com.

Benjamin Franklin House *36 Craven Street, WC2N 5NF (7839 2006, www.benjamin franklinhouse.org). Dramatic re-enactment tours at the home of the future Founding Father.*

ICA (Institute of Contemporary Arts) *The Mall, SW1Y 5AH (7930 3647, www.ica. org.uk). Long-running alternative arts venue.*

Lisson Gallery *7724 2739, www.lissongallery. com; 29 Bell Street, NW1 5BY; 52-54 Bell Street, NW1 5DA. Contemporary art gallery with two spaces on Bell Street.*

London Transport Museum *Covent Garden Piazza, WC2E 7BB (7379 6344, www.ltmuseum.co.uk).*

National Gallery *Trafalgar Square, WC2N 5DN (information line 7747 2885, www.national gallery.org.uk). A national treasure, founded in 1824; now with more than 2,000 pieces spanning virtually every school of art, plus good restaurants.*

National Portrait Gallery *St Martin's Place, WC2H 0HE (7306 0055, www.npg.org.uk). This attractive, manageable museum has fine views from the top-floor restaurant and bar.*

Royal Academy of Arts *Burlington House, Piccadilly, W1J 0BD (7300 8000, www.royal academy.org.uk). Britain's first art school, better known these days for its galleries.*

Serpentine Gallery *Kensington Gardens, W2 3XA (7402 6075, www.serpentinegallery.org). Excellent contemporary art exhibitions.*

Somerset House *Strand, WC2R 0RN (7845 4600, www.somersethouse.org.uk). Contemporary art and design shows, plus the Courtauld Gallery (www.courtauld.ac.uk). The grand courtyard is used for open-air concerts and cinema in summer and ice-skating in winter.*

Tate Britain *Millbank, SW1P 4RG (7887 8888, www.tate.org.uk). The sexier Tate Modern gets all the attention, but don't forget this old stalwart: it contains London's second great collection of art, after the National Gallery.*

Wallace Collection *Hertford House,*
Manchester Square, W1U 3BN (7563 9500,
www.wallacecollection.org). Fine private art
collection, bequeathed to the nation in 1897.

Music & comedy venues

See the weekly *Time Out* magazine or
website (www.timeout.com) for full music
and comedy listings in the borough.

Coliseum *St Martin's Lane, WC2N 4ES*
(7836 0111, www.eno.org). Home of the
English National Opera.
Ronnie Scott's *47 Frith Street, W1D 4HT*
(7439 0747, www.ronniescotts.co.uk). Famous,
long-running jazz venue.
Royal Opera House *Bow Street, WC2E 9DD*
(7304 4000, www.royaloperahouse.org).
Wigmore Hall *36 Wigmore Street, W1U 2BP*
(7935 2141, www.wigmore hall.org.uk). Top
concert venue for chamber music and song.

Other attractions

Buckingham Palace & Royal Mews
SW1A 1AA (7766 7300, www.royal.gov.uk).
Houses of Parliament *Parliament Square,*
SW1A 0AA (Commons information 7219 4272,
Lords information 7219 3107, tours 0870 906
3773, www.parliament.uk).
London Zoo *Outer Circle, Regent's Park,*
NW1 4RY (0844 225 1826, www.zsl.org).
Royal Courts of Justice *Strand, WC2A 2LL*
(7947 6000, www.justice.gov.uk). Members of
the public are allowed to attend certain trials.
St Martin-in-the-Fields *Trafalgar Square,*
WC2N 4JJ (7766 1100, www.stmartin-in the-
fields.org). Landmark 18th-century church,
known for its classical concerts.
Westminster Abbey *20 Dean's Yard,*
SW1P 3PA (7222 5152, tours 7654 4834,
www.westminster-abbey.org).
Westminster Cathedral *Victoria Street,*
SW1P 1QW (7798 9055, www.westminster
cathedral.org.uk).

Sport & fitness

Prices in council-run centres are high,
matching those found in private clubs in
most other boroughs, but the facilities tend
to be well maintained and of high quality.
The independents are correspondingly
pricey, but if you want personal attention
and celeb-spotting opportunities, these
exclusive clubs (some in five-star hotels)
should deliver.

RECYCLING

Household waste recycled &
composted 24%
Main recycling centre the nearest
large sites are outside the borough,
in Battersea and Wandsworth;
otherwise, there are three small
sites in Marylebone (the biggest
is on Paddington Street)
Other recycling services green waste
collection; home composting; collection
of white goods and furniture; computer
recycling scheme
Council contact Environment & Leisure
Department (Environmental Services),
City Hall, 64 Victoria Street, SW1E 6QP
(7641 2000)

COUNCIL TAX

A	up to £40,000	£458.41
B	£40,001-£52,000	£534.82
C	£52,001-£68,000	£611.12
D	£68,001-£88,000	£687.62
E	£88,001-£120,000	£840.42
F	£120,001-£160,000	£993.23
G	£160,001-£320,000	£1,146.03
H	over £320,000	£1,375.24

Gyms & leisure centres

Agua at The Sanderson *50 Berners Street,*
W1T 3NG (7300 1414, www.sanderson
london.com). Private.
Bannatyne Spa *4 Millbank, SW1P 3JA*
(7233 3579, www.bannatynespa.com/spa/
millbank). Private.
Berkeley Health Club & Spa *The Berkeley,*
Wilton Place, SW1X 7RL (7201 1699,
www.theberkeleyhotellondon.com). Private.
Cannons *www.cannons.co.uk; Endell Street,*
WC2H 9SA (7240 2446); 2 Sheldon Square,
W2 6EZ (7289 4686). Private.
Dolphin Fitness Club *Dolphin Square Hotel,*
Dolphin Square, SW1V 3LX (7798 8686,
www.dolphinfitnessclub.co.uk). Private.
Dorchester Spa *The Dorchester, 53 Park*
Lane, W1A 2HJ (7319 7109, www.dorchester
hotel.com). Private.
Fitness First *www.fitnessfirst.co.uk; 6 Bedford*
Street, WC2E 9HD (0844 571 2818); Berkeley
Square House, Berkeley Square, W1J 6BR (0844
571 2813); Concourse Level, 1 Embankment
Place, WC2N 6NN (0844 571 2859); 15 Great
Marlborough Street, W1V 1AF (0844 571
2914); 59 Kingly Street, W1B 5QJ (0844 571

2888); Roebuck House, Cardinal Place, Palace Street, SW1E 5BA (0844 571 2838); 136-150 Victoria Street, SW1E 5LD (0844 571 2951). Private.

Health Club at St James's Court Crowne Plaza Hotel, 51 Buckingham Gate, SW1E 6AF (7963 8307, www.london.crowneplaza.com). Private.

Hilton Fitness by Precor London Hilton, 22 Park Lane, W1K 1BE (7493 8000). Private.

Jubilee Hall 30 The Piazza, WC2E 8BE (7836 4007, www.jubileehallclubs.co.uk). Private.

Jubilee Sports Centre Caird Street, W10 4RR (8960 9629, www.gll.org).

LA Fitness www.lafitness.co.uk; 7 Balcombe Street, NW1 6NA (7723 5757); Bayswater House, 6 Moscow Place, W2 4AP (0843 170 1004); 49 Hallam Street, W1W 6JW (7436 2881); Portland House, Bressenden Place,

SW1E 5BH (7233 8444); Rex House, 4-12 Lower Regent Street, SW1Y 4PE (7839 8448); Waldorf Hilton, Aldwych, WC2B 4DD (7379 5606). Private.

LivingWell Hilton London Metropole, 225 Edgware Road, W2 1JU (7616 6486, www.livingwell.com). Private.

Porchester Centre Queensway, W2 5HS (7792 2919, www.gll.org).

Queen Mother Sports Centre 223 Vauxhall Bridge Road, SW1V 1EL (7630 5522, www.gll.org).

Seymour Leisure Centre Seymour Place, W1H 5TJ (7723 8019, www.gll.org).

Virgin Active www.virginactive.co.uk; Hereford House, 64 North Row, W1K 6DA (7659 4350); 120 Oxford Street, W1D 1LT (7436 0500); Shell Mex House, 80 The Strand, WC2R 0DT (7395 9595). Private.

Other facilities

Paddington Recreation Ground Randolph Avenue, W9 1PD (7641 3642, www.gll.org). Facilities for tennis, cricket, football and athletics, plus a gym.

Queens Ice Rink & Bowling 17 Queensway, W2 4QP (7229 0172, www.queensiceand bowl.co.uk).

Westminster Boating Base 136 Grosvenor Road, SW1V 3JY (7821 7389, www.westminster boatingbase.co.uk).

Spectator sports

Lord's Cricket Ground St John's Wood Road, NW8 8QN (Marylebone Cricket Club 7616 8500, tickets 7432 1000, www.lords.org).

Schools

Primary

There are 38 state primary schools in the City of Westminster, 26 of which are church schools. There are also 16 independent primaries, including one American, one French, one International and one Jewish school. See www.westminster.gov.uk, www.edubase.gov.uk and www.ofsted.gov.uk for more information.

Secondary

Grey Coat Hospital Girls' School St Andrew's Building, Grey Coat Place, SW1P 2DY (7969 1998, www.gch.org.uk). Church of England; girls only.

King Solomon Academy Penfold Street, NW1 6RX (7563 6900, www.kingsolomonacademy.org).

STATISTICS

BOROUGH MAKE-UP
Population 253,100 (during the day, it exceeds 1,000,000)
Ethnic origins
  White 69.5%
  Mixed 4.0%
  Asian or Asian British 12.8%
  Black or Black British 7.2%
  Chinese or other 6.6%
Students 11.9%
Retirees 7.9%

HOUSING STOCK
Borough size (hectares) 2,203
Population density per hectare 107.0
No. of households 119,486
Houses (detached, semi-detached or terraced) 11%
Flats (converted or purpose-built) 89%

CRIME PER 1,000 OF POPULATION
Burglary 5
Robbery 7
Theft of vehicle 2
Theft from vehicle 10
Violence against the person 36
Sexual offences 2

MPs
Cities of London & Westminster Mark Field (Conservative); Holborn & St Pancras Frank Dobson (Labour); Westminster North Karen Buck (Labour); Kensington Sir Malcolm Rifkind (Conservative)

Paddington Academy *50 Marylands Road, W9 2DR (7479 3900, www.paddington academy.org.uk).*

Pimlico Academy *Lupus Street, SW1V 3AT (7828 0881, www.pimlicoacademy.org).*

Portland Place *56-58 Portland Place, W1B 1NJ (7307 8700, www.portland-place.co.uk). Private.*

Queen's College *43-49 Harley Street, W1G 8BT (7291 7000, www.qcl.org.uk). Girls only; private.*

Quintin Kynaston School *Marlborough Hill, NW8 0NL (7722 8141, www.qkschool.org.uk).*

St Augustine's CE School *Oxford Road, NW6 5SN (7328 3434, www.staugustines high.org). Church of England.*

St George's Catholic School *Lanark Road, W9 1RB (7328 0904, www.stgeorgesrc.org). Roman Catholic.*

St Marylebone CE School *64 Marylebone High Street, W1U 5BA (7935 4704, www.stmaryleboneschool.com). Church of England; girls only; mixed sixth form.*

Sylvia Young Theatre School *1 Nutford Place, W1H 5YZ (7258 2330, www.sylviayoung theatreschool.co.uk). Private.*

Westminster Academy *255 Harrow Road, W2 5EZ (7121 0600, www.westminster academy.biz).*

Westminster City Boys' School *55 Palace Street, SW1E 5HJ (7641 8760, www.wcsch.com). Boys only; private.*

Westminster School *Little Dean's Yard, SW1P 3PF (7963 1000, www.westminster. org.uk). Boys only; mixed sixth form; private.*

Property

WHAT THE AGENTS SAY:

'Over the past 15-20 years I've been handling property in Westminster, I've seen a huge increase in the number of flats coming on to the market. Developers are taking old offices and blocks of flats and converting them. The area's closeness to central London is its selling point; people want two-bedroom flats they can use during the week for business, and that's what developers are giving them. Security is a big pull – having Scotland Yard and MI5 in the area makes people feel secure and watched over. Unlike areas such as Mayfair and Knightsbridge, Westminster has kept its light under a bushel in terms of prices. I've seen them rise steadily over the years, but never skyrocket.'

Laurence Benson, Bensons, Westminster

Average property prices

Detached £1,467,281
Semi-detached £1,507,003
Terraced £1,438,752
Flat £643,039

Local estate agents

Bensons *106 Horseferry Road, SW1P 2EF (7222 7020, www.bensonsestateagents. co.uk).*

Fox Gregory *102-104 Allitsen Road, NW8 7AY (7586 1500, www.foxgregory. co.uk).*

James Taylor Property *7 New Quebec Street, W1H 7RH (7724 4777, www.jamestaylor property.com).*

Manors *1A Baker Street, W1U 8ED (7486 5982, www.manors.co.uk).*

Marsh & Parsons *53 Warwick Way, SW1 1QS (7828 8100, www.marshand parsons.co.uk).*

Robert Irving & Burns *23-24 Margaret Street, W1W 8LF (7637 0821, www.rib.co.uk).*

Wallsway *22 Devonshire Street, W1G 6PF (7224 0959, www.wallsway.co.uk).*

York Estates *81-82 Crawford Street, W1H 4AT (7724 0335, www.yorkestates.co.uk).*

Other information

Council

Westminster City Council *PO Box 240, Westminster City Hall, 64 Victoria Street, SW1E 6QP (7641 6000, www.westminster. gov.uk).*

Legal services

Central London Law Centre *14 Irving Street, WC2H 7AF (7839 2998, www.london lawcentre.org.uk).*

Westminster CAB *0844 477 1611, www.adviceguide.org.uk. Phone advice only.*

Local information

Fitzrovia Neighbourhood Association 39 Tottenham Street (7580 4576, www.fitzrovia.org.uk). www.londonlocals.co.uk. www.marylebonevillage.com.

Open spaces & allotments

Allotments *There are no allotments in Westminster.*

Open spaces *www.westminster.gov.uk; www.royalparks.org.uk (Green Park, Hyde Park, Regent's Park, St James's Park).*

'I really love living in the City. There are Roman remains beneath my building, Wren churches around the corner, fabulous contemporary architecture and bell-ringing every Sunday. It's a very special place.'

Cathy Ross, Director of Collections and Learning, Museum of London

City of London

New developments and prestigious buildings continue to go up in the Square Mile, despite the economic downturn, and the area bustles with energy during the working week. Visitors come for the history and architecture, and the unique atmosphere of this very independent borough.

Neighbourhoods

The City

One of the joys of the City is the population ebb and flow that ensures it never stays the same. By day, it's mobbed by over 300,000 office workers, plus a veritable army of tourists, white-van drivers, cycle couriers and City of London police officers. By night (and at weekends), the streets are less busy – though nowhere near as deserted as they were ten years ago, thanks to the increase in shops, bars and restaurants. This is especially apparent at the One New Change complex – which offers a great view of the dome of St Paul's and beyond from its rooftop viewing area – and around redeveloped Paternoster Square, where the

knock-on effect of the crowds surging over the Millennium Bridge gives the place a definite buzz at weekends.

The boundaries of the City are roughly delineated by the Roman city walls, but the 8,000 full-time residents of the district are squeezed into a much smaller area. Most of the elegant townhouses built after the Great Fire of London were destroyed by German bombing in World War II, or transformed into offices by generations of town planners, leaving residents to make the best of small pockets of residential housing tucked away between the tower blocks, Wren churches and national monuments. With the massive focus on office space, amenities such as parks and children's play areas are in short supply, though the City is home to over 150 small 'city gardens' (see

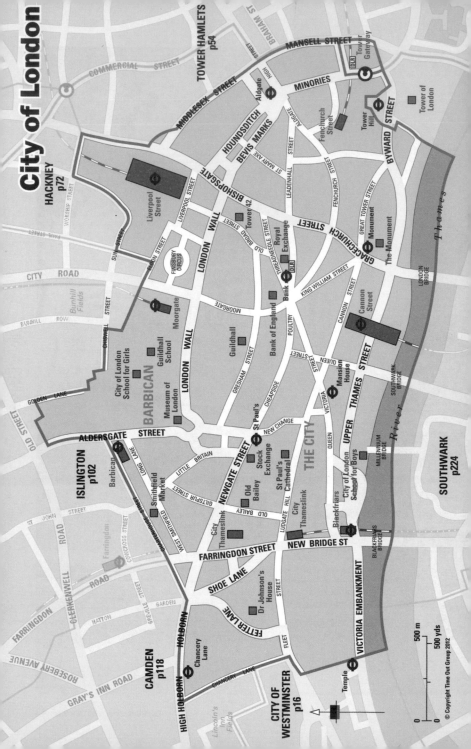

Highs & Lows

▲
Hear the sound of Bow bells Want to be part of historic London? This is the place to live.

No more commutes Live and work in the City and remove the hell of commuting.

Few burglaries Homes in the City are rarely broken into, thanks to some 1,200 police officers roaming the streets.

Chain stores It's rare to find an independent shop – instead it's just one chain after another.

Anti-social drinking Pity the City's street cleaners, who have to clean up the mess left by some after-work drinkers.

Inflated property prices Apartment prices and rents are well above the London norm.
▼

Another inconvenience is that, due to the tidal nature of the daytime population, many shops, pubs and restaurants close over the weekend. On the other hand, this is one of the easiest places in London to flag down a black cab, and with plentiful buses, and train and tube stations every few hundred yards, it's transport heaven. The glitzy new Blackfriars tube and rail station now extends over Blackfriars Bridge, with an entrance on the southern side of the river. The Crossrail project is having a big impact on the area around Moorgate, but by its completion in late 2018 the City will be even better connected.

London's oldest (and richest) local authority, the City has its peculiarities: it has its own police force, numerous archaic traditions and owns land well beyond its borders (Hampstead Heath and Epping Forest, for example). Unlike anywhere else in the UK, local elections are non-party political, and businesses as well as individuals are allowed to vote.

www.cityoflondon.gov.uk), and there's always the river to gaze at. What's more, the architecture is the most fascinating in London, with the showily modern (the Gherkin, Lloyd's of London) sitting alongside the beautifully ancient (St Bartholomew-the-Great is London's oldest parish church), and statues and other public artworks are plentiful.

The most desirable residences are the handful of Georgian townhouses that escaped the fire-storm of the Blitz, found in clusters around Fleet Street, Fenchurch Street and Liverpool Street Station. Most of the townhouses are broken up into luxury apartments, attracting young high-flyers who enjoy the proximity of the bars and restaurants in Islington and Tower Hamlets.

Inflated property prices tend to restrict the City to the wealthier sections of society. Gardens and parking spaces are almost unheard of, but most residents are happy to trade the luxury of space for the convenience of living so centrally. The congestion charge isn't really an issue; few bother with cars when the only available parking is in private car parks (besides, residents are eligible for a 90 per cent discount). With 1,200 police officers patrolling the streets, crime of the kind that affects home-owners is well below the London average. However, after-work binge drinking is one black mark on this otherwise enviable record.

Smithfield and Barbican

In recent years, renovation of the area around Smithfield Market has provided

The **Barbican Estate**. See p46.

plenty of loft apartments in converted warehouses and office buildings. The plan to demolish a set of Victorian buildings on the west side of Smithfield Market (running along Farringdon Road) and replace them with shops and offices has been the subject of much (ongoing) debate. Many of the buildings are by Horace Jones, the architect who designed the rest of the market, but they have been allowed to lie derelict for many years.

The atmosphere in this area most resembles next-door Clerkenwell (in the borough of Islington); there are still local shops and small businesses, as well as destination restaurants and bars. Aside from the handsome meat market, the main landmark is historic St Bartholomew's Hospital. The pretty streets between St Barts and Aldersgate contain some very covetable houses – the area oozes character.

The Barbican is easily the City's most famous residential address. The Barbican Estate was built on space largely created by wartime bomb damage; the government wanted to repopulate the City (down to around 5,000 residents in the 1950s), even though far more money could have been made by using the land for commercial purposes. Designed by architects Chamberlain, Powell & Bon, the Barbican terraces and towers were built between 1964 and 1975 (though the complex was officially opened in 1969 and the Barbican arts centre not finished until 1982).

The Estate covers around 40 acres and has just over 2,000 apartments (of well over 100 different types, ranging from studio flats to penthouses). It also contains the City of London School for Girls, the Museum of London (subject of a £20 million refurbishment in 2010) and the Guildhall School of Music & Drama (the last is building new premises on the site of Milton Court, next to the Barbican, due for completion in 2013). Opinion about the landmark concrete complex (now Grade II listed) has always been divided, and the layout can be confusing to visitors, but its stark charms are currently in fashion and the flats are much sought after; as they grow more and more expensive, the Golden Lane Estate (just to the north, on Fann Street) is becoming increasingly popular. Designed by the same architects (and also Grade II listed), Golden Lane was completed in the mid 1960s and holds 557 flats.

Butcher at Leadenhall, for meat lovers.

Restaurants & cafés

Many City eateries are only open Monday to Friday, though weekend opening is more common than it was. Smithfield is the most fruitful location: the four-storey Smiths of Smithfield (the complex holds two bars and two restaurants, which run from casual dining to high-end British) is open daily, for lunch and dinner; Carluccio's is usefully open all day, every day. Other Smithfield restaurants tend to be open on Saturday nights at least: try Café du Marché (traditional French), Club Gascon (deluxe French) and its more casual offshoot Comptoir Gascon, or Morgan M Barbican (more high-end French). The handsome Fox & Anchor has been reborn as a gastropub. The Barbican complex offers several dining options, none of them compelling. Looking like it's part of the estate, but independent, is modern pub-restaurant Wood Street, though the most appealing choice close to the Barbican is the Chiswell Street Dining Rooms.

The area around St Paul's and Paternoster Square has also become lively at weekends. The smartest options here are bar-restaurants Paternoster Chop House (British, and actually on the Square) and the Restaurant at St Paul's (also British, and housed within the Cathedral). Jamie Oliver and Gordon Ramsay have gone head to head at One New Change with Barbecoa and Bread Street Kitchen, respectively.

Inevitably, the City is not a cheap place to eat. Expense-account dining at its most obvious is represented by the likes of Bonds, Le Coq d'Argent, L'Anima, 1 Lombard Street, Lutyens, Prism and Sauterelle – all serve top-notch food in impressive spaces. Gary Rhodes' place, Rhodes Twenty Four, has the added attraction of amazing views from the 24th floor of Tower 42. The Andaz hotel has several restaurants and bars, including Miyako (Japanese). Hawksmoor Guildhall has joined the ranks of the steak-centric eateries that include Butcher at Leadenhall, Gaucho, Goodman City, High Timber and Le Relais de Venise l'entrecôte.

An antidote to all this monied dining can be found at the Café Below, where breakfasts and brasserie dishes are served in the courtyard and crypt of St Mary-le-Bow church, and Bea's of Bloomsbury, an OTT tearoom in One New Change. Ethnic restaurants also tend to be more affordable: try Haz (Turkish, with several City-based branches); K-10, Moshi Moshi Sushi and Tsuru (all Japanese); Ceena (Korean); and Kenza (Middle Eastern). Exceptions are the pricier Imperial City (Chinese) and Cinnamon Kitchen (Indian), while the most interesting newcomer is City Câphé, a small Vietnamese café serving great bánh mì. The gastropub part of the White Swan also qualifies as a budget option, though its lovely first-floor Dining Room does not. Grazing is part-caff, part sandwich shop, and takes meat very seriously, while Hilliard is a self-styled 'gastro-café'. In addition, the City has more than enough chains – there are Pizza Expresses, Wagamamas, sandwich bars and coffee shops all over (the branch of Paul next to St Paul's Cathedral is particularly well located). Of the chains, Bodeans, Byron, Côte, Gourmet Burger Kitchen and Leon are all worth noting, though none are quite as welcome as the branch of Hummus Bros on Cheapside. Coffee specialists include Dose and Taylor St Baristas.

Interesting one-offs include: Vivat Bacchus, where a serious wine list is balanced by an easy-going attitude and South African-influenced food; Rosemary Lane, an intimate French place at the eastern edge of the City; and Bevis Marks Restaurant, a stylish kosher venue next to the 18th-century synagogue of the same name. Sandeman's port, sherry and wine company was housed in what is now the appealing Don Bistro & Restaurant. And there's nowhere more characterful than our favourite City haunt – trad fish restaurant Sweetings. Only open for lunch on weekdays, it's unpretentious and charming, and merits a special trip, even if you don't live here.

Andaz *40 Liverpool Street, EC2M 7QN (7961 1234, www.london.liverpoolstreet.andaz.com).*
L'Anima *1 Snowden Street, EC2A 2DQ (7422 7000, www.lanima.co.uk).*
Barbecoa *20 New Change Passage, EC4M 9AG (3005 8555, www.barbecoa.com).*
Bea's of Bloomsbury *83 Watling Street, EC4M 9BX (7242 8330, www.beasof bloomsbury.com).*

Locals' Tips

Around the edges of Smithfield Market are several late-night/early-morning or 24-hour cafés, serving clubbers, market traders, couriers and taxi drivers at all hours. Try Ferrari's, 8 West Smithfield, EC1A 9JR.

For a stress-free high-street shop, go to Marks & Spencer, Moorgate (a few steps from the tube). It's a large store, with a basement food hall, and is very quiet on Saturdays.

If you're looking for a queue-free cashpoint near Spitalfields Market, try the Broadgate Centre on the north side of Bishopsgate.

Take advantage of one of the many free lunchtime concerts in the City's churches.

Skate at Broadgate Ice Rink. It's open for more months (mid October to mid February) than the temporary outdoor rinks, is often less crowded and you don't have to book in advance.

Listen to a talk or join in a debate at the Bishopsgate Institute. All sorts of topics are covered: full details at www.bishopsgate.org.uk.

Bevis Marks Restaurant *Bevis Marks, EC3A 5DQ (7283 2220, www.bevismarksthe restaurant.com).*

Bonds *Threadneedle Hotel, 5 Threadneedle Street, EC2R 8AY (7657 8090, www.theeton collection.com).*

Bread Street Kitchen *10 Bread Street, EC4M 9AJ (3030 4050, www.breadstreetkitchen.com).*

Butcher at Leadenhall *6-7 Leadenhall Market, EC3V 1LR (7283 1662).*

Café Below *St Mary-le-Bow Church, Cheapside, EC2V 6AU (7329 0789, www.cafebelow.co.uk).*

Café du Marché *22 Charterhouse Square, Charterhouse Mews, EC1M 6DX (7608 1609, www.cafedumarche.co.uk).*

Carluccio's *12 West Smithfield, EC1A 9JR (7329 5904, www.carluccios.com).*

Ceena *13 St Bride Street, EC4A 4AS (7936 4941).*

Chiswell Street Dining Rooms *56 Chiswell Street, EC1Y 4SA (7614 0177, www.chiswell streetdining.com).*

Cinnamon Kitchen *9 Devonshire Square, EC2M 4YL (7626 5000, www.cinnamon-kitchen.com).*

City Câphé *17 Ironmonger Lane, EC2V 8EY (http://citycaphe.com).*

TRANSPORT

Tube stations *Central* Chancery Lane, St Paul's, Bank, Liverpool Street; *Circle* Temple, Blackfriars, Mansion House, Cannon Street, Monument, Tower Hill, Aldgate, Liverpool Street, Moorgate, Barbican; *District* Temple, Blackfriars, Mansion House, Cannon Street, Monument, Tower Hill; *DLR* Bank, Tower Gateway; *Hammersmith & City* Liverpool Street, Moorgate, Barbican; *Metropolitan* Aldgate, Liverpool Street, Moorgate, Barbican; *Northern* Bank, Moorgate; *Waterloo & City* Bank

Rail stations *c2c* Fenchurch Street; *Greater Anglia* Liverpool Street; *Southeastern Trains* Cannon Street; *First Capital Connect* Blackfriars, City Thameslink, Moorgate

Main bus routes dozens of buses run through the City of London – for a full list, visit www.tfl.gov.uk/buses; *night buses* N8, N11, N15, N21, N26, N35, N47, N55, N63, N76, N133; *24-hour buses* 23, 25, 43, 149, 214, 242, 243, 271, 344

River commuter and leisure boat services running east and west, with a pier at Blackfriars

---

Club Gascon *57 West Smithfield, EC1A 9DS (7796 0600, www.clubgascon.com).*

Comptoir Gascon *63 Charterhouse Street, EC1M 6HJ (7608 0851, www.comptoir gascon.com).*

Coq d'Argent *No.1 Poultry, EC2R 8EJ (7395 5000, www.coqdargent.co.uk).*

Don Bistro & Restaurant *The Courtyard, 20 St Swithin's Lane, EC4N 8AD (7626 2606, www.thedonrestaurant.com).*

Dose *70 Long Lane, EC1A 9EJ (7600 0382, www.dose-espresso.com).*

Fox & Anchor *115 Charterhouse Street, EC1M 6AA (7250 1300, www.foxandanchor. com).*

Gaucho *1 Bell Inn Yard, EC3V 0BL (7626 5180, www.gauchorestaurants.co.uk).*

Grand Café *The Royal Exchange, EC3V 3LR (7618 2480, www.theroyalexchange.com).*

Grazing *19-21 Great Tower Street, EC3R 5AR (7283 2932, www.grazingfood.com).*

Goodman City *11 Old Jewry, EC2R 8DU (7600 8220, www.goodmanrestaurants.com).*

Hawksmoor Guildhall *10 Basinghall Street, EC2V 5BQ (7397 8120, www.thehawksmoor. co.uk).*

Haz *www.hazrestaurant.co.uk; 9 Cutler Street, E1 7DJ (7929 7923); 6 Mincing Lane, EC3M 3BD (7929 3173); 34 Foster Lane, EC2V 6HD (7600 4172); 112 Houndsditch, EC3A 7BD (7623 9143).*

High Timber *8 High Timber Street, EC4V 3PA (7248 1777, www.hightimber.com).*

Hilliard *26A Tudor Street, EC4Y 0AY (7353 8150, www.hilliardfood.co.uk).*

Hummus Bros *128 Cheapside, EC2V 6BT (7726 8011, www.hbros.co.uk).*

Imperial City *The Royal Exchange, EC3V 3LL (7626 3437, www.orientalrestaurantgroup.co.uk).*

Kenza *10 Devonshire Square, EC2M 4YP (7929 5533, www.kenza-restaurant.com).*

K-10 City *20 Copthall Avenue, EC2R 7DN (7562 8510, www.k10.net).*

Lutyens *85 Fleet Street, EC4Y 1AE (7583 8385, www.lutyens-restaurant.com).*

Morgan M Barbican *50 Long Lane, EC1A 9EJ (7609 3560, www.morganm.com).*

Moshi Moshi Sushi *Upper Level, Liverpool Street Station, EC2M 7QH (7247 3227, www.moshimoshi.co.uk).*

1 Lombard Street *1 Lombard Street, EC3V 9AA (7929 6611, www.1lombardstreet.com).*

Paternoster Chop House *Warwick Court, Paternoster Square, EC4M 7DX (7029 9400, www.paternosterchophouse.co.uk).*

Prism *147 Leadenhall Street, EC3V 4QT (7256 3888, www.harveynichols.com).*

Le Relais de Venise l'entrecôte
5 Throgmorton Street, EC2N 2AD (7638 6325, www.relaisdevenise.com).
Restaurant at St Paul's *St Paul's Cathedral, St Paul's Churchyard, EC4M 8AD (7248 2469, www.restaurantatstpauls.co.uk).*
Rhodes Twenty Four *24th floor, Tower 42, Old Broad Street, EC2N 1HQ (7877 7703, www.rhodes24.co.uk).*
Rosemary Lane *61 Royal Mint Street, E1 8LG (7481 2602, www.rosemarylane.btinternet.co.uk).*
Sauterelle *The Royal Exchange, EC3V 3LR (7618 2483, www.sauterelle-restaurant.co.uk).*
Smiths of Smithfield *67-77 Charterhouse Street, EC1M 6HJ (7251 7950, www.smithsof smithfield.co.uk).*
Sweetings *39 Queen Victoria Street, EC4N 4SA (7248 3062, www.sweetingsrestaurant.com).*
Taylor St Baristas *www.taylor-st.com; 1A New Street, EC2M 4TP (7929 2207); Unit 3, 125 Old Broad Street, EC2N 1AR (7256 8665).*
Tsuru *Aldermary House, 10 Queen Street, EC4N 1TX (7248 1525).*
Vivat Bacchus *47 Farringdon Street, EC4A 4LL (7353 2648, www.vivatbacchus.co.uk).*
White Swan Pub & Dining Room *108 Fetter Lane, EC4A 1ES (7242 9696, www.thewhiteswan london.com).*
Wood Street *Wood Street, EC2Y 5EJ (7256 6990, www.woodstreetbar.com).*

Bars & pubs

Bar and pub chains have a very strong presence in the City, but there are some wonderfully historic boozers and wine bars, and one or two excellent cocktail bars too. On and around Fleet Street, try the Viaduct Tavern (whose cellars are believed to be the last surviving cells of Newgate Prison), the Old Bell Tavern (which reputedly stands on the site of London's first print shop), the Black Friar (with its original 1905 interior) and labyrinthine Ye Olde Cheshire Cheese.

Impressive buildings include the Old Bank of England, now a Fuller's pub. For great views, the Samuel Pepys has a sweeping view of the Thames towards the South Bank. El Vino is a family-run group of wine bars that specialises in claret; fans of Guinness might like Tipperary, London's first Irish pub and the first to sell the black stuff outside Ireland.

On Chancery Lane (the border between the Cities of London and Westminster), the prevailing sight is lawyers getting sloshed.

Focus on the architecture instead; standouts include two ancient pubs: Ye Olde Mitre (dating from 1546) and the Cittie of Yorke (1430). Rather different is Volupté, a neo-burlesque bar serving cocktails.

Around Mansion House, Monument and Bank, wine and champagne top the menu at old-timer Bow Wine Vaults and newcomer

Newcomer **Hawksmoor Guildhall**.

Bar Battu. Leadenhall Market is home to the fine Lamb Tavern (a Young's pub); for more historic venues, try the rambling Williamson's Tavern, legend-heavy Ye Olde Watling, unpretentious Hatchet, and the atmospheric, half-timbered Bell – thought to be the City's oldest pub (the Swan Tavern has a different claim to fame, as the City's smallest).

The area around Liverpool Street heaves with City workers on Thursday and Friday nights, all with annihilation on their minds. A safer bet might be adjacent Spitalfields in Tower Hamlets, though the George (part of the Andaz hotel) and Hamilton Hall (a former ballroom restored to some kind of glory by JD Wetherspoon) are worth trying.

For a little more glamour, head to Vertigo 42 – situated on the 42nd floor of the tallest edifice in the City – or the bars at Prism or 1 Lombard Street (for both, see p48). More recent additions include the Anthologist, the Folly and Drift, all huge, contemporary cocktail bars owned by Drake & Morgan, and the Skylounge, a spacious rooftop hotel

bar. A kitsch night out can be guaranteed at tiki bar Kanaloa, while 28°-50° Wine Workshop & Kitchen offers a more serious space for quaffing.

Or opt for Smithfield: thanks to Fabric (the destination club that draws enormous weekend queues), the bars on Charterhouse Street pull in a vibrant crowd – wedge-shaped Charterhouse, kookily designed Fluid and the multifaceted Smiths of Smithfield (see p49) are all popular pre-club pit-stops. There are some decent, underused pubs on the south side of the market too, such as the Bishops Finger and Hand & Shears, plus stellar wine bar Cellar Gascon.

Anthologist *58 Gresham Street, EC2V 7BB (0845 468 0101, www.theanthologistbar.co.uk).*
Bar Battu *48 Gresham Street, EC2V 7AY (7036 6100, www.barbattu.com).*
Bell *29 Bush Lane, EC4R 0AN (7929 7772).*
Bishops Finger *9-10 West Smithfield, EC1A 9JR (7248 2341).*
Black Friar *174 Queen Victoria Street, EC4V 4EG (7236 5474).*
Bow Wine Vaults *10 Bow Churchyard, EC4M 9DQ (7248 1121, www.bowwinevaults.com).*
Cellar Gascon *59 West Smithfield, EC1A 9DS (7600 7561, www.cellargascon.com).*
Charterhouse *38 Charterhouse Street, EC1M 6JH (7608 0858, www.charterhousebar.co.uk).*
Cittie of Yorke *22 High Holborn, WC1V 6BN (7242 7670).*
Drift *Heron Tower, 110 Bishopsgate, EC2N 4AY (0845 468 0103, www.thedriftbar.co.uk).*
Fabric *77A Charterhouse Street, EC1M 3HN (7336 8898, www.fabriclondon.com).*
Fluid *40 Charterhouse Street, EC1M 6JN (7253 3444, www.fluidbar.com).*
Folly *41 Gracechurch Street, EC3V 0BT (0845 468 0102, www.thefollybar.co.uk).*
George *Andaz Hotel, 40 Liverpool Street, EC2M 7QN (7618 7300, www.andaz.com).*
Hamilton Hall *The Concourse, Liverpool Street Station, EC2M 7PY (7247 3579, www.jdwetherspoon.co.uk).*
Hand & Shears *1 Middle Street, EC1A 7JA (7600 0257).*
Hatchet *28 Garlick Hill, EC4V 2BA (7236 0720).*
Kanaloa *18 Lime Office Court, Shoe Lane, EC4A 3BQ (7842 0620, www.kanaloaclub.com.*
Lamb Tavern *10-12 Leadenhall Market, EC3V 1LR (7626 2454, www.lambtavernleadenhall.com).*
Old Bank of England *194 Fleet Street, EC4A 2LT (7430 2255, www.fullers.co.uk).*

Old Bell Tavern *95 Fleet Street, EC4Y 1DH
(7583 0216, www.nicholsonspubs.co.uk).*
Samuel Pepys *Stew Lane, High Timber
Street, EC4V 3PT (7489 1871, www.thesamuel
pepys.co.uk).*
Skylounge *Doubletree by Hilton Hotel,
7 Pepys Street, EC3N 4AF (7709 1000,
http://doubletree1.hilton.com).*
Swan Tavern *Ship Tavern Passage, 77-80
Gracechurch Street, EC3V 1LY (7929 6550,
www.fullers.co.uk).*
Tipperary *66 Fleet Street, EC4Y 1HT (7583 6470).*
28°-50° Wine Workshop & Kitchen
*140 Fetter Lane, EC4A 1BT (7242 8877,
www.2850.co.uk).*
Vertigo 42 *Tower 42, 25 Old Broad Street,
EC2N 1HQ (7877 7842, www.vertigo42.co.uk).*
Viaduct Tavern *126 Newgate Street, EC1A
7AA (7600 1863, www.fullers.co.uk).*
El Vino *www.elvino.co.uk; 47 Fleet Street,
EC4Y 1BJ (7353 6786); 30 New Bridge Street,
EC4V 6BJ (7236 4534); 125 London Wall,
EC2Y 5AP (7600 6377).*
Volupté *7-9 Norwich Street, EC4A 1EJ
(7831 1622, www.volupte-lounge.com).*
Williamson's Tavern *1 Groveland Court,
off Bow Lane, EC4M 9EH (7248 5750,
www.nicholsonspubs.co.uk).*
Ye Olde Cheshire Cheese *145 Fleet Street,
EC4A 2BU (7353 6170).*
Ye Olde Mitre *1 Ely Court, Ely Place (beside
8 Hatton Gardens), EC1N 6SJ (7405 4751).*
Ye Olde Watling *29 Watling Street, EC4M
9BR (7248 8935, www.nicholsonspubs.co.uk).*

Shops

City retailing has undergone a huge shake-
up: the biggest transformation has been
at the western end of Cheapside, with the
arrival of the One New Change centre. But,
as elsewhere in the Square Mile, although
the architecture (courtesy of Jean Nouvel)
may be interesting, the shops are identikit.
Fashion chains predominate (All Saints,
Topshop, Reiss and so on, though there's
also a hairdresser and a dry cleaner) at
One New Change, while at the swanky
Royal Exchange complex there's a raft
of jewellers (Tiffany, Boodles, De Beers,
Omega, Watches of Switzerland and so on),
perfumers (Penhaligon's, Jo Malone), deluxe
brands (Hermès, Gucci, Cartier, Montblanc)
and more quirky – though by no means
budget – names such as Agent Provocateur,
Lulu Guinness and Paul Smith.

Moving slightly downmarket, there's a
useful mini version of House of Fraser just
north of London Bridge. Otherwise, high-
street chains abound: on Moorgate you'll
find a big Marks & Spencer; on Moorfields
there's a huge New Look; in and around
Liverpool Street and the Broadgate Centre
there are branches of Hobbs, Reiss, Molton
Brown and Space NK, plus a big Tesco and
independent wine retailer Uncorked.
Cheapside has yet more clothing chains
and another big Tesco, but some originality
is added to the mix with Daunt Books; for a
little more charm, wander down Dickensian
Bow Lane for Jones the Bootmaker and a
branch of Jigsaw. Near St Paul's, Paternoster
Square looks a treat, but the shops are run
of the mill. Along Holborn Viaduct and Fleet
Street, it's chain stores all the way, enlivened
only by shops for the legal profession. More
scenic is historic Leadenhall Market, to the
east, which is packed with shops and stalls.
The occasional one-off gem remains – visit
F Flittner barbers (est. 1904) on Moorgate for
a glimpse of how things used to be.

Daunt Books *61 Cheapside, EC2V 6AX
(7248 1117, www.dauntbooks.co.uk).*
F Flittner *86 Moorgate, EC2M 6SE
(7606 4750, www.fflittner.com).*
House of Fraser *68 King William Street, EC4N
7HR (0844 800 3718, www.houseoffraser.co.uk).*
Leadenhall Market *Whittington Avenue, off
Gracechurch Street, EC3V 1LR (7929 1073,
www.leadenhallmarket.co.uk).*
One New Change *One New Change, EC4M
9AF (7002 8900, www.onenewchange.com).*
Royal Exchange *Cornhill & Threadneedle
Street, EC3V 3LR (www.theroyalexchange.com)*
Uncorked *Exchange Arcade, Broadgate Centre,
EC2M 3WA (7638 5998, www.uncorked.co.uk).*

Arts & attractions

Cinemas & theatres
Barbican Centre *Silk Street, EC2Y 8DS (7638
8891, www.barbican.org.uk). Major arts centre,
with theatres, an art gallery and one cinema
(two more screens are planned to open in 2012).
Also the home of the LSO (London Symphony
Orchestra) and the BBC Symphony Orchestra.*

Galleries & museums
Bank of England Museum *Entrance on
Bartholomew Lane, EC2R 8AH (7601 5545,
www.bankofengland.co.uk/museum).*

Barbican Art Gallery *Level 3, Barbican Centre, Silk Street, EC2Y 8DS (7638 8891, www.barbican.org.uk). Contemporary art and photography exhibitions.*

Clockmakers' Museum *Guildhall Library, Aldermanbury, EC2V 7HH (7332 1868, www.clockmakers.org). Well-presented horological exhibition.*

Dr Johnson's House *17 Gough Square, EC4A 3DE (7353 3745, www.drjohnsons house.org). Wonderfully atmospheric museum celebrating the life and works of Samuel Johnson.*

Guildhall Art Gallery *Guildhall Yard, off Gresham Street, EC2V 5AE (7332 3700, www.guildhallartgallery.cityoflondon.gov.uk). Works by Constable, Reynolds and Rossetti.*

Museum of London *London Wall, EC2Y 5HN (7001 9844, www.museumoflondon.org.uk). The history of the capital.*

Museum of Methodism & John Wesley's House *Wesley's Chapel, 49 City Road, EC1Y 1AU (7253 2262, www.wesleys chapel.org.uk).*

Tower Bridge Exhibition *Tower Bridge, SE1 2UP (7403 3761, www.towerbridge.org.uk). The history of the bridge. Stunning views from the high-level walkways.*

Tower of London *Tower Hill, EC3N 4AB (0844 482 7777, www.hrp.org.uk). The Crown Jewels, ravens, Beefeaters, tourists… and nearly 1,000 years of British royal history in this fortress on the Thames (actually within the borough of Tower Hamlets).*

Other attractions

College of Arms *Queen Victoria Street, EC4V 4BT (7248 2762, www.college-of-arms.gov.uk). Heraldic and genealogical history.*

Guildhall *Gresham Street, EC2P 2EJ (7606 3030, www.guildhall.cityoflondon.gov.uk). Home of the Corporation of London. The cathedral-like Great Hall is used mainly for ceremonial events.*

Monument *Monument Street, EC3R 8AH (7626 2717, www.themonument.info). Built in 1677 to commemorate the Great Fire of London. Spectacular views from the top.*

Old Bailey *Central Criminal Court, corner of Newgate Street & Old Bailey, EC4M 7EH (7248 3277, www.justice.gov.uk). The public galleries allow viewing of trials in session.*

St Bartholomew-the-Great *West Smithfield, EC1A 9DS (7606 5171, www.greatstbarts.com). The City's finest medieval church.*

St Paul's Cathedral *Ludgate Hill, EC4M 8AD (7246 8357, www.stpauls.co.uk). Wren's masterpiece.*

Sport & fitness

The City is dominated by big-name private chains. The one public centre is a charmer, though: Golden Lane Leisure Centre offers an oasis of unpretentious calm amid high salaries and high towers, and underwent major refurbishment in 2011.

Gyms & leisure centres

Barbican YMCA *2 Fann Street, EC2Y 8BR (7628 0697, www.cityymca.org). Private.*

Cannons *Cousin Lane, EC4R 3XJ (7283 0101, www.cannons.co.uk). Private.*

Citypoint Club *Citypoint, 1 Ropemaker Street, EC2Y 9AW (7920 6200, www.thecitypointclub. co.uk). Private.*

Fitness First *www.fitnessfirst.co.uk; Unit 12, Liverpool Street Station, EC2M 7PY (7247 5511); 55 Gracechurch Street, EC3V 0EE (7621 0911); 5-11 Fetter Lane, EC4A 1QX (7353 2311); 1 Thavies Inn, EC4A 1AN (7822 0990); 1 America Square, EC3N 2LB (7488 9311). Private.*

COUNCIL TAX

A	up to £40,000	**£626.12**
B	£40,001-£52,000	**£730.48**
C	£52,001-£68,000	**£834.82**
D	£68,001-£88,000	**£939.18**
E	£88,001-£120,000	**£1,147.88**
F	£120,001-£160,000	**£1,356.60**
G	£160,001-£320,000	**£1,565.30**
F	over £320,000	**£1,878.36**

RECYCLING

Household waste recycled & composted 35%

Main recycling centre The City of London does not have a site within the borough, so residents are directed to: Northumberland Wharf, Yabsley Street, Isle of Dogs, E14 9RG (7538 4526)

Other recycling services clear sack recycling service; Christmas tree recycling; collection of white goods and furniture; IT equipment disposal; hazardous waste collection

Council contact The Recycling Team Cleansing Services, City of London, Walbrook Wharf, Upper Thames Street, EC4R 3TD (7606 3110, www.cityof london.gov.uk/recycling)

Golden Lane Leisure Centre *Golden Lane Estate, Fann Street, EC1Y 0SH (7250 1464, www.cityoflondon.gov.uk).*

LA Fitness *www.lafitness.co.uk; 20 Little Britain, EC1A 7DH (7600 0900); 48 Leadenhall Street, EC3A 2BE (7488 2934); 48 London Wall, EC2M 5QB (7628 9876); Cutlers Gardens, Devonshire Square, EC2M 4YA (7626 3161); 1 Broadgate, EC2M 7HA (7920 0192); 106 Fenchurch Street, EC3M 5JE (7369 0700).*

Slim Jim's Health Club *1 Finsbury Avenue, EC2M 2PF (7247 9982, www.slim-jims.co.uk). Private.*

Vie *122 Clerkenwell Road, EC1R 5DL (7278 8070, www.viehealthclubs.co.uk). Private.*

Virgin Active *www.virginactive.co.uk; 97 Aldersgate, EC1A 4JP (7374 0091); 1 Exchange Place, Appold Street, EC2M 2QT (7422 6400); Ibex House, 1 Haydon Street, EC3N 1HP (7680 5000). Private.*

Other facilities

Broadgate Ice Rink *Broadgate Circle, EC2M 2QS (7505 4068, www.broadgateinfo.net). Seasonal ice skating.*

Schools

Primary

There is only one state primary school within the City of London, the Sir John Cass's Foundation Primary School, and two independent schools, St Paul's Cathedral School and the Charterhouse Square School. See www.cityoflondon.gov.uk and www.edubase.gov.uk for more information.

Secondary

There are no state secondary schools, but the borough has an arrangement with Tower Hamlets to provide places. Local children also gain priority admission to the City of London Academy in Southwark.

City of London School for Boys *Queen Victoria Street, EC4V 3AL (7489 0291, www.clsb.org.uk). Boys only; private.*

City of London School for Girls *St Giles' Terrace, EC2Y 8BB (7847 5500, www.clsg.org.uk). Girls only; private.*

Property

WHAT THE AGENTS SAY:

'The City is becoming an ever more popular place to live, for a widely mixed community ranging from young professionals to retirees. The Barbican Estate makes up about half the residential population and is highly sought after; despite the architecture not being to everyone's taste, it is continually growing in retro kudos. The advantages are: it's very central, with fantastic transport links, yet quiet and peaceful at weekends; it's renowned as a safe place to live; and there's a growing number of attractive shops, bars, cafés and restaurants, as well as many cultural attractions nearby. Looking ahead, the Crossrail development will improve links to Canary Wharf and Heathrow airport, which will no doubt push up further the cost of buying or renting. Downsides are becoming fewer, but residential property is scarce and apartments are generally on the small side. Plus some places can be on noisy roads and there is a lack of greenery compared to the leafy suburbs.'
Kris Deichler, Frank Harris & Company

Average property prices

Detached, Semi-detached, Terraced n/a
Flat £418,093

Local estate agents

Bridge Estates *98A Curtain Road, EC2A 3AA (7749 1400, www.bridge.co.uk).*

Frank Harris & Company *87 Long Lane, EC1A 9ET (7600 7000, www.frankharris.co.uk).*

Hamilton Brooks *73 Long Lane, EC1A 9ET (7606 8000, www.hamiltonbrooks.co.uk).*

Scott City *122 Newgate Street, EC1A 7AA (7600 0026, www.scottcity.co.uk).*

Spencer Thomas *1B Britton Street, EC1M 5NW (7566 0052, www.spencerthomas.co.uk).*

Square Mile Property Management *Global House, 5A Sandys Row, E1 7HW (7392 0111, www.m2fm.com).*

Other information

Council

City of London Corporation *PO Box 270, Guildhall, EC2P 2EJ (7606 3030, www.cityoflondon.gov.uk).*

Legal services

Royal Courts of Justice Advice Bureau *Strand, WC2A 2LL (0844 856 3534, www.rcjadvice.org.uk). There's no longer a CAB in the City; this is the nearest.*

Local information

www.barbicanliving.co.uk.
www.londonlocals.co.uk.

'I love this area because all the world is here, and has been for centuries. And the 2012 Games are just the cherry on a rich, diverse and very vibrant cake.'

Rhian Harris, Director, V&A Museum of Childhood

Tower Hamlets

Nowhere in London has regeneration and gentrification been more rapid, profound and localised than in Tower Hamlets. But beyond the mini-Manhattan of Docklands and the middle-class paradise of boutiques and gourmet eats around Spitalfields, you'll find a borough still wrestling with the sort of problems Dickens described.

Neighbourhoods

Spitalfields and Brick Lane

You know a neighbourhood has lost its edge when groups of clipboard-wielding schoolchildren filling out local history worksheets can be seen trailing the streets. Indeed, apart from a few prostitutes on Commercial Street after-hours, the seedier side of Spitalfields has become something of a distant memory. The City has crept ever closer over the last few years, bringing with it new public spaces, a market refurb with accompanying Foster & Partners redevelopment, and a variety of other lofty, mostly uninspiring office blocks.

Spitalfields has long been a first place of refuge for communities new to London. Over the years, it has housed groups such as French Huguenots evading persecution by Catholics, and Ashkenazi Jews escaping Russian pogroms. Today, the neighbourhood's most prominent immigrant community is the Bangladeshi one on and around Brick Lane. Central to life here is the Brick Lane Mosque (opened 1976), previously a French Protestant church (1743), Methodist chapel (1819) and the Spitalfields Great Synagogue (1889). Meanwhile, the cheap studio space that once drew arty and creative types to the area has become a thing of the past. Property prices in this part of town have risen exponentially of late, and Spitalfields' role as a home for transient populations has almost certainly come to an end.

It's easy to see why house prices are so high – if you can get past the film crews shooting period dramas, peep through the

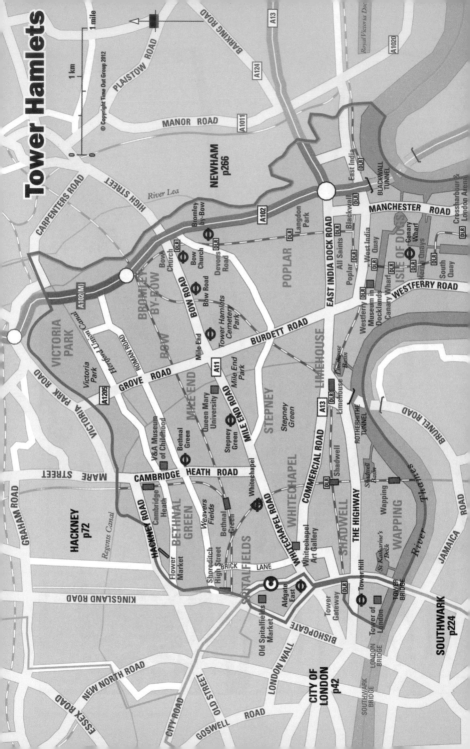

windows at the exquisite interiors of the houses on Hanbury, Princelet and Fournier Streets (in the shadow of Hawksmoor's masterpiece Christ Church). Tracey Emin and Jeanette Winterson are among those who followed early pioneers Gilbert and George in restoring once-dilapidated Huguenot houses to Georgian splendour.

Evidence of the more gruesome elements of Spitalfields' history has all but vanished – though inescapable Jack the Ripper walking tours in the area offer locals the occasional overheard reminder of its murky past.

Sunday is when the neighbourhood's markets come to life. As well as Spitalfields Market itself, there's the Sunday (Up)Market and, of course, the cheap tat and banter of Brick Lane Market. To the west, Dray Walk, by the Old Truman Brewery (a handy short cut between Brick Lane and Spitalfields Market), has embraced café society; on Sunday afternoons the street overflows with young hipsters recovering from hangovers. It also appeals to grown-up money: taxidermy-infested culinary pioneer Les Trois Garçons has been joined by both Conran (Boundary) and Soho House (Shoreditch House and Pizza East); you know the area's days as artsville are pretty much gone.

Whitechapel and Stepney

The lower end of Brick Lane turns into Osborn Street, which merges into the traffic-clogged Whitechapel Road (A11). Tune out the horn-tooting chaos and you'll find there's more to this hectic thoroughfare than first meets the eye. For starters, there's the excellent Whitechapel Gallery, which has expanded into the former library next door, doubling its size and creating enough space for a fine restaurant. Opposite, Altab Ali Park – established in honour of a young machinist murdered by racists in 1978 – has had a splendid redesign, marking out the original White Chapel's foundations and refurbishing the replica of a Dhaka martyrs' monument.

Up the road, the Whitechapel Bell Foundry, maker of Big Ben, has been in continuous operation since 1570. Also serving the needs of the local community are the East London Mosque & London Muslim Centre, Whitechapel Road's street market and the first of the borough's several glass-walled Idea Stores, which have done a great job of bringing people into what were 'dull old' public libraries. It's still a pretty run-down road, but a spot of Queen Anne architecture jollies things up, along with some interesting pockets of terraced housing off the main street and the obligatory new flat developments. There's also a huge branch of Sainsbury's.

Most of the East End boozers that aren't already fried chicken shops look likely to become dessert bars or betting shops, though you'll still encounter local drunks slurring their way into the A&E department of the Royal London Hospital – a Victorian monstrosity that once gave succour to the Elephant Man, but is now undergoing vast refurbishment. There are some great restaurants in the vicinity (Tayyab's, Needoo Grill), but for enjoyable drinking, head to the George

Highs & Lows

▲ **Market mix** The borough has the best range of markets in the capital, from fashion at Spitalfields and fabulous flowers on Columbia Road to handbags and pillow cases on Petticoat Lane. Brick Lane has old-fashioned junk as well as new designer-maker creations.
Ohle eats The combination of cash and cachet has given lower Hamlets some exciting places to eat.
Cultural mix Successive waves of immigration over the centuries have made this one of the most vibrant and varied areas in London

House prices Good luck getting on the housing ladder anywhere in the vicinity of the City or Canary Wharf. And can Spitalfields hold its character against an influx of people who regard property as no more than an investment?
Hell on two wheels At the Bow Flyover, Tower Hamlets has London's most dangerous crossing for cyclists. Of 2011's 16 cycling fatalities, two happened here – less than a month apart.
Olympic legacy Many locals are wondering exactly what benefit the borough is going to get from the 2012 Games in return for all the upheavals. ▼

Columbia Road Flower Market on a Sunday morning.

on Commercial Road, rather than the infamous Blind Beggar.

In Stepney, things have improved since Dr Barnardo set up his first refuge in 1870. Albert Gardens and Arbour Square are well-hidden green spots. Stepney Green is also pleasant, with the adjoining Stepney City Farm and charming St Dunstan church and churchyard – notwithstanding Crossrail disruption. What had been a slum for almost as long as it was part of the city is now full of cranes building new flats (many aimed at teachers and nurses). Nearby, the palatial art deco Troxy, a former cinema, puts on terrific gigs, MMA bouts and elaborate weddings.

Bethnal Green

As in much of east London, World War II bomb damage has left an architectural patchwork in Bethnal Green, with no single style or period monopolising. The result is a neighbourhood that operates on a human scale and streets that each seem to have their own character. Newcomers are often pleasantly surprised when they realise how central Bethnal Green is – much of the area is in Zone 1, and it's a quick Central line

journey from Bethnal Green tube station into the middle of town. The social attractions of Brick Lane and Shoreditch are within walking distance too. The area has its own green space, Weavers Fields, and the vast expanse of Victoria Park is not far away, at the end of Old Ford Road.

On Sundays, Columbia Road Flower Market is a multicoloured frenzy, and the terraced cottages around neighbouring Jesus Green are the most highly prized in the area, despite being on the poky side. As rising housing costs pushed creative types out of areas such as Spitalfields, Bethnal Green's art scene flourished. Property here is decidedly more affordable and, on the edge of Hackney, Vyner Street has its own mini-scene of galleries, musing artists and funky cafés. Even the old Town Hall, just north of the V&A Museum of Childhood, has become a boutique hotel and the high-ticket Viajante restaurant.

It's not all bleeding-edge cool, though. On the main thoroughfare, Bethnal Green Road, you can also still sit down for old-fashioned pie and mash or a proper fry-up at time-honoured local caff Pellicci's.

Mile End

The City may only be a mile away, but its glittering towers on the horizon seem to be in a different world. Mile End still feels considerably down-at-heel, with few of the pockets of cool found in neighbouring Bethnal Green. The legacy of wartime bomb damage and slum clearances means property here is a hotch-potch of 18th-century terraces and expansive housing estates, inspiration for much of Dizzee Rascal's grimy oeuvre. Social housing and rentals make up a large proportion of the area's housing stock, but for those who do choose to buy here, prices remain lower than many other parts of Tower Hamlets.

Mile End may lack glamour, but it offers excellent transport connections (with the Hammersmith & City, District and Central tube lines, as well as numerous bus routes), as well as Mile End Park – a series of green areas adjacent to the canal. The park crosses busy Mile End Road by means of an ingenious Green Bridge, with grass and trees growing out of it; beneath is a handy hub of restaurants, coffee shops and a Budgens. Residents also make good use of the pleasant canal path, the Mile End Climbing Wall, the leisure centre and the outdoor karting track.

Opposite the park, Queen Mary, University of London, gives a studenty feel to this stretch of Mile End Road, with majestic older buildings sitting alongside the award-winning modern architecture of the university's Student Village.

Victoria Park

The area around Victoria Park has gone the way of much of Tower Hamlets and become a serious property hotspot. Described by Dickens as a place 'No student of London life should miss seeing,' the park is London's third largest cultivated green space, after Hyde Park and Regent's Park. Shaped like a wellington boot, it was developed in the mid 19th century in an attempt to bring health and vigour to the working classes. Sadly, its lido is no longer in use, but the lakes, deer enclosure and fine café compensate, as do annual events such as music festivals, outdoor film screenings and firework displays.

Grove Road slices the park in two. If you follow it north as it turns into Lauriston Road, a wonderful hidden 'village' appears (across the borough boundary in Hackney). There's a cluster of shops around the very pleasant junction with Victoria Park Road – not to mention a bevy of estate agents, cashing in on the area's family-friendly layout. The spacious Victorian houses and villagey feel have made this one of the most sought-after pockets of east London, despite

The popular Pavilion Café, next to the lake in **Victoria Park.**

STATISTICS

BOROUGH MAKE-UP

Population 237,900
Ethnic origins
  White 57.1%
  Mixed 2.8%
  Asian or Asian British 30.6%
  Black or Black British 6.3%
  Chinese or other 3.1%
Students 12.3%
Retirees 7.7%

HOUSING STOCK

Borough size (hectares) 2,157
Population density per hectare 102.0
No. of households 108,190
**Houses (detached, semi-detached
or terraced)** 16%
Flats (converted or purpose-built) 84%

CRIME PER 1,000 OF POPULATION

Burglary 5
Robbery 4
Theft of vehicle 4
Theft from vehicle 7
Violence against the person 27
Sexual offences 1

MPs

Bethnal Green & Bow Rushanara Ali
(Labour); *Poplar & Limehouse* Jim
Fitzpatrick (Labour)

Bow, Bromley-by-Bow and Poplar

Poplar, once a crucial suburb of docks and dockers, is now riven by major thoroughfares – the approach to the Blackwall Tunnel, Aspen Way and the nascent A13, the East India Dock Road. Fast-food debris flutters along the last – testament to the predominant style of restaurant – and while the occasional Georgian terrace exists, much of the housing is of the brutalist post-war variety. One notable landmark is Ernö Goldfinger's modernist Balfron Tower, a block of flats with a chimney-like lift shaft stuck on one side; the building mirrors Goldfinger's more famous Trellick Tower in west London.

Poplar's High Street itself has little to recommend it, good (and busy) though its greasy spoon is. North of here is Chrisp Street Market, site of Britain's first pedestrian shopping centre (built for the 1951 Festival of Britain), and one of the borough's Idea Stores.

Bow itself, named as long ago as 1110 for the bridge over the River Lee, has, in keeping with Mile End, some excellent Victorian housing, particularly in the Tredegar conservation area, up and across Roman Road to Zealand and Chisenhale roads – where the Chisenhale building comprises artists' studios, a dance space and an art gallery. A newer artistic initiative is the Nunnery gallery, run by Bow Arts Trust. Roman Road offers pie and mash shops and a vibrant street market that's been in operation since 1843. The defining testament to the area's development is Bow Quarter – a complex of luxury apartments in the vast former Bryant & May match factory, where in 1888 a strike by female workers signalled the beginning of the suffragette movement. Other new-build developments have sprung up in hopes of benefitting from the 'Olympic effect'.

East of Bow sits Bromley-by-Bow. Historically just called Bromley, the 'by-Bow' suffix was dreamed up by London Underground to avoid confusion with the borough of Bromley, eight miles to the south. The area is dominated by ugly urban sprawl – industry, supermarkets, two- and three-lane highways and council estates – but just across Bow Creek (and the border with Newham) are the charming cobbles and historic buildings of Three Mills Island.

the nearest tube station (Bethnal Green) being a long walk down the Roman Road.

The Hertford Union Canal runs along the south of the park, bordered by a variety of new-build flats and houses. Follow the canal path east to Cadogan Terrace and you'll find some fine four-storey houses. Unfathomable council clearances in the 1960s robbed these houses of some of their neighbours, and those that remain have their backs to another unpleasant 1960s phenomenon – the A12 flyover, beyond which the canal connects to the River Lee Navigation.

Where the waterways meet, Fish Island has had something of a pre-Olympic revival: its post-industrial warehouses and swanky new apartments are complemented by Formans restaurant and salmon smokery, as well as the excellent hangout the Counter Café, both of which have great views of the Olympic Stadium.

Wapping, Shadwell and Limehouse

The glass-fronted apartments of Wapping and Limehouse sit at odds with much of the world around them. Affluent incomers who buy flats off-plan might be shocked to see what exists outside the picture frame: endless estates and a brutal, noisy main thoroughfare, the Highway, sucking traffic into the Rotherhithe Tunnel.

At least one half of Wapping has retained a villagey feel; the waterside area, with its atmospheric old pubs, is one of the lovelier examples of restoration in east London – but often feels oddly empty. The other half of the district is another matter: the prison-like enclosure of the News International office complex and its all-night-chugging printing press dominates (although attempts to sell the site are ongoing). King Edward VII Memorial Park, beside the river, is the subject of a local campaign against Thames Water, who want to dig it up for the capital's new 'supersewer'. Hawksmoor's church St George-in-the-East, rebuilt after Blitz damage inside the shell of its original walls, may outlive both park and publisher.

Nearby Shadwell is an incongruous mix of smart new housing and pockets of social deprivation, though of late there has been some welcome regeneration around the DLR station and Watney Street Market. In addition, Shadwell Basin is an excellent watersports and adventure centre.

Further east, Limehouse Basin marina has a similar feel, with some expensive new architecture and old buildings. The Narrow, Gordon Ramsay's popular gastropub, is here – and a postprandial walk along the beautifully scenic (though annoyingly interrupted) riverside path will take you past the historic Grapes pub, now co-owned by local resident Sir Ian McKellen.

Back westwards, towards the City, lie Tower Bridge and the Tower of London. Next door, in glossy St Katharine's Dock, the sense of history all but disappears – this modern yacht-filled marina is overlooked by pricey penthouses, coffee chains, pubs and restaurants.

Docklands and the Isle of Dogs

Very few peaceful cities ever have the chance to regenerate an area the size of the Docklands. And very few people gave such a project a chance of working in London. And yet, 20 years after building began on the site of the disused West India Quay, Canary Wharf is a successful, busy, bustling part of the city – a hub for business, a destination for shopping and an increasingly popular place to live. For much of the 19th century these were the busiest docks in the world, employing up to 50,000 people. The project that Margaret Thatcher's government started in 1981 is now the workplace for around 95,000 people.

The Wharf is featured in just about every film about London. Want a shot that sums up London as a business centre? Go to Canary Wharf. Want a cool-looking underground station? Look no further than the cathedral-like, Norman Foster-designed version here. There is, however, an undeniable sterility to the place – a feeling of not really being in London – particularly when the wind blows down the skyscraper-lined streets. And those skyscrapers no longer dominate the city like they did: Canary Wharf once had the UK's three tallest buildings, but they've

Waterfront **Limehouse**.

been outstripped by the City's Heron Tower and London Bridge's the Shard.

Local residents have plentiful amenities – supermarkets, gyms, shops galore, a cinema, a good museum, some fun public art – and weekends are no longer the lonely experience they were in the 1990s. But it does all feel very corporate: there is a lack of good independent eateries and cool boutiques, and a complete absence of corner shops. But then Canary Wharf never pretended to be edgy – take it as it is, and there's plenty to enjoy.

If the ripples of prosperity were expected to be felt all the way down the Isle of Dogs, they've taken a long time to arrive. New housing developments are being built, but only the privileged few are able to afford a piece of the waterfront. Although there are more shops, more places to go out and better transport links, this area remains in the shadow (literally and metaphorically) of its high-rise neighbours. The pubs are far from gastro (with the exception of the Gun on Coldharbour) and the estates are grim. But 'the Island' has a wonderful green space at its heart in Mudchute Park – a fabulous resource for both residents and visitors, and home to Mudchute City Farm.

Idiosyncratic **Wapping Food**.

Restaurants & cafés

Barely an inch of space remains near Spitalfields Market that hasn't been redeveloped or earmarked for development, resulting in serious smartening-up of the neighbourhood's restaurants and cafés. For locals, the increased choice – branches of Leon, Giraffe and Canteen – is a definite plus, as is the fact that most places are now open on Saturdays, but the too-glossy redevelopment of the covered market left a bitter taste in the mouths of many, and unaffordable commercial rents for some. However, gems such as St John Bread & Wine (British) and Hawksmoor (steak and great cocktails) are still going strong, as is the Market Coffee House; relative newcomers include Poppies (fish and chips) and Moo! (Argentinian).

Brick Lane Beigel Bake (a 24-hour, non-kosher Jewish bakery) is one of the best places to grab a quick, cheap bite on Brick Lane. Few of the Bangladeshi restaurants offer much more than formulaic curries: for real-deal Pakistani grills (and queues

serious enough to attest to the quality), head south, into Whitechapel, for Tayyab's and its offshoot Needoo Grill. For classy Modern European fare, there's the Whitechapel Gallery Dining Room.

On Bethnal Green Road, at the junction with Shoreditch High Street, is Pizza East, run by Soho House. Nearby, the Rochelle Canteen – co-owned by Margot Henderson, wife of St John's Fergus – serves excellent British food for lunch. Conran's Boundary hotel is also here, which features the winning Albion café (as well as a posher restaurant and a rooftop bar), while on Club Row there's fabulously OTT French restaurant Les Trois Garçons.

Along and around Columbia Road there's Jones Dairy Café, natural wine specialist Brawn, gastropub the Royal Oak, tapas bar Laxeiro and StringRay Globe Café, Bar & Pizzeria. Moving east, Bistrotheque provides a delightful cocktail of Anglo-French food, great attitude and a groovy bar in a converted warehouse. Astonishingly inventive cooking is to be had at Viajante (and its no-bookings, budget offshoot, the Corner Room), set in the former Town Hall, now a high-style hotel. British restaurant Palmers, isolated on the Roman Road, is another good option.

There are several old fashioned pie and mash shops in the borough, including G Kelly and S&R Kelly on Bethnal Green Road (also the home of ace greasy spoon E Pellicci). Vicky Park has some reliable dining choices: the Royal Inn on the Park, the Pavilion Café (inside the park, next to the pond) and the Empress of India gastropub (officially just over the border in Hackney). Further south, in Bow, is the Morgan Arms gastropub.

Towards the river, Wapping has its fair share of chains (including a handsome Pizza Express), but also pizza and pasta joint Il Bordello and Wapping Food, a fascinating arts space and Modern European restaurant in a former hydraulic power station. Almost in the City (on the Whitechapel/Wapping borders), Rosemary Lane offers excellent French cuisine in a relaxed setting. Limehouse has Gordon Ramsay's Narrow gastropub.

Docklands is packed with smart chains (Jamie's Italian, Carluccio's Caffè, Itsu, Wagamama, Wahaca) and slick venues designed with suits and their credit cards in mind. Many have fabulous waterfront settings, including the laudable Royal China (Chinese), Curve (North American) and Gaucho (Argentinian steaks). The Gun gastropub also overlooks the Thames, though not from the dining room, while Plateau (restaurant, grill and bar) looks out over Canary Wharf. At the bottom of the Isle of Dogs, Mudchute Kitchen is the city farm's café.

Albion at the Boundary Project
2-4 Boundary Street, E2 7DD (7729 1051, www.albioncaff.co.uk).
Bistrotheque 23-27 Wadeson Street, E2 9DR (8983 7900, www.bistrotheque.com).
Boisdale Canary Wharf Cabot Place, E14 4QT (7715 5818, www.boisdale-cw.co.uk).
Il Bordello 81 Wapping High Street, E1W 2YN (7481 9950).
Brawn 49 Columbia Road, E2 7RG (7729 5692, www.brawn.co).
Brick Lane Beigel Bake 159 Brick Lane, E1 6SB (7729 0616).
Canteen 2 Crispin Place, off Brushfield Street, E1 6DW (0845 686 1122, www.canteen.co.uk).
Corner Room Town Hall Hotel, Patriot Square, E2 9NF (no phone, www.cornerroom.co.uk).

Counter Café Stour Space, 7 Roach Road, E3 2PA (07834 275920, www.thecountercafe.co.uk).
Curve London Marriott Hotel, West India Quay, 22 Hertsmere Road, E14 4ED (7517 2808).
Elephant Royale Locke's Wharf, Westferry Road, E14 3AN (7987 7999, www.elephant royale.com).
Empress of India 130 Lauriston Road, E9 7LH (8533 5123, www.theempressofindia.com).
E Pellicci 332 Bethnal Green Road, E2 0AG (7739 4873).
Forman's Restaurant & Bar Stour Road, E3 2PA (8525 2365, www.formans.co.uk/restaurant).
Gaucho Grill 29 Westferry Circus, E14 8RR (7987 9494, www.gauchorestaurants.co.uk).
G Kelly 414 Bethnal Green Road, E2 0DJ (7739 3603, www.gkellypieandmash.co.uk).
Gun 27 Coldharbour, E14 9NS (7515 5222, www.thegundocklands.com).
Hawksmoor 157 Commercial Street, E1 6BJ (7247 7392, www.thehawksmoor.com).
Jones Dairy Café 23 Ezra Street, E2 7RH (7739 5372).
Laxeiro 95 Columbia Road, E2 7RG (7729 1147, www.laxeiro.co.uk).
Market Coffee House 52 Brushfield Street, E1 6AG (7247 4110).
Moo! 4 Cobb Street, E1 7LB (7377 9276, www.moogrill.co.uk).
Morgan Arms 43 Morgan Street, E3 5AA (8980 6389, www.capitalpubcompany.com).

Fish and chips at **Popples**.

Tower Hamlets

Mudchute Kitchen *Mudchute Park & Farm, Pier Street, E14 3HP (3069 9290, www.mudchutekitchen.org).*
Narrow *44 Narrow Street, E14 8DP (7592 7950, www.gordonramsay.com).*
Needoo Grill *87 New Road, E1 1HH (7247 0648, www.needoogrill.co.uk).*
Palmers *238 Roman Road, E2 0RY (8980 5590, www.palmersrestaurant.net).*
Pavilion Café *Victoria Park, Crown Gate West, E9 7DE (8980 0030, www.the-pavilion-cafe.com).*
Pizza East *56 Shoreditch High Street, E1 6JJ (7729 1888, www.pizzaeast.com).*
Plateau *Canada Place, Canada Square, E14 5ER (7715 7100, www.danddlondon.com).*
Poppies *6-8 Hanbury Street, E1 6QR (7247 0892, www.poppiesfishandchips.co.uk).*
Rochelle Canteen *Old School Building, Arnold Circus, E2 7ES (7729 5677, www.arnoldand henderson.com).*
Rosemary Lane *61 Royal Mint Street, E1 8LG (7481 2602, www.rosemarylane.btinternet.co.uk).*

Royal China *30 Westferry Circus, E14 8RR (7719 0888, www.royalchinagroup.co.uk).*
Royal Inn on the Park *111 Lauriston Road, E9 7HJ (8985 3321, www.remarkable restaurants.co.uk).*
Royal Oak *73 Columbia Road, E2 7RG (7729 2220).*
S&R Kelly *284 Bethnal Green Road, E2 0AG (7739 8676).*
St John Bread & Wine *94-96 Commercial Street, E1 6LZ (3301 8069, www.stjohnbread andwine.com).*
StringRay Globe Café, Bar & Pizzeria *109 Columbia Road, E2 7RL (7613 1141, www.stringraycafe.co.uk).*
Tayyab's *83-89 Fieldgate Street, E1 1JU (7247 6400, www.tayyabs.co.uk).*
Les Trois Garçons *1 Club Row, E1 6JX (7613 1924, www.lestroisgarcons.com).*
Viajante *Patriot Square, E2 9NF (7871 0461, www.viajante.co.uk).*
Wapping Food *Wapping Hydraulic Power Station, Wapping Wall, E1W 3ST (7680 2080, www.thewappingproject.com).*
Whitechapel Gallery Dining Room *77-82 Whitechapel High Street, E1 7QX (7522 7888, www.whitechapelgallery.org/dining-room).*

Locals' Tips

Forget cash machines after 11am on a Sunday in Spitalfields. Market crowds mean hellish (and often fruitless) queues, or no queue, but – curses – an empty machine. **Trinity Buoy Wharf (www.trinitybuoy wharf.com), at the mouth of Bow Creek, is a delight. Creatives labour in warehouses and a village of brightly coloured containers, all overshadowed by London's only lighthouse, now the permanent home of a fabulous sound installation,** *Long Player.*
Don't confuse Commercial *Street* (north–south through Spitalfields) and Commercial *Road* (east–west from Whitechapel to Limehouse). Quite apart from getting lost, everyone will know you're a newcomer. **Take a trip to Greenwich from the Isle of Dogs via the Foot Tunnel. It's much easier than taking the DLR – it's amazing more people don't use it.**
For great views of the Olympic Stadium from across the Lee Navigation, splash out on lunch at Forman's or just grab a coffee at the Counter Café almost next door.

Bars & pubs

It's all about great music and outdoor drinking on Brick Lane. Vibe Bar packs a serious crowd into its courtyard at the first sign of summer. Bar, club and live music venue 93 Feet East (*see p69*) also has a great outside space, as does the Big Chill Bar, off the Lane at Dray Walk. At weekends (particularly on Sunday when the markets are on), the whole area is thronged with hip young things drinking bottled lagers.

On Commercial Street, Public Life offers a haphazard roster of club nights and events, while just off Hanbury Street, Corbet Place has serious Sunday sessions and creative goings-on. Pub fans should head for the unpretentious Pride of Spitalfields, the fabulous Golden Heart or the quirky Commercial Tavern. Or head up Brick Lane to Cheshire Street and the Carpenter's Arms (once owned by the Krays, but now a pub that welcomes all comers). At the top of Brick Lane, on Bethnal Green Road, the Redchurch is a fine place to while away an evening (good music, late opening, minimal attitude); beer fans will enjoy Mason & Taylor across the road.

Bethnal Green also has its share of rough, no-frills hostelries – sprinkled with tastier bars. Trendies who can't be bothered to journey to Hoxton frequent the bar attached to hip restaurant Bistrotheque (*see p63*), or head to one of the roster of unusual nights and gigs at the Bethnal Green Working Men's Club (*see p69*). Also good are the Approach Tavern (with its upstairs art gallery) and done-up old boozer the Camel. Just up from Vyner Street, the little bar attached to Viajante (*see left*) serves good cocktails.

Further south, bar and club life is hidden but promising. On Whitechapel Road, Indo offers a laid-back vibe, pizza and late opening, while Rhythm Factory puts on a varied roster of quality gigs, as well as comedy nights. The George on Commercial Road runs a crazily broad range of events, from pirate rock 'n' roll to jumble sales and classical music.

Limehouse and Wapping have a selection of riverside pubs, many of which have existed in some form or another for centuries; prime examples are the Grapes (built 1720) in Limehouse, and the Prospect of Whitby (built 1520) and Town of Ramsgate (which dates from at least the 17th century), both in Wapping. Gordon Ramsay's gastropub the Narrow (*see left*) offers more fine drinking. Further east towards Poplar, the Greenwich Pensioner attracts a youthful (if not entirely fashionable) crowd.

No longer considered the netherland between the fashionable East End and the wilder expanses of east London, Mile End and Bow have some excellent boozers to offer the discerning drinker. Highlights include the Morgan Arms gastropub (*see p63*) and the time-warped Palm Tree (with 1950s cash register, piano and old-school regulars). Residents also head up to Victoria Park to the Royal Inn on the Park (*see left*).

Eccentric touches are missing from the Docklands scene, though there are enough standard pubs and chain wine bars to get the local office workers so drunk they won't notice. The standout remains classy gastropub the Gun (*see p63*), with its spectacular Thames views.

Approach Tavern *47 Approach Road, E2 9LY (8980 2321, www.remarkablerestaurants.co.uk).*
Big Chill Bar *Dray Walk, Old Truman Brewery, Brick Lane, E1 6QL (7392 9180, www.bigchill.net).*

Artist at work in the **Nunnery**. See p68.

Camel *277 Globe Road, E2 0JD (8983 9888).*
Carpenter's Arms *73 Cheshire Street, E2 6EG (7739 6342, www.carpentersarmsfreehouse.com).*
Commercial Tavern *142 Commercial Street, E1 6NU (7247 1888).*
Corbet Place *Old Truman Brewery, 15 Hanbury Street, E1 6QR (7770 6028).*
George Tavern *373 Commercial Road, E1 0LA (7790 7335, www.thegeorgetavern.co.uk).*
Golden Heart *110 Commercial Street, E1 6LZ (7247 2158).*
Grapes *76 Narrow Street, E14 8BP (7987 4396, www.thegrapes.co.uk).*
Greenwich Pensioner *2 Bazely Street, E14 0ES (7987 4414).*
Indo *133 Whitechapel Road, E1 1DT (7247 4926).*
Mason & Taylor *51-55 Bethnal Green Road, E1 6LA (7749 9670, www.masonandtaylor.co.uk).*
Palm Tree *127 Grove Road, E3 5BH (8980 2918).*
Pride of Spitalfields *3 Heneage Street, E1 5LJ (7247 8933).*
Prospect of Whitby *57 Wapping Wall, E1W 3SH (7481 1095).*
Public Life *82A Commercial Street, E1 6LY (7375 1631, www.publiclife.org.uk).*
Redchurch *107 Redchurch Street, E2 7DL (7749 7844, www.theredchurch.co.uk).*

The new **Labour & Wait** store on hip Redchurch Street. See p68.

Rhythm Factory *16-18 Whitechapel Road, E1 1EW (7375 3774, www.rhythmfactory.co.uk).*
Town of Ramsgate *62 Wapping High Street, E1W 2PN (7481 8000).*
Vibe Bar *Old Truman Brewery, 91-95 Brick Lane, E1 6QL (7247 3479, www.vibe-bar.co.uk).*

Shops

In Tower Hamlets, Sunday is a day of retail, not rest. It's the day that stallholders at Spitalfields, Sunday (Up)Market, Brick Lane and Columbia Road set up shop. Columbia Road Flower Market is the pick of the bunch for atmosphere and entertainment, but starts early (the 8am crowd gets the choice blooms). It's testimony to the market's success that trading on Sunday mornings alone is enough to sustain many of the shopkeepers that line the streets either side of the stalls. These include children's shop Bob & Blossom, perfumier Angela Flanders and numerous homewares shops.

In the five years since the redevelopment around Spitalfields covered market, the area has moved distinctly upmarket and is now busy all week. Names such as Whistles, All Saints, Dower & Hall, Benefit and Sniff are all here, but the real stars remain the

independents: tea specialist Tea Smith, toy and fancy dress shop Wood 'n' Things and fashion boutique Precious. Vintage clothing specialists include Absolute Vintage and Blondie; delis A Gold and Verde & Co, and Wine Bargains of Spitalfields are also local favourites. Between Brick Lane and Spitalfields is Dray Walk, home to record shop Rough Trade East and creative fashion store Junky Styling.

Brick Lane itself – and side street Cheshire Street – come up trumps for vintage fashion: rummage for second-hand clobber in Rokit and everything from 1950s to '90s wear at Beyond Retro. Find new independent fashion at the Laden Showroom and jewellery from Serbian designer Dragana Perisic, plus ukuleles galore at Duke of Uke. The real jewel these days, though, is Redchurch Street, whose boutiques (the likes of Sunspel, Maison Trois Garçons and Sick) have been joined by Labour & Wait (retro homewares) and the flagship branch of Aubin & Wills (with its own boutique cinema). On Bethnal Green Road, check out the 123 Boutique.

At the opposite end of the retail scale, Brick Lane and Petticoat Lane markets are a throwback to a different era, with geezers selling cheap pants and fruit and veg by the bowlful. Towards the top of Brick Lane and its junction with Bethnal Green Road, makeshift stalls set up on blankets on the pavement (selling chipped teapots, '80s videos and stolen bikes) are another quirk of the East End. North of Bethnal Green Road, head for hip jeweller Tatty Devine and affordable, innovative furniture-maker Unto This Last. Alternatively, take a walk east along Bethnal Green Road. Here, a string of nondescript discount stores and cheap supermarkets is brightened up by Asian clothes shops, wedding shops and jewellers. The street markets on Bethnal Green Road and Roman Road are lively places to buy the usual mix of household goods and food. Tatty shops are the norm as Bethnal Green Road gives way to Roman Road, but there are a few above-average clothes shops, such as Rockafella and Zee & Co.

The nicest shopping enclave near Victoria Park is just over the borough line in Hackney. Here, along and off Lauriston Road, small, independent shops such as friendly boutique Sublime and excellent children's bookshop Victoria Park Books, plus a handful of gift and antiques shops, provide succour to well-heeled locals.

Stepney and Whitechapel offer more Asian clothes stores and grocers, plus the stalls of Whitechapel Market and a huge Sainsbury's. On Mile End Road in Stepney Green, a very different shopping experience awaits: a giant retail park, with branches of PC World, Halfords and Currys. Over in St Katharine's Docks sits a large Waitrose.

East into the Isle of Dogs, the best shopping can be found in the complex of subterranean malls around Canary Wharf, where pretty much every high-street chain you can think of (Boots, Topshop, Reiss, the White Company, mobile-phone shops galore) has set up to cater to the legions that flood the place on their lunch breaks. There's also a large branch of Waitrose (with eat-in food stalls).

Just north of Canary Wharf is a shopping centre from a different age – the giant Billingsgate fish market (you'll see its great plastic sign from Trafalgar Way at the east end of the Canary Wharf complex). Catering mainly to wholesale customers, there are nevertheless great stalls here for the individual, selling seafood, snacks, accessories and cooking utensils. The market still maintains old porterage traditions – there were protests in 2010 over Corporation of London attempts to change an 1876 licensing bylaw.

After the sheen of Canary Wharf, the street market on Chrisp Street in Poplar is a real contrast: it offers the usual cheap clothes and fruit and veg, and bottom-dollar caffs with outside seating where you can fill up on faggots and pease pudding for little more than spare change.

Absolute Vintage *15 Hanbury Street, E1 6QR (7247 3883, www.absolutevintage.co.uk).*
A Gold *42 Brushfield Street, E1 6AG (7247 2487, www.agoldshop.com).*
Angela Flanders *96 Columbia Road, E2 7QB (7739 7555, www.angelaflanders-perfumer.com).*
Aubin & Wills *64-66 Redchurch Street, E2 7DP (3487 0066, www.aubinandwills.com).*
Beyond Retro *110-112 Cheshire Street, E2 6EJ (7613 3636, www.beyondretro.com).*
Billingsgate Market *Trafalgar Way, E14 5ST (7987 1118, www.cityoflondon.gov.uk).*
Blondie *114-118 Commercial Street, E1 6NF (7247 0050, www.blondievintage.co.uk).*
Bob & Blossom *140 Columbia Road, E2 7RG (7739 4737, www.bobandblossom.com).*
Brick Lane Market *Brick Lane (north of railway bridge), Cygnet Street, Sclater Street, E1; Bacon Street, Cheshire Street, E2 (7364 1717, www.visitbricklane.org).*

TRANSPORT

Tube stations Central Bethnal Green, Mile End; District Tower Hill; District/Hammersmith & City Aldgate East, Whitechapel, Stepney Green, Mile End, Bow Road, Bromley-by-Bow; DLR Tower Gateway, Shadwell, Limehouse, Westferry, Poplar; All Saints, Langdon Park, Devons Road, Bow Church; Blackwall, East India; West India Quay, Canary Wharf, Heron Quays, South Quay, Crossharbour, Mudchute, Island Gardens; Jubilee Canary Wharf
Rail stations c2c Limehouse; Greater Anglia Bethnal Green, Cambridge Heath; London Overground Wapping, Shadwell, Whitechapel, Shoreditch High Street
Main bus routes into central London 8, 15, 25, 26, 48, 55, 100, 108, 205, 388; night buses N8, N15, N26, N55, N108; 24-hour buses 8, 25, 26, 108, 277
River commuter and leisure boat services to/from central London, with piers at St Katharine's Dock, Masthouse Terrace and Canary Wharf

Tower Hamlets

Columbia Road Flower Market *Columbia Road, between Gosset Street & Royal Oak pub, E2 (www.columbiaroad.info).*

Dragana Perisic *30 Cheshire Street, E2 6EH (7739 4484, www.draganaperisic.com).*

Duke of Uke *88 Cheshire Street, E2 6EH (3583 9728, www.dukeofuke.co.uk).*

Junky Styling *12 Dray Walk, Old Truman Brewery, Brick Lane, E1 6RF (7247 1883, www.junkystyling.co.uk).*

Labour & Wait *85 Redchurch Street, E2 7DJ (7729 6253, www.labourandwait.co.uk).*

Laden Showroom *103 Brick Lane, E1 6SE (7247 2431, www.laden.co.uk).*

Maison Trois Garçons *45 Redchurch Street, E2 7DJ (07879 640858, www.loungelover. co.uk/shop).*

Old Spitalfields Market *Commercial Street, between Lamb Street & Brushfield Street, E1 (7247 8556, www.oldspitalfields market.om).*

123 Boutique *123 Bethnal Green Road, E2 7DG (7729 8050, www.123bethnalgreen road.co.uk).*

Petticoat Lane Market *Middlesex, Goulston, New Goulston, Toynbee, Wentworth, Old Castle, Cobb, Leyden and Strype streets, E1 (7364 1717, www.towerhamlets.gov.uk).*

Precious *16 Artillery Passage, E1 7LJ (7377 6668, www.precious-london.com).*

Rockafella *81 Roman Road, E2 0QN (8981 0011).*

Rokit *101 & 107 Brick Lane, E1 6SE (7375 3864, 7247 3777, www.rokit.co.uk).*

Roman Road Market *Roman Road, between Parnell Road & St Stephen's Road, E3 (7364 1717).*

Rough Trade East *Dray Walk, Old Truman Brewery, Brick Lane, E1 6QL (7392 7788, www.roughtrade.com).*

Sick *105 Redchurch Street, E2 7DL (7033 2961).*

Sublime *225 Victoria Park Road, E9 7HJ (8986 7243).*

Sunday (Up)Market *Old Truman Brewery, entrances on Brick Lane & Hanbury Street, E1 (7770 6028, www.sundayupmarket.co.uk).*

Sunspel *7 Redchurch Street, E2 7DJ (7739 9729, www.sunspel.com).*

Tatty Devine *236 Brick Lane, E2 7EB (7739 9191, www.tattydevine.com).*

Tea Smith *6 Lamb Street, E1 6EA (7247 1333, www.teasmith.co.uk).*

Unto This Last *230 Brick Lane, E2 7EB (7613 0882, www.untothislast.co.uk).*

Verde & Co *40 Brushfield Street, E1 6AG (7247 1924).*

Victoria Park Books *174 Victoria Park Road, E9 7HD (8986 1124, www.victoriaparkbooks. co.uk).*

Wine Bargains of Spitalfields *139 Commercial Street, E1 6BJ (7375 2628).*

Wood 'n' Things *57 Brushfield Street, Old Spitalfields Market, E1 6AA (7247 6275, www.woodnthings.uk.com).*

Zee & Co *454 Roman Road, E3 5LU (8983 3383, www.zeeandco.co.uk).*

Arts & attractions

Cinemas & theatres

Aubin Cinema *64-66 Redchurch Street, E2 7DP (0845 604 8486, www.aubincinema.com).*

Cineworld West India Quay *Hertsmere Road, E14 4AL (0871 200 2000, www.cineworld.co.uk).*

Mile End Genesis Cinema *93-95 Mile End Road, E1 4UJ (7780 2000, www.genesis-cinema.co.uk).*

Rich Mix *35-47 Bethnal Green Road, E1 6LA (7613 7498, www.richmix.org.uk).*

Galleries & museums

Centre of the Cell *Blizard Building, 4 Newark Street, E1 2AT (7882 2562, www.centreofthe cell.org). A science education 'pod', suspended so you can watch medical researchers at work in their labs below.*

Chisenhale Gallery *64-84 Chisenhale Road, E3 5QZ (8981 4518, www.chisenhale.org.uk).*

Dennis Severs' House *18 Folgate Street, E1 6BX (7247 4013, www.dennissevershouse.co.uk). Curious but fascinating period reconstruction: a 'still-life drama' in a splendid Huguenot house.*

Museum of London Docklands *No.1 Warehouse, West India Quay, Hertsmere Road, E14 4AL (7001 9844, www.museumoflondon. org.uk). Huge museum covering everything from slavery and London Bridge to the Blitz and Docklands development.*

Nunnery *181 Bow Road, E3 2SJ (8709 5292, www.bowarts.org/nunnery). Bow Arts Trust gallery, splendidly located in a former Carmelite nunnery.*

Ragged School Museum *46-50 Copperfield Road, E3 4RR (8980 6405, www.raggedschool museum.org.uk). A look at Dr Barnardo's Victorian education of the East End's urchins.*

Royal London Hospital Museum & Archives *St Phillip's Church, Newark Street, E1 2AA (7377 7608, www.medicalmuseums.org).*

V&A Museum of Childhood *Cambridge Heath Road, E2 9PA (8983 5200, www.museumof childhood.org.uk). The V&A's East End offshoot.*

Whitechapel Art Gallery *77-82 Whitechapel High Street, E1 7QX (7522 7888, www. whitechapel.org). Leading contemporary gallery.*

Music & comedy venues

Bethnal Green Working Men's Club *42-44 Pollard Row, E2 6NB (7739 7170, www.workersplaytime.net).*

East Wintergarden *43 Bank Street, E14 5NX (7418 2725, www.canarywharf.com).*

93 Feet East *150 Brick Lane, E1 6QL (7770 6006, www.93feeteast.co.uk).*

Troxy *490 Commercial Road, E1 0HX (7790 9000, www.troxy.co.uk).*

Other attractions

Chisenhale Dance Space *64-84 Chisenhale Road, E3 5QZ (8981 6617, www.chisenhale dancespace.co.uk).*

East London Mosque & London Muslim Centre *46-92 Whitechapel Road, E1 1JX (7650 3000, www.eastlondonmosque.org.uk).*

Mudchute Park & Farm *Pier Street, E14 3HP (7515 5901, www.mudchute.org).*

Spitalfields City Farm *Buxton Street, E1 5AR (7247 8762, www.spitalfieldscity farm.org).*

Stepney City Farm *Stepney Way, E1 3DG (7790 8204, www.stepneycityfarm.org).*

Whitechapel Gallery, Tayyabs and **Whitechapel Road's street market.** See p57.

Whitechapel Bell Foundry *32-34 Whitechapel Road, E1 1DY (7247 2599, www.whitechapel bellfoundry.co.uk).*

Sport & fitness

Tower Hamlet's leisure facilities continue to improve. York Hall's facelift, completed a few years back, included a makeover of its Turkish baths – now budget spa facility Spa London. The Docklands Sailing & Watersports Centre on Millwall Dock offers everything from dragon-boat racing to Royal Yachting Association courses.

Gyms & leisure centres

Bodylines *461 Bethnal Green Road, E2 9QH (7613 1631, www.bodylinesfitness.co.uk). Private.*

Fitness First *www.fitnessfirst.co.uk; 1 America Square, EC3N 2LB (7488 9311); Bow Wharf, Grove Road, E3 5SN (8980 2442); 15 Thomas More Square, E1W 1YW (7702 2777). Private.*

Island Sports Trust *100 Manchester Road, E14 3DW (7537 4762, www.islandsports trust.co.uk).*

John Orwell Sports Centre *Tench Street, E1W 2QD (7488 9421, www.gll.org).*

LA Fitness *West India Quay, 5 Hertsmere Road, E14 4AN (0843 170 1005, www.lafitness.co.uk). Private.*

Langdon Park Leisure Centre *35 Byron Street, E14 0RZ (7987 3575, www.ukfitness network.org).*

Mile End Park Leisure Centre *190 Burdett Road, E3 4HL (8709 4420, www.gll.org).*

Mile End Park Stadium *Rhodeswell Road, E14 7TW (8980 1885, www.gll.org).*

Muscle Works *2 Hague Street, E2 6HN (7256 0916, www.muscleworksgym.co.uk). Private.*

Reebok Sports Club *16-19 Canada Square, E14 5ER (7970 0900, www.reeboksportsclub london.com). Private.*

St George's Swimming Pool *221 The Highway, E1W 3BP (7709 9714, www.gll.org).*

Tiller Centre *Tiller Road, E14 8PX (7987 5211, www.gll.org).*

Titan Fitness Centre *164-170 Mare Street, E8 3RD (8985 1287). Private.*

Virgin Active *Westferry Circus, E14 8RR (7513 2999, www.virginactive.co.uk). Private.*

Whitechapel Sports Centre *55 Durwood Street, E1 5BA (7247 7538, www.gll.org).*

York Hall Leisure Centre *Old Ford Road, E2 9PJ (8980 2243, www.gll.org). Also includes Spa London (8709 5845, www.spa-london.org).*

Other facilities

Docklands Sailing & Watersports Centre *235A Westferry Road, Millwall Dock, E14 3QS (7537 2626, www.dswc.org).*

Mile End Climbing Wall *Haverfield Road, E3 5BE (8980 0289, www.mileendwall.org.uk).*

Mile End Karting Track *418-419 Burdett Road, Mile End Park, E3 4AA (7005 0318, www.gokartinglondon.co.uk).*

Schools

Primary

There are 65 state primary schools in Tower Hamlets, 16 of which are church schools. There are also three independent primaries: one Muslim school and two Montessori schools. See www.towerhamlets.gov.uk, www.edubase.gov.uk and www.ofsted.gov.uk for more information.

Secondary

Bethnal Green Technology College *Gosset Street, E2 6NW (7920 7900, www.bgtc.org.uk).*

Bishop Challoner Catholic Collegiate School *352 Commercial Road, E1 0LB (boys 7791 9500, girls 7791 9593, www.bishop-learningvillage.towerhamlets.sch.uk). Roman Catholic; mixed sixth form.*

Bow School *Paton Close, Fairfield Road, E3 2QD (8980 0118, www.bow-school.org.uk). Boys only.*

Central Foundation Girls' School *College Terrace, E3 5AN (8983 1015, www.central. towerhamlets.sch.uk). Girls only.*

George Green's School *100 Manchester Road, E14 3DW (7987 6032, www.george greens.com).*

Langdon Park School *Byron Street, E14 0RZ (7987 4811, www.langdonparkschool.co.uk).*

Morpeth School *Portman Place, E2 0PX (8981 0921, www.morpethschool.org.uk).*

Mulberry School for Girls *Richard Street, E1 2JP (7790 6327, www.mulberry.tower hamlets.sch.uk). Girls only.*

Oaklands School *Old Bethnal Green Road, E2 6PR (7613 1014, www.oaklands.tower hamlets.sch.uk).*

Raines Foundation School *Approach Road, E2 9LY (8981 1231, www.rainesfoundation. org.uk).*

St Paul's Way Trust School *Shelmerdine Close, E3 4AN (7987 1883, www.stpaulsway.org).*

Sir John Cass Foundation & Redcoat Church of England Secondary School *Stepney Way, E1 0RH (7790 6712, www.sjcr.net).*

Stepney Green Maths & Computing College *Ben Jonson Road, E1 4SD (7790 6361, www.stepneygreen.towerhamlets.sch.uk). Boys only.*
Swanlea School *31 Brady Street, E1 5DJ (7375 3267, www.swanlea.towerhamlets.sch.uk).*

Property

WHAT THE AGENTS SAY:
'As one of the host boroughs for the 2012 Games, Tower Hamlets has experienced a boom in property prices. The rental market is extremely busy too, and although there are pockets where houses are the residence of choice, the main demand is for flats and apartments in the Brick Lane/Shoreditch area. Here, prices for a one-bedroom apartment can easily scale £430 per week. The roads around Bethnal Green station are becoming more popular with commuting professionals. The Central line and overground services provide efficient connections to the City and West End, while Victoria Park offers appealing respite from the hustle and bustle.'
Chris Odysseas, Peach Properties, Bethnal Green

Average property prices
Detached £444,000
Semi-detached £349,312
Terraced £374,639
Flat £344,203

Local estate agents
Alex Neil Property Agents
www.alexneil.co.uk; 3 offices in the borough (Bow 8980 7431, Docklands 7537 9859).
Atkinson Mcleod *www.atkinsonmcleod.com; 2 offices in the borough (Canary Wharf 7001 9680, Aldgate 7488 5050).*
Ellis & Co *www.ellisandco.co.uk; 2 offices in the borough (Bethnal Green 7729 1815, Bow 8981 7999).*
Felicity J Lord *644-646 Mile End Road, E3 4LH (8981 3666, www.fjlord.co.uk).*
Future Pad *70 Commercial Street, E1 6LT (7247 0066, www.futurepadlondon.com).*
Hurford Salvi Carr *9 Branch Road, Limehouse Basin, E14 7JH (7791 7000, www.hurford-salvi-carr.co.uk).*
Peach Properties *53 Bethnal Green Road, E1 6LA (7739 6969, www.peachproperties.com).*
Tarn & Tarn *53 Commercial Street, E1 6BD (7377 8989, www.tarn-tarn.co.uk).*

Other information

Council
Tower Hamlets Borough Council
Town Hall, Mulberry Place, 5 Clove Crescent, E14 2BG (7364 5020, www.towerhamlets.gov.uk).

Legal services
Whitechapel CAB *32 Greatorex Street, E1 5NP (0844 826 9699, www.citizensadvice.org.uk).*

Local information
www.eastlondonadvertiser.co.uk.
www.spitalfieldslife.com.
www.towerhamlets.gov.uk/news/east_end_life.aspx.

Open spaces & allotments
Reeves Road Allotment Society
1 Tibbetts Road, E3 (Mr T Fletcher 7515 7833).
Stepping Stones Farm Allotments
Stepping Stones Farm, Stepney Way, E1 3DG (Lynne Bennett 7790 8204).
Open spaces *www.towerhamlets.gov.uk.*

COUNCIL TAX
A	up to £40,000	£796.90
B	£40,001-£52,000	£929.71
C	£52,001-£68,000	£1,062.53
D	£68,001-£88,000	£1,195.34
E	£88,001-£120,000	£1,460.97
F	£120,001-£160,000	£1,726.60
G	£160,001-£320,000	£1,992.24
H	over £320,000	£2,390.68

RECYCLING
Household waste recycled & composted 32%
Main recycling centre Northumberland Wharf, Yabsley Street, Isle of Dogs, E14 9RG (7538 4526)
Other recycling services furniture collection; home composting; pink sack kerbside collection; garden & food waste collection
Council contact London Borough of Tower Hamlets, Town Hall, Mulberry Place, Clove Crescent, E14 2BG (7364 5004)

'Hackney remains an island that is all the world. An argument of opposites: green spaces, active markets, shabby marvels. A theme park of the discontinued, the decommissioned and the resurrected. The ultimate metaphor for urban living (and dying).'

Iain Sinclair, author of *Hackney, That Rose-Red Empire* (2009)

Hackney

One of the capital's most exciting boroughs, Hackney suffers its share of inner-city problems (unemployment, crime and urban decay). But it's a district that's been on its way up over the past decade, with large pockets that are now well and truly gentrified. It has a cutting-edge creative scene, fantastic Vietnamese and Turkish food, animated bars and clubs, and countless devoted locals who wouldn't dream of living anywhere else.

Neighbourhoods

Shoreditch and Hoxton

Edging into the City at the southern end of Hackney, Shoreditch and Hoxton straddle the boundary between loft-living and life on the estate. Some of the most expensive warehouse apartments in north-east London look out over tracts of community housing and boarded-up pubs and shops. Residents on both sides of the economic divide put up with the slightly decrepit surroundings for the location – just minutes from the City – and the urban vibe of the bars, clubs, shops, galleries and restaurants around Shoreditch High Street, Redchurch Street, Hoxton Square and Old Street.

The area has experienced highs and lows in its long and chequered history. In the 16th century, this was a bustling theatre district, attracting artists whose work was considered too avant-garde for the City (including one W Shakespeare). This sense of being outside the mainstream survived the post-industrial decline of the Victorian era and the double body blows of World War II bombing and 1960s urban planning.

Hoxton's renaissance began in the early 1990s, when artists, designers and other creatives bought cheap units in the fading Victorian warehouses around Hoxton Square to use as studios and live-work

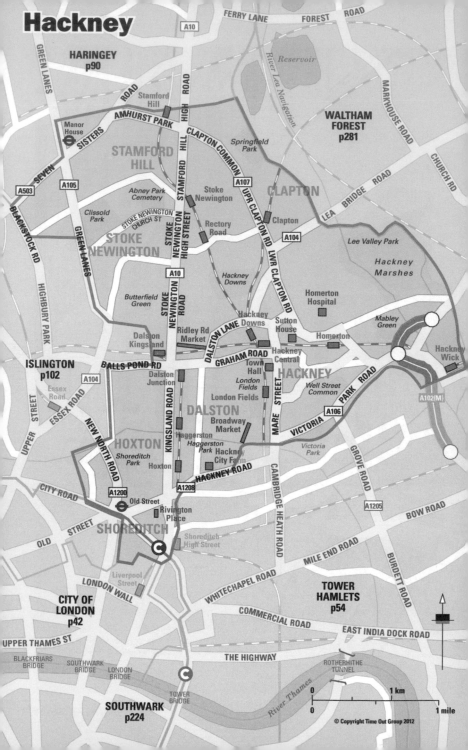

The night-time scene in **Shoreditch**.

spaces. The scene lured in YBAs such as Damien Hirst and Gary Hume, fashion designer Alexander McQueen and counter-culture icons such as Jarvis Cocker before falling victim to its own success. With rising fame came soaring house prices, driving the impoverished artists north to London Fields, Alexander McQueen summed up the decline of Hoxton in a *Guardian* interview back in 2003 – 'One day we looked out of the window and saw lots of people with mullets. The next day the landlord came round and doubled the rent.'

Nevertheless, this remains a desirable neighbourhood, particularly if you rate being close to the City. There are still some solid-gold places to eat and drink, and transport links have improved significantly with the opening of the Shoreditch High Street and Hoxton stations on the London Overground line in 2010. The art scene also received a boost with the opening of Rivington Place a few years ago (a space for 'artists from culturally diverse backgrounds'), joining more established galleries such as the White Cube on Hoxton Square.

North of Hoxton Square, high-rise council estates stretch to the fringes of De Beauvoir. It's not the most salubrious place to live, but the location counts for something; plus Hoxton Street has a modest street market and one of London's last pie and mash shops. Although neglected and run-down, the area benefits from the blisteringly authentic Vietnamese canteens on Kingsland Road and the elegant Geffrye

Highs & Lows

The world on a plate The best Vietnamese, Turkish and Kurdish restaurants in London.

Village vibrations Locals love the neighbourhood vibe of gentrified Stoke Newington Church Street, Broadway Market and Victoria Park.

Public transport The arrival of London Overground in 2010 – bringing four new stations – has made Hackney much more connected to the rest of the city.

Seediness Urban grit is a lure for some, but swathes of the borough are still very grim and intimidating.

Education Hackney is home to some of the worst-performing schools in Britain. Parents who can afford it look to private schools; higher-performing state students venture out of the borough.

So hip it hurts You can't move in Dalston these days for hipsters in skinny jeans and stupid hats. Super-cool status also means rents have gone through the roof.

Museum, which showcases changes in domestic design through the centuries.

Despite the spread of affluence, and a spruced up shopping scene – most visible on boutique-heavy Redchurch Street and at the new Boxpark 'pop-up mall' outside Shoreditch Overground station – much of this area maintains its original gritty vibe. There are still pound-in-a-pint-pot strip clubs on Hackney Road and Shoreditch High Street, and many walls and shopfronts are plastered with graffiti (including numerous works by Banksy, and A-Z letters by local graffiti artist Eine) – which has led to the creation of graffiti tours for tourists keen to sample a slice of urban 'edginess'. Of course, for many the perceived grime is all part of the appeal – if you want a big garden and posh schools, move to Muswell Hill.

Hackney

The original working-class London suburb, Hackney was founded in Roman times near a ford across the River Lee. Once a rural idyll, it grew into a busy industrial centre in the Victorian era before sliding into decline after World War II. Over the next few decades, Hackney became the heartland of social disintegration in the capital; stark housing estates mushroomed, unemployment soared and Hackney Council picked up the European record for most demolitions by a local authority.

These days, large pockets of gentrification are drawing young, wealthy professionals to the area, but Hackney still attracts superlatives. In recent years, newspapers have lambasted the borough for having the worst car crime in London, the worst-performing local council in England, the worst schools in Britain and one of the highest rates of dognapping in Europe. Hackney's Mare Street was one of the hotspots for the 2011 riots, while London Fields and its surrounds have been the location for teenage gang-related shootings in the past couple of years. But if you were hoping to beat the house-price inflation that has blighted Stoke Newington, Victoria Park and De Beauvoir, you've already missed the boat. Hackney has its problems, but most people who live here wouldn't want to live anywhere else.

The bustling heart of Hackney is Mare Street, which runs south past the stately art deco Hackney Town Hall to Bethnal Green

A chilled Saturday on **Broadway Market**.

and Whitechapel. The area is known locally as Hackney Central, after the nearby train station. Following years of deprivation, the centre got a boost from the creation of the 'Hackney Cultural Quarter' in 2001. The modernist Technology & Learning Centre (housing a library and the Hackney Museum) and the impressively restored Hackney Empire theatre (one of the best community theatres in London) are still going, and the new high-profile Hackney Picturehouse (part of the Picturehouse cinema group, known for its indie film focus) has brought a new vitality to this stretch of Mare Street. Open since autumn 2011, in the old Ocean music venue, this impressive new space has four auditoria and multiple bars and event spaces.

Artistic endeavour in Hackney is focused on London Fields – a very popular green space just west of Mare Street that is rammed with hipsters in the summer – and, more recently, further east in Hackney Wick.

Driven from Old Street by soaring rents, painters and sculptors colonised the warehouses and factories around London Fields, creating their own mini-Hoxton, complete with cutting-edge art spaces such as Flowers East and the Hothouse 'creative cluster' on Richmond Road (home to the Free Form Arts Trust). Further evidence of regeneration in the area can be found at the London Fields Lido, which reopened with great aplomb in 2006 after 20 years of neglect; in the new wave of independent shops and cafés on Wilton Way, just north of London Fields; and in the railway arches next to London Fields rail station, which now harbour one of the city's best bakeries – E5 Bakehouse – as well as the new artisan London Fields Brewery.

Out of hours, freelancers hang out in the Pub on the Park on the edge of London Fields or in the pubs and cafés on über-trendy Broadway Market. The Saturday market is one of the liveliest in London, attracting many of the gourmet food stalls that set up at Spitalfields. Wealthier market regulars might live in the grand Victorian town houses to the west of London Fields, or the warehouse apartments that line the Regent's Canal (which provides a handy back route to Islington and Victoria Park).

On the other (east) side of Mare Street, Hackney Wick and Homerton up until recently had never quite recovered from the collapse of their Victorian industries. Both areas offer a mix of council estates and factory warehouses, the latter now inhabited by a new international breed of young creatives, who love the areas precisely because of their remoteness and industrial grit (and correspondingly cheaper rents). Annual arts festival Hackney Wicked (www.hackneywicked festival.co.uk) is emblematic of Hackney Wick's brave new era. However, with Stratford practically on the doorstep, residents are already seeing big changes from the Olympic regeneration programme and while some of this might be positive (new housing developments, cleaned-up streets), there are also fears that many locals will be priced out of the area and that its distinctive character may be lost.

In the far south-east of Hackney, Well Street Common nudges up against Victoria Park, just over the borough border in Tower Hamlets. Houses here are grand and expensive, and residents take full advantage of the park, pubs, cafés and restaurants along villagey, family-friendly Lauriston Road.

Like most of the borough, Hackney is tube-less, so options are the bus or train.

Dalston

Long considered the poor cousin of Stoke Newington, Dalston received a major boost when the Dalston Junction rail station opened in 2010, and is now one of London's most happening nightlife zones. Like much of north-east London, this area has its share of run down council estates and problems with unemployment, crime and poor schools. Despite this, Dalston is changing fast and has plenty worth shouting about – and it's no longer half as tough as some residents like to pretend.

Food and nightlife are now the undisputed highlights of Dalston living. Kingsland High Street and the southern end of Stoke Newington Road are home to some fantastic

Hackney

Countryside pursuits at **Hackney City Farm**. See p82.

Turkish ocakbaşi restaurants, while the area's Vietnamese canteens serve addictive soups and noodle dishes. The African and Caribbean community is represented by an array of specialist hair and beauty shops, numerous restaurants, takeaways and bars. Then there's the excellent Ridley Road Market, one of the best places in London to buy African and Caribbean ingredients. And nightlife has kicked off in a big way since the opening of gay/metrosexual hangout Dalston Superstore.

Though many of the shops and buildings on Dalston's main thoroughfares still look like they could do with a spruce-up, Stoke Newington Road is now home to several interesting independent shops, as well as a huge new branch of vintage emporium Beyond Retro. It also offers roomy Victorian houses, a few interesting new-builds and, despite the increasing gentrification of the area, a properly useful high street.

Jazz bars, theatres and politically minded cafés have been added to the more down-to-earth businesses in recent times. The most interesting new developments are Gillett Square (a futuristic precinct flanked by the Dalston Culture House art space and Vortex jazz bar), and the converted paint and print factory complex on Ashwin Street – near to the flash new Dalston Square apartment block – that now houses the Arcola Theatre, left-field music venue Café Oto and, in the summer months, the trendy Dalston Roof Park. Between the two public spaces is another highlight, the Rio cinema, a gorgeous art deco movie-house screening everything from European arthouse to Hollywood schmaltz.

Away from the hustle of the high street, Dalston is surprisingly quiet and residential, particularly south of Balls Pond Road. To the south-west is De Beauvoir, a leafy area with grand Dutch-gabled houses, the name marking the former country estate of the aristocratic de Beauvoir family. The air of grandeur extends to parts of somewhat less des-res Haggerston on the east side of Kingsland Road, in particular peaceful and lovely Albion Square.

Hackney

Dalston sits at the intersection of several transport lines. Overland trains run east to Stratford (and the new Olympic Park), west to Highbury, Camden, Hampstead and Richmond, and south to Haggerston, Hoxton, Wapping and New Cross. Regular buses serve Clapton, Stoke Newington and the City, and the faithful no.38 runs day and night between Dalston, Islington and the West End.

Stoke Newington

Before it was gobbled up by the expanding suburbs, Stoke Newington was a peaceful country village. A little of that vibe still survives today, aided by enviable open spaces left over from the vast country estates that once sprawled across this part of town. Of course, not all the greenery survived (much of it vanished under bricks and mortar in the late 1860s); by the turn of the 19th century, Stokey had evolved into a bustling suburb, home to hordes of commuters riding the trolleybuses down to Liverpool Street station each morning.

Today, Stoke Newington is a tale of two suburbs. The affluent middle classes congregate around Stoke Newington Church Street, a bijou strip of boutiques, second-hand bookshops, cafés, restaurants and estate agents shamelessly pushing up prices on account of the neighbourhood's family friendliness vibe. A disproportionate number of Church Street residents seem to be employed in the media, and almost everyone has a baby – sitting in front of one of the many cafés with a cappuccino and an all-terrain pushchair is positively de rigueur. However, families tend to move on when confronted by the poor standards of local secondary schools.

In contrast, Stoke Newington High Street is rougher and edgier, with a string of excellent Anatolian ocakbaşı restaurants and all-night Turkish grocers, and a decent selection of high-street shops and amenities. This split personality is partly a consequence of location: Church Street leans towards Islington while the High Street looks to Dalston and Hackney Central. The change in atmosphere at the intersection is quite striking.

Regardless of where they live, residents are united by their love of Clissold Park, a vast tree-lined expanse with tennis courts, an enclosure for deer, duck ponds and a kids' paddling pool. A two-year restoration

has brought a new playground, two new ponds, improved landscaping and a smart new café inside the restored 18th-century Mansion House. Another popular spot for a promenade is the atmospheric and overgrown Abney Park Cemetery, final resting place of the founder of the Salvation Army.

Stoke Newington residents are also known for their environmentally conscious leanings – hence the weekly organic market and thriving Whole Foods Market superstore – and community spirit. This was the home of the Angry Brigade in the 1970s, and bus shelters are still routinely plastered with flyers for demos, protests and fringe causes.

Locals' Tips

Bicycles are the preferred method of transport for many residents – take the backstreet cycle paths (20 minutes to the City, door to door) to beat the traffic. **Many of Hackney's cashpoints charge you to access your money; if you come across one that doesn't, take out more dosh than you think you'll need, so that you don't have to go hunting for another fee-free one later on.**
The pop-up trend has been particularly prolific in Hackney; pop-up shops, bars, restaurants and cinemas were in abundance all around the borough in the summer of 2011. Look out for more. **Broadway Market is bicycle gridlock every Saturday, so come on foot: London Fields station is just across the park, or you can take a scenic boat route via the Regent's Canal**
Tired of the urban crush? Pop over the borough boundary for peaceful riverbank strolls through Walthamstow Marshes. **Parts of Hackney still have a bohemian atmosphere, and you can't get more bohemian than life on a narrowboat – there are berths for hire all along the Regent's Canal and the River Lee. Contact British Waterways (7985 7200, london@britishwaterways.co.uk) for more information.**
Sports facilities in Clapton are limited, but you can exercise your heart out on the River Lee with the Lea Rowing Club (www.learc.co.uk), one of the oldest rowing clubs in London.

Most of the housing stock in Stokey is made up of Victorian terraces, though cheap houses in need of modernisation (which have drawn countless first-time buyers in the area in recent years) are few and far between these days. Stoke Newington also loses points for limited parking, car crime and poor transport links. Reaching the City or the West End involves a 40-minute bus journey or a 20-minute train ride. The nearest tube stations are Finsbury Park and Manor House on the border with Haringey. On the other hand, buses pass through every few minutes, day and night, and you can cycle to Islington in ten minutes and the City in 20.

Stamford Hill

Few districts are as strongly associated with one community as Stamford Hill. The streets between Clapton Common and Seven Sisters Road are home to most of London's 25,000 Hasidic Jews.

Driven from continental Europe by pogroms and fascism, the Hasidim follow a strict form of Judaism, adhering to specific codes of dress and behaviour. On Saturdays, neatly turned-out families on their way to synagogue are a familiar sight. This is a culturally fascinating area, though there's little mixing between the Hasidic community and the rest of the local population.

On Stamford Hill, the area's main traffic-clogged thoroughfare, kosher food shops and bakeries join a typical London high-street melange of launderettes, dodgy-looking outlets selling mobile phone accessories and fast-food joints. The road is hemmed in by ugly council blocks, but the surrounding terraces are bright and inviting, with numerous Hasidic schools, synagogues and community centres.

The prettiest area is north of Manor Road and Lordship Park; houses are positively palatial and the adjacent reservoir has the popular Castle Climbing Centre and the West Reservoir, a centre for watersports and environmental education. Most of the shops and services are clustered around the intersection of Stamford Hill and Clapton Common; Seven Sisters tube station is a short hop north, and Stamford Hill rail station is just west of the main junction.

Clapton

Squeezed between Hackney Central and Walthamstow Marshes, Clapton has an unenviable reputation for inner-city violence. Until recently, the district held the British record for the highest number of bullets shot per head of population. The good news is that the closure of the notorious Chimes and Palace Pavilion nightclubs several years ago seems to have helped reduce the number of shootings in the area. The bad news is that yellow police signs appealing for witnesses to violent crimes are still fairly common, particularly along unappealing, kebab shop-lined Upper and Lower Clapton roads – still sometimes referred to as 'Murder Mile'.

Recently, Hackney Council has spent some money on Clapton, tidying up the roundabout area and beautifying the grubby park at the top of Lower Clapton Road. There have also been signs of gentrification, now that nearby London Fields and Dalston have become more expensive: new bars and trendy cafés have sprung up among the jerk-chicken outlets at the Hackney Central end of Lower Clapton Road, while Chatsworth Road Market – selling gourmet food, vintage bric-a-brac, and crafts on Sundays – has been reinstated following its demise in the 1980s; locals hope the market will do for Clapton what the reintroduction of Broadway Market has done for London Fields.

Housing stock in Clapton is dominated by council estates and Victorian terraces, but there are a few historic gems – most notably, the gorgeous Georgian terraces around Sutton House (on the edge of Homerton).

Flanked by the well-funded but academically middling BSix Brooke House Sixth Form College, the massive Lea Bridge roundabout splits Clapton in two. Lower Clapton has the best of the shops and amenities, while Upper Clapton has the main train station (on the overland line to Hackney Central and Liverpool Street). Parking is in short supply, and the tell-tale piles of glass next to recently vacated bays provide a compelling case for using public transport. Frequent day and night buses connect Clapton with the City and surrounding districts. Perks of living in Clapton include comparatively low property prices, the proximity of the revitalised Hackney town centre and the green open spaces of Springfield Park, Hackney Downs, Hackney Marshes and, across the River Lee in the borough of Waltham Forest, Walthamstow Marshes.

Abney Park Cemetery. See p79.

Restaurants & cafés

Hackney's restaurant scene (the affordable side of it at least) owes a massive debt to the borough's Turkish, Kurdish and Vietnamese communities. The borough has an impressive selection of Vietnamese canteens and Anatolian ocakbaşi grills serving superior food at bargain prices.

For a filling bowl of pho (Vietnamese noodle soup), head for Kingsland Road or Mare Street, where the lion's share of Vietnamese restaurants and cafés are located. Recommendations include Green Papaya and Tre Viet (on Mare Street) and Hanoi Café, Viet Grill, Mien Tay, Viet Hoa and Sông Quê (on Kingsland Road). Also worth hunting down are Cây Tre on Old Street and Huong-Viet on Englefield Road.

The Turkish food on offer in Hackney is mainly Anatolian, which means lots of kebabs served straight from the ocakbasi (charcoal grill). The best of the Turkish and Kurdish restaurants are strung out along Kingsland Road and Stoke Newington High Street. For no-nonsense kebabs, pide and lunchtime stews, try Tava and Testi in Stoke Newington or Sömine and late-opening Istanbul Iskembecisi in Dalston. Also in Dalston, Mangal II is a step upmarket from both the rather spartan (and now legendary) original Mangal Ocakbasi around the corner and its Mangal Turkish Pizza sister across the way. Another successful local chain is grill expert 19 Numara Bos Cirrik, with branches in Dalston, Stoke Newington and Hackney Central.

These sit-down restaurants have been joined by a string of casual Turkish café-bars, many offering live music and cultural events; among them Bodrum Café, Dervish Bistro and Café Z Bar in Stoke Newington, and Evin Café Bar in Dalston. Other good Turkish choices include Anatolia Ocakbaşi and Tad Restaurant in Hackney Central.

Indian restaurants are less well represented, but you'll find superior South Indian vegetarian cuisine at Rasa and sister outfit Rasa Travancore (which also serves meat and fish dishes) on Stoke Newington Church Street, and reliable favourites at nearby Anglo-Asian Tandoori. Thai cooking is available at the stylish but variable Yum Yum on Stoke Newington High Street, and at numerous pub kitchens throughout the borough. For decent Chinese fare, try Shanghai (in a refurbished Dalston pie and mash shop) or Fang Cheng (on Mare Street).

Stoke Newington also has a selection of Mediterranean cafés – Il Bacio (Italian), Clicia (mixed Mediterranean) and Blue Legume (sandwiches, salads and bakes) are neighbourhood favourites. And the Dalston end of Kingsland Road is now home to excellent Modern European brunch/dinner spot A Little of What You Fancy – a symbol of the area's gentrification. Homerton's equivalent is newcomer Railroad, which mixes European with Asian and Middle Eastern influences in an arty space (music and poetry are also performed here). Welcome arrivals in Clapton over the past few years include Italian café Parioli E5 and coffee shop Venetia's, while Hackney Wick is now home to some top-notch cafés, including Counter Café, which has great views of the Olympic Stadium.

Fans of gastropubs should make a beeline for the Fox or the Princess (both on Paul

Hackney

Street in Shoreditch), the Scolt Head in De Beauvoir, the Cat & Mutton on Broadway Market, or the Prince Arthur, on the other side of London Fields. Buen Ayre specialises in carnivorous Argentinian grills. Budget local restaurants include the quirky, Egyptian-styled LMNT, fish and chips specialist Faulkner's, family-friendly Frizzante at Hackney City Farm, Bella Vita pizza parlour, old-fashioned pie and mash shop F Cooke (with branches on Hoxton Street and Broadway Market), and East European eaterie Little Georgia.

Shoreditch has a scattering of more high-end restaurants. Best-known is Jamie Oliver's Fifteen, but Hoxton Apprentice also trains unemployed young people to prepare fine Modern European food. Other contenders for a serious gastronomic experience include Eyre Brothers (Iberian) and Will Ricker's Great Eastern Dining Room (oriental). Newer arrivals include Water House, next to the Regent's Canal, and Pizza East, located in the Tea Building.

A Little of What You Fancy *464 Kingsland Road, E8 4AE (7275 0060, www.alittleofwhat youfancy.info).*
Anatolia Ocakbaşi *253 Mare Street, E8 3NS (8986 2223).*
Anglo-Asian Tandoori *60-62 Stoke Newington Church Street, N16 0NB (7254 3633).*
Il Bacio *61 Stoke Newington Church Street, N16 0AR (7249 3833, www.ilbaciostokey.co.uk).*
Bella Vita *53-55 Broadway Market, E8 4PH (7249 4772, www.bellavitabroadway.com).*

Blue Legume *101 Stoke Newington Church Street, N16 0UD (7923 1303, www.theblue legume.co.uk).*
Bodrum Café *61 Stoke Newington High Street, N16 8EL (7254 6464).*
Buen Ayre *50 Broadway Market, E8 4QJ (7275 9900, www.buenayre.co.uk).*
Café Z Bar *58 Stoke Newington High Street, N16 7PB (7275 7523, www.zcafebar.com).*
Cat & Mutton *76 Broadway Market, E8 4QJ (7254 5599, www.catandmutton.com).*
Cây Tre *301 Old Street, EC1V 9LA (7729 8662, www.vietnamesekitchen.co.uk).*
Clicia *97 Stoke Newington Church Street, N16 0UD (7254 1025).*
F Cooke *9 Broadway Market, E8 4PH (7254 6458); 150 Hoxton Street, N1 6SH (7729 7718).*
Counter Café *Stour Space, 7 Roach Road, E3 2PA (07834 275920, www.thecountercafe.co.uk).*
Dervish Bistro *15 Stoke Newington Church Street, N16 0NX (7923 9999).*
Evin Café Bar *115 Kingsland High Street, E8 2PB (7254 5634, www.evincafe.co.uk).*
Eyre Brothers *70 Leonard Street, EC2A 4QX (7613 5346, www.eyrebrothers.co.uk).*
Fang Cheng *239-243 Mare Street, E8 3NS (8986 0072).*
Faulkner's *424-426 Kingsland Road, E8 4AA (7254 6152).*
Fifteen *15 Westland Place, N1 7LP (3375 1515, www.fifteen.net).*
Fox *28-30 Paul Street, EC2A 4LB (7729 5708, www.thefoxpublichouse.co.uk).*
Frizzante@City Farm *Hackney City Farm, 1A Goldsmith's Row, E2 8QA (7739 2266, www.frizzanteltd.co.uk).*
Great Eastern Dining Room *54-56 Great Eastern Street, EC2A 3QR (7613 4545, www.rickerrestaurants.com).*
Green Papaya *191 Mare Street, E8 3QE (8985 5486, www.green-papaya.com).*
Hanoi Café *98 Kingsland Road, E2 8DP (7729 5610, www.hanoicafe.co.uk).*
Hoxton Apprentice *16 Hoxton Square, N1 6NT (7749 2828, www.hoxtonapprentice.com).*
Huong-Viet *An Viet House, 12-14 Englefield Road, N1 4LS (7249 0877).*
Istanbul Iskembecisi *9 Stoke Newington Road, N16 8BH (7254 7291).*
Little Georgia *87 Goldsmiths Row, E2 8QR (7739 8154, www.littlegeorgia.co.uk).*
LMNT *316 Queensbridge Road, E8 3NH (7249 6727, www.lmnt.co.uk).*
Loong Kee *134G Kingsland Road, E2 8DY (7729 8344).*
Mangal Ocakbaşi *10 Arcola Street, E8 2DJ (7275 8981, www.mangal1.com).*

TRANSPORT

Tube stations *Northern* Old Street; *Piccadilly* Manor House
Rail stations *Greater Anglia* London Fields, Hackney Downs, Clapton, Rectory Road, Stoke Newington, Stamford Hill; *London Overground* Dalston Kingsland, Hackney Central, Homerton, Hackney Wick; Shoreditch High Street, Hoxton, Haggerston, Dalston Junction
Main bus routes *into central London* 4, 8, 19, 21, 26, 29, 30, 35, 38, 43, 48, 55, 56, 73, 76, 106, 141, 149, 153, 205, 214, 242, 243, 253, 259, 271, 341, 388, 394, 476; *night buses* N8, N19, N26, N29, N35, N38, N41, N55, N73, N76, N253, N279; *24-hour buses* 43, 149, 214, 242, 243, 271, 341

Mangal II *4 Stoke Newington Road, N16 8BH (7254 7888, www.mangal2.com).*

Mangal Turkish Pizza *27 Stoke Newington Road, N16 8BJ (7254 6999).*

Mien Tay *122 Kingsland Road, E2 8DP (7729 3074, www.mientay.co.uk).*

19 Numara Bos Cirrik *34 Stoke Newington Road, N16 7XJ (7249 0400, www.cirrik1.co.uk).*

19 Numara Bos Cirrik II *194 Stoke Newington High Street, N16 7JD (7249 9111).*

19 Numara Bos Cirrik III *1-3 Amhurst Road, E8 1LL (8985 2879, www.cirrikhackney.com).*

Parioli E5 *90 Lower Clapton Road, E5 0QR (7502 3288, www.vecchioparioli.com).*

Pizza East *56 Shoreditch High Street, E1 6JJ (7729 1888, www.pizzaeast.com).*

Prince Arthur *95 Forest Road, E8 3BH (7249 9996, www.theprincearthurlondon fields.com).*

Princess of Shoreditch *76-78 Paul Street, EC2A 4NE (7729 9270, www.theprincessof shoreditch.com).*

Railroad *120-122 Morning Lane, E9 6LH (8985 2858, www.railroadhackney.co.uk).*

Rasa *55 Stoke Newington Church Street, N16 0AR (7249 0344, www.rasarestaurants.com).*

Rasa Travancore *56 Stoke Newington Church Street, N16 0NB (7249 1340, www.rasarestaurants.com).*

Scolt Head *107A Culford Road, N1 4HT (7254 3965, www.thescolthead.co.uk).*

Shanghai *41 Kingsland High Street, E8 2JS (7254 2878, www.shanghaidalston.co.uk).*

Sömine *131 Kingsland High Street, E8 2PB (7254 7384).*

Sông Quê *134 Kingsland Road, E2 8DY (7613 3222, www.songque.co.uk).*

Tad Restaurant *261 Mare Street, E8 3NS (8986 2612, www.tadrestaurant.co.uk).*

Tava *17 Stoke Newington Road, N16 8BH (7249 3666).*

Testi *38 Stoke Newington High Street, N16 7XJ (7249 7151).*

Tre Viet *251 Mare Street, E8 3NS (8533 7390, www.treviet.co.uk).*

Venetia's *55 Chatsworth Road, E5 0LH (8986 1642, www.venetias.co.uk).*

Viet Grill *58 Kingsland Road, E2 8DP (7739 6686, www.vietnamesekitchen.co.uk).*

Viet Hoa *70-72 Kingsland Road, E2 8DP (7729 8293, www.viethoarestaurant.co.uk).*

Water House Restaurant *10 Orsman Road, N1 5QJ (7003 0123, www.waterhouse restaurant.co.uk).*

Yum Yum *187 Stoke Newington High Street, N16 0LH (7254 6751, www.yumyum.co.uk).*

Bars & pubs

It may now be London's mainstream nightlife zone (as the regular weekend hen and stag dos attest), but Shoreditch – and particularly the triangle made up by Old Street, Great Eastern Street and Shoreditch High Street – still has dozens of decent bars to choose from, from old faves such as Prague and Catch, to party dens like Favela Chic and club/live music venue Cargo (*see p88*), to smart newer venues such as the Boundary Rooftop, at Terence Conran's Boundary hotel on Redchurch Street. There really isn't a lack of choice here: whether it be for classy cocktails (Loungelover), local legends (Mother), decent real ale (Wenlock Arms), hidden gems (the Kenton), table football (Bar Kick), or Victoriana (Worship Street Whistling Shop). Bar-rammed Hoxton Square is a great focal point in summer, and there are even a few decent gastropubs: try the Princess or the Fox (for both, *see p81*), or William IV on Shepherdess Walk.

Dalston has now arguably taken over from Shoreditch as Hackney's hottest nightlife hub, with a wave of openings over the past couple of years. Dalston Superstore was one of the first to put the area on the late-night hipster map; principally a gay venue, it nevertheless draws a mixed crowd and remains a standout on Kingsland High Street. For live music, head to the Dalston Jazz Bar, or the Shacklewell Arms (*see p88*); the former Caribbean boozer runs a dynamic roster of band and club nights, with the colourful dancefloor a nod to the pub's previous incarnation. Further south, on Kingsland Road, the Junction Room and the Haggerston are popular late-night haunts.

Heading north, Stoke Newington is well stocked with fine pubs: Church Street boasts the best, appealing to everyone from wine-lovers (Fox Reformed) to Guinness drinkers (Auld Shillelagh), and the child-laden (Prince) to the child-avoiding (Rose & Crown). New arrival Mercado adds a boisterous Latin vibe. Around the corner on Stoke Newington High Street, quality dips. The best here is probably the White Hart, despite the sometimes obnoxious crowd at weekends – its large beer garden is gorgeously green in summer.

East of Dalston Junction, towards London Fields, the Spurstowe Arms is one of a

19 Numara Bos Cirrik – the original branch of the excellent mini-chain.

clutch of the borough's rejuvenated boozers; it's been in the hands of Columbia Road's Royal Oak team since 2011, who brought with them a more hipster-biased clientele. As with its sister pub, food is a good bet here. A new fashionable, arty crowd has also colonised the Prince George on Parkholme Road, though the period Victorian interior, much-loved jukebox and real ales remain intact – and a few old locals still prop up the bar. The Shakespeare is part of the same group.

With the opening of the new Hackney Picturehouse, Hackney Central has become more of a go-to area for an evening drink. The cinema's bars serve decent light meals and drinks, and live music is also scheduled. Over in London Fields, reliable watering holes include the Pub on the Park, and the Dove and Cat & Mutton gastropub (*see p82*) on Broadway Market.

Clapton isn't as blessed when it comes to drinking options, but don't write it off. Biddle Bros is a curious bar in the shell of a former builders' merchants, popular with a mixed crowd, while the Elderfield is a supremely likeable boozer. Hackney Downs corner boozer the Pembury Tavern is equally egalitarian, and known for its real ales and bar billiards table.

Auld Shillelagh *105 Stoke Newington Church Street, N16 0UD (7249 5951, www.theauld shillelagh.com).*

Bar Kick *127 Shoreditch High Street, E1 6JE (7739 8700, www.cafekick.co.uk).*

Biddle Bros *88 Lower Clapton Road, E5 0QR (no phone).*

Boundary Rooftop *2-4 Boundary Street, E2 7DD (7729 1051, www.theboundary.co.uk/ rooftop).*

Catch *22 Kingsland Road, E2 8DA (7729 6097, www.thecatchbar.com).*

Dalston Jazz Bar *4 Bradbury Street, N16 8JN (7254 9728).*

Dalston Superstore *117 Kingsland High Street, E8 2PB (7254 2273, www.dalston superstore.com).*

Dove *24-28 Broadway Market, E8 4QJ (7275 7617, www.dovepubs.com).*

Elderfield *57 Elderfield Road, E5 0LF (8986 1591).*

Favela Chic *91-93 Great Eastern Street, EC2A 3HZ (7613 5228, www.favelachic.com).*

Fox Reformed *176 Stoke Newington Church Street, N16 0JL (7254 5975, www.fox-reformed.co.uk).*

Haggerston *438 Kingsland Road, E8 4AA (7923 3206).*

Junction Room *578 Kingsland Road, E8 4AH (7241 5755, www.junctionroom.co.uk).*

Kenton *38 Kenton Road, E9 7AB (8533 5041, www.kentonpub.co.uk).*
Loungelover *1 Whitby Street, E1 6JU (7012 1234, www.loungelover.co.uk).*
Mercado *26-30 Stoke Newington Church Street, N16 0LU (7923 0555, www.mercado-cantina.co.uk).*
Mother Bar *333 Old Street, EC1V 9LE (7739 5949, www.333mother.com).*
Pembury Tavern *90 Amhurst Road, E8 1JH (8986 8597, www.individualpubs.co.uk/pembury).*
Prague Bar *6 Kingsland Road, E2 8DA (7739 9110, www.barprague.com).*
Prince *59 Kynaston Road, N16 0EB (7923 4766, www.theprincepub.com).*
Prince George *40 Parkholme Road, E8 3AG (7254 6060, www.remarkablerestaurants.co.uk).*
Pub on the Park *19 Martello Street, E8 3PE (7923 3398, www.pubonthepark.com).*
Rose & Crown *199 Stoke Newington Church Street, N16 9ES (7254 7497, www.roseand crownn16.co.uk).*
Shakespeare *57 Allen Road, N16 8RY (7254 4190, www.remarkablerestaurants.co.uk).*
Spurstowe Arms *68 Greenwood Road, E8 1AB (7254 4316).*
Wenlock Arms *26 Wenlock Road, N1 7TA (7608 3406, www.wenlock-arms.co.uk).*
White Hart *69 Stoke Newington High Street, N16 8EL (7254 6626, www.antic-ltd.com).*
William IV *7 Shepherdess Walk, N1 7QE (3119 3012, www.williamfour.co.uk).*
Worship Street Whistling Shop *63 Worship Street, EC2A 2DU (7247 0015, www.whistling shop.com).*

Shops

Hackney's shopping scene has become more established in recent years, with Shoreditch's Redchurch Street now very much a focal point for on-trend boutiques (Sunspel, APC) and retro-inspired homewares stores (Labour & Wait). Indie labels and streetwear brands rub shoulders at nearby Boxpark (www.boxpark.co.uk), the world's first 'pop-up mall', which opened at the end of 2011 underneath Shoreditch High Street Overground station. Composed of shipping containers sitting side by side, the Boxpark site is the first of a series of retail, office and housing developments planned for the former wasteland.

Head north for a handful of top-notch clothing/accessories boutiques on and around Shoreditch High Street, including Present, Start, No-one, Goodhood, CA4LA and Ally Capellino, while over on Curtain Road there's a much-visited branch of American Apparel. Hoxton design sensibilities inform the stock of nearby designer furniture and interior accessories store SCP. High-quality groceries (often organic) are on offer at Kingsland Road's excellent Grocery (open until 10pm daily, it usefully stocks magazines, booze and household items as well as fancy cheeses), at Food Hall on Old Street and at Leila's shop, where's there's also a popular café.

Broadway Market in London Fields is another food-fanatic's must. The street's phenomenally popular Saturday market – where wealthier Hackneyites stock up on artisan olive oil, fancy bread and freshly made gourmet lunches – is joined by the kind of appealing boutiques that have already colonised Bethnal Green's Columbia Road Market. Standouts include French deli L'Eau à la Bouche, shoe and accessory outlet Black Truffle, and Fabrications, which deals in 'eco-friendly' textiles and cool gifts. Fabulous bakery E5 Bakehouse is on the other side of London Fields.

Foodies looking for a break from all things artisan will find a wealth of Turkish/Kurdish ingredients in the shops along Stoke Newington High Street, Kingsland Road and Green Lanes. Dalston's Ridley Road Market offers a cornucopia of African and Caribbean ingredients, with fish stalls and fruit and veg the highlights. The Turkish Food Centre here is another must. Mare Street, meanwhile, is home to numerous Vietnamese supermarkets:

Hackney

Huong-Nam, Vietnam Supermarket and the beautifully presented London Star Night Supermarket & Video make for excellent browsing. French deli L'Epicerie@56 is a positive sign on Clapton's Chatsworth Road.

Dalston's Stoke Newington Road is now also graced with some exciting new independents, including Kristina Records and a huge new Beyond Retro vintage clothing emporium. It's still not as bijou as Stoke Newington's Church Street, but change is definitely afoot here. On Church Street itself, there's a big branch of Whole Foods Market, along with several Italian delis and a popular Saturday farmers' market. And this being kiddie-central, there are also numerous shops targeting parents and children; Route 73 Kids is an excellent toy shop, and several outlets specialise in trendy kids' clothes (Born, Olive Loves Alfie). Ribbons & Taylor and Casino carry an excellent stock of vintage clothes, and there are several good spots for second-hand books, including Church Street Bookshop, as well as the independent Stoke Newington Bookshop on the High Street. Nearby Rouge sells eye-catching imported Chinese furniture and ornaments.

Finally, randomly dotted about the borough, but useful in their different ways, are North One Garden Centre, the Burberry Factory Shop and London Fields Cycles.

Ally Capellino 9 Calvert Avenue, E2 7JP (7033 7843, www.allycapellino.co.uk).
American Apparel 123-125 Curtain Road, EC2A 3BX (7012 1112, www.american apparel.net).
APC 5 Redchurch Street, E2 7DJ (7729 7727, www.apc.fr).
Beyond Retro Dalston 92-100 Stoke Newington Road, N16 7XB (7923 2277, www.beyondretro.com).
Black Truffle 4 Broadway Market, E8 4QJ (7923 9450, www.blacktruffle.com).

Born 168 Stoke Newington Church Street, N16 0JL (7249 5069, www.borndirect.com).
Broadway Market Broadway Market, E8 (www.broadwaymarket.co.uk).
Burberry Factory Shop 29-53 Chatham Place, E9 6LP (8328 4287).
CA4LA 23 Pitfield Street, N1 6HB (7490 0055, www.ca4la.com).
Casino 136 Stoke Newington Church Street, N16 0JU (7923 2225, www.casinovintage.com).
Church Street Bookshop 142 Stoke Newington Church Street, N16 0JU (7241 5411).
L'Eau à la Bouche 35-37 Broadway Market, E8 4PH (7923 0600, www.labouche.co.uk).
E5 Bakehouse Arch 395, Mentmore Terrace, E8 3PH (07548 300244, www.e5bakehouse.com).
L'Epicerie@56 56 Chatsworth Road, E5 0LS (7503 8172, www.lepicerie56.com).
Fabrications 7 Broadway Market, E8 4PH (7275 8043, www.fabrications1.co.uk).
Food Hall 374-378 Old Street, EC1V 9LT (7729 6005).
Goodhood 41 Coronet Street, N1 6HD (7729 3600, www.goodhood.co.uk).
Grocery 54-56 Kingsland Road, E2 8DP (7729 6855, www.thegroceryshop.co.uk).
Huong-Nam Supermarket 185-187 Mare Street, E8 3QE (8985 8050).
Kristina Records 44 Stoke Newington Road, N16 7XJ (7254 2130, www.kristinarecords.com).
Labour & Wait 85 Redchurch Street, E2 7DJ (7729 6253, www.labourandwait.co.uk).
Leila's 17 Calvert Avenue, E2 7JP (7729 9789).
London Fields Cycles 281 Mare Street, E8 1PJ (8525 0077, www.londonfieldscycles.co.uk).
London Star Night Supermarket & Video 213 Mare Street, E8 3QE (8985 2949).
No-one 1 Kingsland Road, E2 8AA (7613 5314, www.no-one.co.uk).
North One Garden Centre 25A Englefield Road, N1 4EU (7923 3553, www.n1gc.co.uk).
Olive Loves Alfie 84 Stoke Newington Church Street, N16 0AP (7241 4212, www.olive lovesalfie.co.uk).
Present 140 Shoreditch High Street, E1 6JE (7033 0500, www.present-london.com).
Rebel Rebel 5 Broadway Market, E8 4PH (7254 4487, www.rebelrebel.co.uk).
Ribbons & Taylor 157 Stoke Newington Church Street, N16 0UD (7254 4735, www.ribbonsandtaylor.co.uk).
Rouge 158 Stoke Newington High Street, N16 7JL (7275 0887, www.rouge-shop.co.uk).
Route 73 Kids 92 Stoke Newington Church Street, N16 0AP (7923 7873, www.route73kids.co.uk).
SCP 135-139 Curtain Road, EC2A 3BX (7739 1869,www.scp.co.uk).

COUNCIL TAX		
A	up to £40,000	£872.18
B	£40,001-£52,000	£1,017.54
C	£52,001-£68,000	£1,162.91
D	£68,001-£88,000	£1,308.27
E	£88,001-£120,000	£1,599.00
F	£120,001-£160,000	£1,889.73
G	£160,001-£320,000	£2,180.45
H	over £320,000	£2,216.54

Dalston's much-used **Ridley Road Market**. See p78.

Start *www.start-london.com; womenswear
42-44 Rivington Street, EC2A 3BN (7729
3334); Menswear 59 Rivington Street, EC2A
9QQ (7739 3030); Mr Start 40 Rivington Street,
EC2A 3LX (7729 6272)*
Stoke Newington Bookshop *159 Stoke
Newington High Street, N16 0NY (7249 2808,
www.stokenewingtonbookshop.co.uk).*
Stoke Newington Farmers' Market *St
Paul's Church, Stoke Newington Road, N16 7UY
(7503 7688, www.growingcommunities.org).*
Sunspel *7 Redchurch Street, E2 7DJ
(7739 9729, www.sunspel.com).*
Turkish Food Centre *89 Ridley Road, E8 2NH
(7254 6754, www.tfcsupermarkets.com).*
Vietnam Supermarket *193A Mare Street,
E8 3QE (8525 1655).*
Whole Foods Market *32-40 Stoke Newington
Church Street, N16 0LU (7254 2332, www.
wholefoodsmarket.com).*

Arts & attractions

Cinemas & theatres
Arcola Theatre *Ashwin Street, E8 3DL
(7503 1646, www.arcolatheatre.com).
Enterprising fringe theatre.*

Courtyard Theatre *Bowling Green Walk,
40 Pitfield Street, N1 6EU (7729 2202,
www.thecourtyard.org.uk).*
Hackney Empire *291 Mare Street, E8 1EJ
(8985 2424, www.hackneyempire.co.uk).
Restored Edwardian music hall; shows run
from stand-up comedy to Shakespeare.*
Hackney Picturehouse *270 Mare Street,
E8 1HE (0871 902 5734, www.picturehouses.
co.uk).*
Rio Cinema *107 Kingsland High Street,
E8 2PB (7241 9410, www.riocinema.org.uk).*

Galleries & museums
Flowers East *82 Kingsland Road, E2 8DP
(7920 7777, www.flowerseast.com).*
Geffrye Museum *136 Kingsland Road, E2
8EA (7739 9893, www.geffrye-museum.org.uk).
Domestic interiors from the 1600s to the present,
housed in Georgian almshouses. The annual
Christmas exhibition is a must-see.*
Hackney Museum *Technology & Learning
Centre, 1 Reading Lane, off Mare Street,
E8 1GQ (8356 3500, www.hackney.gov.uk).*
Rivington Place *Rivington Place, EC2A 3BA
(7749 1240, www.rivingtonplace.org). Public
gallery and library dedicated to visual arts
and photography.*

Sutton House *2 & 4 Homerton High Street, E9 6JQ (8986 2264, www.nationaltrust.org.uk). This atmospheric red-brick Tudor mansion is the oldest home in east London.*
Victoria Miro Gallery *16 Wharf Road, N1 7RW (7336 8109, www.victoria-miro.com).*
White Cube *48 Hoxton Square, N1 6PB (7930 5373, www.whitecube.com).*

Music & comedy venues
Café Oto *18-22 Ashwin Street, E8 3DL (7923 1231, www.cafeoto.co.uk).*
Cargo *83 Rivington Street, EC2A 3AY (7739 3440, www.cargo-london.com).*
Comedy Café *66-68 Rivington Street, EC2A 3AY (7739 5706, www.comedycafe.co.uk).*
Shacklewell Arms *71 Shacklewell Lane, E8 2EB (7249 0810, www.shacklewellarms.com).*
Vortex Jazz Club *11 Gillett Square, N16 8AZ (7254 4097, www.vortexjazz.co.uk).*

Other attractions
Abney Park Cemetery *Stoke Newington High Street, N16 0LH (www.abney-park.org.uk).*

Sport & fitness

Hackney's council-owned leisures centres – including the renovated London Fields Lido and long-awaited Clissold Leisure Centre – are run by Greenwich Leisure. Canoeing and sailing take place at the West Reservoir Sports Centre, while the old waterworks next door houses the Castle Climbing Centre. More watersports are possible at Clapton's Lea Rowing Club.

Gyms & leisure centres
Britannia Leisure Centre *40 Hyde Road, N1 5JU (7729 4485, www.gll.org).*
Clissold Leisure Centre *63 Clissold Road, N16 9EX (7254 5574, www.gll.org).*
Kings Hall Leisure Centre *39 Lower Clapton Road, E5 0NU (8985 2158, www.gll.org).*
Queensbridge Sports & Community Centre *30 Holly Street, E8 3XW (7923 7773, www.gll.org).*
Space *31 Falkirk Street, N1 6HQ (7613 9525, www.hackneysportscentre.com). Private.*
Sunstone Health & Leisure Club for Women *16 Northwold Road, N16 7HR (7923 1991, www.sunstonewomen.com). Private.*

Other facilities
Hackney Marshes has numerous football, rugby and cricket pitches.

Cycling in **London Fields**. See p76.

Castle Climbing Centre *Green Lanes, N4 2HA (8211 7000, www.castle-climbing. co.uk).*
Lea Rowing Club *The Boathouse, Spring Hill, E5 9BL (8806 8282, www.learc.org.uk).*
London Fields Lido *London Fields Westside, E8 3EU (7254 9038, www.hackney.gov.uk). Dating from 1936, this art deco lido reopened in autumn 2006 after lying derelict for 20 years.*
West Reservoir Sports Centre *Green Lanes, N4 2HA (8442 8116, www.gll.org).*

Schools

Primary
There are 53 state primary schools in Hackney, 11 of which are church schools and two of which are Jewish schools. There are also 21 independent primaries, including eight Jewish schools and two Muslim schools. See www.learningtrust.co.uk, www.edubase.co.uk and www.ofsted.gov.uk for more information.

Secondary

Bridge Academy *Laburnum Street, E2 8BA (7749 5240, www.bridgeacademy.hackney. sch.uk).*

BSix Brooke House Sixth Form College *Brooke House, Kenninghall Road, E5 8BP (8525 7150, www.bsix.ac.uk).*

Cardinal Pole Catholic School *Kenworthy Road, E9 5RB (8985 5150, www.cardinal pole.co.uk). Roman Catholic.*

Clapton Girls' Academy *Laura Place, Lower Clapton Road, E5 0RB (8985 6641, www.clapton.hackney.sch.uk). Girls only.*

Haggerston School *Weymouth Terrace, E2 8LS (7739 7324, www.haggerston. hackney.sch.uk).*

Mossbourne Community Academy *100 Downs Park Road, E5 8JY (8525 5200, www.mossbourne.hackney.sch.uk).*

Our Lady's Convent High School *6-16 Amhurst Park, N16 5AF (8800 2158, www.ourladys.hackney.sch.uk). Roman Catholic; girls only; mixed sixth form.*

Petchey Academy *Shacklewell Lane, E8 2EY (7275 1500, www.petcheyacademy. org.uk).*

Skinners' Academy *Woodberry Grove, N4 1SY (8800 7411, www.skinnersacademy. org.uk).*

Stoke Newington School *Clissold Road, N16 9EX (7241 9600, www.sns.hackney. sch.uk).*

Urswick School *Paragon Road, E9 6NR (8985 2430, www.theurswickschool.co.uk). Church of England.*

Yesodey Hatorah Secondary School for Girls *Egerton Road, N16 6UB (8826 5500). Jewish; girls only.*

Property

WHAT THE AGENTS SAY:

'The area around Victoria Park and Lauriston Road has been popular for years. Families are drawn by the exceptional schools and the area's villagey feel. The abundance of open green space is a real draw too. More recently, the streets around Chatsworth Road, to the north of Homerton Hospital, have become incredibly desirable. A few good cafés have opened, along with some nice restaurants and a market, and prices have been steadily increasing; three- to four-bedroom houses now cost in the region of half a million pounds.'

Simon Randal, Sovereign House, Hackney

Average property prices

Detached £608,507
Semi-detached £587,229
Terraced £469,768
Flat £327,693

Local estate agents

City & Urban *www.cityandurbaninternational.com; 2 offices in the borough (Hackney 7275 7878, Shoreditch 7729 3344).*

Courtneys *544 Kingsland Road, E8 4AH (7275 8000, www.courtneys-estates.com).*

Excel Properties *140 Albion Road, N16 9PA (7923 2211, www.xlproperties.com).*

Homefinders *86 Amhurst Road, E8 1JH (8533 6461, www.homefinders-uk.com).*

PG Estates *47 Fashion Street, E1 6PX (7375 1515, www.pgestates.com).*

Phillips Estates *7 Stoke Newington Church Street, N16 0NX (7241 0292, www.phillips estates.co.uk).*

Shaw & Co *29 Lower Clapton Road, E5 0NS (8986 7327, www.shawco.com).*

Sovereign House *www.sovereign-house.com; 2 offices in the borough (Hackney 8533 9500, Victoria Park 8985 5800).*

Other information

Council

London Borough of Hackney Council *Town Hall, Mare Street, E8 1EA (8356 3000, www.hackney.gov.uk).*

Legal services

Dalston CAB *491-493 Kingsland Road, E8 4AU (7249 8027, www.citizensadvice.org.uk).*

Hackney Community Law Centre *8 Lower Clapton Road, E5 0PD (8985 5236, www.hclc.org.uk).*

Mare Street CAB *300 Mare Street, E8 1HE (0844 499 1195, www.citizensadvice.org.uk).*

Local information

www.chatsworthroade5.co.uk.
www.hackneycitizen.co.uk.
www.hackneygazette.co.uk.
www.hackney.gov.uk/w-hackneytoday.htm.
www.n16mag.com.

Open spaces & allotments

Hackney Allotment Society *www.hackneyallotments.org.uk.*

Open spaces *www.hackney.gov.uk/parks; www.clissoldpark.com.*

Hackney

'Haringey is the most vibrant, diverse borough in London. And it's home to Tottenham Hotspur FC, London's best football team (although some Arsenal fans might disagree!).'

David Lammy, MP for Tottenham

Haringey

Leafy suburban splendour meets grim deprivation in what is one of the capital's most multicultural boroughs. The grubbier parts of Green Lanes and Bruce Grove may well lower the tone set by villagey Muswell Hill and Crouch End, but this is a borough with much to recommend it – the international shops of Green Lanes, Grade II-listed 'Ally Pally' and pockets of affordable property, for starters.

Neighbourhoods

Finsbury Park and Stroud Green

In common with much of the southerly end of the borough, Finsbury Park, an area that straddles the Haringey/Islington border, is not the most beautiful of environs. That's not to say that efforts aren't being made to improve things. The 112-acre, Grade II-listed park (opened in 1869) that gives the area its name is looking much better thanks to major restoration. It has won Green Flag status for the last five years, plenty of young trees are growing rapidly and there's yet another new café on the Manor House corner of the park. Sports facilities include a new outdoor gym, a new skatepark and revamped tennis courts. The four-mile Parkland Walk, which runs along a disused railway line from the park via Highgate to Alexandra Palace, is lovely.

The area's other major feature is the train station (confusingly, this offically falls into the borough of Islington), upon which local bus, rail and tube services converge. However, despite a string of improvements a few years ago – cycle parking and so on – it retains a shabby, down-at-heel feel.

Other amenities include a slew of grotty, late-opening grocery shops and takeaways, but towards Stroud Green Road (which lies on the Islington border), shopping improves, with traditional boozers flanking late-opening Turkish and Caribbean grocers,

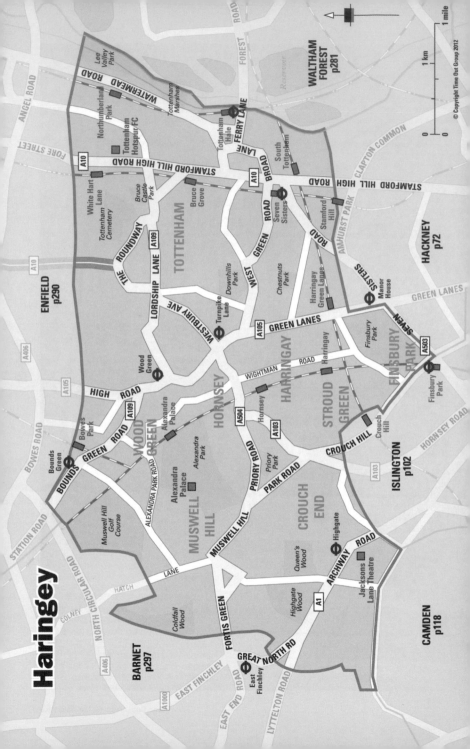

Italian delis, and Latin American and Thai restaurants. Such is the international demographic of this popular residential area, whose location on the borders of Crouch End sees Victorian and Edwardian buildings mixed with council blocks. The terraced houses of Woodstock, Perth and Ennis roads, near popular backstreet local pub the Faltering Fullback, sell for upwards of £425,000. Further up towards Crouch End, prices get higher still.

Another key feature of the district is the North London Central Mosque. Previously called Finsbury Park Mosque (which it continues to be known as locally), the mosque's rebranding began in 2005 following a media link with terrorism created by Abu Hamzah's extremist preaching and the attendance of shoe bomber Richard Reid. It was later reclaimed by the Muslim Association of Britain in the name of the mainstream Muslim community in north London. If only they'd also do something about the horrible modern building it's housed in, then they'd really be on to something.

Crouch End

Initially developed as a settlement due to its location at the junction of four locally important roads, Crouch End's farmsteads made it an early centre of cultivation for the borough. Nowadays, it's still one of Haringey's leafier areas (with easy access to Highgate Wood and Queen's Wood). And, as in much of London, leafy means wealthy.

Today, Crouch End's money comes largely from the crop of young middle-class families, media and arty types who inhabit the neighbourhood's pricey townhouses (most of spoof horror film *Shaun of the Dead* was shot here, and in previous years the Eurythmics' Dave Stewart had his studio in the area – now rumoured to be owned by David Gray). They're drawn to the neighbourhood's proper local shops (bakers, grocers and the like), family-friendly ethos and villagey feel. Gathered on the streets surrounding the landmark clock tower (built in 1895 as a monument to a local councillor) are cosy, multicultural restaurants and cafés, pubs and gyms. As the gaggles of pram-pushing yummy mummies that throng the streets might suggest, a night on the tiles isn't at the forefront of most residents' priority lists, so nightlife isn't a major feature.

Highs & Lows

▲ **Kebabs** Green Lanes has the best in London bar none, and many shops are open very late or even 24 hours.
Multicultural shopping Grabbing something for dinner from a local shop here is a pleasure – most stock an array of tasty, exotic fare.
Local beer Tottenham-based Redemption (www.redemption brewing.co.uk) is gaining quite a reputation. And where better to quaff a London ale than the borough in which it was brewed.

Dirty streets Rubbish collections have improved over the last few years, but many streets are still grotty – there's a long way to go.
The N29 A great regular bus service, but packed with alarmingly confrontational late-night drunks. The change from overcrowded bendy bus to double-decker has improved things slightly.
Lack of nightlife Although Green Lanes and Stroud Green Road have an increasing choice of pubs in which to waste away an evening, you'll need to go to Islington or Camden for a proper night out.

Residents are far more likely to spend their free time deciphering the area's confusing parking system. There's also no tube here: locals who work in central London have to join the throng at Finsbury Park station to catch the W3 or W7 bus up Stroud Green Road to get home.

Where Tottenham Lane runs up to Turnpike Lane tube, things become less gentrified, with the appearance of the area's estates. A large plot on the east side of Crouch End Hill is taken up by the staunchly pro-common-man Trades Union Congress's National Education Centre, providing training and development services for professional trade unionists. All in all, though, it's probably telling that despite a lack of a proper local supermarket (Little Waitrose, Tesco Express and Budgens are the closest options), there's still a Marks & Spencer food store here.

Pavilion Café, **Highgate Wood**. See p93.

Muswell Hill

Haringey may be the tenth most deprived district in England, but you wouldn't know it in Muswell Hill. Sitting atop a steep hill leading up from Crouch End, this is the borough's own Hampstead. One of Haringey's two MPs, Lynne Featherstone (Lib Dem representative for Hornsey and Wood Green, and member of the wealthy family behind the Ryness electrical chain), lives in the area. And when polonium-210-poisoned ex-spy Alexander Litvinenko was installed in a residence by his billionaire Russian oligarch boss, it was Osier Crescent that he picked (residents had to wait seven months for a £15,000 Haringey Council inquiry to conclude that there was no health risk to neighbours).

Among the area's leafy avenues and stately semi-detached residences (those without a spare million or so can forget about buying one) lies Alexandra Palace – the home of TV. Opened in 1873, it had to be rebuilt after burning to the ground just 16 days later. Reopened two years later, it went on to become the site of the first BBC television broadcast, in 1936). Nowadays, there are 196 acres of grounds, an ice-rink at the building's north end and a bar with stunning views of north London. Events are what it does best: it has a tradition of mass-capacity gigs that

includes a legendary 1967 Pink Floyd performance (though the famed fireworks displays are no more). The accompanying Alexandra Palace train station provides a swift link to central London.

Muswell Hill's commercial hub is centred around the bustling, villagey Broadway, largely made up of independent shops and restaurants, although a humongous O'Neill's (replete with massive Guinness pelican hanging from the ceiling), a Tardis-like Sainsbury's and an Odeon cinema (housed in a striking Grade II-listed art deco building) do their bit for the chains.

Wood Green and Bounds Green

Very much the borough's nerve centre, Wood Green contains Haringey's main courthouse (the beautiful Georgian townhouse-style Wood Green Crown Court), Haringey Council's major administrative headquarters, and numerous bus routes. Once upon a time, higher rail fares compared with the rest of the borough made it home to Haringey's moneyed residents, but the fact that its current main purpose is as the borough's retail heart has been a great social leveller.

There are two multi-screen cinemas, a shopping centre with over 80 retailers and a high street crammed with major in stores. The streets are regularly thronged with a

TRANSPORT

Tube stations *Piccadilly* Finsbury Park, Manor House, Turnpike Lane, Wood Green, Bounds Green; *Northern* Highgate, East Finchley; *Victoria* Finsbury Park, Seven Sisters, Tottenham Hale
Rail stations *Greater Anglia* Stamford Hill, Seven Sisters, Bruce Grove, White Hart Lane, Tottenham Hale, Northumberland Park; *London Overground* Crouch Hill, Harringay Green Lanes, South Tottenham; *First Capital Connect* Finsbury Park, Harringay, Hornsey, Alexandra Palace, Bowes Park
Main bus routes *Into central London* 4, 19, 29, 43, 76, 91, 134, 141, 149, 153, 214, 243, 253, 259, 271, 341, 476; *night buses* N19, N29, N41, N76, N91, N253, N279; *24-hour buses* 43, 134, 149, 214, 243, 271, 341

The Parkland Walk is underused by locals. The section just below Muswell Hill (accessible from Muswell Hill Road) offers stunning views of London that you can enjoy in peace and quiet. **Always take the back seat on the upper deck of the bus from Finsbury Park up to Muswell Hill. It may be a bit bumpy, but the views across the city are unrivalled, from the BT Tower via the Gherkin to Canary Wharf.** Appreciate the borough's musical heritage: over the years, Southern Studios (www.southern.net) on Myddleton Road has played host to some of the world's best alt-rock bands. Fugazi, Jesus and Mary Chain and the Buzzcocks have all recorded here. **Pick up late-in-the-day bargains at the Mall Shopping City market in Wood Green. Towards the end of Saturday trading, you'll find the already cheap fruit and veg being offered for jaw-droppingly low prices.**

crowd that varies from well-heeled Muswell Hillites kitting out the kids to sportswear-clad B-boys. A collection of drunken tramps loiter outside Morrison's, seemingly revelling in the area's grotty greyness.

Indeed, diversity is the watchword nowadays: in a recent survey of the West Green neighbourhood, 51 per cent of residents described themselves as hailing from ethnic groups including Caribbean, African, Asian, Chinese, Albanian, Greek, Irish and Turkish Cypriot. (It's estimated that over 200 languages are spoken in Haringey.) Property here is a good deal more affordable than in the borough's swankier neighbourhoods – you might pick up a one-bed for around £220,000. In the desirable New River development to the south (between Wood Green and Harringay), prices are higher, around £300,000.

Bounds Green is a more residential area and a far quieter proposition. The grocery shops and takeaways punctuating the suburban roads (lots of decent-sized semis with gardens) are as exciting as things get around here – the area's very much a middle-class bolthole for when braving the Wooders' crush gets too much.

Harringay

Harringay (confusingly, spelled differently from the borough in which it sits) might have its low points – in 2003 Green Lanes was the site of Operation Narita, a police crackdown on the road's heavy involvement in the UK's heroin trade, only months after a 40-man turf war between two Kurdish and Turkish gangs that saw three men shot – but it has its highs too. With a mixed community of Turks, Kurds, Albanians, Italians, South Americans, Indians and Greeks, Green Lanes has an astonishingly cosmopolitan mix of food shops. The western side of the district is largely an extension of boho neighbour Crouch End, with some of the locale's only green streets and large £500,000 family homes.

Over the past few years, a mini retail park has sprung up, encompassing a Homebase and a Sainsbury's that is open round the clock – as are most of the international grocers and kebab shops. A series of terraced Victorian streets runs horizontally between the two major north–south roads (Green Lanes and Wightman Road) and is known to locals, inevitably, as 'the Ladder'. Many of the period houses have been split into flats by canny investors.

There are good bus links to Camden, but Harringay's main transport link is Manor House tube station, whose grotty collection of fried chicken shops and newsagents is very much par for the course when it comes to the beauty of the neighbourhood.

Tottenham

Tottenham never had the best reputation, but thanks to the events of August 2011, it's more notorious than ever. The area was splashed over the news when local resident Mark Duggan was shot dead by police; a small local protest exploded into rioting across London, which spread to other cities over the following few days. Although the aftermath of the violence is still visible in key locations – the destroyed Carpetright store on the High Road, for example – residents seem to have pulled together, and the council is making progress on the desperately needed repairs.

Of course, the other well-known aspect of Tottenham is its football team. Riding high in the Premier League, Spurs get a lot of attention and are a particular point of pride for locals. The club is currently planning to build a glitzy new stadium

Haringey

adjacent to its current White Hart Lane home. The area also has its fair share of history: the 16th-century Bruce Castle manor house occupies the site of a castle once owned by Robert the Bruce (it now includes a small museum).

The glut of Spurs merchandise shops, tawdry takeaways and uninviting pubs are dispiriting: in general, Tottenham looks like it's been left to decay slowly for the better part of a century. The preponderance of densely packed terraced housing (the best surviving examples are largely on the west side of the High Road, particularly in Church Road and Cemetery Road) has led to a surfeit of low-income residents.

However, money is being pumped into regeneration, and new homes are being built, to bring in more first-time buyers and young professionals. Almost finished is Hale Village, a £400 million development opposite Tottenham Hale station, by Lee Valley Estates and the Newlon Housing Trust. It will include more than 500 affordable homes, as well as private housing, a hotel, shopping and eating facilities and an 'eco' park. Improvements are also planned for the mess that is Tottenham Hale Gyratory, including a larger bus station, a new public square and improved traffic flow. Work is scheduled to start in late 2012, and finish in 2014.

Restaurants & cafés

There's a stark east–west divide where Haringey dining is concerned. You'd be hard-pressed to find anything beyond standard takeaway fodder in down-at-heel Tottenham, while at the other end of the scale, affluent Crouch End's array of eating-out options, mainly clustered around Tottenham Lane and Park Road, seems almost excessive. Together with neighbouring Hornsey, it boasts a trio of good French restaurants – Les Associés, Bistro Aix and Le Bistro. Middle Eastern restaurant Kassaba occupies a converted industrial building in Hornsey, while Crouch End brasserie Banners still draws crowds with its global menu and excellent weekend brunches. International options include Khoai Café (Vietnamese), 2..Sixteen (Caribbean), La Bota (Spanish) and Wow Simply Japanese (obvious).

Muswell Hill is a bit chain-dominated, with branches of child-friendly Giraffe, Pizza Express and ASK, as well as Carluccio's and Maison Blanc, but it also has famed fish and chip shop Toff's, gastropub Victoria Stakes (*see p98*) and relaxed brasserie Café on the Hill.

There's plenty of Turkish fare in Harringay: among the numerous cheap ocakbaşi joints on Green Lanes, Antepliler is one of the best. On a corner by Harringay train station is friendly tapas bar La Vina. The dry-cleaner's next door is now sweet Café Moka; although the prices are more suited to Crouch End, the homemade fare is delicious and there's a cute courtyard too.

In Finsbury Park, Yildiz and Petek (both Turkish) are worth seeking out, while Chez Liline serves terrific Mauritian seafood.

Stroud Green Road offers a variety of ethnic cuisines, including South Indian (and vegetarian) Jai Krishna and a branch of lively mini-chain La Porchetta. The Triangle café serves everything from steak and chips to more exotic North African-influenced fare, while Cats offers an eccentric interior (rickshaws, waterfalls) and tasty Thai food. There's also a constantly busy Nando's.

Wood Green's dining scene has improved with the opening of Fatisa pizzeria in Woodside Park, but, other than cosy Greek restaurant Vrisaki and Modern European bar-brasserie Mosaica @ the factory, there is little else beyond cheap chain offerings.

Antepliler *46 Grand Parade, Green Lanes, N4 1AG (8802 5588, www.antepliler.co.uk).*
Les Associés *172 Park Road, N8 8JT (8348 8944, www.lesassocies.co.uk).*
Banners *21 Park Road, N8 8TE (8348 2930).*
Le Bistro *36 High Street, N8 7NX (8340 2116).*
Bistro Aix *54 Topsfield Parade, Tottenham Lane, N8 8PT (8340 6346, www.bistroaix.co.uk).*
La Bota *31 Broadway Parade, Tottenham Lane, N8 9DB (8340 3082, www.labota.co.uk).*
Café Moka *5 Wightman Road, N4 1RQ (8340 8664).*
Café on the Hill *46 Fortis Green Road, N10 3HN (8444 4957).*
Cats Café des Artistes *79 Stroud Green Road, N4 3EG (7281 5557, www.cats-cafe-des-artistes.co.uk).*
Chez Liline *101 Stroud Green Road, N4 3PX (7263 6550, www.chezliline.co.uk).*
Fatisa Café Pizzeria *292 High Road, N22 8JZ (8888 9008, www.fatisa.co.uk).*

Handsome terraces, **Crouch End**. See p93.

Jai Krishna *161 Stroud Green Road,
N4 3PZ (7272 1680).*
Kassaba *1 New River Avenue, N8 7QD
(8340 0400, www.kassaba.co.uk).*
Khoai Café *6 Topsfield Parade, Tottenham
Lane, N8 8PR (8341 2120, www.khoai.co.uk).*
Mosaica @ the factory *Unit C005,
The Chocolate Factory, Clarendon Road,
N22 6XJ (8889 2400, www.mosaica
restaurants.com).*
Petek *96 Stroud Green Road, N4 3EN
(7619 3933).*
La Porchetta *147 Stroud Green Road,
N4 3PZ (7281 2892, www.laporchetta.net).*
Toff's *38 Muswell Hill Broadway, N10 3RT
(8883 8656, www.toffsfish.co.uk).*
Triangle *1 Ferme Park Road, N4 4DS
(8292 0516, www.thetrianglerestaurant.co.uk).*
2..Sixteen *216 Middle Lane, N8 7LA
(8348 2572, www.2sixteen moonfruit.com)*
La Viña *3 Wightman Road, N4 1RQ
(8340 5400, www.la-vina.co.uk).*
Vrisaki *73 Myddleton Road, N22 8LZ
(8889 8760).*
Wow Simply Japanese *18 Crouch End
Hill, N8 8AA (8340 4539, www.wowsimply
japanese.co.uk).*
Yildiz *163 Blackstock Road, N4 2JS
(7354 3899, www.yildizocakbasi.co.uk).*

Bars & pubs

There isn't a massive choice of good boozers
in Haringey, but that's not to say there are
none. On Green Lanes, the stately Victorian
Salisbury Hotel offers a strong list of real
ales, live jazz, a Monday night quiz and
tasty roasts by the fireside. Nearby, the
Garden Ladder, once an Indian restaurant,
is now a firm favourite, with themed nights,
and ales from Tottenham's very own
Redemption brewery.

Stroud Green has capacious gastropub
the Old Dairy and, on Perth Road, steady
local pub the Faltering Fullback. Closer to
Finsbury Park station, the World's End is
the most appealing pub in which to watch
the footie – far enough from the hardcore
Arsenal pubs to avoid trouble, but local
enough to still have a great atmosphere
on match days. The Triangle (*see left*) is
wonderfully atmospheric for a Casablanca
beer or glass of Moroccan merlot. The ever-
popular Harringay Arms attracts a blokey
but friendly crowd with its 1950s decor,
while the King's Head, best known for
its stand-up, has a relaxed bar upstairs.

In Crouch End, the huge Queen's is
a comfortable boozer serving tarted-up
pub grub, while, in Hornsey, the Three
Compasses has pool, darts, a Monday
quiz and a good range of real ale.
Then there are the steep slopes into
Muswell Hill, offering beautiful views –
the best are from the picnic tables outside
Alexandra Palace's Bar & Kitchen. Near
the centre of Muswell Hill is handsome
gastropub Victoria Stakes. Chain bars
are kept to a minimum here, although
there is an All Bar One in Crouch End
and an O'Neill's in a converted church in
Muswell Hill. To the east, in Tottenham,
drinking options are mostly insalubrious
or unremarkable.

Bar & Kitchen *Alexandra Palace Way, N22
7AY (8365 4256, www.alexandrapalace.com).*
Faltering Fullback *19 Perth Road, N4 3HB
(7272 5834, www.falteringfullback.com).*
Garden Ladder *501 Green Lanes, N4 1AL
(8348 8553, www.thegardenladder.co.uk).*
Harringay Arms *153 Crouch Hill, N8 9QH
(8340 4243, www.theharringayarms.com).*
King's Head *2 Crouch End Hill, N8 8AA
(8340 1028, www.thekingsheadcrouchend.
co.uk).*

Haringey

Old Dairy *1-3 Crouch Hill, N4 4AP*
(7263 3337, www.theolddairyn4.co.uk).
Queen's *26 Broadway Parade, N8 9DE*
(8340 2031, www.thequeenscrouchend.co.uk).
Salisbury Hotel *1 Grand Parade,*
Green Lanes, N4 1JX (8800 9617).
Three Compasses *62 High Street, N8 7NX*
(8340 2729, www.threecompasses.com).
Victoria Stakes *1 Muswell Hill, N10 3TH*
(8815 1793, www.victoriastakes.co.uk).
World's End *21-23 Stroud Green Road, N4*
3EF (7281 8679, www.capitalpubcompany.com).

Shops

Unsurprisingly, the bulk of the borough's
more interesting shops are in well-heeled
Muswell Hill and Crouch End. The former
even has a branch of empire-building
skincare emporium Space NK, plus the
original outpost of expanding upmarket
shoe chain Kate Kuba. Other shops cater
to the family-oriented demographic: toys
and kids' clothes, high-quality foodstuffs
and homewares. Lovely Feast Deli and
the self-explanatory Cheeses rub shoulders
with toyshop Fagin's and the Children's
Bookshop on Fortis Green Road, where
you'll also find superior charity shop North
London Hospice, proudly independent
Muswell Hill Bookshop, Frocks Away
mums' and kids' boutique and Les Aldrich's
redoubtable classical music shop. The
Broadway has superior fishmonger
Walter Purkis & Sons (there's a branch
in Crouch End, complete with century-
old smokehouse), old-fashioned grocer
W Martyn and the Scullery kitchen shop.

There's more kids' stuff in Crouch End:
Soup Dragon, born out of a market stall,
sells unusual clothes and toys for babies
and children; Mini Kin has natural bath
products and merino wool babygros, as
well as a kids' hairdressing salon; Red
Shoes offers footwear from Birkenstock
to Start-rite. Treehouse sells globally
sourced treats for adults, such as
embroidered cushions from India and
Venetian glass jewellery, and Indish is
great for home accessories. Residents
are well served by an organic butcher,
a friendly greengrocer and the venerable
Dunn's Bakery (established 1820). Floral
Hall contains furniture sourced from
France, as well as overmantel mirrors
and even chandeliers.

Among the wig shops and multicultural
food stores of Stroud Green Road is
excellent fishmonger France Fresh Fish;
nearby you'll find long-established picture
framer and art centre John Jones.

The Mall Shopping City dominates
Wood Green; it's a useful local resource
with branches of Argos, TK Maxx and
Boots alongside high-street fashion
(Topshop, New Look, Next, H&M), as well
as numerous smaller shops. Outside the
mall, on the High Road, are branches of
Primark and Lidl, while just off the main
drag, the Big Green Bookshop is a great
local independent. The large Sirwan Food
Centre on Green Lanes (officially just over
the borough border in Enfield) is the place
to go for amazing Turkish flatbreads, good-
value olives, halloumi and fresh produce.
There's also a farmers' market on most
Sunday mornings at Alexandra Palace.

The stretch of Green Lanes in Harringay
is known for its Turkish and Middle
Eastern food shops – try Turkish Food
Market and Yasar Halim. Nearby, the
unpromising-looking Andreas Michli
& Son stocks brilliant Greek, Cypriot and
Turkish specialities such as figs flown in
from Cyprus. Baldwins butcher/deli has
superb produce – try the Welsh Dragon
sausages with leek and chilli. Dandies
without Gieves & Hawkes budgets can
get outfitted by Savile Row-trained tailor
George Christodoulou, on Wightman Road.

Given the low income of most of
Tottenham's denizens, it's hardly surprising
that it isn't exactly a shoppers' paradise –
although fans of its football team may be
tempted by the abundance of replica kit,
leisurewear and accessories at the Spurs
Megastore. There's also an excellent reggae
shop, Body Music, in south Tottenham.
If you do decide to buy and renovate a
bargain property, the B&Q and other
home-related superstores of Tottenham
Hale Retail Park will no doubt become
a regular weekend fixture.

Alexandra Palace Farmers' Market
Hornsey Gate Entrance, Alexandra Palace
Way, Wood Green, N22 7AY (8365 2121,
www.alexandrapalace.com, www.weareccfm.
com).
Andreas Michli & Son *405-411 St Ann's*
Road, N15 3JL (8802 0188).
Baldwins *469 Green Lanes, N4 1AJ*
(8340 5934, www.baldwinsfoods.com).

Big Green Bookshop *Brampton Park Road, N22 6DG (8881 6767, www.biggreenbookshop.com).*
Body Music *261 High Road, N15 4RR (8802 0146).*
Cheeses *13 Fortis Green Road, N10 3HP (8444 9141).*
Children's Bookshop *29 Fortis Green Road, N10 3HP (8444 5500, www.childrensbookshop london.com).*
Dunn's Bakery *6 The Broadway, N8 9SN (8340 1614, www.dunns-bakery.co.uk).*
Fagin's Toys *84 Fortis Green Road, N10 3HN (8444 0282).*
Feast Deli *56 Fortis Green Road, N10 3HN (8883 0117).*
Floral Hall *Corner of Crouch Hill & Haringey Park, N8 9DX (8348 7309).*
France Fresh Fish *99 Stroud Green Road, N4 3PX (7263 9767).*
Frocks Away *81-83 Fortis Green Road, N10 3HP (8444 9309, www.frocksaway.co.uk).*
George's Tailors *50 Wightman Road, N4 1RU (8341 3614).*
Indish *16 Broadway Parade, N8 9DE (8342 9496, www.indish.co.uk).*
John Jones *4 Morris Place, off Stroud Green Road, N4 3JG (7281 5439, www.johnjones.co.uk).*
Kate Kuba *71 Muswell Hill Broadway, N10 3HA (8444 1227, www.katekuba.co.uk).*
Les Aldrich *98 Fortis Green Road, N10 3HN (8883 5631, www.lesaldrich.co.uk).*
Mall Shopping City *159 High Road, N22 6YQ (8888 6667, www.themall.co.uk).*
Mini Kin *22 Broadway Parade, N8 9DE (8341 6898).*
Muswell Hill Bookshop *70-72 Fortis Green Road, N10 3HN (8444 7588).*
North London Hospice *44 Fortis Green Road, N10 3HN (8444 8131).*
Red Shoes *30 Topsfield Parade, N8 8PT (8341 9555, www.theredshoes.co.uk).*

Scullery *123 Muswell Hill Broadway, N10 3RS (8444 5236).*
Sirwan Food Centre *5 11 Green Lanes, N13 4TN (8888 8696).*
Soup Dragon *27 Topsfield Parade, Tottenham Lane, N8 8PT (8348 0224, www.soup-dragon.co.uk).*
Space NK *238 Muswell Hill Broadway, N10 3SH (8883 8568, www.spacenk.com).*
Spurs Megastore *1-3 Park Lane, N17 0AP (8365 5042, www.tottenhamhotspur.com).*
Treehouse *7 Park Road, N8 8TE (8341 4326).*
Turkish Food Market *38 Green Lanes, N4 1EU (8340 4547).*
Walter Purkis & Sons *www.purkis4fish.com; 17 The Broadway, N8 8DU (8340 6281); 52 Muswell Hill Broadway, N10 3RT (8883 4355).*
W Martyn *135 Muswell Hill Broadway, N10 3RS (8883 5642, www.wmartyn.co.uk).*
Yasar Halim *493 Green Lanes, N4 1AL (8340 8090).*

Arts & attractions

Cinemas & theatres
Cineworld Wood Green *Wood Green Shopping City, off Noel Park Road, N22 6LU (0871 200 2000, www.cineworld.co.uk).*
Jacksons Lane Theatre *269A Archway Road, N6 5AA (8341 4421, www.jacksonslane.org.uk). Arts centre in a converted Edwardian church, offering activities and workshops.*
Odeon Muswell Hill *Fortis Green Road, N10 3HP (0871 224 4007, www.odeon.co.uk).*
Vue Wood Green *Hollywood Green, High Road, N22 6EJ (08712 240240, www.myvue.com).*

Galleries & museums
Bruce Castle Museum *Lordship Lane, N17 8NU (8808 8772, www.haringey.gov.uk). Tottenham's local history museum.*

Music & comedy venues
Alexandra Palace *Alexandra Palace Way, Wood Green, N22 7AY (8365 2121, www.alexandrapalace.com).*
Downstairs at the King's Head *2 Crouch End Hill, N8 8AA (8340 1028, www.downstairsatthekingshead.com)*

Sport & fitness

Haringey has five large and well-equipped public leisure centres. There are also some desirable private options, such as the luxurious (and pricey) Laboratory Spa

& Health Club and the small but lovingly formed Factory Gym & Dance Centre. For a lower price tag, try the first London branch of easyGym (from the founders of easyJet), next to Wood Green Shopping Centre.

Gyms & leisure centres

Bodyworks Gym *Fountayne House, Fountayne Road, N15 4QL (8808 6580, www.bodyworksgym.co.uk). Private.*
easyGym *The Mall, 98-100 High Street, N22 6YG (www.easygym.co.uk).*
Factory Gym & Dance Centre *407 Hornsey Road, N19 4DX (7272 1122, www.factory london.com). Private.*

Finsbury Park Track & Gym *Hornsey Gate, Endymion Road, N4 0XX (8802 9139, www.haringey.gov.uk).*
Fitness First *Arena Shoppping Park, Green Lanes, N4 1DT (0844 571 2871, www.fitness first.co.uk). Private.*
Flex Fitness *Cypress House, 2 Coburg Road, N22 6UJ (8881 8222, www.flexfitness.co.uk). Private.*
Hornsey YMCA Fitness Centre *184 Tottenham Lane, N8 8SG (8340 6088, www.ymcahornsey.org.uk). Private.*
Laboratory Spa & Health Club *The Avenue, N10 2QJ (8482 3000, www.labspa.co.uk). Private.*
LA Fitness *Hillfield Park, N10 3PJ (0843 170 1016, www.lafitness.co.uk). Private.*
Park Road Leisure Centre *Park Road, N8 8JN (8341 3567, www.haringey.gov.uk).*
Selby Centre *Selby Road, N17 8JL (8885 5499). Private.*
Tottenham Green Leisure Centre *1 Philip Lane, N15 4JA (8489 5322, www.haringey.gov.uk).*
Virgin Active *31 Topsfield Parade, Tottenham Lane, N8 8PT (0845 270 4089, www.virginactive.co.uk). Private.*
White Hart Lane Community Sports Centre *White Hart Lane, N22 5QW (8881 2323, www.haringey.gov.uk).*

Other facilities

Muswell Hill Golf Club *Rhodes Avenue, N22 7UT (8888 1764, www.muswellhill golfclub.co.uk). Private.*
Rowans Tenpin Bowl *10 Stroud Green Road, N4 2DF (8800 1950, www.rowans.co.uk).*

Spectator sports

Tottenham Hotspur FC *Bill Nicholson Way, 748 High Road, N17 0AP (0844 499 5000, ticket office 0844 844 0102, www.tottenham hotspur.com).*

Schools

Primary

There are 54 state primary schools in Haringey, 17 of which are church schools. There are also ten independent primaries, including one Muslim school, one Montessori school and one Steiner school. See www.haringey.gov.uk, www.edubase.gov.uk and www.ofsted.gov.uk for more information.

Haringey

Secondary

Alexandra Park School *Bidwell Gardens, N11 2AZ (8826 1880, www.alexandrapark. haringey.sch.uk).*

Channing School for Girls *The Bank, Highgate, N6 5HF (8340 2328, www. channing.co.uk). Girls only; private.*

Fortismere School *8365 4400, www.fortismere. haringey.sch.uk; South Wing, Tetherdown, N10 1NE; North Wing, Creighton Avenue, N10 1NS.*

Gladesmore Community School *Crowland Road, N15 6EB (8800 0884, www.gladesmoreit academy.co.uk).*

Greig City Academy *High Street, N8 7NU (8609 0100, www.greigcityacademy.co.uk). Church of England.*

Heartlands High School *Station Road, N22 7ST (8826 1213, www.heartlands.haringey.sch.uk).*

Highgate School *North Road, N6 4AY (8340 1524, www.highgateschool.org.uk). Private.*

Highgate Wood School *Montenotte Road, N8 8RN (8342 7970, www.hws.uk.com).*

Hornsey School for Girls *Inderwick Road, N8 9JF (8348 6191, www.hornseyschool.com). Girls only.*

John Loughborough School *Holcombe Road, N17 9AD (8808 7837). Seventh Day Adventist.*

Northumberland Park Community School *Trulock Road, N17 0PG (8801 0091, www.northumberlandpark.haringey.sch.uk).*

Park View Academy *Langham Road, N15 3RB (8888 1722, www.parkview.haringey.sch.uk).*

St Thomas More Catholic School *Glendale Avenue, N22 5HN (0090 7122, www.stthomas moreschool.org.uk). Roman Catholic.*

Woodside High School *White Hart Lane, N22 5QJ (8889 6761, www.woodsidehighschool.co.uk).*

Property

WHAT THE AGENTS SAY:

'The area between Green Lanes and Wightman Road, known as the Harringay Ladder, remains very popular. House prices here continue to go against the the economic tide, with three- to four-bedroom houses often going for around £650,000. Harringay Gardens, just to the east, is also popular, with lower prices than on the Ladder. Mid-terrace houses and garden flats are always wanted, but there's been an increase in interest in first-floor flats. New-build developments are always over-subscribed.

Also, a recent crackdown by the local authority on HMOs (Houses of Multiple Occupation) has meant more pressure on landlords, drastically increasing the quality of rental properties.'
Steve Hatch, Castles, Turnpike Lane

Average property prices

Detached £1,036,061
Semi detached £479,150
Terraced £358,788
Flat £295,598

Local estate agents

Black Katz *1 Topsfield Parade, Middle Lane, N8 8PR (8347 3335, www.black-katz.co.uk).*

Browne & Nathan *697 Seven Sisters Road, N15 5LA (8800 7677, www.browneandnathan estates.com).*

Castles *5 Turnpike Lane, N8 0EP (8341 6262, www.castles.uk.com).*

Davies & Davies *85 Stroud Green Road, N4 3EG (7272 0986, www.daviesdavies.co.uk).*

Liberty *www.libertyproperty.co.uk; 2 offices in the borough (Crouch End 8348 6669, Finsbury Park 7281 3773).*

Tatlers *www.tatlers.co.uk; 2 offices in the borough (Crouch End 8341 4050, Muswell Hill 8444 1771).*

Thomas & Co *415 High Road, N17 6QN (8801 6068, www.thomasproperty.net).*

WJ Meade *1 Gladstone House, Gladstone Avenue, N22 6JS (8888 9595, www.wjmeade.co.uk).*

Other information

Council

London Borough of Haringey
Civic Centre, High Road, N22 8LE (8489 0000, www.haringey.gov.uk).

Legal services

Tottenham CAB *551B Tottenham High Road, N17 6SD (0044 026 9715, www.citizensadvice. org.uk).*

Turnpike Lane CAB *14A Willoughby Road, N8 0JJ (0844 826 9713, www.citizensadvice.org.uk).*

Local information

www.caschresidents.org.
www.greenn8.org.
www.haringeyindependent.co.uk.
www.harringayonline.com.
www.hornseyjournal.co.uk.
www.mymuswell.com
www.tottenham-today.co.uk
www.welovemuswellhill.co.uk.

Open spaces & allotments

Council allotments *There are 26 sites in the borough, most with long waiting lists. Contact the council's parks services on 8489 1000.*

Open spaces
www.haringey.gov.uk/greenspaces.

'My Islington is a ten-minute stroll, where I find the quaint atmosphere of a small town, with delightful canalside walks, London's finest organic pub and some of the most reputable art galleries in the world.'

Ziba Ardalan, Director, Parasol Unit

Islington

Once a resolutely working-class neighbourhood, Islington today seems to be all swanky boutiques, trendy DJ pubs and increasingly stratospheric property prices. Spirited reminders of its roots remain – a Premiership football team and banter-filled street market – but its child-mobbed beer gardens and terraces of refurbished Victorian and Georgian houses show this is a borough that's definitely up and come, though pockets of deprivation are not hard to find.

Neighbourhoods

Angel and Pentonville

Angel is a pretty name for the rather dull traffic interchange where Upper Street meets Pentonville Road and St John Street. There's a not-unpleasant hustle and bustle around Angel tube station, a buzzy area that's popular as an after-work meeting place due to all the local bars and restaurants. The name comes from a famous Victorian pub that's now a Co-op bank. Look out for the giant halo and wings that adorn the N1 Centre, a miniature shopping centre that's home to one of the area's two cinemas (the other, the Everyman Screen on the Green, further along Upper Street, shows more independent films and is a real looker when lit up at night).

The Angel end of Upper Street is probably best known as a night-out destination, and this creates mixed feelings for local residents. Though the number and

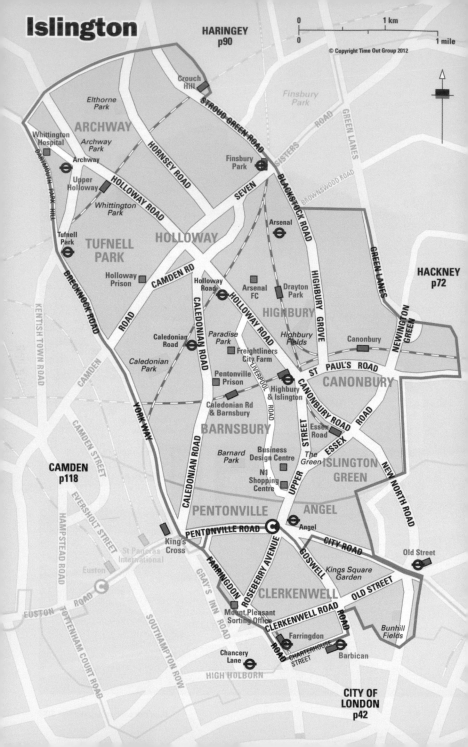

variety of decent restaurants are a boon, the chain pubs that now dominate the area bring with them a brash, often intimidating crowd. A sober walk along the main road at closing time can be a grim experience, and fights are not uncommon. During the day, Angel is equally frenetic, though mostly with crowds rushing from the tube to work and to lunch and back.

As well as excellent eating options, Angel has other compensations for the crowds. Camden Passage is a gorgeous pedestrianised strip, home to a clutch of nice cafés, pubs and shops, as well as a flea market at weekends. Islington Green, at the junction of Upper Street and Essex Road, has been spruced up and now has more benches and (another) halo-themed sculpture. Chapel Market, meanwhile, is a gloriously downmarket run of stalls hawking everything from posh cheese to hair gel. The street also contains some busy late-opening bars at its far end. This, combined with the early-morning traders, makes it best suited to heavy sleepers as a residential location.

Pentonville Road itself is a rather soulless, sloping route towards King's Cross; the latter neighbourhood's process of gentrification has not spread this far yet. Dotted with numerous newsagents and cafés, plus an acting school, purpose-built student accommodation and a few tower blocks, the road is almost entirely without character except at the Angel end, where the hard edges are softened by a Georgian terrace and the Crafts Council headquarters.

Islington Green and Canonbury

An area separate from the like-named green space mentioned above, Islington Green is one of many residential satellites surrounding Upper Street. In parts, it's beautiful (leafy Packington Square). In others, it's hard-bitten and ugly (particularly the run-down roads around Islington Green School). Roving gangs of prank-pulling kids who never seem to be in school are a particular menace. In all, Islington Green is a prime example of the borough's dual personality: the swanky and the shit, side by side. One further oddity is the regularity of mounted police: the Met often use its wide, quiet roads to train officers on horseback. For similar reasons, the area is also popular with local driving instructors.

Noisy, polluted, but with a certain charm, Essex Road is the bane of all those who crawl up and down it on a bus twice a day. On foot, there's a lot to see – better bars than on Upper Street, old-fashioned traders such as a butcher, a baker and a fishmonger, and quirky shops selling everything from vinyl to taxidermy. New North Road (half of which is in Islington), running south towards the City, has less to recommend it: it's a bleak, traffic-strewn route, notable only for trendy blocks of flats, such as the Gainsborough Studios next to the Regent's Canal (on the Islington/ Hackney border) – formerly the site of film studios where Hitchcock worked. Accommodation on and around both these main roads – as well as offshoots Balls Pond Road and Southgate Road – is rarely quiet. Living on principal bus arteries means residents must put up with chugging engines that run all through the night.

Running north from Essex Road rail station to Highbury Corner, residential Canonbury is markedly more peaceful. With a smattering of posh Georgian

Entertainment and shopping all under one roof: Islington's **N1 Centre**.

squares – in particular, Canonbury Square, once home to George Orwell and Evelyn Waugh – it commands huge property prices (well over the £1.5 million mark) and is much hawked by estate agents.

Highbury and Newington Green

Arsenal FC's relocation in 2006 from Highbury Stadium to the Emirates Stadium in Ashburton Grove may have quietened this corner of Islington on match days, but it remains resolutely 'Gooner'. Near kick-off on a Saturday or Sunday, those in red and white shirts outnumber all others. Since the move, the old stadium (bordered by the now distinctly more tranquil Aubert Park, Highbury Hill, Gillespie and Avenell Roads) has been transformed into luxury flats; the pitch is now a communal garden.

Roughly encompassing the postal district of N5, Highbury is often overlooked in favour of its gentrifying neighbours Canonbury and Stoke Newington, but the area has much to offer. Highbury Fields, Islington's largest green space, has tennis courts, football pitches, children's play areas and a well-equipped pool. Lesser-known is Gillespie Park, notable for its range of beautiful wildlife habitats and Ecology Centre (very popular with kids). Highbury

Barn is a fashionable enclave with food shops, restaurants and cafés.

On the eastern edge of Islington – a gateway of sorts to next-door Stoke Newington in Hackney – Newington Green is an area slowly on the up, centred around its eponymous park. This thriving, community-driven green space is in the middle of a busy roundabout (traversed via a network of zebra crossings), but nevertheless draws families with its well-maintained play area and regular events. Surrounding the Green are a number of food shops and cafés.

Barnsbury

A residential refuge tucked to the north of Angel, Barnsbury is served by Liverpool Road, running parallel to Upper Street from the N1 Shopping Centre and the glass-fronted Business Design Centre, all the way up to Holloway Road. Packed with Edwardian terraces, it's generally much quieter than Upper Street – lacking the buzz as well as the sleaze – but can be noisy due to the regular presence of police cars using it as a short cut to trouble in Angel and beyond. The roads connecting the two parallel thoroughfares make for some of Islington's choicest residences (fairly quiet, with easy access to amenities).

Almeida Street is particularly appealing home to both a classy theatre and a smart French restaurant of the same name.

Caledonian Road is scruffier, but has good travel options (including both Piccadilly line and rail stations), making it a popular spot for lower-end renters and buyers. Many properties on the 'Cally Road' itself are above the likes of bookies and kebab shops; elsewhere, expect to find mostly ex-local authority conversions. The other principal residents of note are those serving at Her Majesty's pleasure in Pentonville Prison. No, this is not a part of town for the glamorous

Archway, Tufnell Park and Holloway

The meat around an arterial traffic route, Holloway is a rather transient place, rarely stopped in by drivers chugging up and down the A1 (Holloway Road) to and from central London. Though far from pretty, the area does have London Metropolitan University and a vast Odeon cinema. Tufnell Park itself is pleasant enough, with reasonably priced property that, like Archway, is growing in popularity with London's up-and-comers, as well as parents looking to edge closer to desirable schools in north London. It is, after all, within sniffing distance of Hampstead and Highgate.

Scruffy Archway is seeing various improvements. Though unlovely around its Northern line station and throbbing traffic hub – not to mention the rather ugly Archway Tower - the area is being slowly dragged from the mire. Proximity to both classy, suburban Highgate and buzzy, urban Islington makes it an increasingly alluring proposition for buyers and renters; council discussion regarding major redevelopment of the area seems endless.

Clerkenwell and Farringdon

South from Angel towards the City lies the mystery province of Finsbury (near Rosebery Avenue), an area designation that's been all but abandoned but occasionally crops up on maps and in the names of public buildings, causing confusion with Finsbury Park some way to the north. Some locals refer to it as Clerkenwell, a few as Mount Pleasant (after the large Royal Mail sorting office, itself named after an old rubbish dump), while most stick to the safer 'Islington'.

Regardless, it's a lively, attractive area – kept young thanks to City University and its various sites around Northampton Square, and kept classy thanks to world-renowned dance theatre Sadler's Wells. In Exmouth Market, the area also has one of Islington's jewels: a thriving pedestrianised strip that boasts great bars, restaurants and shops.

To the south lies Clerkenwell proper, bordered by the rather blank Farringdon Road to the west and Smithfield meat market to the south. Running from east to west is the area's main artery, Clerkenwell Road, once home to all sorts of craftsmen, but now filled with pricey furniture shops and expensively renovated flats. The developers haven't finished with this part of town, either – close to the City and situated near some of London's best restaurants, this is a hugely desirable place to live. Prices follow suit.

Clerkenwell Green is an attractive local focal point; good-natured pub crowds

STATISTICS

BOROUGH MAKE-UP
Population 190,900
Ethnic origins
  White 72.7%
  Mixed 3.9%
  Asian or Asian British 9.4%
  Black or Black British 10.1%
  Chinese or other 3.9%
Students 11.1%
Retirees 7.9%

HOUSING STOCK
Borough size (hectares) 1,486
Population density per hectare 128.5
No. of households 82,281
Houses (detached, semi-detached or terraced) 20%
Flats (converted or purpose-built) 80%

CRIME PER 1,000 OF POPULATION
Burglary 9
Robbery 5
Theft of vehicle 5
Theft from vehicle 13
Violence against the person 31
Sexual offences 1

MPs
Islington North Jeremy Corbyn (Labour);
Islington South & Finsbury Emily Thornberry (Labour)

Islington

Fabulous fusion at **Modern Pantry**.

spill out on to the expansive paving during the summer. Indeed, the area is well known for its nightlife, with the enormously popular Fabric, among other nightclubs, just south on Charterhouse Street (in the City of London). This means a non-stop flow of people at weekends – hence 24-hour diner Tinseltown, one of the few places in London to serve through the night.

The area east around Old Street is a bit of a hinterland between the bustling areas of Clerkenwell and Shoreditch. It is sometimes referred to as St Luke's (for the gorgeous Hawksmoor church of the same name, home of the London Symphony Orchestra) but most refer to it simply as Old Street, after the Northern line station that serves as a well-used meeting point. However, it's becoming known as Silicon Roundabout, a reference to the large number of tech companies in the area. The busy roundabout above the station is a local landmark of sorts, with its arching advertising hoardings – this isn't an area big on architectural beauty. As you travel south towards Moorgate and the City along City Road, the view becomes more pleasant, taking in the likes of Bunhill Fields Cemetery and Finsbury Circus, before arriving at historic London Wall.

Restaurants & cafés

The area of Islington around Angel has several upper-end gastropubs: Barnsbury's Drapers Arms, the Albion, Canonbury's House, and organic specialist the Duke of Cambridge, close to Angel itself. There is also an army of chains: branches of Pizza Express, Nando's, Byron's, Thai Square and Carluccio's Caffè, plus Yo! Sushi and Wagamama in the N1 Centre. But there's more to Islington restaurants than that. The Almeida (part of D&D London) offers excellent Gallic prix-fixe menus. Sa Sa Sushi serves under-represented Japanese food; while the Gallipoli empire, with three outlets along Upper Street, provides well-priced Turkish food in party-friendly surroundings. In fact, there are plenty of Turkish restaurants in the vicinity, with Antepliler and Pasha both good choices.

Afghan Kitchen (Afghan) and Sabor (Latin American) on Essex Road, and Maghreb (Moroccan), Isarn (Thai), Rodizio Rico (Brazilian barbecue) and a branch of Masala Zone (Indian) on Upper Street, touch other corners of the globe. For a world of flavours on one plate, visit café Ottolenghi (also Upper Street); for warming Austrian dishes and cakes, try Kipferl in Camden Passage.

North and east from Angel and Upper Street, options thin out a little. Highbury has superb Turkish eaterie İznik, Italian foodie favourite Trullo and easy-going Argentinian Garufa; on the Blackstock Road, there's ice-cream parlour Cremeria Vienna and Good for Food Café; Newington Green has attractive French-accented café Belle Epoque and kid-centred That Place on the Corner. Holloway Road's budget Georgian venue Tbilisi and relaunched Korean Busan are worth seeking out too. In Archway, gastropubs the Landseer and St John's are decent places to dine, while Lalibela brings injera, wots and other Ethiopian delicacies to Tufnell Park locals. Holloway and Tufnell Park residents are also well placed for the myriad dining options offered by Camden.

MasterCard Priceless Tip

Get exclusive access to Priceless London dining offers at www.pricelesslondon.co.uk

Moving south to Clerkenwell and Farringdon reveals some absolute gems. Exmouth Market has an embarrassment of riches: the modish global food at Caravan; Japanese options Necco and Bincho; British restaurant and bar Medcalf; and marvellous Spanish-North African dining room Moro, plus offshoot Morito tapas bar. Round the corner, the handsome ex-Quality Chop House premises are now home to Meatballs. Nearby gastropubs the Easton, the Eagle and the Coach & Horses are yet more fine examples of the genre in the borough. Budget options include Tinseltown, which serves burgers and milkshakes 24 hours a day, chic little Vietnamese café Pho and a branch of La Porchetta pizzeria. Coffee bars and cafés are also a Clerkenwell strength: favourites include Brill, J&A Café and St Ali.

A glut of classy restaurants can be found in the stretch from Clerkenwell to Smithfield Market (where Islington meets the City of London). On St John's Square are Bistrot Bruno Loubet (French) and the Modern Pantry (Fusion); moving south along St John Street there's Portal (high-end Portuguese food), North Road (Scandinavian), St John (the seminal British restaurant) and Vinoteca (new-wave wine bar with food).

Afghan Kitchen 35 Islington Green, N1 8DU (7359 8019).
Albion 10 Thornhill Road, N1 1HW (7607 7450, www.the-albion.co.uk).

Almeida 30 Almeida Street, N1 1AD (7354 4777, www.almeida-restaurant.co.uk).
Antepliler 139 Upper Street, N1 1QP (7226 5441, www.anteplilerrestaurant.com).
Belle Epoque Pâtisserie 37 Newington Green, N16 9PR (7249 2222, www.belleepoque.co.uk).
Bincho 55 Exmouth Market, EC1R 4QL (7837 0009, www.bincho.co.uk).
Bistrot Bruno Loubet 86-88 Clerkenwell Road, EC1M 5RJ (7324 4444, www.bistrotbrunoloubet.com).
Brill 27 Exmouth Market, EC1R 4QL (7833 9757).
Busan 38 Holloway Road, N7 8JP (7697 9889).
Caravan 11-13 Exmouth Market, EC1R 4QD (7833 8115, www.caravanonexmouth.co.uk).
Coach & Horses 26-28 Ray Street, EC1R 3DJ (7278 8990, www.thecoachandhorses.com).
Cremeria Vienna 145 Blackstock Road, N4 2JS (no phone).
Drapers Arms 44 Barnsbury Street, N1 1ER (7619 0348, www.thedrapersarms.com).
Duke of Cambridge 30 St Peter's Street, N1 8JT (7359 3066, www.dukeorganic.co.uk).
Eagle 159 Farringdon Road, EC1R 3AL (7837 1353).
Easton 22 Easton Street, WC1X 0DS (7278 7608, www.theeastonpub.co.uk).
Gallipoli 102 Upper Street, N1 1QP (7359 0630, www.cafegallipoli.com).
Gallipoli Again 120 Upper Street, N1 1QP (7359 1578/7226 8099, www.cafegallipoli.com).
Gallipoli Bazaar 107 Upper Street, N1 1QP (7226 5333, www.cafegallipoli.com).

Islington

Transporting you to a tapas bar in Spain: **Morito**, on Exmouth Market.

Garufa *104 Highbury Park, N5 2XE (7226 0070, www.garufa.co.uk).*
Good for Food *16 Blackstock Road, N4 2DW (7503 0034, www.goodfor food.org.uk).*
House *63-69 Canonbury Road, N1 2DG (7704 7410, www.themeredithgroup.co.uk).*
Isarn *119 Upper Street, N1 1QP (7424 5153, www.isarn.co.uk).*
İznik *19 Highbury Park, N5 1QJ (7354 5697, www.iznik.co.uk).*
J&A Café *4 Sutton Lane, EC1M 5PU (7490 2992, www.jandacafe.com).*
Kipferl *20 Camden Passage, N1 8ED (7704 1555, www.kipferl.co.uk).*
Lalibela *137 Fortress Road, NW5 2HR (7284 0600).*
Landseer *37 Landseer Road, N19 4JU (7263 4658).*
Maghreb *189 Upper Street, N1 1RQ (7226 2305, www.maghreb-restaurant.com).*
Masala Zone *80 Upper Street, N1 0NU (7359 3399, www.masalazone.com).*
Meatballs *92-94 Farringdon Road, EC1R 3EA (3490 6228, www.meatballs.co.uk).*

Medcalf *40 Exmouth Market, EC1R 4QE (7833 3533, www.medcalfbar.co.uk).*
Modern Pantry *47-48 St John's Square, EC1V 4JJ (7553 9210, www.themodern pantry.co.uk).*
Morito *32 Exmouth Market, EC1R 4QE (7278 7007).*
Moro *34-36 Exmouth Market, EC1R 4QE (7833 8336, www.moro.co.uk).*
Necco *52-54 Exmouth Market, EC1R 4QE (7713 8575, www.necco.co.uk).*
North Road *69-73 St John Street, EC1M 4AY (3217 0033, www.northroadrestaurant.co.uk).*
Ottolenghi *287 Upper Street, N1 2TZ (7288 1454, www.ottolenghi.co.uk).*
Pasha *301 Upper Street, N1 2TU (7226 1454, www.pashaislington.co.uk).*
Pho *86 St John Street, EC1M 4EH (7253 7624, www.phocafe.co.uk).*
La Porchetta *84-86 Rosebery Avenue, EC1R 4QY (7837 6060, www.laporchetta.net).*
Portal *88 St John Street, EC1M 4EH (7253 6950, www.portalrestaurant.com).*
Rodizio Rico *77-78 Upper Street, N1 0NU (7354 1076, www.rodiziorico.com).*
Sa Sa Sushi *422 St John Street, EC1V 4NJ (7837 1155, www.sasasushi.co.uk).*
Sabor *108 Essex Road, N1 8LX (7226 5551, www.sabor.co.uk).*
St Ali *27 Clerkenwell Road, EC1M 5RN (7253 5754, www.stali.co.uk).*
St John *26 St John Street, EC1M 4AY (3301 8069, www.stjohnrestaurant.com).*
St John's *91 Junction Road, N19 5QU (7272 1587, www.stjohnstavern.com).*
Tbilisi *91 Holloway Road, N7 8LT (7607 2536).*
That Place on the Corner *1-3 Green Lanes, N16 9BS (7704 0079, www.thatplaceon thecorner.co.uk).*
Tinseltown *44-46 St John Street, EC1M 4DF (7689 2424, www.tinseltown.co.uk).*
Trullo *300-302 St Paul's Road, N1 2LH (7226 2733, www.trullorestaurant.com).*
Vinoteca *7 St John Street, EC1M 4AA (7253 8786, www.vinoteca.co.uk).*

Locals' Tips

Bus users, beware: the slow crawl up and down Essex Road during busy times is the stuff of commuter nightmares. Avoid if possible by using alternative routes – Southgate Road is one possibility.

Make the most of Regent's Canal – the stretch from Noel Road out towards Hackney makes a great walk – though not at rush hour when cyclists dominate.

Visit Freightliners City Farm (7609 0467, www.freightlinersfarm.org.uk) just behind King's Cross; the farm is involved in many community ventures, and has a lovely café, the Strawbale.

Arsenal match days cause havoc in the area. Parking is suspended for miles around and the Victoria, Northern and Piccadilly lines that run through Islington get rammed with home fans before and after the game. Whatever your feelings about football, get a fixture list.

Discover the New River – the covered waterway makes an attractive linear park through Islington. It takes under half an hour to wander from Essex Road to Newington Green.

Bars & pubs

When most people think of drinking in Islington, they think of Upper Street – chain bar-filled and home to many a drunken fight after closing time. There's the odd decent haunt here – Albert & Pearl bar and popular theatre pub the King's Head – but the best options are located on surrounding streets.

Islington's most rock 'n' roll boozer, **Filthy McNasty's**.

Essex Road has plenty of bars too, including Latino DJ bar Barrio North, and revamped pubs New Rose and the Old Queen's Head. Venturing on to side roads reveals gastropub the Duke of Cambridge (*see p108*), friendly neighbourhood pub the Marquess Tavern, tiny cocktail bar Four Sisters, quirky theatre pub the Rosemary Branch, and refurbed, pizza-serving Earl of Essex. Only streets apart, the Island Queen and the Charles Lamb couldn't be more different, but they're both delightful. For a more straightforward pint, try the fuss-free Camden Head, canalside Narrow Boat or the Hemingford Arms.

The roads to the west of Upper Street are equally well stocked with options. The Angelic is an attractive, two-floored bar, popular with a thirtysomething crowd; Chapel Market has the Compass pub and late-opening cocktail bar Anam.

Further north to Holloway, options get grubbier, but the Swimmer at the Grafton Arms is a cosy, worthy boozer, and the Duchess of Kent – at the Holloway end of Liverpool Road – is a locals' favourite. Archway drinkers have gastropubs the Landseer and St John's (for both, *see p108*) – but little in terms of bars. Best to head

to Tufnell Park, for dive bar Aces & Eights (on the border with the borough of Camden).

Business picks up as you head towards Clerkenwell. Just past the Angel there's another historic theatre pub, the Old Red Lion, handsome gastropub the Peasant and music pub Filthy McNasty's. Pedestrianised Exmouth Market goes from strength to strength, offering everything from table-football thrills (Café Kick) to cocktails (Dollar Bar & Grill). The Exmouth Arms has been reborn as a hip local boozer, just yards away from the Easton, the Eagle (for both, *see p109*) and lively local the Wilmington Arms.

Clerkenwell proper is littered with great pubs, from must-visit Jerusalem Tavern (the only London outpost of fine Suffolk brewery St Peter's) to the jocular Three Kings of Clerkenwell, tucked away in a secluded side street. Also of note are gastropub the Green, after-work drinkers' magnet and music pub the Slaughtered Lamb and, for Belgian beer, the Dovetail. On Clerkenwell Road, Giant Robot is a café-bar with a cocktail menu; more cocktails are available at nearby Zetter Townhouse. Or head to St John Street for a superior bottle of wine at St John (*see p108*) or Vinoteca (*see p109*).

Aces & Eights *156-158 Fortess Road, NW5 2HP (7485 4033, www.acesandeights saloonbar.com).*

Albert & Pearl *181 Upper Street, N1 1RQ (7704 1070, www.albertandpearl.com).*

Anam *3 Chapel Market, N1 9EZ (7278 1001, www.anambar.com).*

Angelic *57 Liverpool Road, N1 0RJ (7278 8433, www.theangelic.co.uk).*

Barrio North *45 Essex Road, N1 2SF (7688 2882, www.barrionorth.com).*

Café Kick *43 Exmouth Market, EC1R 4QL (7837 8077, www.cafekick.co.uk).*

Camden Head *2 Camden Walk, N1 8DY (3582 4516, www.taylor-walker.co.uk).*

Charles Lamb *16 Elia Street, N1 8DE (7837 5040, www.thecharleslambpub.com).*

Compass *58 Penton Street, N1 9PZ (7837 3891, www.thecompassn1.co.uk).*

Dollar Bar & Grill *2 Exmouth Market, EC1R 4PX (7278 0077, www.dollargrills.com).*

Dovetail *9-10 Jerusalem Passage, EC1V 4JP (7490 7321, www.dovepubs.com).*

Duchess of Kent *441 Liverpool Road, N7 8PR (7609 7104, www.geronimo-inns.co.uk).*

Earl of Essex *25 Danbury Street, N1 8LE (7424 5828).*

Exmouth Arms *23 Exmouth Market, EC1R 4QR (7837 5622).*

Filthy McNasty's *68 Amwell Street, EC1R 1UU (8617 3505, www.filthymacnastys.co.uk).*

Four Sisters *25 Canonbury Lane, N1 2AS (7226 0955, www.thefoursistersbar.co.uk).*

Giant Robot *45-47 Clerkenwell Road, EC1M 5RS (7065 6810, www.gntrbt.com).*

Green *29 Clerkenwell Green, EC1R 0DU (7490 8010, www.thegreenec1.co.uk).*

Hemingford Arms *158 Hemingford Road, N1 1DF (7607 3303, www.capitalpub company.com).*

Island Queen *87 Noel Road, N1 8HD (7354 8741, www.theislandqueen islington.co.uk).*

Jerusalem Tavern *55 Britton Street, EC1M 5UQ (7490 4281, www.stpeters brewery.co.uk).*

King's Head *115 Upper Street, N1 1QN (7226 4443, www.kingsheadtheatrepub.co.uk).*

Marquess Tavern *32 Canonbury Street, N1 2TB (7354 2975, www.marquess tavern.co.uk).*

Narrow Boat *119 St Peter's Street, N1 8PZ (7288 0572, www.thenarrowboatpub.com).*

New Rose *84-86 Essex Road, N1 8LU (7226 1082, www.newrose.co.uk).*

Old Queen's Head *44 Essex Road, N1 8LN (7354 9993, www.theoldqueenshead.com).*

Old Red Lion *418 St John Street, EC1V 4PD (7837 7816, www.oldredliontheatre.co.uk).*

Peasant *240 St John Street, EC1V 4PH (7336 7726, www.thepeasant.co.uk).*

Rosemary Branch *2 Shepperton Road, N1 3DT (7704 2730, www.rosemary branch.co.uk).*

Slaughtered Lamb *34-35 Great Sutton Street, EC1V 0DX (7253 1516, www.theslaughtered lambpub.com).*

Swimmer at the Grafton Arms *13 Eburne Road, N7 6AR (7281 4632).*

Three Kings of Clerkenwell *7 Clerkenwell Close, EC1R 0DY (7253 0483).*

Wilmington Arms *69 Rosebery Avenue, EC1R 4RL (7837 1384, www.thewilmington arms.co.uk).*

Zetter Townhouse *49-50 St John's Square, EC1V 4JJ (7324 4545, www.thezettertown house.com).*

Shops

There's plenty of scope in this neck of the woods for both the practical and pleasure-seeking shopper. At the very south of the borough, Clerkenwell Green is a crafts hub, with the Lesley Craze Gallery for jewellery and textiles, and a building occupied by Craft Central (formerly the Clerkenwell Green Association), which supports hundreds of designer-makers and holds regular open-studio events.

Pedestrianised Exmouth Market has a selection of independents. Highlights include Clerkenwell Tales bookshop, Family Tree (idiosyncratic gifts and clothes), EC One (modern jewellery), Bagman & Robin (characterful, colourful bags of all sizes) and Sweet (bread and pâtisserie). Just to the north, pretty Arlington Way has Jacqueline Byrne's exquisite bridal gowns, while Amwell Street has accessories boutique Lie Down I Think I Love You and eco-friendly food store Unpackaged.

The undoubted retail hotspot of the borough, however, is shop-packed Upper Street. High-street chains (Waitrose, Gap, Next, Monsoon, M&S, et al) are clustered in and around the shiny N1 Centre. Head out of the back of the mall to find the food, clothing and household goods stalls of old-fashioned Chapel Market, which on Sundays hosts the Islington Farmers' Market (10am-2pm).

Tucked behind Upper Street's east side is Camden Passage, a pedestrian alleyway once lined with antiques shops. Its character is evolving, though, with an influx of new independent shops, including gourmet confectioner Paul A Young Fine Chocolates, contemporary womenswear designer Susy Harper, lovely home accessories and gift store Smug, charming yarn shop Loop, and, at the northern end, the African Waistcoat Company (an utterly original fusion of Nigerian and British traditions). Some antiques dealers remain, especially in the idiosyncratic Pierrepont Arcade, and the antiques market still operates on Wednesday and Saturday (plus a book market on Thursday and vintage clothes on Sunday). Annie's Vintage Clothing is a notable survivor.

On Upper Street proper, the more interesting shops tend to be towards Highbury, past Islington Green. Well-heeled locals kit out their refurbished Georgian terraces in contemporary style with purchases from Aria (on Barnsbury Street), Atelier Abigail Ahern and Scandinavian specialist Twentytwentyone. Aficionados of 20th-century design also have plenty of choice at Fandango (on Cross Street), while After Noah has some unusual vintage pieces amid the reproductions, gifts and kids' toys.

There are also some great boutiques: Diverse and Sefton (menswear) for designer gear, Labour of Love for more avant-garde looks, jeweller Stephen Einhorn and, just off the main strip, Palette London, which mixes vintage and new fashion to hip effect. As you'd expect in a family-friendly area, there are some good kids' shops, including all-rounder Igloo. Cross Street has a few interesting shops, including Tallulah Lingerie.

Nip over to unlovely Essex Road for second-hand record stores such as Flashback, plus Handmade & Found, an affordable womenswear boutique. It's also home to superior fishmonger Steve Hatt – there's often a queue out the door on Saturdays. Other notable food shops in the locale include the Euphorium Bakery and, up on Highbury Park, deluxe deli/cheese shop La Fromagerie and prime butcher Frank Godfrey. Further north, Blackstock Road has plenty of shops with a Middle Eastern or Mediterranean flavour, many of them open late. There's fruit and veg nirvana at the amazingly well-stocked Newington Green Fruit & Vegetables; while you're there, pop into second-hand furniture shop, the Peanut Vendor.

To the west, Holloway Road doesn't offer much in the way of retail excitement, apart from D&A Binder, a fascinating repository of reclaimed shop fittings; further up there's a big Waitrose. On Archway Road, check out Second Layer, home to more than 3,000 CDs, LPs, DVDs and books. There aren't many browsing opportunities in Tufnell Park, but you can buy *MasterChef* winner Julie Friend's own-made dishes and fine foodstuffs at her deli, Flavours.

African Waistcoat Company *33 Islington Green, N1 8DU (7704 9698, www.african waistcoatcompany.com).*
After Noah *121 Upper Street, N1 1QP (7359 4281, www.afternoah.com).*
Annie's Vintage Clothing *12 Camden Passage, N1 8ED (7359 0796, www.anniesvintageclothing.co.uk).*
Aria *Barnsbury Hall, 2 Barnsbury Street, N1 1PN (7704 6222, www.ariashop.co.uk).*
Atelier Abigail Ahern *137 Upper Street, N1 1QP (7354 8181, www.atelierabigailahern.com).*
Bagman & Robin *47 Exmouth Market, EC1R 4QL (7833 8780, www.bagmanandrobin.com).*
Clerkenwell Tales *30 Exmouth Market, EC1R 4QE (7713 8135, www.clerkenwell-tales.co.uk).*

Loop is a joy to browse.

Craft Central *33-35 St John's Square, EC1M 4DS (7251 0276, www.craftcentral.org.uk).*
D&A Binder *101 Holloway Road, N7 8LT (7609 6300, www.dandabinder.co.uk).*
Diverse *294 Upper Street, N1 2TU (7359 8877, www.diverseclothing.com).*
EC One *41 Exmouth Market, EC1R 4QL (7713 6185, www.econe.co.uk).*
Euphorium Bakery *www.euphorium bakery.com; 79 Upper Street, N1 0NU (7288 8788); 202 Upper Street, N1 1RQ (7704 6905); 26A Chapel Market, N1 9EN (7837 7010).*
Family Tree *53 Exmouth Market, EC1R 4QL (7278 1084, www.familytreeshop.co.uk).*
Fandango *2 Cross Street, N1 2BL (07979 650805, www.fandangointeriors.co.uk).*
Flashback *50 Essex Road, N1 8LR (7354 9356, www.flashback.co.uk).*
Flavours *9 Campdale Road, N7 0EA (7281 5552).*
Frank Godfrey *7 Highbury Park, N5 1QJ (7226 2425, www.fgodfrey.co.uk).*
La Fromagerie *30 Highbury Park, N5 2AA (7359 7440, www.lafromagerie.co.uk).*
Handmade & Found *109 Essex Road, N1 2SL (7359 3898, www.handmadeandfound.co.uk).*
Igloo *300 Upper Street, N1 2TU (7354 7300, www.iglookids.co.uk).*
Islington Farmers' Market *Chapel Market, between Penton & Baron Streets, N1 9PZ (7833 0338, www.lfm.org.uk).*
Jacqueline Byrne *18 Arlington Way, EC1R 1UY (7278 7014, www.jacquelinebyrne.co.uk).*
Labour of Love *193 Upper Street, N1 1RQ (7354 9333, www.labour-of-love.co.uk).*
Lesley Craze Gallery *33-35A Clerkenwell Green, EC1R 0DU (7608 0393, www.lesley crazegallery.co.uk).*
Lie Down I Think I Love You *33 Amwell Street, EC1R 1UR (7833 1100, www.liedown ithinkiloveyou.com).*
Loop *15 Camden Passage, N1 8EA (7288 1160, www.loopknitting.com).*
Newington Green Fruit & Vegetables *109 Newington Green Road, N1 4QY (7354 0990).*
N1 Centre *21 Parkfield Street, N1 0PS (7359 2674, www.n1islington.com).*
Palette London *21 Canonbury Lane, N1 2AS (7288 7428, www.palette-london.com).*
Paul A Young Fine Chocolates *33 Camden Passage, N1 8EA (7424 5750, www.paula young.co.uk).*
Peanut Vendor *133 Newington Green Road, N1 4RA (7226 5727, www.thepeanut vendor.co.uk).*
Second Layer *323 Archway Road, N6 5AA (07878 051726, www.secondlayer.co.uk).*

Sefton *196 Upper Street, N1 1RQ (7226 7076, www.seftonfashion.com).*
Smug *13 Camden Passage, N1 8EA (7354 0253, www.ifeelsmug.com).*
Stephen Einhorn *210 Upper Street, N1 1RL (7359 4977, www.stepheneinhorn.co.uk).*
Steve Hatt *88-90 Essex Road, N1 8LU (7226 3963).*
Susy Harper *35 Camden Passage, N1 8EA (7704 0688, www.susyharper.co.uk).*
Sweet *64 Exmouth Market, EC1R 4QP (7713 6777, www.sweetdesserts.co.uk).*
Tallulah Lingerie *65 Cross Street, N1 2BB (7704 0066, www.tallulah-lingerie.co.uk).*
Twentytwentyone *274-275 Upper Street, N1 2UA (7288 1996, www.twentytwentyone.com).*
Unpackaged *42 Amwell Street, EC1R 1XT (7713 8368, http://beunpackaged.com).*

Arts & attractions

Cinemas & theatres

Almeida Theatre *Almeida Street, N1 1TA (7359 4404, www.almeida.co.uk). Award-winning theatre with a world-class reputation.*
Everyman Screen on the Green *Islington Green, Upper Street, N1 0NP (0871 906 9060, www.everymancinema.com).*
King's Head *115 Upper Street, N1 1QN (7478 0160, www.kingsheadtheatre.org).*

A pioneer of the pub theatre scene.
Little Angel Theatre *14 Dagmar Passage, off Cross Street, N1 2DN (7226 1787, www. littleangeltheatre.com). This acclaimed puppet theatre celebrated its 50th birthday in 2011.*
Odeon Holloway *419-427 Holloway Road, N7 6LJ (0871 224 4007, www.odeon.co.uk).*
Pleasance Theatre Islington *Carpenters Mews, North Road, N7 9EF (7609 1800, www.pleasance.co.uk). Sister venue to the Edinburgh Pleasance.*
Rosemary Branch *2 Shepperton Road, N1 3DT (7704 6665, www.rosemarybranch.co.uk). Friendly, eccentrically decorated freehouse with a 60-seat theatre upstairs.*
Sadler's Wells *Rosebery Avenue, EC1R 4TN (0844 412 4300, www.sadlerswells.com). One of the world's premier dance venues.*
Vue Islington *Parkfield Street, N1 0PS (0871 224 0240, www.myvue.com).*

Galleries & museums
Cubitt *8 Angel Mews, N1 9HH (7278 8226, www.cubittartists.org.uk). Artist-run gallery and studio space.*
Estorick Collection of Modern Italian Art *39A Canonbury Square, N1 2AN (7704 9522, www.estorickcollection.com). Work by Italian painters such as Balla, Boccioni and Carra; also a museum, bookshop and cafe.*
London Canal Museum *12-13 New Wharf Road, N1 9RT (7713 0836, www.canal museum.org.uk). Housed in a former 19th-century ice warehouse, which was built for the ice-cream maker Carlo Gatti.*
Museum & Library of the Order of St John *St John's Gate, St John's Lane, EC1M 4DA (7324 4005, www.museumstjohn.org.uk). Recently revamped museum charting the evolution of the medieval Order of Hospitaller Knights to its modern incarnation as the world-renowned ambulance service.*
Parasol Unit *14 Wharf Road, N1 7RW (7490 7373, www.parasol-unit.org). Contemporary art venue.*

Music & comedy venues
Hen & Chickens *109 St Paul's Road, N1 2NA (7704 2001, www.henandchickens.com). Well-established comedy joint.*
LSO St Luke's *161 Old Street, EC1V 9NG (7638 8891, www.lso.co.uk/lsostlukes). Restored Hawksmoor church used for rehearsals by the London Symphony Orchestra, and for gigs.*
O2 Academy Islington *N1 Centre, 16 Parkfield Street, N1 0PS (7288 4400,*

Enjoy the fresh air in leafy **Highbury Fields**. See p106.

www.o2academyislington.co.uk). Slightly soulless shopping mall venue; however, the capital's lack of midsize spaces means it's become a default haunt for international cult acts.

Other attractions

Bunhill Fields *City Road, EC1. Famous residents in this small, Nonconformist cemetery include Daniel Defoe, John Bunyan and William Blake and his wife.*

Business Design Centre *52 Upper Street, N1 0QH (7359 3535, www.businessdesign centre.co.uk). Trade fairs and conferences, including some major art and design shows.*

Candid Arts Trust *3-5 Torrens Street, EC1V 1NQ (7837 4237, www.candidarts.com). Two Victorian warehouses behind Angel tube, with exhibition and rehearsal space, artists' studios, a film-screening room and an excellent café.*

Crafts Council *44A Pentonville Road, N1 9BY (7278 7700, www.craftscouncil.org.uk). Reference library open Wednesday and Thursday.*

Sport & fitness

Islington has a good range of public and private leisure facilities. Aquaterra Leisure, which runs seven of Islington's eight public centres, is a charity organisation that invests the money spent by the public back into the facilities. Saddlers Sports Centre, affiliated to the nearby City University, is closed for redevelopment until at least 2013.

Gyms & leisure centres

Archway Leisure Centre *McDonald Road, N19 5DD (7281 4105, www.aquaterra.org).*
Cally Pool *229 Caledonian Road, N1 0NH (7278 1890, www.aquaterra.org).*
Dowe Dynamics Gym *1-2 Central Hall Buildings, Archway Close, N19 3UB (7281 2267, www.dowedynamics.com). Private.*
Factory *407 Hornsey Road, N19 4DX (7272 1122, www.factorylondon.com). Private.*
Finsbury Leisure Centre *Norman Street, EC1V 3PU (7253 2346, www.aquaterra.org).*
Fitness First *www.fitnessfirst.co.uk; 60-63 Bunhill Row, EC1Y 8NQ (7490 3555); 67-83 Seven Sisters Road, N7 6BU (7281 8585). Private.*
Highbury Pool *Highbury Crescent, N5 1RR (7704 2312, www.aquaterra.org).*
Ironmonger Row Baths *1-11 Ironmonger Row, EC1V 3QF (7253 4011, www.aqua terra.org). Closed for refurbishment until mid 2012.*

Maximum Fitness *144 Fortess Road, NW5 2HP (7482 3941, www.maxfit.co.uk). Private.*
Ozone *Holiday Inn Hotel, 1 King's Cross Road, WC1X 9HX (7698 4039, www.ozonehealth andfitness.co.uk). Private.*
Sequin Park *240 Upper Street, N1 1RU (7704 9844, www.sequinpark.co.uk). Private.*
Sobell Leisure Centre & Ice Rink *Hornsey Road, N7 7NY (7609 2166, www.aquaterra.org).*
Virgin Active *www.virginactive.co.uk; 333 Goswell Road, EC1V 7DG (7014 9700); 33 Bunhill Row, EC1Y 8LP (7448 5454); Islington Green, 27 Essex Road, N1 2SD (7288 8200); Colinwood Business Centre, Mercers Road, N19 4PJ (7561 5200). Private.*

Other facilities

Islington Tennis Centre *Market Road, N7 9PL (7700 1370, www.aquaterra.org).*

Spectator sports

Arsenal FC *Emirates Stadium, Highbury House, 75 Drayton Park, N5 1BU (7619 5003, tours 7619 5000, www.arsenal.com).*

Schools

Primary

There are 45 state primary schools in Islington, 15 of which are church schools. There are also seven independent primaries, including one Montessori school and one Steiner school. See www.islington.gov.uk, www.edubase.gov.uk and www.ofsted.gov.uk for more information.

Secondary

Central Foundation Boys' School *Cowper Street, EC2A 4SH (7253 3741, www.central foundationboys.co.uk). Boys only.*
City of London Academy *Prebend Street, N1 8PQ (7226 8611, www.cityacademy islington.org.uk).*
Elizabeth Garrett Anderson Language College *Donegal Street, N1 9QG (7837 0739, www.egaschool.co.uk). Girls only.*
Highbury Fields School *Highbury Hill, N5 1AR (7288 1888, www.highburyfields. islington.sch.uk). Girls only.*
Highbury Grove School *Highbury New Park, N5 2EG (7288 8900, www.highburygrove. islington.sch.uk).*
Holloway School *Hilldrop Road, N7 0JG (7607 5885, www.holloway.islington.sch.uk).*
Islington Arts & Media School *Turle Road, N4 3LS (7281 5511, www.iamschool.co.uk).*

RECYLING

Household waste recycled & composted 29%
Main recycling centre Household Reuse & Recycling Centre, 40 Hornsey Street, N7 8HU (8884 5645)
Other recycling services green and kitchen waste collection; home composting; white goods collection; real nappies scheme
Council contact Contact Islington, 222 Upper Street, N1 1XR (7527 2000, www.islington.gov.uk/recycling)

COUNCIL TAX

A	up to £40,000	£847.80
B	£40,001-£52,000	£989.09
C	£52,001-£68,000	£1,130.40
D	£68,001-£88,000	£1,271.69
E	£88,001-£120,000	£1,554.29
F	£120,001-£160,000	£1,836.89
G	£160,001-£320,000	£2,119.49
H	over £320,000	£2,543.38

Italia Conti Academy of Theatre Arts
23 Goswell Road, EC1M 7AJ (7253 1430, www.italiaconti.com). Former pupils at this private theatre school (founded in 1911) include Noël Coward and Patsy Kensit.
Mount Carmel Technology College for Girls *Holland Walk, Duncombe Road, N19 3EU (7281 3536, www.mountcarmel.islington.sch.uk). Girls only.*
St Aloysius RC College *30 Hornsey Lane, N6 5LY (7263 1391, www.sta.islington.sch.uk). Roman Catholic, boys only.*
St Mary Magdalene Academy *Liverpool Road, N7 8PG (7697 0123, www.smm academy.org).*

Property

WHAT THE AGENTS SAY:

'People living in Islington enjoy the best of both worlds. Despite its inner-city location and proximity to the capital's financial district, it's also a desirable location for families seeking a taste of small-town life. From the lively buzz of Upper Street's bars and restaurants to the open space of Highbury Fields, Islington strikes the perfect balance between work and play. And it's well served by bus routes and tube lines. The price of so called suburbia is reflected in the cost of the pretty Victorian and Georgian properties; new-build flats are cheaper Barnsbury, Canonbury and Highbury Fields are the most popular areas at present, and there's no prospect of prices going down.'
Christian Thomas, Currell Residential

Average property prices
Detached £1,133,900
Semi-detached £749,228
Terraced £713,256
Flat £394,795

Local estate agents
APS Estates *210 212 Caledonian Road, N1 0SQ (7837 0203, www.apsestates.com)*
Currell Residential *321 Upper Street, N1 2XQ (7226 4200, www.currell.com).*
Jeffrey Nicholas *JN House, 71 Cross Street, N1 2BB (7354 0707, www.jeffreynicholas.co.uk).*
JTM Homes *695 Holloway Road, N19 5SE (7272 1090, www.jtmhomes.co.uk).*
Moving On Property Services *79 Pitfield Street, N1 6BT (3375 3694, www movingon london.com).*
myspace *328 Caledonian Road, N1 1BB (7609 3598, www.myspaceuk.com).*
PG Estates *350 Upper Street, N1 0PD (7226 4994, www.pgestates.com).*
Urban Spaces *10 Clerkenwell Road, EC1M 5QA (7251 4000, www.urbanspaces.co.uk)*

Other information

Council
Islington Council *222 Upper Street, N1 1XR (7527 2000, www.islington.gov.uk).*

Legal services
Islington CAB *222 Upper Street, N1 1XR (7947 7771, www.rcjadvice.org uk).*

Local information
www.islingtongazette.co.uk.
www.islingtontribune.com.

Open spaces & allotments
Council allotments *The waiting list for a council allotment is at least ten years, and thus closed to new applicants until further notice. For more information, contact the Greenspace & Leisure Support Services Team on 7527 2000.*
Open spaces *www.islington.gov.uk/ environment.*

Islington

*'Europe's youth capital,
Camden hustles and bustles,
creates and re-creates. It is an
ever-evolving soup of many
flavours, colours and smells.'*

Marcus Davey, Chief Executive, Roundhouse

Camden

It's all change in certain Camden quarters, with the multi-million-pound development of Stables Market nearly complete and King's Cross's grimy-to-glossy reinvention in full flow. All this seems a world away from the tranquillity of the borough's more exclusive enclaves: in the monied mews of Hampstead, tree-lined avenues of Belsize Park and Georgian squares of Bloomsbury, life proceeds at a more measured pace.

Neighbourhoods

Bloomsbury and Fitzrovia

After the rush of the West End, it's a relief to turn into the well-ordered streets and squares (Bedford and Tavistock Squares are much admired) of Bloomsbury. The neighbourhood has long been a retreat for the literati, and there's a blue plaque at every turn. Yeats, Eliot and Dickens are among its illustrious former residents – though it was Virginia Woolf's gatherings in the drawing room at 46 Gordon Square that assured its literary immortality.

It's still a proudly cultural area – celebrated in October's arty Bloomsbury Festival. Towering sculpture installations occasionally occupy the corner of Bedford Square, home to the Architectural Association, while in-the-know locals join budding thespians in RADA's pleasant café on Malet Street for lunch. Here, too, is the brooding, art deco Senate House (George Orwell's inspiration for the Ministry of Truth in *1984*) – the University of London's library.

Map-toting tourists also mingle with Bloomsbury's students and well-heeled residents. Hotels and upmarket B&Bs dot the area, while the domed British Museum on Great Russell Street, with Norman Foster's magnificent, light-filled Great Court at its heart, is a visitor magnet.

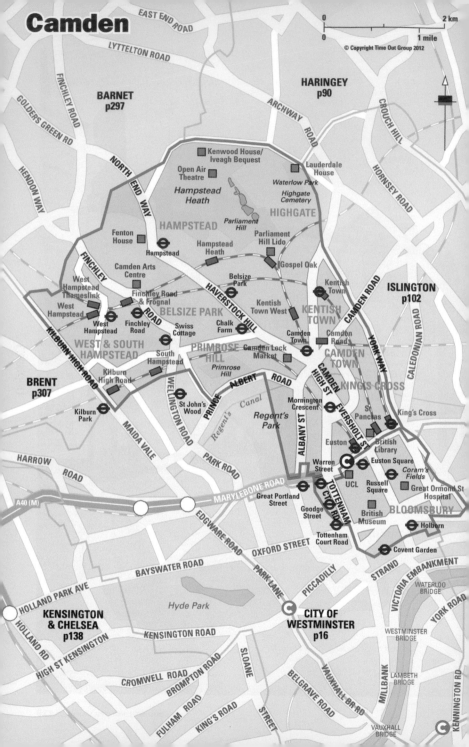

Most of Bloomsbury's charm, though, lies in quieter pleasures: browsing the specialist bookshops and art-supply shops around the British Museum, or wandering along the elegant, colonnaded establishments on nearby Sicilian Avenue.

Another unassuming delight is boutique-lined Lamb's Conduit Street – also home to a small but superb bicycle repair shop and the much-loved Lamb pub. At the end of the road, Coram's Fields was the 18th-century site of philanthropist Thomas Coram's Foundling Hospital. Today, it's a seven-acre child's paradise, with playgrounds and a pets' corner; adults are banned unless accompanied by a child.

Nearby, the stark 1960s Brunswick Centre houses flats and a shopping centre – all now very swish, after a multi-million-pound facelift, with some upmarket names (Coast, Carluccio's, Waitrose). Happily, delightful second-hand bookshop Skoob survived the revamp, as did the Renoir arthouse cinema. Nearby Russell Square, one of Bloomsbury's loveliest gardens, with a café and fountains at the centre, has also had a makeover.

To the west, busy Tottenham Court Road marks Bloomsbury's border with Fitzrovia. Cut-price electrical shops and charity collectors jostle for shoppers' attention at its southern end, while Heals and Habitat sit side-by-side near Goodge Street tube. Running parallel to Tottenham Court Road, Charlotte Street is given over to an array of restaurants and bars. Just behind Centre Point (and on the border with Westminster), is Renzo Piano's new Central St Giles high-rise development of offices and apartments, bringing some (very) vibrant colouring to a formerly drab hinterland.

Camden Town

Famed for its musical links and markets, Camden Town is a shameless clash of alternative culture and commercialism. The drug dealers who once clustered around the tube station murmuring promises of good gear and nice prices have been moved on, but some things never change: on Chalk Farm Road, colourful shopfronts sport huge sculptures of their wares (Doc Marten boots, leather jackets), scowling teenagers shop for stripy tights and vintage tees, and tourists cram the pavements at weekends.

The nightlife scene here has always been self-consciously cool. Britpop may be long

The streets of **Kentish Town**. See p122.

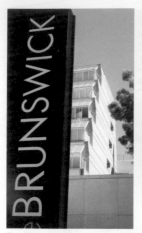

The revamped, revitalised **Brunswick Centre**. See p121.

gone, but a new wave of scenesters have taken up residence in the likes of the Hawley Arms. Up-and-coming bands still take to the stage at the Barfly, the sticky-floored launch pad for acts including the Strokes and Coldplay, and the Camden Crawl remains a booze-fuelled annual institution – though at £58, tickets aren't the bargain they once were.

Nothing is sacred, though. Emanating incense fumes and an air of vague disrepute, Camden Market has been an integral part of the local landscape since the 1970s. Locals may moan about the weekend crowds and chaos, but they were distraught when the north side of the market was damaged by fire in 2008 – it reopened in 2009. There was also opposition to the redevelopment scheme for Stables Market (the biggest of the six markets in the area), but now, almost complete, it's proving popular, with a combination of fashion and food that's focused around bar/music venue Proud Camden.

There's always been another side to the Camden of 'Tapas, fracas, alcohol, tobaccos/Bongs, bongo bingo, Portuguese maracas' that Suggs sang about in 'Camden Town'. Local residents aged over 30 tend to give the market a wide berth: unless you live on Chalk Farm Road, it's easy to avoid getting entangled. Older, more discerning Camdenites prefer to stroll across the bridge to serene Primrose Hill, or meander along the canal to Regent's Park. At the northern

end of Chalk Farm Road, the iconic, historic Roundhouse draws an arty crowd with its programme of music, dance and theatre. And there's always the Lock Tavern for a quick pint afterwards – because, deep down, every Camden resident still prides themselves on being a little bit hip.

Kentish Town

Often overshadowed by its raucous neighbour Camden, Kentish Town has an appeal all of its own. Gentrification has crept in as property prices have risen, but it's still endearingly tatty in places and has a genuinely diverse community. Take the high street, whose line-up includes down-at-heel greasy spoons, a homely Sardinian trattoria, Rio's naturist spa and a tasteful organic food emporium. Polished-up gastropubs are present and correct, but so too are unreconstructed boozers with the football on the telly, frequented by men with dogs on bits of string. By the station, a fruit and veg stall sells everything from globe artichokes and fresh figs to bowls of apples for a pound; towards Chalk Farm, the chaotic Queen's Crescent street market opens on Thursday and Saturday.

Off the main drag, there's some big-scale beauty in the buildings, with crescents of attractive Victorian terraces and the recently refurbished, Grade II-listed St Pancras Public Baths on Prince of Wales Road, now called the Kentish Town Sports Centre. Also here is the Zabludowicz

The café in **Russell Square** in full swing. See p121.

Collection, a great contemporary art gallery and one of the leading lights of the undersized north London arts scene. Meanwhile, side streets lined with diminutive, pastel-painted terraced houses have a sweetly seaside feel – and not so sweet price tags.

Green spaces include Cantelowes Gardens, with its skate park and children's play area, and the spacious City Farm, founded in 1972. For those craving more greenery, Hampstead Heath is a mere 15 minutes' walk away.

King's Cross

Despite its regal moniker, King's Cross has had a less than salubrious reputation for years. Notorious for its drug deals and prostitution, and crowded with tacky takeaways and massage parlours, it wasn't a place to linger – unless you were heading to one of its bars, or the cluster of clubs that occupied York Way Goods Depot.

But times have changed, and an immense regeneration project is well under way. The centrepiece is the renovated St Pancras International station – Eurostar's London terminal. The glass-and-iron Victorian train shed has been painstakingly restored to its former glory, and sculptures, boutiques and a swish champagne bar have been installed. Next door, the gorgeously romantic Gothic Revival railway hotel, closed for almost 80 years, has also been reborn with a whopping £200-million makeover; it's now the five-star St Pancras Renaissance, run by Marriott.

On York Way, Kings Place houses a concert hall, art galleries and restaurant behind its rippling glass façade – along with the *Guardian* newspaper's offices.

Highs & Lows

The Eurostar connection Step on the train in north London; two hours and 15 minutes later you could be quaffing coffee in Paris.
Green retreats Hampstead Heath, Primrose Hill and Highgate Cemetery all beckon if the crowds get too much
Live music Camden is still a big player on the music scene, with venues such as the Forum, Barfly, Jazz Café and the Roundhouse at residents' disposal.

Celebrity overkill We like spotting a celebrity as much as the next person, but not when they're blocking the way to the bar.
Elevated housing costs The higher the area, the higher the prices: multi-millionaires only need apply to buy in Hampstead and Highgate.
Tourist hell Weekends are a roadblock in Camden Town. Locals tend to stick to backstreets and give the market a wide berth.

The latest arrival, in autumn 2011, is Central Saint Martins College of Art & Design, which moved from its grotty Charing Cross Road premises to the revamped Granary building. Development continues on the unlovely industrial wasteland to the north of the station, and will eventually bring 25 large office buildings and 2,000 homes and apartments as well as 20 new streets and ten public squares.

Other cultural establishments in the area include the British Library and the Wellcome Trust, both on Euston Road. The latter houses medical exhibits and modern art in an upstairs gallery, and has a splendid café run by Peyton & Byrne. The old municipal garages on Britannia Street are now the Gagosian Gallery, a vast, starkly impressive showcase for contemporary art.

For its inhabitants, King's Cross's charm lies in its convenience. Islington, Bloomsbury and Camden are a mere stroll away, and transport connections are superb. The constant stream of foot traffic passing through means it rarely feels threatening, even late at night – though it does have a slightly anonymous feel. That said, a close-knit Italian community has spread across from Clerkenwell; an unofficial social hub is KC Continental Stores at 26 Caledonian Road, where parmesan and salumi prices, like the decor, seem frozen in time. There are also some unexpectedly quiet streets tucked off the main thoroughfares; walking along quaintly cobbled Keystone Crescent, you could be in Islington. And if it all gets too much, there's always Camley Street Natural Park, a two-acre oasis of water and woodland.

Belsize Park

Halfway up the hill to Hampstead from Camden Town, Belsize Park was a Victorian development of the notorious 18th-century pleasure gardens that once surrounded Belsize House (now demolished). Much of the estate had been owned by Eton College since the Middle Ages. Grand white stuccoed terraces and red-brick mansions, most now converted into expensive one- or two-bed flats, were designed to compete with Kensington. The area acquired a rather seedy reputation, but is now more staid and salubrious than Camden Town and more bohemian than Hampstead. Celebrity

residents include Gwyneth Paltrow, Helena Bonham-Carter and Bobby Gillespie.

The tube emerges on the area's high street, the top end of Haverstock Hill, with banks, Budgens, chain restaurants, an organic grocer (Pomona), a great bookshop (Daunt) and the Everyman cinema (formerly the Screen on the Hill). England's Lane, at the lower end of Haverstock Hill, is more quirky and rarefied, with a slew of fine local pubs. Most delightful of all is Belsize Village, a pedestrianised oasis off Belsize Lane, with a good vet, excellent pharmacy and a deli among other attractions.

Hampstead

First fashionable for its spa waters in the 18th century, Hampstead has long been London's most gorgeous hilltop hideaway. It resisted the Victorian expansion of the city by conserving Hampstead Heath, a

Camden

wonderful high tract of open countryside, and by preserving its own rural character.

Now many of the houses here cost as much as a farm. Though these may only be within reach of professional footballers and investment bankers, the area's artistic, literary and bohemian reputation is safe in the hands of a critical mass of genteel paupers. The likes of John Constable, John Keats and Robert Louis Stevenson started it; less genteel, Sid Vicious and John Lydon continued it (at a squat on Lutton Terrace, off Heath Street); and much less poor, Jamie Oliver and Jonathan Ross carry it on.

A relatively large area, Hampstead has several different districts. South End Green is the most affordable, close to Hampstead Heath station, and given a rougher edge by its proximity to the Royal Free Hospital, Gospel Oak and Kentish Town. Fitzjohn's, on the other side of Rosslyn Hill, has avenues of fine red-brick Victorian villas and lots of private schools. Freud settled in Maresfield Gardens after fleeing Vienna, and his home is now a museum. Christchurch, east of Heath Street, is particularly delightful; close to the Heath, it's a warren of steep, winding lanes with raised pavements, old houses and fabulous views. Burgh House is the headquarters of the influential residents' association, the Heath & Hampstead Society. Hampstead tube emerges in Hampstead Village, where the High Street and Heath Street provide most of the area's shops and nightlife, including the luxurious Everyman Cinema. Just above is Holly Hill, another charming enclave.

The Heath is, of course, one of the area's biggest assets; at its north end lies the elegant neoclassical Kenwood House. It also contains three open-air swimming ponds: one for men, one for women and the third mixed. Local swimmers have won their battle to keep them open. There's a surfeit of schools in the area, many of them private, so congestion is hellish during the school run, the streets clogged with SUVs.

West and South Hampstead

Separated from Hampstead by the busy Finchley Road, West Hampstead is very much a district in its own right. Since West End Lane became a restaurant magnet, the area has emerged as a firm favourite with middle-class, pre-marriage-and-kids couples who aren't rich… yet. Slightly shabby in parts, surprisingly grand in others, much of West Hampstead is still on the up. If you want to move to north-west London and live this side of Kilburn and Willesden, you might still get lucky here.

Few Londoners know of the existence of South Hampstead as an area, unless they're familiar with the London Overground station (which takes you one stop to Euston in 12 minutes). Closer to St John's Wood, at the top end of Abbey Road, the place should be famous for the Maryon Wilson Estate, which was built in the late 19th century

Camden

The concourse at **St Pancras International** station. See p123.

The view from **Hampstead Heath**. See p124.

and contains some of the area's most expensive housing. Property in South Hampstead consists mainly of stately red-brick mansion blocks or large detached villas such as those around Priory Road and Compayne Gardens. Several houses here remain gloriously spacious family homes, but many were converted into flats in the 1970s. Some of these are now quite scruffy and are one of the cheapest ways to buy into the area. Further north, around Fortune Green, the smaller Victorian terraces are popular with young families.

Primrose Hill and Swiss Cottage

The quickest way to make enemies with Primrose Hill dwellers is to accuse them of living in Camden. This district is a genteel and well-heeled world away from its more raucous, easterly neighbour – and residents don't like you to forget it.

From within a smallish park – an extension of Regent's Park beyond London Zoo and the canal – there are lovely hilltop views of the city. Regent's Park Road and Gloucester Avenue are the local focal points, containing a pretty sprinkling of boutiques, cafés and some constantly busy gastropubs. Most of the diminutive area that constitutes Primrose Hill, however, is residential and this remains the chief draw for the beautiful

people who set up home here. Rather like Hampstead, the neighbourhood has a reputation as a sanctuary for bohemian types. In reality, it's too pricey for most such folk, but they still just about outnumber the banking whizzes who fancy a change from Kensington.

The large, three-storey stuccoed houses close to the park – not only Primrose Hill but the much larger Regent's Park to the south-east – fetch over £2 million if they haven't been converted into flats. Two-bed apartments in the same coveted streets, such as Regent's Park Road and the Chalcots (Crescent, Road and Square), go for more than £500,000; one-beds leave you little change from the same amount. An alternative is to bag a flat in one of the area's few post-war blocks; it might not look as grand, but it's the cheapest way of getting your foot in a Primrose Hill door.

Up the hill from here is Swiss Cottage (named after a 19th-century inn fashioned after a chalet), a bit of a non-area that's wedged north of St John's Wood, south-east of West Hampstead and west of Belsize Park. Housing prices are pretty similar to West Hampstead; public transport is excellent (Swiss Cottage and Finchley Road tubes, plus several bus routes). The Cottage apart, the most notable buildings are the modernist landmark of Swiss Cottage Library (designed by Sir Basil Spence), and the state-of-the-art Swiss Cottage Leisure Centre, with its fine swimming pool, Spa London outpost, climbing wall and popular café.

Highgate and Dartmouth Park

Spilling out from the borough of Camden into Haringey, Highgate is known for its wild and wonderful cemetery (the West Cemetery) and the more ordered, municipal one (the East Cemetery), wherein lies Karl Marx. The area is far from dead, though, with a buoyant property market and one of the capital's most active community groups, the Highgate Society. The locality isn't quite as expensive to live in as Hampstead, but it's not far behind. Highgate also shares many of Hampstead's advantages, such as its elevation and, of course, the lovely Heath (lying to the south-west).

Dartmouth Park is east of the Heath, just south of the cemetery – but isn't a park at all. The land bought by and named after the 18th-century Earl of Dartmouth is a residential area on the slopes up to Highgate, characterised by late 19th-century terraced and semi-detached houses. Both Dartmouth Park and Highgate are close to Parliament Hill, with its protected view over London. Once called Traitor's Hill, this elevation is now affectionately known as Kite Hill, for obvious reasons.

Highgate Village is the prime place to reside in this neck of the woods – and talking of woods, Highgate Wood and Queen's Wood (both across borough boundaries in Haringey, but close) are very lovely. The Village's gated roads housing wealthy families are virtually free of the background hum of traffic. Such semi-rural serenity comes at a price, as does living anywhere very close to the Village, with its pretty shops and famous pub, the Flask. Around Pond Square, most houses are Victorian or Georgian, while some even older properties, built around the time of Charles II, can be glimpsed on the Grove. Five-bedroom, 18th-century piles command almost £3 million in this select enclave. High end estates, such as the Holly Lodge Estate, are also popular, while Berthold Lubetkin's Highpoint flats, intended for workers in the 1930s, now house the chattering classes.

Public transport is a downside. The Northern line station is a hike from the Village on congested Archway Road. Still, you can't argue with the locals: you're doing all right if you've made it to N6.

Restaurants & cafés

Camden Town's cosmopolitan feel extends to the array of restaurants and cafés, cuisines and specialities on offer in the neighbourhood. Check out the classic Lebanese cooking at Le Mignon, reliable tapas at El Parador (or the rowdier Bar Gansa), homely Greek at Andy's Taverna or superior Caribbean at Mango Room. This is also the home of Haché, for top-notch burgers; if comfort food is your thing, also try Castle's for trad pie and mash. Market

Camden

serves excellent modern British food, and offers pretty much everything you could want from a local restaurant.

Also worth a try are Gilgamesh, an opulent Babylonian temple to excess, with pan-Asian food (though the drinking tends to be better than the eating), Cambodian eaterie Lemongrass, and an outpost of the Belgian chain restaurant, Belgo Noord. For ice-cream with a molecular gastronomy twist, try tiny newcomer Chin Chin Laboratorists, or – for more conventional methods and flavours – visit Chalk Farm institution Marine Ices.

In classy Primrose Hill, things take a price hike and pubs swing towards gastro. Most of the dining options are to be found along the villagey Regent's Park Road. Lemonia continues to serve a bustling crowd with its excellent Greek-Cypriot cuisine (though older sister Limani has closed and is now a wine bar); Polish staple Trojka is close by, as is Odette's, the showcase restaurant for TV chef Bryn Williams. Vegetarians, vegans and even meat-eaters love the tasty raw delights at Madder Rose Café within the Triyoga centre; charming Manna is also a good herbivorous option. All this is before you get to Primrose Hill's top-notch gastropubs, the Queens (*see p132*) and the Landsdowne (*see p131*).

Belsize Park's the Hill (*see p131*) is also a good gastropub; the rest of the area's culinary scene is dominated by chains (among them the Gourmet Burger Kitchen), though Greek restaurant Retsina is effortlessly authentic, hugely popular and very good value.

Things aren't great further up the hill in Hampstead: the feeble choice of eateries is always a surprise considering the money locals have to spend. Base meets its Mediterranean criteria well, though, and Jin Kichi (Japanese) and the Coffee Cup Café are long-time favourites. Off Haverstock Hill to the east, you'll find unpretentious and efficient Turkish Zara and family-friendly Fratelli la Bufala. Away from the busy streets, enjoy tea and cake at the charming Brew House café in Kenwood House.

Westwards in busy Swiss Cottage, Eriki impresses with its Indian fare. In South Hampstead, old-timer Singapore Garden remains popular.

In West Hampstead, West End Lane keeps the resident middle classes well fed

Roka on Charlotte Street.

with Italian La Brocca, Modern European Walnut and tapas bar Sirous. A little further afield, on Fortune Green Road, is Nautilus, a proper chippie (eat-in or takeaway). Over in Highgate and its surrounds, gastropubs rule: the Bull in Highgate (in a stunning listed building), spacious Junction Tavern in Dartmouth Park (for both, *see p131*), and the Oxford on Kentish Town Road (*see p132*).

Typical of the transformed King's Cross are Rotunda, a canalside bar-restaurant inside Kings Place, and, in the Regent Quarter complex, a large, ambitious Spanish venture that encompasses restaurant Camino and diminutive Bar Pepito, a rustic sherry and tapas bar. Not far from the Euston Road are the myriad delights of the Queen's Head & Artichoke gastropub, intimate African Kitchen Gallery, and acclaimed chippie North Sea Fish Restaurant.

Directly south of Euston, Bloomsbury houses a concentration of restaurants between Guilford Street and Theobald's Road: try good-value pizza at La Porchetta or great Spanish at Cigala; or good pub grub at the Perseverance (*see p132*).

On Goodge Street, often-packed Salt Yard serves superior Spanish/Italian tapas. Nearby, Lantana has brought a touch of Antipodean café culture to the area. Also west of Tottenham Court Road and just within Camden borders is restaurant hotspot Charlotte Street; best bets here are Tex-Mex shack La Perla, Indian Rasa Samudra, superior tapas joint Fino, classy Japanese Roka and Sicilian Mennula. The Crazy Bear (see p131) restaurant and bar in Whitfield Street is stylish, decadent and supremely comfortable. Mini-chains Busaba Eathai (on Store Street) and dim t café are also good, while Hakkasan, tucked away in the borough's south-west corner on Hanway Place, serves some of the best Chinese food in town. Behind Centre Point are some decent cut-price Korean restaurants and, in the Central St Giles development, the first branch of Jamie Oliver's Union Jacks chain, serving 'British pizza' in a retro setting.

African Kitchen Gallery *102 Drummond Street, NW1 2HN (7383 0918).*

Andy's Taverna *81-81A Bayham Street, NW1 0AG (7485 9718, www.andystaverna.com).*

Bar Gansa *2 Inverness Street, NW1 7HJ (7267 8909).*

Base *71 Hampstead High Street, NW3 1QP (7431 2224, www.baserestaurant.com).*

Belgo Noord *72 Chalk Farm Road, NW1 8AN (7267 0718, www.belgo-restaurants.co.uk).*

Brew House *Kenwood House, Hampstead Lane, NW3 7JR (8341 5384, www.company ofcooks.com).*

La Brocca *273 West End Lane, NW6 1QS (7433 1989, www.labrocca.co.uk).*

Busaba Eathai *22 Store Street, WC1E 7DS (7299 7900, www.busaba.com).*

Camino & Bar Pepito *3 Varnishers Yard, Regent Quarter, N1 9FD (7841 7331, www.camino.uk.com).*

Castle's *229 Royal College Street, NW1 9LT (7485 2196).*

Chin Chin Laboratorists *49-50 Camden Lock Place, NW1 8AF (07885 604284, www.chinchinlabs.com).*

Cigala *54 Lamb's Conduit Street, WC1N 3LW (7405 1717, www.cigala.co.uk).*

Coffee Cup Café *74 Hampstead High Street, NW3 1QX (7435 7565, www.villa biancanw3.com).*

dim t *32 Charlotte Street, W1T 2NQ (7637 1122, www.dimt.co.uk).*

Eriki *4-6 Northways Parade, Finchley Road, NW3 5EN (7722 0606, www.eriki.co.uk).*

Fino *33 Charlotte Street, entrance on Rathbone Street, W1T 1RR (7813 8010, www.fino restaurant.com).*

Fratelli la Bufala *45A South End Road, NW3 2QB (7435 7814, www.fratellila bufala.com).*

Gilgamesh *Camden Stables Market, Chalk Farm Road, NW1 8AH (7428 4922, www.gilgameshbar.com).*

Haché *24 Inverness Street, NW1 7HJ (7485 9100, www.hacheburgers.com).*

Hakkasan *8 Hanway Place, W1T 1HD (7927 7000, www.hakkasan.com).*

Jin Kichi *73 Heath Street, NW3 6UG (7794 6158, www.jinkichi.com).*

Lantana *13 Charlotte Place, W1T 1SN (7637 3347, www.lantanacafe.co.uk).*

Lemongrass *243 Royal College Street, NW1 9LT (7284 1116).*

Lemonia *89 Regent's Park Road, NW1 8UY (7586 7454, www.lemonia.co.uk).*

Madder Rose Café *6 Erskine Road, NW3 3AJ (7483 3344, www.triyoga.co.uk).*

Mango Room *10-12 Kentish Town Road, NW1 8NH (7482 5065, www.mangoroom.co.uk).*

Manna *4 Erskine Road, NW3 3AJ (7722 8028, www.manna-veg.com).*

Marine Ices *8 Haverstock Hill, NW3 2BL (7482 9003, www.marineices.co.uk).*

Market *43 Parkway, NW1 7PN (7267 9700, www.marketrestaurant.co.uk).*

Mennula *10 Charlotte Street, W1T 2LT (7636 2833, www.mennula.com).*

Le Mignon *98 Arlington Road, NW1 7HT (7387 0600).*

Nautilus *27-29 Fortune Green Road, NW6 1DU (7435 2532).*

North Sea Fish Restaurant *7-8 Leigh Street, WC1H 9EW (7387 5892, www.northseafish restaurant.co.uk).*

Odette's *130 Regent's Park Road, NW1 8XL (7586 8569, www.odettesprimrosehill.com).*

El Parador *245 Eversholt Street, NW1 1BA (7387 2789, www.elparadorlondon.com).*

La Perla *11 Charlotte Street, W1T 1RQ (7436 1744, www.cafepacifico-laperla.com).*

La Porchetta *33 Boswell Street, WC1N 3BP (7242 2434, www.laporchetta.net).*

Queen's Head & Artichoke *30-32 Albany Street, NW1 4EA (7916 6206, www.the artichoke.net).*

Rasa Samudra *5 Charlotte Street, W1T 1RE (7637 0222, www.rasarestaurants.com).*

Retsina *48-50 Belsize Lane, NW3 5AN (7431 5855, www.retsina-london.com).*

Roka *37 Charlotte Street, W1T 1RR (7580 6464, www.rokarestaurant.com).*

Rotunda Bar & Restaurant *Kings Place,*
90 York Way, N1 9AG (7014 2840,
www.rotundabarandrestaurant.co.uk).
Salt Yard *54 Goodge Street, W1T 4NA*
(7637 0657, www.saltyard.co.uk).
Singapore Garden *83 Fairfax Road, NW6*
4DY (7624 8233, www.singaporegarden.co.uk).
Sirous *268 West End Lane, NW6 1LJ (7435*
8164, www.sirous.co.uk).
Trojka *101 Regent's Park Road, NW1 8UR*
(7483 3765, www.trojka.co.uk).
Union Jacks *4 Central St Giles Piazza,*
WC2H 8AB (3597 7888, www.unionjacks
restaurants.com).
Walnut *280 West End Lane, NW6 1LJ*
(7794 7772, www.walnutwalnut.com).
Zara *11 South End Road, NW3 2PT*
(7794 5498).

Bars & pubs

In Camden Town, the Hawley Arms
is famed for its excellent jukebox and
fashionable following: packed in like
sardines, Camdenites studiously feign
indifference as members of Razorlight
neck beers, or Rhys Ifans squeezes past
to the bar (this was also one of Amy
Winehouses's favourite haunts). Drinking
dens line nearby Inverness Street, from
record-peddling Bar Vinyl to Britpop
hangout of yesteryear the Good Mixer,
but some of Camden's best bars are in its
backstreets. Just off the high street, the
dimly lit Crown & Goose serves unexpectedly
accomplished food from its tiny kitchen;
just off Camden Road, the Lord Stanley
is a quality local serving decent, if pricey,
food. Venues at the revamped Stables
Market include Proud Camden, which has
live music and a smoker-friendly terrace,
and Gilgamesh (*see p129*) with its wildly
theatrical decor and expensive cocktails.
Further up towards Chalk Farm tube, the
Lock Tavern hosts an eclectic line-up of
DJs, while Joe's Bar dishes up hot dogs
and burgers to a rock 'n' roll soundtrack.

If the Camden scene is all about seeing
and being seen, Kentish Town offers
welcome respite. On the high street, Quinn's
and O'Reilly's are battered, no-nonsense
boozers of the old school. For those that
like their floorboards a touch more polished,
lively local gastropubs include the Oxford,
Vine and Abbey – the last famed for its
evening acoustic sets. The grande dame of

the neighbourhood, though, is the Pineapple.
A local institution since 1868, it's a vision
of Victorian splendour, with an ornate bar
counter and an impressive array of beery
options (beer festivals each Easter further
extend the choice). A short stagger away, the
Bull & Gate is getting a little rough around
the edges, but remains a great old-timer.

Despite their proximity to Camden Town,
Belsize Park and Primrose Hill are more
geared towards a quiet drink and a meal
than riotous nights out, with stately
gastropubs such as the Lansdowne, the
Queens and the Hill catering for a well-off
clientele. The down-to-earth Princess of
Wales is also gaining a good reputation
for its food, and is known for its Sunday
jazz sessions. On Haverstock Hill, the Sir
Richard Steele is another pleasingly old-
fashioned drinking den with a cosily
cluttered interior and regular quiz night.

Up the hill, historic pubs dot the tangled
backstreets and leafy lanes of Hampstead.
The oldest is the wonderfully atmospheric,
16th-century Spaniard's Inn; equally snug
is the warren of wood-panelled rooms at
the Holly Bush – also a good spot for a
roast meal after a hike over the Heath. The
Wells offers classy gastro fare, while at the
Horseshoe you can match lunch with one
of its own Camden Town Brewery beers.

North-west, in hilly West Hampstead,
the nightlife is concentrated around West
End Lane. Bars – local favourites include
the Gallery – predominate over traditional
pubs, though the Railway remains a handy
spot for a pint, close to the tube.

Over in Highgate, upmarket boozers
filled with cliquey locals are the norm. The
Wrestlers and Angel Inn are pleasant spots
for a pint, although traditionalists prefer
the low-ceilinged, intimate Flask, set by
Highgate Village's tiny green. The Bull has
turned into a brewpub, with a wonderful
array of beers and US-style grub. Along
Archway Road, the late-licensed Boogaloo
marks a total change of pace with its superb
jukebox, eclectic DJ nights and occasional
celebrity clientele (the likes of Pete Doherty
and Shane McGowan).

Until a few years ago, King's Cross was
better known for its clubs than its pubs, but
all (except EGG, tucked away on York Way)
been swept away by the area's regeneration.
But it's not all doom and gloom: the Big
Chill House offers relaxed daytime drinking
on its roof terrace and late-night DJ sets,

while 06 St Chad's Place, housed in a stripped-out warehouse space, epitomises self-conscious urban cool. Cosier options include the King Charles I, with its open fire and rotating guest bitters, and the out-of-the-way Harrison.

In Camden's most southern reaches, Bloomsbury contains a clutch of dignified old-timers, where the local literati once supped; the Museum Tavern, opposite the British Museum, counts Orwell and Marx among its former customers. Further off the tourist trail, on Lamb's Conduit Street, the 18th-century Lamb serves well-kept Young's beers; gastropub the Perseverance is just down the road. If you're feeling energetic, boozing and bowling are on offer at Bloomsbury Bowling Lanes and the swankier All-Star Lanes. Towards bar-studded Covent Garden, atmospheric and intimate basement bar Freud mixes a mean cocktail, or there's Belgium-themed Lowlander with its impressive range of draught and bottled beers. For something smarter, hotel bar Brasserie Max offers a lovely environment in which to sip cocktails and munch on snacks – but at a price.

West of Tottenham Court Road sees the beginning of Fitzrovia (half of which falls within Camden's bounds). The area's namesake, the Fitzroy Tavern, was infamous for the bohemian crowd of writers and poets who drank here in the 1930s; these days, their modern equivalents head for the endearingly scruffy Bradley's Spanish Bar. Sleek bars are increasingly par for the course around these parts, though, with modish hotel bar Oscar, subterranean Crazy Bear and slick Shochu Lounge (beneath Roka) vying for affections.

Abbey Tavern *124 Kentish Town Road, NW1 9QB (7267 9449, www.abbey-tavern.com).*
All Star Lanes *Victoria House, Bloomsbury Place, WC1B 4DA (7025 2676, www.allstar lanes.co.uk).*
Angel Inn *37 Highgate High Street, N6 5JT (8341 5913, www.theangelhighgate.co.uk).*
Bar Vinyl *6 Inverness Street, NW1 7HJ (7482 9318, www.barvinyl.com).*
Big Chill House *257-259 Pentonville Road, N1 9NL (7427 2540, www.bigchill.net/house.html).*
Bloomsbury Bowling Lanes *Basement, Tavistock Hotel, Bedford Way, WC1H 9EU (7183 1979, www.bloomsburylive.com).*
Boogaloo *312 Archway Road, N6 5AT (8340 2928, www.theboogaloo.co.uk).*

Bradley's Spanish Bar *42-44 Hanway Street, W1T 1UT (7636 0359).*
Brasserie Max *10 Monmouth Street, WC2H 9HB (7806 1007, www.coventgarden hotel.co.uk).*
Bull *13 North Hill, N6 4AB (8341 0510, www.thebullhighgate.co.uk).*
Bull & Gate *389 Kentish Town Road, NW5 2TJ (7485 5358, www.bullandgate.co.uk).*
Crazy Bear *26-28 Whitfield Street, W1T 2RG (7631 0088, www.crazybeargroup.co.uk).*
Crown & Goose *100 Arlington Road, NW1 7HP (7485 8008, www.crownandgoose.co.uk).*
Fitzroy Tavern *16 Charlotte Street, W1T 2LY (7580 3714).*
Flask *77 Highgate West Hill, N6 6BU (8348 7346).*
Freud *198 Shaftesbury Avenue, WC2H 8JL (7240 9933, www.freudliving.com).*
Gallery *190 Broadhurst Gardens, NW6 3AY (7625 9184, www.ilovethegallery.com).*
Good Mixer *30 Inverness Street, NW1 7HJ (7916 6176).*
Harrison *28 Harrison Street, WC1H 8JF (7278 3966, www.harrisonbar.co.uk).*
Hawley Arms *2 Castlehaven Road, NW1 8QU (7428 5979, www.thehawleyarms.co.uk).*
Hill *94 Haverstock Hill, NW3 2BD (7267 0033, www.thehilllondon.com).*
Holly Bush *22 Holly Mount, NW3 6SG (7435 2892).*
Horseshoe *28 Heath Street, NW3 6TE (7431 7206).*
Joe's Bar *78-79 Chalk Farm Road, NW1 8AR (7916 0595, www.joescamden.co.uk).*
Junction Tavern *101 Fortess Road, NW5 1AG (7485 9400, www.junctiontavern.co.uk).*
King Charles I *55-57 Northdown Street, N1 9BL (7837 7758).*
Lamb *94 Lamb's Conduit Street, WC1N 3LZ (7405 0713, www.youngs.co.uk).*
Lansdowne *90 Gloucester Avenue, NW1 8HX (7483 0409, www.thelansdownepub.co.uk).*
Lock Tavern *35 Chalk Farm Road, NW1 8AJ (7482 7163, www.lock-tavern.co.uk).*
Lord Stanley *51 Camden Park Road, NW1 9BH (7428 9488, www.thelordstanley.co.uk).*
Lowlander *36 Drury Lane, WC2B 5RR (7379 7446, www.lowlander.com).*
Museum Tavern *49 Great Russell Street, WC1B 3BA (7242 8987, www.taylor-walker.co.uk).*
O'Reilly's *289-291 Kentish Town Road, NW5 2JS (7267 4002).*
Oscar *Charlotte Street Hotel, 15 Charlotte Street, W1T 1RJ (7806 2000, www.charlottestreet hotel.com).*

Camden

COUNCIL TAX

A	up to £40,000	£887.57
B	£40,001-£52,000	£1,035.49
C	£52,001-£68,000	£1,183.43
D	£68,001-£88,000	£1,331.35
E	£88,001-£120,000	£1,627.21
F	£120,001-£160,000	£1,923.06
G	£160,001-£320,000	£2,218.92
H	over £320,000	£2,662.70

06 St Chad's Place *6 St Chad's Place, WC1X 9HH (7278 3355, www.6stchadsplace.com).*

Oxford *256 Kentish Town Road, NW5 2AA (7485 3521, www.theoxfordnw5.co.uk).*

Perseverance *63 Lamb's Conduit Street, WC1N 3NB (7405 8278, www.the-perseverance. moonfruit.com).*

Pineapple *51 Leverton Street, NW5 2NX (7284 4631).*

Princess of Wales *22 Chalcot Road, NW1 8LL (7722 0354).*

Proud Camden *Horse Hospital, Stables Market, Chalk Farm Road, NW1 8AH (7482 3867, www.proudcamden.com).*

Queens *49 Regent's Park Road, NW1 8XD (7586 0408, www.thequeensprimrosehill.co.uk).*

Quinn's *65 Kentish Town Road, NW1 8NY (7267 8240).*

Railway *100 West End Lane, NW6 2LU (3603 5457, www.originalpubco.com).*

Shochu Lounge *37 Charlotte Street, W1T 1RR (7580 6464, www.shochulounge.com).*

Sir Richard Steele *97 Haverstock Hill, NW3 4RL (7483 1261).*

Spaniards Inn *Spaniards Road, NW3 7JJ (8731 8406, www.thespaniardshampstead.co.uk).*

Vine *86 Highgate Road, NW5 1PB (7209 0038, www.thevinelondon.co.uk).*

Wells *30 Well Walk, NW3 1BX (7794 3785, www.thewellshampstead.co.uk).*

Wrestlers *98 North Road, N6 4AA (8340 4297).*

Shops

Although the borough's retail hotspots are Hampstead, Primrose Hill and the fringes of the West End, for most people, the words 'Camden' and 'shopping' evoke the sprawling, eponymous market – which is, in fact, made up of several distinct entities. Camden Lock Market, with its artisans' shops, retains its boho character, while the adjacent Stables Market has undergone redevelopment. The markets are also open during the week, when they're considerably quieter, but be prepared for a tourist scrum at weekends. Nearby is vintage clothes specialist Rokit, and Traid, a quality charity shop stocking a huge mix of good vintage, high-street and designer clothes. Chinalife, the well-being arm of long-standing Chinese medicine clinic AcuMedic, is also worth checking out. The iconic Camden Coffee Shop, where George Constantinou has been roasting beans for more than 30 years, and health food store Earth Natural Foods, in Kentish Town, are local assets. Other gems on workaday Kentish Town Road are the Owl Bookshop and Phoenicia Food Hall, for Mediterranean foods of all kinds.

In Primrose Hill, Regent's Park Road is a contender for London's most picture-perfect high street, with a mix of practical traditional shops (hardware store, pet shop, greengrocer and the excellent Primrose Hill Books), plus delis, cafés, and a smattering of fashionable boutiques, including Anna, Press (just off the main drag), yummy-mummy heaven Elias & Grace and Spice for fashion-led footwear. Residents don't have to travel far to furnish their coveted properties; there's a clutch of home-related shops, including Graham & Green. Gloucester Avenue is sprinkled with gems: Shikasuki for well-preserved vintage clothing and accessories; delicate jewellery at Sweet Pea; the Primrose Bakery, which has tables for eating in; and superior deli Melrose & Morgan. Around the corner is a new outpost of much-loved Herne Hill children's bookshop Tales on Moon Lane.

On Haverstock Hill, which links Belsize Park to Hampstead, is a branch of Daunt Books; there's also one in the charming enclave of South End Green. This part of London has no shortage of delis, including Belsize Village Deli and Hampstead Butcher, a butcher/deli/wine shop. Beetroot, a Polish food shop, makes for a welcome change. Also of eastern European extraction (but of over 40 years' standing), Louis' Pâtisserie provides Hungarian-style cakes. Hampstead has plenty of fashion too; as well as branches of upmarket brands such as Jigsaw, there are less ubiquitous labels at boutique Cochinechine. Little girls love Mystical Fairies, while kids in general can be indulged at traditional toyshop Happy Returns. Further east in (otherwise barren) Gospel Oak is Kristin Baybars'

Always popular **Camden Market**.

fascinating shop, full of exquisite miniaturist scenes and dolls' house kits.

Back in the centre of town, Tottenham Court Road has too many electrical goods shops to mention, plus a line-up of homeware stores, including stalwarts Heal's and one of the few remaining branches of Habitat. Near Warren Street tube is an outpost of shoe shop Black Truffle, which also runs footwear- and accessory-making classes downstairs. Further south-east lie the joys of Bloomsbury: here are James Smith & Son, venerable vendor of umbrellas, and, in the streets around the British Museum, small shops selling everything from books to antiquarian maps and rubber stamps. The revamped Brunswick Centre contains a Waitrose, assorted high-street fashion stores and Skoob second-hand bookshop. Lamb's Conduit Street has blossomed into a well-rounded shopping destination, offering everything from hip mens/womenswear at Folk, handmade bags at Susannah Hunter and women's fiction at niche publisher Persephone Books to affordable food at the community-run People's Supermarket.

Anna *126 Regent's Park Road, NW1 8XL (7483 0411, www.shopatanna.co.uk).*

Beetroot *92 Fleet Road, NW3 2QX (7424 8544, www.beetrootdeli.co.uk).*
Belsize Village Deli *39 Belsize Lane, NW3 5AS (7794 4258).*
Black Truffle *52 Warren Street, W1T 5NJ (7388 4547, www.blacktruffle.com).*
Camden Coffee Shop *11 Delancey Street, NW1 7NL (7387 4080).*
Camden Markets *www.camdenmarkets.org.*
Chinalife *99-105 Camden High Street, NW1 7JN (7388 5783, www.acumedic.com).*
Cochinechine *74 Heath Street, NW3 1DN (7435 9377, www.cochinechine.com).*
Daunt Books *www.dauntbooks.co.uk: 193 Haverstock Hill, NW3 4QL (7794 4006); 51 South End Road, NW3 2QB (7794 8206).*
Earth Natural Foods *200 Kentish Town Road, NW5 2AE (7482 2211, www.earth naturalfoods.co.uk).*
Elias & Grace *158 Regent's Park Road, NW1 8XN (7449 0574, www.eliasandgrace.com).*
Folk *49 Lamb's Conduit Street, WC1N 3NG (7404 6458, www.folkclothing.com).*
Graham & Green *164 Regent's Park Road, NW1 8XN (7586 2960, www.grahamand green.co.uk).*
Hampstead Butcher *56 Rosslyn Hill, NW3 1ND (7794 9210, www.hampsteadbutcher.com).*
Happy Returns *36 Rosslyn Hill, NW3 1NH (7435 2431).*
James Smith & Son *53 New Oxford Street, WC1A 1BL (7836 4731, www.james-smith. co.uk).*
Kristin Baybars *7 Mansfield Road, NW3 2JD (7267 0934).*
Louis' Pâtisserie *32 Heath Street, NW3 6DU (7435 9908).*
Melrose & Morgan *42 Gloucester Avenue, NW1 8JD (7722 0011, www.melroseand morgan.com).*
Mystical Fairies *12 Flask Walk, NW3 1HE (7431 1888, www.mysticalfairies.co.uk).*
Owl Bookshop *209 Kentish Town Road, NW5 2JU (7485 7793).*
People's Supermarket *72-78 Lamb's Conduit Street, WC1N 3LP (7430 1836, www.thepeoplessupermarket.org).*
Persephone Books *59 Lamb's Conduit Street, WC1N 3NB (7242 9292, www. persephonebooks.co.uk).*
Phoenicia Food Hall *186-192 Kentish Town Road, NW5 2AE (7267 1267, www.phoenicia foodhall.co.uk).*
Press *3 Erskine Road, NW3 3AJ (7449 0081, www.pressprimrosehill.com).*
Primrose Bakery *69 Gloucester Avenue, NW1 8LD (7483 4222, www.primrosebakery.org.uk).*

Primrose Hill Books *134 Regent's Park Road, NW1 8XL (7586 2022, www.primrosehillbooks. com).*

Rokit *225 Camden High Street, NW1 7BU (7267 3046, www.rokit.co.uk).*

Shikasuki *67 Gloucester Avenue, NW1 8LD (7722 4442, www.shikasuki.com).*

Skoob *Unit 66, The Brunswick Centre, WC1N 1AE (7278 8760, www.skoob.com).*

Spice Shoes *162 Regent's Park Road, NW1 8XN (7722 2478, www.spiceshu.co.uk).*

Susannah Hunter *84 Lamb's Conduit Street, WC1N 3LR (7692 3798, www.susannah hunter.com).*

Sweet Pea *77 Gloucester Avenue, NW1 8LD (7449 9292, www.sweetpeajewellery.com).*

Traid *154 Camden High Street, NW1 0NE (7485 5253, www.traid.org.uk).*

Arts & attractions

Cinemas & theatres

Camden People's Theatre *58-60 Hampstead Road, NW1 2PY (7419 4841, bookings 0844 477 1000, www.cptheatre.co.uk).*

Drill Hall *16 Chenies Street, WC1E 7EX (7307 5060, www.drillhall.co.uk). Lesbian- and gay-focused performance art and activities.*

Etcetera Theatre *265 Camden High Street, NW1 7BU (7482 4857, www.etceteratheatre. com). Mini theatre above the Oxford Arms pub.*

Everyman Cinema *0871 906 9060, www. everymancinema.com; 203 Haverstock Hill, NW3 4QG; 5 Holly Bush Vale, NW3 6TX.*

Hampstead Theatre *Eton Avenue, NW3 3EU (7722 9301, www.hampsteadtheatre.com).*

Horse Hospital *Colonnade, WC1N 1JD (7833 3644, www.thehorsehospital.com). Offbeat arts venue.*

Kings Place *90 York Way, N1 9AG (7520 1490, www.kingsplace.co.uk). Purpose-built cultural venue, with a concert hall and two galleries.*

New Diorama Theatre *15-16 Triton Street, NW1 3BF (tickets 7383 9034, www.newdiorama. com). New 80-seat performance space presenting drama, music and comedy.*

Odeon *0871 224 4007, www.odeon.co.uk; 14 Parkway, NW1 7AA; 96 Finchley Road, NW3 5EL.*

The Place *17 Duke's Road, WC1H 9PY (7121 1100, www.theplace.org.uk). Leading contemporary dance centre.*

Renoir Cinema *Brunswick Square, WC1N 1AW (0871 703 3991, www.artificial-eye.com).*

Shaw Theatre *100-110 Euston Road, NW1 2AJ (0844 248 5075, www.theshawtheatre.com).*

Theatro Technis *26 Crowndale Road, NW1 1TT (7387 6617, www.theatrotechnis.com). Fringe theatre established in 1957.*

Upstairs at the Gatehouse *Corner of Hampstead Lane & North Road, Highgate Village, N6 4BD (8340 3488, www.upstairs atthegatehouse.com). Theatre pub.*

Vue Finchley Road *O2 Centre, 255 Finchley Road, NW3 6LU (0871 224 0240, www.my vue.com).*

Galleries & museums

British Museum *Great Russell Street, WC1B 3DG (7323 8000, www.thebritish museum.ac.uk).*

Camden Arts Centre *Arkwright Road, NW3 6DG (7472 5500, www.camdenartscentre.org). Galleries, studios, a café and landscaped gardens.*

Cartoon Museum *Old Dairy, 35 Little Russell Street, WC1A 2HH (7580 8155, www.cartoon centre.com).*

Fenton House *Windmill Hill, NW3 6RT (7435 3471, information 01494 755563, www.nationaltrust.org.uk). Collection of antique musical instruments and porcelain; the sunken gardens and orchard are a delight.*

Freud Museum *20 Maresfield Gardens, NW3 5SX (7435 2002, www.freud.org.uk). Former home of Sigmund and his daughter Anna.*

Keats House *Keats Grove, NW3 2RR (7332 3868, www.keatshouse.cityoflondon. gov.uk). Recently restored, this was the Romantic poet's last British home.*

Kenwood House *Hampstead Lane, NW3 7JR (8348 1286, www.english-heritage.org.uk). Impressive neoclassical house on Hampstead Heath; displays the Iveagh Bequest art collection.*

Sir John Soane's Museum *13 Lincoln's Inn Fields, WC2A 3BP (7405 2107, www.soane.org). Atmospheric home of 18th-century architect showcasing his collection of art and artefacts.*

Camden

Zabludowicz Collection *176 Prince of Wales Road, NW5 3PT (7428 8940, www.zabludowicz collection.com). Contemporary art in an impressive, restored Methodist chapel.*

Music & comedy venues

Barfly *49 Chalk Farm Road, NW1 8AN (7688 8994, www.barflyclub.com). Music venue.*
Dublin Castle *94 Parkway, NW1 7AN (7485 1773, www.bugbearbookings.com). Music venue and pub.*
Electric Ballroom *184 Camden High Street, NW1 8QP (7485 9006, www.electricballroom. co.uk). Music venue and club.*
HMV Forum *9-17 Highgate Road, NW5 1JY (7428 4099, www.meanfiddler.com). Music venue.*
Jazz Café *5 Parkway, NW1 7PG (7485 6834, www.meanfiddler.com). Music venue.*
Koko *1A Camden High Street, NW1 7JE (0870 432 5527, www.koko.uk.com). Music venue and club.*
Monkey Business Comedy Club *07932 338203, www.monkeybusinesscomedyclub.co.uk). Held at the Sir Richard Steele pub on Haverstock Hill and the Oxford on Kentish Town Road.*
Monto Water Rats *328 Gray's Inn Road, WC1X 8BZ (7837 7269, www.themonto.com). Music venue.*

Persephone Books. See p133.

Roundhouse *Chalk Farm Road, NW1 8EH (0844 482 8008, www.roundhouse.org.uk). Pioneering arts venue.*
Scala *275 Pentonville Road, N1 9NL (7833 2022, www.scala-london.co.uk). Music venue and club.*

Other attractions

Bloomsbury Festival *www.bloomsburyfestival.org.uk.*
British Library *96 Euston Road, NW1 2DB (0843 208 1144, www.bl.uk). One of the greatest libraries in the world. Access to the Reading Rooms requires a Reader Pass.*
Kentish Town City Farm *1 Cressfield Close, NW5 4BN (7916 5421, www.ktcityfarm.org.uk).*
Pirate's Castle *Oval Road, NW1 7EA (7267 6605, www.thepiratecastle.org). Canalside activity centre for young people.*

Sport & fitness

Camden has a good selection of public facilities, including the Talacre Community Sports Centre, the open-air swimming ponds of Hampstead Heath and the Oasis centre with its heated outdoor pool. In the private sector, the borough is blessed with the Central YMCA, one of the top sports centres in London.

Gyms & leisure centres

Armoury *25 Pond Street, NW3 2PN (7431 2263, www.jubileehallclubs.org). Private.*
Central YMCA *112 Great Russell Street, WC1B 3NQ (7343 1700, www.ymca.co.uk). Private.*
Fitness First *www.fitnessfirst.co.uk; 128 Albert Street, NW1 7NE (7284 2244); 81-84 Chalk Farm Road, NW1 8AR (7284 0004); Coram Street, WC1N 1HB (7833 1887). Private.*
Gymbox *100 High Holborn, WC1V 6RD (7400 1919, www.gymbox.co.uk). Private.*
Kentish Town Sports Centre *Grafton Road, NW5 3DU (7974 7000, www.gll.org).*
Kieser Training *Greater London House, Hampstead Road, NW1 7DF (7391 9980, www. kieser-training.co.uk). Back specialists; private.*
LA Fitness *www.lafitness.co.uk; 53-79 Highgate Road, NW5 1TL (0843 170 1015); Lacon House, 84 Theobald's Road, WC1X 8RW (0843 170 1011). Private.*
Mallinson Sports Centre *Bishopswood Road, N6 4NY (8342 7272, www.highgate school.org.uk). Private.*
Mornington Sports & Fitness Centre *142-150 Arlington Road, NW1 7HP (7267 3600, www.camden.gov.uk).*

Oasis Sports Centre *32 Endell Street, WC2H 9AG (7831 1804, www.gll.org).*
Soho Gym *www.sohogyms.com; 193 Camden High Street, NW1 7JY (7482 4524); 12 Macklin Street, WC2B 5NF (7242 1290). Private.*
Spring Health Leisure Club *81 Belsize Park Gardens, NW3 4NJ (7483 6800, www.spring health.net). Private.*
Swiss Cottage Leisure Centre *1 Adelaide Road, NW3 3NF (7974 2012, www.gll.org, www.spa-london.org).*
Talacre Community Sports Centre *Dalby Street, off Prince of Wales Road, NW5 3AF (7974 8765, www.camden.gov.uk).*
Virgin Active *www.virginactive.co.uk; 50 Triton Square, NW1 3XB (7388 5511); O2 Centre, 255 Finchley Road, NW3 6LU (7644 2400). Private.*

Other facilities
Hampstead Heath Swimming Ponds *Hampstead Heath, NW5 1QR (7485 4491).*
Parliament Hill Lido *Parliament Hill Fields, Gordon House Road, NW5 2LT (7485 5757, www.cityoflondon.gov.uk/openspaces).*
Triyoga *6 Erskine Road, NW3 3AJ (7483 3344, www.triyoga.co.uk).*

Schools

Primary
There are 39 state primary schools in Camden, 20 of which are church schools. There are also 22 independent primaries, including one French school, one international school and two Montessori schools. See www.camden.gov.uk, www.ofsted.gov.uk and www.edubase.gov.uk for more information.

Secondary
Acland Burghley School *Burghley Road, NW5 1UJ (7485 8515, www.aclandburghley. camden.sch.uk).*
Camden School for Girls *Sandall Road, NW5 2DB (7485 3414, www.camdengirls. camden.sch.uk). Girls only.*
Collège Français Bilingue de Londres *87 Holmes Road, NW5 3AX (7993 7400, www.cfbl.org.uk). Bilingual school, opened September 2011. Private.*
Great Ormond Street Hospital for Children School *Great Ormond Street, WC1N 3JH (7813 8269, www.gosh.camden.sch.uk).*
Hampstead School *Westbere Road, NW2 3RT (7794 8133, www.hampsteadschool.org.uk).*
Haverstock School *24 Haverstock Hill, NW3 2BQ (7267 0975, www.hampsteadschool.org.uk).*

British Library. See p135.

Maria Fidelis Convent School *34 Phoenix Road, NW1 1TA (7387 3856, www.mariafidelis. camden.sch.uk). Roman Catholic; girls only.*
Parliament Hill School *Highgate Road, NW5 1RL (7485 7077, www.parliamenthill. camden.sch.uk). Girls only; mixed sixth form.*
The Royal School Hampstead *65 Rosslyn Hill, NW3 5UD (7794 7708, www.royal schoolhampstead.net). Girls only; private.*
La Sainte Union Catholic Secondary School *Highgate Road, NW5 1RP (7428 4600, www.lasainteunion.org.uk). Roman Catholic; girls only.*
South Camden Community School *Charrington Street, NW1 1RG (7387 0126, www.sccs.camden.sch.uk).*
South Hampstead High School *3 Maresfield Gardens, NW3 5SS (7435 2899, www.shhs.gdst. net). Girls only; private.*
The UCL Academy *Adelaide Road, NW3 3AQ (www.uclacademy.com). Due to open Sept 2012.*
University College School *Frognal, NW3 6XH (7435 2215, www.ucs.org.uk). Boys only; mixed sixth form; private.*
William Ellis School *Highgate Road, NW5 1RL (7267 9346, www.williamellis.camden. sch.uk). Boys only; mixed sixth form.*

Property

WHAT THE AGENTS SAY:

'The property market in Camden is buoyant and exciting, spanning sought-after ex-council flats to multi-million pound houses. Prices here have certainly bucked the downward trend in the rest of England and continue to rise steadily. We get a constant flow of applicants for both sales and lettings, ranging from students to investors to families. Camden itself is an ideal spot in which to invest; it's within walking distance of the West End and the universities, and extremely well connected, thanks to stations at St Pancras, King's Cross, Mornington Crescent and Camden Town. The King's Cross regeneration area has brought in a huge influx of British and overseas buyers, and the opening of the French School in Kentish Town has seen a rise in the demand for family homes in the area.'

Liana Loporto, London Residential, Camden

Average property prices

Detached £1,646,414
Semi-detached £1,218,809
Terraced £923,982
Flat £507,770

Local estate agents

Alexanders *337 West End Lane, NW6 1RS (7431 0666, www.alexanders-uk.com).*
Black Katz *www.black-katz.com; 2 offices in the borough (Camden 7284 3111, West Hampstead 7624 8131).*
Christo & Co *148 Kentish Town Road, NW1 9QB (7482 1203, www.christo.co.uk).*
Day Morris Associates *www.daymorris.co.uk; 2 offices in the borough (Hampstead 7482 4282, Highgate 8348 8131).*
Jeremy Bass *50 Chalcot Road, NW1 8LS (7722 8686, www.jeremybass.co.uk).*
London Residential *103 Parkway, NW1 7PP (7424 3222, www.londonresidential.uk.com).*
Olivers *189 Kentish Town Road, NW5 2JU (7284 1222, www.oliverstown.com).*
Ringley *Ringley House, 349 Royal College Street, NW1 9QS (7267 2900, www.ringley.co.uk).*

Other information

Council

Camden Council *Camden Town Hall, Judd Street, WC1H 9JE (7974 4444, www.camden. gov.uk).*

Camden Direct Information Service
7974 5974.

Legal services

Camden Community Law Centre
2 Prince of Wales Road, NW5 3LQ (7284 6510, www.lawcentres.org.uk).
Holborn CAB *3rd floor, Holborn Library, 32-38 Theobald's Road, WC1X 8PA (0844 856 3700, www.citizensadvice.org.uk).*

Local information

www.camdennewjournal.co.uk.
www.hamhigh.co.uk.
www.heathandhampsteadsociety.org.uk.
www.highgatesociety.com.
www.kingscrossenvironment.com.

Open spaces & allotments

Council allotments *Allotments Officer, c/o Parks & Open Spaces Section, Crowndale Centre, 218 Eversholt Street, NW1 1BD (7974 1564).*
Open spaces *www.camden.gov.uk/parks.*

Camden

'With London's best-dressed buildings and luxuries on every corner, Kensington and Chelsea flies the flag for English elegance and is the epitome of city glamour.'

**Tarek Malouf, founder and owner
of the Hummingbird Bakery**

Kensington & Chelsea

The Royal Borough certainly lives up to its illustrious name, with palatial properties, world-class museums, sumptuous shopping, green space galore and the highest life expectancy in the country. Unfortunately, it will cost you a king's ransom to buy a piece of the action, and away from the posh postcodes there are still large areas of economic deprivation.

Neighbourhoods

Kensington and Holland Park

Kensington High Street, once the site of offbeat shopping (legendary Biba, funky indoor Kensington Market) and independent shops, has long been lined with chain stores: a big M&S, lots of mid-range fashion outlets and the flagship branch of Whole Foods. For a glimpse of a more traditional Kensington, walk up Kensington Church Street, where the pricier boutiques and antiques parlours seem more suited to the grand stucco-fronted houses that line the backstreets. The other end of Kensington High Street is marked by the former Commonwealth Institute. This behemoth, which introduced many a young child to the Empire's furthest outposts, abuts Holland Park. The Grade II* listed building, having lain dormant for many years, is to become the home of the Design Museum (relocated from Tower Bridge) by 2014.

Outdoor types, especially in-line skaters and cyclists, gravitate towards Kensington

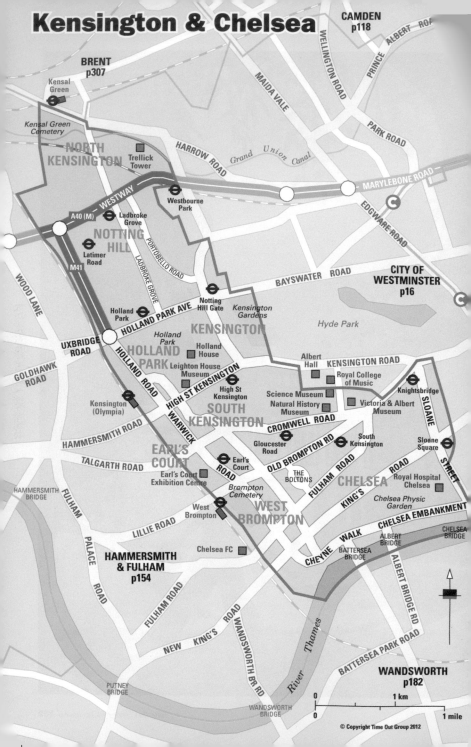

Gardens (which merges with Hyde Park). There, families head for the brilliant Diana, Princess of Wales Memorial Playground, replete with near life-size pirate ship and urban beach, while a stroll around the Round Pond is a traditional Sunday afternoon jaunt. It's easy to forget the dense traffic of Kensington Road.

Kensington also incorporates Holland Park, a relatively tranquil area full of extravagant Georgian and Victorian terraces; wealthy residents support myriad posh delis, beauty salons and upmarket boutiques (most of them on Holland Park Avenue or Portland Road). Holland Park itself is an impressively planned and surprisingly untouristy public space, with a Japanese garden, an art gallery, a summer open-air opera season and one of the city's most handsomely situated youth hostels. It's also one of London's wildest parks, with plenty of squirrels and roaming peacocks. Located just a short stroll away, Leighton House Museum was once the residence of the Victorian artist Frederic, Lord Leighton. Visit for the lavish marble and tiled interior and collection of paintings.

South Kensington, Earl's Court and West Brompton

Between Kensington High Street and Cromwell Road rests South Kensington, a distinctly elegant part of the capital. The updating of South Ken tube station has been the subject of much ongoing wrangling, but the surrounding cluster of shops, cafés and restaurants manages to make this area welcoming, with just the hint of a French accent (the Lycée Français and Institut Français are both nearby). This is also museum mile. A triumvirate of world-famous (and free) museums stand cheek by jowl: the V&A, the Science Museum and the Natural History Museum (the latter replete with outdoor ice-rink between November and January).

There's architectural splendour at nearly every turn in this neighbourhood, from the florid Italianate Brompton Oratory Catholic church to the iconic Royal Albert Hall (technically, just outside the borough – but this whole neighbourhood is sometimes referred to as 'Albertopolis' due to its Victorian heritage). Exhibition Road, named after the 1851 Great Exhibition and a direct route to Hyde Park, is lined with grand 19th- and 20th-century buildings –

Highs & Lows

⬆ **Holland Park** The actual park. It's a real urban adventure, just two minutes from Notting Hill, with peacocks, rabbits and well-heeled nippers all running wild.

Capital museums It's education, education, education all the way, with the Science Museum, Natural History Museum and V&A all lined up for learning.

Portobello Market The fruit and veg traders – go on Friday to beat the crowds.

Notting Hill Carnival Still the best party in town, every August bank holiday weekend...

Notting Hill Carnival ...but it can be a headache for home-owners, not to mention those local businesses that board up their shopfronts against the mob.

Property prices Want something bigger than a broom cupboard? Then it's time to move to W12.

Disappointed tourists Wandering the streets looking for the 'real' Notting Hill.

the Exhibition Road project, completed in 2011, is designed to enhance the area by pedestrianising much of the street-space, limiting cars to 20mph and cutting back on street clutter; the whole area is kerb-free. Besides tourists and wealthy residents, South Kensington is home to a sizeable student population (the Royal College of Art, Royal College of Music, Imperial College and numerous language schools are all here) and lots of embassies.

Directly north from the Royal Albert Hall is the Albert Memorial, unveiled in 1872. Commissioned by Queen Victoria in memory of her late husband, it is now sparkling thanks to a lengthy restoration project by English Heritage. On the corner of Exhibition Road and Kensington Gore sits the venerable Royal Geographical Society, which was formed in 1892 to advance geographical science and along the way absorbed such groups as the 'Association for Promoting the Discovery of the Interior Parts of Africa'.

It's a safe bet that almost every Londoner has taken a journey through the capital that involved passing through Earl's Court, with its busy District and Piccadilly line interchange. Above ground, Earl's Court connects with South Kensington via the very busy Cromwell Road (A4). Further local amenities can be found dotted around Gloucester Road, but the area otherwise remains a sprawl of side streets, hotels, private garden squares, youth hostels and bedsits; the last often have sadly crumbling interiors behind their imposing stuccoed façades. There's a transient spirit to the district, which does at least make for an appealing cultural mix; Hogarth Road, for example, has some interesting Filipino groceries and cafés. Twelve acres of the area are covered by the Earl's Court Exhibition Centre (which is facing the threat of demolition if the ambitious – and contentious – Earl's Court redevelopment masterplan gets the go-ahead).

In contrast to Earl's Court, neighbouring West Brompton is a classy residential area, incorporating plenty of high-value property, including the facing crescents of the Boltons. The district's most memorable landmark is Brompton Cemetery, on Fulham Road, worth a visit for its 19th-century design; the many famous graves include that of the suffragette pioneer Emmeline

Pankhurst. From here, it's a short walk to Stamford Bridge, home of Chelsea FC – just over the border in Hammersmith & Fulham.

Chelsea

This fancy neighbourhood is bisected by the King's Road. Originally Charles II's private route from St James's Palace, this traffic-clogged artery has subsequently been the epicentre of 1960s swinging London and home to the punk explosion, but now acts as a catwalk for Chelsea's smartest men and machines, the perfect place for an upmarket *passeggiata*.

High-end designers and private galleries are concentrated towards the Sloane Square end of the King's Road and on luxurious Sloane Street, which connects Chelsea to Knightsbridge. Sloane Square, named after its 18th-century owner, Sir Hans Sloane, features a central fountain depicting Venus. Dominating the square is Peter Jones, still the spiritual home of upper middle-class life in SW3. John Betjeman once said that, when the end of the world came, he wanted to be in the haberdashery department, 'because nothing unpleasant could ever happen there.'

The Royal Court Theatre, next to Sloane Square tube station, sent shockwaves around the world with its première of John Osborne's *Look Back in Anger* in 1956, and productions continue to err on the side of edgy. Opposite Peter Jones is Duke of York Square (www.dukeofyorksquare.com), home to a smart shopping development and the Saatchi Gallery; a further attraction is the 'fine food' market on Saturdays.

At the other end of the King's Road is the once-notorious World's End estate, a large council development of tower blocks and a shopping complex, built in the 1970s. The estate is slowly but surely shaking off its reputation for drug-related crime – and estate agents are certainly keen to tout the area – but it's still very evidently the poorest pocket of Chelsea.

There's a wealth of English Heritage blue plaques hereabouts. The composer Thomas Arne is believed to have conceived 'Rule Britannia' at his home, 215 King's Road. For truly famous neighbours, check out the quaint riverside Cheyne Walk, which dates back to the 18th century; residents have ranged from George Eliot, JMW Turner and Dante Gabriel Rossetti to the Rolling Stones' Keith Richards and Mick Jagger

Natural History Museum. See p141.

Chelsea catwalk the **King's Road.**

(at nos.3 and 48, respectively). Nearby
Cadogan Pier provides boat services up
and down the Thames.

If you're not spotting names, look out
for the Chelsea Pensioners in their dapper
scarlet uniforms and tricorne hats. These
retired servicemen live at the Royal
Hospital Chelsea, which was designed by
Sir Christopher Wren and Sir John Soane,
among others; the grounds host the lavish
Chelsea Flower Show (www.rhs.org.uk)
every May, as well as hiding some of
the most peaceful public tennis courts in
London. Another great secret haven is the
Chelsea Physic Garden. Founded in 1673,
its four acres are filled with plants dedicated
to the science of healing.

Knightsbridge

While much of Knightsbridge technically
falls under the aegis of the City of
Westminster, it seamlessly continues on
from Sloane Street as a ritzy, label-saturated
enclave. The main drag is dominated by
two temples to conspicuous consumption:
the over-the-top Harrods, and the more
restrained, fashion-conscious Harvey
Nicks. The talking point of the last few
years, residental complex One Hyde Park
has finally been completed. Located next
to the Mandarin Oriental hotel, its 80 or
so flats have broken records for the most
expensive property in London, with the

cheapest said to start at £20 million. There
isn't much affordable housing in SW7,
although some people manage to rent tiddly
bedsits in the area's tucked-away streets.

Notting Hill

Emerging for the first time at Notting Hill
Gate tube, you might wonder what all the
fuss is about. Traffic-clogged Notting Hill
Gate isn't a particularly attractive high
street, lined as it is with unexceptional chain
stores and eateries. But get off the main
drag and the appeal of the area is plain to
see, with rows of imposing stuccoed houses
and myriad garden squares – although any
attempt to re-enact Hugh Grant's jumping
over the fence from the film *Notting Hill*
will be met by stern faces, since the gardens
are only accessible to resident key holders
who can muster an annual fee of up to
£1,500. Money is no object for many of
Notting Hill's present incumbents, making
it hard to imagine the slum conditions here
only 50 years ago.

The district is otherwise best known for
hosting Europe's largest street party, the
Notting Hill Carnival, a raucous celebration
of the neighbourhood's Afro-Caribbean
heritage. The Carnival emerged as a
positive stand against the race riots of
the 1960s. Four decades later, it draws
around a million revellers to these streets
and neighbouring North Kensington every
August bank holiday weekend.

There are, however, enough fashionable
shops and hangouts to keep the crowds
flocking here throughout the year. Film
buffs head to Notting Hill's atmospheric
arty cinemas, the Gate, the Coronet and the
Electric. Fashionistas head to label-heavy
Ledbury Road, while Westbourne Grove is
awash with seriously smart antiques shops
and more couture creations – even the
public toilet is designer.

Hilly Ladbroke Grove, named after its
affluent 19th-century landowners, branches
into curved parades of Victorian townhouses.
The top of the hill was once home to a
racecourse, but waterlogging meant the
venture only lasted from 1837 to 1841, when
the owners decided to build houses instead.
Some of the borough's hippest streets are to
its east: Westbourne Grove, Portobello Road
and self-consciously upmarket All Saints
Road. Powis Square was the setting for the
cult 1960s film *Performance*, starring Mick
Jagger and James Fox.

Kensington & Chelsea

Famous **Portobello Road Market**.

Portobello Road Market is still a good place to find antiques and emerging designers, although there's a fair amount of tat and fakes, and a huge number of tourists. The threat of encroaching chain stores on this happy mix is a current hot topic (with mass protests in 2010 when one of the antiques arcades was replaced by a giant branch of All Saints). Most of the antiques stalls are at the Notting Hill Gate end; the most interesting clothing stalls are crammed beneath the Westway flyover, which carries travellers in and out of central London on the A40(M). The Westway now has its own development trust (www.westway.org), which runs the well-equipped Westway Sports Centre.

North Kensington

On the northern side of the Westway, North Kensington has the edgiest feel of any neighbourhood in the borough. Ladbroke Grove, so gentrified at the Holland Park end, is here lined with late-night shops and fast-food joints, though there are also some handsome houses, long since converted into flats and grimy from decades of traffic fumes.

The district was built around the local St Charles and Princess Louise hospitals, giant Victorian edifices that have been softened slightly with recent revamps. Buildings in the area certainly contrast with each other; take Barlby Road, which has snug-looking terraced houses as well as the imposing 1911 Pall Mall Depository, which now contains office units and a café. North Kensington is also the spiritual home to the 'Notting Hill Set', a powerful clique of Conservatives that includes David Cameron and George Osborne.

At the area's northernmost boundary, you'll find the green oasis of Kensal Green Cemetery, the first of London's grand Victorian burial grounds and final resting place of Trollope, Thackeray and Isambard Kingdom Brunel. Also here are the striking canalside studios of Kensal Town and the borough-run Canalside Activity Centre, which focuses on youth recreation.

Finally, mention should be made of what is surely North Kensington's most famous building: Hungarian Ernö Goldfinger's 31-storey Trellick Tower, originally designed as cheap social housing in 1972. It has shrugged off a troubled reputation in recent years to become one of the most sought-after addresses in the area – now Grade II* listed, it is a modernist icon.

Restaurants & cafés

There's no shortage of restaurants in the Royal Borough. What follows is a taste; for a full menu of options, consult the *Time Out London Eating & Drinking Guide*.

Chelsea brims with quality. Tom Aikens has two restaurants in the area: haute cuisine Tom Aikens and the simpler, cheaper Tom's Kitchen. Both are excellent. Gordon Ramsay, too, has an eponymous restaurant – his first, and still one of his best. Bluebird on the King's Road and Gallery Mess in the Saatchi Gallery offer more affordable Modern European fare. The Pig's Ear and Lots Road Pub & Dining Room help Chelsea rival Islington for gastropub excellence, while Chutney Mary, Rasoi Vineet Bhatia and Painted Heron are all Modern Indian heavyweights – though none could be described as cheap.

The restaurant scene in Knightsbridge is similar: high quality, high prices. The Capital serves haute cuisine in the exclusive environs of the Capital hotel; the Mandarin Oriental has Dinner by Heston Blumenthal and the less expensive Bar Boulud. There's also first-rate French restaurant Racine, sleek Japanese bar-restaurant Zuma, sleekly appointed Indian and Pakistani restaurant Amaya, and Chinese destination Mr Chow, which still draws a pedigree crowd despite being a little passé. Ramsay-affiliated Pétrus and the Berkeley hotel's Koffman's consistently impress for haute cuisine; at the other end of the scale entirely is O Fado, a homely basement restaurant that's London's oldest Portuguese eaterie. Located inside Harvey Nichols and Harrods, respectively, the stylish Fifth Floor (for Modern European) and Ladurée (for superb cakes) prove that dining in department stores needn't be dreary.

The range of high-end options doesn't diminish in South Ken. Bibendum (Modern European) has an excellent location in the Michelin Building; sister operation Bibendum Oyster Bar occupies the lovely tiled foyer. Elsewhere, Cambio de Tercio serves some of the city's best new-wave (or *nueva cocina*) Spanish cooking, while Gessler at Daquise breathes life into East European dishes. On Gloucester Road, L'Etranger (Modern European) and Pasha (North African) offer wonderful food, at a price.

Launceston Place and Clarke's are the best bets in Kensington, alongside Yashin, winner of Time Out's Eating & Drinking Award for Best Sushi Bar in 2011. The Kensington Palace Orangery (for coffee and cake) and Sticky Fingers (for ribs and the like) are great places to take the family. In Holland Park – actually in the park – is smart French restaurant the Belvedere.

Notting Hill is crammed with options: try near-perfect French restaurant the Ledbury, Tex-Mex diner Taqueria, Geales for posh fish and chips or the original (tiny) Ottolenghi.

A string of terrific cafés marks out Ladbroke Grove: Portuguese pair Café Oporto and Lisboa Pâtisserie; cupcake specialist Hummingbird Bakery; and newcomer Lowry & Baker (great for all-day brunch). Just off Portobello Road is the café within cookbook shop Books for Cooks (*see p149*). For people-watching while eating, try Pizza East or pan-Asian bar-restaurant E&O; ice-cream fans will love Dri Dri Gelato. Further up, on the canal, is the Dock Kitchen, set in designer Tom Dixon's HQ. Over on Westbourne Grove, there's kid-friendly pizzeria Mulberry Street and first-rate Lebanese restaurant Al Waha,

plus a busy branch of Daylesford Organic. Tom Conran is the brains behind four operations: gastropub the Cow (officially in Westminster, *see p29*); laid-back US-style diner Lucky 7; Mexican joint Crazy Homies (*see p147*); and brunch favourite Tom's Deli.

Al Waha *75 Westbourne Grove, W2 4UL (7229 0806, www.alwaharestaurant.com).*
Amaya *15 Motcomb Street, Halkin Arcade, SW1X 8JT (7823 1166, www.amaya.biz).*
Bar Boulud *Mandarin Oriental Hyde Park, 66 Knightsbridge, SW1X 7LA (7201 3899, www.danielnyc.com/barboulud_hub.html).*
Belvedere *Holland House, off Abbotsbury Road, in Holland Park, W8 6LU (7602 1238, www.belvedererestaurant.co.uk).*
Bibendum & Bibendum Oyster Bar *Michelin House, 81 Fulham Road, SW3 6RD (Bibendum 7581 5817, Oyster Bar 7589 1480, www.bibendum.co.uk).*
Bluebird *350 King's Road, SW3 5UU (7559 1000, www.danddlondon.com).*
Café Oporto *62A Golborne Road, W10 5PS (8968 8839).*
Cambio de Tercio *163 Old Brompton Road, SW5 0LJ (7244 8970, www.cambiodetercio.co.uk).*

TRANSPORT

Tube stations *Bakerloo* Kensal Green; *Central* Notting Hill Gate, Holland Park; *Circle* Sloane Square, South Kensington, Gloucester Road, High Street Kensington, Notting Hill Gate; *District* Sloane Square, South Kensington, Gloucester Road, High Street Kensington, Notting Hill Gate, Earl's Court, Kensington (Olympia), West Brompton; *Hammersmith & City* Westbourne Park, Ladbroke Grove, Latimer Road; *Piccadilly* Knightsbridge, South Kensington, Gloucester Road, Earl's Court
Rail stations *London Overground* Kensal Green, West Brompton, Kensington (Olympia); *Southern* West Brompton, Kensington (Olympia)
Main bus routes *into central London* 7, 9, 10, 11, 14, 18, 19, 22, 23, 27, 74, 94, 137, 148, 390; *night buses* N7, N9, N11, N18, N19, N22, N52, N74, N97, N137, N207; *24-hour buses* 7, 10, 14, 18, 23, 27, 94, 148, 390
River Commuter and leisure boat services running to/from central London, with stops at Cadogan Pier (under Albert Bridge) and Chelsea Harbour Pier

The Capital *22-24 Basil Street, SW3 1AT (7589 5171, www.capitalhotel.co.uk).*
Chutney Mary *535 King's Road, SW10 0SZ (7351 3113, www.chutneymary.com).*
Clarke's *124 Kensington Church Street, W8 4BH (7221 9225, www.sallyclarke.com).*
Daylesford Organic *208-212 Westbourne Grove, W11 2RH (7313 8050, www.daylesford organic.com).*
Dinner by Heston Blumenthal *Mandarin Oriental Hyde Park, 66 Knightsbridge, SW1X 7LA (7201 3833, www.dinnerbyheston.com).*
Dock Kitchen *Portobello Docks, 342-344 Ladbroke Grove, W10 5BU (8962 1610, www.dockkitchen.co.uk).*
Dri Dri Gelato *189 Portobello Road, W11 2ED (3490 5027, www.dridrigelato.com).*
E&O *14 Blenheim Crescent, W11 1NN (7229 5454, www.rickerrestaurants.com).*
L'Etranger *36 Gloucester Road, SW7 4QT (7584 1118, www.etranger.co.uk).*
Fifth Floor *Harvey Nichols, Knightsbridge, SW1X 7RJ (7235 5250, www.harveynichols.com).*
Gallery Mess *Saatchi Gallery, Duke of York's HQ, King's Road, SW3 4LY (7730 8135, www.saatchi-gallery.co.uk).*
Geales *www.geales.com; 1 Cale Street, SW3 3QT (7965 0555); 2 Farmer Street, W8 7SN (7727 7528).*
Gessler at Daquise *20 Thurloe Street, SW7 2LT (7589 6117, www.gesslerat daquise.co.uk).*
Gordon Ramsay *68 Royal Hospital Road, SW3 4HP (7352 4441, www.gordonramsay.com).*
Hummingbird Bakery *7851 1795, www.hummingbirdbakery.com; 47 Old Brompton Road, SW7 3JP; 133 Portobello Road, W11 2DY.*
Kensington Palace Orangery *The Orangery, Kensington Palace, Kensington Gardens, W8 4PX (3166 6112, www.hrp.org.uk).*
Koffman's *The Berkeley, Wilton Place, SW1X 7RL (7235 1010, www.the-berkeley.co.uk/ koffmanns.aspx).*
Ladurée *Harrods, entrance on Hans Road, SW1X 7XL (3155 0111, www.laduree.com).*

Launceston Place *1A Launceston Place, W8 5RL (7937 6912, www.danddlondon.com).*
Ledbury *127 Ledbury Road, W11 2AQ (7792 9090, www.theledbury.com).*
Lisboa Pâtisserie *57 Golborne Road, W10 5NR (8968 5242).*
Lots Road Pub & Dining Room *114 Lots Road, SW10 0RJ (7352 6645, www.lotsroad pub.com).*
Lowry & Baker *339 Portobello Road, W10 5SA (8960 8534, www.lowryandbaker.com).*
Lucky 7 *127 Westbourne Park Road, W2 5QL (7727 6771, www.lucky7london.co.uk).*
Mr Chow *151 Knightsbridge, SW1X 7PA (7589 7347, www.mrchow.com).*
Mulberry Street *84 Westbourne Grove, W2 5RT (7313 6789, www.mulberrystreet.co.uk).*
O Fado *50 Beauchamp Place, SW3 1NY (7589 3002, www.ofado.co.uk).*
Ottolenghi *www.ottolenghi.co.uk; 63 Ledbury Road, W11 2AD (7727 1121); 1 Holland Street, W8 4NA (7937 0003).*
Painted Heron *112 Cheyne Walk, SW10 0DJ (7351 5232, www.thepaintedheron.com).*
Pasha *1 Gloucester Road, SW7 4PP (7589 7969, www.pasha-restaurant.co.uk).*
Pétrus *1 Kinnerton Street, SW1X 8EA (7592 1609, www.gordonramsay.com).*
Pig's Ear *35 Old Church Street, SW3 5BS (7352 2908, www.thepigsear.info).*
Pizza East *310 Portobello Road, W10 5TA (8969 4500, www.pizzaeastportobello.com).*
Racine *239 Brompton Road, SW3 2EP (7584 4477, www.racine-restaurant.com).*
Rasoi Vineet Bhatia *10 Lincoln Street, SW3 2TS (7225 1881, www.rasoi-uk.com).*
Sticky Fingers *1A Phillimore Gardens, W8 7QG (7938 5338, www.stickyfingers.co.uk).*
Taqueria *139-143 Westbourne Grove, W11 2RS (7229 4734, www.coolchiletaqueria.co.uk).*
Tom Aikens *43 Elystan Street, SW3 3NT (7584 2003, www.tomaikens.co.uk).*
Tom's Deli *226 Westbourne Grove, W11 2RH (7221 8818).*
Tom's Kitchen *27 Cale Street, SW3 3QP (7349 0202, www.tomskitchen.co.uk).*
Yashin *1A Argyll Road, W8 7DB (7938 1536, www.yashinsushi.com).*
Zuma *5 Raphael Street, SW7 1DL (7584 1010, www.zumarestaurant.com).*

COUNCIL TAX

A	up to £40,000	£719.42
B	£40,001-£52,000	£839.31
C	£52,001-£68,000	£959.22
D	£68,001-£88,000	£1,079.12
E	£88,001-£120,000	£1,318.93
F	£120,001-£160,000	£1,558.73
G	£160,001-£320,000	£1,798.54
H	over £320,000	£2,158.24

Bars & pubs

Kensington is relatively short of decent drinking venues – try the Scarsdale Tavern or the Elephant & Castle – but in South

Kensington you're spoilt for choice. Catering to the area's curious mix of Sloanes, rootless cosmopolitans and dodgy geezers are options ranging from hotel bar 190 Queensgate to historic boozer the Anglesea Arms, once a favourite of DH Lawrence and Charles Dickens.

Hopping over to the King's Road, options in Chelsea are almost as good. The star performers, gastropubs Lots Road Pub & Dining Room and the Pig's Ear (for both, *see p146*), are offset by glamorous cocktail bars such as Apartment 195, which is so discreet you need to press a buzzer to get in, and the revamped Hollywood Arms, now a smart bar and eaterie.

To the north-east, on Old Brompton Road, ancient boho den the Troubadour delights locals in its various roles as a café, wine bar and performance venue. Though close geographically, bars in Knightsbridge are a million miles away in terms of clientele and ethos. Expect to find London's elite, ordering only the best in the cracking Mandarin Bar and super-chic Japanese bar-restaurant Zuma (*see p146*).

A batch of quality cocktail bars in Notting Hill includes Montgomery Place, the Lonsdale, subterranean hotspot Trailer Happiness and cinema-affiliated Electric Brasserie; the refurbished Hillgate serves a decent range of beers, and the Mall Tavern is a smart gastropub, while boho boozers Portobello Gold and Sun in Splendour round out the choices. East to Holland Park, we like the Ladbroke Arms, a pub with a front garden that's gorgeous in summer.

North towards Westbourne Grove and the Westway, is the Cow gastropub (*see p29*). Also run by Tom Conran is vampish, Mexican-themed venue Crazy Homies; if you really want crazy, however, look no further than Tiroler Hut, a bonkers bar that celebrates everything Tyrolean (including lederhosen and cowbells). In Westbourne Park, converted pub Grand Union has a fine view over Regent's Canal. To the east of Chepstow Road, there's a clutch of fine bars and pubs that fall into the neighbouring borough of the City of Westminster.

Anglesea Arms *15 Selwood Terrace, SW7 3QG (7373 7960, www.capitalpubcompany.com).*
Apartment 195 *195 King's Road, SW3 5ED (7349 4468, www.apartment195.co.uk).*

Crazy Homies *125 Westbourne Park Road, W2 5QL (7727 6771, www.crazyhomies.com).*
Electric Brasserie *191 Portobello Road, W11 2ED (7908 9696, www.the-electric.co.uk).*
Elephant & Castle *40 Holland Street, W8 4LT (7937 6382, www.nicholsonspubs.co.uk).*
Grand Union *45 Woodfield Road, W9 2BA (7286 1886, www.grandunionlondon.co.uk).*
Hillgate *24 Hillgate Street, W8 7SR (7727 8566, www.thehillgate.com).*
Hollywood Arms *45 Hollywood Road, SW10 9HX (7349 7840, www.hollywoodarms chelsea.com).*
Ladbroke Arms *54 Ladbroke Road, W11 3NW (7727 6648, www.capitalpubcompany.com).*
Lonsdale *48 Lonsdale Road, W11 2DE (7727 4080, www.thelonsdale.co.uk).*
Mall Tavern *71-73 Palace Gardens Terrace, W8 4RU (7229 3374, www.themalltavern.com).*
Mandarin Bar *Mandarin Oriental Hyde Park, 66 Knightsbridge, SW1X 7LA (7235 2000, www.mandarinoriental.com).*
Montgomery Place *31 Kensington Park Road, W11 2EU (7792 3921, www.montgomery place.co.uk).*
190 Queensgate *The Gore, 190 Queensgate, SW7 5EX (7584 6601, www.gorehotel.co.uk).*
Portobello Gold *95-97 Portobello Road, W11 2QB (7460 4910, www.portobellogold.com).*
Scarsdale Tavern *23A Edwardes Square, W8 6HE (7937 1811).*
Sun in Splendour *7 Portobello Road, W11 3DA (7792 0914, www.suninsplendour pub.co.uk).*
Tiroler Hut *27 Westbourne Grove, W2 4UA (7727 3981, www.tirolerhut.co.uk).*
Trailer Happiness *177 Portobello Road, W11 2DY (7727 2700, www.trailerhappiness.com).*
Troubadour *265 Old Brompton Road, SW5 9JA (7370 1434, www.troubadour.co.uk).*

Shops

Kensington & Chelsea has some of the capital's prime consumer destinations: Knightsbridge, the King's Road, Notting Hill. Knightsbridge may be a tourist-clogged nightmare on a Saturday afternoon, but weekday mornings are quiet enough for you to appreciate the extravagantly tiled Edwardian food halls at Harrods. For the latest designer fashion, though, head for coolly sophisticated Harvey Nichols, then stroll down Sloane Street for more international superbrands. On a corner of Sloane Square is Peter Jones department store, John Lewis's posh western sibling. Continue on to Lower Sloane Street for L'Artisan du Chocolat's 'couture' confections.

After its 1960s and '70s heyday, the King's Road had become a bland, chain-dominated strip, but it was given a boost a few years back when the old Duke of York barracks were reborn as an attractive shopping square. Notable retailers within its confines include cult favourite Liz Earle Naturally Active Skincare, denim boutique Trilogy and Italian food specialist Manicomio. Don't miss wonderful indie bookshop John Sandoe, tucked away on a side street. On the King's Road itself, there's US store Anthropologie's second London branch and, further west, the restaurant/retail complex in the landmark Bluebird garage, including the Shop at Bluebird – which sells a combination of designer clobber, furniture, books and gadgets – and posh deli Bluebird Epicerie. Nearby, Austique has a lovely collection of stylish clothes, lingerie and accessories for women. You have to walk further (it may really feel like World's End by the time you get there) for Vivienne Westwood's original shop, which she opened with Malcolm McLaren in 1970 as Let It Rock. Walk even further to arrive at Lots Road Auctions, on the border with Hammersmith & Fulham, which holds sales every Sunday.

In South Kensington, designer boutiques and glossy contemporary furniture stores cluster around Brompton Cross. The Conran Shop flagship is located in the spectacular art nouveau Michelin Building, and there's a spacious branch of Skandium nearby. A mix of upmarket children's stores and

interior designers' showrooms line pretty Walton Street, where you'll also find Farmacia Santa Maria Novella for old-world herbal products. Interiors shops cluster on nearby Elystan Street.

Chain-choked Kensington High Street is another former fashion star that has lost its sparkle, although the iconic Barkers department store is now occupied by swanky US organic superstore Whole Foods Market. From the high street, Kensington Church Street – lined with rarefied antiques shops – leads up to Notting Hill. The area around the intersection of Westbourne Grove and Ledbury Road (on the border with the City of Westminster) is boutique central: Aimé (with Petite Aimé next door), Feathers, JW Beeton, Matches… the list goes on. Also worth a look are J&M Davidson for beautifully crafted bags, British perfumery Miller Harris, and Ben Day's striking jewellery. The stunning post-war and contemporary furniture and decorative art at Themes & Variations would make striking additions to the area's expansive 19th-century properties. No doubt catering to the area's jet-set demographic, there's not one but three shops in the locality dedicated to year-round swimwear: Heidi Klein, Odabash and (technically in Westminster) Pistol Panties.

Clarendon Cross in Holland Park is a lovely shopping spot: browse in well-loved boutique the Cross, stock up on fine kitchenware at Summerill & Bishop or have lunch and a pedicure at the London outpost of Babington House's Cowshed spa, which doubles as a café.

Around Portobello Road, there's a funky mix of vintage clothes shops, hip boutiques, Paul Smith's stucco-mansion flagship, specialist stores (Spice Shop, Books for Cooks) and record shops, notable among them Rough Trade, Honest Jon's and, for rare vinyl, Intoxica! The famous Travel Bookshop has, sadly, closed, but Lutyens & Rubinstein makes a stylish addition. Honeyjam, co-owned by former-model mum Jasmine Guinness, sells toys that won't jar with stylish interiors. In addition to numerous delis, local food stores include picturesque butcher Kingsland and fishmonger Golborne Fisheries. Locals are fighting to keep the area's unique mix and to resist encroaching chain stores – see www.friendsofportobello.com for more information.

On Saturdays, popular – and tourist-mobbed – Portobello Road Market comprises three parts: the antiques stalls and arcades at the Notting Hill end, food stalls further north and, under the Westway flyover, up-and-coming designers and vintage clothes sellers (also on Fridays). Here, the Portobello Green Arcade contains an interesting selection of units (many only open at weekends). Shoppers who keep walking are rewarded by celebrated vintage emporium Rellik, on characterful Golborne Road.

Aimé *32 Ledbury Road, W11 2AB (7221 7070, www.aimelondon.com).*
Anthropologie *131-141 King's Road, SW3 4PW (7349 3110, www.anthropologie.co.uk).*
L'Artisan du Chocolat *0845 270 6996, www.artisanduchocolat.com; 81 Westbourne Grove, W2 4UL; 89 Lower Sloane Street, SW1W 8DA.*
Austique *330 King's Road, SW3 5UR (7376 4555, www.austique.co.uk).*
Ben Day *3 Lonsdale Road, W11 2BY (3417 3873, www.benday.co.uk).*
Bluebird Epicerie *350 King's Road, SW3 5UU (7559 1140, www.bluebird-restaurant.co.uk).*
Books for Cooks *4 Blenheim Crescent, W11 1NN (7221 1992, www.booksforcooks.com).*
Conran Shop *Michelin House, 81 Fulham Road, SW3 6RD (7589 7401, www.conranshop.co.uk).*

Cowshed *119 Portland Road, W11 4LN (7078 1944, www.cowshedclarendoncross.com).*
The Cross *141 Portland Road, W11 4LR (7727 6760, www.thecrossshop.co.uk).*
Farmacia Santa Maria Novella *117 Walton Street, SW3 2HP (7460 6600).*
Feathers *www.feathersfashion.com; 42 Hans Cresent, SW1X 0LZ (7589 5802); 176 Westbourne Grove, W11 2RW (7243 8800).*
Golborne Fisheries *75-77 Golborne Road, W10 5NP (8960 3100).*
Harrods *87-135 Brompton Road, SW1X 7XL (7730 1234, www.harrods.com).*
Harvey Nichols *109-125 Knightsbridge, SW1X 7RJ (7235 5000, www.harvey nichols.com).*
Heidi Klein *www.heidiklein.com; 174 Westbourne Grove, W11 2RW (7243 5665); 257 Pavilion Road, SW1X 0BP (7259 9418).*
Honest Jon's *278 Portobello Road, W10 5TE (8969 9822, www.honestjons.com).*
Honeyjam *2 Blenheim Crescent, W11 1NN (7243 0449, www.honeyjam.co.uk).*
Intoxica! *231 Portobello Road, W11 1LT (7229 8010, www.intoxica.co.uk).*
J&M Davidson *97 Golborne Road, W10 5NL (8969 2244, www.jandmdavidson.com).*
John Sandoe *10 Blacklands Terrace, SW3 2SR (7589 9473, www.johnsandoe.com).*
JW Beeton *48-50 Ledbury Road, W11 2AJ (7229 8874, www.jwbeeton.co.uk).*

Kensington & Chelsea

Harrods Food Hall: classy comestibles in swanky surroundings. See p147.

Kingsland, the Edwardian Butcher
140 Portobello Road, W11 2DZ (7727 6067,
www.kingslandbutchers.co.uk).
Liz Earle Naturally Active Skincare *38-39*
Duke of York Square, King's Road, SW3 4LY
(7730 9191, www.lizearle.com).
Lots Road Auctions *71-73 Lots Road,*
SW10 0RN (7376 6800, www.lotsroad.com).
Lutyens & Rubinstein Bookshop
21 Kensington Park Road, W11 2EU (7229
1010, www.lutyensrubinstein.co.uk).
Manicomio *85 Duke of York Square,*
King's Road, SW3 4LY (7730 3366,
www.manicomio.co.uk).
Matches *60-64 & 85 Ledbury Road, W11 2AJ*
(7221 0255, www.matchesfashion.com).
Miller Harris *14 Needham Road, W11 2RP*
(7221 4370, www.millerharris.com).
Odabash *48B Ledbury Road, W11 2AJ*
(7229 4299, www.odabash.com).
Paul Smith *Westbourne House, 120 & 122*
Kensington Park Road, W11 2EP (7727 3553,
www.paulsmith.co.uk).
Peter Jones *Sloane Square, SW1W 8EL*
(7730 3434, www.peterjones.co.uk).
Pistol Panties *75 Westbourne Park Road,*
W2 5QH (7229 5286, www.pistolpanties.com).
Portobello Green Arcade *281 Portobello*
Road, W10 5TZ (8960 2277, www.portobello
designers.com).
Portobello Road Market
www.portobelloroad.co.uk, www.rbkc.gov.uk.
Rellik *8 Golborne Road, W10 5NW (8962*
0089, www.relliklondon.co.uk).
Rough Trade *130 Talbot Road, W11 1JA*
(7229 8541, www.roughtrade.com).
Shop at Bluebird *350 King's Road, SW3 5UU*
(7351 3873, www.theshopatbluebird.com).
Skandium *245-249 Brompton Road, SW3 2EP*
(7584 2066, www.skandium.com).
Spice Shop *1 Blenheim Crescent, W11 2EE*
(7221 4448, www.thespiceshop.co.uk).
Summerill & Bishop *100 Portland Road,*
W11 4LQ (7229 1337, www.summerilland
bishop.com).
Themes & Variations *231 Westbourne*
Grove, W11 2SE (7727 5531, www.themes
andvariations.com).
Trilogy *33 Duke of York Square, King's Road,*
SW3 4LY (7730 6515, www.trilogystores.co.uk).
Whole Foods Market *The Barkers Building,*
63-97 Kensington High Street, W8 5SE (7368
4500, www.wholefoodsmarket.com).
World's End (Vivienne Westwood)
430 King's Road, SW10 0LJ (7352 6551,
www.viviennewestwoodonline.co.uk,
www.worldsendshop.co.uk).

Arts & attractions

Cinemas & theatres

Ciné Lumière *Institut Français, 17 Queensbury*
Place, SW7 2DT (7871 3515, www.institut-
francais.org.uk). Mostly screens films in French,
with English subtitles.
Cineworld *0871 200 2000, www.cineworld.*
co.uk; 279 King's Road, SW3 5EW; 142 Fulham
Road, SW10 9QR.
Coronet Cinema *103 Notting Hill Gate,*
W11 3LB (7727 6705, www.coronet.org).
Curzon Chelsea *206 King's Road, SW3 5XP*
(7351 3742, www.curzoncinemas.com).
Electric Cinema *191 Portobello Road, W11*
2ED (7908 9696, www.electriccinema.co.uk).
Gate Cinema *87 Notting Hill Gate, W11 3JZ*
(0871 902 5731, www.picturehouses.co.uk).
Gate Theatre *11 Pembridge Road, W11 3HQ*
(7229 0706, www.gatetheatre.co.uk).
Odeon Kensington *263 Kensington*
High Street, W8 6NA (0871 224 4007,
www.odeon.co.uk).
Royal Court Theatre *Sloane Square, SW1*
8AS (7565 5000, www.royalcourttheatre.com).
Science Museum IMAX *Science Museum,*
Exhibition Road, SW7 2DD (0870 870 4868,
www.sciencemuseum.org.uk).

Galleries & museums

Carlyle's House *24 Cheyne Row, SW3 5HL*
(7352 7087, www.nationaltrust.org.uk).
The home of writer Thomas Carlyle offers
an intriguing snapshot of Victorian life.
Leighton House Museum & Art Gallery
12 Holland Park Road, W14 8LZ (7602 3316,
www.rbkc.gov.uk/leightonhousemuseum).
National Army Museum *Royal Hospital Road,*
SW3 4HT (7730 0717, www.national-army-
museum.ac.uk). Exhibits run from 15th-century
Agincourt to present-day peacekeeping.
Natural History Museum *Cromwell Road,*
SW7 5BD (information 7942 5011, switchboard
7942 5000, www.nhm.ac.uk).
Saatchi Gallery *Duke of York's HQ, King's*
Road, SW3 4LY (www.saatchi-gallery.co.uk).
Science Museum *Exhibition Road, SW7 2DD*
(0870 870 4868, www.sciencemuseum.org.uk).
Victoria & Albert Museum *Cromwell Road,*
SW7 2RL (7942 2000, www.vam.ac.uk).

Music & comedy venues

Cadogan Hall *5 Sloane Terrace, SW1X 9DQ*
(7730 4500, www.cadoganhall.com). This fine
classical concert hall is home to the Royal
Philharmonic.

Notting Hill Arts Club 21 Notting Hill Gate, W11 3JQ (7460 4459, www.nottinghillarts club.com). Specialist music and arts venue.

Royal Albert Hall Kensington Gore, SW7 2AP (7589 8212, www.royalalberthall.com). World-famous concert hall known for classical performances, including the Proms; also hosts pop and rock concerts.

Royal College of Music Prince Consort Road, SW7 2BS (7591 4314, www.rcm.ac.uk).

Other attractions

Brompton Oratory Thurloe Place, Brompton Road, SW7 2RP (7808 0900, www.brompton oratory.com). England's second largest Catholic church (after Westminster Cathedral).

Chelsea Physic Garden 66 Royal Hospital Road, SW3 1HS (7349 6458, www.chelsea physicgarden.co.uk).

Earl's Court Exhibition Centre Warwick Road, SW5 9TA (7385 1200, www.eco.co.uk)

Goethe-Institut 50 Princes Gate, Exhibition Road, SW7 2PH (7596 4000, www.goethe.de/ london). German cultural institute.

Institut Français 17 Queensberry Place, SW7 2DT (7871 3515, www.institut-francais.org.uk). French cultural institute, which includes Ciné Lumière.

Kensington Palace W8 4PX (0844 482 7777, bookings 0844 482 7799, www.hrp. org.uk). Reopened spring 2012 after major renovation, with restored gardens and a new courtyard terrace and café.

Notting Hill Carnival www.thenottinghillcarnival.com

Royal Hospital Chelsea Royal Hospital Road, SW3 4SR (7881 5200, www.chelsea-pensioners.co.uk).

Sport & fitness

Leisure centres here tend towards private, highly polished and pricey. Exceptions include the no-nonsense Club Kensington, while Portobello Green Fitness Club defies expectations (and its somewhat reedy location) with a good range of community-driven, family-friendly activities at affordable prices. The borough also has two of the capital's premier public facilities. Kensington Leisure Centre (a brilliant design and a major pull of activities) and the Westway Sports Centre (everything from all-weather sports pitches to a large indoor climbing wall).

Gyms & leisure centres

Aquilla Health Club 11 Thurloe Place, SW7 2DS (7225 0225, www.spaclub.com/aquilla). Private.

Bodyworkswest 11 Lambton Place, W11 2SH (7229 2291, www.bodyworkswest.co.uk). Private.

Chelsea Club Chelsea Village, Fulham Road, SW6 1HS (7915 2200, www.thechelseaclub.com). Private.

Chelsea Sports Centre Chelsea Manor Street, SW3 5PL (7352 6985, www.gll.org). Private.

Club Kensington 201-207 Kensington High Street, W8 6BA (7937 5386, www.clubkensington.com). Private.

David Lloyd 116 Cromwell Road, SW7 4XR (7341 6400, www.davidlloydleisure.co.uk). Private.

Earl's Court Gym 254 Earl's Court Road, SW5 9AD (7370 1402, www.soho-gyms.com). Private.

STATISTICS

BOROUGH MAKE-UP
Population 169,500
Ethnic origins
 White 74.0%
 Mixed 4.0%
 Asian or Asian British 9.7%
 Black or Black British 6.6%
 Chinese or other 5.7%
Students 10.2%
Retirees 8.3%

HOUSING STOCK
Borough size (hectares) 1,239
Population density per hectare 146.0
No. of households 90,850
Houses (detached, semi-detached or terraced) 17%
Flats (converted or purpose-built) 83%

CRIME PER 1,000 OF POPULATION
Burglary 5
Robbery 3
Theft of vehicle 3
Theft from vehicle 10
Violence against the person 17
Sexual offences 1

MPs
Kensington Sir Malcolm Rifkind (Conservative); *Chelsea & Fulham* Greg Hands (Conservative); *Westminster North* Karen Buck (Labour)

Fitness First *Petersham House, 29-37 Harrington Road, SW7 3HD (0844 571 2933, www.fitnessfirst.co.uk). Private.*
The Harbour Club *Watermeadow Lane, SW6 2RR (7371 7700, www.harbourclub.co.uk). Private.*
Kensington Leisure Centre *Walmer Road, W11 4PQ (7727 9747, www.gll.org).*
LA Fitness *63-81 Pelham Street, SW7 2NJ (0843 170 1021, www.lafitness.co.uk). Private.*
Portobello Green Fitness Club *3-5 Thorpe Close, W10 5XL (8960 2221, www.pgfc.org.uk). Private.*
Virgin Active *www.virginactive.co.uk; 3rd floor, 17A Old Court Place, W8 4HP (0845 270 9128); 188A Fulham Road, SW10 9PN (0845 270 4085); 119-131 Lancaster Road, W11 1QT (0845 270 2102). Private.*

Other facilities
Canalside Activity Centre *Canal Close, W10 5AY (8968 4500, www.rbkc.gov.uk).*

Westway Sports Centre & Climbing Wall *1 Crowthorne Road, W10 5XL (8969 0992, www.westwaysportscentre.org.uk).*

Schools

Primary
There are 26 state primary schools in Kensington & Chelsea, 15 of which are church schools. There are also 25 independent primaries, including one Spanish school and one French school. See www.rbkc.gov.uk, www.edubase.gov.uk and www.ofsted.gov.uk for more information.

Secondary
Cardinal Vaughan Memorial School *89 Addison Road, W14 8BZ (7603 8478, www.cvms.co.uk). Roman Catholic; boys only.*
Chelsea Academy *Lots Road, SW10 0AB (7376 3019, www.chelsea-academy.org). Church of England.*
Francis Holland School *39 Graham Terrace, SW1W 8JF (7730 2971, www.fhs-sw1.org.uk). Girls only; private.*
Holland Park School *Airlie Gardens, Campden Hill Road, W8 7AF (7908 1000, www.hollandparkschool.co.uk).*
Queen's Gate *133 Queen's Gate, SW7 5LE (7589 3587, www.queensgate.org.uk). Girls only; private.*
St Thomas More Language College *Cadogan Street, SW3 2QS (7589 9734, www.stm.rbkc.sch.uk). Roman Catholic.*
Sion Manning RC Girls' School *75 St Charles Square, W10 6EL (8969 7111, www.sion-manning.com). Roman Catholic; girls only.*

Property

WHAT THE AGENTS SAY:
'Portobello is still an interesting mix of trendy, arty types living alongside bankers and those working in the City, while Holland Park is as popular with families as ever, with lots of two- to four-bedroom houses. Currently, the market is pretty stale – prices haven't changed in a long while. The economic downturn has meant many residents are choosing to stay where they are, which means not many properties are coming on to the market – so there's nowhere for anyone to move to should they want to. It's a real Catch-22, but, at the same time, this is keeping the prices supported.'

Anna Greenwood, Carter Jonas, Holland Park

Kensal Green Cemetery, one of London's greatest graveyards. See p144.

Average property prices

Detached £3,621,756
Semi-detached £2,570,401
Terraced £2,152,813
Flat £795,706

Local estate agents

Bruten & Co *4A Wellington Terrace,*
W2 4LW (7229 9262, www.brutens.com).
Carter Jonas
8 Addison Avenue, W11 4QR (7371 1111,
www.carterjonas.co.uk).
Chelsea International
15 Radnor Walk, SW3 4BP (7349 9495,
www.chelseainternational.co.uk).
Coutts de Lisle *66 Pembroke Road,*
W8 6NX (7603 4444, www.cdlestates.co.uk).
Executive Lettings
329 Chelsea Cloisters, Sloane Avenue,
SW3 3EE (07957 170697, www.executive
propertyltd.com).
Marsh & Parsons
www.marshandparsons.co.uk; 5 offices
(Chelsea 7591 5570, Holland Park 7605
6890, Kensington 7368 4450, North
Kensington 7313 8350, Notting Hill
7313 2890).
Westways *20 Great Western Road,*
W9 3NN (7286 5757, www.westwaysuk.com).

Other information

Council

Royal Borough of Kensington & Chelsea
Town Hall, Hornton Street, W8 7NX
(7361 3000, www.rbkc.gov.uk).

Legal services

Chelsea CAB *Old Town Hall, King's Road,*
SW3 5EE (0844 826 9708, www.citizens
advice.org.uk).
Kensington CAB *140 Ladbroke Grove,*
W10 5ND (0844 826 9708,
www.citizensadvice.org.uk).
North Kensington Law Centre *74 Golborne*
Road, W10 5PS (8969 7473, www.nklc.co.uk).
Nucleus Legal Advice Centre *298 Old*
Brompton Road, SW5 9JF (7373 6262/4005,
www.nucleus.org.uk).

Local information

www.londonlocals.co.uk.

Open spaces & allotments

Allotments *There are no allotments in*
Kensington & Chelsea.
Open spaces *ww.rbkc.gov.uk; www.kensal*
green.co.uk (Kensal Green Cemetery);
www.royalparks.org.uk (Kensington Gardens).

> *'Neither city centre nor suburb, the borough is home to three famous football clubs and three world-class theatres. Over 150 languages are spoken and a third of the population was born outside the UK.'*

Andy Slaughter, MP for Hammersmith

Hammersmith & Fulham

Multicultural Shepherd's Bush has a new focus these days with the arrival of the Westfield mega mall, but other parts of the borough haven't changed much in recent years. Hammersmith remains a stopover for renters and new immigrants, while Fulham continues to attract a stream of affluent young professionals with their 4WDs and double buggies.

Neighbourhoods

Shepherd's Bush

Everything's changed at Shepherd's Bush with the arrival of Westfield London – the first of the two mammoth shopping centres the Australian mall company has erected in the capital in the past five years. With it came infrastructure improvements, including two new stations: Wood Lane on the Hammersmith & City line and Shepherd's Bush station on the London Overground rail line. Despite all the razzamatazz – and the fact that hordes of west and south Londoners now head to the Bush, not the West End, for their retail action – other aspects of Shepherd's Bush life don't seem to have altered greatly. The Green itself remains a down-at-heel spot (a revamp is promised, as it has been for years).

Within walking distance of the vast BBC Media Village complex in White City, Shepherd's Bush has other links with the entertainment world, having spawned members of the Who and the Sex Pistols, as well as Pete Doherty. It's also famous for the Shepherd's Bush Empire. Other defining

Hammersmith & Fulham

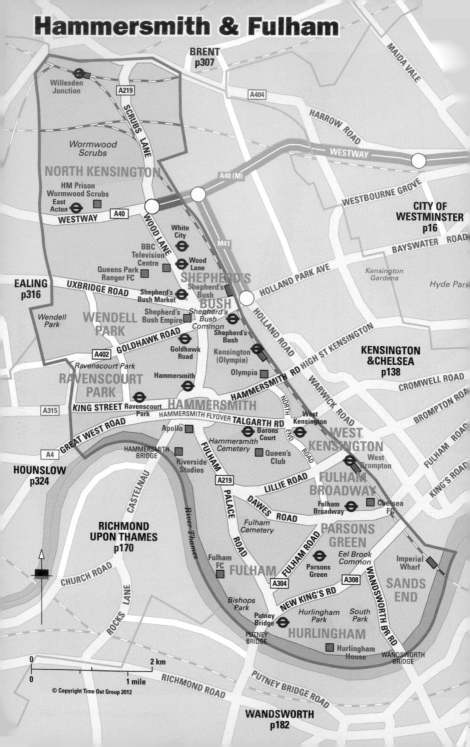

Hammersmith & Fulham

features of the area include football ground Loftus Road, home to the 'Super Hoops' (Queen's Park Rangers). North of the Westway is Wormwood Scrubs common land, the largest open space in the borough, and, adjoining it, the infamous prison.

Hammersmith

The heart of Hammersmith is a congested and noisy mess, thanks to the thundering A4, rickety Hammersmith flyover and the often gridlocked gyratory around Hammersmith Broadway, where the tube (District and Piccadilly lines) and bus station are situated. Changing tubes here is a nuisance, as the Hammersmith & City line station is across the road. Noisy chain pubs dominate the area around the Broadway; far better are the lovely riverside pubs west of green-and-gold Hammersmith Bridge, the city's oldest suspension bridge.

Shopping is centred on busy King Street, which leads west to Chiswick. It's a grubby thoroughfare, providing the usual raft of Dixons, Boots, mobile phone outlets and charity shops, plus an unappealing shopping centre, Kings Mall. Further on lies Lowiczanka Polish Cultural Centre. Home to a theatre, restaurant and the largest Polish library outside Poland, it is a meeting place for Hammersmith's extensive Polish community. Proposals to redevelop the stretch of King Street around the ugly Town Hall Extension – involving new civic offices, a supermarket and two high-rises of luxury apartments – met with fierce local opposition, mainly because of how it would affect the Thameside skyline. The Tory-run council attempted to bulldoze the scheme through regardless, but finally backed down in late 2011 after the intervention of Boris Johnson's office.

Cultural offerings include the HMV Apollo concert venue, Lyric Hammersmith theatre and Riverside Studios, where you can watch edgy performance theatre, an arthouse movie or a TV show being recorded. The Hammersmith Palais, built in 1919 as a dance hall and once a legendary gig venue, closed in 2007 and now stands empty, as wrangles continue about whether to demolish the building to create new student accommodation.

Property is dominated by conversion flats – this is one of the largest private rented sectors in London – and you'll need to venture up Shepherd's Bush Road to leafy Brook Green and Blythe Village for converted family homes, along with medium-sized Victorian houses and modern luxury apartment blocks.

Olympia Exhibition Centre on the border with Kensington & Chelsea hosts a variety of trade shows; locals tend to resent it for the traffic it creates. The extension of the London Overground train link from Shepherd's Bush down to Clapham Junction is a boon, though residents and businesses were angered when the District line service at Kensington (Olympia) was downgraded to weekends only. In general, the area's transport is a plus, especially the fast links

The changing face of Shepherd's Bush, **Westfield**. See p154.

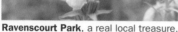
Ravenscourt Park, a real local treasure.

(by road and tube) to Heathrow airport – hence the presence of such multinational companies as Coca-Cola, L'Oréal, Sony Ericsson and Disney.

Brackenbury Village and Ravenscourt Park

This area – bounded by Goldhawk Road to the west and north, King Street to the south and Hammersmith Grove to the east – is an island of middle-class calm in a sea of urban through-traffic. It feels quite distinct from surrounding Hammersmith and Shepherd's Bush. Appealing Ravenscourt Park, a much-needed open space in a very built-up part of the capital, adds to the community feel. Come Guy Fawkes Night, it offers the best fireworks display in west London, and the brilliant Carter's Steam Fair is an annual visitor.

Minimal traffic and one of London's best state primary schools (John Betts) make the area enormously popular with young families, as do the rows of pretty terraced cottages that dominate the area (although prices are pushing many prospective villagers further west to Acton in search of familial space). Wingate Road is probably the area's most desirable address, with its pastel-coloured houses going for well over £1.5 million. Such assets, combined with

clever estate agent marketing (the 'Village' is a recent addition to Brackenbury), also draw BBC staff eager for a quick commute to White City – local celebs include Jeremy Vine and John Humphrys.

Cathnor Park and Wendell Park

This wedge-shaped area west of Shepherd's Bush is hemmed in by two major arteries – Goldhawk Road to the south and Uxbridge Road to the north. It leans towards the ethnic diversity of Shepherd's Bush, with a thriving Muslim community, plus Brackenbury exiles who move across the Goldhawk Road divide in search of extra bedrooms when their bijou cottages fill up.

Uxbridge Road is a wonderfully spicy mix, boasting everything from 24-hour grocers to ethnic restaurants, internet cafés and pound shops, plus quirky music venue Bush Hall, which has spent the last 100 years variously as a dance hall, a soup kitchen, a bingo hall and a snooker den. Goldhawk Road, meanwhile, is torn between two worlds, simultaneously hosting smart bar-restaurants and old-style greasy caffs and Subway franchises.

During the day, smallish Wendell Park can make an adequate setting for a sit or a stroll, but it is beset by its reputation as a hangout for the area's troublemaker teens.

West Kensington and Barons Court

West Ken is the part of Kensington that fashionistas ignore; the name might sound posh to outsiders, but most residents know this is the wrong side of the tracks. The area sits awkwardly between the sprawling concrete of Hammersmith to the west and well-heeled Kensington & Chelsea to the east, with the thundering Talgarth Road (aka the A4) slicing through its centre, notable solely for a row of stunning Grade II-listed artists' studios built in the 1890s. The long spine of the North End Road – pebble-dashed with kebab shops, minimarts and a lively street market – cuts through from Olympia Exhibition Centre in the north to Fulham Broadway in the south.

The district is primarily residential, consisting mainly of Victorian terraces, plus newer apartment blocks. Properties become larger and smarter the nearer you get to Barons Court, which is also home to the Queen's Club, one of the capital's most exclusive tennis clubs. Transport is a strong point, with easy access to the A4 and three tube stations: Barons Court to the west, West Kensington in the centre, and Kensington (Olympia) to the north.

Fulham

Leafy Fulham has changed radically since the 1960s. The former Labour stronghold's tightly packed terraces, once home to working-class families employed in the heavy industry that dominated the riverside, are now full of young, affluent professionals. The population is much less diverse than in Hammersmith next door: there's truth to the clichéd image of private-school-educated, Porsche-driving young men who work in the City and their blonde-bobbed spouses. Yet the area is just as popular with families, thanks to relatively crime-free streets and an abundance of private nurseries and prep schools.

Originally a market garden area, its architecture is largely Victorian, offering row upon row of neat terraced houses and converted flats. Gardens tend to be tiny (a drawback for families), except for the 'alphabet' streets between Fulham Palace Road and the river. Middle-class needs are met by a range of exclusive boutiques, antiques shops, gyms, upmarket bars and restaurants – many clustered along Fulham Road, the main retail street. Two major bugbears are a lack of parking spaces (mainly controlled by resident parking permits) and traffic congestion. Public transport can also be a problem. There is no overground rail service, and the nearest tubes (Putney Bridge, Parsons Green and Fulham Broadway) are all a bit of a hike.

The only green area of any size is hugely popular Bishops Park. Bordering the river, and with views across to Putney, it includes some much-used tennis courts, an ornamental park, and Grade I-listed Fulham Palace museum (the summer home of the Bishops of London from around 700 until 1973) with its adjacent allotments. The Drawing Room café, which spills from the ground floor of the palace on to walled lawns, is popular with well-heeled local mums, as are the playground and paddling pool in the park itself. The annual fireworks display is always packed. A major revamp of the park was completed in 2012.

Next door is Craven Cottage, home of Fulham Football Club since 1896 and still a charmingly old-fashioned ground.

Parsons Green and Fulham Broadway

Avenues lined with stately plane trees give Parsons Green a villagey air. Complete with its own (eponymous) green, a church and the perennially popular White Horse pub, it is slightly more affordable than

Highs & Lows

Westfield London An upmarket mega-mall in the middle of the Bush: what more could W12's ex-Notting Hillbillies want?
Ravenscourt Park Playgrounds, paddling pools, sports pitches and urban peace and quiet – a rare treat in this corner of west London.
Culture club Music and theatre fans are in heaven, thanks to the Apollo, Empire, Lyric, Bush Theatre, Bush Hall and Riverside Studios.

Westfield London With 250 shops, 50 restaurants, thousands of parking spaces and no C-charge, traffic here can only get worse.
King Street Hammersmith's main shopping drag is still grotty and unappealing, with too many bookies and charity shops.
Shepherd's Bush Green There are few less appealing expanses of green in the capital. Despite promises, it's long overdue a clean-up.

neighbouring Chelsea. Eel Brook Common, offering children's play areas, tennis courts, football-cum-netball pitches and dog-free grass sections, is a big draw for families.

The streets north-east of Parsons Green are noticeably busier but also highly desirable. Fulham Broadway itself is a thriving shopping area, with all the standard high-street names, supermarkets, pubs, restaurants and the shiny Fulham Broadway Centre atop the tube station. It has assorted chain shops and eateries, plus a nine-screen cinema complex and a David Lloyd fitness club. Next door is Stamford Bridge, Chelsea FC's ground: congestion on match days is a major downer.

Peterborough Estate and Hurlingham

Lying south of the New Kings Road, this area is a tale of two estates. One is the exclusive Peterborough Estate, built in the 19th century for local workers. Conversions, extensions and increasing gentrification due to the Chelsea overspill have combined to make these elaborately detailed red-brick houses highly sought after (especially the original 500 'Lion' houses, so-named because of their miniature rooftop stone lions). Nearby is the Sullivan Estate – an area known for 'hoodie' street-gang kids and petty crime. The clash can be an uncomfortable one.

Catering to the richest residents is the exclusive Hurlingham Club, located at 18th-century Hurlingham House. Best described as a country mansion (site of many a glittering party), it sits in 42 acres of riverside grounds, which cater for tennis, croquet, cricket, bowls, golf, squash and swimming. Arrivistes, beware – there is currently an eight-year waiting list for membership. Nearby is a smaller green space, South Park (open to all). Both the New Kings Road and more affordable Wandsworth Bridge Road cover the retail side of life. As for transport, Putney Bridge tube and slow buses service the area.

Sand's End and Imperial Wharf

In the south-east corner of the borough and previously seen as Fulham's poor relation, Sand's End is in a state of flux. The fortress-like Imperial Wharf – a dramatic, if rather soulless, residential complex featuring soaring glass towers, a ten-acre park and stunning riverside views – has given the area an aura of glamour that has local estate agents drooling. Transport links have improved substantially with the opening of Imperial Wharf station on the London Overground train line – it's less than ten minutes to Clapham Junction. Moving inland from the river sees a mix of more affordable public and private housing, with facilities for those on lower incomes, such as the Sand's End Community Centre. Wandsworth Bridge Road is the main shopping street, containing upmarket pine furniture and antiques shops, cosy cafés and one of the best butcher's in town (Randalls). Plus, naturally, a slew of estate agents touting for business.

MEDITTERNEAN VOLU-VENT WITH GRILLED HALLOUMI CHEESE 10.00
GNOCCHI WITH BABY PLUM TOMATO + BASIL PESTO
PUF ... ? SEE OUR DESSERT MENU

Uxbridge Road gastropub, the **Queen Adelaide**.

Restaurants & cafés

The variety of places to eat around Shepherd's Bush owes much to its racially mixed population and increasing number of upwardly mobile residents. The neighbourhood has a particular forte in modest ethnic eateries, ranging from Syrian (low-budget, high-quality Abu Zaad) to South-east Asian (unassuming Thai Esarn Kheaw), via Eritrean/Ethiopian (Red Sea), East European (Polish old-timer Patio and newcomer Tatra) and Greek-Cypriot (Vine Leaves). Blah Blah Blah is a well-established veggie haven, while the refurbished Queen Adelaide brings gastro flair to the Uxbridge Road. Westfield shopping centre has brought a slew of chain eateries, including Byron (burgers), Busaba Eathai (Thai), Pho (Vietnamese) and Wahaca (Mexican).

Options near Ravenscourt Park include long-running gastropub the Anglesea Arms, popular Tunisian eaterie Adam's Café and a branch of traiteur Fait Maison (it also runs the café in the park itself).

Travelling south on Shepherd's Bush Road towards Hammersmith, you'll find homely Polish cooking at Malina, sustainable fish and chips at Kerbisher & Malt, deli-café Brook's Counter & Table, and long-running tapas restaurant Los Molinos. In Hammersmith itself, the River Café makes good use of a curvaceous stretch of the Thames; nearby is tiny,

fabulously kitsch, Lebanese caff Mes Amis, while close behind in the fame stakes is excellent vegetarian restaurant the Gate.

At a less exalted level, King Street has long been known for its Polish and Indian restaurants. You'll get the whole East European experience within the concrete block of the Lowiczanka Polish Cultural Centre. As for the South Asian contenders, the best choices are low-priced Sagar (South Indian vegetarian), no-frills Shilpa (Keralan) and vibrant Potli (pan-Indian). Other options include Saigon Saigon (Vietnamese), Tosa (Japanese) and fabulously authentic Iranian restaurant Mahdi. Hammersmith Grove has a branch of Mediterranean brasserie Raoul's, with a deli-café next door.

West Kensington is a good place to look for cheap eats, the market street North End Road being well provided with takeaways (best is Turkish Best Mangal). On the same street is self-explanatory 222 Veggie Vegan. At West Ken's northern boundary is Olympia, where you'll find some great curries at Miran Masala, plus the pared-down Popeseye Steak House, strictly for meat-lovers. The Havelock Tavern and Cumberland Arms gastropubs are neighbourly operations with well-priced menus and a genial air.

Fulham's restaurants mainly cater to the area's young professionals. Off towards Fulham Broadway, My Dining Room is a welcoming French bar-restaurant, while the Harwood Arms, although looking like an ordinary gastropub, offers very superior

British fare, plus a superb wine list and great real ales – booking is essential. Around Fulham Broadway, Blue Elephant (Thai) and pizzeria Napulé are recommended, while further west is British eaterie Manson and Thai restaurant Sukho.

Abu Zaad *29 Uxbridge Road, W12 8LH (8749 5107, www.abuzaad.co.uk).*
Adam's Café *77 Askew Road, W12 9AH (8743 0572, www.adamscafe.co.uk).*
Anglesea Arms *35 Wingate Road, W6 0UR (8749 1291, www.capitalpubcompany.com).*
Best Mangal *104 North End Road, W14 9EX (7610 1050, www.bestmangal.com).*
Blah Blah Blah *78 Goldhawk Road, W12 8HA (8746 1337).*
Blue Elephant *4-6 Fulham Broadway, SW6 1AA (7385 6595, www.blueelephant.com).*
Cumberland Arms *29 North End Road, W14 8SZ (7371 6806, www.thecumberland armspub.co.uk).*
Esarn Kheaw *314 Uxbridge Road, W12 7LJ (8743 8930, www.esarnkheaw.com).*
Fait Maison *www.fait-maison.co.uk; 245 Goldhawk Road, W12 8EU (8222 8755); Tea House, Ravenscourt Park, W6 0UL (8563 9291).*
Gate *51 Queen Caroline Street, W6 9QL (8748 6932, www.thegaterestaurants.com).*
Harwood Arms *Corner of Walham Grove & Farm Lane, SW6 1QP (7386 1847, www. harwoodarms.com).*

TRANSPORT

Tube stations *Central* Shepherd's Bush, White City, East Acton; *District* Kensington (Olympia); West Kensington, Barons Court, Hammersmith, Ravenscourt Park; West Brompton, Fulham Broadway, Parsons Green, Putney Bridge; *Circle, Hammersmith & City* Wood Lane, Shepherd's Bush Market, Goldhawk Road, Hammersmith; *Piccadilly* Barons Court, Hammersmith
Rail stations London Overground, *Southern* Willesden Junction, Shepherd's Bush, Kensington (Olympia), West Brompton, Imperial Wharf
Main bus routes *into central London* 7, 9, 10, 11, 14, 22, 27, 74, 94, 148, 211, 414; *night buses* N7, N9, N10, N11, N22, N28, N74, N97, N207; *24-hour buses* 14, 27, 94, 148

Havelock Tavern *57 Masbro Road, W14 0LS (7603 5374, www.thehavelocktavern.co.uk).*
Kerbisher & Malt *164 Shepherd's Bush Road, W6 7PB (3556 0228, www.kerbisher.co.uk).*
Lowiczanka Polish Cultural Centre *1st floor, 238-246 King Street, W6 0RF (8741 3225, www.lowiczankarestaurant.co.uk).*
Mahdi *217 King Street, W6 9JT (8563 7007).*
Malina *166 Shepherd's Bush Road, W6 7PB (7603 8881, www.malinarestaurant.com).*
Manson *676 Fulham Road, SW6 5SA (7384 9559, www.mansonrestaurant.co.uk).*
Mes Amis *1 Rainville Road, W6 9HA (7385 5155).*
Miran Masala *3 Hammersmith Road, W14 8XJ (7602 4555, www.miranmasala.com).*
Los Molinos *127 Shepherd's Bush Road, W6 7LP (7603 2229, www.losmolinosuk.com).*
My Dining Room *18 Farm Lane, SW6 1PP (7381 3331, www.mydiningroom.net).*
Napulé *585 Fulham Road, SW6 5UA (7381 1122, www.madeinitalygroup.co.uk).*
Patio *5 Goldhawk Road, W12 8QQ (8743 5194, www.patiolondon.com).*
Popeseye Steak House *108 Blythe Road, W14 0HD (7610 4578, www.popeseye.com).*
Potli *319 King Street, W6 9NH (8741 4328, www.potli.co.uk).*
Queen Adelaide *412 Uxbridge Road, W12 0NR (8746 2573, www.thequeenadelaide w12.co.uk).*
Raoul's *113 Hammersmith Grove, W6 0NQ (8741 3692, www.raoulsgourmet.com).*
Red Sea *382 Uxbridge Road, W12 7LL (8749 6888).*
River Café *Thames Wharf, Rainville Road, W6 9HA (7386 4200, www.rivercafe.co.uk).*
Sagar *157 King Street, W6 9JT (8741 8563, www.sagarveg.co.uk).*
Saigon Saigon *313-317 King Street, W6 9NH (8748 6887, www.saigon-saigon.co.uk).*
Shilpa *206 King Street, W6 0RA (8741 3127, www.shilparestaurant.co.uk).*
Sukho *855 Fulham Road, SW6 5HJ (7371 7600, www.sukhogroups.com).*
Tatra *24 Goldhawk Road, W12 8DH (8749 8193, www.tatrarestaurant.co.uk).*
Tosa *332 King Street, W6 0RR (8748 0002, www.tosauk.com).*
222 Veggie Vegan *222 North End Road, W14 9NU (7381 2322, www.222veggievegan.com).*
Vine Leaves Taverna *71 Uxbridge Road, W12 8NR (8749 0325, www.vineleaves taverna.co.uk).*

Hammersmith & Fulham

Bars & pubs

Shepherd's Bush's inexorable push upmarket is not yet reflected in the area's pubs, which remain a fairly insalubrious collection. Venues such as the Defector's Weld, with its smart pub, 'snug' cocktail bar and unobtrusive DJ sounds, bucks the trend, as does the Queen Adelaide gastropub (*see left*), further west along the Uxbridge Road. On the other side of Goldhawk Road is top gastropub the Anglesea Arms (*see left*), while the Thatched House is a relaxed local with more standard pub food. Nestled on a quiet residential road near Brook Green is the long-running Havelock Tavern, one of the first pubs in the neighbourhood to go gastro. Fans of Young's beers can try the modern-looking Brook Green Hotel, on the main road.

The cluster of pubs on the western side of Hammersmith Bridge includes the Old Ship, with its happy marriage of Thames views and outside space, and the 17th-century Dove. Both serve Fuller's beers, and are prime spots for watching the Boat Race in spring. The ornate Salutation, also a Fuller's pub, is the best of King Street's dismal choice of hostelries (it's got a garden too). Just to the north are the Stonemasons Arms, one of the original gastro brigade, and the Dartmouth Castle, with guest ales and a great front patio.

Even though Fulham covers such a large area, from the riverside to the busy lower stretches of the King's and Fulham roads, there's not a great deal to shout about,

though the Crabtree, next to Fulham FC's ground and part of the Realpubs empire, is a welcome addition. Its large riverside terrace is rammed in good weather.

In Parsons Green, well-heeled locals hang out at the White Horse, one of London's finest ale pubs. Aragon House on New Kings Road is a fine neo-Georgian boozer with an ivy-clad exterior and a lovely garden. Just east of the borough, on the far side of Fulham Broadway tube and near Chelsea's football ground, are the King's Arms (part of the ever-expanding Geronimo chain) and – endearingly untouched by modern drinking or design trends – the unpretentious little Fox & Pheasant.

Aragon House *247 New Kings Road, SW6 4XG (7731 7313, www.aragonhouse.net).*
Brook Green Hotel *170 Shepherd's Bush Road, W6 7PB (7603 2516, www.brookgreen hotel.co.uk).*
Crabtree *Rainville Road, W6 9HA (7385 3929, www.thecrabtreew6.co.uk).*
Dartmouth Castle *26 Glenthorne Road, W6 0LS (8748 3614, www.thedartmouthcastle.co.uk).*
Defector's Weld *170 Uxbridge Road, W12 8AA (8749 0008, http://defectors-weld.com).*
Dove *19 Upper Mall, W6 9TA (8748 9474, www.fullers.co.uk).*
Fox & Pheasant *1 Billing Road, SW10 9UJ (7352 2943).*
King's Arms *190 Fulham Road, SW10 9PN (7351 5043, www.kingsarmschelsea.co.uk).*
Old Ship *25 Upper Mall, W6 9TD (8748 2593, www.oldshipw6.co.uk).*
Salutation *154 King Street, W6 0QU (8748 3668).*

Hammersmith & Fulham

The maritime-themed **Old Ship**, in prime position by the Thames.

Stonemasons Arms *54 Cambridge Grove, W6 0LA (8748 1397, www.stonemasons-arms.co.uk).*
Thatched House *115 Dalling Road, W6 0ET (8748 6174, www.thatchedhouse.com).*
White Horse *1-3 Parsons Green, SW6 4UL (7736 2115, www.whitehorsesw6.com).*

Shops

The arrival of shiny mega-mall Westfield London has transformed west London's shopping scene. A vast structure, stretching from the top of Shepherd's Bush Green up to White City, it dominates the immediate skyline. Within – a much brighter, airier experience than most malls – you'll find more than 250 shops, including large branches of Debenhams, House of Fraser and M&S as well as all the usual high-street names, from Accessorize to Zara. Unusually, there's a special luxury section, the Village, devoted to the likes of Louis Vuitton, Prada and Tiffany & Co.

At the other end of the retail spectrum is the area's celebrated sell-'em-cheap bazaar. Running between Uxbridge and Goldhawk Roads, Shepherd's Bush Market offers an intriguing mix of just about everything you can think of, from fruit and veg and fabrics to reggae music and wedding gowns. There is also an impressive array of food shops on Uxbridge Road, including global supermarket Al-Abbas, and a branch of acclaimed butcher the Ginger Pig on Askew Road. The West 12 mall on the south side of the Green with its basic is looking rather neglected these days, though the Vue multiscreen is a useful asset.

The West 12 mall on the north side of the Green has had a makeover and, so far, has managed to survive the arrival of Westfield.

The small Kings Mall shopping precinct in Hammersmith contains an always crowded Primark, and there are a few more chains at the Broadway mall in the centre of the tube/bus station complex. King Street is uninspiring, though healthy ingredients can be found at Soil Association-registered Bushwacker Wholefoods.

Residents of Hammersmith, West Kensington and Fulham converge to stock up on comestibles at the North End Road street market; it's also worth seeking out Polish deli Prima a few streets north. Unsurprisingly, affluent Fulham has the lion's share of browse-worthy shops, in addition to the Sainsbury's and workaday chains of the Fulham Broadway Centre. Excellent specialist Pure Massage is a serene minimalist sanctuary. Union Market, occupying what was the ticket hall of Fulham Broadway station, has counters selling cheese, meat, fish, wine, deli goods and other produce, and a restaurant.

The stretch of the Fulham Road near Parsons Green has enough upmarket chains (Cologne & Cotton, Cath Kidston) and interesting one-offs (Nomad Books) to occupy the locals on a Saturday afternoon. Men can get fitted out in relaxed, Italian tailoring at Palmer. Towards the river on Fulham High Street is a brace of fine vintage shops: Circa, which specialises in glamorous dresses, and Old Hat, where cash-strapped dandies can pick up a (previously worn) Savile Row suit. On the food front, there's a trio of upmarket delis in the general locality – Elizabeth King, Megan's and Moroccan/Middle Eastern Del'Aziz (next to Aziz restaurant) – plus excellent butcher Randalls.

Catering to the numerous nesters, this end of the King's Road and Wandsworth Bridge Road is known for smart furniture and interiors shops and, increasingly, 20th-century design – Talisman occupies a beautifully restored art deco building, while Core One, a varied group of dealers, has colonised the old gas works in Sand's End.

Lillie Road isn't quite the antiques enclave it used to be, but some unusual shops remain, including Andrew Bewick and Stephen Sprake.

Men's vintage specialist **Old Hat**.

Locals' Tips

Calling all film buffs! Riverside Studios is one of the last arthouse rep cinemas in London. It shows a different double bill almost every night, as well as special seasons devoted to particular directors, countries or movements. **Hop on the Duck Bus (no.283) and head over Hammersmith Bridge for a day at the London Wetland Centre in Barnes, a huge slice of rural tranquility just a flutter away from the chaos of King Street.** Switch off the television set and take a tour round the studios instead. The BBC (www.bbc.co.uk/showsandtours) organises 90-minute tours of Television Centre, during which you can visit BBC News and loosen up in the interactive studio. Lights, camera...

Al-Abbas *258-262 Uxbridge Road, W12 7JA (8740 1932).*

Andrew Bewick *287 Lillie Road, SW6 7LL (7385 9025).*

Broadway Shopping Centre *The Broadway, W6 9YE (8563 0131, www.hammersmith broadway.co.uk).*

Brook's Counter & Table *140 Shepherd's Bush Road, W6 7PB (7602 0664, www.counter andtable.com).*

Bushwacker Wholefoods *132 King Street, W6 0QU (8748 2061).*

Cath Kidston *668 Fulham Road, SW6 5RX (7731 6531, www.cathkidston.co.uk).*

Circa Vintage Clothes *64 Fulham High Street, SW6 3LQ (7736 5038, www.circavintage.com).*

Cologne & Cotton *791 Fulham Road, SW6 5HD (7736 9261, www.cologneandcotton.com).*

Core One *The Gasworks, 2 Michael Road, SW6 2AD (7731 7171, www.coreoneantiques.com).*

Del'Aziz *24-32 Vanston Place, SW6 1AX (7386 0086, www.delaziz.co.uk).*

Elizabeth King *32-34 New Kings Road, SW6 4ST (7736 2826, www.elizabethking.com).*

Fulham Broadway Centre *Fulham Road, SW6 1BW (7385 6965, www.fulhambroadway.co.uk).*

Ginger Pig *137-139 Askew Road, W12 9AU (8740 4297, www.thegingerpig.co.uk).*

Kings Mall Shopping Centre *King Street, W6 0PZ (8741 2121, www.kings-mall.co.uk).*

Megan's Delicatessen *571 King's Road, SW6 2EB (7371 7837, www.megansrestaurant. com).*

Nomad Books *781 Fulham Road, SW6 5HA (7736 4000, www.nomadbooks.co.uk).*

Old Hat *66 Fulham High Street, SW6 3LQ (7610 6558).*

Palmer *771 Fulham Road, SW6 5HA (7384 2044).*

Prima Delicatessen *192 North End Road, W14 9NX (7385 2070).*

Pure Massage *3-5 Vanston Place, SW6 1AY (7381 8100, www.puremassage.com).*

Randalls Butchers *113 Wandsworth Bridge Road, SW6 2TE (7736 3426).*

Shepherd's Bush Market *East side of the railway viaduct, off Goldhawk Road, W12 (www.shepherdsbushmarket.co.uk).*

Stephen Sprake *283 Lillie Road, SW6 7LL (7381 3209, www.stephensprake.com).*

Talisman *79-91 New Kings Road, SW6 4SQ (7731 4686, www.talismanlondon.com).*

Union Market *472 Fulham Road, SW6 1BY (7386 2470, www.unionmarket.co.uk).*

Westfield London *Ariel Way, W12 7SL (http://uk.westfield.com/london).*

West 12 Centre *The Broadway, W12 8PP (8746 0038, www.west12online.com).*

Arts & attractions

Cinemas & theatres

Bush Theatre *7 Uxbridge Road, W12 8LJ (8743 3584, www.bushtheatre.co.uk). Moved in 2011 from its long-running home on Shepherd's Bush Green to the former Passmore Edwards Library, round the corner on Uxbridge Road.*

Cineworld Hammersmith *207 King Street, W6 9JT (0871 200 2000, www.cineworld.co.uk).*

Lyric Hammersmith *Lyric Square, King Street, W6 0QL (0871 221 1729, www.lyric. co.uk). Excellent local theatre.*

Riverside Studios *Crisp Road, W6 9RL (8237 1111, www.riversidestudios.co.uk). Performance arts plus repertory cinema.*

Vue *0871 224 0240, www.myvue.com; Fulham Broadway Centre, Fulham Road, SW6 1BW; West 12 Centre, Shepherd's Bush Green, W12 8PP.*

Galleries & museums

Fulham Palace *Bishop's Avenue, SW6 6EA (7736 8140, www.fulhampalace.org). Museum, gallery, gardens – and a fine café.*

Kelmscott House *26 Upper Mall, W6 9TA (8741 3735, www.morrissociety.org). William Morris's 1878-96 home is a private house, but the basement and coach house are open to the public on Thursday and Saturday afternoons.*

Hammersmith & Fulham

Music & comedy venues

Bush Hall *310 Uxbridge Road, W12 7LJ (8222 6955, www.bushhallmusic.co.uk). Chamber concerts and low-key rock shows.*
HMV Apollo *Queen Caroline Street, W6 9QH (8563 3800, www.livenation.co.uk). Powerhouse music venue with a 5,000 capacity.*
O2 Shepherd's Bush Empire *Shepherd's Bush Green, W12 8TT (0844 477 2000, www.o2shepherdsbushempire.co.uk). Great mid-sized music venue.*

Sport & fitness

The newish Phoenix Fitness Centre & Janet Adegoke Swimming Pool added a much-needed public facility to the borough; the only other public swimming option is Virgin Active's Fulham Pools. In general, the best fitness facilities are private.

The borough is home to three football clubs – Chelsea, Fulham and QPR – as well as the prestigious Queen's tennis club, which hosts the Aegon Championships (an annual, men-only precursor to Wimbledon).

Gyms & leisure centres

Charing Cross Sports Club *Aspenlea Road, W6 8LH (8741 3654, www.ccsclub.co.uk). Private.*
David Lloyd *Unit 24, Fulham Broadway Retail Centre, Fulham Road, SW6 1BW (7386 2202, www.davidlloydleisure.co.uk). Private.*
Fitness First *www.fitnessfirst.co.uk; West 12 Centre, W12 8PP (0844 571 2931); 26-28 Hammersmith Grove, W6 7HA (0844 571 2870). Private.*
Hammersmith Fitness & Squash Centre *Chalk Hill Road, W6 8DW (8741 8028, www.gll.org).*
Lillie Road Fitness Centre *Lillie Road, SW6 7PH (7381 2183, www.gll.org).*
Phoenix Fitness Centre & Janet Adegoke Swimming Pool *Bloemfontein Road, W12 0RQ (8735 4900, www.gll.org).*
Thirtysevendegrees *10 Beaconsfield Terrace Road, W14 0PP (7610 4090, www.thirtyseven degrees.co.uk). Private.*
Virgin Active *www.virginactive.co.uk; Normand Park, Lillie Road, SW6 7ST (0845 270 9124); 181 Hammersmith Road, W6 8BS (0845 270 4083); 188A Fulham Road, SW10 9PN (0845 270 4085). Private.*

Other facilities

Hurlingham Club *Ranelagh Gardens, SW6 3PR (7610 7400, www.hurlinghamclub.org.uk).*

Private members' club with a long history, and even longer waiting list for new members.
Linford Christie Outdoor Sports Centre *Artillery Way, off Du Cane Road, W12 0DF (07908 788739, www.lbhf.gov.uk).*
Queen's Club *Palliser Road, W14 9EQ (7386 3400, www.queensclub.co.uk). Upmarket private tennis club.*

Spectator sports

Chelsea FC *Stamford Bridge, Fulham Road, SW6 1HS (0871 984 1905, www.chelseafc.com).*
Fulham FC *Craven Cottage, Stevenage Road, SW6 6HH (0843 208 1234, www.fulhamfc.com).*
Queen's Park Rangers FC *Loftus Road Stadium, South Africa Road, W12 7PA (0844 477 7007, www.qpr.co.uk).*

Schools

Primary

There are 35 state primary schools in Hammersmith & Fulham, including 12 church schools. There are also 12 independent primaries, including one Muslim school, one French school, one theatre school and one Montessori school. See www.lbhf.gov.uk, www.edubase.gov.uk and www.ofsted.gov.uk for more information.

Secondary

Burlington Danes Academy *Wood Lane, W12 0HR (8735 4950, www.burlington danes.org).*
Fulham Cross *Munster Road, SW6 6BP (7381 0861, www.fulhamcross.lbhf.sch.uk). Girls only.*
Godolphin & Latymer School *Iffley Road, W6 0PG (8741 1936, www.godolphinand latymer.com). Girls only; private.*
Henry Compton School *Kingwood Road, SW6 6SN (7381 3606, www.henrycompton.net). Boys only.*
Hurlingham & Chelsea School *Peterborough Road, SW6 3ED (7731 2581, www.hurlinghamandchelseaschool.com).*
Lady Margaret School *Parsons Green, SW6 4UN (7736 7138, www.ladymargaret. lbhf.sch.uk). Church of England; girls only.*
London Oratory School *Seagrave Road, SW6 1RX (7385 0102, www.london-oratory.org). Roman Catholic; boys only; mixed sixth form.*
Phoenix High School *The Curve, W12 0RQ (8749 1141, www.phoenixhighschool.org).*
Sacred Heart High School *212 Hammersmith Road, W6 7DG (8748 7600, www.sacredhearthighschoolhammersmith.org.uk). Roman Catholic; girls only.*

St Paul's Girls' School *Brook Green, W6 7BS (7603 2288, www.spgs.org). Girls only; private.*
West London Free School *Cambridge Grove, W6 0LB (8600 0670, www.westlondonfree school.co.uk).*
William Morris Sixth Form *St Dunstan's Road, W6 8RB (8748 6969, www.wma.ac.uk).*

Property

WHAT THE AGENTS SAY:

'The area bordering Fulham known as the Crabtree Estate is really on the up at the moment – it's popular with families looking for Edwardian homes, as well as first-time buyers. You won't pay as much as you would to live in Fulham, but you're near the river, and only a short bus ride from Fulham Broadway and half a mile from Hammersmith. Supermarkets such as Waitrose are starting to cotton on that this is an upcoming area. House prices are increasing, but it's still affordable. It's not the same postcode as Fulham – SW6 – but it is W6.'

Massimo Malavasi, Sebastian Estates, Fulham

Average property prices
Detached £1,215,471
Semi-detached £1,003,722
Terraced £807,173
Flat £411,678

Local estate agents
Black Katz *24 Shepherd's Bush Road, W6 7PJ (7371 2333, www.blackkatz.com).*
Chard *www.chard.co.uk; 2 offices in the borough (Brook Green 7603 1415, Fulham 7731 5115).*
Douglas & Gordon *www.douglasandgordon. com; 2 offices in the borough (Hammersmith 8563 7100, Parsons Green 7731 4391).*
Faron Sutaria *www.faronsutaria.co.uk; 2 offices in the borough (Fulham 7610 2080, Shepherd's Bush 8740 7766).*
Lawsons & Daughters *68 Fulham Palace Road, W6 9PL (8563 0202, www.lawsonsand daughters.com).*
Marsh & Parsons *www.marshandparsons. co.uk; 2 offices in the borough (Brook Green 7605 7760, Fulham 7736 9822).*
Ravenscourt Residential *3 Seven Stars Corner, Paddenswick Road, W12 8ET (8740 5678, www.ravenscourtresidential.co.uk).*
Sebastian Estates *190 Fulham Palace Road, W6 9PA (7381 4998, www.sebastian estates.co.uk).*

COUNCIL TAX

A	up to £40,000	£747.74
B	£40,001-£52,000	£872.35
C	£52,001-£68,000	£996.98
D	£68,001-£88,000	£1,121.60
E	£88,001-£120,000	£1,370.85
F	£120,001-£160,000	£1,620.09
G	£160,001-£320,000	£1,869.34
H	over £320,000	£2,243.20

RECYCLING
Household waste recycled & composted 27%
Main recycling centre Western Riverside Waste Authority, Smugglers Way, Wandsworth, SW18 1JS (8871 2788, www.wrwa.gov.uk)
Other recycling services home composting; fridge and freezer collection
Council contact Environmental Services Department, Hammersmith Town Hall, King Street, W6 9JU (8753 1100)

Other information

Council
London Borough of Hammersmith & Fulham Council *8748 3020, www.lbhf.gov.uk; Hammersmith Town Hall, King Street, W6 9JU; Fulham Town Hall, Fulham Broadway, SW6 1ET.*

Legal services
Hammersmith & Fulham CAB *The Pavilion, 1 Mund Street, W14 9LY (0845 458 2515, www.hfcab.org.uk).*

Local information
www.fulhamsociety.org.
www.fulhamsw6.com.
www.hammersmithtoday.co.uk.
www.londonlocals.co.uk.
www.shepherdsbushw12.com.
www.w14london.ning.com.

Open spaces & allotments
Fulham Palace Meadow Allotments Association *c/o Fulham Palace, Bishop's Avenue, SW6 6EA (www.fulham-allotments.org).*
Open spaces *www.lbhf.gov.uk; www.scrubs-online.org.uk.*

'What a place to live! My backyard is the most famous botanic garden in the world. Elsewhere are endless parklands, sumptuous restaurants – and I can even get coffee from an Australian-trained barista.'

Tim Entwisle, Director of Conservation, Living Collections & Estates, Kew Gardens

Richmond upon Thames

Richmond is the only London borough that straddles both sides of the Thames, and its gorgeous riverside location, spacious parks and commons – it's also the capital's greenest borough – abundance of private schools and attractive housing make it a magnet for the affluent. Only the relentless air traffic in and out of Heathrow spoils this sylvan scene.

Neighbourhoods

Barnes, Mortlake and Sheen

Barnes lives up to its semi-rural, villagey reputation. At its centre is a large duck pond and adjoining green (site of a popular annual midsummer fair), surrounded by a mix of independent shops, pubs and restaurants. To the south is the buffer zone of wild and wooded Barnes Common, while the London Wetland Centre (an expansive bird reserve converted from defunct reservoirs) sits to the east of Castelnau, the long spine that leads to Hammersmith Bridge. And enclosing it all is a sharp loop of the Thames, offering riverside walks and rowers aplenty – the Oxford and Cambridge boat crews race this stretch each year, finishing at Mortlake.

Combine such attractions with some of London's best private schools, the proximity of Hammersmith (and its tube station) just over the bridge, and a regular service to Waterloo from Barnes and Barnes Bridge stations, and it's clear why affluent families and retirees love the area so much. Consequently, property prices – there are

Richmond upon Thames

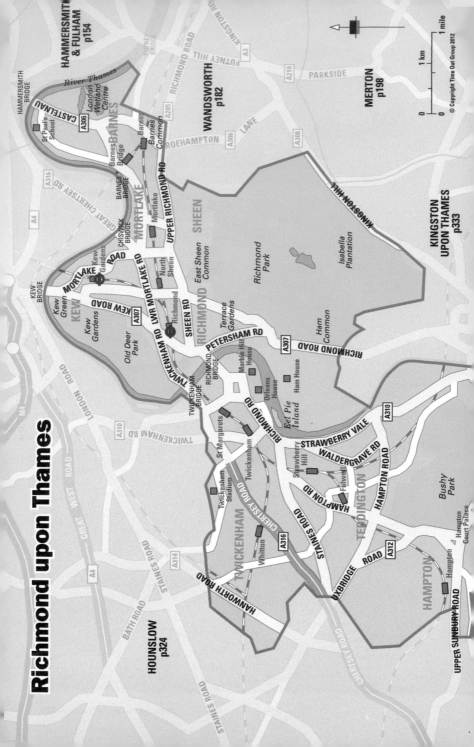

HAMMERSMITH & FULHAM p154

WANDSWORTH p182

MERTON p198

KINGSTON UPON THAMES p333

HOUNSLOW p324

River Thames

HAMMERSMITH BRIDGE

PUTNEY BRIDGE

PUTNEY HILL

PARKSIDE

London Wetland Centre

St Paul's School

CASTLENAU

A306

BARNES

Barnes Bridge

Barnes Common

ROEHAMPTON

LANE

KEW BRIDGE

GREAT CHERTSEY RD

A4

BARNES BRIDGE

CHISWICK BRIDGE

MORTLAKE

UPPER RICHMOND RD

Kew Green

KEW

KEW ROAD

Kew Gardens

Old Deer Park

Mortlake

LWR MORTLAKE RD

North Sheen

East Sheen Common

SHEEN

SHEEN RD

RICHMOND

Richmond Park

Isabella Plantation

KINGSTON HILL

TWICKENHAM RD

Terrace Gardens

PETERSHAM RD

RICHMOND ROAD

A307

Ham Common

RICHMOND BRIDGE

TWICKENHAM BRIDGE

Marble Hill House

Orleans House

Ham House

St Margarets

Twickenham

RICHMOND RD

Eel Pie Island

STRAWBERRY VALE

A310

WALDERGRAVE RD

TWICKENHAM RD

A310

TWICKENHAM

Twickenham Stadium

CHERTSEY ROAD

STAINES ROAD

Strawberry Hill

Fulwell

HAMPTON RD

TEDDINGTON

HAMPTON ROAD

Bushy Park

Whitton

A316

UXBRIDGE ROAD

A312

HANWORTH ROAD

Hampton

HAMPTON

Hampton Court Palace

UPPER SUNBURY ROAD

CHERTSEY ROAD

STAINES ROAD

BATH ROAD

A4

GREAT WEST ROAD

LONDON ROAD

M4

1 mile

1 km

© Copyright Time Out Group 2012

plenty of attractive Edwardian and Victorian houses, and a few grand mansions, including a house near the pond once lived in by writer Henry Fielding – are very high: seven figures is common.

Barnes has an oddly musical heritage: Gustav Holst lived in a bow-fronted riverside property; the Rolling Stones, Jimi Hendrix and Led Zeppelin recorded at the Olympic studios; the Bull's Head pub has been a leading jazz venue since 1959; and Marc Bolan, er, died on Queen's Ride in 1977 (a bronze bust and well-kept shrine mark the spot).

West from Barnes, sandwiched between the Upper Richmond Road and the Thames, is Mortlake, presided over by the mammoth Budweiser brewery (the air is often thick with beery odours). The river is hidden from view here, and the area is split in two by the railway line (hanging around at level crossings is a local pastime). Any village atmosphere disappeared long ago and it feels a bit of a no-man's-land, but property prices are significantly lower than in Barnes; there are some handsome Edwardian terraces, and cute cottages and allotments around the railway tracks. White Hart Lane is the main shopping street, lined with independent boutiques and restaurants.

Highs & Lows

▲ **Greenery** Richmond has more open space than any other London borough, and Richmond Park is the capital's largest royal park.

High price of education Some of the best schools in London are to be found in Richmond and Barnes – but most are private, and very expensive.

A river runs through it The stretch of the Thames Path from Barnes to Hampton Court is the loveliest riverside walk in London.

Plane pain The noise caused by flights to and from Heathrow is non-stop, a persistent local complaint.

Housing costs Property in Richmond, Kew and Barnes is well beyond the reach of all but the wealthiest Londoners.

Cultural diversity Or lack of it. Richmond has the most limited ethnic spread of any London borough.

The brewery is slated for closure, but this has been put back until 2014 – and what will happen with this prime piece of riverside real estate remains unclear. Meanwhile, locals are delighted that the Olympic studios building is returning to its roots as a cinema (details at www.olympiccinema.co.uk).

The residential area of East Sheen sits between the Upper Richmond Road – the main commercial artery, aka the South Circular – and East Sheen Common and the northern fringe of Richmond Park. House prices are as astronomical as in many other parts of the borough, with some grand Victorian and Edwardian villas near the park (the Parkside and Palewell Park areas are sought after). North Sheen is a relatively small pocket abutting Kew, hemmed in by the Lower Richmond Road and Mortlake Road. There's no tube (as is the case in most of the borough), but the overground from North Sheen and Mortlake stations can get commuters to work in a jiffy.

Kew

Everyone knows Kew Gardens (officially the Royal Botanic Gardens, Kew); this exquisitely planned extravaganza of botanical biodiversity, stretching south along the Thames from Kew Bridge, attracts two million visitors a year. But it's not the only chunk of green in this greenest of London boroughs: adjoining the Gardens to the south is the Old Deer Park and the exclusive Royal Mid-Surrey Golf Course, while Kew Green abuts the northern end.

Across Kew Road is the main residential area, with assorted restaurants and shops on Sandycombe Road. Property is relatively varied – Queen Anne to Victorian houses, converted flats and modern purpose-built apartments – and exceedingly popular with prosperous middle-class families who appreciate the highly rated primary schools and good transport connections (tube and train to get into central London, easy access to the A4 and M4 to get out). A villagey vibe remains, especially in the characterful cluster of local shops and restaurants around Kew Gardens station.

Richmond

After Henry VIII built his palace here in the late 15th century, he decided to rename the area, then called Shene, after one of his favourite rural retreats: Richmond, Yorkshire. It was a prescient gesture. Today, Richmond is just what it says in the name: a very, very rich mound (on a hill rising up from the Thames). After Kensington & Chelsea, this is the most affluent borough in England. The pretty riverside setting, huge green spaces and stunning period houses have proved an irresistible lure for monied professionals, especially since the City is scarcely half an hour away by train or tube. Yet Richmond avoids the haughtiness of K&C, retaining a villagey air and a harmonious sense of community. It is clean, safe, peaceful (except for the relentless Heathrow air traffic) and has excellent schools.

North-west of the park is Richmond Hill, where Mick Jagger and Pete Townshend's palatial mansions enjoy an unrivalled, idyllic view over the Thames and the pastures of Surrey. Gracing the hill, on the steeper side, are the Terrace Gardens, another pristine enclosure of parterres and winding stone pathways. Near the top sits a dainty cluster (shops, restaurants, a pub)

STATISTICS

BOROUGH MAKE-UP
Population 180,100
Ethnic origins
  White 84.6%
  Mixed 2.8%
  Asian or Asian British 6.8%
  Black or Black British 3.1%
  Chinese or other 2.8%
Students 7.2%
Retirees 10.0%

HOUSING
Borough size (hectares) 5,877
Population density per hectare 30.6
No. of households 76,146
Houses (detached, semi-detached or terraced) 61%
Flats (converted or purpose-built) 39%

CRIME PER 1,000 OF POPULATION
Burglary 5
Robbery 1
Theft of vehicle 1
Theft from vehicle 6
Violence against the person 12
Sexual offences 1

MPs
MPs *Richmond Park* Zac Goldsmith (Conservative); *Twickenham* Dr Vincent Cable (Liberal Democrat)

known as Richmond Village. The road down the hill takes you into the confusingly planned town centre, a hive of shopping, eating and drinking establishments. The riverside by Richmond Bridge is a buzzing spot, with ducks, swans, fishermen, boats for hire and popular pubs and restaurants perfect for an alfresco meal in good weather.

Tucked away behind George Street (essentially the high street) is Richmond Green, one of the borough's proudest assets. Remnants of Henry VIII's palace still stand in one corner, now converted into lodgings. When the sun's out, the grass is invariably strewn with lounging locals – except when cricket is being played on it, in an authentically casual, village-green fashion. The Green has a diminutive adjunct, the Little Green; opposite this is Richmond's most famous cultural venue, its Victorian theatre – the annual Christmas panto is always a sell-out.

South-east of the town centre is the borough's biggest open space, Richmond Park. In fact, it's London's largest park: 2,500 acres of rolling woodland, ponds, gardens and grassland where the Queen's deer graze. The park was first enclosed for hunting by Charles I and not much has changed since then (though fewer bloodsports take place nowadays). Here you'll find runners, cyclists, kite fliers, birdwatchers, dog walkers, horse riders, picnickers, families out for a stroll – and drivers on the roads that criss-cross it – but there's always a bit of empty space somewhere. The Isabella Plantation, a carefully tended enclosure of azaleas and rhododendrons, is at its best in May (it also has good disabled access). There are also two golf courses adjoining the park's western edge.

Ham & Petersham

The famous view from Richmond Hill of cows grazing on Petersham meadows is preserved by an Act of Parliament, no less (in 1902, the culmination of a public campaign to prevent a housing estate being built here). The meadows once formed part of the estate of Ham House, a spectacular Stuart mansion set further along the river (and also visible from the hill), which is now owned by the National Trust.

Ham and Petersham have maintained their rural character thanks to their secluded location, hemmed in by the

Richmond upon Thames

Glorious **Richmond Park** – London's largest, at 2,500 acres.

Thames on one side, and Ham Common and Richmond Park on the other. There are council estates here, but Petersham also has some particularly fine 17th- and 18th-century mansions (including Rutland Lodge, Montrose House and Petersham House) alongside Victorian cottages and more modern dwellings. Regular polo matches (Ham Polo Club is the only club of its kind left in London) and events such as the Richmond Regatta in June add to the countrified vibe – as does the absence of a train station.

Twickenham

Oval-ball fans around the world revere Twickenham for its connection with rugby,

but there's no shortage of local rugger-buggers too – as evident from the thronged pubs, packed railway station and traffic jams around Twickenham Stadium on match days. South from the stadium lies the town centre, around Heath Road, London Road and King Street. It has none of the grandeur of Richmond across the river, and too many pound shops, but proud residents would assert that they have Church Street instead – a cobbled lane off the main road flanked by restaurants, pubs and independent shops.

Well-kept late Victorian and Edwardian terraces dominate Twickenham's residential districts, and property prices are more palatable, certainly compared to Richmond.

But it's the riverside that is (and has always been) the area's main attraction. Eminently fashionable in the 17th and 18th centuries, this bank of the Thames was lined by posh countryside retreats built by the likes of Horace Walpole and Alexander Pope. Most of these mansions are long gone, though Marble Hill House, Strawberry Hill House and York House (now council offices) remain. Of the once-numerous ferries, only Hammertons Ferry still operates (February to October) – it's the best way to get between Marble Hill House and Ham House.

Watery activities have always been big business: Ferry Road retains old watermen's cottages and boatsheds, while Eel Pie Island (connected by a footbridge to the mainland) is home to Twickenham Rowing Club and Richmond Yacht Club – and about 50 much-prized houses. The island was also the centre of a thriving music scene in the 1950s and '60s, with the likes of George Melly, the Rolling Stones, the Who, Eric Clapton and Rod Stewart all performing here. Local band the Mystery Jets continues the island's musical heritage.

Twickenham lacks the tube, but there are train stations at St Margarets, Twickenham and Strawberry Hill, and easy access to the M3 via the busy Chertsey Road (A316).

A vista at **Kew Gardens**. See p171.

Restaurants & cafés

Eating options aren't as splendid as you might expect, given the amount of money sloshing around in this part of town. Family-friendly chain restaurants are plentiful – you'll find branches of all the leading pizza outlets, as well as Giraffe, Nando's and Wagamama – plus more adult-oriented chains, such as Carluccio's Caffè, Côte, FishWorks and Maison Blanc. Otherwise, expect reliable neighbourhood joints that have built up their reputation and clientele over decades, rather than the latest culinary trends.

In Richmond itself, independents include Don Fernando's for classic Spanish tapas; Breton specialist Chez Lindsay for galettes and cider; Matsuba for Korean and Japanese dishes; and La Buvette for French bistro classics. Java lovers should head for Taylor St Baristas near the station (the original branch of the sucessful Antipodean coffee chain), while fragrant infusions and floral aromas are the order of the day at cosy café Tea Box.

Meaty treats await next to the river, where there's a branch of the popular Argentine grill chain Gaucho, and, further along the towpath, Stein's beer garden, for bratwurst and Bavarian beer (open Easter to Christmas only). Just across Richmond Bridge, in East Twickenham, A Cena provides muscular Italian cuisine. For a tip-top alfresco meal, have lunch amid the boho-chic greenhouses of Skye Gyngell's Petersham Nurseries Café – though such bucolic beauty doesn't come cheap. The Bingham, a boutique hotel with a fine-dining British restaurant, is another option for a special-occasion meal.

Barnes has a trio of excellent, long-running spots: Sonny's (Modern European), Riva (Italian) and the less formal riverside brasserie the Depot – the perfect spot for sunset-viewing. Orange Pekoe is a gem of a café, with pillowy scones and a sterling selection of loose teas. Next door is Mediterranean newcomer Seasalt. Head towards East Sheen for a brace of excellent gastropubs: the Brown Dog and the Victoria (also a hotel).

Elsewhere, the Glasshouse next to Kew Gardens station is an extremely polished

Mod Euro restaurant, while TV chef Antony Worrall Thompson has Kew Grill on Kew Green – visit for quality steaks and burgers and a relaxed, unstuffy vibe. Homely French brasserie Brula in St Margarets keeps the locals happy.

The borough's overwhelmingly white demographic – nearly 90 per cent, the highest in London – means that ethnic restaurants are generally noticeable by their absence. Exceptions include Ragam 2 (Keralan) and Tangawizi (North Indian) – both in Twickenham – and Faanoos (Iranian) and Mango & Silk (pan-Indian) – both in East Sheen.

A Cena *418 Richmond Road, TW1 2EB (8288 0108, www.acena.co.uk).*
Bingham *61-63 Petersham Road, TW10 6UT (8940 0902, www.thebingham.co.uk).*
Brown Dog *28 Cross Street, SW13 0AP (8392 2200, www.thebrowndog.co.uk).*
Brula *43 Crown Road, TW1 3EJ (8892 0602, www.brula.co.uk).*
La Buvette *6 Church Walk, TW9 1SN (8940 6264, www.labuvette.co.uk).*
Chez Lindsay *11 Hill Rise, TW10 6UQ (8948 7473, www.chez-lindsay.co.uk).*
Depot *Tideway Yard, 125 Mortlake High Street, SW14 8SN (8878 9462, www.depot brasserie.co.uk).*
Don Fernando's *27F The Quadrant, TW9 1DN (8948 6447, www.donfernando.co.uk).*
Faanoos *481 Upper Richmond Road West, SW14 7PU (8878 5738, 8876 8938, www.faanoosrestaurant.com).*
Gaucho Richmond *Richmond Towpath, west of Richmond Bridge, TW10 6UJ (8948 4030, www.gauchorestaurants.co.uk).*
Glasshouse *14 Station Parade, TW9 3PZ (8940 6777, www.glasshouserestaurant.co.uk).*
Kew Grill *10B Kew Green, TW9 3BH (8948 4433, www.awtrestaurants.com).*
Mango & Silk *199 Upper Richmond Road West, SW14 8QT (8876 6220, www.mangoandsilk.co.uk).*
Matsuba *10 Red Lion Street, TW9 1RW (8605 3513).*
Orange Pekoe *3 White Hart Lane, SW13 0PX (8876 6070, www.orangepekoeteas.com).*
Petersham Nurseries Café *Church Lane, off Petersham Road, TW10 7AG (8605 3627, www.petershamnurseries.com).*
Ragam 2 *Cross Deep Court, Heath Road, TW1 4QJ (8892 2345, www.ragam2.co.uk).*
Riva *169 Church Road, SW13 9HR (8748 0434).*
Seasalt *5 White Hart Lane, SW13 0PX (8392 1111, www.seasaltgourmet.co.uk).*

Sonny's *92-94 Church Road, SW13 0DQ (8748 0393, www.sonnys.co.uk).*
Stein's *Richmond Towpath, rear of 55 Petersham Road, TW10 6UX (8948 8189, www.stein-s.com).*
Tangawizi *406 Richmond Road, TW1 2EB (8891 3737, www.tangawizi.co.uk).*
Taylor St Baristas *Westminster House, Kew Road, TW9 2ND (07969 798650, www.taylor-st.com).*
Tea Box *7 Paradise Road, TW9 1RX (8940 3521, www.theteabox.co.uk).*
Victoria *10 West Temple Sheen, SW14 7RT (8876 4238, www.thevictoria.net).*

Refurbished **Strawberry Hill House**.

Sausages and Bavarian beer at **Stein's**, on Richmond Towpath. See p174.

Bars & pubs

Real ales, rugby and riverside settings are the three Rs of Richmond's drinking scene. If you want a well-kept Young's or Fuller's pint in an old-fashioned inn that could be in the countryside, you're in the right part of town; if you're after a sophisticated cocktail bar or a late-night urban dive, tough.

Typical is the White Cross on the riverside near Richmond Bridge: Young's beers on tap, pies and sausages on the menu, real fires inside, tables outside overlooking the water. Sometimes too much water, in fact: the towpath here gets flooded regularly, and there's a special entrance for high tide. Away from the river, on the edge of spacious Richmond Green, are two handsome hostelries: the Cricketers (a Greene King establishment) and the Prince's Head (Fuller's). Cricket matches are a common occurrence in summer – get your pint in a plastic glass and stretch out by the boundary for a few wickets.

Barnes and Mortlake also have pubs overlooking the Thames. The former's Ye White Hart offers a perfect view of the Varsity boat race once a year; the latter's Ship, dwarfed by the Budweiser brewery next door, is a pleasant enough place, made special by its sun-drenched patio. Also in Barnes is the Bull's Head; a legendary jazz venue since the late 1950s, it still has gigs every night, alongside Young's ales and a well-priced Thai restaurant in the former stables at the back. More modern – in looks, food and drink (a global selection of bottled beers and a good wine list) – is the Sun Inn, idyllically positioned opposite the duck pond. The outdoor tables at the front get packed in good weather.

Gastro-fication has come to Kew too. If you're visiting the Botanic Gardens, there's a trio of handy pubs to choose from. The Inn at Kew Gardens, on Sandycombe Road, is spacious and airy, and also has bedrooms. Next to Kew Green are the Coach & Horses, a congenial Young's pub offering traditional Sunday roasts, and the Botanist, a more modern affair with its own microbrewery and poshed-up pub grub. The latter is part of the Convivial mini chain, which also owns the historic White Swan next to the river in Twickenham. Towpath flooding is a factor here too – hence the steep steps up to the entrance. Opposite lies the countercultural bastion of Eel Pie Island; nearby, on pretty Church Street, is the low-key and very popular Eel Pie, serving fine Hall & Woodhouse beers.

Botanist *3-5 Kew Green, TW9 3AA (8948 4838, www.thebotanistkew.com).*
Bull's Head *373 Lonsdale Road, SW13 9PY (8876 5241, www.thebullshead.com).*
Coach & Horses *8 Kew Green, TW9 3BH (8940 1208, www.coachhotelkew.co.uk).*

Cricketers *The Green, TW9 1LX (8940 4372, www.greeneking.co.uk).*

Eel Pie *9-11 Church Street, TW1 3NJ (8891 1717, www.theeelpie.co.uk).*

Inn at Kew Gardens *292 Sandycombe Road, TW9 3NG (8940 2220, www.theinnatkew gardens.com).*

Prince's Head *28 The Green, TW9 1LX (8940 1572, www.fullers.co.uk).*

Ship *10 Thames Bank, SW14 7QR (8876 1439).*

Sun Inn *7 Church Road, SW13 9HE (8876 5256, www.thesuninnbarnes.co.uk).*

White Cross *Water Lane, TW9 1TH (8940 6844, www.youngs.co.uk).*

White Swan *Riverside, TW1 3DN (8744 2951, www.whiteswantwickenham.com).*

Ye White Hart *The Terrace, SW13 0NR (8876 5177, www.youngs.co.uk).*

Shops

Richmond residents don't need to head into the West End to do their shopping: they've got pretty much every high-street chain on their doorstep (or they can pop to the smart Bentall Centre in neighbouring Kingston). From Richmond station, a confusing tangle of streets around the main drag of the Quadrant/George Street houses numerous familiar names (Boots, French Connection, Gap, HMV, Jigsaw, Joules, Monsoon, Reiss and many more) plus a Habitat, Topshop, Waterstone's and M&S. Anchoring it all is department store House of Fraser.

Head up Hill Street and its extension Hill Rise to drop some serious dosh on antiques or top-end fashion from the likes of Joseph, Matches, MaxMara and Whistles. Elsewhere, more posh frocks can be found at Margaret Howell, while the sweet-toothed can splurge at acclaimed chocolatier William Curley. If you have youngsters in tow, placate them with a visit to toyshop Toy Station or fabulous kids' bookshop the Lion & Unicorn.

Further along the Thames is Petersham Nurseries, a supremely picturesque and upmarket outlet for all things horticultural, with a lovely café (*see p175*). Over on the Twickenham side of the river, the Real Ale Shop specialises in real ales, ciders, perries and beers from British microbreweries.

There's no candlestick-maker in Barnes, but it's still got a butcher and a baker – plus a fishmonger, a greengrocer, a handy hardware shop, the well-run Barnes

Bookshop and the lovely Real Cheese Shop. All are located on Barnes High Street/Church Street. There's a smattering of upmarket fashion boutiques such as Question Air, and Nina for tasteful Swedish clothing and knick-knacks. The main shopping street in adjoining Mortlake is White Hart Lane, home to posh deli Gusto & Relish and a couple of swanky interiors shops: Tobias & the Angel and the Dining Room Shop.

East Sheen offers a less attractive retail experience, with shoppers having to negotiate the constant traffic on the busy Upper Richmond Road. But there are plenty of useful chains (Superdrug, Boots, WH Smith, an expanded Waitrose, Kew for womenswear, Oliver Bonas for gifts) alongside charity shops and furniture and kitchen suppliers.

In Kew, there's a cluster of independent outlets around Kew Gardens station. For high-street brands, visit user-friendly Kew Retail Park, off the A205, which has

Locals' Tips

Don't miss the Friday morning sale of home-made cakes and savouries at Rose House on Barnes High Street. There's often a queue waiting for the doors to open at 10am.

Twickenham & Thames Valley Bee-Keepers' Association (8568 2869, www.twickenham-bees.org.uk), founded 1919, runs courses from March to September for budding bee-keepers, and hosts free lectures in winter. Old-fashioned fairs and fêtes abound in this countrified part of town. There's the Twickenham Festival in June, Barnes Fair and St Margarets Fair in July, and Kew Fayre in September. New in autumn 2011 – and a big success – was the Barnes Food Fair.

The annual Christmas panto at Richmond Theatre is one of the best in town, with quality thesps such as Simon Callow, Nigel Havers and Robert Powell appearing in recent years. It's very popular, though, so book well ahead.

The child-friendly café in Marble Hill's Coach House is handy for breakfast, lunch and tea. You can also bribe youngsters with the promise of three decent playgrounds (each with refreshments) on the walk from Richmond Bridge to Twickenham.

TRANSPORT

Tube stations *District* Kew Gardens, Richmond
Rail stations *South West Trains* Barnes, Barnes Bridge, Mortlake, North Sheen, Richmond, St Margarets, Twickenham, Whitton, Strawberry Hill, Hampton Wick, Teddington, Fulwell, Hampton; *London Overground* Kew Gardens, Richmond
Bus routes night buses N22, N74; 24-hour buses 65, 72, 281, 285
River leisure boat services (Apr-Oct), with piers at Kew Gardens, Richmond and Hampton Court Palace

branches of M&S, Gap, Boots, TK Maxx, Next and lots of parking.

Middle-class sensibilities and incomes mean there are no fewer than three farmers' markets in the borough, in Barnes (opposite the pond), Richmond (Heron Square) and Twickenham (Holly Street car park). All are held on Saturday.

Barnes Bookshop *60 Church Road, SW13 0DQ (8741 0786).*
Dining Room Shop *62-64 White Hart Lane, SW13 0PZ (8878 1020, www.thediningroom shop.co.uk).*
Gusto & Relish *56 White Hart Lane, SW13 0PZ (8878 2005).*
Joseph *28 Hill Street, TW9 1TV (8940 7045, www.joseph.co.uk).*
Lion & Unicorn Bookshop *19 King Street, TW9 1ND (8940 0483, www.lionunicorn books.co.uk).*
Margaret Howell *7-8 Duke Street, TW9 1HP (8948 5005, www.margarethowell.co.uk).*
Matches *13 Hill Street, TW9 1FX (8332 9733, www.matchesfashion.com).*
MaxMara *32 Hill Street, TW9 1TW (8332 2811, www.maxmara.com).*
Nina *55 Church Road, SW13 9HH (8240 0414).*
Petersham Nurseries *Church Lane, off Petersham Road, TW10 7AG (8940 5230, www.petershamnurseries.com).*

MasterCard Priceless Tip

Get exclusive access to Priceless London music and theatre offers at www.pricelesslondon.co.uk

Question Air *86 Church Road, SW13 0DQ (8741 0816, www.question-air.com).*
Real Ale Shop *371 Richmond Road, TW1 2EF (8892 3710, www.realale.com).*
Real Cheese Shop *62 Barnes High Street, SW13 9LF (8878 6676).*
Tobias & the Angel *68 White Hart Lane, SW13 0PZ (8878 8902, www.tobiasandtheangel.com).*
Toy Station *6 Eton Street, TW9 1EE (8940 4896, www.toy-station.co.uk).*
Whistles *19 Hill Street, TW9 1SX (8332 1646, www.whistles.co.uk).*
William Curley *10 Paved Court, TW9 1LZ (8332 3002, www.williamcurley.co.uk).*

Arts & attractions

Cinemas & theatres

Curzon Richmond *3 Water Lane, TW9 1TJ (0330 500 1331, www.curzoncinemas.com).*
Odeon Richmond *0871 224 4007, www.odeon.co.uk; 72 Hill Street, TW9 1TW; 6 Red Lion Street, TW9 6RE.*
Orange Tree Theatre *1 Clarence Street, TW9 2SA (8940 3633, www.orangetreetheatre.co.uk).*
Richmond Theatre *The Green, TW9 1QJ (8332 4500, box office 0844 871 7651, www.atgtickets.com/richmond).*
Vue Staines *Two Rivers, Mustard Mill Road, TW18 4BL (0871 224 0240, www.myvue.com).*

Galleries & museums

Museum of Richmond *Old Town Hall, Whittaker Avenue, TW9 1TP (8332 1141, www.museumofrichmond.com). A loyal parade of Richmond's regal history.*
Orleans House Gallery *Riverside, TW1 3DJ (8831 6000, www.richmond.gov.uk/arts). The borough's principal art gallery, located right on the river in Twickenham.*
Twickenham Museum *25 The Embankment, TW1 3DU (8408 0070, www.twickenham-museum.org.uk). Local history museum.*

Music & comedy venues

Bull's Head *373 Lonsdale Road, SW13 9PY (8876 5241, www.thebullshead.com).*
Cabbage Patch *67 London Road, TW1 3SZ (8892 3874, www.cabbagepatch.co.uk). Family-run pub with regular music nights hosted by the Eel Pie Club (www.eelpieclub.com).*

Other attractions

Ham House *Ham Street, TW10 7RS (8940 1950, www.nationaltrust.org.uk). Lavish riverside mansion built in 1610, with gardens and a café.*

Horticultural and edible treats await at **Petersham Nurseries** and **Café**.

Hampton Court Palace *East Molesey, KT8 9AU (information 0844 482 7777, www.hrp.org. uk). Dazzling Tudor palace with a famous maze, changing interior exhibitions and a winter ice-rink.*
London Wetland Centre *Queen Elizabeth Walk, SW13 9WT (8409 4400, www.wwt.org.uk).*
Marble Hill House *Richmond Road, TW1 2NL (8892 5115, www.english-heritage.org.uk). Elegant Palladian house built in 1724 by George II for his mistress, Henrietta Howard.*
National Archives *Ruskin Avenue, TW9 4DU (8876 3444, www.nationalarchives.gov.uk). Accessible archives office in Kew, housing 1,000 years of official government and law records.*
Royal Botanic Gardens, Kew *TW9 3AB (8332 5655, www.rbgkew.org.uk).*
Strawberry Hill House *St Mary's College, Waldegrave Road, TW1 4ST (8744 1241, www.strawberryhillhouse.org.uk). After a two-year, £9 million restoration, Horace Walpole's Grade I-listed 'little Gothic castle' reopened in 2012.*

Sport & fitness

Surprisingly, Richmond is not the best equipped borough for sports facilities. The council-run centres are decent, but not state of the art. However, as you'd expect, no one gets short-changed on quality at Richmond's private health clubs.

Gyms & leisure centres

Cannons *Richmond Athletic Ground, Kew Foot Road, TW9 2SS (8948 3743, www.cannons. co.uk). Private.*
Fitness First *1st floor, 20-28 Broad Street, TW11 8QZ (8614 6650, www.fitnessfirst.co.uk). Private.*
Hampton Sport, Arts & Fitness Centre *Hanworth Road, TW12 3HB (8090 0668, www.richmond.gov.uk).*
Nuffield Health *Stoop Memorial Ground, Langhorn Drive, TW2 7SX (8892 2251, www.nuffieldhealth.com). Private.*

Pools on the Park, Springheath Leisure Club *Old Deer Park, Twickenham Road, TW9 2SF (8940 0561, www.springhealth.net).*
Richmond Hill Health Club *Lewis Road, TW10 6SA (8948 5523, www.fit4ever.co.uk). Private.*
Shene Sports & Fitness Centre *Park Avenue, SW14 8RG (8878 7578, www.richmond.gov.uk).*
Teddington Pools & Fitness Centre *Vicarage Road, TW11 8EZ (8977 9911, www.richmond.gov.uk).*
Teddington Sports Centre *Teddington School, Broom Road, TW11 9PJ (8977 0598, www.richmond.gov.uk).*
Virgin Active *Twickenham Club, South Stand, Twickenham Rugby Stadium, 196 Whitton Road, TW2 7BA (8892 4500, www.virginactive.co.uk). Private.*
Whitton Sports & Fitness Centre *Percy Road, TW2 6JW (8898 7795, www.richmond.gov.uk).*

Other facilities

Ham Polo Club *The Polo Office, Petersham Road, TW10 7AH (8334 0000, www.hampoloclub.com).*
Hampton Pool *High Street, TW12 2ST (8255 1116, www.hamptonpool.co.uk). Open-air heated pool – 36m long, open 365 days a year – on the edge of Bushy Park.*

Spectator sports

Rugby rules in Richmond; clubs in the borough include Harlequins (www.quins.co.uk), London Welsh (www.london-welsh.co.uk), London Scottish (www.londonscottish.com) and Rosslyn Park (www.rosslynpark.co.uk).
Twickenham Stadium *Rugby Road, TW1 1DZ (0871 222 2120, www.rfu.com). Home of the England rugby team and the Museum of Rugby; stadium tours are run on non-match days.*

Schools

Primary

There are 41 state primary schools in Richmond, including 15 church schools. There are also 18 independent primaries, including one German and one Swedish school. See www.richmond.gov.uk, www.edubase.gov.uk and www.ofsted.gov.uk for more information.

Secondary

There is also the Swedish School (www.swedishschool.org.uk) in Barnes, and the German School (www.dslondon.org.uk) in Petersham. The Royal

London Wetland Centre. See p179.

Ballet School (www.royal-ballet-school.org.uk) is in the middle of Richmond Park.
Christ's School *Queen's Road, TW10 6HW (8940 6982, www.christs.richmond.sch.uk).*
Grey Court School *Ham Street, TW10 7HN (8948 1173, www.greycourt.richmond.sch.uk).*
Hampton Academy *Hanworth Road, TW12 3HB (8979 3399, www.hamptonacademy.org.uk).*
Hampton School *Hanworth Road, TW12 3HD (8979 5526, www.hamptonschool.org.uk). Boys only; private.*
Harrodian School *Lonsdale Road, SW13 9QN (8748 6117, www.harrodian.com). Private.*
Lady Eleanor Holles School *102 Hanworth Road, TW12 3HF (8979 1601, www.lehs.org.uk). Girls only; private.*
Orleans Park School *Richmond Road, TW1 3BB (8891 0187, www.orleanspark.richmond.sch.uk).*
Richmond Park Academy *Park Avenue, SW14 8RG (8876 8891, www.richmondparkacademy.org).*
St Catherine's School *Cross Deep, Twickenham, TW1 4QJ (8891 2898, www.stcatherineschool.co.uk). Girls only; private.*
St Paul's *Lonsdale Road, SW13 9JT (8748 9162, www.stpaulsschool.org.uk). Boys only; private.*
Teddington School *Broom Road, TW11 9PJ (8943 0033, www.teddington.richmond.sch.uk).*

Waldegrave School *Fifth Cross Road, TW2 5LH (8894 3244, www.waldegrave.richmond. sch.uk). Girls only.*
Whitton School *Percy Road, TW2 6JW (8894 4503, www.whittonsecondary.com).*

Property

WHAT THE AGENTS SAY:

'The river, the parks, the pubs, the schools, the people – Richmond really does have it all. Buying a property here is a long-term investment these days, and, as a result, there's a significant shortage of housing stock for sale. Property prices reflect this and are very high, as is council tax, but the housing market is far from quiet. The rental scene is booming too; you can expect to pay from £1,450 upwards per month for a two-bedroom flat. It's a very affluent neighbourhood, with a vibrant mix of families and young professionals attracted by the leafy surroundings and great train links into the city centre – just 20 minutes to Waterloo. Safe, clean – it's difficult to find a bad word to say about the borough.'
Stuart Mackenzie, Stuart Mackenzie, East Sheen

Average property prices

Detached £875,550
Semi-detached £603,278
Terraced £511,271
Flat £332,939

Local estate agents

Antony Roberts *www.antonyroberts.co.uk; 2 offices in the borough (Kew 8940 9401, Richmond 8940 9403).*
Boileaus *135 Church Road, SW13 9HR (0741 7400, www.boileaus.com).*
Jackson-Stops & Staff *3 Lichfield Terrace, TW9 1AS (8940 6789, www.jackson stops.co.uk).*
Major Son & Phipps *5A The Square, TW9 1DX (8940 2233, www.major-estate agents.com).*
Marquis & Co *Marquis House, 54 Richmond Road, TW1 3BE (8891 0222, www.marquis andco.co.uk).*
Philip Hodges *191 & 193 High Street, TW12 1NL (8783 1007, www.philip-hodges.co.uk).*
Stuart Mackenzie *212B Upper Richmond Road West, SW14 8AH (8876 4445, www. pemberstone.co.uk).*
W Hallet & Co *6 Royal Parade, Station Approach, TW9 3QD (8940 1034).*

Other information

Council

London Borough of Richmond upon Thames Council *Civic Centre, 44 York Street, Twickenham, TW1 3BZ (0845 612 2660, out of office hours 8744 2442, www.richmond.gov.uk).*

Legal services

Richmond upon Thames CAB *223 Lower Mortlake Road, TW9 2LL (0844 826 9700, www.rcabs.org).*

Local information

www.barnesvillage.com.
www.richmondandtwickenhamtimes.co.uk.
www.totallyrichmond.co.uk.

Open spaces & allotments

Council allotments *The Allotments Officer, Civic Centre, 44 York Street, TW1 3BZ (8831 6110, www.richmond.gov.uk/allotments).*
Open spaces *www.richmond.gov.uk/parks; www.royalparks.org.uk.*
Royal Paddocks Allotments *www.paddocks-allotments.org.uk.*

COUNCIL TAX

A	up to £40,000	£1,064.81
B	£40,001-£52,000	£1,242.27
C	£52,001-£68,000	£1,419.74
D	£68,001-£88,000	£1,597.21
E	£88,001-£120,000	£1,952.15
F	£120,001-£160,000	£2,307.08
G	£160,001-£320,000	£2,662.02
H	over £320,000	£3,194.42

RECYCLING

Household waste recycled & composted 43%
Main recycling centre Townmead Road Reuse & Recycling Centre, Kew, TW9 4EL (8876 3281)
Other recycling services Richmond Scrapstore (scrapstore@richmond. gov.uk) for scrap materials to be used in art projects; reusable paint collection; kitchen waste collection; home composting; collection of white goods and furniture; adopt-a-recycling-site scheme
Council contact Recycling Office, Central Depot, Langhorn Drive, Twickenham, TW2 7SG (8891 7329, www.ecoaction.richmond.gov.uk)

Richmond upon Thames

'With a fascinating industrial heritage, green spaces, river walks, grand buildings and cutting-edge architecture, Wandsworth's past is captivating and its present alluring'

Claire Longworth, Curator, De Morgan Centre

Wandsworth

After Westminster and Kensington & Chelsea, Wandsworth has the largest number of million-pound residential properties in London. It's not just the mellow Victorian villas of Putney and Clapham fetching these prices, either. Frenetic gentrification of Wandsworth Town and the reinventing of its Thames-side area as the Riverside Quarter has attracted new money. It's the Chelsea overspill, apparently, although we'd say there's more than a river separating the old money from the new.

Neighbourhoods

Battersea

Battersea is attractive to all comers, be they young families, speculators or monied pied-à-terre hunters. There's no tube station, but connections to central London are fast thanks to Battersea Park and Queenstown Road rail stations, and Chelsea is a short walk away over the Battersea, Albert or Chelsea bridges. The district's name is renowned around the world for two sights: Battersea Dogs & Cats Home (proof, if any were needed, that the British are pet-obsessed) and Battersea Power Station, one of the capital's most iconic buildings.

Sprawling Battersea Park, with its fountain-filled lake, peace pagoda, children's zoo, sports pitches and Thames vistas is the area's most valuable asset (and gives blessed relief from all the new riverside apartment developments).

At the eastern edge of the park, on the other side of Queenstown Road, looms the roofless hulk of the power station. Designed in 1930 by Sir Giles Gilbert Scott and occupying a sprawling chunk of prime riverside territory, it has been slowly falling apart for years – despite being listed Grade II* in October 2007. Since the station ceased functioning in 1983, various developers have proposed schemes, from theme parks to hotels, circuses to cinemas – all to no avail.

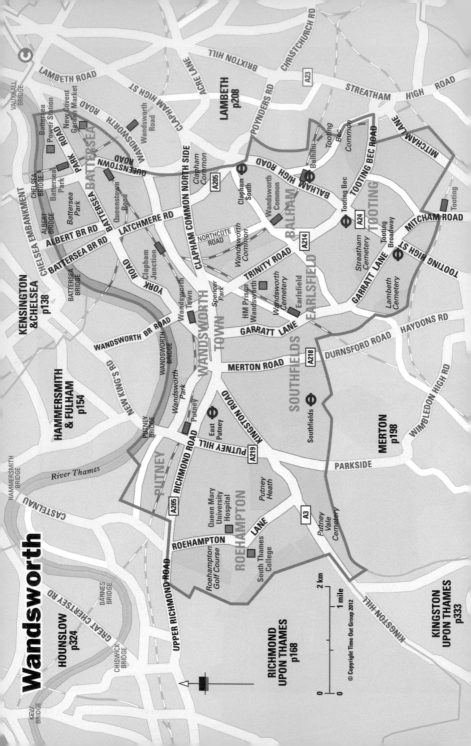

Forlorn icon **Battersea Power Station**. See p182.

To the south, across Battersea Park Road, the area's marshy beginnings as a fertile spot for market gardens are remembered in the ultimate garden market, Nine Elms, where fruit, veg and flower wholesalers were moved from Covent Garden in 1974. This area is also the chosen site for the new American Embassy – set for completion in 2017, the complex will transform the surrounding area, most notably by sparking improved transport links. The proposed Northern Line extension has stations at Nine Elms and Battersea.

The triangle formed by Queenstown and Silverthorne roads, known as the Parktown Estate conservation area – 'the Diamond', to locals – is much in demand, with townhouses and Victorian terraced cottages that sell for upwards of half a million. Away from the Diamond, the Park and chichi little desirables such as Battersea Square, there are plenty of high-rises and estates, particularly around the Clapham Junction side of Battersea.

Walk west along the Thames (where you can) and there's a seemingly endless ribbon of high-tech luxury flats all the way to Wandsworth Bridge. Victorian warehouses that were once hives of industry, such as Price's Candles on York Road, have also been converted into top-end apartments, but there are increasing numbers of boat moorings too, especially around the Heliport (quite a sight in itself, with helicopters landing and taking off between 7am and 11pm), just west of Battersea Railway Bridge. By way of contrast, Battersea High Street, just inland from here, offers a more villagey vibe.

Clapham Junction and Clapham Common

An area defined by its famously frenetic railway station, Clapham Junction is, in fact, in Battersea (rather than Clapham proper); when it was developed in the 1860s, the powers-that-be decided that Clapham's salubrious connotations were better suited to such a major transport interchange. For years, the station has driven commuters potty with its run-down subways and

Highs & Lows

▲ **Council tax** My, it's cheap, isn't it? You'll pay less here than anywhere else in central London.
Eating and drinking Old boozers and smart gastros, top-notch Mod Euro restaurants and characterful curry houses – this is a great borough for food-lovers
The great outdoors Battersea Park; Clapham, Wandsworth and Tooting Bec commons; Putney Heath: Wandsworth is full of green spaces. And it's not bad for cycle paths either, thanks to the likes of the Wandsworth Cycling Campaign (www.wandsworth cyclists.org.uk).

Transport congestion Too many 4WDs, traffic jams everywhere, nowhere to park, crowded tubes and trains – the list goes on.
House prices Up, up and away! First-time buyers haven't a hope in most of the borough, and even Tooting and Balham are getting beyond the pale. ▼

Wandsworth

fiendishly confusing platform information system; a major overhaul is slowly coming along and a second connection to the London Overground line is set to be completed in late 2012.

North of the station, around Grant Road, is the Winstanley Estate, often in the local news for all the wrong reasons. Its main claim to fame is that the founding members of So Solid Crew were brought up here. In contrast is the Shaftesbury Park Estate, south-east of the Junction, containing about 1,200 homes, mostly two-storey cottages plus a few larger houses, all with Gothic Revival flourishes, built by the Artisans', Labourers' & General Dwellings Company in 1873-77. Many are owned by the Peabody Trust, which has limited the changes residents can make to properties in this conservation zone.

Just outside Clapham Junction, there are plenty of shops along St John's Hill and Lavender Hill, as well as performing arts powerhouse Battersea Arts Centre.

The most sought-after housing is not up the Junction, but south of Battersea Rise (A3) – 'between the commons', as the estate agents say. Here are big houses, green spaces, access to the tube, and the numerous shops, bars and restaurants of Northcote Road. Wealthy thirtysomethings who have made a mint in law or finance come here to raise families. Clapham's prep schools, which feed the capital's public schools, do good business. Those who prefer to send children to a state primary tend to invest in private tutors to get their children through the entrance exams. Just to the west is Lambeth: the borough cuts through the middle of Clapham Common, from Wix's Lane to Clapham South station.

Wandsworth Town

For years, the borough's flagship town centre has been a bit of an embarrassment: a traffic-clogged mess of roads, without a proper centre, that forever harked back to past glories. The smell of hops from the famous Young's Brewery ceased to blow across Ram Street in 2006, when Young's sent its brewing operations up to Bedford. Now the biggest business in Wandsworth Town is property development. The Ram Brewery is earmarked to be a new residential and retail quarter, part of a multi-million-pound regeneration of the area, but one that has been the subject of planning wrangles for several years.

Wandsworth Town has some positives, including Southside, the regenerated shopping centre that used to be a ghastly Arndale. More attractive is the residential area known as the Tonsleys, near the river and town centre, with picturesque shops and cafés along largely traffic-free Old York Road. The gorgeous Victorian houses around here command high prices.

Sky-high premiums are, of course, paid for river views in Wandsworth's ever-developing Thames-side quarter. Mega-developments include Battersea Reach, which dominates the riverfront at the south end of Wandsworth Bridge, and Point Pleasant, next to Wandsworth Park and once a rather unpleasant industrial area, dominated by a waste-transfer station. Little Victorian terraces and the antique Cat's Back pub add charm, but, mostly, Wandsworth Riverside is like a whole new town, daunting in its shininess.

Tooting Bec Lido. See p189.

The council pledges affordable housing will be developed alongside the swanky penthouses, and developers are having to improve play areas in local parks and contribute to the upkeep of the promised riverside walkway. But locals are worried that the current level of transport and leisure provision will not be enough for all the new residents, and not all improvements have been quick to appear – the footpath under Wandsworth Bridge was left closed and derelict for years.

Putney

A reputation for wholesomeness – more than 20 rowing clubs are based on the Thames at Putney Embankment and there's plenty of open space – sells Putney to the middle classes. The riverside area has pubs and a path rather than apartment blocks; there's also a heath, a busy high street and shopping centre, and some fantastic houses with mature gardens. What's not to like? Easy: planes, trains and automobiles.

Namely, the incessant noise of the Heathrow flight path, the oversubscribed rush-hour train services into Waterloo, the lack of tube stations in the westerly reaches, and the clogged South Circular (A205) and Roehampton Lane (A306). Other turn-offs are the stupidly high house prices (for some really quite boring terraced three-beds) and a sense of being lost in the suburbs.

The rest of London turns its gaze on Putney every spring, when the Boat Race attracts huge crowds – though the Great River Race (in autumn) is much more fun to watch. The riverside path provides glorious walking to Barnes and beyond. Away from the Thames, Putney Heath, together with nearby Wimbledon Common, accounts for half of all London's heathland.

Putney remains aloof from too much new housing development because about 50 per cent of its current stock is in a designated conservation area. The streets between Upper Richmond Road (aka the South Circular) and Chartfield Avenue contain the most spacious and expensive abodes. Coalecroft Road and Parkfields, with their terraced Victorian cottages, original lamp-posts and herringbone brick roads, rank among the most attractive. Of more interest, however, is the area near the river, including idiosyncratic Lower Common South on the edge of Putney Lower Common, and the quaint, cosy streets around Cardinal Place.

Popular developments include the Sir Giles Gilbert Scott building, a handsome Grade II-listed red-brick construction in Whitelands Park, just off Sutherland Grove from West Hill. It contains some fancy flats, plus a communal gym, grounds and parking. Also in the park, the new build Hannay House is part of the council's shared ownership scheme for key workers.

Roehampton

Wandsworth's most westerly outpost is Roehampton, which in parts is more like down at-heel Surrey suburbia. Alton Estate, one of the largest council estates in the country – a vast swathe of concrete, mixing low- and high-rise modernist architecture – lies in the south-east corner of Richmond Park. West Alton, inspired by French architect Le Corbusier, is now Grade II listed. Elsewhere are smaller spatterings of council housing and some attractive tree-lined roads. One of London's tallest plane trees can be seen in Minstead Gardens.

There are students galore here – studying at Roehampton University, South Thames College and Queen Mary's Hospital, the main structure of which was built in 1712 and later enlarged by Sir Edwin Lutyens.

The Grade I-listed Roehampton House and other parcels of ex-hospital land are being turned into smart housing schemes, designed to be in keeping with the gracious buildings hereabouts.

The Putney Heath district is the poshest neighbourhood, with huge elaborate Edwardian houses that seem to belong more in the stockbroker belt. Off the north-west edge of the heath, Roehampton Village is also a desirable quarter, with families living in picturesque terraced buildings, near a high street that has a good mix of independent shops, a pub and a parish church. Famous names buried in Putney Vale Cemetery, on the other side of the A3, include Howard Carter, discoverer of Tutankhamen's tomb, writer Enid Blyton, footballer Bobby Moore and racing driver James Hunt.

Earlsfield and Southfields

Earlsfield, once considered a rather nondescript residential area, has become a far more attractive prospect – mainly because it contains spacious homes with gardens that hit the spot for well-paid Londoners who don't want to sever their links with the Smoke. There are also three large council estates: the Aboyne, the Burtop and the Henry Prince.

Garratt Lane, which parallels the flow of the River Wandle from Summerstown, is Earlsfield's main road. This is where you'll find most of the restaurants, bars and pubs, as well as a few old-fashioned businesses. Magdalen Road, behind the rail station, is a cheerily middle-class area. Gorgeous King George's Park, along which the Wandle flows, separates Earlsfield from the well-established pocket of posh that is Southfields.

Southfields has plenty of handsome Victorian terraces and semis with large mature gardens; the neatly appointed properties in 'the Grid' (south-east of the station) are most sought after. Similar houses around Wimbledon Park Road are also popular. The agreeable cafés and shops on low-key Replingham Road give the place the peaceful air of a Home Counties town. Southfields has a tube, but it's on the slow District line – it's quicker to use Earlsfield's excellent overground station. Nonetheless, Southfields trumps Earlsfield on the grounds that the houses are bigger and grander; consequently, the whole atmosphere is rather smug.

Balham

If the presence of a Waitrose, an organic butcher and two weekend farmers' markets signals gentrification, Balham long ago reached the sunny uplands of desirability – certainly as far as estate agents are concerned. High house prices are a given. Bars and restaurants continue to open apace, but Balham's workaday town centre and High Road (Iceland, Nando's), despite various council initiatives to sex them up,

Tooting Bec Common, one of Wandsworth's many green spaces.

evoke a sense of grinding tedium rather than metropolitan cool.

Balham can boast of a huge stock of Victorian houses of good proportions (even if the gardens are a bit tiddly). It also has a train and tube station (albeit on the often troublesome Northern line), and a close relationship with Wandsworth, Tooting Bec and Clapham commons. Young professionals untroubled by plans for procreation invest in serviced flats in Du Cane Court, a distinctive 1937 art deco apartment block on Balham High Road.

Tooting

House prices are pushing the well-to-do further and further south and west, but Tooting will never really be highfalutin. This agreeably diverse area, familiar to telly addicts of all ages (from viewers of *Citizen Smith* to *Little Britain*) is defined by the stretch of Upper Tooting Road between the Bec and Broadway tube stations – the curry corridor. Tooting is the only area in London where you can find good East African Asian, Gujarati, South Indian, Pakistani and Sri Lankan restaurants within a ten-minute walk of one another. There are plenty of Asian greengrocers, too, for exotic fruit, veg, snacks, spices and sweets.

St George's Hospital is one of the biggest employers in Wandsworth, and dominates the ebb and flow of people around Tooting Broadway. The preponderance of low-paid health workers with nowhere to live has led to frantic demands for the council to create more affordable housing for key workers. This it is doing, and proudly trumpeting the fact, but plenty of property speculators have focused on Tooting too – numerous tiny expensive flats are being squeezed into defunct commercial buildings all over the district. House hunters favour Furzedown (near Tooting Bec) and the more affordable Edwardian terraces of Tooting Broadway. The residential roads around the two local commons (Wandsworth and Tooting Bec) are very smart, with plenty of million-pound houses.

The other reason for living in Tooting is the easy access to large green spaces and sports facilities. Tooting Bec Common has football pitches, tennis courts and the lovely Tooting Bec Lido. Built in 1906, it's London's most beautiful open-air pool, and its biggest: an exhausting 100 yards by 33 yards.

Restaurants & cafés

You're in the right borough for sociable grazing. Wandsworth has dining options galore, from upmarket French restaurants to budget Indian caffs, family-oriented chains to riverside gastropubs. Fashionable eating streets, such as Northcote Road, fill up quickly at weekends, but there's plenty of choice elsewhere.

A focal point for good food for families, Northcote Road has plenty of chain restaurants (Gourmet Burger Kitchen, Nando's) and child-friendly café Crumpet. Young couples gaze romantically over Italian dishes in Osteria Antica Bologna or innovative tapas at modern Spanish hangout Lola Rojo. Newcomer Bistro Délicat adds Austrian dishes to the mix. Around the corner on Webbs Road is French café Couleur, while Battersea Rise has French bistro Le Bouchon Bordelais, jolly Pizza Metro and budget orientalist Banana Tree, as well as a branch of Strada. Most excitingly, it's also the site of hip wine bar Soif. A couple of options are found on St John's Hill – delightful Birdhouse café, and top-notch fish and chips at the Fish Club.

Further north, Battersea High Street has excellent neighbourhood brasserie Galapagos, while nearby Battersea Square is lined with bars and restaurants, including Bennett, an oyster-bar-cum-brasserie. Near Battersea Park, Ransome's Dock is the epitome of a relaxed neighbourhood restaurant, with a varied Modern European menu and a stellar wine list. Next door is Butcher & Grill, combining shop, bar and brasserie. Queenstown Road also has a couple of standouts, namely Tom Ilic – the first go-it-alone venture for a talented young chef acclaimed for his adventurous Modern European cooking – and cheerful Argentine grill Santa Maria del Sur.

On the Balham edge of Wandsworth Common, well-regarded French veteran Chez Bruce is king of all it surveys on Bellevue Road. Wandsworth Town's riverside developments are blessed with the Waterfront, a splendid modern gastropub run by Young's, and Marco Polo, a lively Italian restaurant that appeals to all age groups. For fish and chips, try posher-than-average Brady's near the train station.

Restaurants in Putney tend to cluster on Upper Richmond Road and Putney High

Iberian specialist **Lola Rojo**, on busy Northcote Road.

Street. The former contains Ma Goa, which showcases Portuguese-influenced Goan specialities; family-run French bistro L'Auberge; long-running Japanese Chosan; and Wallace & Co café, owned by Greg Wallace of *MasterChef* fame. Further towards Barnes is a branch of steak specialist Popeseye. The High Street tends towards chain restaurants, but also has family-oriented Eddie Catz, Spanish outpost La Mancha, and Enoteca Turi, a classy Italian with a superb wine list. Just off the High Street, Royal China is reliable for dim sum and daily specials. Head towards the river, and on Lower Richmond Road you'll find the flagship branch of the Thai Square chain, housed in a striking modern building next to Putney Bridge.

Earlsfield's eateries are found mainly along Garratt Lane. Wine bar Willie Gunn (*see p193*) has a restaurant attached. Across St George's Park to Southfields, the very splendid Earl Spencer gastropub still hits all the right buttons, with its wide-ranging menu, big portions and fine ales.

Eating in Balham is getting better. The area's finest restaurant is still Lamberts, a Modern European stalwart, but Harrison's (slick bar-brasserie), Avalon (a grown-up gastropub with a lovely garden) and Balham Bowls Club (charming bar-restaurant, *see p192*) draw the crowds too. Ever-popular Ciullo's is a family-friendly Italian option.

Tooting has long been famed for Indian cuisine, with many different regions represented. A favourite is Radha Krishna Bhavan (South Indian), while Indian sweets are the speciality of Pooja. Good, cheap and fiery-hot food can be had at local Sri Lankan cafés Apollo Banana Leaf and Jaffna House. European alternatives are provided by Rick's Restaurant (Mod Euro with a Spanish edge) and Harrington's (pie and mash).

Apollo Banana Leaf *190 Tooting High Street, SW17 0SF (8696 1423).*
L'Auberge *22 Upper Richmond Road, SW15 2RX (8874 3593, www.ardillys.com).*
Avalon *16 Balham Hill, SW12 9EB (8675 8613, www.theavalonlondon.com).*
Banana Tree *75-79 Battersea Rise, SW11 1HN (7228 2828, www.bananatree.co.uk).*
Bennett *7-9 Battersea Square, SW11 3RA (7223 5545, www.bennettsbrasserie.com).*
Birdhouse *123 St John's Hill, SW11 1SZ (7228 6663, www.birdhou.se).*
Bistro Délicat *124 Northcote Road, SW11 6QU (7924 3566, www.bistrodelicat.com).*
Le Bouchon Bordelais *5-9 Battersea Rise, SW11 1HG (7738 0307, www.lebouchon.co.uk).*
Brady's *513 Old York Road, SW18 1TF (8877 9599, www.bradysfish.co.uk).*
Butcher & Grill *39-41 Parkgate Road, SW11 4NP (7924 3999, www.thebutcherandgrill.com).*
Chez Bruce *2 Bellevue Road, SW17 7EG (8672 0114, www.chezbruce.co.uk).*

Chosan *292 Upper Richmond Road, SW15 6TH (8788 9626).*

Ciullo's *31 Balham High Road, SW12 9AL (8675 3072).*

Couleur *32 Webbs Road, SW11 6SF (7924 3030).*

Crumpet *66 Northcote Road, SW11 6QL (7924 1117, www.crumpet.biz).*

Earl Spencer *260-262 Merton Road, SW18 5JL (8870 9244, www.theearlspencer.co.uk).*

Eddie Catz *68-70 Putney High Street, SW15 1SF (0845 201 1268, www.eddiecatz.com).*

Enoteca Turi *28 Putney High Street, SW15 1SQ (8785 4449, www.enotecaturi.com).*

Fish Club *189 St John's Hill, SW11 1TH (7978 7115, www.thefishclub.com).*

Galapagos *169 Battersea High Street, SW11 3JS (8488 4989, www.galapagosfoods.co.uk).*

Harrington's *3 Selkirk Road, SW17 0ER (8672 1877).*

Harrison's *15-19 Bedford Hill, SW12 9EX (8675 6900, www.harrisonsbalham.co.uk).*

Jaffna House *90 Tooting High Street, SW17 0RN (8672 7786, www.jaffnahouse.co.uk).*

Lamberts *2 Station Parade, Balham High Road, SW12 9AZ (8675 2233, www.lambertsrestaurant.com).*

Lola Rojo *70 Northcote Road, SW11 6QL (7350 2262, www.lolarojo.net).*

Ma Goa *242-244 Upper Richmond Road, SW15 6TG (8780 1767, www.ma-goa.com).*

La Mancha *32 Putney High Street, SW15 1SQ (8780 1022, www.lamancha.co.uk).*

Marco Polo *6-7 Riverside Quarter, Eastfields Avenue, SW18 1LP (8874 7007, www.marco polo.uk.net).*

Osteria Antica Bologna *23 Northcote Road, SW11 1NG (7978 4771, www.osteria.co.uk).*

Pizza Metro *64 Battersea Rise, SW11 1EQ (7228 3812, www.pizzametropizza.com).*

Pooja *168-170 Upper Tooting Road, SW17 7ER (8672 4523, www.poojasweets.com).*

Popeseye *277 Upper Richmond Road, SW15 6SP (8788 7733, www.popeseye.com).*

Radha Krishna Bhavan *86 Tooting High Street, SW17 0RN (8682 0969, www.tooting southindian.co.uk).*

Ransome's Dock *35-37 Parkgate Road, SW11 4NP (7223 1611, www.ransomesdock.co.uk).*

Rick's Restaurant *122 Mitcham Road, SW17 9NH (8767 5219, www.ricks-restaurant.co.uk).*

Royal China *3 Chelverton Road, SW15 1RN (8788 0907, www.royalchinaputney.co.uk).*

Santa Maria del Sur *129 Queenstown Road, SW8 3RH (7622 2088, www.santamariadel sur.co.uk).*

Soif *27 Battersea Rise, SW11 1HG (7223 1112).*

Thai Square *2-4 Lower Richmond Road, SW15 1LB (8780 1811, www.thaisq.com).*

Tom Ilic *123 Queenstown Road, SW8 3RH (7622 0555, www.tomilic.com).*

Wallace & Co *146 Upper Richmond Road, SW15 2SW (8780 0052, www.wallaceand co.com).*

Waterfront *Baltimore House, Juniper Drive, SW18 1TS (7228 4297, www.waterfront london.co.uk).*

Bars & pubs

Old and new money sloshes around Wandsworth, making this a great district for drinking, whatever your tipple. In the established honeypots of Battersea and Clapham – especially Northcote Road – young, loud professionals gather at a range of bars. The easy-going Northcote pub has been joined by the Draft House, a beer specialist with a dining room. The Holy Drinker, Frieda B and Underdog bars all appeal to twentysomethings.

Elsewhere in Battersea, there's established pub theatre the Latchmere, cocktail bar Alchemist and sibling bars Lost Angel and Lost Society.

Wandsworth Town's most famous watering hole is the beautiful, green tiled Alma, now a Young's pub with a dining room that peddles gargantuan portions of gastro favourites. The Ship, also part of the Young's empire, has a riverside setting (but

TRANSPORT

Tube stations *District* East Putney, Southfields; *Northern* Clapham South, Balham, Tooting Bec, Tooting Broadway

Rail stations *London Overground* Clapham Junction; *Southern* Battersea Park, Wandsworth Road, Clapham Junction, Wandsworth Common, Balham; *South West Trains* Queenstown Road, Clapham Junction, Wandsworth Town, Putney, Earlsfield

Main bus routes *into central London* 14, 19, 22, 35, 44, 74, 77, 87, 137, 344, 414; *night buses* N19, N22, N35, N44, N74, N87, N133, N137, N155; *24-hour buses* 14, 344

Development plans The London Overground extension, connecting Clapham Junction and Surrey Quays, should open at the end of 2012

Balham Bowls Club, one of the area's quirkier hangouts.

not overly inspiring views), a garden and barbecue. Pubs away from the river include the East Hill and the cramped former lighterman's pub Cat's Back.

In Putney, the cavernous Duke's Head (another handsome Young's hostelry, recently refurbished) insists it offers views of the Thames, although these are hard to achieve given the numbers of drinkers outside on a summer evening. The nearby Half Moon (*see p195*), now part of the Geronimo Inns stable, is a prime venue for bands of all musical persuasions. There's also the Coat & Badge, the unpretentious Whistle & Flute (a rare Fuller's outpost in these parts) and Putney Station, a bright, modern wine bar with good food.

Many of Balham's pubs lead a double life, catering for both sides of the gentrification divide, though the Devonshire has been gastopubbed beyond recognition. Otherwise, there's the Bedford, which hosts top comedy nights and low-key acoustic sets while maintaining a noisy bar. Exhibit offsets its unappealing location (adjoining a supermarket car park) with a trendy cinema space, comfort food and a relaxed, cocktail bar vibe. The Balham Bowls Club was indeed a bowls club; now it's an eccentric bar with original fixtures and fittings intact. The Tooting Tram & Social is by the same owners, and equally oddball.

Tooting also offers the likeable, laid-back Antelope, and the Selkirk, which feels like

a proper local pub, with amiable staff, not overly poncey food and great beers. The Trafalgar Arms has a huge garden and close connections with St George's Hospital next door.

Further south, in Earlsfield, is wine bar Willie Gunn, and the food-focused Jolly Gardeners, where the only shame is that there are no ales on tap.

Alchemist *225 St John's Hill, SW11 1TH (7801 9650, www.thealchemistbar.co.uk).*
Alma *499 Old York Road, SW18 1TF (8870 2537, www.almawandsworth.com).*
Antelope *76 Mitcham Road, SW17 9NG (8672 3888, www.theantelopepub.com).*
Balham Bowls Club *7-9 Ramsden Road, SW12 8QX (8673 4700, www.antic-ltd.com).*
Bedford *77 Bedford Hill, SW12 9HD (8682 8940, www.thebedford.co.uk).*
Cat's Back *86-88 Point Pleasant, SW18 1NN (8877 0818, www.thecatsback.co.uk).*
Coat & Badge *8 Lacy Road, SW15 1NI (8788 4900, www.geronimo-inns.co.uk).*
Devonshire *39 Balham High Road, SW12 9AN (8673 1363, www.dukeofdevonshire balham.com).*
Draft House *94 Northcote Road, SW11 6QW (7924 1814, www.drafthouse.co.uk).*
Duke's Head *8 Lower Richmond Road, SW15 1JN (8788 2552, www.dukesheadputney.co.uk).*
East Hill *21 Alma Road, SW18 1AA (8874 1833, www.geronimo-inns.co.uk).*
Exhibit *12 Balham Station Road, SW12 9SG (8772 6556, www.theexhibit.co.uk).*

Frieda B 46 Battersea Rise, SW11 1EE
(7228 7676, www.frieda-b.co.uk).
Holy Drinker 59 Northcote Road, SW11 1NP
(7801 0544, www.holydrinker.co.uk).
Jolly Gardeners 214 Garratt Lane, SW18
4EA (8870 8417, www.thejollygardeners.co.uk).
Latchmere 503 Battersea Park Road, SW11
3BW (7223 3549).
Lost Angel 339 Battersea Park Road, SW11
4LS (7622 2112, www.lostangel.co.uk).
Lost Society 697 Wandsworth Road, SW8
3JF (7652 6526, www.lostsociety.co.uk).
Northcote 2 Northcote Road, SW11 1NT
(7223 5378).
Putney Station 94-98 Upper Richmond Road,
SW15 2SP (8780 0242, www.brinkleys.com).
Selkirk 60 Selkirk Road, SW17 0ES (8672
6235, www.theselkirk.co.uk).
Ship 41 Jew's Row, SW18 1TB (8870 9667,
www.theship.co.uk).
Tooting Tram & Social 46-48 Mitcham Road,
SW17 9NA (8767 0278, www.antic-ltd.com).
Trafalgar Arms 148-158 Tooting High Street,
SW17 0RT (8767 6199, www.trafalgararms.
com).
Underdog 8-10 Northcote Road, SW11 1NT
(7924 6699, www.theunderdogbar.co.uk).
Whistle & Flute 46-48 Putney High Street,
SW15 1SQ (8780 5437, www.fullers.co.uk).
Willie Gunn 422 Garratt Lane, SW18 4HW
(8946 7773, www.williegunn.co.uk).

Shops

The most picturesque (if not the most useful
or economical) way to shop for food has to
be basket over arm, down Northcote Road.
Select local honey from the Hive, traceable
steak from butcher Dove and cheese from
Hamish Johnston, to be washed down with
wine from Philglas & Swiggot. On parallel
Webbs Road, there's romantic florist La
Maison des Roses and hi-fi and home
cinema equipment at Oranges & Lemons.
With a small antiques market for collectable
china and restored furniture, along with a
traditional street market, Northcote Road
is all about living the dream, family style.

Fashion-wise, there are branches of White
Stuff, Kew, Question Air and Iris, plus shoes
and bags at Opus and high-quality toiletries
at Verde. For children, there's JoJo Maman
Bébé, then mini-fashions from Quackers,
shoes from One Small Step One Giant
Leap, toys from QT and Letterbox, and the
wherewithal for a musical education from

Northcote Music. Bolingbroke Bookshop
has a large kids' section and is also the
lifeline for local reading groups.

Elsewhere, Battersea does all right
for independents, and benefits from
vicarious Sloaniness thanks to its proximity
to Chelsea. Designer Alterations specialises
in alterations and repairs, and offers a
wardrobe 'detox' service, while milliner
Edwina Ibbotson will do you a titfer for
Ascot. Anita's Vintage Fashion Fairs sport
vintage clothing from Biba, Ossie Clark,
Dior and more, and take place six times a
year, sometimes at Battersea Arts Centre.
Interiors specialists include the London
Door Company and Tablemakers – both
on St John's Hill.

Apart from unlovely retail parks
at either end of Wandsworth Bridge,
Wandsworth Town's retail resources
are boosted by the Southside Shopping
Centre, which has a Waitrose, a Virgin
Active health club, a 14-screen Cineworld
and 65 high-street stores, from H&M to
HMV. There's a food market near the
train station on Saturdays.

Balham and Tooting run the gamut of
shopping experiences. Both are loath to
let go of their scruffy high streets and
local markets. Tooting, in particular, still
specialises in African and Asian produce,
available in the covered 1930s arcades of
Broadway Market and Tooting Market.
Deepak Food is the place for Asian staples
and spices. Balham tries harder to appease
the incomers, with affordable modern
furniture at Dwell, organic meat at
Chadwick's and two food markets: at
Chestnut Grove School on Saturdays,
and Hildreth Street on Sundays. Amid
the Bedford Hill cafés and bars sits
Lucas Bond, a kookily elegant gift shop.

Putney High Street is traffic-clogged
and lined with unenticing chains, though
the Exchange Shopping Centre is a pleasant,
well-appointed mall with a Waitrose. At
Will's Art Warehouse – which has been
dubbed the 'Oddbins of the art world' –
you can pick up affordable artworks to
decorate your home.

Anita's Vintage Fashion Fairs 8325 5789,
www.vintagefashionfairs.com.
Balham Farmers' Market Chestnut Grove
Primary School, junction of Chestnut Grove
& Hearnville Road, SW12 8JZ (www.lfm.org.uk/
markets/balham).

Bolingbroke Bookshop *147 Northcote Road, SW11 6QB (7223 9344).*
Chadwick's Organic Butchers *109 Balham High Road, SW12 9AP (8772 1895, www. chadwicksbutchers.co.uk).*
Deepak Food *953-959 Garratt Lane, SW17 0LR (8767 7819).*
Designer Alterations *220A Queenstown Road, SW8 4LP (7498 4360, www.designer alterations.com).*
Dove *71 Northcote Road, SW11 6PJ (7223 5191, www.doveandson.co.uk).*
Dwell *264 Balham High Road, SW17 7AN (0845 675 9076, www.dwell.co.uk).*
Edwina Ibbotson *45 Queenstown Road, SW8 3RG (7498 5390).*
Exchange Shopping Centre *High Street, SW15 1TW (8780 1056, www.theexchange sw15.com).*
Hamish Johnston *48 Northcote Road, SW11 1PA (7738 0741).*
Hildreth Street Market *www.hildrethstreetmarket.co.uk.*
Hive Honey Shop *93 Northcote Road, SW11 6PL (7924 6233, www.thehivehoneyshop.co.uk).*
Iris *97 Northcote Road, SW11 6PL (7924 1836, www.irisfashion.co.uk).*
JoJo Maman Bébé *www.jojomamanbebe.co.uk; 68 Northcote Road, SW11 6DS (7228 0322); 72 Northcote Road, SW11 6DS (7223 8510); Unit 30, The Exchange, SW15 1TW (8780 5165).*
Kew *58 Northcote Road, SW11 1PA (7223 5378, www.kew159.com).*

Letterbox *99 Northcote Road, SW11 6PL (0844 573 4561, www.letterbox.co.uk).*
London Door Company *155 St John's Hill, SW11 1TQ (7801 0877, www.londondoor.co.uk).*
Lucas Bond *45 Bedford Hill, SW12 9EY (8675 9300, www.lucasbond.com).*
La Maison des Roses *48 Webbs Road, SW11 6SF (7228 5700, www.maison-des-roses.com).*
Northcote Music *155C Northcote Road, SW11 6QB (7228 0074).*
Northcote Road Antiques Market *155A Northcote Road, SW11 6QB (7228 6850, www.spectrumsoft.net/nam.htm).*
One Small Step One Giant Leap *www.onesmallsteponegiantleap.com; 49 Northcote Road, SW11 1NJ (7223 9314); Unit D2, The Exchange, SW15 1TW (8789 2046).*
Opus *57 Northcote Road, SW11 1NP (7978 4240, www.opusshoes.co.uk).*
Oranges & Lemons *61-63 Webbs Road, SW11 6RX (7924 2040, www.oandlhifi.co.uk).*
Philglas & Swiggot *21 Northcote Road, SW11 1NG (7924 4494, www.philglas-swiggot. com).*
QT Toys *90 Northcote Road, SW11 6QN (7223 8637).*
Quackers *155D Northcote Road, SW11 6QB (7978 4235).*
Question Air *143-145 Northcote Road, SW11 6PX (7924 6948, www.question-air.com).*
Southside Shopping Centre *Wandsworth High Street, SW18 4TF (8870 2141, www.southsidewandsworth.com).*

Local hub **Tooting Market**. See p193.

Tablemakers *153 St John's Hill, SW11 1TQ (7223 2075, www.tablemakers.co.uk).*
Verde *133A Northcote Road, SW11 6PJ (7223 2095, www.verde.co.uk).*
White Stuff *39 Northcote Road, SW11 1NJ (7228 7129, www.whitestuff.com).*
Will's Art Warehouse *180 Lower Richmond Road, SW15 1LY (8246 4840, www.willsart.com).*

Arts & attractions

Cinemas & theatres

Battersea Arts Centre (BAC) *Lavender Hill, SW11 5TN (7223 6557, www.bac.org.uk). Forward-thinking theatre specialising in new writers and companies.*
Cineworld Wandsworth *Southside Shopping Centre, Wandsworth High Street, SW18 4TF (0871 200 2000, www.cineworld.co.uk).*
Odeon Putney *26 Putney High Street, SW15 1SN (0871 224 4007, www.odeon.co.uk).*
Putney Arts Theatre *Ravenna Road, SW15 6AW (8788 6943, www.putneyartstheatre. org.uk).*
Tara Arts Theatre *356 Garratt Lane, SW18 4ES (8333 4457, www.tara-arts.com). Cross-cultural (British Asian) enterprise producing quality community theatre.*
Theatre 503 *The Latchmere, 503 Battersea Park Road, SW11 3BW (7978 7040, www. theatre503.com).*

Galleries & museums

De Morgan Centre *38 West Hill, SW18 1RZ (8871 1144, www.demorgan.org.uk). Works by William De Morgan, the Victorian ceramic artist, and his wife Evelyn, the painter.*
Hua *Unit 7B, 8 Hester Road, SW11 4AX (7738 1215, www.hua-gallery.com). Stunning riverside art gallery near Battersea Park specialising in contemporary Chinese art.*
Pump House Gallery *Battersea Park, SW11 4NJ (8871 7572). Tiny art gallery in a 19th-century building.*
Wandsworth Museum *38 West Hill, SW18 1RZ (8870 6060, www.wandsworthmuseum. co.uk). State-of-the-art local history museum on the site of the old West Hill Library.*

Music & comedy venues

Bedford *77 Bedford Hill, SW12 9HD (8682 8949, www.thebedford.com).*
Half Moon *93 Lower Richmond Road, SW15 1EU (8780 9383, www.halfmoon.co.uk). One of London's longest-running music venues, this*

pub – recently revamped – has hosted almost everyone over the years (the Stones, Elvis Costello, the Who, U2).

Other attractions

Battersea Dogs & Cats Home *4 Battersea Park Road, SW8 4AA (7622 3626, www.dogs home.org). Casual visitors are welcome at this world-famous animal sanctuary.*
Battersea Park Children's Zoo *Entrance at Chelsea Gate, Queenstown Road, SW11 4NJ (7924 5826, www.batterseaparkzoo.co.uk).*

Sport & fitness

The council's sports centres (run by DC Leisure) are excellent, among the best in London. A £15 million overhaul of all the centres in the borough was completed with the reopening of Roehampton Sport & Fitness Centre in early 2008. The private sector is dominated by the big-name chains.

Wandsworth

COUNCIL TAX

		Main borough area	Commons area
A	up to £40,000	£454.43	£471.01
B	£40,001-£52,000	£530.16	£549.50
C	£52,001-£68,000	£605.90	£628.01
D	£68,001-£88,000	£681.64	£706.51
E	£88,001-£120,000	£833.11	£863.51
F	£120,001-£160,000	£984.59	£1,020.51
G	£160,001-£320,000	£1,136.06	£1,177.51
H	over £320,000	£1,363.27	£1,413.01

Gyms & leisure centres

Balham Leisure Centre *Elmfield Road, SW17 8AN (8772 9577, www.dcleisure centres.co.uk).*

Fitness First *www.fitnessfirst.co.uk; 34 St John's Hill, SW11 1SA (0844 571 2844); 279-291 Balham High Road, SW17 7BA (0844 571 2804); 276-288 Lavender Hill, SW11 1LJ (0844 571 2843). Private.*

Latchmere Leisure Centre *Burns Road, SW11 2DY (7207 8004, www.dcleisurecentres.co.uk).*

Nuffield Health *www.nuffieldhealth.com; King George's Park, Burr Road, SW18 4SQ (8874 1155); Sheepcote Lane, Burns Road, SW11 5BT (7228 4400). Private.*

Physical Culture Studios *21-22 The Arches, Winthorpe Road, SW15 2LW (8780 2172, www.physicalculture.co.uk). Private.*

Putney Leisure Centre *Dryburgh Road, SW15 1BL (8785 0388, www.dcleisurecentres.co.uk).*

Roehampton Sport & Fitness Centre *Laverstoke Gardens, SW15 4JB (8785 0535, www.dcleisurecentres.co.uk).*

Tooting Leisure Centre *Greaves Place, off Garratt Lane, SW17 0NE (8333 7555, www.dcleisurecentres.co.uk).*

Virgin Active *www.virginactive.co.uk; 154-160 Upper Richmond Road, SW15 2SW (8246 6676); Smugglers Way, SW18 1DG (8875 2222). Private.*

Wandle Recreation Centre *Mapleton Road, SW18 4DN (8871 1149, www.dcleisure centres.co.uk).*

Yorky's *24-28 York Road, SW11 3QA (7228 6266, www.yorkys-gym.com). Private.*

Other facilities

There are plenty of sports pitches in Battersea Park, and numerous rowing clubs along the Thames in Putney.

Sivananda Yoga Vedanta Centre *51 Felsham Road, SW15 1AZ (8780 0160, www.sivananda.co.uk). Long-established yoga centre offering numerous classes.*

Tooting Bec Lido *Tooting Bec Road, SW16 1RU (8871 7198, www.dcleisurecentres.co.uk). The second-largest open-air pool in Europe, open from the end of May to September. Home of the South London Swimming Club (www.slsc.org.uk).*

Schools

Primary

There are 55 state primary schools in the borough, including 17 church schools and one Muslim school. There are also 22 independent primaries, including one French school, one Montessori school and one Steiner school. See www.wandsworth.gov.uk, www.edubase.gov.uk and www.ofsted.gov.uk for more information.

Secondary

Ashcroft Technology Academy *100 West Hill, SW15 2UT (8877 0357, www.atacademy.org.uk).*

Battersea Technology College *401 Battersea Park Road, SW11 5AP (7622 0026, www.batterseaparkschool.org).*

Burntwood School *Burntwood Lane, SW17 0AQ (8946 6201, www.burntwoodschool.com). Girls only; mixed sixth form.*

Chestnut Grove School *45 Chestnut Grove, SW12 8JZ (8673 8737, www.chestnutgrove. wandsworth.sch.uk).*

Elliott School *Pullman Gardens, SW15 3DG (8788 3421, www.elliott-school.org.uk).*

Emanuel School *Battersea Rise, SW11 1HS (8870 4171, www.emanuel.org.uk). Private.*

Ernest Bevin College *Beechcroft Road, SW17 7DF (8672 8582, www.ernestbevin. org.uk). Boys only; mixed sixth form.*

Graveney School *Welham Road, SW17 9BU (8682 7000, www.graveney.org).*

Putney High School *35 Putney Hill, SW15 6BH (8788 4886, www.putneyhigh.gdst.net). Private; girls only.*

St Cecilia's, Wandsworth School
Sutherland Grove, SW18 5JR (8780 1244, www.saintcecilias.wandsworth.sch.uk). Church of England.
Saint John Bosco College *Princes Way, SW19 6QE (8246 6000, www.sjbc.wandsworth. sch.uk). Roman Catholic.*
Southfields Community College
333 Merton Road, SW18 5JU (8875 2600, www.southfields.wandsworth.sch.uk).

Property

WHAT THE AGENTS SAY:
'We deal mainly with property in the area known as 'Between the Commons', named, predictably, for its position between Clapham and Wandsworth commons. Battersea Park is not far either, and these green spaces are a big draw for young families. Schooling in the area is superb too – places at the two local primaries are highly sought after. There's a great mix of families and young professionals, which creates a buzzing social hub. The housing stock consists mostly of pretty Victorian terraced properties, usually with three or four bedrooms. More new-builds have cropped up in the past few years, but these are located towards the river and are more popular with young couples who work in central London, rather than families.'
Tom Crouch, John Thorogood, Battersea

Average property prices
Detached £1,118,227
Semi-detached £664,869
Terraced £545,921
Flat £330,316

Local estate agents
Andrews *www.andrewsonline.co.uk; 4 offices in the borough (Battersea 7326 8171, Balham 8675 2244, Southfields 8874 6686, Putney 8780 2233).*
Cochrane & Wilson *78 St John's Hill, SW11 1SF (7924 5444, www.cochraneandwilson.com).*
Craigie & Co *309 Garratt Lane, SW18 4DX (8874 7475, www.craigie-co.co.uk).*
First Union *www.first-union.co.uk; 2 offices in the borough (Battersea 7771 7100, Wandsworth 8480 4444).*
Jacksons Estate Agents
www.jacksonsestateagents.com; 5 offices in the borough (Balham 8675 6565, Battersea 7924 2255, Earlsfield 8971 7070, Tooting 8767 0522, Wandsworth 8875 8899).

John Thorogood *140 Northcote Road, SW11 6QZ (7228 7474, www.john-thorogood.co.uk).*
Rolfe East *168 Putney High Street, SW15 1RS (8780 3355, www.rolfe-east.com).*
Time2move *28 London Road, SW17 9HW (8640 0146).*

Other information

Council
Wandsworth Borough Council *The Town Hall, Wandsworth High Street, SW18 2PU (8871 6000, www.wandsworth.gov.uk).*

Legal services
Battersea CAB *125 Bolingbroke Grove, SW11 1DA (8333 6960, www.wandsworthcabx.org.uk).*
Battersea Law Centre *125 Bolingbroke Grove, SW11 1DA (7585 0716, www.lawcentres.org.uk).*
Roehampton CAB *166 Roehampton Lane, SW15 4HR (8333 6960, www.wandsworth cabx.org.uk).*
Tooting & Balham CAB *4th floor, Bedford House, 215 Balham High Road, SW17 7BQ (8333 6960, www.wandsworthcabx.org.uk).*

Local information
www.putneysw15.com.
www.southlondonpress.co.uk.
www.wandsworthguardian.co.uk.
www.wandsworthsw18.com.

Open spaces & allotments
Council allotments *8871 6441, www.wandsworth.gov.uk.*
Roehampton Garden Society *Paula Alderson 8789 5836, www.roehampton allotments.co.uk.*
Open spaces *www.wandsworth.gov.uk/parks.*

RECYCLING
Household waste recycled & composted 28%
Main recycling centres
www.wrwa.gov.uk; Western Riverside Civic Amenity Site, Smugglers Way, SW18 1JS (8871 2788); Cringle Dock Civic Amenity Site, Cringle Street, SW8 5BX (7622 1046)
Other recycling services green waste collection; home composting
Council contact Waste Services, Room 57A, Town Hall, Wandsworth High Street, SW18 2PU (8871 8558, www. wandsworth.gov.uk/wastemanagement)

'Merton's got a great cultural buzz. It has lots of theatres and arts festivals, the old textile works at Merton Abbey Mills, a medieval chapter house and a beautiful Buddhist temple. It confounds most people's expectations.'

Stephen Midlane, Associate Director, Polka Theatre

Merton

The name Merton – meaning 'farmstead by the pool' – dates from the tenth century, and while this is a fairly modern London borough (it was formed in 1965), it hasn't completely relinquished its prettily bucolic, old-fashioned feel. Despite its reserved spirit, Merton is a borough of bustling amenities and burgeoning town centres, handy transport links and intriguing contrasts.

Neighbourhoods

Wimbledon, Wimbledon Village and Wimbledon Park

Every year in late June, Wimbledon becomes the focus of international attention as its All England Lawn Tennis Club hosts the championship fortnight. The area blossoms during the tournament, but at any time of year Wimbledon town centre is the buzzing hub of Merton, with excellent transport links (train, tube, tram and lots of buses).

The main thoroughfare, the Broadway, is a shopping hotspot by day – you'll find most chain retailers here, concentrated in the Centre Court shopping centre, formerly the town hall, adjoining Wimbledon station. There's a glut of new-build property developments in the area; some, like the flats on the site of the former Wimbledon football ground, have been controversial.

Property has never been cheap in Wimbledon, and there are plenty of razzle-dazzle houses located around Wimbledon Village and the Common, where prices

easily soar into the millions. You'll find interesting architectural variety on the upper reaches of hilly Arthur Road, adjacent Vineyard Hill Road and the parkside stretch of Wimbledon Park Road (which overlooks a golf club) - but it will cost you.

Residents are also well provided with cultural amenities. Theatregoers have the pick of three venues on the Broadway: the plushly restored New Wimbledon Theatre; its intimate Studio space; it's a child-friendly jewel that is the Polka Theatre. The area has also spawned some acclaimed musicians – both Jamie T and MIA grew up around here – so it's a shame that the nightlife, including a cinema and numerous bars and restaurants, mostly comprises identikit chains.

Wimbledon Village, up the hill from the town centre, is the smartest and most desirable district, with the boutique-lined High Street running through it to Wimbledon Common. A strangely rustic sight for London is the horses that regularly stop the traffic: there's been a riding stables here for over 100 years.

Of Merton's many green spaces, Wimbledon Common (the stamping ground of Elisabeth Beresford's loveable eco-warriors the Wombles) offers 1,140 acres of woodland, including its own windmill and golf club. It has also proved popular with fungus foragers, although there has been a clampdown on wild mushroom picking. Less famous, but equally unmissable, are the romantic landscaped gardens of Cannizaro House hotel (West Side Common); it's a quaint (if pricey) place to take afternoon tea, while Cannizaro Park features an aviary and sculptures, and hosts various events. One tube stop along the District line, the compact satellite of Wimbledon Park provides another local green haven, including kids' playgrounds, tennis courts, bowling greens, football pitches and a boating lake.

South Wimbledon and Colliers Wood

History hasn't been as well preserved in these neighbourhoods – a shame, as they conceal some of the most interesting local stories. You'd never guess that, in 1963, the Beatles played at the Wimbledon Palais on Merton High Street – a site that now consists of fairly bland residences.

Merton's new-build phenomenon is most pronounced in South Wimbledon, traditionally the more rough and ready end of the Broadway, but increasingly home to young professionals who've taken advantage of the cheaper property prices. The side streets off Haydons Road are worth checking out for Victorian and Edwardian terraces, while in the so-called 'Poet's Corner' (a quiet enclave from Tennyson Road to Wilfred Owen Close) houses tend to be newer.

Moving towards Colliers Wood, you'll find evidence of the area's cultural mix, from Asian grocers to Irish pubs, plus a few late-night bars and soulless but convenient retail parks. One dubious landmark is the Tower, a 19-storey 1960s concrete office block, which featured in a Channel 4 programme about Britain's worst buildings; it currently lies empty and its future is the subject of ongoing debate.

The 12th-century Merton Abbey once educated the likes of Thomas Becket; its ruins can be seen behind the Savacentre supermarket car park. The new apartments here have brought a chain gym and more

Highs & Lows

Wimbledon Common Nature trails, horse tracks, cycle paths, sports grounds – and Wombles, of course.
Tennis For two weeks a year, the nation's attention turns to SW19 for the Wimbledon tournament; enterprising residents set up stalls on their driveways.
Global tastes Merton is more cosmopolitan than you might think: foodies can feast on treats from eastern Europe, the Middle East, South Africa and more.

Grim patches There's a reason Colliers Wood was so often used as the location for episodes of The Bill
Morden and Mitcham Morden Hall Park is pleasant, but the streets of these two districts are not massively welcoming, especially at night.
New-builds Yes, it's 'progress', but many locals feel new-build developments are sapping the character from the borough. And who exactly is supposed to afford all these 'luxury apartments'?

TRANSPORT

Tube stations *District* Wimbledon Park, Wimbledon; *Northern* Colliers Wood, South Wimbledon, Morden
Rail stations *South West Trains* Wimbledon, Raynes Park, Motspur Park; *First Capital Connect* Tooting, Haydons Road, Wimbledon, Wimbledon Chase, South Merton, Morden South, St Helier, Mitcham Junction
Tram stops *London Tramlink* Wimbledon, Dundonald Road, Merton Park, Morden Road
Main bus routes *into central London* no direct service; *night buses* N44, N133, N155

fast-food outlets to the area – give these a miss, and instead head to the former Liberty silk works at Abbey Mills, which hosts a weekend craft and book market. On summer evenings, this is a convivial spot to drink and catch jazz and folk acts, alongside the River Wandle.

Morden, Mitcham and Raynes Park

Acclaimed young indie rockers the Good Shoes promoted a 2007 song about their home town with the slogan: 'Morden Life Is Rubbish'. Morden might date back further than the Domesday Book (just 14 occupants were recorded here in 1086), but it's seen little improvement since the 1980s.

Located at the southernmost end of the Northern line, this is where Merton Council is based, in the grim Crown House tower block on traffic-clogged London Road. There's no specific town centre, and time was called on its best-known pub, the Crown Inn (apparently for 'additional office space'), in summer 2007; you're better off heading into Wimbledon for nightlife.

Morden Hall Park, run by the National Trust, is a welcome retreat, with meadows, wetlands, waterways and the Old Snuff Mill environmental education centre. There's a café in the old stables, and a well-stocked garden centre. Head to the park's northern side for Deen City Farm, a big hit with kids.

Like Morden, Mitcham's streets don't seem particularly welcoming after dark – perhaps unsurprisingly, ITV's police drama *The Bill* was filmed around here (and in neighbouring South Wimbledon)

for years. Still, its local shops offer a few treats, including lots of South Asian groceries.

It might be hard to believe that this sprawling suburb was once full of lavender fields (expansive Mitcham Common is now the main local green space), or that remains of a Roman settlement were unearthed near the gasworks. But Mitcham still lays claim to the world's oldest cricket green (dating back to 1730); these days, players have to cross the busy Cricket Green Road to reach the pavilion. It was also home to the pioneering Surrey Iron Railway, between 1803 and 1846; the modern transport links aren't nearly as grand.

Another commuter enclave with rural roots is Raynes Park. Taking its name from 19th-century landowners, it's clearly the most affluent district, with the biggest family residences outside of Wimbledon Village (particularly on Grand Drive), and the lowest crime rates. Developed as a garden suburb (like nearby Merton Park), Raynes Park is sometimes referred to as 'West Wimbledon' by estate agents.

Restaurants & cafés

Merton offers pretty much every kind of chain restaurant on a plate – including such staples as Wagamama, Carluccio's, Pizza Express (two branches – on the Broadway and in Wimbledon Village) and family-friendly Giraffe. In fact, it's even the launch pad for prototype chains – this is where French brasserie Côte started, from the team who conceived the Strada pizza chain (naturally, there's a Strada here too, on Wimbledon High Street). Argentinian grill Buenos Aires and meat specialist Butcher & Grill are also both part of small chains.

There are a few welcome individual establishments too. As this guide went to press, old-school chippie Broadway Place Fish Bar was closed due to illness – it's to be hoped it reopens. La Nonna and Al Forno, meanwhile, are both popular Italian eateries. Opposite Wimbledon Park tube, Dalchini specialises in Hakka Indo-Chinese cuisine. Further north, Café 377 serves full English breakfasts and fresh smoothies to a mix of builders and local yummy mummies. The big developments, however are the Lawn Bistro (French) and the Fox & Grapes (smart restaurant posing

Cah Chi Korean restaurant.

as a gastropub), both of which caused huge excitement when they opened in 2011.

Other finds include Watch Me – a cosy and reasonably priced Sri Lankan restaurant on busy Morden Road (the restaurant's name refers to its open kitchen) – and Cah Chi, a convivial Korean canteen in Raynes Park (close to the established Korean community of New Malden; for more, *see p337*). Cocum offers decent South Indian cuisine.

Al Forno *2A Kings Road, SW19 8QN (8540 5710, www.alfornowimbledon.com).*
Broadway Place Fish Bar *8-10 Hartfield Road, SW19 3TA (8947 5833).*
Buenos Aires *62 Wimbledon Hill Road, SW19 7PA (8947 7544, www.barestaurant. com).*
Butcher & Grill *33 High Street, SW19 5BY (8944 8269, www.thebutcherandgrill.com).*
Café 377 *377 Durnsford Road, SW19 8EF (8946 7733, www.cafe377.com).*
Cah Chi *34 Durham Road, SW20 0TW (8947 1081, www.cahchi.com).*
Cocum *9 Approach Road, SW20 8BA (8540 3250, www.cocumrestaurant.co.uk).*
Côte *8 High Street, SW19 5DX (8947 7100, www.cote-restaurants.co.uk).*
Dalchini *147 Arthur Road, SW19 8AB (8947 5966, www.dalchini.co.uk).*
Fox & Grapes *9 Camp Road, SW19 4UN (8619 1300, www.foxandgrapeswimbledon.co.uk).*

Lawn Bistro *67 High Street, SW19 5EE (8947 8278, www.thelawnbistro.co.uk).*
La Nonna *213-217 The Broadway, SW19 1NL (8542 3060, www.lanonna.co.uk).*
Watch Me *108 Morden Road, SW19 3BP (8286 7900).*

Bars & pubs

Chain bars and pubs dominate Wimbledon town centre. Standouts include quirky cocktail bar Sia and the youthful Suburban Bar & Lounge. The Alexandra occupies a grand 19th-century building; it has a bijou 'roof garden', but the interior is pretty unexceptional. For drinks with real character, head further into Wimbledon Village – beyond the chains, you'll find the supposedly haunted Hand in Hand, which draws crowds to the lawn outside in the summer, and the Rose & Crown, a spruced-up Young's hotel that dates from 1659. Also on the High Street is Hemingways, a cocktail bar.

For real ale fans, the Sultan pub in South Wimbledon remains a homely hotspot, much lauded by CAMRA. The William Morris, near the Merton Abbey Mills crafts enclave, has a beer garden next to the River Wandle.

Locals' Tips

Open spaces are what make Merton special – so make the most of them. There are plenty of suburban playgrounds with kids' facilities, but Cannizaro Park is also lovely for family picnics or romantic dates. **The traditional haunt for star-spotting during Wimbledon fortnight is San Lorenzo restaurant (38 Wimbledon Hill Road, SW19 7PA, 8946 8463, www.labyrintos.com). It's definitely the closest the town centre gets to old-fashioned playboy style.**
Heading into town, the overground train is generally faster than the long haul of the District line – even if the tube does give you a lovely view over Putney Bridge.
It's worth rising early to get to Wimbledon Stadium's car boot sales, held on Saturday and Sunday mornings. There's plenty to buy – clothes, toys, crockery, furniture – but plenty of eagle-eyed bargain hunters too.

Alexandra *33 Wimbledon Hill Road, SW19 7NE (8947 7691, www.alexandrawimbledon. com).*
Bar Sia *105-109 The Broadway, SW19 1QG (8540 8339, www.barsia.com).*
Hand in Hand *6 Crooked Billet, SW19 4RQ (8946 5720, www.thehandinhandwimbledon. co.uk).*
Hemingways *57 High Street, SW19 5EE (8944 7722, www.hemingwaysbar.co.uk).*
Rose & Crown *55 High Street, SW19 5BA (8947 4713, www.roseandcrown wimbledon.co.uk).*
Suburban Bar & Lounge *27 Hartfield Road, SW19 3SG (8543 9788, www.suburbanbar.com).*
Sultan *78 Norman Road, SW19 1BT (8542 4532).*
William Morris *20 Watermill Way, SW19 2RD (8540 0216, www.faucetinn.com).*

Shops

Merton offers a mixed bag for shopaholics. Wimbledon town centre is the main retail area, with a wide range of high-street chain stores (plus a handful of independent retailers and charity shops) located on the Broadway. Centre Court shopping mall has plenty of familiar names, including a branch of Debenhams. Local department store Elys was revamped in 2007, but retains an old-fashioned atmosphere. There are bigger branches of chains in the Priory Retail Park on Merton High Street.

Even Wimbledon Village, once a bastion of high-end boutiques, is now becoming increasingly chain-led (although these are still of the exclusive mini-chain variety, such as Question Air and the long-established Matches boutique). Also worth a browse on the High Street are Bayley & Sage (speciality foods), Cath Kidston (colourful retro homewares), Diane von Furstenberg (one of just two stand-alone DVF shops in London), Luella's Boudoir (bridal boutique) and MaxMara.

The borough's compact farmers' market, held every Saturday (9am-1pm) in the playground of Wimbledon Park Primary School, is popular. The pedestrianised area outside Morrison's supermarket (so-called 'Wimbledon Piazza') also hosts regular continental food markets. And for a more down-to-earth street market experience, Wimbledon Stadium's vast car park features weekend stalls – fruit and veg,

Wimbledon Stadium car boot sale.

clothing and groceries on Sunday, plus a popular car boot sale on Saturday and Sunday, with second-hand furniture, clothes and music.

The industrial estates off busy Durnsford Road conceal the marvellous Vallebona Sardinian Gourmet, open for public tastings most Saturdays between 9.30am and 4pm. It's worth a visit for the climate-controlled cheese room alone.

On the High Street in Colliers Wood, Burge & Gunson is a bathroom centre with strikingly designed furniture and fittings, as well as high-tech toys for those who want to take bathing to a new level. Nearby, the Boat Harbour is a well-stocked nautical shop – and the only place you can get your jet-skis fixed in this neck of the Wood. Near South Wimbledon tube, Architectural Salvage is a good place for unusual interior fittings, including fireplaces and doors.

For gifts and collectibles, stroll around the Merton Abbey Mills market at the weekend; there's a hotchpotch of antiques and crafts (scented candles, jewellery, second-hand books), plus food stalls selling everything from noodle dishes to Belgian waffles. Indulge your inner hippie at Charlie's Rock Shop, purveyor of healing crystals, wind chimes and the like.

Architectural Salvage 83 Haydons Road, SW19 1HH (8543 4450).
Bayley & Sage 60 High Street, SW19 5EE (8946 9904, www.bayley-sage.co.uk).
Boat Harbour 40 High Street, SW19 2AB (8540 6815).
Burge & Gunson 13-27 High Street, SW19 2JE (8543 5166, www.burgeandgunson.co.uk).
Cath Kidston 3 High Street, SW19 5DX (8944 1001, www.cathkidston.co.uk).
Centre Court 4 Queens Road, SW19 8YA (8944 8323, www.centrecourtshopping.co.uk).
Charlie's Rock Shop The 1929 Shop, Merton Abbey Mills, 18 Watermill Way, SW19 2RD (8544 1207, www.charliesrock shop.com).
Diane von Furstenberg 38B High Street, SW19 5DE (8944 5995, www.dvf.com).
Elys of Wimbledon 16 St Georges Road, SW19 4DP (8946 9191, www.elysofwimbledon. co.uk).
Luella's Boudoir 18 High Street, SW19 5DX (8879 7744, www.luellasboudoir.co.uk).
Matches 34 High Street, SW19 5BY (8947 8707, www.matchesfashion.com).
MaxMara 37 High Street, SW19 5BY (8944 1494, www.maxmara.com).
Merton Abbey Mills Watermill Way, SW19 2RD (7287 1766, www.mertonabbey mills.com).
Question Air 77-78 High Street, SW19 5EG (8946 6288, www.question-air.com).
Vallebona Sardinian Gourmet Unit 14, 59 Weir Road, SW19 8UG (8944 5665, www.vallebona.co.uk).
Wimbledon Farmers' Market Wimbledon Park First School, Havana Road, SW19 8EJ (7833 0338, www.lfm.org.uk).
Wimbledon Stadium Market Wimbledon Stadium Car Park, Plough Lane, SW17 0BL (7240 5405).

Arts & attractions

Cinemas & theatres
Colour House Theatre Merton Abbey Mills, Watermill Way, SW19 2RD (8542 5511, www.colourhousetheatre.co.uk).
New Wimbledon Theatre & Studio Theatre The Broadway, SW19 1QG (0844 871 7646, www.atgtickets.com).
Odeon Wimbledon 39 The Broadway, SW19 1QB (0871 224 4007, www.odeon.co.uk).
Polka Theatre for Children 240 The Broadway, SW19 1SB (8543 4888, www. polkatheatre.com).

Galleries & museums
Wimbledon Lawn Tennis Museum Centre Court, All England Lawn Tennis & Croquet Club, Church Road, SW19 5AE (8946 6131, www.wimbledon.org/museum). Costumes, memorabilia and film footage.
Wimbledon Society Museum of Local History 22 Ridgway, SW19 4QN (8296 9914, www.wimbledonmuseum.org.uk). Charts the 3,000-year history of the area.
Wimbledon Windmill Museum Windmill Road, Wimbledon Common, SW19 5NR (8947 2825, www.wimbledonwindmill.org.uk). This old dear, built in 1817, is still working, but only on high days and holidays.

Other attractions
Buddhapadipa Temple 14 Calonne Road, Wimbledon Parkside, SW19 5HJ (8946 1357, www.buddhapadipa.org). London's first Buddhist temple.
Cannizaro House West Side, Wimbledon Common, SW19 4UE (8879 1464, www. cannizarohouse.com, www.cannizaropark.com).

Merton

COUNCIL TAX

		Main borough	Wimbledon Common area
A	up to £40,000	£941.88	£958.46
B	£40,001-£52,000	£1,098.85	£1,118.19
C	£52,001-£68,000	£1,255.84	£1,277.94
D	£68,001-£88,000	£1,412.81	£1,437.68
E	£88,001-£120,000	£1,726.77	£1,757.17
F	£120,001-£160,000	£2,040.73	£2,076.65
G	£160,001-£320,000	£2,354.69	£2,396.14
H	over £320,000	£2,825.62	£2,875.36

Huge Queen Anne mansion, now a hotel; the fabulous gardens are open to the public.

Deen City Farm *39 Windsor Avenue, SW19 2RR (8543 5300, www.deencityfarm.co.uk). Tidy-sized community farm on the edge of the beautiful Morden Hall Park Estate.*

Merton Priory *off Merantun Way, Merton Abbey, SW19 2RD (8946 4141, www.merton priory.org). Twelfth-century Augustinian priory.*

Morden Hall Park *Morden Hall Road, SM4 5JD (8545 6850, www.nationaltrust.org.uk).*

Southside House *3-4 Woodhayes Road, Wimbledon Common, SW19 4RJ (8946 7643, www.southsidehouse.com). Grand house, open to visitors (April-Sept) and the site of occasional concerts and lectures.*

Sport & fitness

Greenwich Leisure manages Merton's public fitness centres. Merton's private health clubs have to battle for business with the popular chains, but there's enough elitism among the racket-loving Wimbledon Village locals for a continued reign by the independent clubs.

Gyms & leisure centres

Canons Leisure Centre *Madeira Road, CR4 4HD (8640 8543, www.gll.org.uk).*

Christopher's Squash & Fitness Club *Wimbledon Stadium, Plough Lane, SW17 0BL (8946 4636, www.christopherssquash.com). Private.*

David Lloyd *Bushey Road, SW20 8TE (8543 8020, www.davidlloydleisure.co.uk). Private.*

King's Club *Woodhayes Road, SW19 4TT (8255 5401, www.sportkings.org). Private.*

Morden Park Pool *Morden Park, London Road, SM4 5HE (8640 6727, www.gll.org.uk).*

Nuffield Health *The Broadway, SW19 1QB (8947 9627, www.cannons.co.uk). Private.*

Virgin Active *www.virginactive.co.uk; North Road, SW19 1AQ (0845 270 2108); 21-33 Worple Road, SW19 4JS (8545 1717). Private.*

Wimbledon Club *Church Road, SW19 5AG (8971 8090, www.thewimbledonclub.co.uk). Private.*

Wimbledon Leisure Centre *Latimer Road, SW19 1EW (8542 1330, www.gll.org.uk).*

Wimbledon Racquets & Fitness Club *Cranbrook Road, SW19 4HD (8947 5806, www.wimbledonclub.co.uk). Private.*

YMCA *200 The Broadway, SW19 1RY (8542 9055, www.kwymca.org.uk). Private.*

Other facilities

Wimbledon Village Stables *24A/B High Street, SW19 5DX (8946 8579, www.wvstables.com).*

Spectator sports

All England Lawn Tennis Club *Church Road, SW19 5AE (8944 1066, www.wimbledon.org). Site of the annual Wimbledon tournament.*

Wimbledon Stadium *Plough Lane, SW17 0BL (0870 840 8905, www.lovethedogs.co.uk). Greyhound and speedway racing.*

Schools

Primary

There are 43 state primary schools in Merton, including 12 church schools. There are also eight independent primaries, including one Norwegian school. See www.merton.gov.uk, www.edubase.gov.uk and www.ofsted.gov.uk for more information.

Secondary

Bishopsford Arts College *Lilleshall Road, SM4 6DU (8687 1157, www.bishopsford.org).*

Harris Academy Merton *Wide Way, CR4 1BP (8623 1000, www.harrismerton.org.uk).*

King's College School *Southside, Wimbledon Common, SW19 4TT (8255 5300, www.kcs. org.uk). Private; boys only.*

RECYCLING

Household waste recycled & composted 32%
Main recycling centres Weir Road Recycling Centre, 36 Weir Road, SW19 8UG (8274 4902); Merton Refuse & Recycling Centre, 63-69 Amenity Way, Garth Road, SM4 4NJ (8274 4902)
Other recycling services green waste collection; home composting; collection of white goods and furniture. Squirrels (8641 1881) takes unwanted materials for use by local groups in arts play
Council contact Waste Services, Environment & Regeneration, 63-69 Amenity Way, Morden, SM4 4NJ (8274 4902)

Perseid School *Bordesley Road, SM4 5LT (8648 9737, www.perseid.merton.sch.uk).*
Raynes Park High School *Bushey Road, SW20 0JL (8946 4112, www.raynespark. merton.sch.uk).*
Ricards Lodge High School *Lake Road, SW19 7HB (8946 2208, www.ricardslodge. merton.sch.uk). Girls only.*
Rutlish School *Watery Lane, SW20 9AD (8542 1212, www.rutlish.merton.sch.uk). Boys only.*
St Mark's Academy *Acacia Road, CR4 1SF (8648 6627, www.stmarksacademy.com). Church of England.*
Ursuline High School *Crescent Road, SW20 8HA (8255 2688, www.ursulinehigh.merton. sch.uk). Roman Catholic; girls only; mixed sixth form with Wimbledon College.*
Wimbledon College *Edge Hill, SW19 4NS (8946 2533, www.wimbledoncollege.org.uk). Boys only; mixed sixth form with Ursuline High School.*
Wimbledon High School *Mansel Road, SW19 4AB (8971 0900, www.wimbledonhigh. gdst.net). Private; girls only.*

Property

WHAT THE AGENTS SAY:

'The housing stock in Wimbledon is of the highest quality. We deal mainly with two- to three-bedroom Victorian terraced houses, which sell easily for £550,000 to £700,000. All types of property get snapped up quickly, but the main interest is in houses, rather than flats and apartments. The new St Anne's Mews development, located on the Downs, is testament to this – three of the eight luxury homes, costing from £1.7 million to £2.5 million, were reserved before the site was launched. The South Park Gardens area is another prime location, where prices are forever creeping upwards. It's hard for first-time buyers; many purchasers work in finance or marketing in the City.'
Harrie Vischjager, Ellisons, Wimbledon

Average property prices
Detached £1,164,636
Semi-detached £422,870
Terraced £323,071
Flat £263,524

Local estate agents
Christopher St James *61 High Street, SW19 2JF (8296 1270, www.csj.eu.com).*
Dicksons *194 Merton High Street, SW19 1AX (8542 8595).*
Eddison White *www.eddisonwhite.co.uk; 2 offices in the borough (Colliers Wood 8540 9828, Wimbledon 8540 5544).*
Ellisons *www.ellisons.uk.com; 3 offices in the borough (Wimbledon 8944 9494, Raynes Park 8944 9595, Morden 8543 1166).*
Goodfellows *44 Coombe Lane, SW20 0LD (8946 6511, www.goodfellows.co.uk).*
Hawes & Co *www.hawesandco.co.uk; 3 offices in the borough (Wimbledon Village 8946 1000, Wimbledon Broadway 8542 6600, Raynes Park 8946 3000).*

Other information

Council
London Borough of Merton Council *Civic Centre, London Road, SM4 5DX (8274 4901, www.merton.gov.uk).*
Out-of-hours Social Services *Sutton Civic Offices (8543 9750).*

Legal services
Merton Law Centre *112 London Road, SM4 5AX (8543 4069, www.lawcentres. org.uk).*

Local information
www.merton.gov.uk/mymerton.
www.wimbledonguardian.co.uk.

Open spaces & allotments
Council allotments *8545 3665, www.merton.gov.uk/allotments.*
Open spaces *www.merton.gov.uk/parks.*

'Lambeth encompasses such a multitude of people and places that it feels both extremely exciting and reassuringly normal. Incredible history, the best Caribbean food markets in London and a beautiful art deco lido – it certainly keeps you on your toes.'

Zoe Jewell and Tim Dickens, Editors, www.brixtonblog.com

Lambeth

A multicultural microcosm of everything London has to offer, Lambeth mixes some of the capital's most exciting nightlife with sprawling open spaces, gastropubs with greasy spoons, and luxurious Victorian refurbs with crime-crippled estates, then adds a spectacular riverside retreat that's as popular with locals as it is with tourists. When a man is tired of Lambeth, he is truly tired of life.

Neighbourhoods

South Bank, Waterloo and Lambeth North

Though it has Lambeth's lowest population, the South Bank remains one of the best bets in town for weekend unwinding or entertaining out-of-towners. The stretch between Westminster Bridge and Blackfriars Bridge is where most of the tourist money gets spent – there's the London Aquarium, the London Eye, Royal Festival Hall, the Hayward Gallery, the IMAX Cinema, BFI Southbank, the National Theatre and, in the summer, the Udderbelly comedy tent, hard to miss as it's in the shape of an upside-down inflatable purple cow. There's also a huge range of places to eat and drink, with some of the most popular clustered outside the refurbished Royal Festival Hall and around terraced Gabriel's Wharf.

Assorted festivals and open-air events take place throughout the year, from summer music and arts festivals and play fountains, to food fairs and a Christmas market. There are occasional raves on the banks of the Thames, while beneath Queen Elizabeth Hall, you'll find the spiritual home of London skateboarding.

Living here, however, remains prohibitively expensive, and not just on the river itself; the 'South Bank Effect' is creeping south and eradicating the character of what was once one of London's

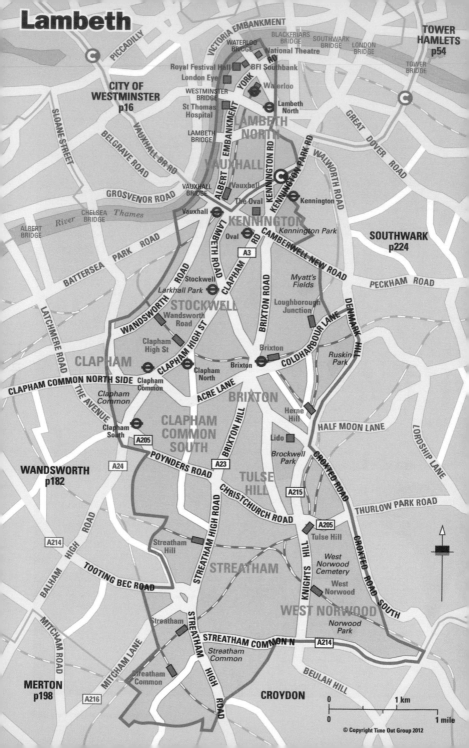

seediest but most soulful areas. Baylis
Road retains some less smart local authority
housing, but gone are the legendary market
stalls of Lambeth Walk, now home to
modern flat developments that make it
hard to believe the famous promenade
ever existed at all. Opposite Lambeth
North Tube station is Morley College,
highly regarded for its adult education
courses and evening classes.

Between Lambeth North and the South
Bank sits Waterloo, best known to tourists
for Terry and Julie's legendary sunset
encounter and for its train station, although
the latter's importance suffered a major
blow in 2007 when the international
Eurostar service moved to refurbished
St Pancras station. Waterloo features
everything from the community market
stalls and specialist shops of Lower Marsh
to the gastropubs of the Cut – the latter
popular with those anticipating, or
reflecting on, a night of theatrical
entertainment at either the Old or Young
Vic. Waterloo Bridge, meanwhile, continues
to offer one of the best views of the capital,
and not just at sunset.

Vauxhall

All that is left of the sprawling Vauxhall
Pleasure Gardens, which drew visitors
from all over the world between the 17th
and 19th centuries, is a miniature park
called Spring Gardens, the area having
traded green for grey following the
completion of Vauxhall Bridge in 1816
and the subsequent establishment of
heavy industrial centres for Royal Doulton,
Marmite and Vauxhall Iron Works (which
later became the car manufacturer).

The Vauxhall of today is a smog-
shrouded criss-cross of major roads and
underpasses, a hectic interchange with a
strangely forlorn air despite its central
location and riverside views of Tate Britain
and Millbank Tower. Heavy industry gave
way to offices long ago – most noticeably
the bizarre structure housing the MI6
headquarters – and the local demographic
includes a large number of MPs and civil
servants thanks to the proximity of
Parliament. Since the Greater London
Plan designated Vauxhall an 'Opportunity
Area' ripe for high-density construction,
developers have been circling with
proposals for skyscrapers. Along with
the forthcoming move of the US Embassy

from Mayfair to Nine Elms (in the borough
of Wandsworth), this could really shake
up the area.

Vauxhall is also home to one of the most
thriving gay communities in London, with
clubs such as Fire and pubs such as the
legendary Royal Vauxhall Tavern at its
core. The resulting carnival of madness
regularly stretches weekends into Mondays
and even Tuesdays, giving sedated suits
and ties something to ogle in disbelief as
they shuffle into work.

And while the area isn't the most
aesthetically inspired corner of the capital
(the soaring silver planes of the bus station
are a bit love-'em-or-hate-'em), it also has
various charming corners, including lovely
pubs and cafés, atmospheric Brunswick
House (home to architectural salvage
company Lassco, and reputedly haunted),
the wonderful Vauxhall City Farm and
some well-tended allotments.

Kennington

Traditionally a working-class area,
Kennington was once blighted by the

Highs & Lows

▲ **Arts attack** Music, theatre, film,
art: culture vultures are spoilt for
choice at the numerous world-class
venues around the South Bank.
Never a dull moment Smaller
independent venues also abound,
offering hip clubs, edgy music,
community arts, film clubs, new
theatre, arts festivals and more.
Room to breathe Clapham Common,
Streatham Common, Kennington
Park, West Norwood Cemetery –
Lambeth has more than its fair
share of sprawling open spaces.

Crime Lambeth has a disturbing level
of everything from muggings and drug
dealing to gang-related murders.
Clapham High Street at night The
bars filled with rugby boys, the barely
dressed girls passed out in doorways,
the grown men in suits relieving
themselves by the cashpoint – it's
not very pleasant.
Streatham High Road What claims
to be the longest high street in the
UK is also one of the most polluted,
thanks to the heavy and constant
▼ volume of traffic.

fumes of countless factories (the Hayward's pickle factory's acrid smell plagued a young Charlie Chaplin) and largely bereft of entertainment save the Lambeth Walk, an evening promenade immortalised in Noel Gay's song of the same name from the 1937 musical *Me and My Girl*.

These days, Kennington is increasingly popular with first-time buyers, thanks to its tube station and the wide variety of housing (from LCC estates of various vintages to the Duchy of Cornwall cottages west of Kennington Cross). It's also a political hangout of sorts – the faces of Charles Kennedy and John Prescott feature prominently in the windows of the Kennington Tandoori. Nor is the place's relationship with politics limited to the mainstream, with incidents of political dissent dating from the Chartist rally of 1848 all the way up to the final eviction in 2005 of squatters who had occupied the entirety of St Agnes Place for more than 30 years.

That said, and despite its location on a major crossroads at the edge of the congestion charge zone, Kennington remains a peaceful place to live. There's Kennington Park (home to an excellent concrete skate bowl dating from the late 1970s) and a range of local amenities, including the White Bear pub theatre, Ovalhouse theatre, a Saturday farmers' market at St Mark's Church (opposite Oval tube), and Cleaver Square, a secluded space lined with gorgeous Georgian houses. For many, however, Kennington is all about cricket, with the nearby Kia Oval ground sending the place into a beer-fuelled hysteria that can often be felt (and heard) for miles around.

Stockwell and South Lambeth

Dogged by higher than average crime levels and an overabundance of unattractive concrete blocks, Stockwell nevertheless remains a good spot for first-time buyers unable to afford Clapham but keen to avoid the bustle of Brixton. There are various amenities; most of them – including charming Larkhall Park, tree-lined Victorian streets, a real-life Albert Square and the monthly South Lambeth Market at the Cavendish Arms – lying west of Clapham Road. There's also the local air-raid-shelter-turned-war-memorial complete with colourful murals, 19th-century St Michael's Church with its stained-glass windows by John Trinick, and Grade II*-listed Stockwell Bus Garage, built in 1952, with a vaulting concrete ribbed roof.

And while the district may have remained largely in the margins of London's history books since its days as a 17th-century village green, it was once home to Vincent Van Gogh, whose former house on Hackford Road is marked by a blue plaque. It's a short walk from the Type Museum (currently closed for refurbishment), a favourite with font fanatics the world over.

Stockwell is also home to one of London's best skateparks, a rare example of 1980s concrete-wave construction that draws skaters from across the country and provides an excellent resource for kids from the surrounding estates. Local boozers vary from sweat-box meat markets to more genteel establishments; eateries from tatty takeaways to the numerous restaurants, bars and bakeries of South Lambeth Road,

Lambeth

known as Little Portugal thanks to its sizeable Portuguese contingent.

Property-wise, Stockwell is a mix of Victorian terraces jostling for space with council and ex-council blocks – not the most visually attractive place, perhaps, but somewhere with a strong sense of community that causes many to stick around longer than they'd intended.

Brixton

Few places embody the potential harmony of London's multicultural make-up like Brixton, yet its name retains a certain notoriety (usually among those who have never set foot in the place), thanks to decades of social unrest that ghettoised its large Caribbean contingent and led to widespread rioting in the 1980s. Nor has the area emerged entirely unscathed: drug-peddling remains rife on certain streets, and the blaring of police sirens is a constant reminder of the gun and knife crime between gangs on less salubrious estates. Its prominence in the London-wide riots of August 2011 did little to help dispel its negative image.

Not that this is something that overly bothers the influx of (mostly) white, middle-class professionals staking a claim on the place thanks to its affordable housing, ease of access and seemingly limitless capacity to entertain. Gentrification continues apace, especially in the charming Victorian housing forking off Acre Lane and Effra Road, but seems destined never to completely uproot the Caribbean character. Sure, there are occasional stabs at exclusivity – Modern European restaurant Upstairs, for example – but for the most part it's a case of community in action, from the West Indian foods and wares of the market stalls behind the railway station (including those on Electric Avenue, the first shopping street in London to boast electric lighting) to the wealth of cross-cultural bars and eateries.

And Brixton is big on community these days. It has its own currency – the Brixton Pound – aimed at encouraging people to shop locally. In the restyled 'Brixton Village' (formerly Granville Arcade), small independent traders, many of them food-oriented, have taken over long-empty units to create a buzzing atmosphere that's attracting visitors from across the capital. Piano House, on Brighton Terrace, is another creative hub, home to literary

agents, sewing schools and the London Printworks Trust.

There's been lots of investment in Brixton of late, both in terms of public money and personal commitment. Landscaping of Windrush Square has provided a versatile public piazza with fountains and seating. Public art has started popping up – look out for Maggie Hambling's heron weathervane on the corner of Brixton Road and Coldharbour Lane. And there's the Brixton Windmill, a working 19th-century mill, newly restored by enthusiasts and tucked in an unassuming park just off Brixton Hill.

The local music scene still thrives (those to namecheck Brixton in their songs include Pink Floyd, Eddy Grant and the Clash, who cut their teeth in the back room of the Telegraph pub), thanks to venues such as Brixton Academy, which hosts international stars and souped-up clubnights, and indie favourite the Windmill pub; plus there's jazz at the Effra, and experimental and international music upstairs at the Ritzy cinema. These, along with big clubs such as Electric Brixton ensure that the High Street is often as busy at 6am as it is at 6pm.

If central Brixton is too noisy for you, consider the popular group of terraces known as 'the Poets' (because they're named after bards), which runs alongside Brockwell Park up to Herne Hill; east towards Denmark Hill, the area around Ruskin Park has larger family homes.

Clapham and Clapham North

Everyone has an opinion on Clapham, from embittered locals raging at the braying rugger-buggers cluttering up their High Street on weekends, to aspiring near-neighbours who see it as an idyllic mix of the sleepily suburban and the fiercely forward-thinking. Whatever the angle, there's no denying the increasingly lurid diplays of wealth – the fleets of bankers in their soft-top Porsches, some of them barely out of university; their WAGish companions weighed down with bags from the local boutiques – but there's a real community feel to Clapham that no amount of money can erase. Its Picturehouse is one of the most comfortable cinemas in London, and the Landor one of the best pub theatres.

The cream of Clapham's society types tends to settle around Old Town, a genteel quadrangle of posh shops, tarted-up pubs and premium-value Victorian property –

there are even three Queen Anne-style houses (nos.39, 41 and 43) – that also doubles as a bus depot. Not that it's all swank and celebrity-spotting. Clapham can also be seen as something of a cultural melting pot, with million-pound dream houses sited a stone's throw from council estates harking back to the area's less upwardly mobile era.

An eye-catching new landmark has arrived on the High Street in the shape of the white undulating façade of Clapham One (www.clapham-one.com), housing a library, health centre, café and performance space. Nearby, the leisure centre and swimming pool at Clapham Manor Street has also got shiny new accommodation.

For the most part, however, Clapham is more up-and-come than up-and-coming, its High Street crammed with faceless bars pumping lobotomised house music and packed on weekends with obnoxiously

New shops and restaurants are pulling crowds to **Brixton Village**. See p213.

inebriated young professionals on the pull. That said, there are plenty of more enigmatic establishments off the beaten track, from bohemian local pubs (Bread & Roses) and hip bars (Secondo) to quirky clubs (Lost Society), and there's no shortage of decent restaurants.

Clapham Common South and Clapham Park

Clapham Common South straddles the border of Lambeth and Wandsworth – the line runs through the Common, although Lambeth technically controls the area – and enjoys an aesthetic that manages to be neither entirely Balham nor Clapham proper, but a strange mix of mundane and magnificent. Clapham's regenerative tendrils have taken hold along the South Side itself, host to increasingly swanky eating and drinking options, while Abbeville Road, with its flower-shrouded Victorian houses, shops and restaurants, was a destination for society types long before the fancy franchises of the High Street started turning a trade. However, not all locals live a charmed life: the nearby Clapham Park Estate was notorious enough for journalist Polly Toynbee to settle here in 2003 while researching her book *Hard Work: Life in Low-Pay Britain*.

Regardless of income, however, Clapham Common itself remains a democratic place to rest, recharge or run riot – reason enough to want to live here. Sure, summer months see informal public school reunions determined to turn the entire common into one big beer garden, but it's not all moronic chanting and yummy mummies – you're just as likely to see a full cross-section of south London living, from Jamaican barbecue parties and children flying kites to bell-ringing weed dealers, sunbathing kids from the surrounding estates and, later in the evening, gay cruisers straying momentarily from the bijou wooded stretch to the west.

Streatham

Streatham's reputation is inextricably bound up with its High Road, often voted one of the worst streets in Britain due to its mix of damaged paving, downtrodden (and occasionally downright empty) shopfronts and less discerning nightlife options, including Caesars, a rite of passage for button-down boys and their criminally under-clothed girlfriends. Then there are the albums of negative press cuttings: most notably the prostitutes loitering around St Leonard's (the area has been tied with the sex trade since Cynthia Payne set up her notorious brothel on Ambleside Avenue) and the woefully regular incidents of gun and knife crime.

Not that it puts off first-time buyers: Streatham has been an initial rung on the property ladder for decades, something attributable to its relative ease of access (estate agents often refer to it as 'Brixton Hill' to make the Victoria line sound closer than it is, though Streatham is well served by buses and three rail stations) and affordable house prices. That said, there is a growing diversity among both the types of properties (from Victorian terraces to spacious 20th-century housing estates) and their prices – those around the Telford Park conservation area tend to go for a third more than those in Streatham Vale, for example. And while crime may make the headlines, there remains a widespread community spirit (seen in pubs like the Earl Ferrers, meetings of the popular Streatham Society and occasional residents' street parties, bunting and all).

Streatham's famous Ice Arena is closed until 2013 (replaced by a temporary rink on Brixton Station Road), when it will reopen as part of the Streatham Hub, along with a new 'state-of-the-art leisure centre' being built in partnership with Tesco.

Beyond the pollution and congestion of the High Street lies the relative tranquillity of Streatham Common, an underrated open space at the southern tip of the borough, with woodland, wild flower meadows, a playground, a cricket crease and football pitches, plus the attractive formal gardens of the Rookery.

Tulse Hill and West Norwood

Tulse Hill is the embodiment of south London suburbia: it feels peaceful and settled, even in the less picturesque estates. Housing tends to cluster in identikit rows of net-curtained semis, although the whole spectrum is represented, from affordable flats on the site of the former Tulse Hill School (erstwhile educator of Ken Livingstone) to the Regency style parkside houses and apartments where the Dick Shepherd School used to be. That is not to say that all the local schools have been turned into residences: West Norwood has

Lambeth

plenty, both private and state, encouraging an influx of young families.

There's a real sense of community here, with active local churches, the L'Arche centre for disabled residents, a mix of local pubs and restaurants, and the excellent South London Theatre. The artisanal spirit is strong, celebrated in the monthly West Norwood Feast, which brings local arts and crafts, a food fair, vintage clothes and furniture, and live music. Light industrial units house everything from old-fashioned printers to Rococo's chocolate kitchen. Grand Victorian municipal buildings such as the South London Botanical Institute and the Old Library (designed by Sidney Smith of Tate Britain fame) are complemented by open spaces such as child-friendly Norwood Park and sprawling West Norwood Cemetery, one of the most noteworthy in the capital.

Eating and drinking is still a weak point, but probably not for long. While there's no tube line, West Norwood is well connected by trains and buses to the West End and beyond, and the installation of a CCTV system has made it a safer place to stroll after the night bus drops you off.

Restaurants & cafés

There's plenty of choice on the South Bank. For classy Modern European fare and fantastic Thames views, try Skylon, or, for cheaper British dishes, Canteen – both attached to the Royal Festival Hall. Just outside, next to the river, are assorted chain options, including Giraffe, Ping Pong, Strada and Wagamama, as well as Latin American at Las Iguanas. Diners here tend to be tourists or theatregoers, with a resulting tendency for large crowds and above-average prices – especially within the clutter of terraced bars and restaurants in Gabriel's Wharf. Old-timer wine bar-restaurant the Archduke has decent pre-theatre options, while Japanese Ozu is the best of the various eateries inside County Hall (although locals tend to prefer the less showy Inshoku, on Lower Marsh).

Near Waterloo station, the Cut has long-standing gastropub the Anchor & Hope and branches of Pizza Paradiso and Tas, while Troia is a decent Turkish on the blind side of the London Eye. Budget choices include standout chippie Masters Super Fish, curry specialist Marsh Ruby, and Scootercaffe for a stiffening cup of coffee. Otherwise, there are unpretentious cafés closer to Lambeth North – Perdoni's, with its all-day breakfasts and Italian standards, is pick of the crop.

Vauxhall is a less assured dining destination, although there is a decent Portuguese port of call in the form of the Madeira Pâtisserie and a popular BYO vegetarian diner, the Bonnington Centre Café, but both have been outclassed by the opening of the Brunswick House Café amid the architectural curios of salvage company Lassco. Nearby Kennington is better served, from the nautical but nice French fish restaurant Lobster Pot and Eritrean outpost Adulis, to the cheap and cheerful Windmill Fish Bar. The Kennington Tandoori is favoured by high-profile political types.

Further south, Stockwell has an excellent Spanish restaurant, Rebato's, and quality Indian and West African curries at Hot Stuff. The area is also predictably heavy on Portuguese cuisine, with Bar Estrela (*see p219*) the best for flawless puddings and a party vibe, and nearby Grelha d'Ouro nipping closely at its heels.

Brixton keeps the area's large African and West Indian communities smiling,

Lambeth

Savour the architectural setting of **Brunswick House Café**.

thanks to places such as Eritrean restaurant Asmara and Caribbean hotspots Bamboula and Negril. For a smart evening out, there's artful Modern European cuisine at the unmarked Upstairs. But for foodie credentials, the new place to visit is the reinvented section of the covered market known as 'Brixton Village'. At one point in 2011, it seemed that each week another excellent small-scale operator was opening another delicious venue: Honest Burgers, local and seasonal Cornercopia, Pakistani street food at Elephant, Thai at KaoSarn… Elsewhere in the market, there's acclaimed Franco Manca, now rapidly becoming a London-wide pizza chain.

The joy of the Brixton market eateries is their rough-and-ready vibe; for something a little more upmarket, Clapham is still king in Lambeth. The High Street restaurants tend to be branches of upmarket chains, but there's much more interesting dining to be had if you know where to look. Clapham North offers excellent Japanese restaurant Tsunami and sophisticated Modern European eaterie Fouronine. In the Old Town, expect French flair at award-winning Trinity; near Clapham Common tube are adventurous internationalist Rapscallion and Gallic stalwart Gastro. Over in Clapham Park, long-standing brasserie Newtons continues to serve the bohemian baby-boomers of Abbeville Road.

Streatham has a few alternatives to the High Street's faceless takeaways, including party-hearty Tex-Mex favourite El Chicos,

vegetarian café Wholemeal and Perfect Blend, café by day, bar-restaurant by night. A very welcome addition to the area is the Manor Arms gastropub. There are also a couple of good Asian options, Slurp and Oishii, with staff at the latter notorious for drawing out games of Chinese poker long after they've drawn the blinds.

Adulis *11-16 Brixton Road, SW9 6BT (7587 0055, www.adulis.co.uk).*

Anchor & Hope *36 The Cut, SE1 8LP (7928 9898).*

Archduke *153 Concert Hall Approach, SE1 8XU (7928 9370, www.thearchduke.co.uk).*

Asmara *386 Coldharbour Lane, SW9 8LF (7737 4144).*

Bamboula *12 Acre Lane, SW2 5SG (7737 6633, www.bamboulas.net).*

Bonnington Centre Café *11 Vauxhall Grove, SW8 1TD (7820 7466).*

Brunswick House Café *Brunswick House, 30 Wandsworth Road, SW8 2LG (7720 2926. www.brunswickhousecafe.co.uk).*

Canteen *Royal Festival Hall, Belvedere Road, SE1 8XX (0845 686 1122, www.canteen.co.uk).*

El Chicos *62 Streatham High Road, SW16 1DA (8677 5100).*

Cornercopia *65 Brixton Village Market, Coldharbour Lane, SW9 8PS (07919 542233, http://brixtoncornercopia.ning.com).*

Elephant *55 Brixton Village Market, Coldharbour Lane, SW9 8PS (07590 389684).*

Fouronine *409 Clapham Road, SW9 9BT (7737 0722, www.fouronine.co.uk).*

Gastro *67 Venn Street, SW4 0BD (7627 0222).*

Grelha d'Ouro *151 South Lambeth Road, SW8 1XN (7735 9764, www.grelhadouro.net).*
Honest Burgers *12 Brixton Village Market, Coldharbour Lane, SW9 8PR (7733 7963, www.honestburgers.co.uk).*
Hot Stuff *19 Wilcox Road, SW8 2XA (7720 1480, www.welovehotstuff.com).*
Las Iguanas *Festival Terrace, Belvedere Road, SE1 8XX (7620 1328, www.iguanas.co.uk).*
Inshoku *23-24 Lower Marsh, SE1 7RJ (7928 2311).*
KaoSarn *2 & 96 Brixton Village Market, Coldharbour Lane, SW9 8PR (7095 8922).*
Kennington Tandoori *313 Kennington Road, SE11 4QE (7735 9247, http://kennington tandoori.com).*
Lobster Pot *3 Kennington Lane, SE11 4RG (7582 5556, www.lobsterpotrestaurant.co.uk).*
Madeira Pâtisserie *46A-C Albert Embankment, SE1 7TL (7820 1117, www.madeiralondon.co.uk).*
Manor Arms *13 Mitcham Lane, SW16 6LQ (3195 6888, www.themanorarms.com).*
Marsh Ruby *30 Lower Marsh, SE1 7RG (7620 0593, www.marshruby.com).*
Masters Super Fish *191 Waterloo Road, SE1 8UX (7928 6924).*
Negril *132 Brixton Hill, SW2 1RS (8674 8798).*
Newtons *33-35 Abbeville Road, SW4 9LA (8673 0977, www.newtonsrestaurants.co.uk).*
Oishii *70 Streatham Hill, SW2 4RD (8674 6888).*
Ozu *County Hall, Westminster Bridge Road, SE1 7BH (7928 7766, www.ozulondon.com).*
Perdoni's *18-20 Kennington Road, SE1 7BL (7928 6846).*
Perfect Blend *8-9 Streatleigh Parade, Streatham High Road, SW16 1EQ (8769 4646).*
Pizza Paradiso *61 The Cut, SE1 8LL (7261 1221, www.pizzaparadiso.co.uk).*
Rapscallion *75 Venn Street, SW4 0BD (7787 6555, www.therapscallion.co.uk).*
Rebato's *169 South Lambeth Road, SW8 1XW (7735 6388, www.rebatos.com).*
Scootercaffe *132 Lower Marsh, SE1 7AE (7620 1421).*
Skylon *Southbank Centre, Belvedere Road, SE1 8XX (7654 7800, www.danddlondon.com).*
Slurp *104-106 Streatham High Road, SW16 1BW (8677 7786, www.slurprestaurant.co.uk).*
Tas *33 The Cut, SE1 8LF (7928 2111, www.tasrestaurants.co.uk).*
Trinity *4 The Polygon, Clapham Old Town, SW4 0JG (7622 1199, www.trinityrestaurant. co.uk).*
Troia *3F Belvedere Road, SE1 7GQ (7633 9309, www.troia.co.uk).*

Tsunami *5-7 Voltaire Road, SW4 6DQ (7978 1610, www.tsunamirestaurant.co.uk).*
Upstairs Bar & Restaurant *89B Acre Lane, SW2 5TN (7733 8855, www.upstairs london.com).*
Wholemeal *1 Shrubbery Road, SW16 2AS (8769 2423, www.wholemealcafe.com).*
Windmill Fish Bar *211 Kennington Lane, SE11 5QS (7582 5754).*

Bars & pubs

There are few places more fertile for nightlife venues to prosper than Brixton, a result of its blend of street cred and increasingly moneyed young professionals on the prowl for a good time. The list of clubs seems never-ending, from Electric Brixton (formerly legendary trance and techno behemoth the Fridge) and nearby Mass, set in converted St Matthew's Church, to the more upmarket Plan B. Then there's the seemingly endless list of DJ bars and pubs, including the always heaving White Horse and the Dogstar – plus enigmatic institutions such as jazz dive the Effra and the Windmill, an achingly out-there pub stage that has hosted everyone from Hard Fi to Hot Chip. Not that it's all swinging, swaying and records playing: those seeking a quiet pint are well served by characterful pubs including the Trinity Arms.

Options become more limited towards Stockwell, although the brightly painted Queen's Head does fine Sunday roasts, the Priory Arms and Surprise are good local pubs, and there are several places catering to the Portuguese contingent – the best is Bar Estrela, which heaves during Portuguese football games. The Swan, a cavernous meat market hosting tribute bands, is popular with Antipodeans.

Streathamites are best off trekking down Brixton Hill, although local alternatives include aspiring cocktail bar Mint and a handful of locals' locals, including the Earl Ferrers. Nor are Tulse Hill or West Norwood exactly drinking destinations, although Kennington is developing nicely as a self-contained nightspot, with community boozers such as the Beehive and the Prince of Wales on charming Cleaver Square, upbeat melting pots such as the Dog House, the Tommyfield and the Three Stags (now unrecognisable as the pub in which Charlie Chaplin's father drank himself to death), and even a courageously camp Hawaiian theme bar, South London Pacific.

Vauxhall's gay scene tends to wet its whistle at the Royal Vauxhall Tavern, while the Fentiman Arms fills the gastro gap and the Riverside has floor to-ceiling windows and a contemporary piazza setting. Then, of course, there's Clapham, where, come weekends, it's hard to take a step without tripping over a casualty from one of the various joyless vodka and cocktail bars along the High Street. There are more personable places to drink, including lefties' favourite Bread & Roses, the Windmill on the Common, and the Abbeville, plus a handful of quirky venues such as Secondo (tucked into a railway arch by Clapham North and doubling as a vintage shop by day) and Lost Society.

Waterloo has more than its fair share of fine drinking establishments, from gastropub the Anchor & Hope (see p217) and real ale favourite the King's Arms to Cubana and theatre bars at the Old and Young Vics (Pit Bar and the Cut Bar). Finally, poor weather notwithstanding, drinking on the South Bank is its own reward: there may be an absence of characterful bars, but few people-watching experiences beat a pint from Benugo, drunk outside the BFI Southbank, beneath Waterloo Bridge.

Abbeville *67-69 Abbeville Road, SW4 9JW (8675 2201, www.theabbeville.co.uk).*
Bar Estrela *111-115 South Lambeth Road, SW8 1UZ (7793 1051).*
Beehive *51 Durham Street, SE11 5JA (7582 7608).*
Benugo Bar & Kitchen *BFI Southbank, Belvedere Road, SE1 8XT (7401 9000, www.benugobarandkitchen.com).*
Bread & Roses *68 Clapham Manor Street, SW4 6DZ (7498 1779, www.breadandroses pub.com).*
Cubana *48 Lower Marsh, SE1 7RG (7928 8778, www.cubana.co.uk).*
Cut Bar *Young Vic, 66 The Cut, SE1 8LZ (7928 4400, www.thecutbar.com).*
Dog House *293 Kennington Road, SE11 6BY (7820 9310).*
Dogstar *389 Coldharbour Lane, SW9 8LQ (7733 7515, www.antic-ltd.com/dogstar).*
Earl Ferrers *22 Ellora Road, SW16 6JF (8835 8333, www.earlferrers.co.uk).*
Effra *38A Kellet Road, SW2 1EB (7274 4180).*
Electric Brixton *1 Town Hall Parade, Brixton Hill, SW2 1RJ (7274 2290, www.electricbrixton.com)*
Fentiman Arms *64 Fentiman Road, SW8 1LA (7793 9796, www.geronimo-inns.co.uk).*
King's Arms *25 Roupell Street, SE1 8TB (7207 0784, www.windmilltaverns.com).*
Lost Society *697 Wandsworth Road, SW8 3JF (7652 6526, www.lostsociety.co.uk).*
Mass *St Matthew's Church, Brixton Hill, SW2 1JF (7738 7875, www.mass-club.com).*
Mint *5 Streatham High Road, SW16 1EF (8677 0007, www.mintstreatham.co.uk).*
Pit Bar *Old Vic, The Cut, SE1 8NB (7928 2651, www.oldvictheatre.com).*
Plan B *418 Brixton Road, SW9 7AY (7737 7372, www.plan-brixton.co.uk).*
Prince of Wales *48 Cleaver Square, SE11 4EA (7735 9916, www.shepherd neame.co.uk).*
Priory Arms *83 Lansdowne Way, SW8 2PB (7622 1884, www.theprioryarms.co.uk).*
Queen's Head *144 Stockwell Road, SW9 9TQ (7737 3519).*
Riverside *5 St George's Wharf, SW8 2LE (7735 8129, www.riversidelondon.com).*
Royal Vauxhall Tavern *372 Kennington Lane, SE11 5HY (7820 1222, www.rvt.org.uk).*
Secondo *642 Voltaire Road, SW4 6DH (7720 7059, www.secondouk.com).*

TRANSPORT

Tube stations *Bakerloo* Waterloo, Lambeth North; *Jubilee* Waterloo; *Northern* Waterloo, Kennington, Oval, Stockwell, Clapham North, Clapham Common, Clapham South; *Victoria* Vauxhall, Stockwell, Brixton; *Waterloo & City* Waterloo

Rail stations *Southeastern* Brixton, Herne Hill; Waterloo East; *Southern* Wandsworth Road, Clapham High Street; Streatham Common, Streatham, Tulse Hill, West Norwood, Streatham Hill; *South West Trains* Waterloo, Vauxhall; *First Capital Connect* Loughborough Junction, Herne Hill, Tulse Hill, Streatham

Main bus routes *into central London* 1, 2, 3, 4, 12, 26, 35, 42, 45, 59, 68, 76, 77, 87, 88, 133, 137, 139, 159, 168, 171, 172, 176, 188, 243, 341, 344, 436, 521, RV1, X68; *night buses* N1, N2, N3, N35, N44, N68, N76, N133, N137, N155, N171, N343, N381; *24-hour buses* 12, 88, 139, 159, 176, 188, 243, 341, 344

COUNCIL TAX

A	up to £40,000	£823.41
B	£40,001-£52,000	£960.64
C	£52,001-£68,000	£1,097.88
D	£68,001-£88,000	£1,235.11
E	£88,001-£120,000	£1,509.58
F	£120,001-£160,000	£1,784.05
G	£160,001-£320,000	£2,058.52
H	over £320,000	£2,470.22

RECYCLING

Household waste recycled & composted 27%
Main recycling centre Vale Street Recycling Centre, Vale Street, SE27 9PH (7926 8026)
Other recycling services green waste collection; home composting; furniture and white goods collection; food waste pilot scheme
Council contact Sustainable Waste Unit, 1st floor, Service Team House, 185-205 Shakespeare Road, SE27 0PZ (Callpoint Environmental Services 7926 9000, www.lambeth.gov.uk/recycling)

South London Pacific 340 Kennington Road, SE11 4LD (7820 9189, www.southlondon pacific.com).
Surprise 16 Southville, SW8 2PP (7622 4623).
Swan 215 Clapham Road, SW9 9BE (7978 9778, www.theswanstockwell.co.uk).
Three Stags 67-69 Kennington Road, SE1 7PZ (7928 5974, www.thethreestags.org).
Tommyfield 185 Kennington Lane, SE11 4EZ (7735 1061, www.thetommyfield.com).
Trinity Arms 45 Trinity Gardens, SW9 8DR (7274 4544, www.trinityarms.co.uk).
White Horse 94 Brixton Hill, SW2 1QN (8678 6666, www.whitehorsebrixton.com).
Windmill Clapham Common South Side, SW4 9DE (8673 4578, www.windmillclapham.co.uk).
Windmill 22 Blenheim Gardens, SW2 5BZ (8671 0700, www.windmillbrixton.co.uk).

Shops

Lambeth is not the most obvious of retail destinations, though its culturally diverse food shops are well worth seeking out. Vauxhall's Portuguese offerings include Madeira Pâtisserie (see p218), which turns out the finest custard tarts in town, and, next door, the Luis Deli for cold cooked meats and sandwiches. Also in Vauxhall is Lassco, an intriguing clutter of architectural antiques and relics in a haunted Georgian mansion.

The Old Post Office Bakery in Clapham North stocks a huge selection of breads, while Breads Etcetera, on the High Street, supplies various upmarket restaurants. Closer to Clapham Common, Macaron is an authentic French pâtisserie and M Moen & Sons a well-respected organic butcher. The North Street Deli offers top-quality charcuterie, breads and cakes.

Brixton Market remains an enormously enjoyable (if strikingly unorganised) food shopping experience. The stalls along Electric Avenue are piled high with yams, plantains, mangoes and other exotic items, while on Atlantic Road there's clothes, towels and wallets, and on Brixton Station Road second-hand clobber (Saturday) and a farmers' market (Sunday). In Brixton Village, African, Caribbean and South American stores have been joined by enthusiastic new crafts and homewares shops as part of the arcade's renaissance. One of the market's strongest suits is music, with two of the best specialist record shops in the capital: reggae, gospel and soca at Supertone, and soul and roots at Selectors. Coldharbour Lane has African and West Indian record stores, as well as new-age bookstore Book Mongers.

For literature elsewhere, Soma Books in Kennington imports a wide range of texts from India. There's also the fantastic Riverside Walk Book Market under the arches of Waterloo Bridge and a branch of Foyles beneath the Royal Festival Hall. Lower Marsh is a treasure trove of specialist outlets, from Top Wind flute shop and classical music shop Gramex, to I Knit (the clue's in the name) and vintage emporium Radio Days.

In Clapham, tiny Places & Spaces has one of the most interesting selections of furniture, lighting and accessories in London, Lisa Stickley deals in beautiful textiles and Clapham Books is a charming independent.

Norwood High Street has all the necessities, as well as excellent specialists such as paint paradise the South London Decorators Merchants. Streatham High Road has a great many charity shops.

More interesting is vintage clothing store Cenci, in West Norwood: once based in Covent Garden, it's got a fantastic collection from the 1960s.

Book Mongers *439 Coldharbour Lane, SW9 8LN (7738 4225, www.bookmongers.com).*
Breads Etcetera *127 Clapham High Street, SW4 7SS (07717 642812, www.breads etcetera.com).*
Brixton Market *Electric Avenue, Pope's Road, Brixton Station Road, Atlantic Road, SW9 (www.brixtonmarket.net).*
Cenci *4 Nettlefold Place, SE27 0JW (8766 8564, www.cenci.co.uk).*
Clapham Books *120 Clapham High Street, SW4 7UH (7627 2797, www.clapham books.com).*
Foyles *Festival Riverside, South Bank Centre, SE1 8XX (7440 3212, www.foyles.co.uk).*
Gramex *25 Lower Marsh, SE1 7RJ (7401 3830).*
I Knit *106 Lower Marsh, SW6 1TE (7261 1338, www.iknit.org.uk).*
Lassco *Brunswick House, 30 Wandsworth Road, SW8 2LG (7394 2100, www.lassco.co.uk).*
Lisa Stickley *74 Landor Road, SW9 9PH (7737 8067, www.lisastickleylondon.com).*
Luis Deli *46 Albert Embankment, SE1 7TL (7820 0314).*
Maoaron *22 The Pavement, SW4 0HY (7498 2636).*
M Moen & Sons *24 The Pavement, SW4 0JA (7622 1624, www.moen.co.uk).*
North Street Deli *26 North Street, SW4 0HB (7978 1555).*
Old Post Office Bakery *76 Landor Road, SW9 9PH (7326 4408, www.oldpostoffice bakery.co.uk).*
Places & Spaces *30 Old Town, SW4 0LB (7498 0998, www.placesandspaces.com).*
Radio Days *87 Lower Marsh, SE1 7AB (7928 0800, www.radiodaysvintage.co.uk).*
Selectors Music Emporium *100B Brixton Hill, SW2 1AH (7771 2011).*
Soma Books *38 Kennington Lane, SE11 4LS (7735 2101, www.somabooks.co.uk).*
South Lambeth Market *Cavendish Arms, 128 Hartington Road, SW8 2HJ (www.south lambethmarket.com).*
South London Decorators Merchants *547 Norwood Road, SE27 9DL (8655 9595).*
Supertone Records, Videos & CDs *110 Acre Lane, SW2 5RA (7737 7761, www.supertonerecords.co.uk).*
Top Wind *2 Lower Marsh, SE1 7RJ (7401 8787, www.topwind.com).*

Arts & attractions

Cinemas & theatres

BFI London IMAX *1 Charlie Chaplin Walk, SE1 8XR (7199 6000, www.bfi.org.uk/whatson/bfi_imax). 3-D spectaculars at the UK's biggest cinema screen.*
BFI Southbank *Belvedere Road, South Bank, SE1 8XT (7928 3232, www.bfi.org.uk). London's best cinema, with an unrivalled programme of retrospective seasons and previews.*
Clapham Picture House *76 Venn Street, SW4 0AT (0871 902 5727, www.picture houses.co.uk).*
Landor *70 Landor Road, SW9 9PH (7737 7276, www.landortheatre.co.uk).*
National Theatre *South Bank, SE1 9PX (7452 3400, box office 7452 3000, www.nationaltheatre.org.uk). Three theatres (Olivier, Lyttleton, Cottesloe) present an eclectic mix of news plays and classics.*
Odeon Streatham *47-49 Streatham High Road, SW16 1PW (0871 224 4007, www.odeon.co.uk).*
Old Vic *The Cut, SE1 8NB (0844 871 7628, www.oldvictheatre.com). Kevin Spacey continues as artistic director at this historic theatre.*
Ovalhouse *52-54 Kennington Oval, SE11 5SW (7582 7680, www.ovalhouse.com). Theatre and gallery with strong community and young persons' programme.*
Ritzy *Brixton Oval, Coldharbour Lane, SW2 1JG (0871 902 5739, www.picture houses.co.uk). Much-loved local cinema, with café and jazz bar.*
South London Theatre *2A Norwood High Street, SE27 9NS (box office 8670 3474, members' club 8670 4661, www.southlondon theatre.co.uk).*
Young Vic *66 The Cut, SE1 8LZ (7922 2922, www.youngvic.org).*

Galleries & museums

Florence Nightingale Museum *St Thomas' Hospital, 2 Lambeth Palace Road, SE1 7EW (7620 0374, www.florence-nightingale.co.uk). Honours the remarkable life and Crimean War work of 'the lady with the lamp'.*
Garden Museum *Lambeth Palace Road, SE1 7LB (7401 8865, www.gardenmuseum.org.uk). The world's first horticultural museum.*
Hayward Gallery *South Bank Centre, SE1 8XX (7960 4200, www.southbankcentre. co.uk/hayward). One of London's leading art galleries, presenting a mix of contemporary and older work.*

Museum of the Royal Pharmaceutical Society *1 Lambeth High Street, SE1 7JN (7572 2211, www.rpharms.com). A permanent collection of objects relating to the history of pharmaceuticals, plus regular special events.*

Music & comedy venues

O2 Academy Brixton *211 Stockwell Road, SW9 9SL (7771 3000, www.o2academy brixton.co.uk). Major concert venue.*

Southbank Centre *Belvedere Road, SE1 8XX (7960 4200, www.southbankcentre.co.uk). Three concert halls – the majestic Royal Festival Hall, smaller Queen Elizabeth Hall and diminutive Purcell Room – cover classical and contemporary music and dance.*

Udderbelly *Jubilee Gardens, off Belvedere Road, SE1 8XX (0844 545 8282, www.underbelly.co.uk). Comedy and music; summer only.*

Other attractions

Brixton Windmill *Windmill Gardens, west end of Blenheim Gardens, off Brixton Hill, SW2 5EU (07587 170029, www.brixton windmill.org). The area's last surviving windmill, built in 1816 and restored in 2011 as an educational attraction.*

London Aquarium *County Hall, Riverside Building, Westminster Bridge Road, SE1 7PB (0871 663 1678, www.londonaquarium.co.uk). One of Europe's largest exhibitions of global aquatic life, displayed in giant tanks and touch pools.*

London Eye *Next to County Hall, Riverside Building, Westminster Bridge Road, SE1 7PB (0871 781 3000, www.londoneye.com).*

Vauxhall City Farm *165 Tyers Street, SE11 5HS (7582 4204, www.vauxhallcityfarm.org). Community farm and gardens, with beekeepers and riding lessons.*

Sport & fitness

Lambeth's residents have access to four council-owned sports centres, all run by Greenwich Leisure; the new Clapham Leisure Centre opened in January 2012 with a state-of-the-art gym and 25-metre pool. Private clubs range from small operations squeezed between big buildings and main roads to large facilities in quieter, more remote areas. Also on offer is Vauxhall's Paris Gym, previously a 'gay-only' facility but now also open to straight men who are comfortable in that environment.

Gyms & leisure centres

Brixton Recreation Centre *27 Brixton Station Road, SW9 8QQ (7926 9779, www.gll.org).*

Clapham Leisure Centre *141 Clapham Manor Street, SW4 6DB (7627 7900, www.gll.org).*

Ferndale Community Sports Centre *Nursery Road, SW9 8PB (0845 130 8998, www.gll.org).*

Fitness First *Blue Star House, 234-244 Stockwell Road, SW9 9FP (0844 571 2828, www.fitnessfirst.co.uk). Private.*

Flaxman Sports Centre *Carew Street, SE5 9DF (7926 1054, www.gll.org).*

Paris Gym *73 Goding Street, SE11 5AW (7735 8989, www.parisgym.com). Men only; private.*

Soho Gym *95-97 Clapham High Street, SW4 7TB (7720 0321, www.sohogyms.com). Private.*

South Bank Club *124-130 Wandsworth Road, SW8 2LD (7622 6866, www.southbankclub. co.uk). Private.*

Virgin Active *www.virginactive.co.uk; 4-20 North Street, SW4 0HG (0845 270 4087); 20 Ockley Road, SW16 1UB (0845 270 2106). Private.*

Other facilities

Brixton Ice Arena *49 Brixton Station Road, SW9 8PQ (0845 177 1707, www.brixtonice rink.co.uk). Temporary ice-rink, in use while Streatham's ice-rink and leisure centre are closed for redevelopment (due to be completed in 2013).*

Spectator sports

Kia Oval *Surrey County Cricket Club, Kennington, SE11 5SS (7820 5700, www.kiaoval.com).*

Schools

Primary

There are 59 state primary schools in Lambeth, 21 of which are church schools, and one a Muslim school. There are also nine independent primaries, including two Muslim schools. See www.lambeth.gov.uk, www.edubase.gov.uk and www.ofsted.gov.uk for more information.

Secondary

Archbishop Tenison's School
55 Kennington Oval, SE11 5SR (7735 3771, www.tenisons.com). Church of England; boys only.

Bishop Thomas Grant School *Belltrees Grove, SW16 2HY (8769 3294, www.btg.ac). Roman Catholic.*
Charles Edward Brooke CE School *Langton Road, SW9 6UL (7274 6311, www.charlesedwardbrooke.lambeth.sch.uk). Girls only. Becomes St Gabriel's College from Sept 2012.*
Dunraven School *94-98 Leigham Court Road, SW16 2QB (8677 2431, www.dunraven.org.uk).*
Elmgreen School *Elmcourt Road, SE27 9BZ (8766 5020, www.the-elmgreen school.org.uk).*
Evelyn Grace Academy *255 Shakespeare Road, SE24 0QN (7737 9520, www.evelyn graceacademy.org).*
Lambeth Academy *Elms Road, SW4 9ET (7819 4700, www.lambeth-academy.org).*
Lilian Baylis Technology School *323 Kennington Lane, SE11 5QY (7091 9500, www.lilianbaylis.com).*
London Nautical School *61 Stamford Street, SE1 9NA (7928 6801, www.lns.org.uk). Boys only.*
Norwood School *Crown Dale, SE19 3NY (8670 9382, www.thenorwoodschool.org).*
La Retraite RC School *Atkins Road, SW12 0AB (8673 5644, www.laretraite.lambeth.sch.uk). Roman Catholic; girls only.*
St Martin-in-the-Fields CE School *155 Tulse Hill, SW2 3UP (8674 5594, www.st martins.lambeth.sch.uk). Church of England, girls only.*
Stockwell Park High School *Clapham Road, SW9 0AL (7733 6156, www.stockpark. lambeth.sch.uk).*

Property

WHAT THE AGENTS SAY:

'Kennington is primarily residential, with plenty of shops, bars and restaurants. It's well served by public transport, with the Northern line at Kennington and the Oval, and the Victoria line and mainline trains at Vauxhall. There are fine examples of grand Georgian houses and attractive squares, as well as some smart modern developments. It's also within the Parliamentary 'division bell' – which is why so many MPs live in Kennington.'
Jonathan Lloyd-Ham, Field & Sons, Kennington

Average property prices
Detached £637,703
Semi-detached £501,010
Terraced £438,468
Flat £321,152

Local estate agents
Aspire *www.aspire.co.uk; 2 offices in the borough (Clapham South 8675 1222, North Clapham 7840 3700).*
Beresford Residential *91 Acre Lane, SW2 5TU (7326 7450, www.beresford residential.com).*
Brooks *76 Streatham High Road, SW16 1BS (8769 8000, http://brooksestateagents.com).*
Daniel Cobb *191 Kennington Lane, SE11 5QS (7735 9510, www.danielcobb.co.uk).*
Harmens *www.harmens.co.uk; 2 offices in the borough (Brixton 7737 6000, Streatham 8769 4777).*
Keating Estates *25 Clapham Common South Side, SW4 7AB (7720 2113, www.keating estates.com).*
Martin Barry *4 Acre Lane, SW2 5SG (7738 5866, www.martinbarrypartnership.co.uk).*
Murray Estates *92-96 Stockwell Road, SW9 9HR (7733 4203, www.murrayestates.com).*

Other information

Council
Lambeth Council *Town Hall, Brixton Hill, SW2 1RW (7926 1000, www.lambeth.gov.uk).*

Legal services
Lambeth Law Centre *11 Mowll Street, SW9 6BG (7840 2000, www.lambeth lawcentre.org).*
Streatham Hill CAB *Ilex House, 1 Barrhill Road, SW2 4RJ (0844 243 8430, www.adviceguide.org.uk).*

Local information
www.brixtonblog.com.
www.brixton.makerhood.com.
www.brixtonpound.org
www.claphamhighstreet.co.uk.
www.loveclapham.com.
www.streathamguardian.co.uk.
www.streathamsociety.org.uk.
www.waterlooquarter.org

Open spaces & allotments
Lorn Road Allotments *Lorn Road, SW9 (7926 9000).*
Open spaces *www.lambeth.gov.uk/parks.*
Rosendale Allotments Association *227 Rosendale Road, SE21 8LR (www.rosendale-allotments.org.uk).*
Streatham Vale Allotments *SW16, c/o Streatham Vale Property Occupiers Association (www.svpoa.org.uk).*

Lambeth

'Southwark's properly London.
Bombed out and re-imagined.
Locally international. The art
students in Camberwell put
an installation in the phone box
overnight. And SE5 has its
own nuclear bunker.'

Anneliese Davidsen, Executive Director, Unicorn Theatre

Southwark

Gentrification and widespread regeneration have turned Southwark into a borough of layers: popular cultural attractions and riverside walks to the north; green spaces and smart food shops in the south; and down-on-their-luck housing estates and vibrant high streets across the middle. As reconstruction continues, this is a borough on the move – upwards.

Neighbourhoods

Borough and Bankside

Bankside has historically been a place of entertainment and fun, hedonism and artistic delight. Though associated with light industry until as recently the 1980s, it is once again a vibrant cultural quarter. Shakespeare's Globe theatre was rebuilt with painstaking historical accuracy in 1997, the Oxo cold store converted into small-scale design workshops and a rooftop restaurant with stunning views in 1996, and, most importantly, Tate Modern opened in 2000 in the former Bankside power station – and was an instant hit. The Tate's expansion plans involve new galleries in the underground spaces that once housed the oil tanks (opening summer 2012) and, later, a ten-storey extension.

Norman Foster's Millennium Bridge has changed the geography of this part of London, linking it directly with the City and St Paul's Cathedral. The recent rebuilding of Blackfriars rail station, as neither north nor south of the river but stretching right across it, brings the two banks even closer.

By restyling itself as 'London's Larder' in the late 1990s, Borough Market has become one of the city's top tourist attractions. The market is surrounded by characterful old pubs, and the historic streets around it are often used in period films. Other landmarks include 13th-century Southwark Cathedral, a replica of Francis Drake's flagship the *Golden Hinde*, the Clink Prison, the Old Operating Theatre Museum and, in

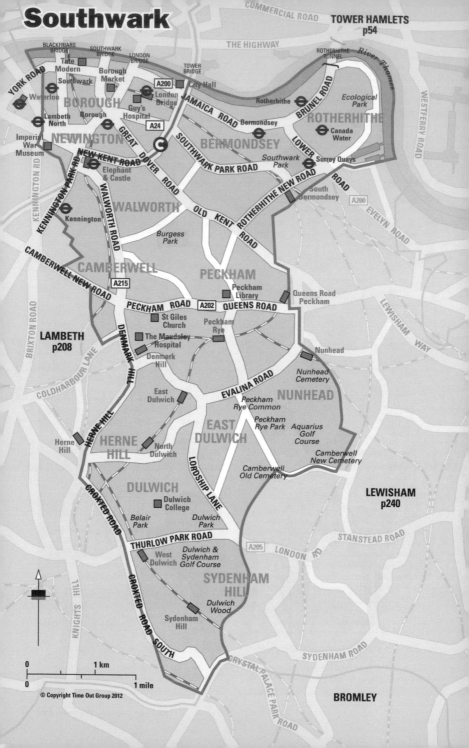

a courtyard off Borough High Street, the 17th-century George Inn, the last galleried coaching inn left in London.

The area to the east of London Bridge has been given new importance by shiny commercial development More London and the relocation of the Greater London Authority to purpose-built City Hall, a glass and steel ovoid with a public viewing space – London's Living Room – at the top. Outdoor amphitheatre the Scoop, next to the Thames, often hosts free performances and film screenings, while new public spaces host specially commissioned artworks. This is also where you'll find two acclaimed theatres: the Menier Chocolate Factory and purpose-built children's theatre Unicorn.

The Dickensian wharfs beyond Tower Bridge were, in the 1980s, the site of some of the first forays into warehouse redevelopment. Here too is the Design Museum, opened in 1989 by Terence Conran as a declaration of optimism for the area (though it is moving to a new home, in 2014, to the former Commonwealth Institute in High Street Kensington).

Behind London Bridge station is Bermondsey Street, spiritually more connected to the prosperity of Borough than down-at-heel Bermondsey on the other side of Tower Bridge Road. There are cool cafés, lauded restaurants, media companies, trendy boutiques, smart galleries, a fancy florist and some hip residents. Designer and local resident Zandra Rhodes chose to open her pink and orange Fashion & Textiles Museum here in 2003 (it's now operated by Newham College). The seal of cultural approval came with the opening of the White Cube's third, and biggest, gallery.

London Bridge station is the key interchange for most Southwark residents, taking trains from all over Kent and south east London and funnelling them into Charing Cross or up through the City, or swapping commuters on to the Jubilee and Northern lines. Looming dramatically over the station, and visible from all across London, is the 'Shard', architect Renzo Piano's pointed glass tower (www.shardlondonbridge.com), scheduled for completion in 2012. It incorporates offices, apartments and a public observation deck that promises breathtaking views across the whole city. But it's also a controversial structure: 1,016 feet high,

it's the tallest building in Europe, and dwarfs all of the capital's other skyscrapers.

Elephant & Castle and Walworth

Once known as the Piccadilly of south London, the busy Elephant & Castle double roundabout is effectively the gateway to south London. Radiating off the roundabout are the New Kent Road and historic Old Kent Road; perennially busy, bus-laden Walworth Road, which runs down to Camberwell; and Newington Butts, heading south-west to Kennington and thence to Clapham. Beneath it is a forbidding warren of foot tunnels.

Dominating everything is the Elephant & Castle shopping centre, the building most Londoners love to hate. Its scheduled demolition, as part of a massive redevelopment of the whole area, keeps being postponed, though some rebuilding has begun. The 43-storey Strata tower, topped with three wind turbines, can be seen for miles but is already as unpopular

Southwark

The **Scoop** amphitheatre, next to City Hall. See p227.

aesthetically as the shopping centre. The Heygate housing estate has been cleared and awaits the wrecking ball. For more details, see www.elephantandcastle.org.uk.

Despite its reputation, the area is not without its charms. There's a vibrant Colombian community who come together at La Bodeguita café, a popular bowling alley (Superbowl) and a street market (daily except Sunday). Two big colleges – South Bank University and London College of Communication – and some large halls of residence bring lots of students into the mix. A colourful playground, new lighting and the replacement of the southern tunnels with pedestrian crossings is already tidying up the streetscape. E&C is also considered central enough to merit Boris bikes.

Towards Lambeth North and the borough boundary, the streets become prettier and return to a more human scale. Highlights include the architecturally exciting Siobhan Davies Dance Studios and the Imperial War Museum. There is also an attempt being made to woo an annexe of the Science Museum to the area, using the Faraday Memorial – a shiny steel box that currently sits stranded in the middle of one of the roundabouts – as an incentive.

At present, the Walworth Road is a hit-and-miss affair, where down-at-heel sofa outlets and high-street chains rub shoulders with local gems such as the Cuming Museum (great for local history), the 24-hour Bagel King, Turkish grocer Oli's (which famously never closes), Dragon Castle dim sum restaurant, one of London's first health shops (G Baldwin & Co), and cheap and cheerful East Street Market. Behind the chaos, there are even pockets of gentility such as Liverpool Grove and Addington Square. The reopening of Burgess Park in summer 2012, following a £6 million facelift, will hopefully provide some much needed beauty, as well as a community space with playgrounds, gardens and sports areas.

Bermondsey

Bermondsey is perhaps the bleakest stretch of Southwark. From medieval times, it was home to the leather industry (witness such addresses as Leathermarket Street), and further light industry developed during the 19th century, causing overcrowding and unsavoury smells. The area became known as 'London's larder' (a moniker now used by the far more salubrious Borough Market) because of the amount of food processing done in the area, with the industrial work continuing until the docks closed in the 1970s. Famous names that had factories here include Sarson's (vinegar), Hartley's (jam), Peek Freans (biscuits) and Crosse & Blackwell (chutney). Now, small independent foodmakers such as Kernel Brewery and Ice Cream Union have moved into the railway arches along Druid and Frean Streets, and there's a popular Saturday food market on Maltby Street.

Eschewing its rough reputation and industrial roots, this part of town has steadily emerged as a fashionable place in which to live. The central swathe of Bermondsey (along Spa Road, between Grange Road and Jamaica Road) is subject to ongoing regeneration. Spa Park has already been landscaped, and new buildings are to welcome shops, key worker housing, live-work units, business space and even penthouse flats. But the housing estates that were built after slum clearances in the 1920s and '30s, and after the Blitz, seem bleak and endless, with more than their share of flags of St George hung in windows.

A little to the south-east, you'll find Southwark Park Road and occasional pretty terraces. By South Bermondsey rail station, 'The Den' – Millwall Football Club's ground – is still a focus of local pride (and occasional violence, although the club itself runs a commendable community programme). To the south, Old Kent Road creaks on, sustaining boxing gyms and Nigerian cafés, intimidating lounge bars and DIY superstores. To the north, families and amateur sports clubs enjoy Southwark Park, which – post-regeneration – features an Italian coffee hut, a great playground and the artist-run Café Gallery. It is London's oldest municipal park.

At the west, Bermondsey Square has been developed and is now touted as one of London's chicest quarters. As well as smart new apartments around an intimate public square, there's a cinema, independent bookshop and hotel, but the world-famous Antiques Market (good for china and silver) is still open 4am to 1pm every Friday.

Rotherhithe

On emerging from Rotherhithe tube station, an eerie silence greets you, a silence that is rarely broken anywhere across this isolated peninsula. The area is rich in maritime history: the Mayflower pub marks the departure point of the Pilgrim Fathers, while the Finnish Church and Seamen's Mission on Albion Street are reminders of more recent Scandinavian seafarers. The diminutive Brunel Museum is housed in the pumping house for the world's first underwater tunnel, which was dug beneath the Thames in 1843.

The fringes of the Rotherhithe peninsula are now marked by riverfront apartments and a Hilton hotel, but you'll rarely see a soul. The best chances of finding life are at the charming Surrey Docks Farm, home to

cows, pigs, sheep, fowl and bees (their honey is available in the farm shop), or at Lavender Pond & Nature Park, where the ponds, reed beds, meadow and marshland are complemented by the Pumphouse Educational Museum. There are also superb Docklands views from Stave Hill Ecological Park on Salter Road.

Most of the docks had been filled in by the 1980s, with the few that remain developed into luxury housing complexes. The swanky South Dock is the capital's largest working marina, with over 200 berths, and there are some great opportunities for watersports. Major regeneration followed the linking of Canada Water to the West End by the arrival of the Jubilee line, and now the extension of the Overground line from Dalston right down to West Croydon has made Canada Water a busy interchange. It's also home to a landmark new library (designed by architect Piers Gough of CZWG) – an inverted pyramid with much of the building actually below ground.

Camberwell

Once a small farming village, Camberwell predates the Domesday Book, which mentions it having a church (a sign of the village's importance). Today's church of St Giles was built on the site of the original by architect Giles Gilbert Scott. It features stained-glass windows by one-time local resident John Ruskin. Rapid expansion in Victorian times bequeathed attractive terraces, but the street that really impresses is the Georgian Camberwell Grove.

As one of the best connected areas in Southwark – lying between central London to the north and southerly Dulwich, east of Vauxhall and west of Peckham – it's natural that Camberwell should have become a social hub. On the downside, this means a depressing amount of police incident tape on Friday and Saturday nights, but also a number of good restaurants and a flourishing gay scene. The most popular eating and drinking places and food shops are on Peckham Road and Camberwell Church Street (and rumour has it that some smart extensions from Soho and Hoxton are on their way). A shopping mecca, it ain't: Camberwell Road and Denmark Hill are lined with evangelical churches, pound shops and bookies, although a council consultation of local people ('Revitalise

Camberwell') could lead to improvements. The presence of Camberwell College of Arts continues Ruskin's aesthetic legacy, and for decades many artists have lived in the area. The South London Gallery has expanded and now has a popular café, as well as high-profile exhibitions and activities for children on Sundays.

Other major institutions are King's College Hospital (technically in Lambeth) and the Maudsley psychiatric hospital, which serve the wider south London community. William Booth College (headquarters of the Salvation Army) is also here. Designed by Giles Gilbert Scott in 1929, the college has an imposing tower that's 190 feet tall and lords it over the poor lost souls of south London.

Dulwich Village, Herne Hill and Sydenham Hill

Dulwich Village is an anomaly – it feels more like rural Kent than a near-neighbour such as Brixton or Peckham. Elizabethan actor Edward Alleyn bought land here and set up Dulwich College to help educate the poor; the trustees still guard against overdevelopment of the area. There are white picket fences, wooden signposts,

Locals' Tips

Theatres such as the Unicorn, Old Vic and Young Vic offer reduced-price tickets for Southwark residents.
Grab an empanada from the Colombian snack shack inside Elephant & Castle shopping centre.
Kids adore the slide that's built into a slope in Southwark Park. Adults love the Italian café and art gallery.
Visit Maltby Street food market in Bermondsey (10am-2pm Saturday) for small but brilliant producers.
Nunhead Cemetery is one of London's seven great Victorian cemeteries. The Friends of Nunhead Cemetery (www.fonc.org.uk) runs guided tours on the last Sunday of every month, starting from the Linden Grove gates at 2.15pm.
The Brunel Museum in Rotherhithe may be one of the capital's lesser-known museums, but it's fascinating.
Follow the number trail round Dulwich Woods/Sydenham Hill Woods, part of the Great North Wood that once stretched from Deptford to Selhurst.

an impressive coaching inn (the Crown & Greyhound) and, on College Road, a functioning toll gate – but nothing useful like a cashpoint. This is a posh area, where you'll find some of the capital's most expensive real estate (Georgian villas, Victorian cottages, 1930s suburban homes) and three top private schools (Dulwich College, Alleyn's and James Allen's Girls).

Attractions include England's first public art gallery, Dulwich Picture Gallery, which was designed by Sir John Soane. It contains an important collection of 17th- and 18th-century masters and has a great café. The area also has extensive green spaces that stretch from the heights of Sydenham Hill (where there are allotments, a golf course, a cricket pitch and ancient woodland) all the way down to Herne Hill (with more sports pitches and the velodrome used for the finals of the 1948 London Olympic Games). Dulwich Park, in the heart of Dulwich Village, is popular and well maintained, with an excellent children's playground, bike hire, tennis courts and a lake.

Herne Hill is characterised by lively independent shops, restaurants and cafés, which mainly cluster around the pedestrianised area in front of the station and on Half Moon Lane. These serve a population of affluent, well-dressed foodies and privately educating families. Property here is generally grander than in East Dulwich or Brixton, with houses commanding large price tags. The area is served by good rail links to Victoria and Blackfriars and plenty of buses, but traffic is still slow at the main junction in spite of recent road improvements.

Brockwell Park (officially in the borough of Lambeth) is the area's green lung. Its charms include the much-loved lido, a walled garden, BMX dirt tracks, a paddling pool, community greenhouses, a Georgian country house and great views. It also hosts Southwark and Lambeth's joint firework display, and the incongruous Lambeth Country Show.

East Dulwich and Nunhead

Somehow, since the millennium, East Dulwich has gone from being a relaxed, vaguely bohemian secret to a caricature of middle-class urban living. The online East Dulwich Forum is one of the most active local area forums in the country, where people get hot under the collar

Family-friendly **Peckham Rye Park**.

Peckham

Peckham suffers from a poor reputation, reinforced by reports of teenage gun crime and the TV legacy of *Only Fools and Horses*. Although the area north of Peckham Road and Peckham High Street is still troubled, the notorious North Peckham estate is being flattened as part of an ongoing £300 million regeneration that has already seen a change in the fortunes of much of the rest of the area. Will Alsop's unconventional, award-winning library and the well-equipped sports centre and swimming pool Peckham Pulse have indicated that planners are willing to embrace new ideas and marked the town centre as a dynamic place.

The most desirable area of Peckham is around Bellenden Road, given a smart but relaxed air by pavement cafés, an arts bookshop, good restaurants and Antony Gormley designed bollards. There are also a few surprises, including delightful Lyndhurst Square and Elm Grove, and the Regency villas of Holly Grove. Plenty of artists have been attracted to the area, with funky art squats lending a frisson of cool.

There's a constant hubbub along Rye Lane, where the wares are as varied and colourful as the patrons. You'll find plantains, yams, hair extensions, Chinese medicine, fish, international phone cards, a Primark, Pentecostal churches, the Wing Tai Chinese supermarket and a very cheap cinema. East of Rye Lane, things are still fairly desolate but the area is definitely on the up, with stylish new housing and even a deli on Consort Road. At Queens Road Peckham, several new residential schemes are adding more apartments for key workers and commuters, while down St Mary's Road the architectural mix includes a 1960s church and the 1930s Pioneer Centre, a gated community with its own swimming pool and tennis courts.

about unsightly advertising hoardings, noise after 10pm, and whether chain shops are welcome (Waitrose only, it seems).

SE22's busy spine, Lordship Lane, is lined with delis, proper old-fashioned food shops, good restaurants, chichi boutiques, florists, a bookshop and eager estate agents. It's possible to get anything you need by shopping locally, and many people do, but there's also a big Sainsbury's up Dog Kennel Hill. North Cross Road offers more of the same, plus an ever-expanding market on Saturday. Goose Green is the old village centre and often hosts local fêtes. The Victorian terraced housing, good primary schools, child-friendly pubs and big open spaces of Dulwich Park and Peckham Rye attract hordes of young families – to the point where you can't move for buggies.

As East Dulwich gets increasingly clichéd, Nunhead – the other side of Peckham Rye – is coming into its own. It's been touted as 'on the up' for years, but the arrival of two delis, a gastropub running comedy nights, and an annual film festival (www.freefilmfestivals.org) suggest it's finally reaching critical mass. Established favourites include Ayres baker, Soper's fishmonger and Ivy House, which hosts a highly regarded programme of music, comedy, film and more. Nunhead's rambling Victorian cemetery (Grade II* listed) and the ancient woods of One Tree Hill loom over the Victorian terraces.

Restaurants & cafés

Southwark has no shortage of quality places to eat, and there are many dining-with-a-view options along the riverfront. Predictable chains abound, but there are exceptions, such as the Oxo Tower and the Tate Modern Café (the family-friendly one on the second floor is our favourite). Past Tower Bridge, near the Design Museum

Southwark

(home to the Blueprint Café), are Butlers Wharf Chop House and Le Pont de la Tour.

Away from the river, near Southwark tube, is stylish east European restaurant Baltic, unpretentious tapas joint Mar i Terra, and relaxed bistro Laughing Gravy. Up on Southwark Street, budget canteen the Table is a definite don't-miss, while the Blue Fin building houses reputable chain eateries such as Leon.

As you might expect, the area surrounding foodie magnet Borough Market holds real culinary gems. Try bustling Tapas Brindisa, British meat specialist Roast, or Wright Brothers Oyster & Porter House. Nearer London Bridge, on Tooley Street, is British restaurant Magdalen. Bermondsey Street has some great options: charming restaurant/gallery Delfina (Mod Euro), Zucca (Italian) and the Garrison gastropub. Spanish newcomers Pizarro and José, from the same chef, are deservedly packed. Tower Bridge Road is home to M Manze – gloriously old-fashioned and probably the oldest extant pie and mash shop in London, dating from 1902.

The Elephant & Castle is an area in flux, but do check out Colombian café La Bodeguita, which, with other South American cafés, is holding on inside the shopping centre. There's excellent Cantonese cuisine at Walworth Road's Dragon Castle, an unusual location in which to find some of London's best dim sum.

Over in Camberwell, you'll find new gastropub the Crooked Well, award-winning Angels & Gypsies (Spanish), Viet Café (Vietnamese) and Silk Road (fiery Chinese and Xinjiang specialities). No 67, the in-house café at the South London Gallery (see p237), has an inventive, daily-changing menu and homemade cakes.

Peckham has less of note, although pie and mash stalwart M Manze (run by the same family as the Tower Bridge Road branch), appealing café Petitou, new café/deli Anderson & Co, and low-key South Indian Ganapati all deserve their fans.

In food-obsessed East Dulwich, locals are spoilt for choice. To start, there's a slew of excellent cafés (full even on weekdays owing to the disproportionate number of homeworkers and pre-school children in the area): Blackbird, Blue Mountain, Homemade, Jack's, Lucas and vegetarian Blue Brick. For simple suppers, there's fish and chips at the Sea Cow, pizza at the

Gowlett and the Actress (for both, see p234), and Asian flavours at Indian Mischief, Thai Corner Café and underrated Café Noodles. For something more upmarket, try the Palmerston gastropub or long-running British restaurant Franklins.

In West Dulwich, the Rosendale is a first-rate gastropub. Herne Hill's finest includes Olley's for fish and chips, and Spanish restaurant Number 22.

Even the parks in Southwark have great eateries. Dulwich Park's Pavilion Café does a roaring trade in quality fry-ups, Southwark Park has a tiny but popular Italian, and the Lido Café in Brockwell Park (Time Out's Best Park Café 2011) trumps the lot with waterside views, solid lunches, gourmet evening meals, special burger nights and occasional residencies by experimental foodists Blanch & Schock.

Anderson & Co 139 Bellenden Road, SE15 4DH (7469 7078).

Angels & Gypsies 29-33 Camberwell Church Street, SE5 8TR (7703 5984, www.angels andgypsies.com).

Baltic 74 Blackfriars Road, SE1 8HA (7928 1111, www.balticrestaurant.co.uk).

Blackbird 208 Railton Road, SE24 0JT (7095 8800).

Blue Brick Café 14 Fellbrigg Road, SE22 9HH (8299 8670).

Blue Mountain Café 18 North Cross Road, SE22 9EU (8299 6953, www.bluemo.co.uk).

Blueprint Café Design Museum, 28 Shad Thames, SE1 2YD (7378 7031, www.dand dlondon.com).

La Bodeguita Unit 222, Elephant & Castle Shopping Centre, SE1 6TE (7701 9166, www.labodeguita.co.uk).

Butlers Wharf Chop House 36E Shad Thames, SE1 2YE (7403 3403, www.dandd london.com).

Café Noodles 159 Lordship Lane, SE22 8HX (8693 4016).

Crooked Well 16 Grove Lane, SE5 8SY (7252 7798, www.thecrookedwell.com).

Delfina 50 Bermondsey Street, SE1 3UD (7564 2400, www.thedelfina.co.uk).

Dragon Castle 110 Walworth Road, SE17 1JL (7277 3388, www.dragoncastle.co.uk).

Franklins 157 Lordship Lane, SE22 8HX (8299 9598, www.franklinsrestaurant.com).

Ganapati 38 Holly Grove, SE15 5DF (7277 2928, www.ganapatirestaurant.com).

Garrison 99-101 Bermondsey Street, SE1 3XB (7089 9355, www.thegarrison.co.uk).

Homemade 44 Barry Road, SE22 0HU
(3490 6474).
Indian Mischief 71 Lordship Lane, SE22 8EP
(8693 1627).
Jack's Tea & Coffee House 85 Pellatt Road,
SE22 9JD (7183 9135, www.chocolateconcrete
andpinkcustard.blogspot.com).
José 104 Bermondsey Street, SE1 3UB
(7403 4902, www.josepizarro.com).
Laughing Gravy 154 Blackfriars Road, SE1
8EN (7998 1707, www.thelaughinggravy.co.uk).
Lido Café Brockwell Lido, Dulwich Road,
SE24 0PA (7737 8183, thelidocafe.co.uk).
Lucas 145 Lordship Lane, SE22 8HX
(8613 6161, www.lucashakery.com).
Magdalen 152 Tooley Street, SE1 2TU
(7403 1342, www.magdalenrestaurant.co.uk).
M Manze 87 Tower Bridge Road, SE1 4TW
(7407 2985, www.manze.co.uk).
M Manze 105 Peckham High Street, SE15 5RS
(7277 6181, www.manze.co.uk).
Mar i Terra 14 Gambia Street, SE1 0XH
(7928 7628, www.mariterra.co.uk).
Number 22 22 Half Moon Lane, SE24 9HU
(7095 9922, www.number-22.com).
Olley's 65-69 Norwood Road, SE24 9AA
(8671 8259, www.olleys.info).

TRANSPORT

Tube stations Bakerloo Elephant &
Castle; Jubilee Southwark, London
Bridge, Bermondsey, Canada Water;
Northern Kennington, Elephant & Castle,
Borough, London Bridge
Rail stations First Capital Connect
Blackfriars, London Bridge, Elephant
& Castle; London Overground
Rotherhithe, Canada Water, Surrey
Quays; Southeastern London Bridge;
Elephant & Castle, Denmark Hill,
Peckham Rye, Nunhead; West Dulwich,
Sydenham Hill; Southern London Bridge,
South Bermondsey, Queens Road
Peckham, Peckham Rye, East Dulwich,
North Dulwich
Main bus routes into central London
1, 12, 17, 21, 35, 36, 37, 40, 42, 43,
45, 47, 48, 53, 63, 68, 100, 133, 141,
148, 149, 171, 172, 176, 188, 453,
521, RV1; night buses N1, N21, N35,
N47, N63, N68, N133, N155, N171,
N343, N381; 24-hour buses 12, 35,
37, 43, 53, 148, 149, 176, 188, 453
Development plans The London
Overground extension, connecting
Clapham Junction and Surrey Quays,
should open at the end of 2012

Oxo Tower Restaurant, Bar & Brasserie
8th floor, Oxo Tower Wharf, Barge House Street,
SE1 9PH (7803 3888, www.harveynichols.com).
Palmerston 91 Lordship Lane, SE22 8EP
(8693 1629, www.thepalmerston.net).
Pavilion Café Dulwich Park, SE21 7BQ
(8299 1383).
Petitou 63 Choumert Road, SE15 4AR
(7639 2613).
Pizarro 194 Bermondsey Street, SE1 3TQ
(7407 7339, www.josepizarro.com).
Le Pont de la Tour 36D Shad Thames, SE1
2YE (7403 8403, www.danddlondon.com).
Roast The Floral Hall, Borough Market,
Stoney Street, SE1 1TL (0845 034 7300,
www.roast-restaurant.com).
Rosendale 65 Rosendale Road, SE21 8EZ
(8761 9008, www.therosendale.co.uk).
Sea Cow 37 Lordship Lane, SE22 8EW
(8693 3111, www.theseacow.co.uk).
Silk Road 49 Camberwell Church Street,
SE5 8TR (7703 4832).
Table 83 Southwark Street, SE1 0HX
(7401 2760, www.thetablecafe.com).
Tapas Brindisa 18-20 Southwark Street,
SE1 1TJ (7357 8880, www.brindisa.com).
Tate Modern Café 2 2nd floor, Tate Modern,
Sumner Street, SE1 9TG (7401 5014,
www.tate.org.uk).
Thai Corner Café 44 Northcross Road, SE22
9EU (0299 1011, www.thaicornercafe.co.uk).
Viet Café 75 Denmark Hill, SE5 8RS
(7703 2531).
Wright Brothers Oyster & Porter House
11 Stoney Street, SE1 9AD (7403 9554,
www.wrightbros.eu.com).
Zucca 184 Bermondsey Street, SE1 3TQ
(7378 6809, www.zuccalondon.com).

Bars & pubs

Lucky Borough. The area is home to the
best concentration of good pubs in London.
The tiny Lord Clyde, the quintessential
backstreet local, has been run immaculately
by the Fitzpatrick family for more than
50 years, while next to Borough Market
are the Rake (run by the folks behind the
Utobeer stall) and the Market Porter, with
its peerless range of ales and 6am opening.
Best of the bunch, though, is the Royal Oak
behind Borough tube; it's the only London
outpost of Sussex brewery Harvey's.

Though Elephant & Castle has a cast-
iron nightlife rep, thanks to world-renowned
club Ministry of Sound, decent bars and

Southwark

pubs are thin on the ground. For boozing in Bermondsey, Hide Bar is an ambitious cocktail bar with an encyclopaedia-like menu, while modern-chic Village East is fine for a less showy drink.

The southern end of the borough has largely gone gastro. Casual drinkers in Camberwell will find a fantastic beer selection at Stormbird, and the transformation of the notorious Silver Buckle pub into the Tiger is a great improvement. Peckham's Victoria Inn seems to be going all out for a family crowd, with a kids' playroom, good food and big screen. It's part of the Capital Pub empire, as are the Actress and the Bishop (both in East Dulwich) and the Florence (Herne Hill).

Overlooking Peckham Rye is the Herne Tavern, with its large, child-friendly garden; further up the hill, newcomer the Rose has an enticing seasonal menu. On nearby Lordship Lane, wine bar Green & Blue is hard to fault, the East Dulwich Tavern (aka EDT) is a decent boozer, and the Palmerston (*see p233*) and Franklins (*see p232*) attract drinkers as well as diners. The relaxed Gowlett pub serves locally adored pizza.

Over in Nunhead, the appropriately named Old Nun's Head does its bit for real ale, good grub and community spirit (regular events include table tennis and comedy). Dulwich and the surrounding area is something of a hotspot for grand pubs with beer gardens: Dulwich Village stalwart the Crown & Greyhound; Sydenham Hill's Dulwich Wood House; and the Rosendale (*see p233*), a textbook example of a fine gastropub.

Actress *90 Crystal Palace Road, SE22 9EY* *(8693 2130, www.capitalpubcompany.com/ the-actress).*
Bar Story *213 Blenheim Grove, SE15 4QL* *(7635 6643, www.barstory.co.uk).*
Bear *296A Camberwell New Road, SE5 0RP* *(7274 7037, www.thebear-freehouse.co.uk).*
Bishop *25-27 Lordship Lane, SE22 8EW* *3994, www.capitalpubcompany.com/the-bishop).*
Crown & Greyhound *73 Dulwich Village, SE21 7BJ (8299 4976, www.thecrownand greyhound.co.uk).*
Dulwich Wood House *39 Sydenham Hill, SE26 6RS (8693 5666, www.dulwichwood house.com).*
East Dulwich Tavern *1 Lordship Lane, SE22 8EW (8693 1316, www.eastdulwich tavern.com).*

Market Porter, at Borough Market.

Florence *131-133 Dulwich Road, SE24 0NG* *(7326 4987, www.capitalpubcompany.com/ the-florence).*
Gowlett *62 Gowlett Road, SE15 4HY* *(7635 7048, www.thegowlett.com).*
Green & Blue *38 Lordship Lane, SE22 8HJ* *(8693 9250, www.greenandbluewines.com).*
Herne Tavern *2 Forest Hill Road, SE22 0RR* *(8299 9521, www.theherne.net).*
Hide Bar *39-45 Bermondsey Street, SE1 3XF* *(7403 6655, www.thehidebar.com).*
Lord Clyde *27 Clennam Street, SE1 1ER* *(7407 3397).*
Market Porter *9 Stoney Street, SE1 9AA* *(7407 2495, www.markettaverns.co.uk).*
Ministry of Sound *103 Gaunt Street, SE1 6DP* *(7740 8809, www.ministryofsound.com).*
Old Nun's Head *15 Nunhead Green, SE15 3QQ* *(7639 4007, www.theoldnunshead.co.uk).*
Rake *14A Winchester Walk, SE1 9AG* *(7407 0557, www.utobeer.co.uk).*
Rose *108 Forest Hill Road, SE22 0RS* *(8693 3838, www.therosedulwich.blogspot.com).*
Royal Oak *44 Tabard Street, SE1 4JU* *(7357 7173).*
Stormbird *25 Camberwell Church Street, SE5 8TR (no phone).*
Tiger *18 Camberwell Green, SE5 7AA* *(7703 5246, www.thetigerpub.com).*
Victoria Inn *77-79 Choumert Road, SE15 4AR* *(7639 5052, www.capitalpubcompany.com/ the-victoria-inn).*
Village East *171-173 Bermondsey Street, SE1 3UW (7357 6082, www.villageeast.co.uk).*

Southwark

Shops

Borough Market is the most famous food market in London, selling everything from organic cakes and breads to Spanish ham from acorn-fed pigs. Fridays and Saturdays are always packed (it's become a major tourist attraction), so visit on Thursdays for a quieter time. Permanent food shops in the area include branches of Spanish food importer Brindisa, cake shop Konditor & Cook and Neal's Yard Dairy. At the other end of the borough, Camberwell, Dulwich and Peckham host regular farmers' markets.

Though Bermondsey Square has been remodelled – bookshop Woolfson & Tay is a friendly place to browse – the Antiques Market (aka the New Caledonian Market) continues on Fridays and specialises in ramshackle Victoriana. There has also been much excitement about Maltby Street Food Market, on Saturdays, where small-scale operations based in the area are joined by other high-quality food stalls. The traditional London street market still thrives in the shape of busy and bustling East Street Market, off the Walworth Road.

Beside the river, the Oxo Tower hosts a community of independent designer makers (details at www.oxostreet.org); look out for Bodo Sperlein's delicate porcelain, and quirky crockery and tea towels from Whitbread Wilkinson W2 Products .

Bermondsey Street has the hippest shops, including Cock & Magpie's cult casuals, men's fashion from the former head of Burberry's menswear at Bermondsey 167, and florist/wine shop Igloo.

Surrey Quays Shopping Centre and Canada Water Retail Park are grim but functional, the latter containing a massive branch of the French sports superstore Decathlon. The Old Kent Road, similarly uninspiring, is home to superstores such as PC World, B&Q and Toys R Us.

In Camberwell, seek out Caribbean bakery Mixed Blessings, Edwardes bikes and Men's Traditional Shoes – in business since 1861, it still sells handmade leather brogues alongside Tricker's, Church's and Loakes.

It's cheap and cheerful down Rye Lane and Peckham High Street, where street life is dominated by the Afro-Caribbean population. This means exotic fish and vegetables, colourful market stalls and plenty of nail and hair shops. Persepolis sells Moroccan food and fancy goods, and Wing Tai supermarket is a useful source of all things oriental. The chichi enclave is Bellenden Road, where you'll find Review bookshop, Melange chocolatier, designer boutique Fenton Walsh and vintage clothing specialist Threads.

In the south of the borough, pretty gift shops suit Dulwich and Herne Hill's genteel air. Dulwich Trader on Croxted Road (the border with Lambeth) has a well-edited array of furniture, clothing, ceramics and textiles, including pieces from Cath Kidston, Lulu Guinness and Lola Rose jewellery. Clustered around the same junction are Dulwich Books and a branch of Cook, purveyor of upmarket ready meals. In Herne Hill, delightful children's bookshop Tales on Moon Lane is a birthday present fail-safe, as is Just William's toyshop across the road. You'll find deli goods at Mimosa, and Blackbird Bakery is superb for bread, cakes, tarts and muffins. A well-stocked Oxfam has been joined by a second outlet, dedicated to books, though the bijou Herne Hill Books by the station is popular for new publications.

Though a few chains (White Company, Oliver Bonas) have snuck in, East Dulwich is still ruled by independent shops that residents will defend to the death. Among

---

COUNCIL TAX

A	up to £40,000	£814.64
B	£40,001-£52,000	£950.41
C	£52,001-£68,000	£1,086.19
D	£68,001-£88,000	£1,221.96
E	£88,001-£120,000	£1,493.51
F	£120,001-£160,000	£1,765.06
G	£160,001-£320,000	£2,036.60
H	over £320,000	£2,443.92

RECYCLING

Household waste recycled & composted 22%
Main recycling centre 43 Devon Street, SE15 1AL (7525 2000)
Other recycling services Food and green waste collection; home composting; white goods, home and office furniture collection
Council contact Waste & Recycling Team, 30-34 Penrose Street, SE17 3DW (7525 2000)

the best are Grace & Favour (chic gifts), Roullier White (lifestyle accessories), Mrs Robinson (interiors), Chener Books and high-end clothes exchange Give & Take.

The area also draws foodies from miles around, only too happy to join the lengthy queues at Moxon's fishmonger, William Rose butcher, the Cheese Block, the East Dulwich Deli, Green & Blue wine shop (see p234), Franklins Farm shop, Pretty Traditional greengrocer, SMBS mini supermarket and Hope & Greenwood's old-school sweet shop. Elsewhere, popular specialist shops include South London Music, Rye Books, BC Bikes, and quirky Dutch paint shop Colour Makes People Happy. On Saturdays, North Cross Road Market offers a mixed bag of stalls, with the emphasis on food, while Ed Warehouse on Zenoria Street brings together a collection of independent traders under one roof.

BC Bikes *36 East Dulwich Road, SE22 9AX (7732 4170, www.bcbikes.co.uk).*
Bermondsey 167 *167 Bermondsey Street, SE1 3UW (7407 3137, www.bermondsey167.com).*
Bermondsey Square Antiques Market *Bermondsey Street & Long Lane, SE1 4QB (7525 6000, www.southwark.gov.uk).*
Blackbird Bakery *208 Railton Road, SE24 0JT (7095 8800).*
Bodo Sperlein *Unit 2.05, Oxo Tower Wharf, Barge House Street, SE1 9PH (7633 9413, www.bodosperlein.com).*
Borough Market *8 Southwark Street, SE1 1TL (7407 1002, www.boroughmarket.org.uk).*
Brindisa *The Floral Hall, Stoney Street, SE1 9AF (7407 1036, www.brindisa.com).*
Cheese Block *69 Lordship Lane, SE22 8EP (8299 3636).*
Chener Books *14 Lordship Lane, SE22 8HN (8299 0771, www.chenerbooks.co.uk).*
Cock & Magpie *96 Bermondsey Street, SE1 3UB (7357 6482, www.cockandmagpie.com).*
Colour Makes People Happy *53 Grove Vale, SE22 8EQ (7207 1120, www.makespeople happy.co.uk).*
Decathlon *Canada Water Retail Park, Surrey Quays Road, SE16 2XU (7394 2000, www.decathlon.co.uk).*
Dulwich Books *6 Croxted Road, SE21 8SW (8670 1920, www.dulwichbooks.co.uk).*
Dulwich Farmers' Market *South Gravel, Dulwich College, Dulwich Common, SE21 7LD (www.weareccfm.com).*
Dulwich Trader *www.rigbyandmac.com; 9-11 Croxted Road, SE21 8SZ (8761 3457);*

41 Northcross Road, SE22 9ET (8299 6938); 89 Dulwich Village, SE21 7BJ (8299 1260).
East Dulwich Deli *15-17 Lordship Lane, SE22 8EW (8693 2525).*
East Street Market *East Street, SE17 1EL (Street Trading Office 7525 6000, www.southwark.gov.uk).*
Edwardes *221-225 Camberwell Road, SE5 0HG (7703 5720, www.edwardescamberwell.co.uk).*
Ed Warehouse *1 Zenoria Street, SE22 8HP (8693 3033, www.edwarehouse.co.uk).*
Fenton Walsh *117 Bellenden Road, SE15 4QY (7635 0033, www.fentonwalsh.com).*
Give & Take *3 Lordship Lane, SE22 8EW (7998 8993, www.giveandtakeshop.co.uk).*
Grace & Favour *35 North Cross Road, SE22 9ET (8693 4400).*
Herne Hill Books *289 Railton Road, SE24 0LY (7998 1673, www.hernehillbooks.com).*
Hope & Greenwood *20 North Cross Road, SE22 9EU (8613 1777, www.hopeand greenwood.co.uk).*
Igloo Flowers *88 Bermondsey Street, SE1 3UB (7403 7774, www.iglooflowers.com).*
Just William's *www.justwilliamstoys.com; 18 Half Moon Lane, SE24 9QP (7733 9995); 106 Grove Vale, SE22 8DR (8299 3444).*
Konditor & Cook *10 Stoney Street, SE1 9AD (0844 854 9363, www.konditorandcook.com).*
Maltby Street Food Market *Maltby Street, SE1 (www.maltbystreet.com).*
Melange Chocolate *184 Bellenden Road, SE15 4BW (07722 650711, www.themelange. com).*
Men's Traditional Shoes *171 Camberwell Road, SE5 0HB (7703 4179).*
Mimosa *16 Half Moon Lane, SE24 9HU (7733 8838, www.mimosafoods.com).*
Mixed Blessings *12-14 Camberwell Road, SE5 0EN (7703 9433).*
Moxon's *149 Lordship Lane, SE22 8HX (8299 1559).*
Mrs Robinson *128-130 Lordship Lane, SE22 8HD (8693 0693, www.mrsrobinsonshop.co.uk).*
Neal's Yard Dairy *6 Park Street, SE1 9AB (7367 0799, www.nealsyarddairy.co.uk).*
Peckham Farmers' Market *Peckham Square, Peckham High Street, SE15 5DT (07961 027324, www.urbanfarmersmarket.co.uk).*
Persepolis *30 Peckham High Street, SE15 5DT (7639 8007, www.foratasteofpersia.co.uk).*
Pretty Traditional *47 North Cross Road, SE22 9ET (8693 7169).*
Review *131 Bellenden Road, SE15 4QY (7639 7400, www.reviewbookshop.co.uk).*
Roullier White *125 Lordship Lane, SE22 8HU (8693 5150, www.roullierwhite.com).*

Rye Books *45 Upland Road, SE22 9EF
(3581 1850, www.ryebooks.co.uk).*
South London Music *29 Grove Vale,
SE22 8EQ (8693 9879, www.slmusic.co.uk).*
Tales on Moon Lane *25 Half Moon Lane,
SE24 9JU (7274 5759, www.talesonmoon
lane.co.uk).*
Threads *186 Bellenden Road, SE15 4BW
(07415 994073).*
Whitbread Wilkinson W2 Products
*Unit 2.01/2.02, Oxo Tower Wharf, Barge
House Street, SE1 9PH (7922 1444, www.
w2products.com).*
William Rose *126 Lordship Lane, SE22 8HD
(8693 9191).*
Wing Tai *Unit 11A, Aylesham Centre,
SE15 5EW (7635 0714).*
Woolfson & Tay *12 Bermondsey Square, SE1
3UN (7407 9316, www.woolfsonandtay.com).*

Arts & attractions

Cinemas & theatres

Menier Chocolate Factory *53 Southwark
Street, SE1 1RU (7378 1713, www.menier
chocolatefactory.com). Gallery, restaurant,
theatre and rehearsal space.*
Odeon Surrey Quays *Surrey Quays Leisure
Park, Redriff Road, SE16 7LL (0871 224 4007,
www.odeon.co.uk).*
Peckham Plex *95A Rye Lane, SE15 4ST
(0844 567 2742, www.peckhamplex.com).*
Shakespeare's Globe *21 New Globe Walk,
SE1 9DT (7401 9919, tours 7902 1500,
www.shakespeares-globe.org).*
Siobhan Davies Dance Studios *85 St
George's Road, SE1 6ER (7091 9650,
www.siobhandavies.com).*
Unicorn Theatre *147 Tooley Street, SE1
2HZ (7645 0560, www.unicorntheatre.com).
A purpose-built theatre for children.*

Galleries & museums

Brunel Museum *Railway Avenue, SE16 4LF
(7231 3840, www.brunelenginehouse.org.uk).*
Clink Prison Museum *1 Clink Street, SE1
9DG (7403 0900, www.clink.co.uk). Prison
exhibition with re-creation of original cells.*
Cuming Museum *Old Walworth Town Hall,
151 Walworth Road, SE17 1RY (7525 2332,
www.southwark.gov.uk/cumingmuseum).
Southwark's local history from Roman times.*
Design Museum *28 Shad Thames, SE1 2YD
(7403 6933, www.designmuseum.org).*
Dulwich Picture Gallery *Gallery Road,
SE21 7AD (8693 5254, www.dulwichpicture*

*gallery.org.uk). An exquisite collection of Old
Masters, housed in England's first purpose-built
art gallery, designed by Sir John Soane in 1811.*
Fashion & Textiles Museum *83 Bermondsey
Street, SE1 3XF (7407 8664, www.ftmlondon.
org).*
Imperial War Museum *Lambeth Road,
SE1 6HZ (7416 5320, www.iwm.org.uk).*
London Dungeon *28-34 Tooley Street, SE1
2SZ (7403 7221, www.thedungeons.com).*
**Old Operating Theatre Museum &
Herb Garret** *9A St Thomas's Street,
SE1 9RY (7188 2679, www.thegarret.org.uk).
A 16th-century herb loft and 17th-century
operating theatre.*
South London Gallery *65-67 Peckham Road,
SE5 8UH (7703 6120, www.southlondon
gallery.org).*
Tate Modern *Bankside, SE1 9TG (7887 8888,
www.tate.org.uk).*
White Cube *144-152 Bermondsey Street,
SE1 3TQ (7930 5373, www.whitecube.com).*
**Winston Churchill's Britain at War
Experience** *64-66 Tooley Street, SE1 2TF
(7403 3171, www.britainatwar.co.uk).*

Other attractions

Dulwich Festival *www.dulwichfestival.co.uk.
Music, theatre, poetry and art; held in May.*
Golden Hinde *Unit 1 & 2, Pickfords Wharf,
Clink Street, SE1 9DG (7403 0123,
www.goldenhinde.com).*
HMS Belfast *Morgan's Lane, Tooley Street,
SE1 2JH (7940 6300, www.iwm.org.uk).*
Southwark Cathedral *London Bridge,
SE1 9DA (7367 6700, tours 7367 6734,
www.southwark.anglican.org).*
Surrey Docks Farm *South Wharf, Rotherhithe
Street, SE16 5ET (7231 1010, www.surrey
docksfarm.org).*

Sport & fitness

Well-organised, grant-funded outfit
Fusion maintains the borough's public
leisure facilities. Many of the borough's
Victorian swimming baths have been
refurbished; Camberwell and East Dulwich
both now look very smart. The private
Miami Health Club is a well-disguised gem,
while the Dojo Physical Arts centre is a
beacon for wannabe Karate Kids and kick-
boxing champions. The nine-hole Aquarius
golf club in Nunhead provides an
unpretentious alternative to the posher
Dulwich & Sydenham Hill club.

Gyms & leisure centres

Camberwell Leisure Centre *Artichoke Place, off Camberwell Church Street, SE5 8TS (0844 893 3888, www.fusion-lifestyle.com).*

Club & Spa at County Hall *County Hall, SE1 7BP (7928 4900, www.marriottleisure.co.uk). Private.*

Colombo Centre *34-68 Colombo Street, SE1 8DP (7261 1658, www.jubileehalltrust.org/ colombo).*

Dojo Physical Arts *10-11 Milroy Walk, Upper Ground, SE1 9LW (7928 3000, www.physical-arts.com). Private.*

Dulwich Leisure Centre *45 East Dulwich Road, SE22 9AN (0844 893 3888, www.fusion-lifestyle.com).*

Elephant & Castle Leisure Centre *22 Elephant & Castle, SE1 6SQ (0844 893 3888, www.fusion-lifestyle.com).*

Fitness First *www.fitnessfirst.co.uk; Cottons Building, Tooley Street, SE1 2QN (0844 571 2847); London Bridge Hotel, 8-81 London Bridge Street, SE1 9SG (0844 571 2896); 1st floor, 332-344 Walworth Road, SE17 2NA (0844 571 2954). Private.*

Hamlets Health Club *Edgar Kail Way, Dog Kennel Hill, SE22 8BD (7274 8707, www.hamletshealthclub.com). Private.*

Kinetic Fitness *127 Stamford Street, SE1 9NQ (7633 2196, www.kclsu.org). Private.*

LivingWell *265 Rotherhithe Street, SE16 5HW (7064 4421, www.livingwell.com). Private.*

Peckham Pulse Healthy Living Centre *10 Melon Road, SE15 5QN (0844 893 3888, www.fusion-lifestyle.com).*

Seven Islands Leisure Centre *Lower Road, SE16 2TU (0844 893 3888, www.fusion-lifestyle.com).*

Surrey Docks Watersports Centre *Rope Street, off Plough Way, Greenland Dock, SE16 7SX (0844 893 3888, www.fusion-lifestyle.com).*

Thirtysevendegrees *2B More London, Riverside, SE1 2AP (7940 4937, www.thirty sevendegrees.co.uk).*

Other facilities

Aquarius Golf Course *Marmora Road, SE22 0RY (8693 1626, www.aquariusgolfclub.co.uk).*

Brockwell Lido *Lido Park Gardens, Brockwell Park, Dulwich Road, SE24 0PA (7274 3088, www.fusion-lifestyle.com). Lovely 1930s lido.*

Dulwich Sports Club *Burbage Road, SE21 7JA (7274 1242, www.dulwichsportsclub.com).*

Herne Hill Velodrome *104 Burbage Road, SE24 9HE (www.hernehillvelodrome.com). An active local campaign has raised funds for ongoing renovations.*

STATISTICS

BOROUGH MAKE-UP
Population 278,000
Ethnic origins
  White 65.9%
  Mixed 3.8%
  Asian or Asian British 8.3%
  Black or Black British 17.4%
  Chinese or other 4.5%
Students 13.3%
Retirees 8.0%

HOUSING STOCK
Borough size (hectares) 2,990
Population density per hectare 93.0
No. of households 105,806
Houses (detached, semi-detached or terraced) 26%
Flats (converted or purpose-built) 74%

CRIME PER 1,000 OF POPULATION
Burglary 7
Robbery 7
Theft of vehicle 4
Theft from vehicle 7
Violence against the person 31
Sexual offences 2

MPs
Camberwell & Peckham Harriet Harman (Labour); *Dulwich & West Norwood* Tessa Jowell (Labour); *Bermondsey & Old Southwark* Simon Hughes (Liberal Democrat)

Schools

Primary
There are 68 state primary schools in the borough of Southwark, 20 of which are church schools. There are also six independent primaries. See www.southwark.gov.uk, www.edubase.gov.uk and www.ofsted.gov.uk for more information.

Secondary
Alleyn's *Townley Road, SE22 8SU (8557 1500, www.alleyns.org.uk). Private.*

Bacon's College *Timber Pond Road, SE16 6AT (7237 1928, www.baconsctc.co.uk).*

Charter School *Red Post Hill, SE24 9JH (7346 6600, www.charter.southwark.sch.uk).*

City of London Academy Southwark *240 Lynton Road, SE1 5LA (7394 5100, www.cityacademy.co.uk).*

Dulwich College *Dulwich Common, SE21 7LD (8693 3601, www.dulwich.org.uk). Boys only; private.*

Globe Academy *Harper Road, SE1 6AG (7407 6877, www.globeacademy.org).*

Harris Academy Bermondsey *55 Southwark Park Road, SE16 3TZ (7237 9316, www.harris bermondsey.org.uk). Girls only.*

Harris Academy Peckham *112 Peckham Road, SE15 5DZ (7703 4417, www.harris peckham.org.uk).*

Harris Girls' Academy East Dulwich *Homestall Road, SE22 0NR (7732 2276, www.hgaed.org.uk). Girls only.*

James Allen's Girls' School *144 East Dulwich Grove, SE22 8TE (8693 1181, www.jags.org.uk). Girls only; private.*

Kingsdale School *Alleyn Park, Dulwich, SE21 8SQ (8670 7575, www.kingsdale. southwark.sch.uk).*

Notre Dame RC Girls' School *118 St George's Road, SE1 6EX (7261 1121, www.notredame.southwark.sch.uk). Roman Catholic; girls only.*

Sacred Heart RC School *Camberwell New Road, SE5 0RP (7274 6844, www.sacredheart. southwark.sch.uk). Roman Catholic.*

St Michael & All Angels Academy *164 Wyndham Road, Camberwell, SE5 0UB (7701 4166, www.smaaa.co.uk). Church of England.*

St Michael's Catholic College *John Felton Road, SE16 4UN (7237 6432, www.stmichaels school.org.uk). Roman Catholic.*

St Saviour's & St Olave's CE School *New Kent Road, SE1 4AN (7407 1843, www.ssso.southwark.sch.uk). Church of England; girls only.*

St Thomas the Apostle College *Hollydale Road, SE15 2EB (7639 0106, www.stac.uk.com). Roman Catholic; boys only.*

Walworth Academy *Shorncliffe Road, SE1 5UJ (7450 9570, www.walworthacademy.org).*

Property

WHAT THE AGENTS SAY:

'Borough is a vibrant area, with a diverse mix of people, property and places of interest. Its proximity to the City means it's become an extremely desirable place to live. Property is varied; there are beautiful period properties in Trinity Church Square, warehouse conversions with delightful original features, and ex-local authority buildings that offer great value and a way on to the property ladder. Schools are rapidly improving, and there are lots of lovely local parks to appeal to families. And London's newest landmark, the Shard, will bring in new business, commerce and tourism.'
Sean McMahon, Field & Sons, Borough

Average property prices
Detached £802,498
Semi-detached £519,743
Terraced £412,982
Flat £358,191

Local estate agents
Alex Neil *146 Lower Road, SE16 2UG (7237 6767, www.alexneil.co.uk).*

Bairstow Eves *29A Denmark Hill, SE5 8RS (7305 7316, www.bairstoweves.co.uk).*

Burnet Ware & Graves *www.b-w-g.co.uk; 2 offices in the borough (East Dulwich 8693 4201, Herne Hill 7733 1293).*

Dulwich & Village Residential *100 Grove Vale, SE22 8DR (8693 7999, www.dulwich homes.com).*

Field & Sons *www.fieldandsons.co.uk; 2 offices in the borough (Borough 7407 1375, Shad Thames 7403 8571).*

Hastings International *www.hastings international.com; 3 offices in the borough (Borough 7378 9000, Rotherhithe 7231 1066, Shad Thames 7407 1066).*

Osbourne Stewart *103 Union Street, SE1 0LA (7922 1113, www.osbourne-stewart.com).*

Roy Brooks *2 Barry Parade, Barry Road, SE22 0JA (8299 3021, www.roybrooks.co.uk).*

Other Information

Council
Southwark Council *PO BOX 64529, SE1P 5LX (7525 5000, www.southwark.gov.uk).*

Legal services
Bermondsey CAB *8 Market Place, Southwark Park Road, SE16 3UQ (0844 499 4134, www.southwarkcabservice.org.uk).*

Cambridge House Law Centre *1 Addington Square, SE5 0HF (7358 7025, www.ch1889.org).*

Peckham CAB *97 Peckham High Street, SE15 5RS (0844 499 4134, www.southwark cabservice.org.uk).*

Local information
www.eastdulwichforum.co.uk.
www.hernehillforum.org.uk.
www.southlondonpress.co.uk.
www.southwarknews.co.uk.
www.westdulwichforum.co.uk.

Open spaces & allotments
Allotments *For details of allotments in the borough, visit www.southwark.gov.uk.*
Open spaces *www.southwark.gov.uk/parks.*

'Sometimes the forgotten borough of south London, Lewisham brims over with cultural talent and diversity – from the artists' quarter in Deptford to the thriving fringe in Catford and Brockley.'

Martin Costello, Artistic Director, Broadway Theatre

Lewisham

With beautiful wooded hills looking out over gritty urban wastes, Lewisham is the original jolie laide borough. Regeneration schemes aplenty – to improve housing, schools, parks and sports facilities – mean its popularity is on an upward trajectory, despite the pockets of deprivation that never seem to make it to the 'to do' list.

Neighbourhoods

New Cross and Telegraph Hill

A happy combination of Goldsmiths art college, a preponderance of affluent, semi-famous, creative types settling and breeding in the big houses around Telegraph Hill Park and a generally anarchic/artistic/idealistic atmosphere has turned New Cross into the epicentre of cool. The area's appealingly nonconformist nature, these days evident in local traders' vociferous rejection of the supermarket chains, is manifested in some delightful one-off shops, cafés, bars and pubs. In days gone by, the independent New Cross spirit rose up in a proud moment in Lewisham's history: in 1977, the biggest street battle against fascists since the Battle of Cable Street in 1936 took place here, on Clifton Rise.

Goldsmiths (part of the University of London) occupies various buildings. The Ben Pimlott Building, a dramatic glass and steel construction, is a Will Alsop creation. Up the steeply climbing wide roads, away from all the hullabaloo of the main drag, Telegraph Hill is a largely unspoilt residential area with some impressive, bay-fronted Edwardian houses. The park of the same name offers inspiring views over the city, has great play facilities (including the best slide in London) and is the site of a monthly farmers' market.

Deptford and St John's

Those who always rejoiced in the hidden pleasures of atmospheric, riverside Deptford now have to acknowledge its officially

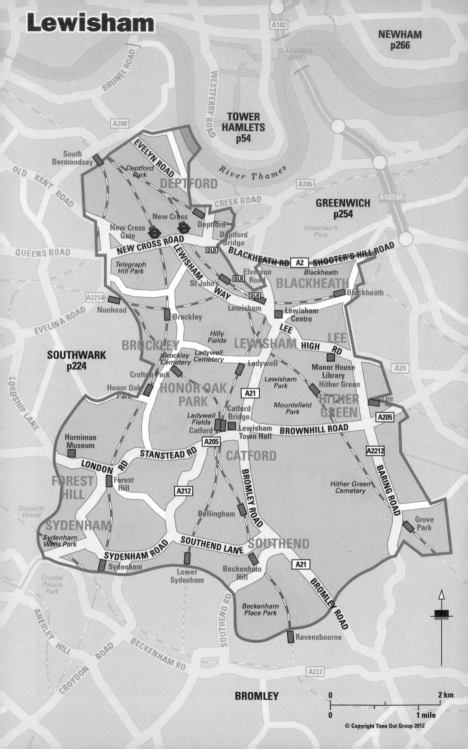

trendy status. Thankfully, some of the cobbled cut-throughs and ancient terraces are protected by preservation orders, but the old wharves and muddy river flats are disappearing under multi-windowed residential developments at Convoys Wharf and Greenwich Reach. Nonetheless, Deptford is still a joy to explore. By way of an introduction, take a stroll down picturesque Tanners Hill before crossing New Cross Road and weaving your way down Deptford High Street. A mish-mash of pound shops and pie and mash caffs, with a lively multicultural market – stalls sell everything from fruit and vegetables to second-hand clothes and household junk – this is a very old-school retail experience. Destination businesses include the Deptford Project, a groovy café-restaurant inside an old railway carriage, with its own attractive decked garden. The Project is a collaborative creative enterprise: it has an open-air cinema, a bespoke bike service and resourceful artists and craftspeople working under the arches. Everyone is waiting for planning permission for a new, permanent creative space next to the revamped rail station.

Veer right for beautiful Albury Street, built in the early 18th century and all the more elegant for its proximity to the chaotic High Street. Between here and Church Street stands the Queen Anne church of St Paul's, where there's a plaque to Myididdee, a Tahitian who sailed with Captain Bligh and died in Deptford in 1793. Follow Church Street riverward to find St Nicholas's Church, where Christopher Marlowe is rumoured to have been buried following his violent end in a Deptford pub, or go east to Creekside, Deptford's artists' quarter. This slightly spooky area, with its mudflats and rotting hulks of old boats, is lit up by sudden flashes of artistic licence. It's home to Cockpit Arts (www.cockpitarts.com) – a charity that supports designer-makers – as well as the studios and workshops of the neighbourhood's many creative souls.

Laban, the contemporary dance centre, is housed in an iridescent, coloured-perspex building that looks like it's been marooned on the muddy creek when you look at it from the Ha'penny Hatch Bridge. New apartment buildings are springing up around it. If you really want to get stuck in to this area's (natural) history, pull on your gumboots and get down to the Creekside

Telegraph Hill Park. See p240.

Centre, which runs some satisfyingly muddy Sunday walks. Twinkle Park, on Watergate Street, provides a much needed children's playspace. Opposite, half hidden behind a high wall, is the master shipwright's house, built in 1708 for Joseph Allen; it was used for many years as a cafeteria for News Corporation employees, but is now privately owned and has been restored. You can carry on to the water's edge via some slimy muddy steps – all very Dickensian.

Away from the river, St John's sits between Deptford and Lewisham town centres. Developed in the the mid 19th century as New Deptford, it's a handsome conservation pocket, with lots of spacious Victorian and Edwardian houses clustered around its own station and church.

Blackheath

One of Lewisham's high points, both topographically and socially, Blackheath is a busy, independently minded village that serves the residents of grand houses set around an expanse of common land. The heath has been witness to significant events in London's history: Wat Tyler assembled his revolting peasants on Blackheath in 1381, and Henry VIII and Anne of Cleves met for the first time here for a right royal picnic in 1540, after which the King escorted

Lewisham

his new bride over to his pad in Greenwich (and not long after kicked her out again). These days, the heath is favoured by dogwalkers, kite-fliers, sporting clubs and travelling circuses; it will see service as a Live Site during the 2012 Games, with a huge screen broadcasting events, an all-weather entertainments tent and numerous stalls. The Blackheath Tea Hut has been serving tea and bacon sandwiches to travellers since the 1950s. The adjacent A2 (formerly Watling Street, the Roman road to Canterbury) sees to it that passing trade is constant.

Bijou Blackheath Village is one of London's oldest recorded settlements, and contains a satisfying mix of quality high-street chains and independent delis, gift shops and grocery stores. The smartest address in the area is the Paragon, near South Row, a semicircle of seven colonnaded houses designed around 1800 by Michael Searles. The southern end of the Village, on the road to Lee, is home to the Blackheath Conservatoire (a long-established music school) and Blackheath Halls (now part of Greenwich's Trinity College of Music).

Lewisham

Sitting at the centre of a major road junction (the A20, A21 and A2211 for the A2 all radiate from the roundabout that dominates the area), with its own bus terminus, busy railway station and DLR station, Lewisham is certainly well connected. Work to make it all hang together a little less chaotically is ongoing, but it's a huge regeneration project that won't be completed before 2014.

Much has been done to make the route from the stations to the town centre more pleasant, including attractively landscaping Cornmill Gardens. The Renaissance scheme provides nearly 800 apartments in various high-rise buildings around the new Loampit Vale Leisure Centre (opening 2013), whose façade will consist of multicoloured glass panels that will change according to the noises within. Over on the High Street, in the shopping centre, the atmosphere is rather less restful. The largest building here is the police station (the biggest in Europe) – which is apt, given the frequency with which things kick off in town. The High Street was trashed during the riots in August 2011.

Catford's **Broadway Theatre**. See p246.

Estate agents urge housebuyers to explore areas around Lewisham Park, Belmont Hill and the roads connecting the High Street to Ladywell. They're seduced by the size and relative cheapness of the houses, easily accessible from town via wide, tree-lined roads.

Ladywell, Brockley and Honor Oak

Ladywell sits as a genteel halfway house between uncouth Lewisham and grotty Catford town centres. Compared to the Primark crowds of Lewisham, the pace is slower and businesses more rarefied; there's a baker, a post office, an art shop, a fine independent hardware store, a florist, a barber and, er, a tattoo and piercing parlour.

From the train station, Ladywell Fields follows the prettily landscaped Ravensbourne River, with its Pooh Sticks bridges and shingly 'beaches' for paddling toddlers, to the recently refurbished Ladywell Arena and running track. With football pitches, a new adventure playground and some handsome play areas, the Fields are a major community resource. The wider Ladywell area is ideal for young families: the open green spaces, the pretty little terraced homes with gardens, the preponderance of school new-builds (both primary and secondary) give off all the right vibes.

Across wide and traffic-calmed Adelaide Avenue rises Hilly Fields, a lovely, airy park with its own mini Stonehenge (erected to mark the new millennium). On the other side is the larger neighbourhood of Brockley, now on the London Overground line. Artistic types tend to settle around here, and have done much to improve Brockley's profile – the Brockley Road is rich in meeting places for the area's creatives and media mummies, especially cupcake/artisan bread shops and tot-friendly cafés (often with a gallery thrown in). Some useful traders remain too. Also here is the famous Brockley Jack pub-theatre managed by Southside Arts, and the grand old Rivoli Ballroom, which started life as the Crofton Park Picture Palace in 1913. The large sprung maple dancefloor dates from its conversion to a ballroom in 1957. The place's old-fashioned good looks have given it London-wide kudos and made it an apt venue for the International Gay Ballroom Dancing Championship. Housing here is dominated by modest Victorian terraces built for local workers.

Brockley Rise, meanwhile, takes you to Honor Oak, a hilly residential area

Highs & Lows

straddling the Lewisham/Southwark border. The Overground train link has given the area a similar boost to that enjoyed by Brockley. The main thoroughfare, Honor Oak Park, is lined with useful independent shops. For great views, climb One Tree Hill, where there's a beacon (last lit for the millennium).

Lee and Hither Green

Residents of Lee are keen for Lewisham Council to spare a bit of its regeneration budget for this rather put-upon section of the borough, whose centre is swamped by heavy traffic and ill-advised building developments. Particularly dismal is Leegate Shopping Centre, dubbed 'Britain's worst shopping district' by the *Evening Standard*; at time of writing, more than a third of its businesses had closed down.

However, there are some beautiful roads between pretty Manor House Gardens, with its wildfowl-filled pond and excellent community café, and Blackheath to the north. Houses here are spacious, well-kept and pricey – as would be expected of a conservation area. Lee High Road and Manor Lane have the kinds of cafés and galleries beloved of a bohemian and well-heeled populace bringing up families

Further west is Hither Green, a densely populated residential area with a major railway junction (London Bridge is 11 minutes away) – it's also a short walk from Lewisham town centre. The thriving array of shops around the rail station is buoyed up by FUSS (Friends and Users of Staplehurst Shops). Up on Hither Green Lane, the Café of Good Hope – set up by the Jimmy Mizen Foundation, in memory of a 16-year-old boy murdered not far from here – is fast becoming a local landmark. Opposite, St Swithun's Church hosts community choir concerts, 1970s disco nights and the occasional film. The FUSS Christmas Fair is always fun, as is the Lee Open Studios fortnight in November.

Catford

Catford's famously ill-favoured looks have been due a makeover for decades. The area took a battering in the August 2011 riots, but it wasn't looking great before that, to be honest. Boarded-up shops line Rushey Green (the main road that starts as Lewisham High Street). The Catford Mews, a hideous shopping centre famous for its giant fibreglass cat, has been taken over by Poundland. Asda and Tesco are competing with each other for permission to dump a superstore on the derelict land that was once the Greyhound Stadium.

Apart from the elegant art deco Broadway Theatre, Catford's dominant architectural theme is brutalist. The town's once-beautiful Broadway market area now cowers behind a 1971 carbuncle containing Lewisham Town Hall and Civic Suite; another culprit, Laurence House (across the dreadful A205 gyratory), houses the local library. More tower blocks – Eros House, Rosenthal House and the horrible council flats known as Milford Towers – complete a depressing picture. Regeneration is needed, and soon. The council started the ball rolling by purchasing Catford Mews in 2010, and, if funding is secured, there are plans to demolish Milford Towers, create new homes and revamp Catford Broadway – but nothing is likely to happen to this neediest of areas until 2014 at the earliest.

Away from the gyratory, green spaces and huge, reasonably priced Edwardian family houses are reasons enough for settling here. Towards Hither Green, the well-made houses of the Corbett Estate (built by Archibald Cameron Corbett MP around 1900) are coveted for their generous proportions. There are no pubs near Corbett houses, though: the developer was a strict Presbyterian. Mountsfield Park, between Rushey Green and Hither Green, is the scene of Lewisham's People's Day every summer. The park now has its own little café, with outside seating, for ice-cream and tea and scones, but – like Catford itself– still feels like the ugly and neglected friend within the borough.

Forest Hill and Sydenham

Traditionally, young professionals hearing the pitter-patter of little feet have traded in their pricey Camberwell and Clapham flats for large family houses in Forest Hill. It's one of the most rewarding parts of Lewisham in which to bring up children, thanks to its accessible green spaces and the delights of the eccentric Horniman Museum, its most famous landmark. There's a cluster of new cafés, as well as interesting independent shops, along Dartmouth Road.

The arrival of the London Overground train link has brought a new sense of purpose to the area, and also to Sydenham, which has seen its fair share of businesses going to the wall in recent years. Luckily, it's in line for some regeneration cash to spruce up the high street and create new homes and businesses around Cobbs Corner – the junction of Westwood Hill and Kirkdale – where the old Greyhound pub is being refurbished. A piazza and new social housing block are part of the scheme, hopefully to be finished by 2013.

Upper Sydenham has gorgeous Sydenham Wells Park and the soon to be spectacular again Crystal Palace Park. Lower Sydenham, beyond Cobbs Corner, has Home Park, with its much loved outdoor gym and community allotments, and the massive Savacentre by the gas containers. The Bell Green end of Sydenham, curving around towards more downmarket Catford, is less than salubrious, but is now undergoing an extensive facelift.

STATISTICS

BOROUGH MAKE-UP
Population 261,600
Ethnic origins
White 66.2%
Mixed 4.2%
Asian or Asian British 6.7%
Black or Black British 19.0%
Chinese or other 3.8%
Students 9.9%
Retirees 8.7%

HOUSING STOCK
Borough size (hectares) 3,532
Population density per hectare 74.1
No. of households 107,412
Houses (detached, semi-detached or terraced) 47%
Flats (converted or purpose-built) 53%

CRIME PER 1,000 OF POPULATION
Burglary 8
Robbery 5
Theft of vehicle 4
Theft from vehicle 9
Violence against the person 29
Sexual offences 1

MPs
Lewisham East Heidi Alexander (Labour); *Lewisham, Deptford* Joan Ruddock (Labour); *Lewisham West & Penge* Jim Dowd (Labour)

Grove Park, Bellingham and Downham

These southernmost reaches of the borough are characterised by large, established council housing estates, well provided for by shops and supermarkets, with green spaces nearby and community-oriented health and leisure facilities. They lack heart, though, and the bustle and chaos of the urban centres of Catford, Sydenham and Lewisham.

Grove Park, especially, plays the marshy backwater card with aplomb. Its main green space is extensive, wildlife-filled Chinbrook Meadows, through which flows the River Quaggy, all cleaned up and prettily channelled to maximise kingfisher and rare wader sightings. The Quaggy is a tributary of the Ravensbourne, and the two meet at Lewisham; the River Quaggy Waterways Action Group is responsible for making Chinbrook lovely.

Green spaces (and easy links to more of them in Kent) are the saving grace of these neighbourhoods. Other highlights are Forster Memorial Park and Beckenham Place Park, whose Grade II-listed mansion house is home to the clubhouse for an excellent municipal pay-and-play golf course. The house, gardens and cottages here are under Lewisham's auspices, and there are moves to address their near-derelict state, although the state of council finances have put these plans, like so many others, on the back burner for a few years.

Restaurants & cafés

Lewisham town centre's refuelling mainstays are daytime chippy Something Fishy and, just near the station, much-loved Maggie's, a 30-year-old Irish-run diner that does a hearty meat stew. For spicier fare, Taste of Lewisham doles out decent curries for indecently low prices, while Everest Curry King, a Sri Lankan specialist, offers raging hot curries and snacks in cramped surroundings.

In New Cross, students tuck into fiery dishes at tiny Thailand, or Turkish barbecued meats, meze and pide at Meze Mangal. Highlights among the many new eateries in the area are the New Cross House gastropub (see p249) and the London Particular café. Deptford's budget eating places include AJ Goddard's and Manze's

pie and mash shops. The Deptford Project Café creates interesting vegetarian meals, and the Big Red Pizzeria is a nostalgic treat, a Routemaster bus-turned-restaurant, where the crunchy-based pizzas match well with local Greenwich Meantime beer. For more exotic flavours, there's Panda Panda (Vietnamese) and Chaconia (Trinidadian).

Blackheath's top dining venue is generally considered to be Chapters, which runs from eggs benedict and coffee for breakfast to quite swanky evening meals. There's also Laicram, a cosy neighbourhood Thai, and Black Vanilla, a new coffee and ice-cream shop.

The biggest noise in Brockley is the smart modern Indian restaurant Babur Brasserie. But there also plenty of cafés and cheaper eateries, many of which welcome children; favourites include the Broca, Browns, the Brockley Mess and Pat-a-Cakes. Toads Mouth Too is a homely little dining room that doubles as an art gallery. For fish and chips, try Brockley's Rock.

Few people would consider eating out in Catford unless they knew about the uncannily good Japanese restaurant Sapporo Ichiban. Catfordites also fill up on noodles at Tai Won Mein, Turkish meze at Mokan and handmade pizzas at La Pizzeria Italiana, which attracts incongruous numbers of middle-class diners to its premises under a block of flats.

Cafés are opening up with gusto in Lee and Hither Green – recommended are With Jam and Bread and Rhubarb & Custard. Elsewhere, Café Oscar's is a super little spot in Ladywell, with a suntrap garden that's perfect for leafing through the weekend papers; and Blue Mountain, at the Cobbs Corner conservation area in Sydenham, is a first-rate café-deli.

AJ Goddard *203 Deptford High Street, SE8 3NT (8692 3601).*
Babur Brasserie *119 Brockley Rise, SE23 1JP (8291 2400, www.babur.info).*
Big Red Pizzeria *30 Deptford Church Street, SE8 4RZ (3490 8346, www.thebigredpizza.com).*
Black Vanilla *32 Tranquil Vale, SE3 0AX (8852 0020, www.black-vanilla.com).*
Blue Mountain Café *260 Kirkdale, SE26 1RS (8659 6016).*
Broca *4 Coulgate Street, SE4 2RW (8691 0833, www.brocafoods.com).*
Brockley Mess *325 Brockley Road, SE4 2QZ (07887 674051, www.thebrockleymess.com).*

Brockley's Rock *317 Brockley Road, SE4 2QZ (8694 1441, www.brockleysrock.co.uk).*
Browns of Brockley *5 Coulgate Street, SE4 2RW (8692 0722).*
Café Oscar's *48 Ladywell Road, SE13 7UX (8690 7920, www.cafe-oscars.com).*
Chaconia *26 Deptford High Street, SE8 4AF (8692 8815).*
Chapters All Day Dining *43-45 Montpelier Vale, SE3 0TJ (8333 2666, www.chapters restaurants.co.uk).*
Deptford Project Café *121-123 Deptford High Street, SE8 4NS (07545 593279, www.thedeptfordproject.com).*
Everest Curry King *24 Loampit Hill, SE13 7SW (8691 2233).*
Laicram *1 Blackheath Grove, SE3 0DD (8852 4710).*
London Particular *399 New Cross Road, SE14 6LA (8692 6149, www.thelondon particular.co.uk).*
Maggie's Café & Restaurant *320-322 Lewisham Road, SE13 7PA (8244 0339, www.maggiesrestaurant.co.uk).*
Manze's *204 Deptford High Street, SE8 3PR (8692 2375, www.manzepieandmash.com).*
Mekan *11-13 Bromley Road, SE6 2TS (7998 1598).*
Meze Mangal *245 Lewisham Way, SE4 1XF (8694 8099).*
Panda Panda *8 Deptford Broadway, SE8 4PA (8616 6922, www.panda-panda.co.uk).*
Pat-a-Cakes *358 Brockley Road, SE4 2BY (07725 641284, www.patacakes.org).*
La Pizzeria Italiana *Eros House, Brownhill Road, SE6 2EF (8461 4606, www.lapizza italia.com).*
Rhubarb & Custard *164 Manor Lane, SE12 8LP (8297 0035, www.rhubarband custardcafe.com).*
St David Coffee House *5 David's Road, SE23 3EP (8291 6646).*
Sapporo Ichiban *13 Catford Broadway, SE6 4SP (8690 8487).*
Something Fishy *117-119 Lewisham High Street, SE13 6AT (8852 7075).*
Tai Won Mein *90-92 Rushey Green, SE6 4HW (8690 8238).*
Taste of Lewisham *19 Lee High Road, SE13 5LD (8297 6452).*
Thailand *15 Lewisham Way, SE14 6PP (8691 4040, www.thailand.foodkingdom.com).*
Toads Mouth Too *188 Brockley Road, SE4 2RN (8469 0043).*
With Jam and Bread *386 Lee High Road, SE12 8RW (8318 4040, www.withjamand bread.com).*

Bars & pubs

New Cross fairly throbs with live-music pubs to satisfy the Goldsmiths students. Currently in favour is New Cross House, which caused so much excitement with its Meateasy pop-up and now does a good line in pizzas. The Hobgoblin remains resolutely studenty. For bands, indie-leaning Amersham Arms (run by the same people behind the Lock Tavern in Camden) is popular. The Old Haberdasher has been gastrofied, and promises an ambitious menu. Further down towards Peckham, the kitsch Montague Arms continues to wow/alarm people with its vast Sunday lunches and eccentric outlook.

In Lewisham, the Fox & Firkin attracts a diverse crowd and does much to further diversify, with knitting evenings and whatnot. Others swear by the Dirty South, which is also renowned for live music, but has more expensive booze. The Jolly Farmers, near the hospital and mostly frequented by its employees, is a popular post-work boozer. Just opposite, the Ravensbourne Arms is a very welcome addition, with its great beer, bar billiards and brilliant skin-on chips. It's part of the Antic stable, who are also responsible for Jam Circus, a drinking and music venue that enlivens Brockley.

In Blackheath, the choice is wide. Of the many fine pubs, the centuries-old Hare & Billet and the Georgian Princess of Wales are the grandest. Livelier options include Zero Degrees, with its microbrewed beers and inventive bar food, the upbeat Railway, and Cave Austin, a slick wine bar with basement club and chill-out room.

In Catford, the sticky-carpeted dive that was the Copperfield is due a gastro makeover – also by Antic – and will reopen as the Catford Bridge Tavern (details on www.antic-ltd.com). Otherwise, the Catford Ram (a Young's pub) is stuck in the shopping centre, but its position near the Broadway Theatre means it attracts a more urbane crowd than you'd think. The Blythe Hill Tavern is a lively, Irish-run local exuding comfort and cheer.

Elsewhere in the borough, down-to-earth Deptford has the real ales, good Sunday lunches and unpretentious charm of the Dog & Bell; Forest Hill has the Dartmouth Arms gastropub and Sydenham its sibling, the Dolphin. Honor Oakies adore their landmark pub, the Honor Oak, for its food, beer, jazz, quiz nights and poker.

Amersham Arms *388 New Cross Road, SE14 6TY (8469 1499, www.amersham-arms.co.uk).*
Blythe Hill Tavern *319 Stanstead Road, SE23 1JB (8690 5176).*
Catford Ram *9 Winslade Way, SE6 4JU (8690 6206, www.youngs.co.uk).*
Cave Austin *7-9 Montpelier Vale, SE3 0TA (8852 0492, www.caveaustin.co.uk).*
Dartmouth Arms *7 Dartmouth Road, SE23 3HN (8488 3117, www.thedartmoutharms.com).*
Dirty South *162 Lee High Road, SE13 5PR (8852 1267, www.dirtysouthlondon.com).*
Dog & Bell *116 Prince Street, SE8 3JD (8692 5664, www.thedogandbell.co.uk).*
Dolphin *121 Sydenham Road, SE26 5HB (8778 8101, www.thedolphinsydenham.com).*
Fox & Firkin *316 Lewisham High Street, SE13 6JZ (8690 8925).*
Hare & Billet *1A Elliot Cottages, Hare & Billet Road, SE3 0QJ (8852 2352, www.gkpubs. co.uk).*
Hobgoblin *272 New Cross Road, SE14 6AA (8692 3193).*

Honor Oak *1 St German's Road, SE23 1RH (8690 8606, www.thehonoroak.com).*
Jam Circus *330-332 Brockley Road, SE4 2BT (8692 3320, www.antic-ltd.com).*
Jolly Farmers *354 Lewisham High Street, SE13 6LE (8690 8402).*
Montague Arms *289 Queens Road, SE14 2PA (7639 4923).*
New Cross House *316 New Cross Road, SE14 6AF (8691 8875, www.thenewcrosshouse.com).*
Old Haberdasher *44 Lewisham Way, SE14 6NP (8305 6560, www.theoldhaberdasher.com).*
Princess of Wales *1A Montpelier Row, SE3 0RL (8297 5911, www.princessofwalespub.co.uk).*
Railway *16 Blackheath Village, SE3 9LE (8852 2390, www.therailwayblackheath.co.uk).*
Ravensbourne Arms *323 Lewisham High Street, SE13 6NR (8613 7070, www.antic-ltd.com).*
Zero Degrees *29-31 Montpelier Vale, SE3 0TJ (8852 5619, www.zerodegrees.co.uk).*

Shops

The borough's retail heart, the Lewisham Centre, is improving, with newish branches of H&M, TK Maxx and the Danish retailing miracle, Tiger. The council promises to continue the regeneration of the town centre and to address the problem of multiplying pound shops and diminishing independents. Outside the shopping centre is a raucous fruit and veg market. For quality over quantity, visit Gennaro, a fine traditional Italian deli run by Antonio and his sister Alba. Rolls & Rems textiles shop is fab for one-off bolts of unusual fabric.

For a proper old fashioned street market, visit Deptford on Wednesday, Friday or Saturday. Numerous stalls – fruit and veg, clothes second-hand and new, household goods and more – cluster along Deptford High Street, Douglas Way and Giffin Street. One of the most established businesses is the excellent Lewisham & Deptford Sewing Machines, where the friendly staff really know their bobbins. New Cross has a well-meaning independent grocer, the Allotment, where as much of the produce as possible is local (or from Kent).

Ladywell's villagey feel is enhanced by its florists, bakers, barber and hardware shops. El's Kitchen and Café Oscar (*see left*) are excellent delis, and newcomer Slater & King has attractive gifts and cards.

Lee High Road has Harlequin, a fancy-dress hire and sales shop, and Snapdragon, which has pots, planters and vases for the garden, as well as gifts and homewares. Keep going to find the legendary Allodi Accordions, with its several rooms of accordions and a repair workshop.

Outside Hither Green train station lie the Staplehurst Road shops, overseen by FUSS (Friends & Users of Staplehurst Shops). These doughty shopkeepers keep the community close. You Don't Bring Me Flowers, a florist that also encompasses a café, knitting group and writers' club, is central to this arty scene. The Education Interactive maths initiative has a shop full of number puzzles and the sort of toys bought by conscientious parents.

Blackheath Village provides the genteel antidote to Lewisham. Independent traders are the norm (discreet chains include Neal's Yard Remedies, Phase Eight, Fat Face and Ryman). Upmarket gourmet shops such as Hand Made Food, the Village Deli and Jade Boulangerie help shunt up the grocery bill. There are far too many gift shops, but 2nd Impressions is a joy, with many floors and an extensive toy department. Near the heath, Cookery Nook is a large kitchen equipment shop; at the Lee end, Hortus is a garden design and maintenance business.

Shopping in Catford is a singular experience. FLK, a bright yellow shop by Catford Bridge station, is excellent for green tea, tofu and noodles of every variety, while, a few doors down, Turkish Food Express has top cheese, olives, bread and baklava. For good horticultural advice, seeds, plants and pets, Phoebes Garden Centre is an institution.

A large ski, snowboard and mountain-bike store, Finches Ski Emporium, hides behind the South Circular on Perry Vale. Sydenham and Kirkdale also have fine shopping areas, strong on arts and antiques. For gewgaws and trinkets, there's Koochie Bazaar. The Kirkdale Bookshop & Gallery provides art and literature, La Bonne Bakery offers proper French bread, Antoinette Costume Hire has fancy dress outfits galore, and the handsome art deco wares at Behind the Boxes include furniture, ceramics, jewellery and glass. Honor Oak is worth visiting for Hills & Parkes deli/bakery. Bunka is a sassy boutique in Forest Hill (with branches in Balham and Earlsfield).

Farmers' markets are popping up all over the borough, with the new Brockley one going down a storm. Most frequented

is the Sunday market at Blackheath rail station; there are also monthly gatherings in Manor House Gardens, Hilly Fields Park and Telegraph Hill Park.

Allodi Accordions *143-145 Lee High Road, SE13 5PF (8244 3771, www.accordions.co.uk).*
Allotment *318 New Cross Road, SE14 6AF (3583 5953).*
Antoinette Costume Hire *High Street Buildings, 134 Kirkdale, SE26 4BB (8699 1913, www.costumehirelondon.com).*
Behind the Boxes *98 Kirkdale, SE26 4BG (8291 6116, www.behindtheboxes-artdeco.co.uk).*
La Bonne Bakery *138 Kirkdale, SE26 4BB (3538 7549, www.labonnebakery.com).*
Boulangerie Jade *44 Tranquil Vale, SE3 0BD (8318 1916, www.boulangeriejade.com).*
Bunka *4 Dartmouth Road, SE23 3XU (8291 4499, www.bunka.co.uk).*
Cookery Nook *32 Montpelier Vale, SE3 0TA (8297 2422).*
Education Interactive *10 Staplehurst Road, SE13 5NB (8318 6380, www.education-interactive.co.uk).*
El's Kitchen *71 Ladywell Road, SE13 7JA (7998 4889, www.elskitchen.co.uk).*
Finches Ski Emporium *25-29 Perry Vale, SE23 2NE (8699 6768, www.finches-ski.com).*
FLK Chinese Groceries *3 Catford Road, SE6 4QZ (8690 0898).*
Gennaro Delicatessen *23 Lewis Grove, SE13 6BG (8852 1370, www.italianfoodexpress.co.uk).*

You Don't Bring Me Flowers.

TRANSPORT

Tube stations *DLR* Lewisham
Rail stations *London Overground*
New Cross Gate, New Cross, Brockley,
Honor Oak Park, Forest Hill, Sydenham;
Southeastern Deptford, Nunhead,
Lewisham, Blackheath, Crofton Park,
Catford, Bellingham, Beckenham Hill,
Ravensbourne; New Cross, St John's,
Ladywell, Catford Bridge, Lower
Sydenham; Hither Green, Grove Park,
Lee; *Southern* South Bermondsey,
New Cross Gate, Brockley, Honor
Oak Park, Forest Hill, Sydenham

Main bus routes *into central London* 21,
47, 53, 171, 172, 176, 185, 188, 436,
453; *night buses* N21, N36, N47, N89,
N171, N343; *24 hour buses* 53, 176,
188, 453

Hand Made Food *40 Tranquil Vale, SE3 0BD
(8297 9966, www.handmadefood.com).*
Harlequin *254 Lee High Road, SE13 5PL
(8852 0193, www.harlequinparty.co.uk).*
Hills & Parkes Delicatessen *49 Honor
Oak Park, SE23 1EA (8699 1996, www.hills
andparkes.com).*
Hortus *26 Blackheath Village, SE3 9SY
(8297 9439, www.hortus.co.uk).*
Kirkdale Bookshop & Gallery *272 Kirkdale,
SE26 4RS (8778 4701, www.kirkdalebookshop.com).*
Koochie Bazaar *140 Sydenham Road, SE26
5JZ (8659 8042).*
Lewisham & Deptford Sewing Machines
*181 Deptford High Street, SE8 3NT (8692
1077, www.sewingmachinesuk.co.uk).*
Lewisham Centre *33A Molesworth Street, SE13
7HB (8852 0094, www.lewishamshopping.co.uk).*
Phoebes Garden Centre *Penerley Road,
SE6 2LQ (8698 4365, www.phoebes.co.uk).*
Rolls & Rems *111 High Street, SE13 6AT
(8852 8686, www.rollsandrems.com).*
2nd Impressions *10 Montpelier Vale, SE3
0TA (8852 6192).*
Slater & King *46 Ladywell Road, SE13 7UZ
(07545 973085).*
Snapdragon *266 Lee High Road, SE13 5PL
(8463 0503, www.snapdragonpots.co.uk).*
Turkish Food Express *5-6 Station Buildings,
SE6 4QZ (8613 9579).*
Village Deli *1-3 Tranquil Vale, SE3 0BU
(8852 2015).*
You Don't Bring Me Flowers *15 Staplehurst
Road, SE13 5ND (8297 2333, www.youdont
bringmeflowers.co.uk).*

Arts & attractions

Cinemas & theatres
Albany *Douglas Way, SE8 4AG (8692
4446, www.thealbany.org.uk). Deptford's
busy community arts centre.*
Blackheath Halls *23 Lee Road, SE3 9RQ
(8463 0100, www.blackheathhalls.com).
Concerts (classical and contemporary),
community events and more.*
Broadway Theatre *Rushey Green, SE6 4RU
(8690 0002, www.broadwaytheatre.org.uk).
Handsome art deco theatre that is scruffy
Catford's pride and joy.*
Brockley Jack Studio Theatre *410 Brockley
Road, SE4 2DH (0844 847 2454, www.brockley
jack.co.uk). Popular theatre (and pub) that
hosts drama productions, plus regular music
and comedy events. Also home to a film club
(www.brockleyjackfilmclub.co.uk).*
Deptford Film Club *Amersham Arms,
388 New Cross Road, SE14 6TY (8469
1499, www.deptfordfilmclub.org).*
Laban *Creekside, SE8 3DZ (8469 9500, www.
trinitylaban.ac.uk). Independent conservatoire
for contemporary dance training, housed in
stunning premises designed by Tate Modern
architects Herzog & de Meuron.*

Galleries & museums
Horniman Museum *100 London Road,
SE23 3PQ (8699 1872, www.horniman.ac.uk).
Eccentric art nouveau museum, with natural
history and anthropological displays, a spacious
café, lovely gardens and an animal enclosure.*
Lewisham Arthouse *140 Lewisham Way,
SE14 6PD (8244 3168, www.lewisham
arthouse.co.uk). Gallery in an impressive
Edwardian hall.*

Other attractions
Age Exchange Reminiscence Centre
*11 Blackheath Village, SE3 9LA (8318 9105,
www.age-exchange.org.uk) Charity that aims
to improve quality of life for elderly people by
emphasising the value of memories. Closed for
redevelopment until end of 2012.*
Creekside Centre *14 Creekside, SE8 4SA
(8692 9922, www.creeksidecentre.org.uk).
Environmental education centre.*
Goldsmiths, University of London *SE14
6NW (7919 7171, www.gold.ac.uk) Famous
art college with various sites around New Cross
and Deptford; the fabulously ornate building
on Lewisham Way (once Deptford Town Hall)
is particularly attractive.*

Manor House Library & Gardens *34 Old Road, SE13 5SY (8314 7794, www.lewisham. gov.uk). One of the grandest local libraries in London, built in 1772.*
Rivoli Ballroom *346-350 Brockley Road, SE4 2BY (8692 5130). Stylish old ballroom used for tea dances and classes.*

Sport & fitness

Fusion Lifestyle runs Lewisham's public sports centres. Forest Hill Pools has had an extensive facelift and should reopen in autumn 2012. In 2013, a new sports and leisure centre will open in Loampit Vale, and Ladywell Leisure Centre will shut.

Gyms & leisure centres

Bridge Leisure Centre *Kangley Bridge Road, SE26 5AQ (8778 7158, www.fusion-lifestyle.com).*
Colfe's Leisure Centre *Horne Park Lane, SE12 8AW (8297 9110, www.colfes.com/leisurecentre). Private.*
Downham Health & Leisure Centre *7-9 Moorside Road, BR1 5EP (8461 9200, www.harpersfitness.co.uk). Located in Bromley, but a Lewisham venture, this much-loved centre has a GP and dentist alongside a library, community hall and sports facilities.*
Fitness First *61-71A High Street, SE13 5JX (8852 4444, www.fitnessfirst.co.uk). Private.*
Ladywell Arena *Silvermere Road, SE6 4QX (8314 1986, www.fusion-lifestyle.com).*
Ladywell Leisure Centre *261 Lewisham High Street, SE13 6NJ (8690 2123, www. fusion-lifestyle.com). Closing in 2013.*
LA Fitness *291 Kirkdale, SE26 4QD (8778 9818, www.lafitness.co.uk). Private.*
Lucky's Gym *19B Marischal Road, SE13 5LE (8318 5630, www.luckysgym.com). Private.*
Skyline Gym *96-102 Rushey Green, SE6 4HW (8314 1167, www.skylinegym.co.uk). Private.*
Wavelengths Leisure Centre *Giffin Street, SE8 4RJ (8694 9400, www.fusion-lifestyle.com).*

Other facilities

Beckenham Place Park *Beckenham Hill Road, BR3 5BP (8650 2292, www.glendale-golf.com). 18-hole public golf course.*
1st Bowl Lewisham *11-29 Belmont Hill, SE13 5AU (0870 118 3021, www.1stbowl.com).*

Spectator sports

Millwall FC *The New Den, Zampa Road, SE16 3LN (7231 9999, www.millwallfc.co.uk).*

Schools

Primary

There are 65 state primary schools in Lewisham, including 20 church schools. There are also six independents, including one Muslim school. See www.lewisham.gov.uk/educationandlearning, www.edubase.gov.uk and www.ofsted.gov.uk for more information.

Secondary

Addey & Stanhope School *472 New Cross Road, SE14 6TJ (8305 6100, www.as. lewisham.sch.uk).*
Bonus Pastor RC School *Winlaton Road, BR1 5PZ (8695 2100, www.bp. lewisham.sch.uk).*
Catford High School *Bellingham Road, SE6 2PS (8697 8911). Was girls only, now mixed.*
Conisborough College *Conisborough Crescent, SE6 2SE (8461 9600, www.conisboroughcollege.co.uk).*
Crossways Academy *Sprules Road, SE4 2NL (7358 2400, www.crossways.ac.uk). Sixth form only.*

COUNCIL TAX

A	up to £40,000	£901.29
B	£40,001-£52,000	£1,051.50
C	£52,001-£68,000	£1,201.72
D	£68,001-£88,000	£1,351.93
E	£88,001-£120,000	£1,652.36
F	£120,001-£160,000	£1,952.79
G	£160,001-£320,000	£2,253.22
H	over £320,000	£2,703.86

RECYCLING

Household waste recycled & composted 17%
Main recycling centre Landmann Way Reuse & Recycling Centre, Landmann Way, off Surrey Canal Road, SE14 5RS (8314 7171)
Other recycling services green garden rubbish collection; home composting; white goods and furniture collection; mattress recycling
Council contact Beth Sowden, Waste Education Officer, Wearside Service Centre, Wearside Road, SE13 7EZ (8314 2053, www.lewisham.gov.uk/recycling)

Deptford Green School *141 Amersham Vale,*
SE14 6LQ (8691 3236, www.deptfordgreen.
lewisham.sch.uk).
Forest Hill School *Dacres Road, SE23 2XN*
(8613 0913, www.foresthillschool.co.uk).
Boys only; mixed sixth form.
Haberdashers' Aske's Hatcham College
Pepys Road, SE14 5SF (7652 9500,
www.haaf.org.uk).
Haberdashers' Aske's Knights Academy
Launcelot Road, BR1 5EB (7652 9500,
www.haaf.org.uk).
Prendergast-Ladywell Fields College
Manwood Road, SE4 1SA (8690 1114,
www.crofton.lewisham.sch.uk).
Prendergast School *Hilly Fields,*
Adelaide Avenue, SE4 1LE (8690 3710,
www.prendergast-school.com). Girls only;
mixed sixth form.
St Dunstan's College *Stanstead Road,*
SE6 4TY (8516 7200, www.stdunstans.org.uk).
Private.
St Matthew Academy *St Joseph's Vale,*
SE3 0XX (8853 6250, www.stmatthew
academy.co.uk).
Sedgehill School *Sedgehill Road, SE6*
3QW (8698 8911, www.sedgehill-
lewisham.co.uk).
Sydenham School *Dartmouth Road,*
SE26 4RD (8699 6731, www.sydenham.
lewisham.sch.uk). Girls only.
Trinity Lewisham *Taunton Road, SE12 8PD*
(8852 3191, www.trinitylewisham.org).

Property

WHAT THE AGENTS SAY:

'The extension of the London Overground has
revitalised the borough, and we're are seeing
an increasing number of professionals seeping
in. In great contrast to every other area in
London, property prices here have remained
relatively steady over the past few years. The
only problem preventing growth is the lack of
housing stock available. The average property
is a turn-of-the-20th-century, three bedroom
terraced house. And although some attempt has
been made to introduce new-build developments,
they're few in number.

Brockley is very popular thanks to its
transport links into central London and
Docklands. The area around the station has
blossomed over recent years, and now has a
fine selection of independent shops and cafés.'
Ken Jones, Saxton & Co, Brockley

Average property prices
Detached £547,823
Semi-detached £353,997
Terraced £286,236
Flat £223,583

Local estate agents
Acorn Estate Agents *153 High Street,*
SE13 6AA (8852 4455, www.acorn.ltd.uk).
Beaumont Residential *111B Rushey Green,*
SE6 4AF (8695 0123,
www.beaumontcatford.co.uk).
Cannon Kallar *www.cannonkallar.co.uk;*
2 offices in the borough (Deptford 8692 0555,
Brockley 8692 9533).
Mark Beaumont *197 Lewisham High Street,*
SE13 6AA (8852 5000,
www.markbeaumont.com).
Property World *4 Sydenham Road, SE26*
5QW (8488 0011, www.propertyworlduk.net).
Rocodells *388 Brockley Road, SE4 2BY*
(8691 8731, www.rocodells.co.uk).
Saxton & Co *369 Brockley Road, SE4 2AG*
(8691 1516, www.saxtonest.co.uk).
Sebastian Roche *www.sebastianroche.com;*
2 offices in the borough (Forest Hill 8291 9441,
Lewisham 8690 8888).

Other information

Council
Lewisham Council *Lewisham Town Hall,*
Catford Road, SE6 4RU (8314 6000,
www.lewisham.gov.uk).

Legal services
Catford CAB *120 Rushey Green, SE6 4TTQ*
(0844 826 9691, www.citizensadvice.org.uk).
Sydenham CAB *299 Kirkdale, SE26 4QD*
(0844 826 9691, www.adviceguide.org.uk).

Local information
www.brockleycentral.blogspot.com.
www.foresthillsociety.com.
www.forum.catford.co.uk.
www.hopandbeyond.com.
www.mercury-today.co.uk.
www.se23.com.
www.southeastcentral.co.uk.

Open spaces & allotments
Council allotments *8314 2277,*
www.lewisham.gov.uk.
One Tree Hill Allotment Society
One Tree Hill, SE23 1NX (www.othas.org.uk).
Open spaces *www.lewisham.gov.uk*

Lewisham

'The panoramic view from the hill outside the Royal Observatory is amazing, it has to be one of the best in London.'

Dr Marek Kukula, Public Astronomer, Royal Observatory

Greenwich

The borough of Greenwich is known for its world-class heritage sites and, more recently, entertainment giant the 02 Arena. It's also one of the six London Olympic boroughs, and in 2012 took on the status of a Royal Borough.

Neighbourhoods

Greenwich

Although its seaside-town feel, sense of community and attractive Georgian and Victorian properties make Greenwich a very desirable residential area, the focus here always falls on the neighbourhood's historic side. Royal, horological and maritime history takes precedence – except in 2012, when three venues in the borough host six Olympic and four Paralympic sports for the London 2012 Games.

Many of Greenwich's main attractions are set around panoramic Greenwich Park or the Thames waterfront, now accessible by a regular Thames Clipper boat service from the West End. The superbly overhauled Royal Observatory is the spectacular don't-miss; the Weller Astronomy Galleries and

the Time Galleries both do justice to the Observatory's influential heritage and provide enough free entertainment for families and school groups to gawp at for a good couple of hours. Shows at the Peter Harrison Planetarium and star-gazing in winter provide affordable alternatives. The nearby Queen's House and National Maritime Museum are also free – the latter now with the glorious new Sammy Ofer Wing.

The fire that swept through the *Cutty Sark* in May 2007 damaged much of the ship, but the artefacts and half the timbers of the famous tea clipper have been stored away as part of a £25 million restoration project – now set for completion in 2012.

The borough's transport links are continuing to improve, though several planned schemes have been cancelled – Crossrail is still on track, however; when

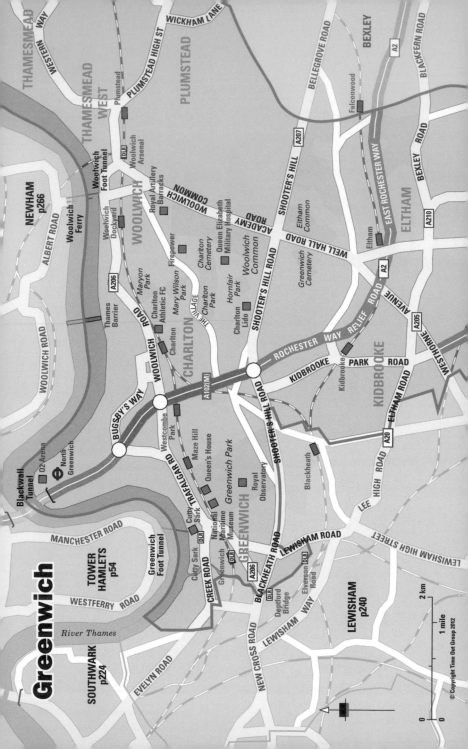

Abbey Wood terminus station on the southeast section of the line opens in 2018/2019, the journey time to Liverpool Street station is expected to be just 17 minutes. Greenwich town centre is well served by overland rail, the DLR, the Thames Clipper and the old Greenwich Foot Tunnel to the Isle of Dogs.

In the middle of Greenwich, the twisting streets on and off focal Greenwich Church Street house second-hand bookshops, independent boutiques and a covered market. At weekends, both the indoor and outdoor markets, and many nearby restaurants, are mobbed.

For culture, there's the plush Greenwich Picture House, Greenwich Theatre, Greenwich Playhouse and quality stand-up comedy at Up the Creek. Atmospheric recitals take place at St Alfege's Church, built in 1714 by Nicholas Hawksmoor. Regular festivals take place throughout the year.

Residents also have Greenwich Park at their disposal. This splendid, undulating space includes a boating lake, a children's play area, flower gardens, a deer enclosure and one of the finest views in – and of – London, from the top of One Tree Hill (where the Observatory stands). Despite some fierce local opposition, the park will host the Olympic and Paralympic equestrian competitions, plus the modern pentathlon's combined running and shooting segment, new for the 2012 Games . The attractions of the Old Royal Naval College, Queen's House and National Maritime Museum spread in historic splendour over the foot of the hill by the park entrance.

Less obvious attractions lie a short bus journey north. The much maligned North Greenwich Peninsula is no longer an industrial wasteland centrepieced by a white elephant Dome. Locals make the most of the Thames Path, which is dotted with lesser-known sculptures by Antony Gormley and Richard Wilson, and culminates in the Greenwich Peninsula Ecology Park, a four-acre wetland awash with birds, plants and insects. The Millennium Village is an inventive residential development centred on a wildlife lake shared with the park. It's not just Greenwich residents who are taking advantage either – the O2 Arena hosts all manner of crowd-pullers, notably gigs and sporting extravaganzas such as

Highs & Lows

the ATP Tennis Tour finals, and will host several events during London 2012. By then, the new cable car across the Thames (sponsored by Emirates, who get their name on the tube map as a result) should be running. Next to the O2 is the new, RIBA award-winning campus of Ravensbourne design college.

Kidbrooke

The lofty and elegant houses at the north-western end of Kidbrooke, by the border with Blackheath, quickly make way for a bleak landscape of 1960s Brutalist architecture and run-down tower blocks south of Kidbrooke rail station. This is not the borough's most desirable area, but a £750 million redevelopment programme is ongoing, including the demolition of 2,000 dwellings on the infamous Ferrier Estate – one of the largest in London. The opening of the Kidbrooke Station

Greenwich

Greenwich Market, for cakes, clothes and much more. See p261.

COUNCIL TAX		
A	up to £40,000	£860.49
B	£40,001-£52,000	£1,003.90
C	£52,001-£68,000	£1,147.32
D	£68,001-£88,000	£1,290.73
E	£88,001-£120,000	£1,577.56
F	£120,001-£160,000	£1,864.39
G	£160,001-£320,000	£2,151.22
H	over £320,000	£2,581.46

Interchange and its network of well-lit footpaths was welcomed by locals, while the David Lloyd Club is a major leisure attraction.

Charlton, Woolwich and Eltham

Charlton offers tree-lined residential streets around Charlton Park and more shady havens of teenage gangland culture elsewhere. Move east towards Woolwich Dockyard and the less affluent part of town and you'll find that soulless surroundings abound. Transport connections have improved, though, thanks to the DLR extension to Woolwich Arsenal. The main regeneration here concerns the eye-catching new Woolwich Centre development in Wellington Street, which provides council services, a modern and expanded library, a café, and an exhibition and meeting space. A new landscaped public square between the Centre offices and a refurbished Town Hall is also planned. Civic development in nearby Eltham includes the council-run Eltham Centre (two swimming pools, a fitness centre, a spa and a crèche), which opened in 2007.

Attractions for locals and visitors in these three neighbourhoods include Charlton House (a magnificent Jacobean mansion set in beautiful grounds) and vestiges of Charlton's village roots, such as St Luke's parish church. The Firepower Royal Artillery Museum and Thames Barrier Learning Centre provide local diversions in Woolwich, while the Royal Artillery Barracks is being used for London 2012 (for Olympic and Paralympic shooting and Paralympic archery). Eltham Palace and its fabulous art deco interiors is another surprise. Open spaces include Charlton Park and Woolwich Common. The art deco Charlton Lido closed in 2011, but it's hoped that it will reopen as a year-round pool in 2012.

Thamesmead

Even Thamesmead, the 1960s' planners' nightmare known for its *Clockwork Orange* backdrops and intimidating high-rises, is undergoing regeneration. Admittedly, its redevelopment has suffered more than its fair share of bureaucratic delays, but a joint commitment by both Greenwich and Bexley councils (which Thamesmead straddles), supported by the only community development charity working in the area, Trust Thamesmead (www.trust-thamesmead. co.uk), offers some hope for the future.

Restaurants & cafés

Much of the borough's local restaurant trade is driven by tourism. Standard pub lunches are the norm, interspersed by uninspiring, catch-all Mexican and Asian eateries, and chain restaurants (Nando's, Pizza Express, Prezzo, Zizzi, Gourmet Burger). Exceptions include contemporary European cuisine at Inside, upmarket British cooking at the Rivington Grill and tasty nibbles at deli-cum-diner Buenos Aires. Bar du Musée, with its diverse dining and drinking spaces, is also very popular, while the Hill is the pick of the gastropubs. Relative newcomer

Greenwich

> ## TRANSPORT
>
> **Tube stations** *DLR* Cutty Sark, Greenwich, Deptford Bridge, Elverson Road; Woolwich Arsenal; *Jubilee* North Greenwich
>
> **Rail stations** *Southeastern Trains* Greenwich, Maze Hill, Westcombe Park, Charlton, Woolwich Dockyard, Woolwich Arsenal, Plumstead; Blackheath, Kidbrooke, Eltham, Falconwood
>
> **Main bus routes** *into central London* 53, 188; *night buses* N1, N21; *24-hour buses* 53, 188
>
> **River** Woolwich Ferry; commuter and leisure boat services to/from central London, including the Thames Clipper (www.thamesclippers.com), with piers at Greenwich, O2 Arena and Woolwich Arsenal
>
> **Development plans** Emirates Air Line, a cable car system crossing the Thames from the O2 Arena on the Greenwich Pensinula to the ExCeL centre at the Royal Docks, should be finished by summer 2012; Crossrail (www.crossrail.co.uk) by 2018/2019.

Old Brewery is a welcome addition: a cavernous restaurant/café/bar in the Old Royal Naval College that serves British dishes and more than 50 ales. The new wing of the Maritime Museum has a decent brasserie, 16" West, with an outdoor terrace and Sunday roasts.

Within the O2 there are chains of all persuasions, from Thai Silk to Gaucho. Still in North Greenwich, but away from the main drag, Chinese restaurant Peninsula occupies the whole ground floor of the Holiday Inn Express. It serves dim sum until 4.45pm, as well as evening meals. In East Greenwich, Efes Meze offers reliable Turkish standards.

Bar du Musée *17 Nelson Road, SE10 9JB (8858 4710, www.bardumusee.com).*
Buenos Aires Café & Deli *86 Royal Hill, SE10 8RT (8488 6764, www.buenosaires ltd.com).*
Efes Meze *170 Trafalgar Road, SE10 9TZ (8293 0626, www.efesmeze.com).*
The Hill *89 Royal Hill, SE10 8SE (8691 3926, www.thehillgreenwich.com).*
Inside *19 Greenwich South Street, SE10 8NW (8265 5060, www.insiderestaurant.co.uk).*
Old Brewery *Pepys Building, Old Royal Naval College, SE10 9LM (3327 1280, www.oldbrewery greenwich.com).*
Peninsula *Holiday Inn Express, Bugsby's Way, SE10 0GD (8269 1638, www.mychinese food.co.uk).*
Rivington Grill *178 Greenwich High Road, SE10 8NN (8293 9270, www.rivington grill.co.uk).*
16" West *National Maritime Museum, Park Row, SE10 9NF (8312 8516, www.16seconds west.co.uk).*

Bars & pubs

Even in Nelson's day, Greenwich was a popular spot for a pint. These days, a handful of attractive, late-opening bars – including Bar du Musée (*see above*) – complement an atmospheric lunchtime and evening scene set around the river and the market. Landmark boozer Gipsy Moth, right beside the *Cutty Sark*, has continental beers and a real buzz about it. Mention must also be made of the Greenwich Union, flagship outlet of Alistair Hook's lauded Meantime Brewing Company, where knowledgeable and

Old Brewery: top beer and British food.

friendly staff serve signature Union, Chocolate, Golden, Raspberry and Stout beers along with decent food (Meantime also runs the Old Brewery – *see left*). Bang next door is exemplary old-school Young's pub Richard I.

Other worthy boozers in the area include the stately Trafalgar Tavern, which has a superb location next to the lapping Thames; the Coach & Horses in Greenwich Market, a key local meeting place; and the Ashburnham Arms, an excellent locals' boozer with Shepherd Neame ales, decent wines, superior pub food and a garden that's popular in the summer.

The North Pole on Greenwich High Road still sees some action: it's a stylish three-floor club-bar-restaurant with DJs downstairs at weekends. Davy's Wine Vaults, part of the London-wide Davy's wine bar chain, is handy for thirsty commuters (it's next to Greenwich train station).

If you're looking further afield, then the Pilot Inn is the perfect place for a pre-show pint within walking distance of the O2. In Charlton, Eltham and Woolwich, it's pretty much a case of finding a trusted local pub and sticking with it.

Ashburnham Arms *25 Ashburnham Grove,
SE10 8UH (8692 2007, www.ashburnham
arms.com).*
Coach & Horses *13 Greenwich Market,
SE10 9HZ (8293 0880, www.greenwich-
inc.com/coach_and_horses).*
Davy's Wine Vaults *161 Greenwich High
Road, SE10 8JA (8858 6011, www.davy.co.uk).*
Gipsy Moth *60 Greenwich Church Street,
SE10 9BL (8858 0786, www.thegipsymoth
greenwich.co.uk).*
Greenwich Union *56 Royal Hill, SE10 8RT
(8692 6258, www.greenwichunion.com).*
North Pole *131 Greenwich High Road, SE10
8JA (8853 3020, www.northpolegreenwich.com).*
Pilot Inn *68 River Way, SE10 0BE
(8858 5910, www.fullershotels.com).*
Richard I *52-54 Royal Hill, SE10 8RT
(0693 2996, http://youngs.co.uk).*
Trafalgar Tavern *Park Row, SE10 9NW
(8858 2909, www.trafalgartavern.co.uk).*

Shops

Greenwich has lots of shops, boutiques and
market stalls to browse – shopping is one
of the area's main attractions. Greenwich
Market is spread over two sites. The
smaller, the Weekend Market, has mostly
bric-a-brac with a handful of traders dealing
in second-hand books and vinyl, with a few
punk bootlegs available. The Crafts Market
is jam-packed with clothes, handicrafts,
jewellery and home furnishings.

The shops on the fringes of the covered
market are worth investigating. Greenwich
Printmakers offers original, affordable
artworks; Music & Video Exchange deals
in CDs in all genres; and Compendia
specialises in games from around the
world, such as Mexican train dominoes and
the Japanese board game Go.

Nearby, the Emporium has a fine stock
of vintage clothes, at much better prices
than in central London. Worth crossing
town for, Pickwick Papers & Fabrics has
a huge selection of wallpapers and fabric.

Greenwich is also known for its
antiquarian and second-hand bookshops;
Halcyon Books is a fine trove, while Naval
& Maritime Books covers naval and
mercantile history up to the end of World
War II, with contemporary and historical
naval magazines to boot. For more Nelson
memorabilia, elegant brass porthole mirrors
and vintage china from an 1822 shipwreck,
visit jaunty little marine shop Nauticalia;
Warwick Leadlay also specialises in antique
maps as well as Nelsonia.

For clothes and accessories, Hide All has
an excellent selection of bags; Bullfrogs
deals in urban footwear and clothes; Johnny
Rocket, purveyor of creative, contemporary
jewellery, has its main outlet in College
Approach; Red Door trades in ceramics
and gifts, and doubles as a café; and
Meet Bernard offers Carhartt and other
streetwear labels. So Organic deals in
beauty treatments, cleaning products,
and bedding and bathwear of every
description, while Biscuit offers the chance
to paint your own ceramics. Niche food
stores include Heaps (gourmet sausages,
plus coffee and cakes), the Creaky Shed
(fruit and veg, herbs, jams and organic
products), Cheeseboard and the Fishmonger.

Bugsby's Way, which links North
Greenwich to Charlton, is lined with huge
supermarkets (Asda, Sainsbury's) and
shopping centres containing fashion stores
(Next, H&M, New Look), Boots, B&Q,
Comet and so on. The heart of Charlton
provides an old-style high street experience,
while Woolwich has a rather run-down
shopping precinct.

Biscuit *3-4 Nelson Road, SE10 9JB (8853
8588, www.biscuit-biscuit.com).*
Bullfrogs *www.bullfrogs.co.uk; 22 Greenwich
Church Street, SE10 9BJ (8305 2404);
12 Nelson Road, SE10 9BJ (8305 1102).*
Cheeseboard *26 Royal Hill, SE10 8RT
(8305 0401, www.cheese-board.co.uk).*
Compendia *10 Greenwich Market, SE10 9HZ
(8293 6616, www.compendia.co.uk).*
Creaky Shed *20 Royal Hill, SE10 8RT
(8269 0333, www.thecreakyshed.co.uk).*

Greenwich

Emporium *330-332 Creek Road, SE10 9SW (8305 1670).*
Fishmonger *Rear of 26 Royal Hill, SE10 8RT (07880 541485, www.thefishmongerltd.com).*
Greenwich Market *8269 5090, www.shopgreenwich.co.uk/greenwich-market.*
Greenwich Printmakers *1A Greenwich Market, SE10 9HZ (8858 1569, www. greenwich-printmakers.org.uk).*
Halcyon Books *1 Greenwich South Street, SE10 8NW (8305 2675, www.halcyon books.co.uk).*
Heaps Sausages *8 Nevada Street, SE10 9JL (8293 9199, http://heapssausages.com).*
Hide All *9 Greenwich Market, SE10 9HZ (8858 6104, www.hideall.co.uk).*
Johnny Rocket *10 College Approach, SE10 9HY (8269 1814, www.johnnyrocketltd.com).*
Meet Bernard *23 Nelson Road, SE10 9JB (8858 4047, www.meetbernard.com).*
Music & Video Exchange *23 Greenwich Church Street, SE10 9BJ (8858 8898, www.mgeshops.com).*

Nauticalia *25 Nelson Road, SE10 9JB (8858 1066, www.nauticalia.com).*
Naval & Maritime Books *66 Royal Hill, SE10 8RT (8692 1794, www.navalandmaritime books.com).*
Pickwick Papers & Fabrics *6 Nelson Road, SE10 9JB (8858 1205, www.pickwickpapers. co.uk).*
Red Door *10 Turnpin Lane, SE10 9JA (8858 2131, www.reddoorgallery.co.uk).*
So Organic *Eagle House, 7 Turnpin Lane, SE10 9JA (8305 5357, www.soorganic.com).*
Warwick Leadlay *1& 2 Nelson Arcade, SE10 9JB (8858 0317, www.warwickleadlay.com).*

Arts & attractions

Cinemas & theatres
Greenwich Picture House *180 Greenwich High Road, SE10 8NN (0871 902 5732, www.picturehouses.co.uk).*
Greenwich Playhouse *189 Greenwich High Road, SE10 8JA (8858 9256, www.galleontheatre.co.uk).*
Greenwich Theatre *Crooms Hill, SE10 8ES (8858 4447, www.greenwichtheatre.org.uk). Musical theatre productions.*
Odeon Greenwich *Bugsby Way, SE10 0QJ (0871 224 4007, www.odeon.co.uk).*

Galleries & museums
Cutty Sark *King William Walk, SE10 9HT (www.cuttysark.org.uk). Due to reopen in 2012.*
Fan Museum *12 Crooms Hill, SE10 8ER (8305 1441, www.fan-museum.org). More than 3,500 fans from around the world.*
Firepower *Royal Artillery Museum, Royal Arsenal, SE18 6ST (8855 7755, www. firepower.org.uk). Artillery through the ages, from catapults to nuclear warheads.*
National Maritime Museum *Romney Road, SE10 9NF (8858 4422, information 8312 6565, tours 8312 6608, www.rmg.co.uk). Explore more than 500 years of maritime history.*
Old Royal Naval College *King William Walk, SE10 9LW (8269 4747, tours 8269 4791, www.greenwichfoundation.org.uk). Built by Sir Christopher Wren at the turn of the 17th-century; originally a hospital, then a naval college, it is set in landscaped grounds in the centre of the Maritime Greenwich World Heritage Site.*
Royal Observatory & Planetarium *Greenwich Park, SE10 9NF (8312 6565, www.rmg.co.uk). Also by Wren, built for Charles II in 1675, and the home of Greenwich Mean Time and the Prime Meridian Line.*

STATISTICS
BOROUGH MAKE-UP
Population 222,900
Ethnic origins
  White 73.9%
  Mixed 3.4%
  Asian or Asian British 8.2%
  Black or Black British 10.9%
  Chinese or other 3.5%
Students 9.5%
Retirees 10.3%

HOUSING STOCK
Borough size (hectares) 5,038
Population density per hectare 44.2
No. of households 92,788
Houses (detached, semi-detached or terraced) 57%
Flats (converted or purpose-built) 43%

CRIME PER 1,000 OF POPULATION
Burglary 9
Robbery 4
Theft of vehicle 4
Theft from vehicle 11
Violence against the person 27
Sexual offences 2

MPs
Eltham Clive Efford (Labour); *Greenwich & Woolwich* Nick Raynsford (Labour); *Erith & Thamesmead* Teresa Pearce (Labour)

The splendid new Sammy Ofer Wing at the **National Maritime Museum**.

**Thames Barrier Information & Learning
Centre** *1 Unity Way, SE18 5NJ (8305 4188,
www.environment-agency.gov.uk). Learn about
London's flood defence system: the world's
largest adjustable dam, built in 1982.*

Music & comedy venues

St Alfego's Church *Church Street, SE10 9BJ
(www.st-alfego.org)*
Up the Creek *302 Creek Road, SE10 9SW
(8858 4581, www.up-the-creek.com).*

Other attractions

Age Exchange Reminiscence Centre
*11 Blackheath Village, SE3 9LA (8318 9105,
www.age-exchange.org.uk). A charity that
emphasises the value of memories through
exhibitions, theatre and educational programmes.*
Charlton House *Charlton Road, SE7 8RE
(8856 3951, www.charlton-house.org). Grand
Jacobean manor house, now used as a community
centre and library.*
Eltham Palace *Court Yard, SE9 5QE
(8294 2548, www.english-heritage.org.uk).
Two sights in one: a medieval royal palace
and an art deco home*
Greenwich & Docklands Festivals
*Royal Hill, SE10 8RE (8305 1818, www.
festival.org.) Runs the highly acclaimed
Greenwich & Docklands International
Festival, in June.*
Greenwich Festivals *www.greenwich
festivals.co.uk. Info on all the local annual
shindigs, from comedy to jazz.*
Greenwich Tourist Information Centre
*Pepys House, 2 Cutty Sark Gardens, SE10 9LW
(0870 608 2000, www.visitgreenwich.org.uk).
Includes an exhibition on the history of
Greenwich.*
The O2 *Peninsula Square, SE10 0DX
(www.theo2.co.uk). Includes the O2 Arena
music venue, IndigO2 (a smaller, more
intimate entertainment venue), an 11-screen
Cineworld cinema, Proud2 nightclub and
various eateries.*
Queen's House *Romney Road, SE10
9NF (8312 6565, www.rmg.co.uk). Palladian
house designed by Inigo Jones in 1616 for
James I's wife. It's now home to the National
Maritime Museum's art collection (including
paintings by Hogarth and Gainsborough) –
and a ghost.*

Greenwich

Ranger's House (Wernher Collection)
*Chesterfield Walk, SE10 8QX (8294 2548,
www.english-heritage.org.uk). Medieval and
Renaissance art, housed in an 18th-century villa.*

Sport & fitness

National Lottery money, and the investment
of Greenwich Leisure (which manages
sports facilities in a number of London
boroughs), has meant an upturn in the
fortunes of the public leisure centres in
Greenwich – they can certainly give the
private clubs a run for their money. The
Waterfront Leisure Centre, in particular,
is outstanding, with excellent swimming
facilities and ample provision for other
sports. The Eltham Centre is also very good.
The private sector can offer PhysioActive,
a gym that specialises in sports injuries.

Charlton Lido – one of just three
remaining lidos in south-east London –
is a local gem, but is currently closed.

Gyms & leisure centres

Arches Leisure Centre *80 Trafalgar Road,
SE10 9UX (8317 5020, www.gll.org).*
Coldharbour Leisure Centre *Chapel Farm
Road, SE9 3LX (8851 8692, www.gll.org).*
David Lloyd *Kidbrooke Park Road, at
Weigall Road, SE12 8HG (8331 3901,
www.davidlloyd.co.uk). Private.*
Eltham Centre *2 Archery Road, SE9 1HA
(8921 4344, www.gll.org).*
FitSpace *Unit 1, Macbean Street, SE1 6LW
(8854 2465, www.fitspacegyms.co.uk). Private.*
PhysioActive *Old Bank House, Mottingham
Road, SE9 4QZ (8857 6000, www.physioactive.
com). Private.*
Thamesmere Leisure Centre *Thamesmere
Drive, SE28 8RE (8311 1119, www.gll.org).*
**Warehouse, Sports & Performing Arts
Centre** *Speranza Street, SE18 1NX (8855 8289,
www.gll.org).*
Waterfront Leisure Centre *High Road,
SE18 6DL (8317 5010, www.gll.org).*

Other facilities

Charlton Lido *Hornfair Park, Shooter's Hill
Road, at Charlton Park Lane, SE18 4LX
(www.gll.org). GLL intends to refurbish the lido as
a 50m heated outdoor pool, open all year round.*
Royal Blackheath Golf Club *Court Road,
SE9 5AF (8850 1795, www.royalblackheath.
com). Reputedly the oldest golf club in England,
established in 1608.*

Shooters Hill Golf Club *Lowood,
Eaglesfield Road, SE18 3DA (8854 6368,
www.shgc.uk.com).*

Spectator sports

Charlton Athletic FC *The Valley, Floyd Road,
SE7 8BL (8333 4000, www.cafc.co.uk).*

Schools

Primary

*Greenwich has 65 state primary schools, 17 of
which are church schools. There are also eight
independents, including a Steiner school and a
theatre academy. See www.greenwich.gov.uk,
www.edubase.gov.uk and www.ofsted.gov.uk
for more information.*

Secondary

Blackheath Bluecoat CE School
*Old Dover Road, SE3 8SY (8269 4300,
www.bbcs.greenwich.sch.uk). Church of
England.*
Colfe's School *Horn Park Lane, SE12 8AW
(8852 2283, www.colfes.com). Private.*
Corelli College *Corelli Road, SE3 8EP
(8516 7977, www.corellicollege.org.uk).*
Crown Woods College *145 Bexley Road, SE9
2PT (8850 7678, www.crownwoods.org.uk).*
Eltham Foundation School *Middle
Park Avenue, SE9 5EQ (8859 0133,
http://elthamfoundation.com).*
Eltham Hill Technology College for Girls
*Eltham Hill, SE9 5EE (8859 2843,
www.elthamhill.greenwich.sch.uk). Girls only.*
John Roan School *Maze Hill, SE3 7UD
(8516 7555, www.thejohnroanschool.co.uk).*
Plumstead Manor School *Old Mill Road,
SE18 1QF (3260 3333, www.plumstead
manor.com). Girls only.*
St Paul's Academy *Finchale Road, SE2 9PX
(8311 3868, www.stpaulsacademy.org.uk).*
**St Thomas More Catholic Comprehensive
School** *Footscray Road, SE9 2SU (8850 6700,
http://stmcomprehensive.org). Roman Catholic.*
St Ursula's Convent School *70 Crooms Hill,
SE10 8HN (8858 4613, www.stursulas.com).
Roman Catholic; girls only.*
Shooters Hill Post-16 Campus *Red Lion
Lane, SE18 4LD (8319 9700, www.shooters
hill.ac.uk). Sixth form only.*
Thomas Tallis School *Kidbrooke Park Road,
SE3 9PX (8856 0115, www.thomastallis.co.uk).*
Woolwich Polytechnic School *Hutchins
Road, SE28 8AT (8310 7000, www.woolwich
poly.greenwich.sch.uk). Boys only.*

Greenwich

The **O2** on the revitalised North Greenwich Peninsula. See p257.

Property

WHAT THE AGENTS SAY:

'Greenwich is still a transient market, with people living in the borough for roughly two to three years before moving on. Demand remains high for two- and three-bedroom period properties, but there has been a steady decline in sales of one and two-bed purpose-built apartments. First time buyers are finding it hard to move into the area due to the current lending market, but Greenwich remains a desirable place to live, helped by its easy connections to the 2012 Olympics as well as it becoming a Royal Borough to mark the Queen's Diamond Jubilee.'
Graham Lawes, Jones Lang LaSalle

Average property prices
Detached £487,246
Semi-detached £313,625
Terraced £257,110
Flat £240,653

Local estate agents
Alan Ives Estates *118 Plumstead High Street, SE18 1SJ (8854 0101, www.alanives.co.uk).*
Cockburn *352 Footscray Road, SE9 2EB (8859 8590, www.cockburn-online.co.uk).*
Harrison Ingram *156 Wellhall Road, SE9 6SN (8859 4419, www.harrisoningram. co.uk).*
Jones Lang LaSalle *22 College Approach, SE10 9HY (8858 9986, www.joneslang lasalle.co.uk).*
Oliver Bond *38 King William Walk, SE10 9HU (8858 9595, www.oliverbond.co.uk).*

Redwood Estates *9 Gunnery House, Gunnery Terrace, SE18 6SW (0316 8000, www.redwoodestates.co.uk).*

Other information

Council
London Borough of Greenwich *The Woolwich Centre, 35 Wellington Street, SE18 6HQ (8054 8888, www.greenwich.gov.uk).*

Legal services
Greenwich (Eltham) CAB *The Eltham Centre, Archery Road, SE9 1HA (8853 9499, www.citizensadvice.org.uk).*
Greenwich (Woolwich) CAB *Old Town Hall, Polytechnic Street, SE18 6PN (8853 9499, www.citizensadvice.org.uk).*
Greenwich Community Law Centre *187 Trafalgar Road, SE10 9EQ (8305 3350).*

Local information
www.allthingsgreenwich.co.uk.
www.thegreenwichphantom.co.uk.
www.mercury-today.co.uk.
www.shopgreenwich.co.uk.

Open spaces & allotments
Council allotments *8921 6885, www.greenwich.gov.uk.*
Kidbrooke Allotments *Kidbrooke Park Road, SE3 (www.kpaa.org.uk).*
Open spaces *www.greenwich.gov.uk/parks; www. urbanecology.org.uk (Greenwich Peninsula Ecology Park); www.royalparks.org.uk (Greenwich Park).*
Prior Street Allotments *www.priorstreetgardens.org.uk.*

Newham

The key host borough for the 2012 Games (providing the gateway to the Olympic Park itself), Newham was also the area of London most in need of regeneration. Two areas of major top-down redevelopment – Stratford, and the long-neglected Royal Docks – may begin to have some effect on long-term unemployment and endemic poverty, and the social problems that come with them.

Neighbourhoods

Stratford, Forest Gate and Manor Park

Stratford has long been Newham's most important district. Amid all the oppressively same-same concrete, there was always a little culture – focused at the doughty Theatre Royal, the Picturehouse Cinema next door and the Stratford Circus arts centre – as well as shedloads of transport possibilities. There was even a kind of shopping mall: the permanently down-at-heel Stratford Centre.

Now, the area prepares for what may be the most-hyped event in sporting history: the London 2012 Olympic & Paralympic Games. The curly-wurly red scaffolding of Anish Kapoor's lofty *Orbit* peers down on Zaha Hadid's Aquatics Centre and the Olympic Stadium – who ever would have suspected starchitects and abstract artists would be at work, and on such a scale, in dear old Stratford? Of course, no one gets inside the Olympic Park until 2013 unless they're clutching one of those hard-to-acquire tickets, but even the hoi polloi are welcome at the Australian megamall Westfield Stratford City – a glossy, well-run, carefully planned, largely atmosphere-free retail behemoth that expects to welcome a daunting 70 per cent of the ten million Games visitors.

A whole heap of cash and expectations, then. But the jury is still out on what it means for E15. That the Olympic Park – and its 2,800 promised houses, its Chobham Academy and polyclinic, even the unquestionably impressive and well-intentioned public parklands that the Games will leave behind – was granted its own postcode (E20, previously the fictional address-footer for *EastEnders* residents) is unintentionally symbolic. There seems a

division between the new and the old that may be bridged by trickle-down effects. Many of the people who bought into the Olympic property bubble never intended to live in the borough – they bought to let; what's left is a feeling of a population in transit: students, City workers and immigrant communities, all renting in east London.

Of course, Stratford's excellent transport links are one of the major reasons for this grandiose sporting arrival. Spectators will be able to choose from a panoply of options:

Highs & Lows

▲ **Redevelopment** Serious money is finally being spent in Newham: the Olympic Park will, at the very least, provide some new homes, a beautiful park and some world-class sporting venues; and, if all goes to plan, the Siemens Pavilion on the Royal Docks could become a major employer.
Connections Stratford has the tube, Overground, trains, the DLR and buses, with serious work done on most of them to service the Olympic hordes. Then there's City Airport and the new, high-speed Javelin.

▼ **Redevelopment** Not everyone is excited about the Olympic shindig, with some asking whether the kind of top-down projects Newham has welcomed will benefit anyone except their investors. Many locals grumble that jobs building the Olympic Park were few and far between, and things won't improve after the Games.
Beckton With a vast sewage works on one side, and the soulless world of Custom House and the ExCeL Exhibition Centre on the other, Beckton is not one of London's most desirable neighbourhoods.

The **Olympic Stadium**, the focal venue in the Olympic Park.

the DLR; the Central and Jubilee tube lines; London Overground; the mainline from Liverpool Street and Essex; and (not cowed by Eurostar's eventual decision to not have a stop here), the high-speed Javelin train. Stansted Airport is less than an hour by coach, and then there's London City Airport in the Royal Docks. Stratford is definitely easy to leave – Canary Wharf is five minutes away, the City ten, the West End no more than 20.

Get on a train towards Essex, however, and within minutes you're in Forest Gate, Manor Park and Little Ilford, on the outer edges of the borough. Alight here and you've arrived in the leafy suburbs. There's certainly less to do in this part of Newham, but there are rows of pleasant enough Victorian semis on tree-lined streets to compensate. There are some wonderful green spaces, too, such as heathy Manor Park, Wanstead Flats (just across the borough border in Redbridge) and even the colossal City of London Cemetery, last resting place of Newham's favourite son, Bobby Moore. In fact, the borough as a whole seems to have a disproportionately high acreage of cemeteries, which may explain why so much of it is so quiet.

Plaistow, Upton Park, and East and West Ham

There is a hard-to-shake feeling that the further south you travel in the borough, and the closer you get to the old docks, the worse everything gets. This isn't the most prosperous part of town, and classic inner-city problems such as crime, pollution, unemployment and overcrowding abound. It's not all bad – far from it – you just have to look a bit harder than you would in some other London areas to find the good parts.

A strong sense of community, particularly in East and West Ham, is one obvious 'good'. Newham was formed in 1965 by the merging of the former Essex county boroughs of East Ham and West Ham into Greater London. Both neighbourhoods have an ethnically diverse – Cockney meets subcontinental – population. On High Street North and, more famously, Green Street, shoppers from India, Sri Lanka, Pakistan, Bangladesh and beyond bustle in and out of sari shops, jewellers, grocers and the like. Meanwhile, Queen's Market provides the sort of trading banter you'd expect from a marketload of East Enders.

In the north-east of the borough, leafy side streets continue off High Street North

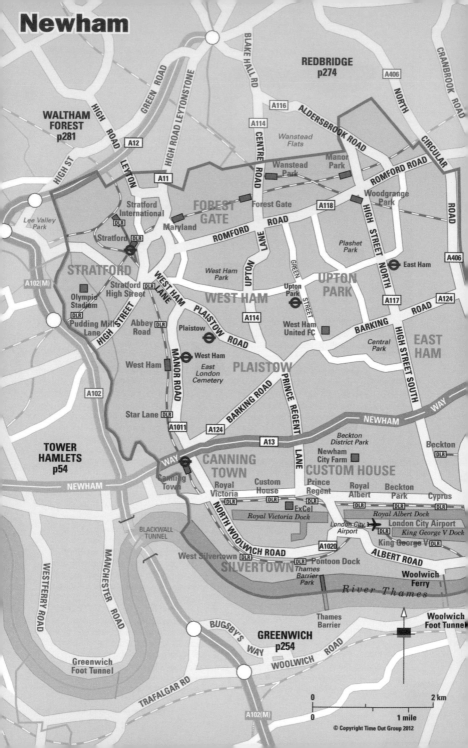

into East Ham; the poet-named streets around Plashet Park and the area known as the Burges Estate, which extends towards the Barking Relief Road, are quiet and anonymous. Central Park, an oasis of greenery that ties together many of the quieter Victorian residential streets in the heart of East Ham, is another popular area. Further west, the area bordering West Ham Park, particularly Ham Park Road, has some excellent housing stock. West Ham Park itself is one of the borough's many fine open spaces, with some good tennis courts, cricket nets and football pitches.

The Hams even have some respectable architecture in the form of the attractive old Town Hall, East Ham's fabulous period Underground station and the ornate Boleyn Cinema, but easily the borough's most famous building, and perhaps the focal point of the whole community, is the Boleyn Ground. This is home to the pride of the East End, West Ham United, although for how much longer is not clear – West Ham remain the most likely anchor-tenant when the Olympic Stadium is leased for public use in 2013.

For now, match days see pubs such as the Duke of Edinburgh on Green Street heave with battalions of the claret and blue army. Yet the pubs are still able to support events such as Diwali, with groups of Indian singers – further evidence of a relaxed, multiracial neighbourhood.

Head further west, into Plaistow, and housing becomes less attractive, places of interest dwindle. But even here you've got the Greenway, a four-mile walking and cycling artery that follows the path of the Northern Outfall Sewer (no, really) linking Hackney and Beckton, as well as the green and pleasant Lee Valley Park, with Three Mills Island (containing film studios and a cluster of historical mill buildings) at the confluence of the area's rivers.

Canning Town, Custom House and the Royal Docks

The view from the Woolwich Ferry as it docks at North Woolwich pier rather sums up the southern third of Newham: brutalist remnants of the docks; unloved and unassimilated modern architecture; and, precariously intermingled, some surprising green spaces. In fact, parks provide the only real highlights in an area dominated by ugliness – the sprawling, war-influenced

estates, the vast ExCeL Exhibition Centre, the huge scar of the Beckton Reach Sewage Treatment Works, and the impressively bleak, underused expanses of the Royal Docks themselves. It is alongside the Docks that Newham Council hopes to develop another economic powerhouse: the Siemens Pavilion 'eco-centre' is rising alongside ExCeL, soon to be connected to the O2 Arena on the Greenwich Pensinsula by the Emirates-sponsored cable car.

Thames Barrier Park, with its good café, sculpted gardens, interesting industrial views and a great kids' play area, is a modern triumph. Just the other side of London City Airport, Beckton District Park stretches beyond the A13, and contains a wonderful hidden gem – a city farm.

Parks aside, Canning Town is really little more than a transport hub amid a maze of mediocre streets – a minor-league Stratford. Silvertown, North Woolwich and Custom

Newham

House form what is essentially a windblown desert of dockland with oases of 'luxury' flats, Premier Inns and Novotels. On the positive side, there's the new main campus of the University of East London (UEL), a good athletics track, and a horse-riding centre. There might, if the developers can find the money, one day be a replacement for the Beckton Alp, once the UK's steepest dry ski slope.

Between the docks and the Thames, the Victorian workers' township of Silvertown (named after the boss of a 19th-century rubber firm) is afflicted by the sickly rotten smell from the Tate & Lyle sugar refinery, and the roar of aeroplanes. Two spurs of the DLR run to this corner of Newham, one of which leads directly to the bijou City Airport.

Restaurants & cafés

Until the arrival of Westfield Stratford City, there were very few good independent eateries, and the borough lacked even a reasonable selection of the above-average chains taken for granted elsewhere. But now the Pizza Express at the Stratford Picturehouse has been joined by Westfield's legion of glossier chains (Jamie's Italian, Wahaca, Busaba Eathai, Real Greek); there's even a Rosa's (Vietnamese), Comptoir Libanais (Mediterranean)

Locals' Tips

The best view of Anish Kapoor's huge Olympic sculpture, *Orbit*, is from the southbound DLR just out of Stratford station.
Unless you support West Ham United, avoid Upton Park on match days – the ensuing chaos can be seriously disruptive... though it'll be sorely missed locally if the club does move into the Olympic Stadium.
Near Upton Park, Newham Bookshop (745-747 Barking Road, E13 9ER, 8552 9993, www.newhambooks.co.uk) is a real community bookstore of 30 years' standing. It organises regular readings and talks with the Bishopsgate Institute, Stratford Circus and Wanstead Library.
Heading south of the river? Use the Woolwich Ferry or the little-known Woolwich Foot Tunnel.

and Franca Manca (pizza). There is the odd place at ExCeL, but the real treat out this way is across the water from London City Airport: Yi-Ban serves brilliant Cantonese food, including dim sum.

A smattering of curry houses exists on Green Street, among them Vijay's Chawalla (Gujarati vegetarian dishes). And while these aren't exactly world-beaters, they at least avoid the tourist circus and pavement hassle of Brick Lane. Other popular local choices include the India Gate (pan-Indian) on the Grove in Stratford, and its oriental counterpart, Chan's, on High Street North.

Alternatively, if you're hankering after a taste of the old East End, try Robins Pie & Mash in East Ham, or Queen's Fish Bar on Green Street. Also worth a mention is Café Mondo at the Stratford Library.

Café Mondo *Stratford Library, 5 The Grove, E15 1EL (8555 1319, www.cafemondo.co.uk).*
Chan's *321 High Street North, E12 6PQ (8472 3384).*
Comptoir Libanais *Westfield Stratford City, E20 1ET (8519 1302, www.lecomptoir.co.uk).*
Franca Manca *Westfield Stratford City, E20 1ET (8522 6669, www.francomanca.co.uk).*
India Gate *150 The Grove, E15 1NS (8534 6565, www.theindiagate.co.uk).*
Queen's Fish Bar *406 Green Street, E13 9JJ (8471 2457).*
Robins Pie & Mash *105 High Street, E6 1HZ (8472 1956, www.robinspieandmash.com).*
Rosa's *Westfield Stratford City, E20 1ET (8519 1302, www.rosaslondon.com).*
Vijay's Chawalla *268-270 Green Street, E7 8LF (8470 3535, www.vijayschawalla.co.uk).*
Yi-Ban *London Regatta Centre, Dockside Road, E16 2QT (7473 6699, www.yi-ban.com).*

Bars & pubs

Good spots for drinking are barely more numerous than those for eating – you won't be coming to Newham on your stag do. Westfield Stratford City again provides a kind of rescue: Tap East is probably too glossy for the pub connoisseur, but does serve superb beer – as you'd expect from the people behind the Rake in Borough Market – and Balans offers cocktails.

King Edward VII, known locally as King Eddie's, is a rare example in Stratford of a proper pub with decent beer and passable food. The next best option is probably the

Queens Market, Upton Park.

two million square feet of it) contains pretty much every high-end chain you can think of, plus some more individual options and enough entertainment (bowling alley, multiscreen cinema, casino) to keep you indoors all day. The place will be hell for many, of course, but is at least committed to paying the 'living wage'. Directly opposite is Newham's other shopping centre – the Stratford Centre. This is no classic of the genre, and may well decline further if the national chains within are sucked across the road into Westfield, leaving the fruit and vegetable stalls and independent shops stranded.

Queens Market at Upton Park tube station is a hustle and bustle of cheap clothes and fresh food. Green Street in West Ham, and the High Street running south from Plashet to East Ham, are busy thoroughfares, fine for basics and excellent if you're looking for jewellery or a sari.

Westfield Stratford City *E20 1ET (8555 4467, http://uk.westfield.com/stratfordcity).*

bar at the Theatre Royal (*see right*), which has free live entertainment every night of the week. If you want a late drink, be aware that the Railway Tavern in Stratford has the borough's only late licence. Drinkers who like to know exactly what they're getting head for the Fox chain bars in Stratford and at ExCeL, or the Golden Grove, part of the Wetherspoon's empire.

Balans *Westfield Stratford City, E20 1ET (8555 5478, www.balans.co.uk)*
Fox ExCeL *Warehouse K, 2 Western Gateway, E16 1DR (7473 2288, www.foxbars.com).*
Fox Stratford *108-110 The Grove, E15 1NS (8221 0563, www.foxbars.com)*
Golden Grove *146-148 The Grove, E15 1NS (8519 0750, www.jdwetherspoon.co.uk).*
King Edward VII *47 Broadway, E15 4BQ (8534 2313, www.kingeddie.co.uk).*
Railway Tavern *131 Angel Lane, E15 1DB (8534 3123, www.railwaytavernhotel.co.uk)*
Tap East *Westfield Stratford City, E20 1ET (8555 4467, http://uk.westfield.com/stratfordcity).*

Shops

Shopping is now all about Westfield Stratford City, which opened in September 2011 and is the largest urban shopping centre in Europe. Anchored by John Lewis and Marks & Spencer, the centre (nearly

Arts & attractions

Cinemas & theatres
Boleyn Cinema *7-11 Barking Road, E6 1PW (8471 4884, www.boleyncinema.com).*
Brick Lane Music Hall *443 North Woolwich Road, E16 2DA (7511 6655, www.bricklane musichall.co.uk).*
Stratford Circus *Theatre Square, E15 1BX (0844 357 2625, www.stratford-circus.com)*
Stratford East Picturehouse *Theatre Square, E15 1BX (8555 3366, bookings 0871 902 5740, www.picturehouses.co.uk).*
Theatre Royal Stratford East *Gerry Raffles Square, E15 1BN (8534 0310, www.stratford east.com).*
Vue Stratford *Westfield Stratford City, E20 1ET (0871 224 0240, www.myvue.com). One of the largest all-digital cinemas in Europe, with 17 screens.*

Other attractions
All Star Lanes *Westfield Stratford City, E20 1ET (3167 2434, www.allstarlanes.co.uk). Bowling alley.*
Discover *383-387 High Street, E15 4QZ (8536 5555, www.discover.org.uk). The UK's first story centre for children.*
ExCeL Exhibition Centre *1 Western Gateway, Royal Victoria Dock, E16 1XL*

(7069 5000, www.excel-london.co.uk). Trade fairs, conferences, sporting events and concerts; during the 2012 Games, this will be the busiest venue outside the Olympic Park, hosting seven Olympic and six Paralympic sports.
Newham City Farm *Stansfield Road, E6 5LT (7474 4960).*

Sport & fitness

By 2013, Newham will have some of the best sporting facilities in the world: the Zaha Hadid-designed Aquatics Centre, the VeloPark, with a BMX and road-riding circuit supplementing the beautiful Velodrome; and the Olympic Stadium itself, still thought likely to become the new home of West Ham football club, albeit now as a long lease rather than outright purchase. However, the four public centres – led by East Ham Leisure Centre and all run by Greenwich Leisure – will continue to see heavy use. Also popular are the various watersports centres in the old docks.

Gyms & leisure centres

Atherton Leisure Centre *189 Romford Road, E15 4JF (8536 5500, www.gll.org).*
Balaam Leisure Centre *Balaam Street, E13 8AQ (7476 5274, www.gll.org).*
East Ham Leisure Centre *324 Barking Road, E6 2RT (8548 5850, www.gll.org).*
Newham Leisure Centre *281 Prince Regent Lane, E13 8SD (7511 4477, www.gll.org).*
Peacock Gymnasium *Peacock House, Caxton Street North, E16 1JL (7476 8427, www.peacockgym.com). Private.*

Other facilities

Docklands Equestrian Centre *2 Claps Gate Lane, E6 6JF (7511 3917, www.newham ridingschool.com). Riding lessons for all ages.*
London Regatta Centre *Dockside Road, E16 2QT (7511 2211, www.london-regatta-centre.org.uk). Training facilities for rowing clubs, a fully equipped gym and boat hire.*
Royal Victoria Dock Watersports Centre *Gate 5, Tidal Basin Road, off Silvertown Way, E16 1AF (7511 2342, www.royaldockstrust. org.uk). The RVDWC offers canoeing and sailing lessons, for individuals and groups.*

Spectator sports

West Ham United FC *Boleyn Ground, Green Street, E13 9AZ (0871 222 2700, www.whufc.com).*

Schools

Primary

There are 62 state primary schools in Newham, including ten church schools. There are also six independent primaries, including three Muslim schools. See www.newham.gov.uk, www.edubase. gov.uk and www.ofsted.gov.uk for information.

Secondary

Brampton Manor School *Roman Road, E6 3SQ (7540 0500, www.bramptonmanor. newham.sch.uk).*
Cumberland School *Oban Close, E13 8SJ (7474 0231, www.cumberland.org.uk).*
Eastlea Community School *Pretoria Road, E16 4NP (7540 0400, www.eastlea.newham. sch.uk).*
Forest Gate Community School *Forest Street, E7 0HR (8534 8666, www.forestgate. newham.sch.uk).*
Kingsford Community School *Kingsford Way, E6 5JG (7476 4700, www.kingsford school.com).*

TRANSPORT

Tube stations *Central* Stratford; *District, Hammersmith & City* West Ham, Plaistow, Upton Park, East Ham; *Jubilee* Stratford, West Ham, Canning Town; *DLR* Pudding Mill Lane (closed to the public for the duration of the Games), Stratford; Stratford International, Stratford High Street, Abbey Road, West Ham, Star Lane, Canning Town, Royal Victoria, Custom House, Prince Regent, Royal Albert, Beckton Park, Cyprus, Gallions Reach, Beckton; West Silvertown, Pontoon Dock; London City Airport, King George V
Rail stations *c2c* West Ham; *Greater Anglia* Stratford, Maryland, Forest Gate, Manor Park; *London Overground* Stratford; Wanstead Park, Woodgrange Park; *Southeastern (Javelin)* Stratford International
Main bus routes *into central London* 25, 115; *night buses* N8, N15; *24-hour buses* 25
River services Woolwich Ferry
Airports London City Airport
Development plans Emirates Air Line, a cable-car system crossing the Thames from the O2 Arena to the ExCeL Centre at the Royal Docks, should be finished by summer 2012

Langdon School *Sussex Road, E6 2PS*
(8471 2411, www.langdon.newham.sch.uk).
Lister Community School *St Mary's Road,*
E13 9AE (8471 3311, www.lister.newham.
sch.uk).
Little Ilford School *Browning Road, E12 6ET*
(8478 8024, www.littleilford.newham.sch.uk).
Newham College of Further Education
High Street South, E6 6ER (8257 4000,
www.newham.ac.uk).
Newham Sixth Form College *Prince Regent*
Lane, E13 8SG (7473 4110, www.newvic.ac.uk).
Plashet School *Plashet Grove, E6 1DG (8471*
2418, www.plashet.newham.sch.uk). Girls only.
Rokeby School *Barking Road, E16 4DD*
(7540 5620, www.rokeby.newham.sch.uk).
Boys only.
Royal Docks Community School *Prince*
Regent Lane, E16 3HS (7540 2700,
www.royaldocks.newham.sch.uk).
St Angela's Ursuline School *St George's*
Road, E7 8HU (8472 6022, www.stangelas-
ursuline.co.uk). Girls only; mixed sixth form.
St Bonaventure's RC School *Boleyn Road,*
E7 9QD (8472 3844, www.stbons.org). Boys only;
mixed sixth form.
Sarah Bonnell School *Deanery Road, E15*
4LP (8534 6791, www.sarahbonnellonline.co.uk).
Girls only.
Stratford School *Upton Lane, E7 9PR*
(8471 2415, www.stratford.newham.sch.uk).

Property

WHAT THE AGENTS SAY:

'After the Olympics, I am expecting both rental
and sales prices to drop considerably, as supply
exceeds demand. But the rejuvenation of the
whole area, including having the new Westfield
development, will, I hope, ensure that prices fall
back to a higher rate than they were before.'
Rashad Cheema, Spencers Property Services,
Forest Gate

Average property prices
Detached *£287,417*
Semi-detached *£250,048*
Terraced *£221,582*
Flat *£266,645*

Local estate agents
Charles Living & Son *14-16 Romford Road,*
E15 4BZ (8534 1163, www.charlesliving.com).
Marvel Estates *367 Katherine Road, E7 8LT*
(8471 0845, www.marvelestates.com).

RECYCLING

**Household waste recycled &
composted** 19%
Nearest recycling centre Jenkins Lane
Reuse & Recycling Centre, Jenkins
Lane, Barking, IG11 0AD (0800 389
9918)
Other recycling services green waste
collection; home composting; collection
of white goods, electrical goods,
furniture and other household items
Council contact Recycling Team,
Central Depot, Folkestone Road, E6
6BX (8430 2000)

McDowalls *54-56 Barking Road, E6 3BP*
(8472 4422, www.mcdowalls.com).
Samuel King *110A Barking Road, E16 1EN*
(7474 6000, www.samuelking.co.uk).
Spencers Property Services *70 Woodgrange*
Road, E7 0EN (8555 5666, www.spencers
property.co.uk).

Other information

Council
London Borough of Newham Council
Newham Town Hall, Barking Road, E6 2RP
(8430 2000, www.newham.gov.uk).

Legal services
Newham CAB *Custom House, 71A Coolfin Road,*
E16 3AP (7540 4941, www.adviceguide.org.uk).

Local information
www.newham.gov.uk/aboutnewham/
newhammag.htm.
www.newhamrecorder.co.uk.

Open spaces & allotments
Council allotments *Parks Services, 1000*
Dockside Road, E16 2QU (8430 2000).
Open spaces *www.newham.gov.uk/parks;*
www.thamesbarrierpark.org.uk.

Redbridge

Between the 'gritty' East End and the hair-gel antics of *The Only Way Is Essex*, you're in the suburbs here: which, when it means green acres, good schools and plenty of space for families, doesn't seems a bad thing at all.

Neighbourhoods

Wanstead

The Green Man roundabout separates Leytonstone (in the borough of Waltham Forest) from Wanstead. It also marks a distinct change in mentality. Where the former remains urban in appearance and attitude, the latter is more typically suburban. It's leafier, visibly prosperous and boasts a wealth of clubs and societies that reflect a life independent of the capital – even though a daily commute on the Central line is the reality for most residents.

The actual county boundary may be a couple of miles further out, but this stretch of E11 is where London fringes into Essex. The result is the occasional lairy mansion and 'East End made good' mentality more commonly found in the so-called 'golden triangle' of Chigwell, Buckhurst Hill and Loughton. However, since Wanstead is popular with City execs, business folk and professional families, it also means there's Saturday socialising in the stylish delis and cafés along the attractive High Street.

Central Wanstead and the Aldersbrook Estate, which is surrounded by historic Wanstead Park (buy a guidebook from the tea stall here for fascinating historical insights) and the vast playing fields of Wanstead Flats, consist predominantly of large, classic late Victorian terraced houses. Most are occupied by families keen to maintain Wanstead's strong community feel; there are active churches, residents' associations and societies. Elsewhere, 18th-century merchants' houses near Snaresbrook Crown Court and a plethora of stylish but pricey blocks of flats reflect the other extremes of the property market.

When the M11-A12 link road was tunnelled through the area in the early

Local landmark the George in **Wanstead**.

Highs & Lows

▲ **Seat of learning** Redbridge's state primary and secondary schools are among the best in the country, making the borough popular with young families.
Wide open spaces Wanstead Park has a fascinating history, Epping Forest is east London's traditional green lung and Woodford Green contains some magnificent trees.

The only way? TOWIE has only intensified a divide in Redbridge: hair-gelled with WAG versus smug about owning a conservation area home.
Brave new world Can 'match funding' meet the £4.6 million required for Roding Valley flood protection regeneration of Barkingside, and
▼ an ambitious new town square?

1990s, with protesters gaining national attention by creating the 'independent republic of Wanstonia', many feared that Wanstead's character would be destroyed. The road, always jammed at the Redbridge roundabout, still arouses fierce passion, but Wanstead has managed to retain the feel of a small town within reach of, but at arm's length from, London.

South Woodford

The reality of life in E18 is rather confused. Its appeal, particularly for well-heeled young City workers, is obvious: a vibrant bar and restaurant scene, a large branch of Waitrose, plus easy access both to London for work and the M11 to put the latest four-wheeled status symbol through its paces. For older and more established South Woodfordians, however, a preponderance of new glass and chrome is damaging what has been a smart but understated residential area since the 19th century.

At one end of E18 is the Drive: the local millionaires' row of 1930s mansions. At the other, London becomes Essex at Woodford Green. In between are streets of large Victorian and Edwardian properties radiating out from the shopping centre in George Lane. The area is popular with families thanks to the good local schools, both state and private. The Odeon, the only

mainstream cinema for miles around, keeps teenagers happy when they're not getting kicked out of the George pub next door.

One downside of South Woodford is the inescapable presence of the North Circular Road. Its six lanes lie in a deep cutting, with the High Road crossing over on a bridge, whose promised public art installation is unlikely to do much to prettify its concrete span – or the vista for residents of the adjacent housing estate. Unlike in next-door Wanstead, where the A12 goes underground through the central town area, the planners of an earlier generation paid less heed to the physical and psychological damage caused by constant heavy traffic.

Woodford Green

As the name implies, Epping Forest is all around you in Woodford Green. Surrounded by ponds and magnificent chestnut trees is the green itself, on which the local cricket club has played since 1735. Entrusted to the care of the City of London by an Act of Parliament in 1878, the forest's protected status has helped to limit development and retain the area's verdant feel. There are few modern blocks of flats, while the large, detached houses in the Woodford Wells neighbourhood, off Monkham's Lane, are extremely desirable.

Sir Winston Churchill was the local MP for 40 years, and his presence is still felt, notably in the famous statue outside Hurst House, the area's grandest residence. Another prime minister, Clement Attlee, also lived here – as did suffragette campaigner Sylvia Pankhurst. Compared to the bustling building site that is South Woodford, Woodford Green is working hard to stay in touch with its history.

Restaurants & cafés

In Wanstead, 2011 was a brutal year for old favourites: first, Hadley House shut down, probably to become an Italian; then, Applebee's became the Green, which closed to become an Indian (so now the selection of Indian restaurants outweighs those for any other type of food). However, Nam An is still serving high-quality Vietnamese food, and a branch of Robins Pie & Mash has opened to satisfy the retro proletariat.

The area does nicely for upmarket food stores and cafés. Nice Croissant started

Redbridge

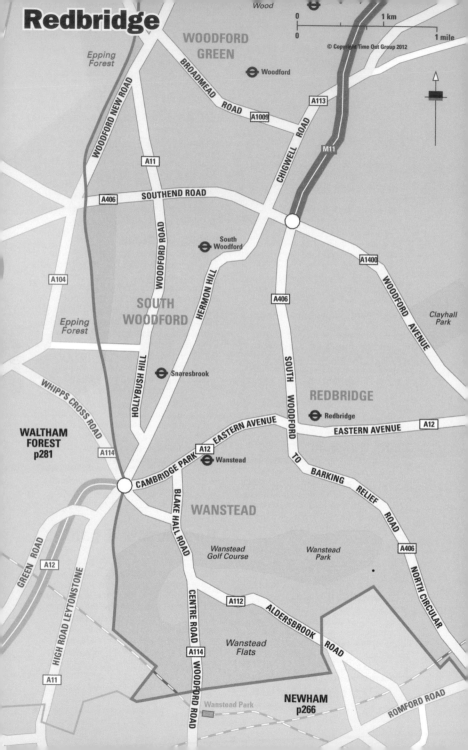

the trend, but both Italian deli Olive Branch and, the pick of the lot, café/deli the Larder, are now well established.

The South Woodford equivalent is the 1950s-styled Soul Stop Café, while good-value fish restaurant Ark offers more substantial fare. You can also check out the fish and chips at George's, though the Greek specialities are the real attraction. You'll need to travel further afield to find the best ethnic options: Curry Special (North Indian) in Newbury Park and Mandarin Palace (Chinese) by the Gants Hill roundabout.

If you've got kids to entertain, don't miss Pizzeria Bel-Sit in Woodford Green. Every inch of wall and ceiling is crammed with signed football shirts, balls and photos.

Ark *142 Hermon Hill, E18 1QH (8989 5345, www.arkfishrestaurant.co.uk).*
Curry Special *2 Greengate Parade, Horns Road, IG2 6BE (8518 3005, www.curryspecial. co.uk).*
George's Fish & Souvlaki Bar *164 George Lane, E18 1AY (8989 3970, www.georgesfish bar.co.uk).*
Larder *30 High Street, E11 2AA (8989 7181).*
Mandarin Palace *559-561 Cranbrook Road, IG2 6JZ (8550 7661).*
Nam An *157 High Street, E11 2RL (8532 2845).*
Nice Croissant *119A High Street, E11 2RL (8530 1129, www.nicecroissant.co.uk).*
Olive Branch *141 High Street, E11 2RL (8530 7500).*
Pizzeria Bel-Sit *439 High Road, IG8 0XF (8504 1164).*
Robins Pie & Mash *14 High Street, E11 2AJ (8989 1988, www.robinspieandmash.com).*
Soul Stop Café *154 George Lane, E18 1AY (8989 1849).*

Bars & pubs

The watering holes along Wanstead's High Street and South Woodford's George Lane attract a young and sometimes brash clientele – so don't turn up at the Cuckfield and Bar Room Bar in E11, or Lizard Lounge and Switch in E18, for a quiet glass of pinot. After-hours, nightclub Funky Mojoe soaks up the minor celebs and those that love them (*TOWIE* filmed here in 2011), with the longer-established Faces catering to a similar clientele in Gants Hill.

More low-key drinking options are found away from the main drag. Fine local pubs include the Nightingale in Wanstead and the Cricketers and the Travellers Friend, both in Woodford Green.

Bar Room Bar *33-34 High Street, E11 2AA (8989 0552, www.barroombar.com).*
Cricketers *299-301 High Road, IG8 9HQ (8504 2734).*
Cuckfield *31 High Street, E11 2AA (8532 2431, www.thecuckfieldwanstead.co.uk).*
Faces *458-462 Cranbrook Road, IG2 6LE (8554 8899, www.facesnightclub.co.uk).*
Funky Mojoe *159-161 High Road, E18 2PA (8506 9703, www.funkymojoe.co.uk).*
Lizard Lounge *186 George Lane, E18 2AY (8989 3991, www.lizardlounge.biz).*
Nightingale *51 Nightingale Lane, E11 2EY (8530 4540).*
Switch *77-81 George Lane, E18 1JJ (8530 5803, www.switchbarlounge.com).*
Travellers Friend *496-498 High Road, IG8 0PN (8504 2435).*

STATISTICS

BOROUGH MAKE-UP
Population 257,600
Ethnic origins
　White 60.1%
　Mixed 3.5%
　Asian or Asian British 23.4%
　Black or Black British 10.4%
　Chinese or other 2.6%
Students 9.2%
Retirees 11.3%

HOUSING STOCK
Borough size (hectares) 5,645
Population density per hectare 45.6
No. of households 92,288
Houses (detached, semi-detached or terraced) 73%
Flats (converted or purpose-built) 27%

CRIME PER 1,000 OF POPULATION
Burglary 10
Robbery 3
Theft of vehicle 5
Theft from vehicle 10
Violence against the person 16
Sexual offences 1

MPs
Chingford & Woodford Green Iain Duncan Smith (Conservative); *Leyton & Wanstead* John Cryer (Labour)

Shops

Ilford is the main destination for Redbridge residents, with the recently reorganised Exchange Mall offering most major names, including a big new Next and medium-sized Marks & Spencer.

Wanstead offers a more low-key experience, with the emphasis on high-end goods. Its villagey ambience is enhanced by an excellent butcher, AG Dennis, and greengrocer, Harvey's (both of which have won awards from residents' association the Wanstead Society for high quality and friendly service). Up the road, South Woodford has a cute old-fashioned sweet shop (Hardys) and branches of Sainsbury's, Waitrose and M&S.

Contemporary style comes in the form of Wanstead's Onedeko, a super-slick lifestyle store that also has a branch in Spitalfields. There's also a home furnishings branch of Laura Ashley in South Woodford. You'll find stylish men's clothes at Santa Fe in Wanstead, though anyone getting ready for a night out may prefer the clobber at brilliant menswear store Jun-Qi in Woodford Green. South Woodford's Source has independent fashion and accessories. To top off your new look, head to Zoology hair salon.

If lugging everything home leaves more than your wallet screaming for mercy, visit the Back Pain Centre, run by Terry Chimes – the Clash's original drummer, he's been a registered chiropractor since 1994.

AG Dennis *3 Clock House Parade, High Street, E11 2AG (8989 2691).*
Back Pain Centre *50 Chigwell Road, E18 1LS (8989 3330, www.chimes-chiropractic.co.uk).*
Exchange Mall *High Road, IG1 1RS (8553 3000, www.exchangeilford.com).*
Hardys Original Sweet Shop *166 George Lane, E18 1AY (8532 2762).*
Harvey's *6 Clock House Parade, High Street, E11 2AG (8989 6369).*
Jun-Qi *172 High Road, IG8 9EF (8559 2122).*
Laura Ashley *12-14 Electric Parade, George Lane, E18 2LY (0871 223 1468, www.lauraashley.com).*
Onedeko *151 High Street, E11 2RL (8989 3377, www.onedeko.co.uk).*
Santa Fe *119 High Road, E11 2RL (8518 8922, www.santafe-menswear.co.uk).*
Source *227 High Road, E18 2PB (8505 6697, www.sourcelifestyle.com).*
Zoology *145 High Street, E11 2RL (8530 3005, www.zoology-hair.com).*

Arts & attractions

Cinemas & theatres

Cineworld Ilford *Clements Road, IG1 1BP (0871 200 2000, www.cineworld.co.uk).*
Kenneth More Theatre *Oakfield Road, IG1 1BT (8553 4466, www.kmtheatre.co.uk).*
Odeon South Woodford *60-64 High Road, E18 2QL (0871 224 4007, www.odeon.co.uk).*

Galleries & museums

Redbridge Museum *Central Library, Clements Road, IG1 1EA (8708 2317, www.redbridge. gov.uk). Local history museum; being refurbished, along with the library, in 2012.*

Other attractions

Valentines Mansion & Gardens *Emerson Road, IG1 4XA (8708 8100, www.valentines*

Locals' Tips

The spine of Redbridge is green – amble up the Roding River Valley when city living gets too much.

Designed in the late 1950s by Frederick Gibberd, Fullwell Cross Library is an extraordinary building. Circular but spiky, with a lofty roof and church-like arched windows, it is exemplary 20th-century modernist architecture.

The Larder café/deli in Wanstead is a must for local foodies, with a great array of savouries and cakes at the weekend. It's been such a success, owner James opened a second branch in Bethnal Green in 2011.

WAG wannabes will find plenty of footballers living in the borough. Funky Mojoes nightclub and Pizzeria Bel-Sit in Woodford Green are two of their haunts.

---

mansion.com, www.valentines.org.uk).
A 17th-century mansion in Valentines Park, with picturesque gardens.
Woodford Festival *ww.woodfordfestival. org.uk. Community knees-up.*

Sport & fitness

This segment of east London suburbia plays host to countless sports clubs amid its green acres. The charitable trust-run Redbridge Sports & Leisure Centre is superb – among the very best fitness clubs in the capital. Physicals is the pick of the private clubs, although the chains are establishing an ever-stronger presence. In contrast, public-sector provision is poor: just one sports centre (Wanstead) and one swimming pool (Fullwell Cross), although Ashton Playing Fields in Woodford Green does have a gym. On the plus side, Fullwell Cross now has a spa (www.thespalondon andessex.co.uk).

Gyms & leisure centres

David Lloyd *Roding Lane, IG9 6BJ (8559 8466, www.davidlloydleisure.co.uk). Private.*
Fitness First *261-275 High Road, IG1 1NJ (8514 7666, www.fitnessfirst.co.uk). Private.*

Fullwell Cross Leisure Centre *High Street, IG6 2EA (8550 2366, www.vision-rcl.org.uk).*
Physicals *327 High Road, IG8 9HQ (8505 4914, www.physicalsfitness.co.uk). Private.*
Redbridge Sports & Leisure Centre *Forest Road, IG6 3HD (8498 1000, www.rslonline.co.uk). Private.*
Wanstead Leisure Centre *Redbridge Lane West, E11 2JZ (8989 1172, www.vision-rcl. org.uk).*

Other facilities

Ashton Playing Fields *598 Chigwell Road, IG8 8AA (8559 0486, www.vision-rcl.org.uk). Athletics track-and-field facilities, plus a full-size AstroTurf football pitch and grass pitches.*
Fairlop Waters *Forest Road, Barkingside, IG6 3HN (8500 9911, www.vision-rcl.org.uk). A driving range, nine- and 18-hole golf courses, fishing and various watersports.*
Redbridge Cycling Centre *Forest Road, Hainault, Ilford, IG6 3HP (8500 9359, www.redbridgecyclingcentre.co.uk). Road cycling circuit (also mountain biking and BMX) known as Hog Hill.*
Wanstead Golf Course *Overton Drive, E11 2LW (8989 3938/0604, www.wansteadgolf. org.uk). Private.*

Schools

Primary

There are 51 state primary schools in Redbridge, including seven church schools and two Jewish schools. There are also 16 independent primaries, including three faith schools. See www.redbridge. gov.uk, www.ofsted.gov.uk and www.edubase. gov.uk for more information.

Secondary

Bancroft's School *High Road, Woodford Green, IG8 0RF (8505 4821, www.bancrofts.org). Private.*
Beal High School *Woodford Bridge Road, IG4 5LP (8551 4954, www.bealhighschool.org.uk).*
Caterham High School *Caterham Avenue, IG5 0QW (8551 4321, www.ecaterham.net).*
Chadwell Heath Academy *Christie Gardens, RM6 4RS (8252 5151, www.chadwellacademy. org.uk).*
Chigwell School *High Road, IG7 6QF (8501 5700, www.chigwell-school.org). Private.*
Forest Academy *Harbourer Road, IG6 3TN (8500 4266, www.theforestacademy.org).*
Forest School *2 College Place, E17 3PY (boys 8520 1744; girls 8521 7477, www.forest.org.uk). Private.*

COUNCIL TAX

A	up to £40,000	£936.90
B	£40,001-£52,000	£1,093.05
C	£52,001-£68,000	£1,249.20
D	£68,001-£88,000	£1,405.35
E	£88,001-£120,000	£1,717.65
F	£120,001-£160,000	£2,029.95
G	£160,001-£320,000	£2,342.25
H	over £320,000	£2,810.70

Ilford County High School for Boys *Fremantle Road, IG6 2JB (8551 6496, www.ichs.org.uk). Boys only.*
Isaac Newton Academy *High Road, Ilford, IG1 1UE (www.isaacnewtonacademy.org). Opens in September 2012.*
King Solomon High School *Forest Road, IG6 3HB (8498 1300, www.kshsonline.com). Jewish.*
Loxford School of Science & Technology *Loxford Lane, IG1 2UT (8514 4666, www.loxford.net).*
Mayfield School *Pedley Road, RM8 1XE (8590 5211, www.mayfieldschool.net).*
Oaks Park High School *45-65 Oaks Lane, IG2 7PQ (8590 2245, www.oakspark.co.uk).*
Palmer Catholic Academy *Aldborough Road South, IG3 8EU (8590 3808, www.canon palmer.redbridge.sch.uk). Roman Catholic.*
Seven Kings High School *Ley Street, IG2 7BT (8554 8935, www.skhs.net).*
Trinity Catholic High School *Mornington Road, IG8 0TP (8504 3419, http://fc.tchs.uk.net). Roman Catholic.*
Ursuline Academy Ilford *Morland Road, IG1 4JU (8554 1995, www.ilfordursuline-high. org.uk). Roman Catholic; girls only.*
Valentines High School *Cranbrook Road, IG2 6HX (8554 3608, www.valentines-sch.org.uk).*
Wanstead High School *Redbridge Lane West, E11 2JZ (8989 2791, www.wansteadhigh.co.uk).*
Woodbridge High School *St Barnabas Road, IG8 7DQ (8504 9618, www.woodbridgehigh. co.uk).*
Woodford County High School for Girls *High Road, IG8 9LA (8504 0611, www.woodford. redbridge.sch.uk). Girls only.*

Property

WHAT THE AGENTS SAY:

'Woodford Green is a popular suburb for people working in London, with fantastic access into town via the Central line and by road. It's also ideal for families, with Epping Forest on the doorstep and good local schools, both private and public. There's a great selection of restaurants too; the Bel-Sit Italian is particularly well liked. South Woodford and Wanstead are close by, offering coffeeshops, bars and pubs, so they're a big draw for the younger generation.'
Adrian Sinclair, Spencers Property Services, Woodford Green

Average property prices
Detached £590,569
Semi-detached £355,212
Terraced £285,197
Flat £234,988

Local estate agents
Churchill Estates *32 High Street, E11 2RJ (8989 0011, www.churchill-estates.co.uk).*
Homes & Co *131 High Road, E18 2PA (8504 8844, www.homesandco.com).*
Knightons *35 The Broadway, IG8 0HQ (8559 2288, www.knightons.co.uk).*
Sandra Davidson *www.sandradavidson.com; 2 offices in the borough (Redbridge 8551 0211, Seven Kings 8597 7372).*
Spencers Property Services *www.spencersproperty.co.uk; 2 offices in the borough (Woodford Green 8559 2110, Ilford 8518 5411).*

Other information

Council
Redbridge Council Town Hall *128-142 High Road, IG1 1DD (8554 5000, www.redbridge.gov.uk).*

Legal services
Loughton CAB *St Mary's Parish Centre, High Road, IG10 1BB (8502 0031, www.citizensadvice.org.uk).*
Redbridge CAB *2nd floor, Broadway Chambers, 1 Cranbrook Road, IG1 4DU (8514 5700, www.citizensadvice.org.uk).*

Local information
www.guardian-series.co.uk.
www.wansteadium.com.

Open spaces & allotments
Council allotments *8th floor, Lynton House, 255-259 High Road, IG1 1NY (8708 3091, www.redbridge.gov.uk).*
Open spaces *www.redbridge.gov.uk; www.cityoflondon.gov.uk (Epping Forest).*

Waltham Forest

One of the six Olympic boroughs, Waltham Forest stands to gain little by way of infrastructure improvements from the Games – apart from swanky new sports facilities at Eton Manor. Perhaps a trickle-down effect and the arrival of more affluent home-buyers priced out of central London can begin to transform remaining areas of endemic neglect in this mainly residential borough.

Neighbourhoods

Walthamstow

Once famous only for a greyhound track and a boy band, Walthamstow is definitely moving upmarket. Although swathes of the area are blighted by grime and industrial eyesores, notably on the North Circular Road, Lea Bridge Road and Forest Road, there remains at Walthamstow's heart a thriving street market – a rarity, indeed, in these days of chain-bland megamalls and all-powerful supermarkets. Reckoned to be the longest in Europe, the market sprawls along the mainly pedestrianised High Street. Open five days a week, it's a bustling and characterful experience, and a truly multicultural affair – there are gor-blimey East Enders selling bowls of bananas for a quid, alongside Tamil, Chinese, east European and Caribbean stallholders, and a multitude of ethnic cafés. It's a great place for high quality English fruit and veg, but you can also purchase cheap clothing, cosmetics and every household item you can think of. On Sunday mornings, organic and free-range produce comes to the fore at the farmers' market in the Town Square.

E17's other point of interest, certainly for middle-class house buyers, is Walthamstow Village. Around the attractively overgrown churchyard of St Mary's huddles a handful of quiet streets with cute cottages; there are decent restaurants and pubs on Orford Road, a rumbling train line and the excellent Vestry House Museum. Residents are proud of the neighbourhood's conservation status and certainly attempt to foster a community spirit; there's an active residents' association and plenty of locally minded groups and gatherings.

Walthamstow was assessed in the Domesday Book at £28 in gold – not bad for a farming village of just 82 people. More recently, first-time buyers have recognised there's value to be had in these parts; while the days when you could buy a four-bedroom house in Walthamstow for the price of a one-bed flat in Stoke Newington have long gone, it is still one of London's more affordable neighbourhoods. Warnings that prices would rocket across the borough once Olympic regeneration work began in nearby Stratford have yet to be realised, though locals insist it's only a matter of time. (There's another connection between E17 and E15: the fictional Walford of *EastEnders* is a combination of 'Wal' from Walthamstow and 'ford' from Stratford.)

Away from the centre, dark-brick terraces and housing estates predominate, home to a mix of young professionals and families. A particular feature are the terraces of

Highs & Lows

▲ **Affordable housing** Although prices are rising, there's still plenty of choice for first-timers in Leytonstone and Walthamstow.
Green scene The southernmost reaches of Epping Forest comprise the eastern boundary of Waltham Forest, the Lea Valley its western edge – good news for both walkers and bikers.

▼ **Dismal shopping** Apart from gentrifying Walthamstow, this is not a borough for retail hounds keen on sniffing out interesting independents.
Poverty Certain wards in Leyton and south Chingford are among the most deprived in Britain.

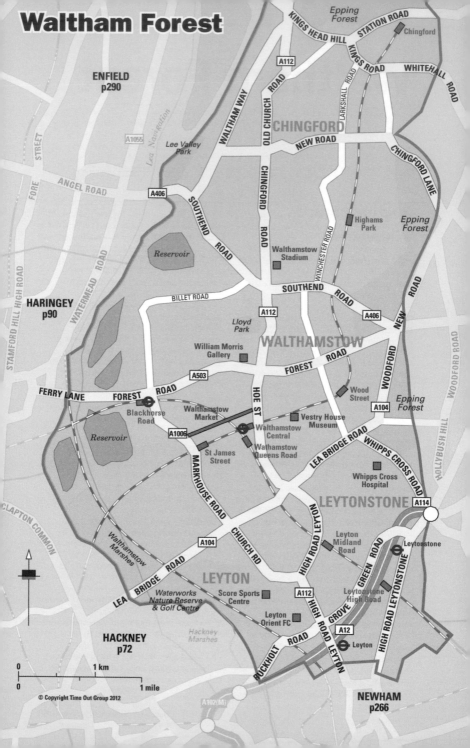

A street of much sought-after **Warner maisonettes**.

purpose-built Warner maisonettes. More than 5,000 were built from the 1880s to the 1930s, a remarkable enterprise by a local family to provide housing for the masses. These one- and two-bedroom properties are popular with first-time buyers, though few are still painted in the original colours of green and cream.

Just off the North Circular, near the sports grounds of Wadham Lodge, is Walthamstow Stadium, once Britain's most famous greyhound racing venue, which closed in 2008. Plans to turn the art deco structure into flats have met with widespread opposition. A few minutes' walk away is pleasant Lloyd Park. The park surrounds the childhood home of the late Victorian designer and socialist William Morris; the attractive gallery here has a collection of his Arts and Crafts fabrics and wallpapers. Ongoing redevelopment (scheduled for completion in summer 2012) will bring new displays and a tea room to the gallery, and major changes to the park, including a new café, toilets and outdoor performance space, better lighting and refurbished sports facilities.

Walthamstow's strong community vibe is evident in numerous local arts events, including September's E17 Art Trail (www.e17arttrail.co.uk). One drawback is the lack of a cinema in the borough; the campaign to revitalise the art deco picture house (owned by an evangelical Christian group since 2003 and currently empty) has made little progress. The council has rejected plans to transform it into a church; the group has refused to sell it to anyone else. Meanwhile, there's a welcome alternative in the shape of Screen 17, run by local film enthusiasts.

Transport connections are excellent: Walthamstow is linked to central London by the Victoria line and no fewer than five rail stations, plus a plethora of buses. Nevertheless, the commute, on the tube in particular, can be a crowded affair.

Leyton

Leyton is also well served for transport, with the Central line whisking commuters to the heart of the City, the A12 running east to Essex and the A102 speeding traffic south across the Thames. However, these very visible rail and road links leave the area feeling less of a destination and more like somewhere people merely pass through. Development in E10 remains piecemeal and nondescript, despite part of it edging into the northernmost corner of the Olympic Park. Proposals for a rail link between Chingford and Stratford, which would involve reopening Lea Bridge station, may yet help improve shopping and stimulate the local economy.

The controversial redevelopment of Leyton Orient's Matchroom Stadium – blocks of flats were built on the corners of the new stands a few years ago – has been overshadowed by what's happening to the south, with sports facilities at Eton Manor a concrete post-Games improvement for Leyton. Until Eton Manor opens to the public, the jewel in Leyton's crown remains the Score centre, tucked away behind the football ground and offering a huge indoor sports hall, high-quality outdoor pitch, a nursery, a primary care centre and the local development trust O-Regen.

For now, Leyton remains more inner-city than suburban. There are some pleasant terraces, and the Coronation Gardens beside the Stadium are still charming after their restoration to Edwardian glory a few years ago, but there are almost as many industrial zones and concrete estates. Shopping options are little better. Along the High Road, you'll find a very limited selection:

there's a run-of-the-mill Tesco at one end and Asda at the other, anchoring the Leyton Mills shopping mall, with its familiar and resolutely downmarket brands.

The western boundary of Walthamstow and Leyton is the Lee Valley Park, a very welcome green space that sprawls north and south along the River Lea (confusingly, both Lea and Lee are acceptable spellings for the waterway). In addition, there's a riding school, an ice rink and marina, and walking trails through the miles of meadows on the Walthamstow Marshes. Also here is the Waterworks Nature Reserve and Golf Centre, on what used to be the Middlesex Filter Beds.

Leytonstone

New-build flats on the High Road confirm Leytonstone's reputation as a target for teachers, nurses and local authority personnel, while the 20-minute Central line journey to Liverpool Street is a strong lure for City workers. Once settled, these newcomers often find they don't want to leave; Leytonstone is scruffy but generally safe, with a surprisingly strong sense of community that shows itself in an annual arts festival (8555 6623 , www.leytonstone festival.org.uk) and arts trail (www. leytonstoneartstrail.org), both in July.

The district is a product of mid 19th-century railway expansion, and the terraces that sprang up as a result are now occupied by middle-class British and Asian families. Upper Leytonstone has a Hindu temple, Bushwood claims the mosque, while the vicar of St John's by the junction of Church Lane and the High Road is a popular figure for his efforts to bring together locals of all faiths and none. There are signs that more youthful residents are beginning to move in: the Red Lion is a hip addition to the old geezer boozers and occasional Essex glitz-trash night spot.

Though first impressions on emerging from the tube station are not very appealing – a handful of independent retailers including Polski Skleps scratching a living alongside bottom-end chain stores and pound shops – E11 greatly benefits from the greenery of Epping Forest and Wanstead Flats, which fringes the popular Bushwood area and straddles the boundary with Redbridge. A boat ride on Hollow Ponds (off Whipps Cross Road) is a popular Sunday afternoon outing. There's even a mooted return for the legendary Leytonstone cows, which until the early 1990s were free to roam and often caused havoc – and hilarity – at the busy Green Man roundabout.

Restaurants & cafés

Walthamstow Village is increasingly a destination for food-lovers. Eat 17 serves excellent, ethically sourced Modern British food and is hugely popular; it's also got a bakery and pizzeria (run out of the adjoining Spar shop), where you can also buy their famed 'bacon jam'. Also on Orford Road are two Italian joints, Trattoria La Ruga and Mondragone (revamped in 2011), and friendly tapas bar Orford Saloon. Further afield, on Forest Road, is the quietly stylish La Cafeteria, while pie and mash shop L Manze on Walthamstow High Street offers a touch of authenticity. Opened in 1929, it's a welcome respite from the otherwise ubiquitous fast-food outlets. Opposite is lively Café Rio, a brilliant little spot with its kitsch, cluttered Americana decor and pavement seating – a boon in summer. Daisy's and newcomer Le Delice are reliable, family-friendly cafés on Hoe Street, while Cinar is an inexpensive Turkish grill restaurant opposite St James's station.

Ye Olde Rose & Crown. See p286.

TRANSPORT

Tube stations *Central* Leyton, Leytonstone; *Victoria* Blackhorse Road, Walthamstow Central
Rail stations *Greater Anglia* St James Street, Walthamstow Central, Wood Street, Highams Park, Chingford; *London Overground* Blackhorse Road, Walthamstow Queens Road, Leyton Midland Road, Leytonstone High Road
Main bus routes *into central London* 48, 55, 56; *night buses* N8, N26, N38, N55, N73

High Road Leyton is a world tour in transient single-room caffs – African, Pakistani, Portuguese and Polish – but the tenor is takeaway or cheap refuelling, not international gourmandism.

In Leytonstone, there are some highlights on the High Road: Petch Sayam, Singburi (both Thai) and Mudra (South Indian). The Eatery (North Indian) on Church Lane is more functional, but popular, not least for its downstairs chillout bar, the Luna Lounge, which hosts gigs, karaoke and occasional screenings.

Café Rio *85 High Street, E17 7DB (www.caferio-london.com).*
La Cafeteria *841 Forest Road, E17 4AT (8527 1926).*
Cinar *18 St James's Street, E17 7PF (8520 2783).*
Daisy's *176 Hoe Street, E17 4QH (8509 8844).*
Le Delice *111 Hoe Street, E17 4QR (8521 0606).*
Eatery *7 Church Lane, E11 1HG (8518 7463).*
Eat 17 *28-30 Orford Road, E17 9NJ (8521 5279, www.eat17.co.uk).*
L Manze *76 Walthamstow High Street, E17 7LD (8520 2855).*
Mondragone *25-27 Orford Road, E17 9NL (8509 1990).*
Mudra *715 High Road Leytonstone, E11 4RD (8539 1700).*
Orford Saloon *32 Orford Road, E17 9NJ (8503 6542).*
Petch Sayam *682 High Road Leytonstone, E11 3AA (8556 6821, www.petchsayamthai restaurant.co.uk).*
Singburi *593 High Road Leytonstone, E11 4PA (8281 4801).*
Trattoria La Ruga *59 Orford Road, E17 9NJ (8520 5008, www.laruga.co.uk).*

Waltham Forest

Bars & pubs

Walthamstow has the best selection of pubs. The Castle gastropub serves its middle-class customers well with its seasonal menu and popular Sunday roasts; we like the open fire and library's worth of books too. On Orford Road, there's the Nag's Head (cats welcome, children less so), which has plenty of seating front and back, and the Village, which is more corporate in feel, but also has a beer garden. On Hoe Street, Ye Olde Rose & Crown is a proper community pub, hosting music, theatre, exhibitions and other events – though it could do with a spruce-up. Near Walthamstow Marshes, the little Coppermill is that rare thing, an old-fashioned local boozer, with Fuller's beers and sport on the telly.

The Birkbeck Tavern is the best pub in Leyton, and home to the terrific What's Cookin' club, which serves regular blues, cajun, country and rock 'n' roll gigs. The handsome William IV has its own microbrewery again, which supplies most of the pub's impressive array of real ales.

In Leytonstone, the focal point of the quiet Browning Road conservation area is the North Star, an excellent traditional boozer that serves food and hosts occasional jazz gigs. The Sir Alfred Hitchcock Hotel (Hitch was born in Leytonstone) recalls a grander age – though the hotel bar's interior is a little unkempt. On the High Road, the Red Lion is a terrific replacement for naughty old Zulu's – with decks, multiple draught ales and slouchy sofas.

Birkbeck Tavern *45 Langthorne Road, E11 4HL (8539 2584, www.whatscookin.co.uk).*
Castle *15 Grosvenor Rise East, E17 9LB (8509 8095, www.thecastlegastropub.co.uk).*
Coppermill *205 Coppermill Lane, E17 7HF (8520 3709).*
Nag's Head *9 Orford Road, E17 9LP (8520 9709, www.thenagshead17.com).*
North Star *24 Browning Road, E11 3AR (no phone).*
Red Lion *640 Leytonstone High Road, E11 3AA (8988 2929, www.theredlionleytonstone.com).*
Sir Alfred Hitchcock Hotel *147 Whipps Cross Road, E11 1NP (8530 3724).*
Village *31 Orford Road, E17 9NL (8521 4398, www.village-walthamstow.com).*
William IV *816 Leyton High Road, E10 6AE (8556 2460, www.williamthefourth.net).*
Ye Olde Rose & Crown *53 Hoe Street, E17 4SA (8509 3880, www.yeolderoseandcrown theatrepub.co.uk)*

Walthamstow Market, which runs for almost a kilometre along the High Street.

Shops

Waltham Forest, sadly, is a shopping desert. Apart from Walthamstow Village and Station Road up in Chingford, specialist stores and attractive independent retailers are few and far between. Most residents head for villagey Wanstead (in Redbridge) instead. Proximity to the North Circular Road at least gives access to IKEA and the major DIY, electrical and home-furnishing superstores, but for a department store or even a Marks & Spencer, it's a trip out of the borough to to Ilford, Romford or, since the arrival of the all-conquering Westfield mall in 2011, Stratford.

Always worth a visit is Walthamstow's epic street market, a teeming strip of some 450 stalls and 300 shops stretching the entire length of the High Street (linking Hoe Street to St James's Street). It's open Tuesday to Saturday; on Sunday, the farmers' market takes over in the Town Square. Some of the shops are true one-offs: the tiny nan bakery near Sainsbury's, for example, where fresh bread is made to order in a traditional oven; and, towards the bottom of the High Street, Eastman Army Camp, which has all kinds of outdoor and camping equipment.

For conventional chain stores, plus Asda and a branch of Waterstones, the Selborne Walk shopping centre at the High Street's top (east) end suffices, while Hoe Street has a continuous line of shops and takeaways running south to High Road Leyton. Davies & Sons, near the Bakers Arms, is the best traditional fishmonger for miles.

In Walthamstow Village, Orford Road offers a great butcher, the East London Sausage Company, and Penny Fielding Beautiful Interiors, which sells homewares, vintage clothes and art – but at a price.

Davies & Sons *494 Hoe Street, E17 9AH (8556 3910).*
East London Sausage Company *57 Orford Road, E17 9NJ (8520 4060).*
Eastman Army Camp *52 High Street, E17 7LD (8521 9266, www.armysurplusuk.net).*
Penny Fielding Beautiful Interiors *34 Orford Road, E17 9NJ (8509 0039, www.penny fielding.com).*
Walthamstow Farmers' Market *Town Square, by Selborne Walk shopping centre, E17 (7833 0338, www.lfm.org.uk).*

Locals' Tips

When the William Morris Gallery reopens in 2012, the new café should make it a perfect stop-off on the way into the park. **Designer-makers are being encouraged to set up stalls in Wood Street Market in Walthamstow – it's a quirky maze of small stalls, artists' workshops and units selling everything from James Bond memorabilia to cake decorations and baby-carrying slings.**
The reopened Red Lion in Leytonstone is a corker, with its cheerfully manned decks, plentiful ales and late-opening at weekends.
To make the most of a sunny Sunday afternoon, take a boat out on Hollow Ponds, off Whipps Cross Road.
The Big Screen, a fixture outside the town hall in Walthamstow Town Square for major sporting events, should come into its own for the 2012 Olympic & Paralympic Games.

Walthamstow Market *High Street, E17 (Street Trading Section 8496 3000).*

Arts & attractions

Cinemas & theatres
Screen 17 *Orford House, 73 Orford Road, E17 9QR (www.screen17.co.uk). 'Walthamstow's Microplex Cinema', with regular film screenings, including plenty for kids.*

Galleries & museums
Stone Space *6 Church Lane, E11 1HG (www.thestonespace.com). Community-run exhibition space.*
Tokarska Gallery *163 Forest Road E17 6HE (8531 5419, www.tokarskagallery.co.uk). Contemporary art gallery opened in 2011.*
Vestry House Museum *Vestry Road, E17 9NH (8496 4391, www.walthamforest.gov.uk). Local history museum.*
William Morris Gallery *Lloyd Park, Forest Road, E17 4PP (8527 3782, www.walthamforest. gov.uk). Closed until July 2012.*

Music venues
Walthamstow Folk Club *07740 612607, www.walthamstowfolk.co.uk. Friendly folk club at Ye Olde Rose & Crown pub.*

Penny Fielding Beautiful Interiors.
See p287.

What's Cookin' *8539 2584, www.whatscookin. co.uk. Birkbeck Tavern hosts cajun, rock and blues.*

Sport & fitness

Waltham Forest's five public centres are managed by Greenwich Leisure and are pleasant and well maintained. The Score complex in Leyton, which offers high-quality facilities for a wide range of sports, will be joined after the Games by Eton Manor, Waltham Forest's little sliver of the Olympic Park. It will have indoor and outdoor tennis courts, pitches for hockey and five-a-side, and a mountain bike trail.

Gyms & leisure centres

Bannatyne's Health & Fitness Club Chingford *2 Morrison Avenue, E4 8SA (8503 2266, www.bannatyne.co.uk). Private.*

Cathall Leisure Centre *Cathall Road, E11 4LA (8539 8343, www.gll.org).*

E4 Fitness & Leisure *14A Hickman Avenue, E4 9JG (8523 5133, www.e4fitnessandleisure. co.uk). Private.*

Fitness First *Unit 6, Leyton Mills Retail Park, Marshall Road, E10 5NH (0844 571 2894, www.fitnessfirst.co.uk). Private.*

Greens Health & Fitness *175 New Road, E4 9EY (8523 7474, www.greensonline.co.uk). Private.*

Kelmscott Leisure Centre *243 Markhouse Road, E17 8RN (8520 7464, www.gll.org).*

Larkswood Leisure Centre *Larkswood Leisure Park, New Road, E4 9EY (8523 8215, www.gll.org).*

Leyton Leisure Lagoon *763 High Road, E10 5AB (8558 8858, www.gll.org).*

Waltham Forest Pool & Track *170 Chingford Road, E17 5AA (8527 5431, www.gll.org).*

Other facilities

Community Pool *Waltham Forest College, 707 Forest Road, E17 4JB (www.collegepool friends.co.uk).*

Lee Valley Ice Centre *Lea Bridge Road, E10 7QL (8533 3154, www.leevalleypark.org.uk).*

Lee Valley Riding Centre *Lea Bridge Road, E10 7QL (8556 2629, www.leevalleypark.org.uk).*

Score *100 Oliver Road, E10 5JY (8539 8474, www.walthamforest.gov.uk, www.o-regen.co.uk/ score.asp).*

Spectator sports

Leyton Orient Football Club *Matchroom Stadium, Brisbane Road, E10 5NF (0871 310 1883, www.leytonorient.com).*

Schools

Primary

There are 52 state primary schools in Waltham Forest, seven of which are church schools. There are also seven independent primaries, including six faith schools and one Montessori school. See www.edubase.gov.uk and www.ofsted.gov.uk for more information.

Secondary

Chingford Foundation School *31 Nevin Drive, E4 7LT (8529 1853, www.chingford- school.co.uk).*

Connaught School for Girls *39 Connaught Road, E11 4AB (8539 3029, www.connaught- school.co.uk). Girls only.*

Frederick Bremer School *Siddeley Road, E17 4EY (8498 3340, www.bremer.org.uk).*

George Mitchell School *192 Vicarage Road, E10 5DX (8539 6198, www.georgemitchell school.co.uk).*

Heathcote School *96 Normanton Park, E4 6ES (8498 5110, www.heathcoteschool.com).*

Highams Park School *34 Handsworth Avenue, E4 9PJ (8527 4051, www.highams park.waltham.sch.uk).*

Holy Family Technology College *34 Shernhall Street, E17 3EA (8520 0482, www.holyfamily.waltham.sch.uk).*

Kelmscott School *245 Markhouse Road, E17
8DN (8521 2115, www.kelmscott.waltham.sch.uk).*
Lammas School *150 Seymour Road, E10 7LX
(8988 5860, www.lammas.waltham.sch.uk).*
Leytonstone School *159 Colworth Road, E11
1JD (8988 7420, www.leytonstoneschool.org).*
Norlington Boys' School *Norlington Road, E10
6JZ (8539 3055, www.norlington.net). Boys only.*
Rushcroft School *57 Rushcroft Road, E4 8SG
(8531 9231, www.rushcroft.waltham.sch.uk).*
Tom Hood School *Terling Close, E11 3NT
(8534 3425).*
Walthamstow Academy *Billet Road, E17
5DP (8527 3750, www.walthamstow-academy.
org).*
Walthamstow Girls' School *60 Church Hill,
E17 9RZ (8509 9446, www.wsfg.waltham.
sch.uk). Girls only.*
Willowfield School *Clifton Avenue, E17 6HL
(8527 4065, www.willowfield-school.net).*

Property

WHAT THE AGENTS SAY:

'Walthamstow Village remains as popular as
ever with first-time buyers. But they are paying a
premium for the mix of Victorian and Edwardian
terraced houses in the area; the restaurants, bars
and shops gives it a villagey feel that people are
willing to pay for. Currently, prices are pretty
stable, and it seems to be a buyer's market.
On the other hand, the rental market across the
borough is going through the roof. People aren't
looking to buy – either they're afraid to commit
or they can't get the finance – so landlords can
pretty much charge any price they like.'
Steve James, Clarke Hillyer, Walthamstow

Average property prices

Detached *£383,811*
Semi-detached *£317,000*
Terraced *£250,127*
Flat *£187,878*

Local estate agents

Alan Harvey *658 High Road, E11 3AA
(8539 9999, www.alanharvey.co.uk).*
Allen Davies & Co *342 High Road, E10 5PW
(8539 2121, www.allendavies.co.uk).*
Central Estate Agents *179 Hoe Street, E17
3AP (8520 0033, www.central-estates.co.uk).*
Clarke Hillyer *163-165 Hoe Street, E17 3AL
(8521 8875, www.clarkehillyer.co.uk).*
Village Estates *54-56 Hoe Street, E17 4PG
(8223 0784, www.villageestates.org.uk).*

Other information

Council

Waltham Forest Council *Town Hall, Forest
Road, E17 4JF (8496 3000, www.waltham
forest.gov.uk).*

Legal services

Waltham Forest CAB *Churchill Business
Centre, 6 Church Hill, E17 3AG (8521 5125).*

Local information

*www.e17foodanddrink.co.uk.
www.guardian-series.co.uk.
www.walthamstownow.org.uk.
www.walthamstowscene.org.uk.
www.walthamstowvillageguide.com.
www.walthamstowvillage.net.*

Open spaces & allotments

Council allotments *Environment and
Regeneration, Low Hall, Argall Avenue, E10
7AS (8496 3000, www.walthamforest.gov.uk/
allotments).*
Open spaces *www.walthamforest.gov.uk/parks.*

RECYCLING

**Household waste recycled &
composted** 28%
Main recycling centres South Access
Road Household Waste & Recycling
Centre, South Access Road, Markhouse
Avenue, E17 8BS; Leyton Household
Waste Recycling Centre, Gateway Road,
off Orient Way, E10 5BY
Other recycling services garden
and kitchen waste collection; home
composting; white goods collection
Council contact Street Services,
London Borough of Waltham Forest,
Low Hall Depot, Argall Avenue, E10
7AS (8496 3000)

COUNCIL TAX

A	up to £40,000	**£974.69**
B	£40,001-£52,000	**£1,137.13**
C	£52,001-£68,000	**£1,299.58**
D	£68,001-£88,000	**£1,462.03**
E	£88,001-£120,000	**£1,786.93**
F	£120,001-£160,000	**£2,111.82**
G	£160,001-£320,000	**£2,436.72**
H	over £320,000	**£2,924.06**

Enfield

The capital's northernmost borough encompasses the down-at-heel grit of urban Edmonton, popular suburb Palmers Green and the family-friendly affluence of Winchmore Hill and Hadley Wood. Generous amounts of open space and proximity to the green belt mean residents have access to their fair share of park life.

Neighbourhoods

Enfield Town and Edmonton

Church Street is Enfield Town's main thoroughfare, a narrow, down-to-earth shopping street with charity shops aplenty. Just off it, historic Enfield Market (established over 700 years ago) bursts into life four days a week, selling a cheap and cheerful mix of clothing, household goods and fresh fruit and veg. The other side of the road sees local trading in its 21st-century form – the Palace Gardens Centre and the Palace Exchange Centre. Avert your eyes from the street-level bargains in Superdrug and New Look and you might notice the *Enfield Word Wall*, a public art installation that uses extracts from Enfield conversations past and present to create a snapshot of local life – 'You don't know names you just know the faces, but everyone says hello when you go past'; 'I was evacuated during the war but back in time for the doodlebugs and our Anderson shelter.' Just a short stroll from here, Gentleman's Row, with its much sought-after large Georgian and Victorian houses, offers a reminder of the town's prosperous past.

Surrounded by huge arterial, traffic-clogged roads and light industrial estates, Edmonton struggles to achieve a distinct identity and suffers from many of the problems traditionally associated with deprived, inner-city areas. Cheap rented housing – much of it in the form of looming twin and triplet towers of council estate flats – is characteristic, rather than owner-occupied houses. The 2005 opening of IKEA on Glover Drive remains lodged in the memories of many locals – and not because it signalled a new dawn in cheap home furnishings. Opening night saw scenes of farcical, near fatal, madness as a flat-pack-crazed mob charged the doors.

Edmonton Green, with its railway station and bus terminal, is the public transport hub of the neighbourhood and home to a shopping centre in the throes of an ongoing £100 million redevelopment. Whether or not this will regenerate the neighbourhood has divided local opinion. Edmonton Green Market is at the heart of the centre, which also holds a selection of standard high-street names.

Palmers Green and Southgate

Found along the stretch of Green Lanes that continues beyond the North Circular, Palmers Green is a popular suburb, home to a substantial Greek Cypriot community. At the heart of the area is Broomfield Park, a much-loved and much-used public green space. With its playing fields, picturesque gardens, tennis courts and bowling green, the park provides many amenities for local people, while its ponds attract both waterfowl and model-boat enthusiasts.

Alongside the park is Alderman's Hill; the peaceful roads laddering off it are

Highs & Lows

▲ **Green spaces** Set on the edge of London, Enfield is ideal for quick and easy days out in the country.
Schools Latymer School is one of the top mixed grammars in the country. Be warned, though: the competition to get in is ferocious.

Lack of decent clubs A desirable nightspot in Enfield has yet to be found. Will the nightlife ever pick up?
Golf bores All these golf courses make getting stuck with a golf bore scarily likely. ▼

STATISTICS

BOROUGH MAKE-UP
Population 287,600
Ethnic origins
White 71.6%
Mixed 3.8%
Asian or Asian British 9.7%
Black or Black British 12.1%
Chinese or other 2.8%
Students 9.3%
Retirees 11.2%

HOUSING STOCK
Borough size (hectares) 8,220
Population density per hectare 35.0
No. of households 110,398
Houses (detached, semi-detached or terraced) 65%
Flats (converted or purpose-built) 35%

CRIME PER 1,000 OF POPULATION
Burglary 10
Robbery 5
Theft of vehicle 4
Theft from vehicle 9
Violence against the person 16
Sexual offences 1

MPs
Edmonton Andrew Love (Labour), *Enfield, Southgate* David Burrowes (Conservative); *Enfield North* Nick de Bois (Conservative)

known as 'the Lakes' (they're named after British lakes). These streets are home to the area's most desirable residences. The stretch of Green Lanes from the Triangle (a junction at the foot of Alderman's Hill) up to St John's Church on Bourne Hill is lined with shops, cafés and restaurants. The usual chain suspects are well represented, but there is also a sprinkling of independents. In contrast to the low-key daytime bustle, evenings see the area become a rougher, tougher kind of place.

Traditionally a stepping stone to suburban life for those leaving Wood Green, Southgate's good transport connections – served by the Piccadilly line and several bus routes – make it a convenient place to live. The pivotal hub of the area is the circular art deco tube station, a classic designed by Charles Holden and opened in 1932.

Students from nearby Southgate College hang out in the assorted cafés and fast-food joints around the station. Shops and eateries here are humdrum on the whole, with a 24-hour Asda the dominant retail presence. Southgate's rough-and-ready feel takes on an edge at night as the streets fill up with boy racers showing off their mock-alloy wheels. Head away from the station, however, and you'll find peaceful residential streets, lined predominantly with mock-Tudor houses. Greenery is plentiful, including Grovelands Park, which has a large boating lake, tennis courts and pitch-and-putt course, and Oakwood Park. Both are well used by local families. For wider green spaces, travel a little further to Trent Country Park for bracing walks through woods and grassland. Near the Bramley Sports Ground (home of Saracens amateur rugby club), the dynamic Chicken Shed Theatre offers true community theatre, running a drama club for able-bodied and disabled children. Shows are often excellent and the annual panto is a regular sell-out.

Winchmore Hill and Hadley Wood

Keeping hold of its village credentials, peaceful Winchmore Hill has a pace of life that suits its family-focused residents down to the ground. The area's overground railway station, Winchmore Hill, is handily positioned by the picturesque old village green. Here, a cluster of independent shops and restaurants mean locals can stock up for Sunday lunch (at the butcher on Wades Hill), choose a new colour palette for their home (at interiors specialist the House) and stop off for drinks or coffee without venturing outside their neighbourhood. A short stroll down the hill to Green Lanes reveals yet more shops, cafés, pubs and eateries. Fresh air is also in ample supply, thanks to nearby Grovelands and Grange parks. Sports-lovers are well served by Winchmore Hill Cricket Club – a local institution that also offers tennis, football and hockey – and Enfield Golf Course.

As one might expect, prices here are notably higher than in other parts of Enfield. Properties are larger and more characterful, with some notably lavish houses along the Broadwalk.

Similarly affluent, though much further north, is Hadley Wood. Discreetly nestling beside picturesque Monken Hadley Common,

Enfield

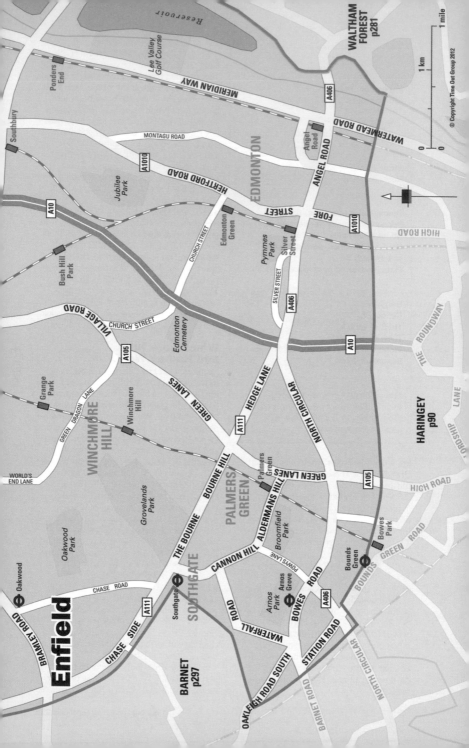

The desirable housing stock of **Gentlemen's Row**. See p290.

this is a small but affluent pocket of Enfield, noted for its high number of local aspirant millionaires. This is the place to find your detached ranch-style house, complete with spacious grounds, swimming pool and electronic gates. Key to the area's social life is Hadley Wood Golf Club, with its prestigious course and imposing clubhouse, a mansion built in 1781.

Kervan Sofrasi *www.kervansofrasi.com; 171 Hertford Road, N9 7EP (8804 5599); 80 Church Street Lower, N9 9PB (8884 4441).*
La Paella *9 Broadway, N14 6PH (8882 7868, www.lapaellatapasbar.com).*
Regatta *10-12 The Green, N21 1AX (8886 5471, www.regattarestaurant.co.uk).*
Vadi *314-316 Ponders End, EN3 4HF (8805 9838, www.vadirestaurant.co.uk).*

Restaurants & cafés

Chains dominate here, so you're never far from a McDonald's, Pizza Express or Starbucks. Southgate's Spanish eaterie La Paella holds fast. Affluent Winchmore Hill has a number of cafés, as well as established favourites such as Italian restaurant Regatta. In Palmers Green, Turkish restaurant Vadi is a popular choice for its charcoal grill, and bohemian tea room Baskervilles is winning fans for its range of teas. Kervan Sofrasi on Church Street in Edmonton is an excellent Turkish restaurant – there's a sister branch on Hertford Road in Ponders End, where you'll also find Sri Lankan Chennai Spice.

Baskervilles *66 Alderman's Hill, N13 4PP (8351 1673, www.baskervillesteashop. co.uk).*
Chennai Spice *217 Hertford Road, N9 7ER (8805 9944).*

Bars & pubs

Many of Enfield Town's boozers have a brash element to them. For a peaceful pint, head to the picturesque Old Wheatsheaf, a friendly, old-fashioned Victorian pub with decent beer and a popular Thursday-night pub quiz that brings in a crowd of regulars. For a more rural setting, try the King & Tinker, parts of which date from the 16th century – these days, you'll find decent ales and a large beer garden.

The Fox – a tarted-up old boozer in Palmers Green – pulls in the youngsters and is a popular meeting place. Unimaginative chain pubs include the Inn on the Green in Palmers Green and the New Crown in Southgate. Nicer is Ye Olde Cherry Tree, which draws a slightly older crowd. In Winchmore Hill, the Green Dragon is an immense old pub with a popular beer garden; it serves oriental grub. Also offering food and drink is the inviting Kings Head, on Palmers Green – it offers excellent, wide-ranging stock and the chance of a serendipitous find. Palmers Green Antiques is another spot for bargain hunters, a down-to-earth business selling miscellaneous antiques, from old china to furniture. For new furniture and homeware, head to IKEA in Edmonton, which, now the frenzy of opening is over, is generally less busy than its older sister store on the North Circular.

Winchmore Hill wins hands down in the individuality stakes, with the likes of interiors shop the House, boutique Katzi and the long-established Mistress Appleby – a charming shop with a selection of contemporary, antique and bespoke jewellery. There are lots of independent food shops too, including Deli on the Green for hot salt-beef sandwiches and Greek dishes.

in a grand Victorian building on Winchmore Hill Green. In Edmonton, the pubs that aren't chain joints tend to be intimidating backwater boozers – try the ones on Church Street if you're desperate, though these are often peopled by the barely legal from local schools.

Fox *413 Green Lanes, N13 4JD (8886 9674, www.thefoxpalmersgreen.com).*
Green Dragon *889 Green Lanes, N21 2QP (8360 0005, www.greendragon-winchmore. co.uk).*
Inn on the Green *295 Green Lanes, N13 4XS (8886 3760).*
King & Tinker *Whitewebbs Lane, EN2 9HJ (8363 6411).*
Kings Head *1 The Green, N21 1BB (8886 1988).*
New Crown *80-84 Chase Side, N14 5PH (8882 8758, www.jdwetherspoon.co.uk).*
Old Wheatsheaf *3 Windmill Hill, EN2 6SE (8363 0516).*
Ye Olde Cherry Tree *22 The Green, N14 6EN (8447 8022, www.vintageinn.co.uk/ yeoldecherrytreesouthgate).*

Shops

Enfield Town's refurbished Palace Gardens and Palace Exchange shopping centres are the place to go for chain stores, especially clothes shops such as H&M, River Island, Monsoon and Next. For upmarket menswear, head to Winchmore Hill's Twenty-One The Green.

Book-lovers will enjoy browsing at the British Red Cross Shop dedicated to books

British Red Cross Shop *383 Green Lanes, N13 4JG (8886 7467).*
Deli on the Green *251 Hoppers Road, N21 3NP (8882 5631).*
House *19 The Green, N21 1AY (8886 3800).*
IKEA *Glover Drive, N18 3HF (0845 355 2255, www.ikea.co.uk).*
Katzi *61 Station Road, N21 3NB (8350 6957, www.katziboutique.co.uk).*
Mistress Appleby *20 The Green, N21 1AY (8886 1303).*
Palace Exchange Shopping Centre *Hatton Walk, EN2 6BP (8362 1934, www.palaceexchange.co.uk).*
Palace Gardens Shopping Centre *Church Street, EN2 6SN (8367 1210, www.palacegardensenfield.co.uk).*
Palmers Green Antiques *482 Green Lanes, N13 5PA (8350 0878).*
Twenty-One The Green *21 The Green, N21 3NL (8882 4298, www.zednet.co.uk/21thegreen).*

Arts & attractions

Cinemas & theatres
Artszone *1st floor, 54-56 Market Square, Edmonton Green Shopping Centre, N9 0TZ (8803 9877, www.artzone-facilities.org.uk). Community theatre, gallery and studio space.*
Chicken Shed *Theatre Chase Side, N14 4PE (8292 9222, www.chickenshed.org.uk).*
Cineworld Enfield *Southbury Leisure Park, 208 Southbury Road, EN1 1YQ (0871 200 2000, www.cineworld.co.uk).*
Millfield Theatre *Silver Street, N18 1PJ (8807 6680, www.millfieldtheatre.co.uk).*

Enfield

Odeon Lee Valley *Lee Valley Leisure Complex, Picketts Lock Lane, N9 0AS (0871 224 4007, www.odeon.co.uk).*

Other attractions

Forty Hall & Estate *Forty Hill, EN2 9HA (8363 8196, www.enfield.gov.uk/fortyhall). Henry VIII's hunting lodge – refurbished in 2011 – has a museum and appropriately regal grounds.*

Sport & fitness

There's a decent spread of sports and leisure facilities in Enfield, both public and private.

Gyms & leisure centres

Albany Leisure Centre *505 Hertford Road, EN3 5XH (8804 4255, www.fusion-lifestyle.com).*
Arnos Pool *Bowes Road, N11 0BD (8361 9336, www.fusion-lifestyle.com).*
David Lloyd *Caterhatch Lane, EN1 4LF (8364 5858, www.davidlloydleisure.co.uk). Private.*
Edmonton Leisure Centre *2 The Broadway, N9 0TR (8375 3750, www.fusion-lifestyle.com).*
Island Fitness *57 Island Centre Way, EN3 6GS (01992 762107, www.islandfitness.co.uk). Private.*
LA Fitness *www.lafitness.co.uk; 18 East Barnet Road, EN4 8RW (0843 170 1018); Winchmore Hill Road, N14 6AA (0843 170 1019). Private.*
Southbury Leisure Centre *192 Southbury Road, EN1 1YP (8245 3201, www.fusion-lifestyle.com).*
Southgate Leisure Centre *Winchmore Hill Road, N14 6AD (8882 7963, www.fusion-lifestyle.com).*
Virgin Active *Tower Point, Sydney Road, EN2 6SZ (8370 4100, www.virginactive.co.uk). Private.*

Other facilities

Lee Valley Athletics Centre *61 Meridian Way, Picketts Lock, N9 0AR (8344 7230, www.leevalleypark.org.uk). Superb athletics centre and a training base for many Olympic hopefuls.*
Lee Valley White Water Centre *Station Road, EN9 1AB (0845 677 0606, www.leevalleypark.org.uk/whitewaterrafting). Brand-new, and the site of the canoe slalom at the 2012 Games, just north of the M25.*
Southgate Hockey Centre *Trent Park, Snakes Lane, EN4 0PS (8441 5855, www.southgatehockeycentre.co.uk). Private.*
Trent Park Equestrian Centre *Trent Park Stables, Bramley Road, N14 4XS (8363 8630, www.trentpark.com). One of the largest riding schools in London.*

Schools

Primary

There are 59 state primary schools in Enfield, including 16 church schools and one Jewish school. There are also six independent primary schools. See www.enfield.gov.uk, www.edubase.gov.uk and www.ofsted.gov.uk for more information.

Secondary

Aylward Academy *Windmill Road, N18 1NB (8803 1738, www.aylwardacademy.org).*
Bishop Stopford's School *Brick Lane, EN1 3PU (8804 1906, www.bishopstopfords.enfield.sch.uk).*
Broomfield School *Wilmer Way, N14 7HY (8368 4710, www.broomfieldschool.co.uk).*
Chace Community School *Churchbury Lane, EN1 3HQ (8363 7321, www.chace.enfield.sch.uk).*
Edmonton County School *Great Cambridge Road, EN1 1HQ (8360 3158, www.edmonton county.co.uk).*

Enfield

Enfield County School *Holly Walk, EN2 6QG (8363 3030, www.enfieldcs.enfield.sch.uk). Girls only; mixed sixth form.*
Enfield Grammar School *Market Place, EN2 6LN (8363 1095, www.enfieldgrammar.com). Boys only.*
Highlands School *148 Worlds End Lane, N21 1QQ (8370 1100, www.highlands. enfield.sch.uk).*
Kingsmead School *196 Southbury Road, EN1 1YQ (8351 5000, www.kingsmead.org).*
Latymer School *Haselbury Road, N9 9TN (8807 4037, www.latymer.co.uk).*
Lea Valley High School *Bullsmoor Lane, EN3 6TW (01992 763666, www.lvhs.org.uk).*
Nightingale Academy *Turin Road, N9 8DQ (8443 8500, www.nightingaleacademy.org).*
Oasis Academy Enfield *9 Kinetic Crescent, EN3 7XH (01992 655400, www.oasisacademy enfield.org).*
Oasis Academy Hadley *Bell Lane, EN3 5PA (8804 6946, www.oasisacademyhadley.org).*
St Anne's Catholic High School for Girls *Oakthorpe Road, N13 5TY (8886 2165, www.st-annes.enfield.sch.uk). Roman Catholic; girls only.*
St Ignatius College *Turkey Street, EN1 4NP (01992 717835, www.st-ignatius.enfield.sch.uk). Roman Catholic; boys only.*
Southgate School *Sussex Way, EN4 0BL (8449 9583, www.southgate.enfield.sch.uk).*
Winchmore School *Laburnum Grove, N21 3HS (8360 7773, www.winchmore.enfield. sch.uk).*

Property

WHAT THE AGENTS SAY:

'A lot of people move to Palmers Green, above the North Circular, for the abundance of characterful Edwardian properties. Many new families come here from the inner boroughs of London, such as Islington, because they realise that, for the same amount of money, they can have access to good local primary schools as well as more space for their growing families. Prices in the area have been steadily on the up since 2007.'

Tony Ourris, Anthony Webb, Palmers Green

Average property prices

Detached £558,822
Semi-detached £337,220
Terraced £250,973
Flat £205,809

COUNCIL TAX

A	up to £40,000	£940.11
B	£40,001-£52,000	£1,096.79
C	£52,001-£68,000	£1,253.48
D	£68,001-£88,000	£1,410.16
E	£88,001-£120,000	£1,723.53
F	£120,001-£160,000	£2,036.90
G	£160,001-£320,000	£2,350.27
H	over £320,000	£2,820.32

Local estate agents

Anthony Webb *348 Green Lanes, N13 5TL (8882 7888, www.anthony webb.co.uk).*
Brien Firmin *www.brienfirmin.com; 2 offices in the borough (Green Lanes 8889 9944, Winchmore Hill 8360 9696).*
James Hayward *181 Chase Side, EN2 0PT (8367 4000, www.james-hayward. co.uk).*
Lanes *www.lanesproperty.co.uk; 3 offices in the borough (Enfield Town 8342 0101, Enfield Southbury Road 8362 7680, Enfield Highway 8804 2253).*
Peter Barry *946 Green Lanes, N21 2AD (8360 4777, www.peterbarry.co.uk).*
Townends *913 Green Lanes, N21 2QP (8360 8111, www.addisontownends. co.uk).*

Other information

Council
Enfield Council *Civic Centre, Silver Street, EN1 3XY (8379 1000, www.enfield. gov.uk).*

Legal services
Enfield CAB *Unit 3, 5 Vincent House, 2E Nags Head Road, EN3 7FN (0844 826 9712, www.enfieldcab.org.uk).*

Local information
www.enfieldindependent.co.uk.
www.enfield-today.co.uk.
www.n21.net.

Open spaces & allotments
Council allotments *Contact the council's Parks Business Unit (8379 1000, www. enfield.gov.uk) for assistance with local allotment sites.*
Open spaces *www.enfield.gov.uk; www.friendsofbroomfieldpark.org.*

Barnet

For London living with an edge, look elsewhere – Barnet's attractions are distinctly suburban. The borough takes in traffic-clogged Hendon, Jewish Golders Green, East, Central and North Finchley, wealthy and leafy Totteridge and, at the northern edge, self-sufficient High Barnet, offering oodles of 1930s semis, golf courses, excellent schools and plentiful parkland along the way.

Neighbourhoods

Golders Green and Hendon

In a classic story of the suburbs, Golders Green was transformed by the introduction of the tube in 1907. The Golders Green Northern line station and a busy bus terminus lie at the neighbourhood's core, by a major junction that sees Golders Green Road crossing Finchley Road. Nearby is the majestic-looking Golders Green Hippodrome, now the El-Shaddai International Christian Centre. Signs at the station point the way to Golders Green Crematorium (opened 1902) where the likes of Sigmund Freud, George Bernard Shaw, Marc Bolan and, most recently, Amy Winehouse were cremated.

The area has become synonymous with Jewish London, hence the presence of numerous kosher businesses (particularly along Golders Green Road and the stretch of Finchley Road by Temple Fortune). In order to observe the Jewish Shabbat, many of the district's businesses close from sunset on Friday to sunset on Saturday. The weekly reopening on Saturday night sees Golders Green buzzing with young people hanging out in the cafés, and local bakeries doing a roaring trade in salmon and cream cheese bagels. Sunday too is a busy shopping day.

Heading up the hill towards Hampstead, you'll find Golders Hill Park, a popular and nicely laid-out patch of greenery. A little further up the hill is the London Jewish Cultural Centre, attractively housed in Ivy House (where ballerina Anna Pavlova once lived).

It's hard to imagine it, but neighbouring Hendon was once a land of fields and stables. These days, brutally bisected by traffic-choked Watford Way (A41) and adjacent to the start of the M1, Hendon's local identity lacks strong definition. In a *Time Out* article in 2006, local writer Naomi Alderman described Hendon's Jewish community, for example, as 'hidden, intentionally half-submerged so as to be almost invisible to outsiders.'

The proximity of the UK's first large enclosed shopping centre, Brent Cross (opened in 1976), has had a draining effect on Hendon's local shops, with Brent Street, the area's supposed high street, a surprisingly down-at-heel affair. Still, the area functions well in practical terms, with an excellent library just by the imposing Town Hall, a pleasantly formal green space in Hendon Park and the Barnet Copthall Leisure Centre.

Hampstead Garden Suburb

Bordered by arterial Falloden Way (A1) and Finchley Road, Hampstead Garden Suburb remains a relatively well-kept secret, although it's growing in popularity. Founded in 1907 by heiress Dame Henrietta Barnett, HGS was an idealistic piece of social engineering that aimed to provide housing for all social classes, from workers' cottages to grand residences for the toffs. Gardens and green spaces played a central part in Dame Barnett's vision: an average density of eight dwellings to an acre allowed for ample gardens. The attractive Arts and Crafts-style houses are much sought after – and, not surprisingly, command premium prices.

The buildings on the central square and at 140-142 Hampstead Way are frequently visited by fans of classic architecture, but, despite the appealing exteriors, there is something stand-offish about the neighbourhood. Even the central square's great Lutyens churches bear stern notices forbidding ball games against their walls. There are no shops within Hampstead

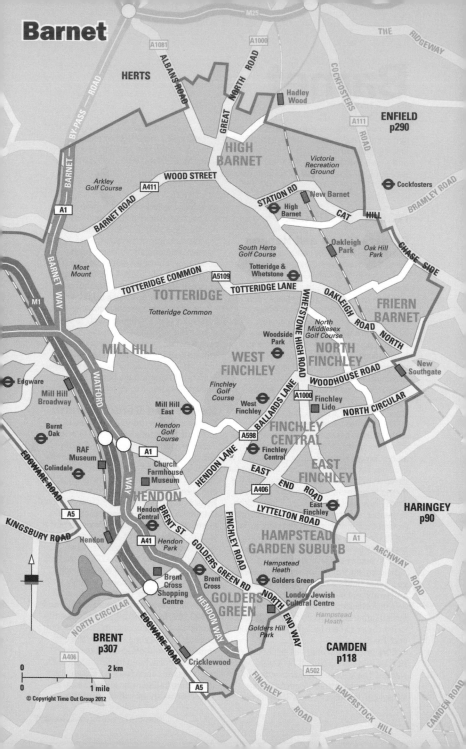

Garden Suburb (let alone pubs or cafés), but residents are well catered for by nearby Temple Fortune.

East Finchley and Finchley Central

Of the several Finchleys, East Finchley offers the strongest sense of place, retaining its identity, local community and even an art deco tube station topped with a striking figure of an archer. Positioned cheek-by-jowl with Highgate and Muswell Hill, and with desirable Victorian and Edwardian housing stock, East Finchley appeals to a liberal, arts crowd. Although the homely high street – part of the Great North Road – is often congested, it is also narrow enough to allow for life on a human scale. Local businesses include such London high-street rarities as a decent fishmonger, greengrocer and bookshop.

Adult learners are amply catered for by the Hampstead Garden Suburb Institute, with its purpose-built Arts Centre around the corner from East Finchley tube. The jewel in the district's crown, however, is the Phoenix Cinema. Opened in 1910 and thought to be the UK's oldest continuously operating picture house, this deco gem is one of the capital's few remaining independent cinemas and is loyally supported by locals. Families, especially those with toddlers, make a beeline for Cherry Tree Wood and its playground. The park hosts a community festival every summer.

The green fields of College Farm, formerly the showcase farm for Express Dairies, is a reminder of Finchley Central's rural past. Any pastoral feel, however, is long gone, with the area now seeing a high volume of traffic pass along its congested high street (Ballards Lane). Good transport links (both tube and buses) have attracted a mixed population, including a sizeable Jewish contingent, Japanese expats (catered for by Japanese food shop Atari-ya) and a recent influx of young Poles. For a much-needed breath of fresh air, residents head to the Victoria Recreation Ground.

West Finchley and North Finchley

Despite having its own tube station, West Finchley exists in Finchley Central's shadow. Primarily residential, it lacks a real shopping centre, but plus points

Highs & Lows

▲ **Real neighbourhoods** Each area has it's own distinct character and loyal inhabitants; people move to a neighbourhood and stay for life, getting to know their neighbours and investing in the community.
Bagels You simply can't beat the bagels found at the best bakeries in Golders Green and Hendon.

Northern line Running through the borough, the Northern line is plagued by signal problems – which can make journeys very slow indeed. Add in upgrade works that often result in whole sections of the line closing at weekends, and you've got a lot of exasperated locals.
▼ **Traffic** Too many huge, traffic-laden roads cut through the borough.

include comparatively peaceful streets, views over the green belt and proximity to Finchley Golf Course.

North Finchley's most prominent landmark is the Artsdepot complex, which towers over Tally Ho Corner. It houses a well-appointed arts centre, a bus depot and luxury apartments. For additional recreation, locals can head to nearby Finchley Lido. This redeveloped 1930s lido now houses a Vue cinema, fast-food outlets, a bowling alley and a swimming pool. The high street offers chains and a handful of down-to-earth independents, including a locksmith, a haberdashery shop and a school uniform store. The most desirable houses are tucked away in the peaceful streets around Woodside Park, location of the nearest tube station.

Totteridge and Whetstone

Drive into Whetstone from the south and it seems distinctly unprepossessing: a B&Q sits opposite a large timber merchant, with Barnet House – the tall, grim tower block that contains Barnet Council's offices – looming in the background. However, turn left into Totteridge Lane, towards Totteridge Village, and you're soon travelling tree-lined lanes between substantial houses. Home to the seriously wealthy (including footballers and their

Barnet

WAGs), the mansions here are discreetly set back from the road and have fine green-belt views. However, despite the area's prosperity, Whetstone High Road shows little sign of conspicuous consumption – unless you count the telltale branches of Waitrose and Marks & Spencer.

The prestigious South Herts Golf Club, its course designed by golf legend Harry Vardon, is among the area's hidden assets. Even further west, flanking Barnet Way, are Scratchwood and Moat Mount, a lovely nature reserve that comprises the largest area of woodland in Barnet.

Friern Barnet

During the 19th century, this part of north London was best known for Colney Hatch, its infamous mental hospital, correctly known as the Middlesex County Pauper Lunatic Asylum. Today, such is the driving force of the property market, the asylum has been reinvented as Princess Park Manor, a gated development of luxurious properties with gyms, a bar and tennis courts. The area's refurbishment, however, stops firmly at the gates. The immediate area is decidedly grim and down-at-heel, although Coppetts Wood on Colney Hatch Lane and, west into North Finchley, the Glebelands Nature Reserve provide some relief. Local commuters head for New Southgate rail, as there's no tube nearby.

The picture improves, albeit along traditional suburban lines, as you head north towards Whetstone. The leafy roads around Friern Barnet Lane are lined with large houses and open on to North Middlesex Golf Course. Just south of the course lies Friary Park, which has landscaped grounds, a popular playground, a skateboard park and a child-friendly café.

High Barnet

Once a staging post on the main road to London, High Barnet still has a bit of an old-fashioned, out-of-town feel, which is much relished by the residents. 'Barnet Church' (actually St John the Baptist) is the dominating local landmark. It marks the start of the high street, a narrow spot known appropriately as 'the squeeze'. The top of the church tower is meant to be the highest point between London and York; be that as it may, the tower certainly commands spectacular views. Historically, Barnet was famous for its fair, a major livestock trading event – 'Barnet (Fair)' became Cockney rhyming slang for 'hair'.

Even today, Barnet has a sense of community to match its parochialism, with events such as Scout parades, church fêtes and cricket on the green. There's even a professional football team (the Bees), which commands a passionate following. Barnet Market, granted a charter by King John in 1199, plied a thriving cattle trade; these days, traders operate on St Albans Road every Wednesday and Saturday, selling fish (R&H Fisheries has been at the Market for more than 40 years), meat, fresh fruit and veg, as well as flowers. Easy access to green spaces is much appreciated by residents, who walk their dogs, cycle and fly kites on the Common and Hadley Green (where the Battle of Barnet was fought in 1471, during the War of the Roses).

One of the many styles of house in **Hampstead Garden Suburb**. See p297.

On the downside, life here in the suburbs can be dull. Other than the flicks at the huge 1930s Odeon down the road, there is little cultural life on offer, and the fact that Barnet's yob element comes to the fore at night makes walking around after dark a depressing experience. Commuters working in central London and using the tube can rely on getting a seat in the morning, but with the Northern line's frequent signal problems, relying on the service itself can be problematic.

Barnet is, however, seeing a steady influx of families from other parts of north London drawn to the more affordable property prices and good schools.

Restaurants & cafés

With Golders Green home to a long-established Jewish community, it is no surprise to learn this is a great place to sample Jewish cuisine. Both Ashkenazi (Russian and east European) and Sephardi (Middle Eastern) dishes are generously represented. Bustling Dizengoff's offers a taste of Israeli cuisine, with generous portions of houmous, grilled meat and excellent salads; Solly's too specialises in Israeli-style food. Other kosher options include La Fiesta (Argentinian), Met Su Yan (Asian), New Yorker Deli and – relocated

from Hendon – Isola Bella brasserie. Over in Hendon, Mr Baker pulls in a steady stream of customers for bagels and sweet pastries, while popular kosher restaurants include contemporary diner Eighty-Six Bistro Bar, Orli's café, homely Sami's and old-style Chinese restaurant Kaifeng.

Of course, it isn't all kosher food round here. Café Japan has long had a loyal following, while sushi restaurant H2O in Hendon is also good. Fine fish and chips and traditional seafood are on offer at Leon and Tony Manzi's perpetually popular fish restaurant, the Two Brothers in Finchley Central; also here is charming Vietnamese Vy Nam Café. Indian restaurants range from Hendon's bustling Lahore Original Kebab House, offering robust Pakistani food, to sedate Gujarati vegetarian restaurant Rani in Finchley Central. North Finchley has a branch of Khoai Café, a good-quality Vietnamese restaurant; East Finchley has the very welcome Bald-Faced Stag gastropub; another gastropub, the Adam & Eve, is in Mill Hill. Brent Cross Shopping Centre has branches of Nando's, Carluccio's, Leon, Yo! Sushi, Pizza Express and Wagamama.

The Din Café at Temple Fortune is deservedly popular with local ladies who lunch. The menu takes in salads, burgers and South African specialities such as grilled boerewors sausages.

Barnet is lacking in upmarket eateries – Whetstone's bar-restaurant the Haven is as glamorous as it gets. Also in Whetstone, El Vaquero draws crowds for its Brazilian/ Argentinian grilled meats (it also has a branch in Mill Hill), while Italian joint Al Fresco is perpetually bustling. The cavernous and coyly named Coffee & Tease café does its bit for the area's harassed mothers, with a handy play area.

Up in High Barnet, Suruchi, despite many rival curry houses, is much visited. Dory's Café serves great fry-ups to appreciative regulars, and family-friendly noodle bar Emchai also pulls in a lively crowd.

Adam & Eve *The Ridgeway, NW7 1RL (8959 1553, www.adamandevemillhill.co.uk).*
Al Fresco *1327 High Road, N20 9HR (8445 8880, www.alfresco-restaurant.co.uk).*
Bald-Faced Stag *69 High Road, N2 8AB (8442 1201, www.thebaldfacedstagn2.co.uk).*
Café Japan *626 Finchley Road, NW11 7RR (8455 6854).*
Coffee & Tease *1379 High Road, N20 9LP (8492 3400, www.coffeeandtease.com).*
Din Café *816 Finchley Road, NW11 6YL (8731 8103, www.dincafe.co.uk).*
Dizengoff's *118 Golders Green Road, NW11 8HB (8458 7003).*
Dory's Café *3 St Albans Road, EN5 4LN (8440 1954).*
Eighty-Six Bistro Bar *86 Brent Street, NW4 2ES (8202 5575).*
Emchai *78 High Street, EN5 5SN (8364 9993).*
La Fiesta *235 Golders Green Road, NW11 9ES (8458 0444, www.lafiestalondon.co.uk).*
Haven Bistro & Bar *1363 High Road, N20 9LN (8445 7419, www.haven-bistro.co.uk).*
H2O *33 Watford Way, NW4 35H (8203 2088).*
Isola Bella Café *111A-113 Golders Green Road, NW11 8HR (8455 2228, www.isola bella.co.uk).*
Kaifeng *51 Church Road, NW4 4DU (8203 7888, www.kaifeng.co.uk).*
Khoai Café *362 Ballards Lane, N12 0EE (8445 2039, www.khoai.co.uk).*
Lahore Original Kebab House *148-150 Brent Street, NW4 2DR (8203 6904, www.originallahore.com).*
Met Su Yan *134 Golders Green Road, NW11 8HP (8458 8088, www.metsuyan.co.uk).*
Mr Baker *119-121 Brent Street, NW4 2DX (8202 6845, www.mrbakeruk.com).*
New Yorker Deli *122 Golders Green, NW11 8HB (8209 0232).*
Orli *96 Brent Street, NW4 2HH (8203 7555).*

Locals' Tips

Not many people know that Arsenal use Barnet FC's Underhill ground for their second-team matches. They're usually on a Monday at 7pm, which makes them good for kids. Admission is free, and you get a smattering of recovering first-team players too. **If you're a housebound new mum, try the screenings for mothers and babies at the Phoenix in East Finchley.** For a Sunday morning treat, have breakfast at the Din Café in Temple Fortune. It does a mean eggs benedict. **The guided walks (Barnet Weekend Walks, 8440 6805) around High Barnet are great. They tell the area's history really well.** For really good poultry and meat in East Finchley, try Graham's, the butcher at 134-136 East End Road, N2 0RZ (8883 6187).

Rani *7 Long Lane, N3 2PR (8349 4386, www.raniuk.com).*
Sami's Kosher Restaurant *157 Brent Street, NW4 4DJ (8203 8088).*
Solly's *148A Golders Green Road, NW11 8HE (8455 0004).*
Suruchi *45 High Street, EN5 5UW (8447 1111, www.suruchibarnet.com).*
Two Brothers Fish Restaurant *297-303 Regents Park Road, N3 1DP (8346 0469, www.twobrothers.co.uk).*
El Vaquero *1105-1111 High Street Whetstone, N20 0PT (8445 1882, www.elvaquero.co.uk).*
Vy Nam Café *371 Regents Park Road, N3 1DE (8371 4222).*

Bars & pubs

Barnet's drinking scene has a distinctly suburban vibe, lacking the variety, edge and glamour of more central London boroughs. It is, however, not short on pubs, be they trad locals or brash bars aimed at a younger crowd.

In Hendon, for example, tucked-away, traditional pub the Greyhound contrasts with the in-your-face Claddagh Ring, which attracts a boisterous crowd with its live music. The Gallery, a former pub reincarnated as a nightclub, bar and restaurant, is aimed at those wanting a West End-style night without the journey into town. Over in Finchley Central, the Catcher in the Rye, with football on its TV screens, reasonably priced pub grub and quiz nights, is also popular. East Finchley has the Bald-Faced Stag gastropub (*see left*), where the beer garden can seat up to 200 people.

One of Totteridge's best-known pubs is the Orange Tree, which gets top marks for its picturesque location down tree-lined Totteridge Lane. Cocktail drinkers should try restaurant-cum-bar the Haven (*see left*) on Whetstone High Road.

Meanwhile, memories of High Barnet's past role as as a staging post linger in a number of traditional pubs; try Ye Olde Monken Holt or the White Lion. The Mitre offers a spruced-up trad pub vibe and the Sebright Arms is a firm local favourite.

Catcher in the Rye *319 Regents Park Road, N3 1DP (8343 4369, www.faucetinn.com).*
Claddagh Ring *10 Church Road, NW4 4EA (8203 2600, www.claddagh-ring.co.uk).*
Gallery *407-411 Hendon Way, NW4 3LH (8202 4000, www.galleryhendon.com).*
Greyhound *Church End, NW4 4JT (8457 9730).*
Mitre *58 High Street, EN5 5SJ (8449 5701).*
Orange Tree *7 Totteridge Village, N20 8NX (8343 7031, www.theorangetreetotteridge.co.uk).*
Sebright Arms *9 Alston Road, EN5 4ET (8449 6869, www.sebrightarmsbarnet.com).*
White Lion *50 St Albans Road, EN5 4LA (8449 4560).*
Ye Olde Monken Holt *193 High Street, EN5 5SU (8449 4280, www.yeoldemonkenholt.com).*

Shops

The borough's shopping scene is, inevitably, dominated by Brent Cross Shopping Centre. The veteran shopping mall (home to some 110 shops and cafés) was the harbinger of the countless out of town retail conglomerations that have opened since. Despite being near a tube station (note that Hendon Central is closer than Brent Cross), the Centre has ample car parks, all heaving with vehicles – the car is very much king here.

For those who prefer to shop on a more human scale, Golders Green offers a few one-offs alongside chains and charity shops – though veteran florist Galton Flowers has moved into the shopping centre. Factory outlet Gold & Son, specialising in bargain suits and shoes, cheerfully advertises itself as 'the big red building on Golders Green Road'. Just up the road, genteel Temple Fortune is home to a number of small independents, including Brian's (kids' shoes), the Bookworm (kids' books) and Joseph's (more books).

High Barnet has the Spires, a pleasant, low-level shopping centre constructed around small open-air squares, which offers the likes of the Body Shop, Monsoon, Waterstone's and WH Smith, plus ice-cream parlour Cremeria Vienna. At the Monken Hadley end of the high street, you'll find Bargain Buys (an Aladdin's cave of household goods), Wanders (chic footwear) and the Present (fancily wrapped gifts).

On the food front, the borough's most distinctive feature is the number of vintage Jewish food shops, including Kosher Wines, classic Jewish deli Platters, fishmonger Sam Stoller and JA Corney, butcher La Boucherie and bustling bagel bakeries Carmelli, Daniel's and Hendon Bagel Bakery. Barnet's Japanese residents are catered for by branches of Atari-ya, while Asian food shops include Goodeats

Atari-ya Foods *www.atariya.co.uk; 595 High Road, N12 0DY (8446 6669); 15-16 Monkville Parade, Finchley Road, NW11 0AL (8458 7626).*
Bargain Buys *4 Hadley Parade, EN5 5SX (8440 7983).*
Black Gull Books *121 High Road, N2 8AC (8444 4717).*
Bookworm *1177 Finchley Road, NW11 0AA (8201 9811, www.thebookworm.uk.com).*
La Boucherie *4 Cat Hill, EN4 8JB (8449 9215).*
Brent Cross Shopping Centre *NW4 3FP (8202 8095, www.brentcross.co.uk).*
Brian's Shoes *3 Halleswelle Parade, Finchley Road, NW11 0DL (8455 7001, www.brians shoes.com).*
Carmelli Bakery *126-128 Golders Green Road, NW11 8HB (8455 2074, www.carmelli.co.uk).*
Daniel's *12-13 Halleswelle Parade, Finchley Road, NW11 0DL (8455 5826, www.daniels catering.co.uk).*
Gold & Son *110 Golders Green Road, NW11 8HB (8905 5721, www.thebigredbuilding.com).*
Goodeats *124 Ballards Lane, N3 2PA (8349 2373).*

Hendon Bagel Bakery *55-57 Church Road, NW4 4DU (8203 6919).*
JA Corney *16 Halleswelle Parade, Finchley Road, NW11 0DL (8455 9588).*
Joseph's Book Store *2 Ashbourne Parade, 1257 Finchley Road, NW11 0AD (8731 7575, www.josephsbookstore.com).*
Kosher Wines *20 Bell Lane, NW4 2AD (8202 2631, www.kosherwineuk.com).*
Platters *10 Halleswelle Parade, Finchley Road, NW11 0DL (8455 7345).*
Present *220-222 High Street, EN5 5SZ (8441 6400, www.thepresentbarnet.co.uk).*
Sam Stoller & Son *28 Temple Fortune Parade, Finchley Road, NW11 0QS (8458 1429).*
Spires Shopping Centre *111 High Street, EN5 5XY (8449 7505, www.thespiresbarnet.co.uk).*
Wanders *180 High Street, EN5 5SZ (8449 2520, www.wanders.co.uk).*

Arts & attractions

Cinemas & theatres

Artsdepot *5 Nether Street, N12 0GA (8369 5454, www.artsdepot.co.uk). Multidisciplinary arts venue, featuring comedy, dance and theatre productions, plus lots of activities for kids.*
Cineworld Staples Corner *Staples Corner Retail Park, Geron Way, NW2 6LW (0871 200 2000, www.cineworld.co.uk).*
Odeon Barnet *Great North Road, EN5 1AB (0871 224 4007, www.odeon.co.uk).*
Phoenix Cinema *52 High Road, N2 9PJ (8444 6789, www.phoenixcinema.co.uk).*
Vue North Finchley *Great North Leisure Park, Chaplin Square, N12 0GL (0871 224 0240, www.myvue.com).*

Galleries & museums

Artsdepot Gallery *5 Nether Street, N12 0GA (8369 5454, www.artsdepot.co.uk).*
Barnet Museum *31 Wood Street, EN5 4BE (8440 8066, www.barnetmuseum.co.uk). Local history museum, holding everything from a fine costume collection to archaeological remains.*
Royal Air Force Museum *Grahame Park Way, NW9 5LL (8205 2266, www.rafmuseum.org.uk). More than 100 aircraft (including a Spitfire and a Lancaster bomber) are displayed on the site of the original London Aerodrome.*

Other attractions

London Jewish Cultural Centre *Ivy House, 94-96 North End Road, NW11 7SX (8457 5000, www.ljcc.org.uk). A Jewish hub, with a range of courses, exhibitions, films, music and lectures.*

Sport & fitness

Barnet has a decent mix of clubs and centres, both public and private. Golfers will also be in their element: there are more golf courses in Barnet than any other London borough.

Gyms & leisure centres

Barnet Burnt Oak Leisure Centre *Watling Avenue, HA8 0NP (8201 0982, www.gll.org).*
Barnet Copthall Leisure Centre *Champions Way, off Great North Way, NW4 1PX (8457 9900, www.gll.org).*
Church Farm Swimming Pool *Church Hill Road, EN4 8XE (8368 7070, www.gll.org).*
Compton Leisure Centre *Porters Way, off Summers Lane, N12 0RF (8361 8658, www.gll.org).*
David Lloyd *Leisure Way, High Road, N12 0QZ (0844 692 0694, www.davidlloydleisure.co.uk). Private.*
Finchley Lido Leisure Centre *Great North Leisure Park, Chaplin Square, N12 0GL (8343 9830, www.gll.org).*
Fitness First *Old Priory Road Shopping Centre, 706 High Road, N12 9QL (0844 571 2910, www.fitnessfirst.co.uk). Private.*
Hendon Leisure Centre *Marble Drive, NW2 1XQ (8455 0818, www.gll.org).*
Laboratory Spa & Health Club *1A Hall Lane, NW4 4TJ (8201 5500, spa 8201 5588, www.labspa.co.uk). Private.*
LA Fitness *www.lafitness.co.uk; East End Road, N3 2TA (0843 170 1013); 152-154 Golders Green Road, NW11 8HE (0843 170 1014). Private.*
Oakleigh Park School of Swimming *100 Oakleigh Road North, N20 9EZ (8445 1911, www.swimoakleighpark.co.uk).*
Virgin Active *www.virginactive.co.uk; 108-110 Cricklewood Lane, NW2 2DS (8453 7200); 260 Hendon Way, NW4 3NL (8203 9421); 264 Princess Park Manor, Friern Barnet Road, N11 3BG (8362 8444). Private.*

Other facilities

Arkley Golf Club *Rowley Green Road, EN5 3HL (8449 0394, www.club-noticeboard.co.uk/arkley).*
Finchley Golf Club *Nether Court, Frith Lane, NW7 1PU (8346 2436, www.finchley golfclub.com).*

Barnet

Hendon Golf Club *Ashley Walk, Devonshire Road, NW7 1DG (8346 6023, www.hendon golfclub.co.uk).*
Hollywood Bowl *Great North Leisure Park, Chaplin Square, N12 0GL (0844 826 1459, www.hollywoodbowl.co.uk).*
Mill Hill Golf Club *100 Barnet Way, NW7 3AL (8959 2339, www.millhillgc.co.uk).*
North Middlesex Golf Course *Friern Barnet Lane, N20 0NL (8445 1604, www.northmiddlesexgc.co.uk).*
Old Fold Manor Golf Club *Old Fold Lane, Hadley Green, EN5 4QN (8440 9185, www.oldfoldmanor.co.uk).*
South Herts Golf Club *Links Drive, Totteridge, N20 8QU (8445 2035, www.southhertsgolfclub.co.uk).*

Spectator sports

Barnet FC *Underhill Stadium, Barnet Lane, EN5 2DN (8441 6932, tickets 8449 6325, www.barnetfc.com).*

Schools

Primary

There are 76 state primaries in Barnet, including 23 church schools and nine Jewish schools. There are also 18 independent primary schools, including nine faith schools and one international school. See www.barnet.gov.uk, www.edubase.gov.uk and www.ofsted.gov.uk for more information.

Secondary

Ashmole Academy *Cecil Road, N14 5RJ (8361 2703, www.ashmoleacademy.org).*

Bishop Douglass School *Hamilton Road, N2 0SQ (8444 5211, www.bishopdouglass.barnet.sch.uk). Roman Catholic.*
Christ's College Finchley *East End Road, N2 0SE (8349 3581, www.ccfplus.com/school/). Boys only; mixed sixth form.*
Compton School *Summers Lane, N12 0QG (8368 1783, www.thecomptonschool.co.uk).*
Copthall School *Pursley Road, NW7 2EP (8959 1937, www.copthallschool.org.uk). Girls only.*
East Barnet School *Chestnut Grove, EN4 8PU (8440 4162, www.eastbarnet.barnet.sch.uk).*
Finchley Catholic High School *Woodside Lane, N12 8TA (8445 0105, www.finchley catholic.org.uk). Roman Catholic; boys only.*
Friern Barnet School *Hemington Avenue, N11 3LS (8368 2777, www.friern.barnet.sch.uk).*
Hasmonean High School *www.hasmonean. co.uk; boys' site Holders Hill Road, NW4 1NA (8203 1411); girls' site 2-4 Page Street, NW7 2EU (8203 4294). Jewish.*
Hendon School *Golders Rise, NW4 2HP (8202 9004, www.hendonschool.co.uk).*
Henrietta Barnett School *Central Square, NW11 7BN (8458 8999, www.hbschool.org.uk). Girls only.*
Jewish Community Secondary School *Castlewood Road, EN4 9GE (8344 2220, www.jcoss.org). Jewish.*
London Academy *Spur Road, HA8 8DE, (8238 1100, www.londonacademy.org.uk).*
Mill Hill County High School *Worcester Crescent, NW7 4LL (0844 477 2424, www.mhchs.org.uk).*
Queen Elizabeth's Girls' School *High Street, EN5 5RR (8449 2984, www.qegschool.org.uk). Girls only.*

Barnet

Queen Elizabeth's School *Queen's Road, EN5 4DQ (8441 4646, www.qebarnet.co.uk). Boys only.*
St James' Catholic High School
Great Strand, NW9 5PE (8358 2800, www. st-james.barnet.sch.uk). Roman Catholic.
St Mary's CE High School *Downage, NW4 1AB (8203 2827, www.st-maryshigh.barnet. sch.uk). Church of England.*
St Michael's Catholic Grammar School *Nether Street, N12 7NJ (8446 2256, www. st-michaels.barnet.sch.uk). Roman Catholic; girls only.*
Totteridge Academy *Barnet Lane, N20 8AZ (8445 9205, www.thetotteridgeacademy.co.uk).*
Whitefield School *Claremont Road, NW2 1TR (8455 4114, www.whitefield.barnet.sch.uk).*
Wren Academy *Warnham Road, N12 9HB (8492 6000, www.wrenacademy.org). Church of England.*

Property

WHAT THE AGENTS SAY:

'Barnet has a great mix of shops, leisure facilities and green spaces, as well as a fantastic education record. East Finchley station is the last stop in Zone 3, and the area's eclectic mix of shops and restaurants attracts a more youthful crowd. Younger families are also drawn to the Victorian or Edwardian properties, which are similar to those in adjoining Muswell Hill and Highgate, but slightly better value for money. Mill Hill, Totteridge and Barnet are known for their open spaces, good walks and diversity of property, ranging from glitzy Totteridge Lane and Hadley Wood to more affordable homes and modest flats. The borough isn't the most exciting place to live in terms of nightclubs and bars, but it feels friendly, comfortable and relatively safe.'
Jeremy Leaf, Jeremy Leaf & Co, Finchley

Average property prices
Detached £796,255
Semi-detached £441,731
Terraced £331,718
Flat £251,354

Local estate agents
Douglas Martin *18 Central Circus, NW4 3AS (8202 6333, www.douglasmartin.co.uk).*
Ellis & Co *www.ellisandco.co.uk; 4 offices in the borough (Barnet 8441 7700, Finchley 8349 3131, Golders Green 8455 1014, Mill Hill 8959 3281).*

COUNCIL TAX		
A	up to £40,000	£948.68
B	£40,001-£52,000	£1,106.79
C	£52,001-£68,000	£1,264.91
D	£68,001-£88,000	£1,423.02
E	£88,001-£120,000	£1,739.25
F	£120,001-£160,000	£2,055.48
G	£160,001-£320,000	£2,371.70
H	over £320,000	£2,846.04

Jeremy Leaf & Co *www.jeremyleaf.co.uk; 2 offices in the borough (East Finchley 8444 5222, North Finchley 8446 4295).*
Martyn Gerrard *www.martyngerrard.co.uk; 5 offices in the borough (East Finchley 8883 0077, Finchley Central 8346 0102, Mill Hill 8906 0660, North Finchley 8445 2222, Whetstone 8446 2111).*
Richard James *52A The Broadway, NW7 3LH (8959 9191, www.richardjames.biz).*

Other information

Council
Barnet Council *North London Business Park, Oakleigh Road South, N11 1NP (8359 2000, www.barnet.gov.uk).*
Barnet Council First Contact Unit *8359 2277, first.contact@barnet.gov.uk.*

Legal services
Finchley CAB *23-25 Hendon Lane, N3 1RT (0844 826 9336, www.barnetcab.org.uk).*
Hendon CAB *40-42 Church End, NW4 4JT (0844 826 9336, www.barnetcab.org.uk).*
New Barnet CAB *30 Station Road, New Barnet, EN5 1PL (0844 826 9336, www. barnetcab.org.uk).*

Local information
www.hgs.org.uk.
www.the-archer.co.uk.
www.times-series.co.uk.

Open spaces & allotments
Barnet Federation of Allotments & Horticultural Societies
www.www.barnetallotments.org.uk.
Council allotments *Greenspaces Development Team, North London Business Park, Oakleigh Road South, N11 1NP (8359 7820, www.barnet. gov.uk).*
Open spaces *www.barnet.gov.uk/parks-and-open-spaces.*

Brent

With one foot firmly lodged in inner-city London, Brent also embraces suburbia. Upmarket media types wanting more bricks for their money rub shoulders with old-school Irish, Asian, Caribbean and Portuguese communities and newer eastern European ones. A vibrant microcosm of London living, Brent offers a mix of industrial and green landscapes plus great transport links.

Neighbourhoods

Kilburn and Brondesbury

Kilburn straddles the traffic clogged thoroughfare of the A5, aka Kilburn High Road, an arterial route in and out of London since Roman times. This grotty but popular high street offers useful if uninspiring chains, such as Boots and Sainsbury's, alongside numerous pound shops and Kilburn Square Market.

Kilburn's long-standing sense of Irish identity is fast fading – the St Patrick's Day Parade now starts in Willesden – as many older residents leave the area, cashing in on house prices as they go. Some Irish pubs remain, but there's been a definite sea change, typified by the closure of McGoverns Irish pub, which once occupied almost an entire block just north of Willesden Lane.

Despite the influx of coffee chains and other indicators of affluence, Kilburn retains a slightly down-at-heel vibe. The housing stock ranges from large estates to handsome Victorian terraces. The good news is that prices remain consistently less painful than those in nearby West Hampstead and Maida Vale – though the stream of young and middle-aged professionals taking advantage means things won't remain as such for long.

Residential Brondesbury stretches north and west of Kilburn, and includes Willesden Lane. It's another area with a varied ethnic mix, reflected in the many food shops proffering Indian, Polish and Persian specialities, alongside some generic greasy-spoon caffs. Historical precedents of the area's diversity can be witnessed at peaceful and pretty Paddington Cemetery. House prices are fairly high, primarily due to the area's popularity with young families.

Kensal Rise and Kensal Green

Neighbouring Harlesden's edgy reputation helps amplify the laid-back feel of Kensal Green. The neighbourhood has an arty, bohemian feel (Kensal Green Cemetery, just over the Kensington & Chelsea border, was a fashionable final resting place for Victorian writers and artists) and its cosy, compact terraces appeal to young professionals who can't afford Notting Hill. In fact, estate agents often call this area 'Notting Hill borders', hence the dramatic increase in house prices in the last few years. At its southernmost tip, this part of Brent really is within spitting distance of Ladbroke Grove where housing stock ranges from swanky conversions and gated complexes to 1960s council estates, loft-style pads and terraces.

West of Kensal Green tube is a popular shopping area that also sports plenty of restaurants and takeaways. Transport links are decent, and the Kensal Rise end of Chamberlayne Road provides more local shopping options.

Kensal Rise itself has blossomed over the last decade. House prices are on the up, though it's still cheaper than Queen's Park. As a result, it's a popular choice with young families. Property consists mainly of large Victorian terraces and 1930s houses, both large and small. The north end of College Road is where most of the retail action happens. It has a bijou, middle-class vibe, with delis, alternative-medicine treatment rooms and quirky boutiques.

Harlesden, Stonebridge and Church End

Despite its often negative reputation, there's plenty to love about Harlesden. Around the famous clock tower is one of Brent's most vibrant shopping areas, with food stores

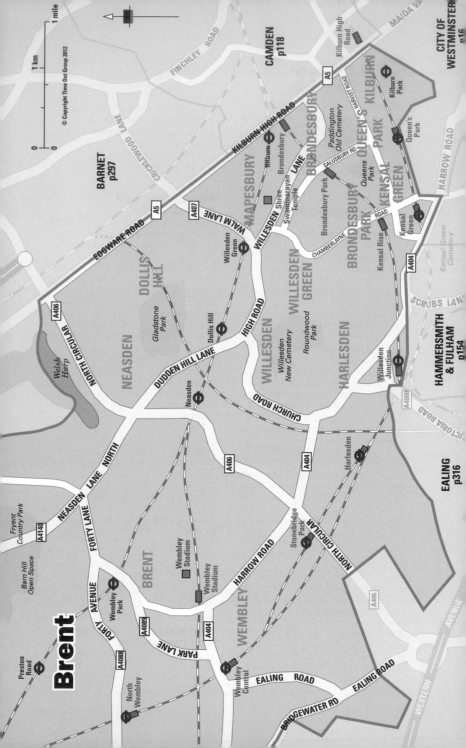

catering for the local Caribbean, Asian and Brazilian communities, as well as discount shops and takeaways.

Brent grew and developed along with the arrival of the railways in the late 1880s, and this is very much reflected in Harlesden's predominantly late Victorian properties. House sizes vary – north of the High Street, some are very large, and quite a few have (pleasingly) not yet been converted into flats. Prices reflect the area's long-standing notoriety and tend to be somewhat lower than you might expect.

Transport links (bus, tube and train) are good, though drivers have a hard time – Harlesden is a controlled parking zone and double-parking along the high street causes frequent gridlock at weekends. Locals can easily escape the hustle and bustle, though. Roundwood Park is a popular gated green space, with a café, play area and some award-winning flowerbeds.

West of Harlesden, Stonebridge has been transformed – at least from the outside – with high-rise blocks almost gone, replaced by new low-rise housing run by a mix of Brent council and a housing association. Improvements include the colourful and contemporary £2.1 million family centre Stonebridge Nursery.

Neighbouring Church End is also (slowly) getting a makeover and, with the new Central Middlesex Hospital in the middle of Park Royal, there's a note of optimism in a formerly bleak urban area. Church End sits between Harlesden, Willesden and Neasden, meeting Stonebridge on the other side of the railway tracks. Here, anonymous prefabs have been replaced with modern low-rise estates.

Willesden, Willesden Green and Cricklewood

Willesden High Road offers an array of restaurants, shops and takeaways. It is, however, a grimy thoroughfare, with slow-moving traffic.

Long favoured by immigrant communities, Willesden has a large rental market as well as plenty of Victorian terraces that appeal to families and young professionals keen to get a foot on the property ladder. The area's Irish influence is less evident than it once was – nowadays eastern European and Antipodean voices are more likely to be heard on the high street than Irish ones.

Landmark Willesden Green Library was a well-used local amenity (home to a bookshop, licensed café and cinema), but has been earmarked for 'redevelopment' and will be closed in 2012 until at least 2014; this is in addition to the six libraries permanently closed by Brent Council (a decision still being battled by community groups).

The Brent side of Cricklewood, meanwhile, shares many features with Kilburn; it's centred around the A5, grew up with the railways and was historically favoured by Irish immigrants. It has, however, a much more suburban feel, with wide roads and terraces. Transport links are good and it has its own bus station, but it's a walk to the nearest tube (Dollis Hill or Willesden Green). Family-friendly Cricklewood Library, home to the Brent Archive, was among those closed by the council in late 2011.

Gladstone Park, which sits between Cricklewood, Willesden and Dollis Hill, is a big green space much used by families and dog walkers, with a café and a friendly neighbourhood feel. To the south of the park are a number of popular culs-de-sac with detached 1930s houses (these command a premium), while to the north are wide avenues of '30s semis. This isn't the most fashionable part of town – Jean Simmons grew up in Cricklewood, but used to say she came from Willesden to appear posher – but with its sizeable (and not entirely unreasonably priced) houses and suburban vibe, it's increasingly populated with young families.

Brent

Queen's Park, Brondesbury Park and Mapesbury

Queen's Park has profited from the Notting Hill knock-on effect and is now beloved of creative folk. The houses around the park command the best views and the highest prices, while the southern end of Salusbury Road provides plenty of upmarket shopping and dining options. Around the park, houses vary in size, with the largest sitting either side of the railway line to the north. The Avenue has some desirable and spacious 1930s houses with large gardens front and back. There are still a few surviving areas of light industry, particularly Lonsdale Mews, although restaurants are fast replacing the spring manufacturers. Prices are lower the further you stray from the park.

Queen's Park itself is gated (and managed by the City of London); dogs are not allowed to roam free, though children – and there are plenty of them in these parts – very much are. The café does brisk business, as does the crazy-golf course and the tennis courts. It gets very crowded in summer, when the playground is packed.

At the top of Salusbury Road is another station, Brondesbury Park (London Overground line). This popular district offers appealing detached houses – many stone-clad and firmly gated – located around Mallorees School. Willesden Lane offers a slightly greyer version, with large Victorian piles, many of which have been turned into flats, and some new-builds and gated estates.

The Mapesbury conservation area, meanwhile, is a world of its own, with 'urban villas' situated on wide avenues. It's favoured by families and has a quiet, safe, suburban feel. Larger houses here have long since passed the £1 million price tag.

Dollis Hill and Neasden

North of Dollis Hill underground station congregates a selection of small Edwardian terraces and a 1930s estate. The area has a sedate but cosmopolitan feel and is popular with British Asian, English and Irish families. There's a marked contrast with nearby Willesden's grimy urban vibe. Local shops are limited to a smattering near the station (most residents scoot off to Willesden, Neasden or Brent Cross for serious supplies); other amenities include imposing Gladstone Park.

Neasden, long the butt of *Private Eye* jokes, was named after its nose-shaped hill, which is today lined with streets of '30s houses. More people are familiar with Neasden's traffic island than its slightly sad shopping centre. Outside the shopping area, this is an area with a distinctly anonymous, suburban feel. For posh boutiques and fancy food, you'll need to look elsewhere, but with the nearby North Circular, plenty of buses and the Jubilee line at residents' disposal, access to neighbouring areas is easy.

The magnificent Shri Swaminarayan Mandir Hindu temple is also in Neasden, and open to visitors. To the north is the open green space of Welsh Harp Reservoir.

Wembley

Best known for its impressive stadium, Wembley sits on the far side of the North Circular. A steady stream of stadium visitors means excellent transport links: locals have access to the Metropolitan and

---

STATISTICS

BOROUGH MAKE-UP
Population 256,600
Ethnic origins
  White 51.7%
  Mixed 4.0%
  Asian or Asian British 24.4%
  Black or Black British 16.2%
  Chinese or other 3.9%
Students 11.9%
Retirees 9.6%

HOUSING STOCK
Borough size (hectares) 4,324
Population density per hectare 63.0
No. of households 111,000
Houses (detached, semi-detached or terraced) 53%
Flats (converted or purpose-built) 47%

CRIME PER 1,000 OF POPULATION
Burglary 11
Robbery 7
Theft of vehicle 3
Theft from vehicle 9
Violence against the person 28
Sexual offences 1

MPs
Brent Central Sarah Teather (Liberal Democrat); *Brent North* Barry Gardiner (Labour); *Hampstead & Kilburn* Glenda Jackson (Labour)

Jubilee lines (Wembley Park), Bakerloo line (Wembley Central and North Wembley), Piccadilly line (Alperton) and Central line (Hanger Lane in neighbouring Ealing).

Wembley High Road itself is a fairly unremarkable affair, dotted with banks, takeaways and chain shops such as Boots, as well as some popular local restaurants (most specialising in South Indian cuisine). Deceptively quiet midweek, restaurants such as dosa specialist Sarashwathy Bavans become a hive of activity at weekends. Also nearby is Copland School, and, up Park Lane towards Wembley Park, is King Edward VII Park.

Wembley has a strong community feel, due largely to the extensive Gujarati and South Indian population. The area's housing stock includes plenty of good-sized family-friendly 1930s semis (particularly in North Wembley) and most residents seem to be in for the long haul, with many children of first- and second-generation immigrants choosing to remain in the area near their parents. A recent influx of eastern European residents has added another dimension to the cultural mix – shops such as Polski Sklep (on Mount Pleasant at the bottom of Ealing Road) are appearing fast.

Ealing Road – stunning by night when it's lit up for the Diwali festival – offers a bustling mix of restaurants, travel agents advertising great deals to Mumbai, and shops selling gold jewellery, fabulous sari fabrics, Bollywood hits, altars and huge piles of exotic fruit and veg. The road is also home to a small but well-used library, the striking Shree Sanatan Hindu Mandir temple (opened 2010), Wembley Central Mosque and the Clay Oven banqueting suites, a popular venue for local wedding receptions. To the south is mainly residential Alperton.

Restaurants & cafés

Though not exactly a hotspot of fine gastronomy, Brent has plenty to satisfy the average appetite. The borough's budget bistros, Small & Beautiful and Little Bay in Kilburn, are now established eateries and deservedly popular with young professionals. On Kilburn High Road, other possibilities are Betsy Smith (global menu with lots of pizzas) and Ariana II (Afghan).

Gritty **Kilburn High Road**. See p307.

In Willesden, Sushi-Say remains a big draw for sushi-lovers – booking is essential. Vijay, Anjanaas and Kovalam are a pleasing cluster of South Indian specialists on Willesden Lane. For a classy coffee, pop into the café at the Tricycle Theatre (see p313); Kensal Rise caffeine needs are best fixed at family-friendly Gracclands, though the Diner is now a popular option too. Minkie's Deli (see p313) also has a café, while Island on the Rise is a Caribbean restaurant on Station Terrace.

As parts of the borough become increasingly fashionable, so too do its gastropubs. Paradise by Way of Kensal Green is an energetic gastropub with lots of entertainment (music, comedy nights). Nearby, the Regent offers excellent organic burgers, and DJs on Friday and Saturday nights. Also of note is Harrow Road's William IV.

Visit Behesht in Kensal Green for great Persian fare (grills, stews and salads). In Queen's Park, Penk's bistro remains consistently charming, and Hugo's has child-friendly brunching appeal, while the Salusbury satisfies those with gastropub leanings. There's also a branch of posh café/bakery Gail's here, and easy-going brasserie Jacks.

In Neasden, Shayona, set in the grounds of the huge Hindu temple, offers pan-Indian vegetarian fare; Oasis provides bargain Polish food in cheery surroundings.

Brent

Wembley has masses of Indian restaurants; try Sakonis for Gujarati cuisine, Sanghaman for pan-Indian dishes and Sarashwathy Bavans for South Indian – all are vegetarian. Mesopotamia is a beacon of homespun Iraqi cooking.

Anjanaas *57-59 Willesden Lane, NW6 7RL (7624 1713, www.anjanaas.co.uk).*
Ariana II *241 Kilburn High Road, NW6 7JN (3490 6709, www.ariana2restaurant.co.uk).*
Behesht *1084 Harrow Road, NW10 5NL (8964 4477, www.behesht.co.uk).*
Betsy Smith *77 Kilburn High Road, NW6 6HY (7624 5793, www.thebetsysmith.co.uk).*
Diner *64-66 Chamberlayne Road, NW10 3JJ (8968 9033, www.goodlifediner.com).*
Gail's *75 Salusbury Road, NW6 6NH (7625 0068, www.gailsbread.co.uk).*
Gracelands *118 College Road, NW10 5HD (8964 9161, www.gracelandscafe.com).*
Hugo's *21 Lonsdale Road, NW6 6RA (7372 1232, www.hugosrestaurant.co.uk).*
Island on the Rise *1 Keslake Mansions, Station Terrace, NW10 5RU (8969 0405).*
Jack's *101 Salusbury Road, NW6 6NH (7624 8925, www.jacks-cafe.com).*
Kovalam *12 Willesden Lane, NW6 7SR (7625 4761, www.kovalamrestaurant.co.uk).*
Little Bay *228 Belsize Road, NW6 4BT (7372 4699, www.littlebay.co.uk).*
Mesopotamia *115 Wembley Park Drive, HA9 8HG (8453 5555, www.mesopotamia.ltd.uk).*
Oasis *236 Neasden Lane, NW10 0AA (8450 5178).*
Paradise by Way of Kensal Green *19 Kilburn Lane, W10 4AE (8969 0098, www.theparadise.co.uk).*
Penk's *79 Salusbury Road, NW6 6NH (7604 4484, www.penks.com).*
Regent *5 Regent Street, NW10 5LG (8969 2184, www.theregentkensalgreen.com).*
Sakonis *127-129 Ealing Road, HA0 4BP (8903 1058, www.sakonis.co.uk).*
Salusbury *50-52 Salusbury Road, NW6 6NN (7328 3286, www.thesalusbury.co.uk).*
Sanghaman *531 High Road, HA0 2DJ (8900 0777, www.sanghamam.co.uk).*
Sarashwathy Bavans *549 High Road, HA0 2DJ (8902 1515, www.sarashwathy.com).*
Shayona *54-62 Meadow Garth, NW10 8HD (8965 3365, www.shayonarestaurants.com).*
Small & Beautiful *351 Kilburn High Road, NW6 2QJ (7328 2637).*
Sushi-Say *33B Walm Lane, NW2 5SH (8459 2971).*

Vijay *49 Willesden Lane, NW6 7RF (7328 1087, www.vijayrestaurant.co.uk).*
William IV *786 Harrow Road, NW10 5LX (8969 5955, www.williamivlondon.com).*

Bars & pubs

Brent's pubs reflect the changing faces of the borough. You can still find Irish boozers on Kilburn High Road, but not as many as there once were. The consistently excellent Black Lion, with its gorgeously ornate Victorian decor, is a must-visit for discerning drinkers and handy for the Tricycle Theatre, while the unpretentious, late-opening Good Ship bar draws a lively crowd to its DJ/music and comedy nights. In Willesden Green, bar-restaurant the Queensbury attracts a classy local crowd.

Kensal Green and Rise offer gastropubs Paradise by Way of Kensal Green and the Regent (for both, *see left*). In Queen's Park, watch sports at Irish pub Corrib Rest, chill out at the Salusbury gastropub (*see left*) or try cocktails at newcomer the Shop.

Harlesden's canalside Grand Junction Arms (just in Ealing) is great in summer. In North Wembley's Mumbai Junction, you can have Indian food with your pint.

Black Lion *274 Kilburn High Road, NW6 2BY (7625 1635, www.blacklionguesthouse.com).*
Corrib Rest *76 Salusbury Road, NW6 6PA (7625 9585, www.claddagh-ring.co.uk).*
Good Ship *289 Kilburn High Road, NW6 7JR (07949 008253, www.thegoodship.co.uk).*

Mumbai Junction *231 Watford Road, HA1 3TU (8904 2255, www.mumbaijunction.co.uk).*
Queensbury *110 Walm Lane, NW2 4RS (8452 0774, www.thequeensbury.net).*
Shop *75 Chamberlayne Road, NW10 3ND (8969 9399, www.theshopnw10.com).*

Shops

Brent residents often pop to Barnet's Brent Cross Shopping Centre for supplies, though there's plenty of good retail action to be had here too. On College Road in Kensal Rise, popular café Gracelands (*see p312*) offers alternative-health treatments at adjoining Gracelands Yard. East on Chamberlayne Road is contemporary floristry courtesy of Flirty Flowers and Scarlet & Violet, new butcher Brooks, children's clothes shop Their Nibs, Supra clothes store, and a number of decent vintage furniture shops including Niche and Howie & Belle. Alongside Chamberlayne Road are charming fashion outlet Lali and Minkie's Deli. Salusbury Road has more shops, including feminine boutique Iris, Queens Park Books, the contemporary Salusbury Wine Store, and, on Sundays, a farmers' market at Salusbury Road Primary School.

Away from the trendy hotspots, things aren't so bright. Chinese and Asian food superstore Wing Yip remains stalwart in Dollis Hill, and in Wembley you'll find a thriving Sunday market around the stadium. Fruit Asia and Fruity Fresh offer top-notch fruit and veg, while Musik Zone offers Bollywood tunes aplenty. Heading round the North Circular, local homeowners have IKEA on their doorsteps. Also a bonus are the salvage yards at Park Royal and Willesden Green. Music fans should check out Hawkeye for reggae and Mandy's for Irish folk. Also in Willesden is Edward's Bakery, in business since 1908. Harlesden is buzzing: visit for some reggae on vinyl, all things African and pound shops.

Brooks Butchers *91 Chamberlayne Road, NW10 3ND (8964 5678, www.brooksbutchers. com).*
Edward's Bakery *269 High Road, NW10 2RX (8459 3001, www.londonbakery.co.uk).*
Flirty Flowers *98A Chamberlayne Road, NW10 3JN (8960 9191).*
Fruit Asia *196 Ealing Road, HA0 4QL (8900 2850).*

Fruity Fresh *111 Ealing Road, HA0 4BP (8902 9797, www.fruityfresh.com).*
Hawkeye Record Store *2 Craven Park Road, NW10 4AB (8961 0866).*
Howie & Belle *52 Chamberlayne Road, NW10 3JH (8964 4553, www.howieandbelle.com).*
IKEA *2 Drury Way, North Circular Road, NW10 0TH (0845 355 1141, www.ikea.co.uk).*
Iris *73 Salusbury Road, NW6 6NJ (7372 1777, www.irisfashion.co.uk).*
Lali *15 Station Terrace, NW10 5RX (8968 9130, http://lalishop.blogspot.com).*
Mandy's Irish Shop *161 High Road, NW10 2SG (8459 2842, www.irishshopatmandys.com).*
Minkie's Deli *3 Unicorn House, Station Terrace, NW10 5RQ (8969 2182, www.minkiesdeli.co.uk).*
Musik Zone *105A Ealing Road, HA0 4BP (8795 1266).*
Niche *70 Chamberlayne Road, NW10 3JJ (3181 0081, www.nicheantiques.co.uk).*
Park Royal Salvage *Acton Lane, NW10 7AB (8961 3627, www.parkroyalsalvage.co.uk).*
Queens Park Books *87 Salusbury Road, NW6 6NH (7625 1008, www.queensparkbooks.co.uk).*
Salusbury Wine Store *54 Salusbury Road, NW6 6NN (7372 6664).*
Scarlet & Violet *76 Chamberlayne Road, NW10 3JJ (8969 9446, www.scarletandviolet.com).*
Supra *71 Chamberlayne Road, NW10 3ND (8968 6868, www.supralondon.com).*
Their Nibs *79 Chamberlayne Road, NW10 3ND (8964 8444, www.theirnibs.com).*
Willesden Green Architectural Salvage *189 High Road, NW10 2SD (8459 2947, www.willesdensalvage.com).*
Wing Yip *395 Edgware Road, NW2 6LN (8450 0422, www.wingyip.com).*

Arts & attractions

Cinemas & theatres
Lexi *194B Chamberlayne Road, NW10 3JU (0871 7042069, www.thelexicinema.co.uk).*
Tricycle *269 Kilburn High Road, NW6 7JR (7328 1000, www.tricycle.co.uk). Theatre and cinema, plus café-bar and art gallery.*

Galleries & museums
Brent Museum *Willesden Green Library Centre, 95 High Road, NW10 2SF (8937 3600, www.brent.gov.uk/museum). Local history museum.*

Other attractions
BAPS Shri Swaminarayan Mandir *105-119 Brentfield Road, NW10 8LD (8965 2651, www.mandir.org).*

Sport & fitness

With the closure of Charteris Road Sports Centre, Brent now has just three council-run sports centres. Willesden Sports Centre is particularly popular – parking can be a problem.

Gyms & leisure centres

Bridge Park Community Leisure Centre *Harrow Road, NW10 0RG (8937 3730, www.brent.gov.uk).*

Cannons *Sidmouth Road, NW2 5JY (8451 7863, www.cannons.co.uk). Private.*

Fitness First *www.fitnessfirst.co.uk; The Atlip Centre, 197 Ealing Road, HA0 4LW (0844 571 2800); 1st floor, 632-640 Kingsbury Road, NW9 9HN (0844 571 2889); 105-109 Salusbury Road, NW6 6RG (0844 571 2886). Private.*

Genesis Gym *333 Athlon Road, HA0 1EF (8566 8687, www.genesisgym.co.uk). Private.*

LivingWell *Wembley Plaza Hotel, Empire Way, HA9 8DS (8795 4118, www.livingwell.com). Private.*

Manor Health & Leisure *307 Cricklewood Broadway, NW2 6PG (8450 6464, www.the manorhealthandleisure.co.uk). Private.*

Vale Farm Sports Centre *Watford Road, HA0 3HG (8908 6545, www.brent.gov.uk).*

Willesden Sports Centre *Donnington Road, NW10 3QX (8955 1120, www.brent.gov.uk).*

TRANSPORT

Tube stations *Bakerloo* Kilburn Park, Queen's Park, Kensal Green, Willesden Junction, Harlesden, Stonebridge Park, Wembley Central, North Wembley, South Kenton, Kenton; *Jubilee* Kilburn, Willesden Green, Dollis Hill, Neasden, Wembley Park, Kingsbury, Queensbury; *Metropolitan* Wembley Park, Preston Road, Northwick Park; *Piccadilly* Alperton, Sudbury Town

Rail stations *Chiltern Railways* Wembley Stadium, Sudbury & Harrow Road; *London Overground* Brondesbury, Brondesbury Park, Kensal Rise; Kilburn High Road, Queen's Park, Kensal Green, Willesden Junction, Harlesden, Stonebridge Park, Wembley Central, North Wembley, South Kenton, Kenton

Main bus routes *into central London* 6, 16, 18, 36, 43, 52, 98, 189; *night buses* N16, N18, N36, N52, N98; *24-hour buses* 6, 43, 189

Spectator sports

Wembley Arena *Arena Square, Engineers Way, HA9 0AA (8782 5500, www.wembley arena.co.uk). Big-name bands and more.*

Wembley Stadium *HA9 0WS (stadium 0844 980 8001, box office 0845 676 2006, www.wembleystadium.com).*

Schools

Primary

There are 51 state primary schools in Brent, 13 of which are church schools, three Jewish and one Muslim. There are also ten independent primaries, including two Muslim schools, one Montessori school, one Jewish school, one Hindu school and one Welsh school. See www.brent.gov.uk, www.edubase.gov.uk and www.ofsted.gov.uk for more information.

Secondary

Alperton Community School *Ealing Road, HA0 4PW (8902 2293, www.alperton.brent. sch.uk).*

Al-Sadiq & Al-Zahra Schools *134 Salusbury Road, NW6 6PF (7372 7706, www.al-sadiqal-zahraschools.co.uk). Muslim.*

Ark Academy *Bridge Road, HA9 9JR (8385 4370, www.arkacademy.org).*

Brondesbury College London *8 Brondesbury Park, NW6 7BT (8830 4522, www.bcbcollege.com). Boys only.*

Capital City Academy *Doyle Gardens, NW10 3ST (8838 8700, www.capitalcityacademy.org).*

Claremont High School *Claremont Avenue, HA3 0UH (0844 850 0093, www.claremont-high.org.uk).*

Convent of Jesus & Mary Language College *Crownhill Road, NW10 4EP (8965 2986, www.cjmlc.co.uk). Roman Catholic; girls only.*

Copland Community School *Cecil Avenue, HA9 7DU (8902 6362, www.copland-school. co.uk).*

Crest Boys' Academy *Crest Road, NW2 7SN (8452 8700, www.thecrestboysacademy.org.uk). Boys only.*

Crest Girls' Academy *Crest Road, NW2 7SN (8452 4842, www.thecrestgirlsacademy.org.uk). Girls only.*

JFS *The Mall, HA3 9TE (8206 3100, www.jfs.brent.sch.uk). Jewish.*

Kingsbury High School *Princes Avenue, NW9 9JR (8204 9814, www.kingsburyhigh.org.uk).*

Menorah High School *105 Brook Road, NW2 7BZ (8208 0500). Girls only.*

Brent

Newman Catholic College *Harlesden Road,*
NW10 3RN (8965 3947, www.ncc.brent.sch.uk).
Roman Catholic; boys only.
Preston Manor High School *Carlton*
Avenue East, HA9 8NA (8385 4040, www.
pmanor.brent.sch.uk).
Queen's Park Community School
Aylestone Avenue, NW6 7BQ (8438 1700,
www.qpcs.brent.sch.uk).
St Gregory's Science College
Donnington Road, HA3 0NB (8907 8828,
www.stgregorys.harrow.sch.uk). Roman Catholic.
School of the Islamic Republic of Iran
100 Carlton Vale, NW6 5HE (7372 8051).
Swaminarayan School *260 Brentfield Road,*
NW10 8HE (8965 8381, www.swaminarayan.
brent.sch.uk). Hindu.
Wembley High Technology College
East Lane, HA0 3NT (8385 4800,
www.whtc.co.uk).

Property

WHAT THE AGENTS SAY:

'Queen's Park and Kensal Rise are very popular.
In both areas, for the same price you'd pay for a
flat in Ladbroke Grove, you can buy a house –
which is attracting a lot of families. Transport
links, such as the Bakerloo line and the
overground services into Euston, mean that the
district is also full of young professionals. Prices
are rising steadily, but there's not a lot on sale
at the moment, as is true of much of London.'
Gary Margo, Margo's, Kensal Rise

Average property prices
Detached £580,356
Semi-detached £391,695
Terraced £369,572
Flat £262,280

Local estate agents
Cameron Stiff & Co
www.cameronsstiff.co.uk, 3 offices in the borough
(Willesden 8459 4395, Willesden 8459 1133,
Willesden Green 8450 9377).
Daniels *www.danielsestateagents.co.uk; 4 offices*
in the borough (Kensal Rise 8969 5999, Neasden
8452 7000, Sudbury 8904 4888, Wembley
8900 2811).
Grey & Co *www.greyandco.net; 2 offices in*
the borough (Wembley Central 8903 3909,
Wembley Park 8904 1235).
Hoopers *258 Neasden Lane, NW10 0AA*
(8450 1633, www.hoopersestateagents.co.uk).

COUNCIL TAX

A	up to £40,000	£912.51
B	£40,001-£52,000	£1,064.59
C	£52,001-£68,000	£1,216.68
D	£68,001-£88,000	£1,368.76
E	£88,001-£120,000	£1,672.93
F	£120,001-£160,000	£1,977.10
G	£160,001-£320,000	£2,281.27
H	over £320,000	£2,737.52

RECYCLING

**Household waste recycled &
composted** 40%
Main recycling centre Brent Reuse
& Recycling Centre, Abbey Road, Park
Royal, NW10 (8965 5497)
Other recycling services green waste
collection; home composting; collection
of white goods and furniture; recycling
of electrical items
Council contact StreetCare, 1st floor
(East), Brent House, 349-357 High
Road, Wembley, HA9 6BZ (8937 5050)

Margo's *62 Chamberlayne Road, NW10 3JJ*
(8960 3030, www.margos.co.uk).

Other information

Council
Brent Council *Town Hall, Forty Lane,*
HA9 9HD (general enquiries 8937 1200,
customer services 8937 1234, www.brent.gov.uk).

Legal services
Brent CAB *270-272 High Road, NW10 2EY*
(0845 050 5250, www.citizensadvice.org.uk).
Brent Community Law Centre *8451 1122,*
www.lawcentres.org.uk.

Local information
www.harrowobserver.co.uk.
www.harrowtimes.co.uk.
www.kilburntimes.co.uk.
www.park-life.org.
www.wembleymatters.blogspot.com.

Open spaces & allotments
Council allotments *Cultural Services,*
Brent House, 349-357 High Road, HA9 6BZ
(8937 5619).
Open spaces *www.brent.gov.uk/parks;*
www.cityoflondon.gov.uk (Queen's Park).

Ealing

It has been called the Queen of Suburbs, and, on the whole, Ealing is pleasant and leafy, with plenty of green spaces and a genteel feel. But the character of the borough is diverse. It also contains bustling, ethnically mixed spots such as Southall and Acton, and has its share of downtrodden housing estates.

Neighbourhoods

Acton

For many, Acton is just a place on the way to Heathrow. But get off the A40 and you'll find a thriving neighbourhood. Not all the area is prospering, though. North Acton is dominated by a business-park-cum-industrial-estate in Park Royal; this is also a road and rail spaghetti junction. The South Acton housing estate, meanwhile, is the largest in west London – one of its tower blocks was used to film *Only Fools and Horses*. But parts of the south and east are profiting from money squeezed out in Acton's direction by the prohibitive property prices of Chiswick and Fulham – hence the smart houses, parks, sports fields and upmarket private schools. An area known for its long-established Polish population, Acton has seen an influx of Somali and Iraqi immigrants and contains a rash of Antipodean pubs, and a Japanese community in West Acton.

In Acton Town, the High Street, which is a conservation area, has all the usual banks, fast-food franchises and supermarkets, plus the imposing Acton Library and Town Hall. Pubs such as the Redback Tavern cater to the large Australian population, while the Belvedere on the High Street is a Polish-owned pub. Halal tandoori places provide for the Pakistani community.

The district is swamped by 1930s mock-Tudor houses, but you can still find some impressive Victorian detached residences and brick terraces, particularly around Creffield Road. Other upmarket areas include South Acton, Acton Green and Bedford Park, which all gain from being near the shops and restaurants of Chiswick High Road (in the borough of Hounslow). Further north, the streets around Acton Park are jammed with Clerkenwell-style

office conversions, while East Acton has long rows of posh semis, sports grounds and the Saudi-sponsored independent school, the King Fahad Academy.

The north and west of Acton are the least attractive places to live in the borough. West Acton is dominated by train tracks and industrial estates, and North Acton is an unappealing jumble of industrial developments and retail parks, cut off from the rest of the district by the traffic mayhem on the A40 (Western Avenue). More pleasantly, Acton Green Common, near Turnham Green tube station, is a nice example of an old village green, though cut in half by a rail bridge. In an area not famous for its green spaces, there's also Acton Park, situated on the Vale.

This is one of the most ethnically mixed areas in west London and also one of the best integrated. There is a panoply of churches and faith centres, all of which seem to pull in large congregations. The transport links are excellent too: numerous tube stops; overground train stations; and the A40 and M4 right on the doorstep.

Ealing and Hanger Hill

By turns elegant, bijou and brash, Ealing has come a long way since Ealing Studios produced its famous comedies on the edge of Walpole Park. Sure, the area has its share of tower blocks and housing estates – most notably around Argyle Road – but Ealing is overwhelmingly upper middle class, and it shows. The district is ultra-suburban, with tree-lined avenues full of independent faith schools and stately detached homes with gravel drives.

From a resident's perspective, the main attractions (apart from the houses) are the schools and transport links. Ealing is packed with primary and secondary schools – mostly of the private, opted-out variety. Commuters have a choice of half a dozen

The popular green space of **Ealing Common**.

train and tube stations, while the A40 and M4 provide easy access to Heathrow and the South-west.

There are numerous parks and sporting clubs too. Lammas Park is a large green lung, complete with playground and tennis courts. Walpole Park near the Broadway is child-friendly and hosts jazz and comedy festivals in summer. Right opposite, well-known Questors Theatre is an Ealing gem: a great venue for children and adults to get involved in the performing arts.

Ealing Green rivals Chiswick in terms of genteel affluence; the most extravagant houses are north of the Broadway towards Hanger Hill. The so-called Pitshanger Village area near the park of the same name exudes a villagey feel and has a parade full of independent shops.

The main civic centre is on Ealing Broadway; the streets around the tube/rail station and Haven Green are packed with banks, cafés, restaurants, chain pubs and shops (some of which were damaged by the rioting in August 2011). Various building/transport projects have fallen by the wayside in recent years, partly because of objections from locals, including the high-rise Arcadia development near the station and the West London Tram scheme along Uxbridge Road – but Crossrail will see several new stations open in the borough (though not until 2018/19).

In recent years, Ealing has been given a new lease of life by immigration from eastern Europe. As you can see from the delis and Polish-language signs in shops, the Polish community has long had a foothold in Ealing – ever since World War II, in fact, when Polish aircrew were based at nearby RAF Northolt.

Things get more residential as you head south, but South Ealing is still well-to-do. Houses may be mock-Tudor, but they're huge, and there are plenty of shops and restaurants along Ealing South Road. The grand housing extends to the streets around Ealing Common. This popular open space is divided in two by train tracks, but from here it's only a short stroll south to huge

Highs & Lows

Community unity With such a mix of nationalities in places such as Greenford and Acton, integration is the pleasing result.

Pitshanger Village It's hard to beat this neighbourhood for desirable property, nearby schools and transport convenience.

Hub trouble Ealing's centre is losing its character as it gets busier and blander.

Road spaghetti It's great to have all the transport links, but the borough is shredded into pieces by roads, railway lines and a canal.

Gunnersbury Park (over the borough border in Hounslow). By contrast, Argyle Road in the north-west is dominated by retirement villages and uninspiring planned housing.

Greenford and Perivale

Greenford is a somewhat overlooked suburb sliced in half by the thundering A40, on either side of the art deco Hoover Building. Residents wanting to be near the shops and private schools of Ealing generally prefer West Ealing and Hanwell, where the property is similar; in Greenford, winding streets of mainly 1930s semis surround the town centre, which has been given a £5 million revamp by the council. Greenford's 'other' town centre and residential area, north of the A40, is posher. The place feels like a backwater, though you wouldn't want to hang around on a street corner here at night: too many 'yoofs'. No single ethnicity dominates, though there are large Polish and Indian communities in the area.

Bonuses include Ravenor Park and Perivale Park. It's also blessed with low property prices and good transport links. But there's not much in the way of restaurants or nightlife. The area's best secret is that crossing the Grand Union Canal leads to Horsenden Hill, which has been compared to Hampstead Heath and feels like open countryside.

Perivale is a kind of satellite to Greenford, an out-of-the-way place that doesn't possess what you could call a proper town centre. But it's right next door to a Tesco superstore, the Westway shopping complex, and is even closer than Greenford to the Grand Union and Horsenden Hill.

Hanwell, Northfields and West Ealing

Bounded by Northfield Avenue and Boston Road, Hanwell is the poorer cousin of Ealing. As you travel west along the Uxbridge Road, from West Ealing to Hanwell to Southall, the area declines in status. Drayton Manor, a much-sought-after secondary school, is here, but it's all a bit grotty. Uxbridge Road cuts through the middle, providing the usual high-street amenities and a Rolls-Royce garage.

Hanwell and Northfields (the next district south) both score highly for green open spaces; there are recreation grounds and sporting clubs galore. Uxbridge Road passes between the vast Kensington and

City of Westminster cemeteries, the final resting places for many of west London's wealthiest residents. For golfers, it's a short putt to the courses of Osterley Park and the Brent Valley. Brent Lodge Animal Centre in Hanwell is a small zoo, endearingly known locally as 'Bunny Park'.

The most appealing streets are east of Northfield Avenue in West Ealing. There are some huge detached houses here, notably around Lammas Park, while the south end of Northfield Avenue boasts an array of restaurants. For travelling to central London, there are tube stops at Boston Manor and Northfields, overland train stations at Hanwell and West Ealing, and the congested M4.

Southall

Southall is a residential area with a large south Asian population, originally due to its proximity to Heathrow (many Punjabis arrived as a source of cheap labour for the airport). It's been estimated that 55 per cent of residents are Indian/Pakistani, and there is also a large Somali community. The Punjabi population is sizeable, hence the Sri Guru Singh Sabha Southall, the largest Sikh temple outside India, the golden dome of which can be seen for miles.

As arguably a kind of capital for the UK's Indian community, Southall boasts a vibrant subculture: it has its own radio station, and is home territory to a number of writers, musicians and film directors, including Gurinder Chadha, director of *Bend it Like Beckham* (which was filmed locally), and playwright Kwame Kwei-Armah. The Chinese-style Himalaya Palace cinema, a Grade II-listed art deco landmark built in 1929, closed its doors to Bollywood fans in 2010, but reopened a year later as an indoor market. The Glassy Junction, which was used as a location in the film *Dhan Dhana Dhan Goal*, was the first pub in Britain to accept rupees.

The Broadway, running through the centre of Southall, is a boisterous slice of the subcontinent. From wedding caterers to sari shops, wholesale grocers to pavement snack stalls, there's little you can't get here. There are also lots of restaurants, mainly Punjabi; even the McDonald's advertises itself as halal. The Broadway hosts a lively market, although its famous Wednesday horse auction (and Tuesday livestock market) finally closed in 2007 after 300 years of trading.

STATISTICS

BOROUGH MAKE-UP
Population 309,000
Ethnic origins
 White 62.7%
 Mixed 3.8%
 Asian or Asian British 20.7%
 Black or Black British 8.9%
 Chinese or other 4.0%
Students 9.4%
Retirees 9.1%

HOUSING STOCK
Borough size (hectares) 5,552
Population density per hectare 55.7
No. of households 118,023
Houses (detached, semi-detached or terraced) 57%
Flats (converted or purpose-built) 42%

CRIME PER 1,000 OF POPULATION
Burglary 9
Robbery 5
Theft of vehicle 3
Theft from vehicle 13
Violence against the person 26
Sexual offences 1

MPs
Ealing Central & Acton Angie Bray (Conservative); *Ealing North* Steve Pound (Labour); *Ealing Southall* Virendra Sharma (Labour)

Restaurants & cafés

The highest concentration of restaurants is in Ealing, reflecting the division of disposable income in the borough. As well as the familiar list of chain options on and around the Broadway (Nando's, Carluccio's, Bella Italia), independent eateries covering a wide ethnic spread are thrown into the mix. Friendly Café Grove serves Polish specialities, tiny Santa Maria provides excellent, authentic Neapolitan pizzas, and Joie de Vivre is a Mediterranean-style gaff that's both relaxed and romantic. Gastropubs include the huge and ever-popular Ealing Park Tavern in South Ealing, with its great back garden, and the Village Inn in Pitshanger Village.

Southall is also a hub for gourmands, with numerous Indian restaurants and cafés. Notables include the New Asian Tandoori Centre (aka Roxy's), purveyor of no-frills North Indian dishes. Sibling restaurants Brilliant and Madhu's specialise in Kenyan-Punjabi food, and Giftos in Karahi cuisine, while Moti Mahal is an all-rounder. Heading towards Acton, what used to be known as Sushi Hiro is now part of the Atari-ya group; little has changed and the sushi remains swimmingly fresh.

Acton has a tiny but authentic Sichuan restaurant, classic Cantonese on offer at North China and a couple of pubs, including the Rocket gastropub, serving above-average fare on budding hotspot Churchfield Road.

Atari-ya *1 Station Parade, Uxbridge Road, W5 3LD (8896 3175, www.atariya.co.uk).*
Brilliant *72-76 Western Road, UB2 5DZ (8574 1928, www.brilliantrestaurant.com).*
Café Grove *65 The Grove, W5 5LL (8810 0364).*
Ealing Park Tavern *222 South Ealing Road, W5 4RL (8758 1879, www.ealingparktavern. com).*
Giftos Lahore Karahi *162 The Broadway, UB1 1NN (8813 8669, www.gifto.com).*
Joie de Vivre *12 St Mary's Road, W5 5ES (8932 5508).*
Madhu's *39 South Road, UB1 1SW (8574 1897, www.madhusonline.com).*
Moti Mahal *94 The Broadway, UB1 1QF (8574 7682, www.motimahal.co.uk).*
New Asian Tandoori Centre *114-118 The Green, UB2 4BQ (8574 2597).*

Ealing

North China *305 Uxbridge Road, W3 9QU (8992 9183, www.northchina.co.uk).*
Rocket *11-13 Churchfield Road, W3 6BD (8993 6123, www.therocketw3.co.uk).*
Santa Maria *15 St Mary's Road, W5 5RA (8579 1462, www.santamariapizzeria.com).*
Si Chuan Restaurant *116 Churchfield Road, W3 6BY (8992 9473, www.sichuan-london. co.uk).*
Village Inn *122-124 Pitshanger Lane, W5 1QP (8998 6810, www.village-inn.co.uk).*

Bars & pubs

Ealing is not the best neighbourhood for a pub crawl, but there are a handful of good drinking holes. The area's oldest and most attractive pubs tend to be found in South Ealing – in the vicinity of St Mary's Road, where the original Ealing village developed. Thames Valley University is nearby, which means that the pubs, for better or worse, are often full of students. The cosy Red Lion is a stone's throw from Ealing Film Studios; a little further south is gastropub Ealing Park Tavern (*see left*).

The Broadway, with its chain shops, coffee bars and fast-food joints, delivers the usual names, Hog's Head and O'Neills included. The North Star is a small gem, while further north, past West Ealing station, is Drayton Court, where punters can relax in the lounge area or landscaped garden, or get rowdy in the sports bar.

Acton's contribution to the pub scene is modest. The best pickings are to be found near the Uxbridge Road/High Street and adjoining Steyne Road, which offer a slew of chain bars and pubs. A couple of boozers on Churchfield Road have been done up, including the Rocket (*see above*). The Grand Junction Arms is an unexpected find in an unpromising industrial area, with seasonal Young's ales and a large beer garden overlooking the Grand Union Canal.

Unsurprisingly, neither Southall nor Greenford contribute much to the drinking scene. A decent pub away from the usual spots is the Plough in Northfields, a friendly local with Fuller's ales and reasonable food.

Drayton Court *2 The Avenue, W13 8PH (8997 1019).*
Grand Junction Arms *Canal Bridge, Acton Lane, NW10 7AD (8965 5670, www.youngs.co.uk).*

North Star *43 The Broadway, W5 5JN (8579 0863, www.thenorthstarealing.co.uk).*
Plough Inn *297 Northfields Avenue, W5 4XB (8567 1416, www.fullers.co.uk).*
Red Lion *13 St Mary's Road, W5 5RA (8567 2541, www.fullers.co.uk).*

Shops

Although it's not an area you would travel to for an afternoon's browse, Ealing has sufficient retail resources for local needs. Ealing Broadway is the borough's undisputed shopping hub, site of the Ealing Broadway Centre and smaller Arcadia Centre, which contain a wide array of chains (Next, Morrisons, M&S, Monsoon and TK Maxx, to name a few), interspersed with smaller units. Outside, there's Polish deli Parade and organic food store As Nature Intended, alongside various other independents – it's worth exploring the streets around the back and sides of the Broadway Centre.

Elsewhere, Stuff Boutique offers women's clothes, while the Pitshanger Village parade offers a choice of independents, including the Pitshanger Bookshop. A bus ride east towards Hanwell will bring you to the well-established Ealing Farmers' Market (9am-1pm Saturday).

Choice is rather more limited in Acton, with a basic, chain-dominated high street – although Churchfield Road is showing signs of a more interesting scene (contemporary florist Heart & Soul is well worth a look). There's a food and crafts market on the Mount, next to Morrison's supermarket, from Thursday to Saturday. Southall is strictly for those wanting an Indian-style shopping experience (think saris, henna and bangles), including the Ambala Sweet Centre. Greenford offers a Tesco superstore.

Acton Market *The Mount/King Street, W3 9NW (8993 9605, www.actonmarket.com).*
Ambala Sweet Centre *107 The Broadway, UB1 1LN (8843 9049, www.ambalafoods.com).*
Arcadia Centre *1-8 The Broadway, W5 2NH (8567 0851).*
As Nature Intended *17-31 High Street, W5 5DB (8840 1404, www.asnatureintended. uk.com).*
Ealing Broadway Centre *101 The Broadway, W5 5JY (8567 3453, www.ealingbroadway shopping.co.uk).*

Ealing

Ealing Farmers' Market *Leeland Road,
W13 (7833 0338, www.lfm.org.uk).*
Heart & Soul *65 Churchfield Road,
W3 6AX (8896 3331, www.heart-n-soul.
co.uk).*
Parade Delicatessen *8 Central Buildings,
The Broadway, W5 2NT (8567 9066).*
Pitshanger Bookshop *141 Pitshanger Lane,
W5 1RH (8991 8131, www.pitshangerbooks.
co.uk).*
Stuff Boutique *7 The Green, W5 5DA
(8567 1385).*

Arts & attractions

Cinemas & theatres

Questors Theatre *12 Mattock Lane, W5 5BQ
(8567 0011, www.questors.org.uk). The largest
community theatre in Europe, presenting around
20 shows a year.*
Vue Acton *Royale Leisure Park, Western
Avenue, W3 0PA (0871 224 0240, www.
myvue.com).*

Galleries & museums

PM Gallery & House *Mattock Lane, W5
5EQ (8567 1227, www.ealing.gov.uk/pm
galleryandhouse). A grand manor house in
Walpole Park, designed by John Soane in
1800, used for various cultural events.*

TRANSPORT

Tube stations *Central* East Acton,
North Acton, West Acton, Ealing
Broadway, Hanger Lane, Perivale,
Greenford, Northolt; *District* Turnham
Green, Chiswick Park, Acton Town,
Ealing Common, Ealing Broadway;
Piccadilly Acton Town, Ealing
Common, North Ealing, Park
Royal, South Ealing, Northfields,
Boston Manor
Rail stations *First Great Western*
Acton Main Line, Ealing Broadway,
West Ealing, Hanwell, Southall,
Drayton Green, Castle Bar Park,
South Greenford, Greenford; *London
Overground* Acton Central, South Acton
Main bus routes *into central London*
7, 70, 94; *night buses* N7, N11, N207;
24-hour buses 94
Development plans Crossrail (www.
crossrail.co.uk) will call at five stations –
Acton Main Line, Ealing Broadway, West
Ealing, Hanwell, Southall – with services
due to start in 2018/19

Sport & fitness

There is a broad choice of public and
private leisure centres, including the Park
Club, a posh country club in Acton.

Gyms & leisure centres

David Lloyd *Greenford Road, UB6 0HX (8422
7777, www.davidlloydleisure.co.uk). Private.*
Dormers Wells Leisure Centre *Dormers
Wells Lane, UB1 3HX (8571 7207, www.gll.org).*
Elthorne Sports Centre *Westlea Road,
off Boston Road, W7 2AD (8579 3226,
www.ealing.gov.uk).*
Featherstone Sports Centre *11 Montague
Waye, UB2 5HF (8813 9886, www.featherstone-
sportscentre.co.uk).*
Fitness First *The Oaks Shopping Centre,
High Street, W3 6RD (8993 0364,
www.fitnessfirst.co.uk). Private.*
Greenford Sports Centre *Ruislip Road,
UB1 2NP (8575 9157, www.ealing.gov.uk).*
Gurnell Leisure Centre *Ruislip Road East,
W13 0AL (8998 3241, www.gll.org).*
LA Fitness *Rowdell Road, UB5 6AG
(8841 5611, www.lafitness.co.uk). Private.*
Park Club *East Acton Lane, W3 7HB
(8743 4321, www.theparkclub.co.uk). Private.*
Twyford Sports Centre *Twyford Crescent,
W3 9PP (8993 9095, www.ealing.gov.uk).*
Virgin Active *5th floor, Ealing Broadway
Centre, Town Square, W5 5JY (8579 9433,
www.virginactive.co.uk). Private.*

Schools

Primary

*There are 61 state primary schools in Ealing,
including 12 church schools. There are also 13
independent primaries. See www.ealing.gov.uk,
www.education.gov.uk and www.ofsted.gov.uk
for more information.*

Secondary

Acton High School *Gunnersbury Lane, W3
8EY (3110 2400, www.actonhighschool.co.uk).*
Brentside High School *Greenford Avenue,
W7 1JJ (8575 9162, www.brentsidehigh.ealing.
sch.uk).*
Cardinal Wiseman RC School *Greenford
Road, UB6 9AW (8575 8222, www.wiseman.
ealing.sch.uk). Roman Catholic.*
Dormers Wells High School *Dormers Wells
Lane, UB1 3HZ (8813 8671, www.dormers-
wells.ealing.sch.uk).*

Drayton Manor High School *Drayton Bridge Road, W7 1EU (8357 1900, www.drayton manorhighschool.co.uk).*
Ellen Wilkinson School for Girls *Queen's Drive, W3 0HW (8752 1525, www.ellen wilkinson.ealing.sch.uk). Girls only.*
Elthorne Park High School *Westlea Road, W7 2AH (8566 1166, www.ephs.ealing.sch.uk).*
Featherstone High School *11 Montague Waye, UB2 5HF (8843 0984, www.featherstone high.ealing.sch.uk).*
Greenford High School *Lady Margaret Road, UB1 2GU (8578 9152, www.greenford. ealing.sch.uk).*
Northolt High School *Eastcote Lane, UB5 4HP (8864 8544, www.northolthigh.org.uk).*
Twyford CE High School *Twyford Crescent, W3 9PP (8752 0141, www.twyford.ealing. sch.uk). Church of England.*
Villiers High School *Boyd Avenue, UB1 3BT (8813 8001, www.villiers.ealing.sch.uk).*
West London Academy *Bengarth Road, UB5 5LQ (8841 4511, www.westlondon academy.co.uk).*

COUNCIL TAX

A	up to £40,000	£913.17
B	£40,001-£52,000	£1,065.36
C	£52,001-£68,000	£1,217.56
D	£68,001-£88,000	£1,369.75
E	£88,001-£120,000	£1,674.14
F	£120,001-£160,000	£1,978.53
G	£160,001-£320,000	£2,282.92
H	over £320,000	£2,739.50

RECYCLING

Household waste recycled & composted 38%
Main recycling centre Acton Reuse & Recycling Centre, Stirling Road, off Bollo Lane, W3 8DJ (8993 7580)
Other recycling services green waste, kitchen waste and plastics collections; home composting; white goods and furniture collection
Council contact Environmental Services, Winchester Room, Acton Town Hall, Winchester Street, W3 6NE (8825 6000)

Property

WHAT THE AGENTS SAY:

'The property market in Acton is very active at the moment. People living in Chiswick and Shepherd's Bush realise that they can get better value for money here, whether it's an extra bedroom or a garden. Schools have improved no end in recent years, and you're never more than a 13 minute walk from a tube station, making it a great location for lots of different people, whatever their needs. Prices have remained stable: I haven't seen a great increase, but nor has there been a decline.'
Phillip Harrison, Robertson Smith & Kempson, Acton

Average property prices
Detached £734,552
Semi-detached £383,161
Terraced £328,999
Flat £256,338

Local estate agents
Adams *22A Northfield Avenue, W13 9RL (8566 3738, www.adamsproperty.co.uk).*
Churchill *18 Old Oak Common Lane, W3 7EL (8749 9798, www.churchillestateagents.co.uk).*
Goodman Estate Agents *12 Market Place, W3 6QS (3479 3178, www.goodmanestates.co.uk).*

Robertson Smith & Kempson *www.rsk homes.co.uk; 4 offices in the borough (Acton 8896 3996, Ealing Broadway 8840 7677/7885, Hanwell 8566 3339, Northfields 8566 2340).*
Sinton Andrews *www.sintonandrews.co.uk; 3 offices in the borough (Ealing 8566 1990, Hanwell 8567 3219, Northfields 8840 5151).*

Other information

Council
Ealing Council *Perceval House, 14-16 Uxbridge Road, W5 2HL (8825 5000, www.ealing.gov.uk).*

Legal services
Southall Rights *54 High Street, UB1 3DB (8571 4920).*

Local information
www.actonw3.com.
www.ealingcivicsociety.org.
www.ealinggazette.co.uk.
www.ealingtimes.co.uk.
www.saveealingscentre.com.

Open spaces & allotments
Council allotments *www.ealing.gov.uk;*
www.ealingallotmentspartnership.co.uk.
Open spaces *www.ealing.gov.uk/parks.*

Hounslow

Leafy Chiswick has long been a favourite of affluent, middle-class families, but development in up-and-coming Brentford and culturally diverse Hounslow is bringing a new lease of life to the western reaches of the borough. Thames views are another local joy – if you're after a riverside pint there are few better places in London in which to sink one.

Neighbourhoods

Chiswick

This swanky part of west London offers easy access to the city centre along with a tranquil, suburban feel. Two main thoroughfares running west to east divide Chiswick: bustling Chiswick High Road (A315), the main shopping hotspot, and the imposing, six-lane A4 (Great West Road), which runs out to Brentford, Isleworth and Hounslow. At the junction of the two roads, and the start of the M4, is Chiswick Roundabout, flanked by car dealerships and usually gridlocked. Some of the area's most affordable property is nearby. Chiswick Village (www.chiswickvillagew4.co.uk), a collection of attractive 1930s flats, has a good sense of community and is popular.

The riverside section of the A4 is anchored by Hogarth Roundabout, named after 18th-century artist and satirist William Hogarth, who lived nearby (his house reopened to the public in late 2011 after a two-year restoration project). Also next to the roundabout is Fuller's, London's oldest brewery.

Lined with upmarket shops, landmark restaurants and Parisian-style pavement cafés, Chiswick High Road is bustling day and night. The traffic of sports cars, 4x4s and all-terrain buggies is testament to the predominance of wealthy, middle-class families. At the west end of the road is Chiswick Business Park, a glassy, high-tech, tree-lined office complex designed by Richard Rogers on the site of the old Gunnersbury bus depot, complete with its own pond and waterfall. Nearby is a triangular green space, confusingly called Turnham Green (Chiswick Common, meanwhile, can be found next to Turnham Green tube station). North of here – and just over the borough border in Ealing – is 19th-century Bedford Park, London's first garden suburb and still an exclusive area. Further west is expansive Gunnersbury Park, site of the hugely popular London Mela.

It's the southern half of Chiswick that is most sought after, however, with notable riverside stretches at Chiswick Mall – whose spectacular Georgian residences have mini-gardens across the road next to the Thames, facing Chiswick Eyot – and Strand-on-the-Green, whose waterside pubs are popular with walkers and cyclists heading along the Thames Path. Tiny Church Street is full of architectural gems, while Corney Reach, just to the south, is a more modern residential complex.

Also in great demand is the Grove Park area. Huge houses from all eras squat on a network of wide, tree-lined streets, with a smattering of shops around Chiswick rail station to break the residential norm. Sutton Court Mansions on Fauconberg Road is popular with renters. To the south lies Dukes Meadows – largely inaccessible to the public unless you have an allotment, belong to the upmarket Riverside health club or can use the Civil Service sports fields – and beyond that Chiswick and

Barnes Bridges. Elegant 18th-century Chiswick House is another local treasure; the recently restored grounds are stunning and there's a striking new café too.

Brentford

Though still very much playing catch-up with its more affluent W4 neighbour, Brentford has undergone significant redevelopment of late. There's certainly plenty of potential: a riverside location, a 20-minute train ride to Waterloo, a strong community spirit and, the clincher, affordable housing. In Old Brentford (south of the A4), Brentford Dock Estate (built in the 1970s on the site of the former docks) has a fantastic location bang next to the Thames. Adjacent is Ferry Quays, the most popular of several new housing developments, containing assorted restaurants as well as swanky apartments. There are also some impressive canalside developments: the Island is an expensive gated community; Heron View is somewhat more affordable. Housing elsewhere consists mainly of Victorian two- and three-bed terraces. There are also two sizeable council estates.

Brentford has strong appeal for families, downsizers and young professionals wanting a foot on the property ladder. GlaxoSmithKline has its global headquarters here, and folding bike maker Brompton Bicycles still designs and builds all its bikes in Brentford. The area also offers decent amenities. While Chiswick lacks a theatre and cinema, Brentford has both in the shape of the trusty riverside Watermans Centre, which offers everything from comedy to panto.

Other attractions include Boston Manor Park (which has a restored Jacobean manor house and hosts the annual Brentford Festival), spacious Syon Park and Kew Gardens (across the Thames, in the borough of Richmond). Then there's retro football stadium Griffin Park (home of Brentford FC), the Kew Bridge Steam Museum and the Musical Museum.

Isleworth and Osterley

Isleworth and Osterley, separated by the thundering Great West Road, are largely residential, with lots of large 1930s homes – both areas are popular with families who find the prices in Chiswick too steep. Isleworth's shops are clustered near

Isleworth rail station (which links to Waterloo) on London Road, St John's Road and Twickenham Road – though they're not much to shout about: a few restaurants and takeaways, betting shops, convenience stores and florists.

Osterley, home to gorgeous Osterley House and Park and the headquarters of BSkyB, is quieter than Isleworth and has a low-key, villagey feel. The nicest part of the area, however, is riverside Old Isleworth, where the landscape is dominated by the small tree-covered island of Isleworth Ait. The Ait opens once a year, offering visitors the opportunity to see rare wildlife in its natural habitat. Situated between Brentford and Isleworth is another local attraction, Syon House.

Hounslow

If excellent transport links are high on your list of priorities, you'll find escape routes galore in Hounslow. Unfortunately, you may well feel the need to use them. What this area lacks in glamour, peace (the constant roar of planes overhead is an issue) and des res addresses, it makes up for in proximity to Heathrow and easy access to central London. Other pluses include cheap houses and a large Asian population that makes this the borough's most diverse corner.

The pedestrianised High Street is run-down, although hints of regeneration are appearing, such as the Blenheim Centre, a huge glass shopping complex with luxury flats. In general, housing stock is not hugely exciting: 1930s and '60s semis and '80s flats. Green spaces include Hounslow Heath and Hounslow Urban Farm, one of the capital's largest community farms.

Hounslow

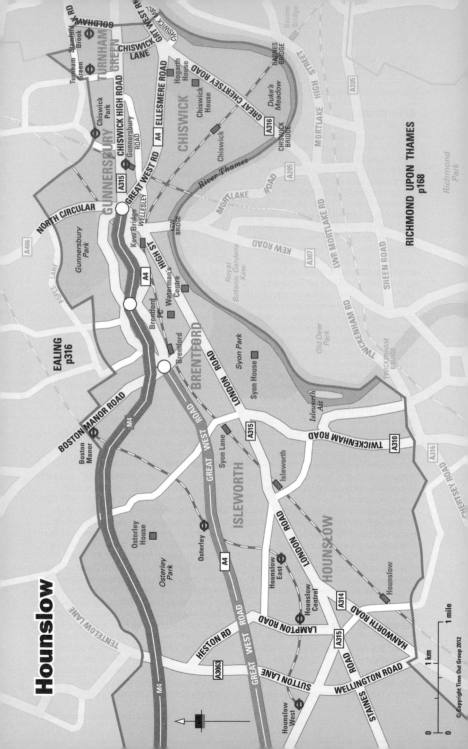

Restaurants & cafés

You're spoilt for choice when it comes to eating out in Chiswick. Family-friendly chains (ASK, Pizza Express, Nando's, Giraffe, Gourmet Burger Kitchen) abound on the High Road, along with a branch of more adult-oriented brasserie Balans, as well as independents such as the High Road Brasserie (part of the High Road House hotel and members' club), Modern European restaurant/wine bar Carvosso's at 210, upmarket chippie the Catch and, towards Gunnersbury, British restaurant Napa. Boys offers Thai/Malaysian treats, but for Asian food you're better off heading east towards Hammersmith or west to Hounslow.

Elsewhere are established local favourites Sam's Brasserie & Bar, Michael Nadra (formerly Fish Hook, but with the same chef/owner) and laid-back café the Copper Cow. Chiswickians also have the choice of two of London's best French restaurants: the near-perfect La Trompette – part of the mini-empire of Nigel Platts-Martin and Bruce Poole – and classic bistro Le Vacherin.

This is also prime gastropub territory, with the Pilot, the Roebuck and the sympathetically restored Duke of Sussex providing ham-hock terrine, cumberland sausages and pints aplenty. The Devonshire Arms – no longer part of the Gordon Ramsay empire – has reverted to being a lovely local, with Harveys bitter and a homely menu.

Venues change hands frequently; recent arrivals on the High Street include Franco Manca (sibling of the much praised Brixton pizzeria), Iranian restaurant Faanoos II (sibling of the East Sheen original), an outpost of café/bakery Gail's and making the biggest splash – haute cuisine eaterie Hedone, helmed by Swedish chef-patron Mikael Jonsson. A second outlet for Jamie Oliver's brand-new British pizza joint, Union Jacks (www.unionjacksrestaurants. com), is about to open here too.

Eating options in the rest of the borough pale by comparison. In Brentford, Ferry Quays is host to two good restaurants: Pappadums (Indian) and Glistening Waters (Caribbean). The High Street itself has little to offer, though Italian La Rosetta is popular and there's an outlet of Thai chain Fat Boys. Watermans arts centre has a pleasant café and Indian restaurant. Osterley is home to Memories of India and the much-loved

Hedone, for Chiswick hedonists.

Greedies (organic greasy-spoon café and deli, now with a conservatory). Hounslow is dominated by big-name chains and fast-food joints, including Pizza Hut and Nando's. There are also plenty of Indian restaurants, including the locally admired Heathrow Tandoori and glitzy newcomer Mantra.

Balans *214 Chiswick High Road, W4 1PD (8742 1435, www.balans.co.uk).*
Boys *95 Chiswick High Road, W4 3EF (8995 7991).*
Carvosso's at 210 *210 Chiswick High Road, W4 1PD (8995 9121, www.carvossos at210.co.uk).*
Catch *303 Chiswick High Road, W4 4HH (8747 9358, www.the-catch.co.uk).*
Copper Cow *2 Fauconberg Road, W4 3JY (8742 8545, www.thecoppercow.co.uk).*
Devonshire Arms *126 Devonshire Road, W4 2JJ (8742 2302, www.devonshirearmspub.com).*
Duke of Sussex *75 South Parade, W4 5LF (8742 8801, www.thedukeofsussex.co.uk).*
Faanoos II *472 Chiswick High Road, W4 5TT (8994 4217, www.faanoosrestaurant.com).*
Franco Manca *144 Chiswick High Road, W4 1PU (8747 4822).*
Glistening Waters *Ferry Quays, Ferry Lane, TW8 0AT (8758 1616, www.glistening waters.org.uk).*
Greedies *49 South Street, TW7 7AA (8560 8562, www.greediesworld.co.uk).*

Heathrow Tandoori *482 Great West Road, TW5 0TA (8572 1772, 8577 2145, www.heathrowtandoori.com).*
Hedone *301-303 Chiswick High Road, W4 4HH (8747 0377, www.hedonerestaurant.com).*
High Road Brasserie *162-170 Chiswick High Road, W4 1PR (8742 7474, www.high roadhouse.co.uk).*
Mantra *253 Bath Road, TW3 3DA (8572 6000, www.mantradining.com).*
Memories of India *160-162 Thornbury Road, TW7 4QE (8847 1548, www.memoriesof india.co.uk).*
Michael Nadra *6-8 Elliott Road, W4 1PE (8742 0766, www.restaurant-michaelnadra.co.uk).*
Napa *626 Chiswick High Road, W4 5RY (8996 5200, www.naparestaurant.co.uk).*
Pappadums *Ferry Quays, Ferry Lane, TW8 0BT (8847 1123, www.pappadums.co.uk).*
Pilot *56 Wellesley Road, W4 4BZ (8994 0828, www.pilot-chiswick.co.uk).*
Roebuck *122 Chiswick High Road, W4 1PU (8995 4392, www.theroebuckchiswick.co.uk).*
La Rosetta *201 High Street, TW8 8AH (8560 3002).*
Sam's Brasserie & Bar *11 Barley Mow Passage, W4 4PH (8987 0555, www.sams brasserie.co.uk).*
La Trompette *5-7 Devonshire Road, W4 2EU (8747 1836, www.latrompette.co.uk).*
Le Vacherin *76-77 South Parade, W4 5LF (8742 2121, www.levacherin.co.uk).*

Bars & pubs

There's no excuse for wasting your time on a below-par pint in Chiswick. The proximity of the Fuller's brewery means plenty of exemplary pubs, though barflies are not quite as well catered for. Located on riverside Strand-on-the-Green are the Bell & Crown and the City Barge: both are child-friendly, with decent pub grub, waterside terraces and real ales. Also here is the Bull's Head, opposite Oliver's Island.

Chiswick High Road has plenty of options. The George IV has the Headliners Comedy Club, while the Packhorse & Talbot draws a younger crowd. The Old Pack Horse (open fires, leather sofas, Thai food, Fuller's beers) is one of the best, but for a pint of Chiswick Bitter within barrel-rolling distance of the brewery, head for the Mawson Arms (also the start of the brewery tour). The Bollo gastropub has a good quiz night (Wed), while the Tabard has a tiny theatre above it.

In Brentford, try the Old Fire Station – Cuban-themed bar downstairs, Persian restaurant upstairs – or the Weir gastropub with its waterside garden. The Lord Nelson in north Brentford is a friendly, cosy choice, while the Magpie & Crown offers an astonishing array of beers, plus good home-cooked food.

Old Isleworth also has some fabulous places to drink. The London Apprentice, just outside Syon Park, opposite Isleworth Ait, was once a favourite of Charles Dickens – now it's a fine place to enjoy a drink by the river in summer. Moving into new Isleworth and Osterley, there's Young's pub the Coach & Horses (also mentioned in Dickens) and the quaint Hare & Hounds (Fuller's). Also of note is the Red Lion: it offers up to nine real ales at any one time, as well as music, quiz nights and beer festivals.

Bell & Crown *11-13 Thames Road, Strand-on-the-Green, W4 3PL (8994 4164).*
Bollo *13-15 Bollo Lane, W4 5LR (8994 6037, www.thebollohouse.co.uk).*
Bull's Head *15 Strand-on-the-Green, W4 3PQ (8994 1204).*
City Barge *27 Strand-on-the-Green, W4 3PH (8994 2148).*
Coach & Horses *183 London Road, TW7 5BQ (8181 5627, www.coachandhorses isleworth.co.uk).*
George IV *185 Chiswick High Road, W4 2DR (8994 4624).*

Gastropub **Duke of Sussex**. See p327.

Hare & Hounds *Windmill Lane, Wyke Green, TW7 5PR (8560 5438).*
London Apprentice *62 Church Street, TW7 6BG (8560 1915, www.thelondonapprentice.co.uk).*
Lord Nelson *9-11 Enfield Road, TW8 9NY (8568 1877, www.thelordnelsonbrentford.co.uk).*
Magpie & Crown *128 High Street, TW8 8EW (8560 4570).*
Mawson Arms *110 Chiswick Lane South, W4 2QA (8994 2936).*
Old Fire Station *55 High Street, TW8 0AH (8568 5999, www.the-firestation.co.uk).*
Old Pack Horse *434 Chiswick High Road, W4 5TF (8994 2872).*
Packhorse & Talbot *145 Chiswick High Road, W4 2DT (8994 0360).*
Red Lion *92-94 Linkfield Road, TW7 6QJ (8560 1457, www.red-lion.info).*
Tabard *2 Bath Road, W4 1LW (8994 3492).*
Weir *22-24 Market Place, TW8 8EQ (8568 3600, www.theweirbar.co.uk).*

Shops

Chiswick's retail action is predominantly located on or near Chiswick High Road. Devonshire Street and Turnham Green Terrace – facing each other on opposite sides of the High Road – also have notable clusters of shops.

Matters domestic hold sway here, so there's an abundance of interiors chains (Cath Kidston also has a store here), while the Old Cinema offers three floors of antiques and retro furniture. Foodies are well catered for, with the excellent Covent Garden Fishmongers; lovely continental deli Mortimer & Bennett; Theobroma Cacao, one of London's best chocolatiers; the Natural Food Store; and organic supermarket As Nature Intended. Near Chiswick Park tube is a huge Sainsbury's.

Reproducing is a popular Chiswick pastime and local tots are a well-dressed lot, thanks to branches of JoJo Maman Bebe, Petit Bateau, Gap Kids and London mini-chain Trotters, as well as charity shop Fara for high-quality second-hand clothes. For adult clothing, women fare better than men, with various upmarket chains (Sweaty Betty, Whistles) and independent women's clothing and jewellery shop Blink. Middle-class surfer wannabes are happy, thanks to branches of Fat Face and White Stuff. Chiswick Farmers' Market is held on Dukes Meadows on Sundays, and the Chiswick

Community School car boot sale is very popular (first Sunday of the month).

On Brentford High Street, there's arty furniture and accessories shop Naked Grain. In Osterley, there's the excellent second-hand Osterley Bookshop; the owners also sell free-range eggs from their own chickens and homemade jam.

Hounslow High Street offers down-at-heel chains as well as the outdated Treaty Centre, which houses a Debenhams plus various chains. A 24-hour Asda has opened in the new Blenheim Centre, but locals generally prefer to get their groceries from smaller independents. Try Ortadogu, which offers Turkish, Greek and Middle Eastern goodies.

As Nature Intended *201 Chiswick High Road, W4 2DR (8742 8838, www.asnatureintended.uk.com).*
Blenheim Centre *86-94 High Street, TW3 1NH (8577 5056, www.blenheimcentre.com).*
Blink *294 Chiswick High Road, W4 1PA (8742 1313, www.blinkfashion.co.uk).*
Cath Kidston *125 Chiswick High Road, W4 2ED (8995 8052, www.cathkidston.co.uk).*
Chiswick Farmers' Market *www.dukesmeadowstrust.org/farmersmarket.html*
Covent Garden Fishmongers *37 Turnham Green Terrace, W4 1RG (8995 9273).*
Eco *213 Chiswick High Road, W4 2DW (8995 7611, www.eco-age.com).*
Fara *www.faracharityshops.org; 40 Turnham Green Terrace, W4 1QP (8994 2287); 78 Turnham Green Terrace, W4 1RG (8994 4724).*

Mortimer & Bennett *33 Turnham Green Terrace, W4 1RG (8995 4145, www.mortimer andbennett.com).*
Naked Grain *192 High Street, TW8 8LB (8758 1456, www.nakedgrain.com).*
Natural Food Store *41 Turnham Green Terrace, W4 1RG (8995 4906).*
Old Cinema *160 Chiswick High Road, W4 1PR (8995 4166, www.theoldcinema.co.uk).*
Ortadogu Supermarket *51-53 High Street, TW3 1RB (8814 1928).*
Osterley Bookshop *168A Thornbury Road, TW7 4QE (8560 6206).*
Theobroma Cacao *43 Turnham Green Terrace, W4 1RG (8996 0431, www.theobroma-cacao.co.uk).*
Treaty Centre *High Street, TW3 1RH (8572 3570, www.treatyshoppingcentre.co.uk).*
Trotters *84 Turnham Green Terrace, W4 1QN (8742 1195, www.trotters.co.uk).*

Arts & attractions

Cinemas & theatres
Cineworld Feltham *Leisure West, TW13 7LX (0871 200 2000, www.cineworld.co.uk).*
Watermans *40 High Street, TW8 0DS (8232 1010, www.watermans.org.uk). Multi-purpose arts centre next to the river in Brentford.*

Galleries & museums
Gunnersbury Park Museum *Popes Lane, W3 8LQ (8992 1612, www.hounslow.info). Local history museum.*
Kew Bridge Steam Museum *Green Dragon Lane, TW8 0EN (8568 4757, www.kbsm.org). Steam engines, in a Victorian pumping station.*
Musical Museum *399 High Street, TW8 0DU (8560 8108, www.musicalmuseum.co.uk). Automatic musical instruments.*
Redlees Studios *Redlees Park, Worton Road, TW7 6DW (www.redlees.org). Council-run artists' studios, set in a former Victorian stable block.*

Other attractions
Brentford Festival
www.brentfordfestival.org.uk. Community festival, held on 1st Sun in Sept.
Chiswick House & Gardens *Burlington Lane, W4 2RP (8995 0508, www.english-heritage.org.uk). A 1725 Palladian villa with interiors by William Kent, and lovely gardens.*
Hogarth's House *Hogarth Lane, Great West Road, W4 2QN (8994 6757, www.hounslow. info). Country home of the great 18th-century painter, engraver and satirist William Hogarth.*

London Mela *www.londonmela.org. South Asian cultural festival, with music, dancing, street theatre, food and more, held at the end of the summer.*
Osterley House & Park *Off Jersey Road, TW7 4RB (8232 5050, www.nationaltrust. org.uk). Former Tudor house turned into a swish neoclassical villa by Robert Adam.*
Syon House & Park *London Road, TW8 8JF (8560 0882, www.syonpark.co.uk). Family seat of the Duke of Northumberland, with interiors by Robert Adam.*

COUNCIL TAX

A	up to £40,000	£933.65
B	£40,001-£52,000	£1,089.25
C	£52,001-£68,000	£1,244.87
D	£68,001-£88,000	£1,400.47
E	£88,001-£120,000	£1,711.69
F	£120,001-£160,000	£2,022.90
G	£160,001-£320,000	£2,334.12
H	over £320,000	£2,800.94

STATISTICS
BOROUGH MAKE-UP
Population 234,200
Ethnic origins
 White 64.6%
 Mixed 3.5%
 Asian or Asian British 23.4%
 Black or Black British 5.3%
 Chinese or other 3.2%
Students 8.7%
Retirees 9.4%

HOUSING STOCK
Borough size (hectares) 5,660
Population density per hectare 39.0
No. of households 96,200
Houses (detached, semi-detached or terraced) 62%
Flats (converted or purpose-built) 38%

CRIME PER 1,000 OF POPULATION
Burglary 9
Robbery 3
Theft of vehicle 3
Theft from vehicle 10
Violence against the person 24
Sexual offences 1

MPs
Brentford & Isleworth Mary Macleod (Conservative); *Feltham & Heston* Seema Malhotra (Labour)

Sport & fitness

Hounslow has several public leisure facilities. There are also private clubs, particularly in well-heeled W4.

Gyms & leisure centres

Brentford Fountain Leisure Centre
658 Chiswick High Road, TW8 0HJ (0845 456 6675, www.fusion-lifestyle.com).
David Lloyd *Southall Lane, TW5 9PE (8573 9378, www.davidlloydleisure.co.uk). Private.*
Hanworth Air Park Leisure Centre
Uxbridge Road, TW13 5EG (0845 456 2865, www.fusion-lifestyle.com).
Heston Community Sports Hall *Heston Road, TW5 0QZ (8570 6544, www.heston communityschool.co.uk).*
Heston Pool *New Heston Road, TW5 0LW (0845 456 6675, www.fusion-lifestyle.com).*
Hogarth Health Club *1 Airedale Avenue, W4 2NW (8995 4600, www.thehogarth.co.uk). Private.*
Isleworth Recreation Centre *Twickenham Road, TW7 7EU (0845 456 6675, www.fusion-lifestyle.com).*
Lampton Sports Centre *Lampton Avenue, TW3 4EP (0845 456 6675, www.fusion-lifestyle.com).*
New Chiswick Pool *Edensor Road, W4 2RG (0845 456 6675, www.fusion-lifestyle.com).*
Roko Chiswick *Chiswick Sports Ground, Hartington Road, W4 3UH (8747 5757, www.roko.co.uk). Private.*
Virgin Active *www.virginactive.co.uk; Riverside Drive, Dukes Meadows, W4 2SX (8987 1800); Chiswick Business Park, 566 Chiswick High Road, W4 5YA (8987 5858). Private.*
West 4 *10A Sutton Lane North, W4 4LD (8747 1713, www.west4healthclub.co.uk). Private.*

Other facilities

Chiswick Tennis Club *Burlington Lane, W4 3EU (07946 096933, www.chiswicktennis club.com). Private.*
Civil Service Sports Club *Riverside Drive, Dukes Meadow, W4 2SH (8994 1202, www.cssc-london.co.uk). Private club for civil servants, with grass tennis courts, and football and cricket pitches.*

Spectator sports

Brentford FC *Griffin Park, Braemar Road, TW8 0NT (0845 345 6442, www.brentfordfc. co.uk). Currently in League One.*

Schools

Primary

There are 45 state primary schools in Hounslow, including eight church schools. There are also six independents, including one international school and one Muslim school. See www.hounslow.gov.uk, www.edubase.gov.uk and www.ofsted.gov.uk for more information.

Secondary

Hounslow has 14 secondary schools, of which ten are comprehensive (eight mixed, one boys only, one girls only) and four are voluntary-aided schools (three Roman Catholic, one Church of England).

Brentford School for Girls *5 Boston Manor Road, TW8 0PG (8847 4281, www.brentford. hounslow.sch.uk). Girls only.*
Chiswick Community School *Burlington Lane, W4 3UN (8747 0031, www.chiswick. hounslow.sch.uk).*
Cranford Community College *High Street, TW5 9PD (8897 2001, www.cranford.hounslow. sch.uk).*
Feltham Community College *Browells Lane, TW13 7EF (8831 3000, www.feltham.hounslow. sch.uk)*
The Green School for Girls *Busch Corner, TW7 5BB (8321 8080, http://thegreenschool.net). Church of England; girls only.*
Gumley House RC Convent School *St John's Road, TW7 6XF (8568 8692, www.gumley. hounslow.sch.uk). Roman Catholic; girls only.*
Gunnersbury Catholic School *The Ride, TW8 9LB (8568 7281, www.gunnersbury.com). Roman Catholic; boys only.*
The Heathland School *Wellington Road South, TW4 5JD (8572 4411, www.heathland.hounslow. sch.uk).*

Heston Community School *Heston Road, TW5 0QR (8572 1931, www.hestoncommunity school.co.uk).*
Hounslow Manor School *Prince Regent Road, TW3 1NE (8572 4461, www.hounslowmanor. hounslow.sch.uk).*
Isleworth & Syon School for Boys *Ridgeway Road, TW7 5LJ (8568 5791, www.isleworthsyon.hounslow.sch.uk). Boys only.*
Lampton School *Lampton Avenue, TW3 4EP (8572 1936, www.lampton.hounslow.sch.uk).*
Rivers Academy *Tachbrook Road, TW14 9PE (8890 0245, www.riversacademy.org.uk).*
St Mark's Catholic School *106 Bath Road, TW3 3EJ (8577 3600, www.st-marks.hounslow. sch.uk). Roman Catholic.*

Property

WHAT THE AGENTS SAY:
'Chiswick is ideally placed for getting in and out of London and has long been favoured by celebrities, families and mobile professionals. The area is cosmopolitan in feel, with a number of highly sought-after schools, chic shops, good restaurants and easy transport. Bedford Park, just to the north, was the original garden suburb; the houses there, built between 1875 and 1886, are now some of the most desirable and prestigious family homes in west London.'
Claire Cooper, Featherstone-Leigh, Chiswick

Average property prices
Detached £537,621
Semi-detached £312,827
Terraced £280,350
Flat £243,249

Local estate agents
Featherstone-Leigh *Chardin House, Chardin Road, W4 1RJ (8994 6567, www.featherstone leigh.co.uk).*
Fletchers *58 Turnham Green Terrace, W4 1QP (8987 3000, www.fletcherestates.com).*
Quilliam Property Services *206 High Street, TW8 8AH (8847 4737, www.quilliam.co.uk).*
River Homes *28 Thames Road, W4 3RJ (8996 0600, www.riverhomes.co.uk).*

Other information

Council
London Borough of Hounslow
Civic Centre, Lampton Road, TW3 4DN (8583 2000, out of hours 8583 2222, www.hounslow.gov.uk).

Legal services
Brentford & Chiswick CAB *Old Town Hall, Heathfield Terrace, W4 4JN (0844 499 4113, www.citizensadvice.org.uk).*
Hounslow CAB *2nd floor, 45 Treaty Centre, High Street, TW3 1ES (0844 499 4113, www.hounslowcabs.org.uk).*

Local information
www.brentforddockresidents.co.uk.
www.brentfordtw8.com.
www.chiswickw4.com.
www.hounslowchronicle.co.uk.

Open spaces & allotments
Council allotments *Lettings Team, CIP, Treaty Centre, High Street, TW3 1ES (0845 456 2796, www.hounslow.info).*
Open spaces *www.hounslow.info/parks.*

Syon House Conservatory: not your average greenhouse. See p330.

Kingston upon Thames

The 'secret' side of south-west London, Kingston doesn't have the tube, so it doesn't get the hype that Richmond and Wimbledon do. Yet for shops, schools, security and river views it is well able to compete with its posher neighbours – and if you live on the right railway line, it's effectively 'closer' to Waterloo than Brixton.

Neighbourhoods

Kingston Town

Kingston loves pedestrians and hates drivers. Well, something has to explain why it takes 15 minutes to get around the town centre on what must be the worst bypass in outer London. The good thing, though, if you're moseying around Kingston's compact yet comprehensive shopping district, is that you'll barely see a bus or car all day.

Kingston was a market town in Saxon times: seven Saxon kings are said to have been crowned on the Coronation Stone, which stands to the right of the Guildhall, on the High Street. Today, Kingston and its immediate environs are a bustling, family-friendly shopping and leisure hub (David Mach's *Out of Order* phone-box sculpture is worth a look on your way up Old London Road). Kingston University attracts a large number of foreign students, which gives a cosmopolitan air to what is largely a white, middle-class town. By night, however, the town centre can be lairy and noisy.

Property here, though more affordable than central London boroughs, can be pricey (especially the desirable riverside properties), with lots of big Victorian detached and semi-detached homes. There are a few sought-after new developments too, such as the Royal Quarter. Residents also benefit from easy access to the expansive greenery of neighbouring Richmond upon Thames (Bushy, Hampton Court and Richmond Parks) as well as spaces such as Thames-side Canbury Gardens.

Norbiton, Coombe and Kingston Vale

Kingston Hospital sprawls around the centre of Norbiton, while the ring road and exit roads to the A3 hack into margins. It's not exactly a pretty place. Housing is a mix of Victorian and Edwardian properties and 1960s and '80s developments. As Kingston's 'inner city', Norbiton is also home to much of the borough's social housing.

In sharp contrast, just up the hill to the east is Coombe, a microcosm of modern, bourgeois gated life. Around the Coombe House conservation area – developed on the land of a demolished manorial estate – it's all culs-de-sac, CCTV, three Mercs per garage and preened pampas grass beside

Highs & Lows

▲ **Riverside locations** Choose between the bars and restaurants in Kingston centre, pleasant parks to the north and Surbiton's serene footpath.
Education Kingston University is one of the most ambitious ex-polys in the UK, and high-performing private and state secondaries make the borough a brainy one.

Private roads Walking round Coombe's lanes and culs-de-sac makes all but well heeled residents feel like burglars on the prowl.
▼ **Limited cultural offerings** OK, there's an impressive brand-new theatre, but this isn't a borough at the cutting edge of culture.

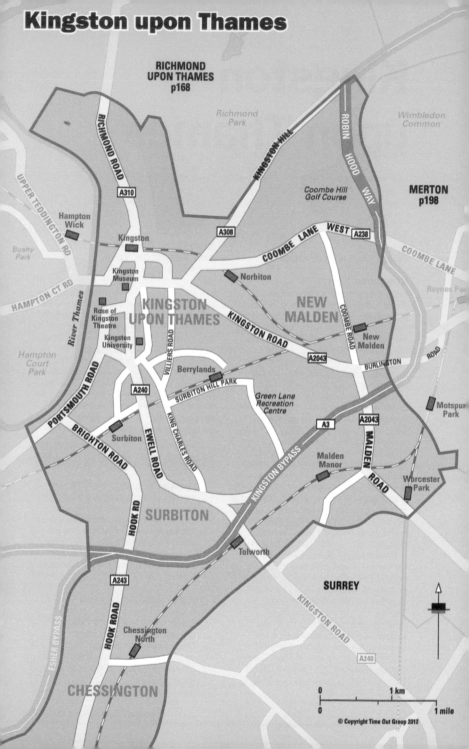
Kingston upon Thames

the porch. The Coombe Hill Golf Course spreads its greens around the private lanes, and the one bus that runs through – the no.57 to Streatham – never needs to stop. The abutting district of Kingston Vale, while slightly less exclusive, is also leafy and stridently suburban – and also utterly bereft of pubs and amenities.

New Malden and Berrylands

New Malden's centre is spread out over Kingston Road, Malden Road, Burlington Road and New Malden High Street, with the great majority of shops and services on the last. Crummy-looking discount stores, charity shops and chains dominate, with the only colour provided by the restaurants and shops that employ and serve the area's large and vibrant Korean community.

The word 'Scoul' features in many of the names of local businesses, but New Malden looks more like Pyongyang, with the grey hulks of the 16-storey Apex and CI Towers looming over the townscape and the A3 throbbing in the background. Developed around the railway station, the area's housing consists predominantly of Victorian and Edwardian terraces. Heading north on Coombe Road – later Traps Lane – things get immediately leafier.

Berrylands, the next stop on the train line to Surbiton, is primarily residential. Apart from a smattering of shops – a florist, a launderette, a picture framer – on Chiltern

STATISTICS

BOROUGH MAKE-UP
Population 169,000
Ethnic origins
White 80.7%
Mixed 2.9%
Asian or Asian British 9.1%
Black or Black British 3.0%
Chinese or other 3.4%
Students 1.3%
Retirees 6.9%

HOUSING STOCK
Borough size (hectares) 3,866
Population density per hectare 43.0
No. of households 64,550
Houses (detached, semi-detached or terraced) 64%
Flats (converted or purpose-built) 36%

CRIME PER 1,000 OF POPULATION
Burglary 4
Robbery 2
Theft of vehicle 1
Theft from vehicle 4
Violence against the person 14
Sexual offences 1

MPs
Kingston & Surbiton Edward Davey (Liberal Democrat); *Richmond Park* Zac Goldsmith (Conservative)

Kingston upon Thames

Messing about on the Thames at **Kingston Bridge**. See p333.

Drive, the neighbourhood is devoted entirely to 19th- and mid 20th-century housing. A good cycle path connects Surbiton, Berrylands and New Malden.

Surbiton

Much as they do about Posh Spice and Simon Cowell, everybody has an opinion about Surbiton – and it's rarely positive. Residents have to put up with tedious ribbing about 1970s sitcom *The Good Life* (filmed in Northwood, but fictionally located here), the notion that it's just a railway junction (it isn't) and the stereotype that it is the definitive suburb (it isn't that, either).

Surbiton is 12 miles from central London, but is closer – in travelling minutes – than many places in Zone 2. Fast trains bound for Surrey and Hampshire stop here after Clapham Junction. The beautiful, white art deco station is a monument to the suburb's role as a commuter town, but conservation areas off Maple Road and along Claremont Road and the Crescent hint at a leafy graciousness that pre-dates the trains.

Surbiton's more sociable residents are happy with their handful of fine eateries and one cool cocktail bar (the Rubicon) – all on Maple Road. There is an excellent, if pricey, gym on the riverside within a former Thames pumphouse, some good charity shops on Victoria Road (the high street) and a few decent pubs – but just as people go to London for work, they go to Kingston for shopping, to Home Park near Hampton Court for greenery and to Thames Ditton for bucolic boozing.

Restaurants & cafés

When Kingston's riverside was redeveloped in the 1990s, the rent on units was set high, inviting in chains (new arrivals include Jamie's Italian) and making for a rather predictable dining experience. Fortunately, you'll also find long-running, idiosyncratic veggie eaterie Riverside Vegetaria, French brasserie Frère Jacques and friendly Italian Al Forno – all by the river, though Al Forno is a hop across the main road.

For a laid-back meal, head to Surbiton, where a handful of places on Maple Road offer something like chic suburbia. Well-priced Italian Da Lucio is good for a low-key bite, the French Table has long been praised by critics from uptown, and Gordon Bennett

Superior chippie **Fish! Kitchen**.

– somewhere between a gastropub and a bar-bistro – is always buzzing.

Elsewhere in the borough, it's hit and miss, though there are a few nice delis and restaurants near Norbiton railway station (classy chippie Fish! Kitchen for one). New Malden is the best place in London (apart from the West End) for Korean food: try Jee Cee Neh's tabletop barbecues and unusual specials, and sophisticated Su La's good-value set lunches and dinners.

Al Forno *1-3A Townsend Parade, High Street, KT1 1LY (8439 7555, www.alforno kingston.co.uk).*
Da Lucio *101 Maple Road, KT6 4AW (8399 5113, http://dalucio.co.uk).*
Fish! Kitchen *58 Coombe Road, KT2 7AF (8546 2886, www.fishkitchen.com).*
French Table *85 Maple Road, KT6 4AW (8399 2365, www.thefrenchtable.co.uk).*
Frère Jacques *10-12 Riverside Walk, Bishops Hall, KT1 1QN (8546 1332, www.frerejacques.co.uk).*
Gordon Bennett *75 Maple Road, KT6 4AG (8390 7222, www.gordonbennetts.co.uk).*
Jee Cee Neh *74 Burlington Road, KT3 4NU (8942 0682).*
Riverside Vegetaria *64 High Street, KT1 1HN (8546 0609, www.rsveg.plus.com).*
Su La *79-81 Kingston Road, KT3 3PB (8336 0121).*

Bars & pubs

Drinkers heading to Kingston town centre or the river have plenty of choice, though most venues get packed at weekends. Saturday night sees the place awash with drunken students and out-of-town youngsters. Locals after a quieter night tend to stay well away, though the Druid's Head is something of a refuge from shopping madness and the crawler circuit.

North of the town and off the main drag, the Willoughby Arms is a proper locals' pub with regular beer festivals, while the Wych Elm is a popular Fuller's pub. The Boaters Inn in Canbury Gardens is one of the nicest places for a summer beer by the river.

In Surbiton, the Rubicon bar (recently revamped) is always lively, while Brave New World has musicians on Thursday nights. The Lamb has bags of character, first-rate cheese platters and a garden that's

perfect for summer boozing. For a decent wine list, head to the Grove. For a great array of beers, try Woodies in New Malden.

Boaters Inn *Canbury Gardens, Lower Ham Road, KT2 5AU (8541 4672, www.capitalpub company.com/the-boaters-inn).*
Brave New World *22-26 Berrylands Road, KT5 8QX (8399 0200).*
Druid's Head *3 Market Place, KT1 1JT (8546 0723).*
Grove *Grove Road, KT6 4BX (8399 1662).*
Lamb *73 Brighton Road, KT6 5NF (8390 9229).*
Rubicon *97 Maple Road, KT6 4AW (8399 5055, www.rubiconbar.com).*
Willoughby Arms *47 Willoughby Road, KT2 6LN (8546 4236, www.thewilloughby arms.com).*
Woodies *Thetford Road, KT3 5DX (8949 5824, www.woodiesfreehouse.co.uk).*
Wych Elm *93 Elm Road, KT2 6HT (8546 3271, www.thewychelm.co.uk).*

Shops

Kingston is the ultimate shopopolis: a stroll from the thriving Ancient Market (in the historic Market Place, open daily except Sunday) to the Bentall Centre (containing all the major chains, from Apple to Zara) and then to the grand John Lewis by the river gives you the range. People come from Chessington, Hounslow and even Richmond to visit the upmarket chain stores, but there are plenty of smaller retailers too, especially along Fife Street and Castle Street. Health freaks can check out the running shoes, clothing and accessories at Lanson Running, while surfers and snowboarders should head to Two Seasons. Just outside the centre, Old London Road is home to around 90 antiques' dealers, courtesy of the Kingston Antiques Centre. Also here is vintage/upcycled interiors shop 37 Old London Road, which was given a TV makeover by Mary Portas.

Pickings are much slimmer elsewhere in the borough. Heading up Coombe Road towards the golf courses, you'll find golf emporium American Golf. On the same road are Japanese food store Atari-Ya, wine merchant Wined Up Here, high-quality fish shop Jarvis and Sicilian deli Sud Ovest. New Malden has numerous Korean food shops, while Surbiton's Shoes at Last has a large local following.

American Golf *11-13 Coombe Road, KT2 7AB (08444 992159, www.americangolf.co.uk).*
Ancient Market *Market Place, KT1 1JS.*
Atari-Ya *44 Coombe Road, KT2 7AF (8547 9891, www.atariya.co.uk).*
Bentall Centre *Wood Street, KT1 1TP (8541 5066, www.thebentallcentre-shopping.com).*
Jarvis the Fishmonger *56-58 Coombe Road, KT2 7AF (8296 0139, www.fishkitchen.com).*
Kingston Antiques Centre *29 Old London Road, KT2 6ND (8549 2004, http://kingston antiquescentre.co.uk).*
Lanson Running *34 High Street, KT1 4DB (8943 4094, www.lansonrunning.com).*
Shoes at Last *81 Maple Road, KT6 4AW (8390 5673, www.shoesatlast.com).*
Sud Ovest *54 Coombe Road, KT2 7AF (8549 0084, www.sudovest.co.uk).*
37 Old London Road *37 Old London Road, KT2 6ND (8541 4774, www.37oldlondon road.co.uk).*
Two Seasons *28 Castle Street, KT1 1SS (8974 8973, www.twoseasons.co.uk).*
Wined Up Here *30 Coombe Road, KT2 7AG (8549 6622, www.wineduphere.co.uk).*

TRANSPORT

Rail stations *South West Trains* New Malden, Norbiton, Kingston; Berrylands, Surbiton; Malden Manor, Tolworth, Chessington North, Chessington South **Main bus routes** *into central London* no direct service; *night buses* N87

Arts & attractions

Cinemas & theatres

Cornerhouse *116 Douglas Road, KT6 7SB (8296 9012, www.thecornerhouse.org). Volunteer-run community arts centre.*
Green Theatre Company *Barton Green Theatre, Elm Road, KT3 3HU (07587 196378, www.greentheatre.com). Youth theatre company, based in a former cricket pavilion.*
Odeon Kingston *The Rotunda, Clarence Street, KT1 1QP (0871 224 4007, www. odeon.co.uk). The Rotunda entertainment complex (www.therotundakingston.co.uk) contains this 14-screen cinema, plus a bowling alley, fitness centre and several chain restaurants.*
Rose Theatre Kingston *24-26 High Street, KT1 1HL (08444 821556, www.rosetheatre kingston.org). A purpose-built theatre (opened 2008), with a populist programme, from Shakespeare and musicals to monthly comedy nights.*

Galleries & museums

Dorich House Museum *67 Kingston Vale, SW15 3RN (8417 5515, www.kingston.ac.uk/ dorich). 1930s house with a large collection of Russian art. Guided tours on certain days only.*
Kingston Museum *Wheatfield Way, KT1 2PS (8547 5006, www.kingston.gov.uk/museum). Local history museum.*
Stanley Picker Gallery *Faculty of Art, Design & Architecture, Kingston University, Knights Park, KT1 2QJ (8417 4074, www.stanleypickergallery.org).*

Music & comedy venues

Grey Horse *46 Richmond Road, KT2 5EE (8541 4328, www.grey-horse.co.uk). Jazz, funk, blues and comedy nights take place at this venerable old boozer.*
Peel *160 Cambridge Road, KT1 3HH (8546 3516, www.peelmuzik.com). Up-and-coming bands galore.*

Other attractions

Chessington World of Adventures & Zoo *Leatherhead Road, KT9 2NE (0870 999 0045, www.chessington.co.uk).*
Coombe Conduit *Coombe Lane West (8541 3108, www.english-heritage.org.uk). Two small Tudor buildings connected by an underground passage that carried water to Hampton Court Palace. Open occasionally.*

Sport & fitness

Kew has plenty of public and private leisure facilities, and lots of golf courses.

Gyms & leisure centres

Chessington Sports Centre *Garrison Lane, KT9 2JS (8974 2277, www.chessingtonsports centre.co.uk).*

David Lloyd *The Rotunda, Clarence Street, KT1 1QJ (8974 7440, www.davidlloyd.co.uk). Private.*

Kingfisher Leisure Centre *Fairfield Road, KT1 2PY (8541 4576, www.dcleisure centres.co.uk).*

Kingsmeadow Fitness & Athletics *422A Kingston Road, KT1 3PB (8547 2198, www.dcleisurecentres.co.uk).*

Malden Centre *Blagdon Road, KT3 4TA (8336 7770, www.dcleisurecentres.co.uk).*

Nuffield Health Surbiton *Simpson Way, KT6 4ER (8335 2900, www.nuffieldhealth.com). Private.*

Tolworth Recreation Centre *Fullers Way, KT6 7LQ (8391 7910, www.dcleisure centres.co.uk).*

Virgin Active *www.virginactive.co.uk; Bentall Centre, Wood Street, KT1 1TP (8549 7700); Richmond Road, KT2 5EN (8481 6060). Private.*

YMCA Hawker Centre *Lower Ham Road, KT2 5BH (8296 9747, www.kwymca.org.uk).*

Other facilities

New Malden Tennis, Squash & Badminton Club *Somerset Close, KT3 5RG (8942 0539, www.newmaldenclub.co.uk).*

Surbiton Racket & Fitness Club *Berrylands, Surbiton, KT5 8JT (8399 1594, www.surbiton.org).*

Spectator sports

AFC Wimbledon/Kingstonian FC *Cherry Red Records Fans' Stadium, Kingsmeadow, Jack Goodchild Way, 422A Kingston Road, KT1 3PB (8547 3528, www.afcwimbledon.co.uk, 8330 6869 www.kingstonian.net). Home to what many fans consider the real Wimbledon FC.*

Schools

Primary

There are 34 state primary schools in Kingston (including 14 church schools), plus eight independent primaries. See www.kingston.gov.uk, www.edubase.gov.uk and www.ofsted.gov.uk.

Secondary

Chessington Community College *Garrison Lane, KT9 2JS (8974 1156, www.chessington communitycollege.co.uk).*

Coombe Boys' School *College Gardens, KT3 6NU (8949 1537, www.coombeboysschool.org). Boys only.*

Coombe Girls' School *Clarence Avenue, KT3 3TU (8942 1242, www.coombegirlsschool.org). Girls only.*

Hollyfield School & Sixth Form Centre *Surbiton Hill Road, KT6 4TU (8339 4500, www.hollyfield.kingston.sch.uk).*

Holy Cross RC School *25 Sandal Road, KT3 5AR (8395 4225, www.holycross. kingston.sch.uk). Girls only.*

The historic **Market Place** in Kingston town centre. See p337.

COUNCIL TAX		
A	up to £40,000	**£1,108.00**
B	£40,001-£52,000	**£1,292.67**
C	£52,001-£68,000	**£1,477.34**
D	£68,001-£88,000	**£1,662.00**
E	£88,001-£120,000	**£2,031.33**
F	£120,001-£160,000	**£2,400.67**
G	£160,001-£320,000	**£2,770.00**
H	over £320,000	**£3,324.00**

RECYCLING

Household waste recycled & composted 47%
Main recycling centre Villiers Road Recycling Centre, KT1 3BE
Other recycling services green waste and kitchen waste collection; collection of furniture and white goods
Council contact Guildhall 2, High Street, KT1 1EU (8547 5560)

Kingston Grammar School *70 London Road, KT2 6PY (8546 5875, www.kingston grammar.com). Private.*
Richard Challoner RC School *Manor Drive North, KT3 5PE (8330 5947, www.richardchalloner.com). Boys only.*
Southborough School *Hook Road, KT6 5AS (8391 4324, www.southborough. kingston.sch.uk). Boys only.*
Tiffin Girls' School *Richmond Road, KT2 5PL (8546 0773, www.tiffingirls. kingston.sch.uk). Girls only.*
Tiffin School *Queen Elizabeth Road, KT2 6RL (8546 4638, www.tiffin.kingston.sch.uk). Boys only.*
Tolworth Girls' School *Fullers Way North, KT6 7LQ (8397 3854, www.tolworth girlsschool.co.uk). Girls only.*

Property

WHAT THE AGENTS SAY:

'Kingston is a fantastic place to live. You have the River Thames and excellent shopping on your doorstep, with Richmond just up the road. Not only that, but it takes less than half an hour to get to central London from Kingston. It's a popular place for commuters with young families, who take advantage of the large open parks and the larger housing available at more affordable prices. The development of Kingston over recent years has increased substantially and allowed a lot of buy-to-let investments to be snapped up by landlords, who accommodate young professionals and students alike.'
Tom Burkinshaw, Thamesview Group (Dexters)

Average property prices

Detached £643,198
Semi-detached £366,008
Terraced £295,078
Flat £251,365

Local estate agents

Carringtons *7 Kingston Hill, KT2 7PW (8549 3366, www.carringtonsproperty.co.uk).*
Dexters *www.dexters.co.uk; 2 offices in the borough (Kingston 8546 3555, Surbiton 8390 3939).*
Hawes & Co *www.hawesandco.co.uk; 2 offices in the borough (New Malden 8949 5856, Surbiton 8390 6565).*
JeJe Barons *5 Kingston Hill, KT2 7PW (8296 9800, www.jejebarons.co.uk).*

Other information

Council

Royal Borough of Kingston upon Thames *The Guildhall Complex, High Street, KT1 1EU (8547 5000, www.kingston.gov.uk).*

Legal services

Chessington & Hook CAB *The Hook Centre, Hook Road, KT9 1EJ (0844 826 9701, www.citizensadvice.org.uk).*
Kingston & Richmond Law Centre *Siddeley House, 50 Canbury Park Road, KT2 6LX (8547 2882).*
Kingston CAB *Neville House, 55 Eden Street, KT1 1BW (0844 826 9701, www.kcabs.org.uk).*
Malden & Coombe CAB *The Malden Centre, Blagdon Road, KT3 4TA (0844 826 9701, www.citizensadvice.org.uk).*

Local information

www.kingstonguardian.co.uk.
www.kingstononline.co.uk.
www.surreycomet.co.uk.

Open spaces & allotments

Council allotments *Quadron Services, Chapel Mill Road, KT1 3GZ (8546 9842, www.kingston.gov.uk/allotments).*
Kingston Federation of Allotment Gardeners *Gloria Wallis 8942 9686, www.kfag.org.uk.*
Open spaces *www.kingston.gov.uk/parks.*

Useful Contacts

SERVICES & TRADESMEN

Directories
020 London www.020.co.uk.
118 www.118.com
BT Directory
www.thephonebook.bt.com.
Rated People
www.ratedpeople.com.
Yellow Pages
www.yell.com.

Builders
Federation of Master Builders www.fmb.org.uk.

Chimneys
National Association of Chimney Sweeps 01785 811732, www.nacs.org.uk.

Electricians
Electrical Contractors' Association 7313 4800, www.eca.co.uk. Electrical engineering and building services.
National Inspection Council for Electrical Installation Contracting (NICEIC) 0870 013 0382, www.niceic.org.uk. NICEIC-approved electricians.

Glazing
Glass & Glazing Federation www.ggf.org.uk. Database of registered glaziers.

Infestation
British Pest Control Association 01332 294288, www.bpca.org.uk. For private pest control. Alternatively, local councils will address most common problems.

Plumbers
Association of Plumbing & Heating Contractors 0121 711 5030, www.aphc.co.uk.
Institute of Plumbing & Heating Engineering 01708 472791, www.iphe.org.uk.

Removals
British Association of Removers 01923 699480, www.bar.co.uk.

HOME EMERGENCIES

Power cuts & electrical enquiries
National Grid 0800 111999, non-emergencies 0845 605 6677, www.nationalgrid.com.

Gas leaks
National Grid 0800 111999, non-emergencies 0845 605 6677, www.nationalgrid.com.

Water leaks
Thames Water leakline 0800 714614, non-emergencies 0845 920 0800, www.thameswater.com.

Locksmiths
Master Locksmiths Association 0800 783 1 100, www.locksmiths.co.uk.

HEALTH & SUPPORT

Complementary medicine
British Homeopathic Association 01582 408675, www.trusthomeopathy.org.
Institute for Complementary Medicine 7922 7980, www.i-c-m.org.uk.

Dentists
Find a Dentist www.bda-findadentist.org.uk.

NHS services
NHS Direct 0845 4647, www.nhsdirect.nhs.uk. Health information. Alternatively, find your nearest NHS health service at www.nhs.uk.

Helplines
Alcoholics Anonymous 0845 769 7555, www.alcoholics-anonymous.org.uk.
ChildLine 0800 1111, www.childline.org.uk.

London Friend 7837 3337, www.londonfriend.org.uk.
London Lesbian & Gay Switchboard 0300 330 0630, www.llgs.org.uk.
Narcotics Anonymous 0300 999 1212, www.ukna.org.
National Missing Persons Helpline 0500 700 700, www.missingpeople.org.uk.
Samaritans 08457 909090, www.samaritans.org.uk.
Rape & Sexual Abuse Support Centre 0808 802 9999, www.rapecrisis.org.uk.
Victim Support 0845 303 0900, www.victimsupport.com.

Pregnancy & birth
British Pregnancy Advisory Service 08457 304030, www.bpas.org.
National Childbirth Trust 0300 330 0700, www.nct.org.uk.
Marie Stopes 0845 300 8090, www.mariestopes.org.uk.

Sexual health
Brook 7284 6040, helpline 0808 802 1234, www.brook.org.uk). For young people.
NHS Choices www.nhs.uk/worthtalkingabout.
Terrence Higgins Trust/ Lighthouse helpline 0808 802 1221, www.tht.org.uk). Advice and counsel for those with HIV/AIDS.

CHILDREN

Childminding
London Au Pair & Nanny Agency www.londonnanny.co.uk
Night Nannies 7731 6168, www.nightnannies.com.
Sitters 0800 389 0038, www.sitters.co.uk.
Universal Aunts 7738 8937, www.universalaunts.co.uk.

Schools
BBC Education www.bbc.co.uk/learning.

Edubase
www.education.gov.uk/edubase.
Ofsted *www.ofsted.gov.uk.*

Support
Family Lives *0808 800 2222,*
www.familylives.org.uk.
London Mums
www.londonmums.org.uk

LEGAL SERVICES

Legal advice
Citizens' Advice Bureau
www.citizensadvice.org.uk.
**Community Legal Service
Direct** *0845 345 4345,*
www.direct.gov.uk.

Legal aid
**Legal Services
Commission** *0300 200 2020,*
www.legalservices.gov.uk.

Solicitors
Law Society *7242 1222 ,*
*www.lawsociety.org.uk. Find
a solicitor in your area.*

PUBLIC TRANSPORT

Information
Transport for London
*7222 1234, www.tfl.gov.uk.
Information, maps and service
updates for tubes, trains, buses,
DLR and river services.*
Journey Planner
*www.journeyplanner.org.
Route advice.*
National Rail Enquiries
*0845 748 4950,
www.nationalrail.co.uk.*
Oyster Card *0845 330 9876,
www.oystercard.com.*

Rail services
Chiltern Railways
www.chilternrailways.co.uk.
c2c *www.c2c-online.co.uk.*
Eurostar *www.eurostar.com.*
First Capital Connect
www.firstcapitalconnect.co.uk
First Great Western
www.firstgreatwestern.co.uk.
Greater Anglia
www.greateranglia.co.uk
London Midland
www.londonmidland.com
Southern
www.southernrailway.com.

South Eastern Trains
www.southeasternrailway.co.uk.
South West Trains
www.southwesttrains.co.uk.

Coaches
Green Line Travel *0844 801
7261, www.greenline.co.uk.*
National Express *0871 781
8178, www.nationalexpress.
com.*

Water transport
Thames Clippers *0870 781
5049, www.thamesclippers.com.*
**Thames Executive
Charters** *www.thames
executivecharters.com.*
Thames River Services
www.westminsterpier.co.uk.

Complaints
Public Carriage Office
*0845 602 7000,
www.tfl.gov.uk/pco.*
Travel Watch *7505 9000,
www.londontravelwatch.org.uk.*

DRIVING & CYCLING

Breakdown services
**AA (Automobile
Association)** *information
0800 085 2721, breakdown
0800 887766, www.theaa.co.uk.*
**ETA (Environmental
Transport Association)**
0800 212 810, www.eta.co.uk.
**RAC (Royal Automobile
Club)** *breakdown 0844 273
7195, office & membership
0844 891 3558, www.rac.co.uk.*

Car clubs
City Car Club *0845 330
1234, www.citycarclub.co.uk.*
Ecurie25 *7278 3010,
www.ecurie25.co.uk.*
Zipcar *0333 240 9000,
www.zipcar.co.uk.*

Clamping
Trace Service *7747 4747.*

Cycling
Barclays Cycle Hire
*www.tfl.gov.uk/roadusers/
cycling/11598.aspx*
London Cycle Network
*www.londoncyclenetwork.
org.uk.*
**London Cycling
Campaign** *7234 9310,
www.lcc.org.uk.*
Sustrans
*www.sustrans.org.uk. Charity
promoting cycling and
sustainable travel across
the country.*

Disabled services
Dial a Ride *0845 999 1999,
www.tfl.gov.uk.*
**Wheelchair Travel &
Access Mini Buses** *01483
233640, www.wheelchair-
travel.co.uk.*

Parking
NCP *0845 050 7080 ,
www.ncp.co.uk.*

Vehicle hire
Alamo *0870 400 4508,
www.alamo.com.*
Avis *0844 581 0147,
www.avis.co.uk.*

CONGESTION CHARGE

Drivers coming into central London between 7am
and 6pm Monday to Friday have to pay a £10 fee.
The charging zone is marked on the borough maps
at the beginning of each chapter of this guide; red
'C' signs painted on the road indicate the zone. The
scheme is enforced by CCTV cameras; expect a fine
of £60 if you fail to pay (rising to £120 if you delay).
You can pay by phone or online at any time during
the day of entry. Payment is also accepted until
midnight on the next charging day – but it rises to
£12. Vauxhall Bridge Road, Grosvenor Place and
Park Lane is the toll-free through-route.
0845 900 1234, www.tfl.gov.uk

EasyCar www.easycar.com.
Enterprise 0800 261 7331,
www.enterprise.com.
HGB Motorcycles 8841
5787, www.hgbmotorcycles.
co.uk.

Taxis Transport for London
(www.tfl.gov.uk) has a licensed
minicab database. Alternatively,
text HOME to 60835 for firms
in your area.
Lady Cabs 7272 3300,
www.ladyminicabs.co.uk.
Women-only minicab drivers.
Radio Taxis 7272 0272,
www.radiotaxis.co.uk.
For black cabs.
Scooterman 0333 666 1999,
www.scooterman.co.uk. Be
driven home in your own car.

Motorbike taxis
Passenger Bikes 0844 561
6147, www.passengerbikes.com.
Taxybikes 7255 4269,
www.addisonlee.com/
passengers/taxybikes.

SPORT

GetActive London
www.getactivelondon.com.
Interactive 7717 1699,
www.interactive.uk.net.
Disability equality in sport.
Pro-Active London
www.pro-activelondon.org.
Encouraging access to
organised sport.
Sport England 08458
508508, www.sport
england.org. Find your local
sports centre.

USEFUL WEBSITES

Time Out London
www.timeout.com/london.
Premier source of information
about what's happening in
the capital.
BBC London
www.bbc.co.uk/london.
Online news, weather, sport
and entertainment.
Fix My Street
www.fixmystreet.com.
Report, view or discuss
problems in your area.
Freecycle www.freecycle.org/

ESTATE AGENTS
London wide chains; locals are listed in each borough.

Bairstow Eves
www.bairstoweves.co.uk
Belvoir
www.belvoirlettings.com
Dexters
www.dexters.co.uk
Douglas Allen
www.douglasallen.co.uk
Douglas & Gordon
www.douglasandgordon.
com
Ellis & Co
www.ellisandco.co.uk
Faron Sutaria
www.faronsutaria.co.uk
Felicity J Lord
www.fjlord.co.uk
Foxtons
www.foxtons.co.uk
Haart
www.haart.co.uk
Hampton's International
www.hamptons.co.uk
John D Wood & Co
www.johndwood.co.uk
Keatons
www.keatons.com
**Kinleigh Folkard &
Hayward**

www.kfh.co.uk
Knight Frank
www.knightfrank.co.uk
Ludlow Thompson
www.ludlowthompson.
com
Regents Estate Agent
www.regents.co.uk
Sequence
www.sequencehome.
co.uk
Spencer Thomas
www.spencerthomas.
co.uk
Wates Residential
www.watesresidential.
co.uk
Winkworth
www.winkworth.co.uk
Your Move
www.yourmove.co.uk

General websites
www.findaproperty.
co.uk
www.hotproperty.co.uk
www.primelocation.com
www.rightmove.co.uk
www.zoopla.oo.uk

group/UK/London. Give stuff
away, get stuff for free.
Greater London Authority
www.london.gov.uk.
See what the mayor and
co are up to.
Gumtree www.gumtree.com.
Online community noticeboard.
IAmMoving.com
www.iammoving.com.
Notify people of your new
address.
Loot www.loot.com.
Buy and sell in London.
Londonist www.londonist.com.
Entertaining and informative
blog about the capital.
London Farmers' Markets
www.lfm.org.uk.
Find your nearest market.
Meteorological Office
www.metoffice.gov.uk.
Weather forecasts.

On a Bus http://onabus.com.
Enter a bus number to map
its route.
Post Office
www.postoffice.co.uk.
Find your nearest post office.
Streetmap
www.streetmap.co.uk.
Useful A-Z-like resource.
StreetSensation
www.streetsensation.co.uk.
Panoramic 'streetscapes' of
over 3,000 London streets.
This is London
www.thisislondon.co.uk.
The Evening Standard online.
UpMyStreet.com
www.upmystreet.com.
Services and info, broken down
by neighbourhood.
Visit London
www.visitlondon.com.
Official tourist board website.

London's Rail & Tube services

Oyster pay as you go

Oyster pay as you go is valid at all stations and on all services shown on this map, except on Southeastern High Speed, Heathrow Express and Heathrow Connect between Hayes & Harlington and Heathrow Airport.

Key to lines and symbols

	Bakerloo
	Central
	Circle
	District
	Hammersmith & City
	Jubilee
	Metropolitan
	Northern
	Piccadilly
	Victoria
	Waterloo & City
	Docklands Light Railway
	London Overground
	London Tramlink
	Chiltern Railways
	c2c
	First Capital Connect
	First Great Western
	Heathrow Connect
	Heathrow Express
	London Midland
	National Express East Anglia
	Southern
	Southeastern
	Southeastern high speed
	South West Trains

Symbol	Meaning
○	interchange stations
✈	Airport
	Riverboat services
Kew Gardens	Station in both fare zones
	Tramlink fare zone

© Transport for London and ATOC   December 2011   Reg. user No. 11/2110/P

Index

Index

Index